New England Institute

D0897659

KIERKEGAARD

Written by one of the world's preeminent authorities on Kierkegaard, this biography is the first to reveal the delicate imbrication of Kierkegaard's life and thought. To grasp the importance and influence of Kierkegaard's thought far beyond his native Denmark, it is necessary to trace the many factors that led this gifted but (according to his headmaster) "exceedingly childish youth" to grapple with traditional philosophical problems and religious themes in a way that later generations would recognize as amounting to a philosophical revolution.

Although Kierkegaard's works are widely tapped and cited, they are seldom placed in context. Nor is due attention paid to their chronology. However, perhaps more than the work of any other contributor to the Western philosophical tradition, these writings are so closely meshed with the background and details of the author's life that knowledge of this is indispensable to their content.

Alastair Hannay solves these problems by following the chronological sequence of events and focusing on the formative stages of Kierkegaard's career, from the success of his first pseudonymous work, *Either/Or,* through to *The Sickness unto Death* and *Practice in Christianity.*

This book offers a powerful narrative account that will be of particular interest to philosophers, literary theorists, intellectual historians, and scholars of religious studies as well as to any nonspecialist looking for an authoritative guide to the life and work of one of the most original and fascinating figures in Western philosophy.

Alastair Hannay is Professor Emeritus in the department of philosophy at the University of Oslo. He is the author of *Mental Images – A Defense* (1971), *Kierkegaard* (1982), and *Human Consciousness* (1990). He has translated several works by Kierkegaard in the Penguin Classics series.

Kierkegaard
A Biography

Alastair Hannay
University of Oslo

CAMBRIDGE
UNIVERSITY PRESS

To whom this may concern

Afflictus vitam in tenebris luctuque trahebam
Et casum insontis mecum indignabar amici.
Aeneid, II.92

PUBLISHED BY THE PRESS SYNDICATE OF THE UNIVERSITY OF CAMBRIDGE
The Pitt Building, Trumpington Street, Cambridge, United Kingdom

CAMBRIDGE UNIVERSITY PRESS
The Edinburgh Building, Cambridge CB2 2RU, UK
40 West 20th Street, New York, NY 10011-4211, USA
10 Stamford Road, Oakleigh, VIC 3166, Australia
Ruiz de Alarcón 13, 28014 Madrid, Spain
Dock House, The Waterfront, Cape Town 8001, South Africa

http://www.cambridge.org

© Alastair Hannay 2001

First published 2001

Printed in the United States of America

Typeface Ehrhardt 10.5/13 pt.   *System* DeskTopPro/ᵤₓ [BV]

A catalog record for this book is available from the British Library.

Library of Congress Cataloging in Publication data
Hannay, Alastair.
Kierkegaard : a biography / Alastair Hannay.
p. cm.
Includes bibliographical references and index.
ISBN 0-521-56077-2
1. Kierkegaard, Søren, 1813–1855.   2. Philosophers – Denmark – Biography.   3.
Theologians – Denmark – Biography.   I. Title.
B4376 .H36 2001
[B]   198'.9 – dc21
00–065082

ISBN 0 521 56077 2 hardback

Contents

v

Preface

ONE AIM of a biography of a famous intellectual figure is to place its subject's works in their historical and cultural context. Another, closer to home, is to see the works in the context of their author's own intellectual development. But we must bear in mind that it is the *bios* of the subject, and not of the works, that the biographer must focus on. Obviously enough, for it is just because the works themselves are still alive, and so don't qualify for biography, that we are interested in their author. Yet it is because they still live that we are curious about the life of their author.

What is the precise link between works and a life that allows biography to be at once both intellectual and biography? Must the biographer's interest in a writer and thinker be confined to those aspects of the life that as it were produce the works? Perhaps, but then of course the actual origins of a thinker's ideas go much further back than to the writer's schooldays or birth; they can be traced as far back as the early histories of the ideas which the works embody. And if the intellectual biographer's task is conceived more particularly, as in Kierkegaard's case, as that of finding out and describing how an intellectual tradition has come to be renewed or transformed by a great thinker, then although the contingencies of time, place, talent, and opportunity that are part of the thinker's biography will enter quite naturally into an account of the genesis of the works, this still doesn't explain why it should be necessary to write a full-blown biography.

Still, it is doubtful whether an academic curiosity about origins is the real reason for the genre. Behind or beside that we may find a simple fascination with history. But other motivations too can make us hanker after biography. Isn't there a more particular curiosity, when it comes down to it, that intellectual biography caters to, a desire to uncover the secret of the person 'behind' the works? Divine spark? Lucky break? Noble mind? Feet of clay? Maybe even a personal fascination with creativity itself, an interest in calculating just how far from Olympus or Parnassus we ourselves are, or how close.

An intellectual biography is not then simply the biography of an intellectual. For reasons of the kind just hinted at it should, as biography, by rights be something less, but on the intellectual side perhaps something more. Calling a biography of a writer 'intellectual' signals the fact that what we have been bequeathed is an edifice of thought. Rather strangely, if the same grounds were given for categorizing a biography of, say, Beethoven or Wordsworth, we would be made to expect in their respective cases a 'musical' and a 'poetic' biography. Apparently, then, as a genre intellectual biography must be in some way sui generis with regard to the nature of its subject's special contribution.

We can say that the biography is intellectual not *just* because its subject was that too, but because through that very fact suitably attuned readers are helped by a suitably erudite biographer to grasp in recapitulation the genesis and substance of the subject's intellectual achievement. Erudition here requires entering somehow into the world of the subject's thought, something which requires in turn a mastery of the words and concepts from the tradition to which the subject has made a significant contribution. The very ability to write and to read such a biography might therefore be taken not only as some indication of the fact that the works do in fact continue to live but also as a measure of the success of the thinker's achievement. We owe it to him or to her that we have or still have the tools to rehearse and appreciate that life's achievement.

That there is still a question, however, of the relationship between an interest in the life and an interest in the works can be seen by asking what would be achieved in regard to the one by simply beginning and ending with the other. Suppose you take your point of departure in the writings. As far as a writer's works are concerned it is only so far as a once-living creator can be revealed in the still-living works that a rehearsal of the history of the works will yield its creator and provide material for that creator's *own* biography. But then facts of biography important enough in the subject's life may have very little bearing or none at all on what we find significant in that subject's works, particularly so, one would think, in the case of those whose contributions are intellectual, unlike warriors, politicians, and statesmen. Not only may there be very few facts of note to relate in any case, writers' lives tending in general to be quite dull – and those of thinkers are hardly likely to be less so – those worth telling may take us no further than explaining how the thinker got started and what sustained him. Suppose, however, that we started and ended with the narrative of a creative writer's or thinker's life. We would risk never getting to the works at all. One need only think of the films and documentaries about famous authors that win audiences and prizes but without, beyond a few ritual quotations out of context, telling their audience anything about the contents of their works.

Some today will say, well and good, let's forget the biographical incident and get on with the works, adding that if you are looking for the life of the author there if anywhere is where you will find it, a life that we note can now even be thought of as still being lived. Followers of Barthes and Foucault would claim, conveniently enough, though in a rather backhanded way, for the credibility of the intellectual biography as a genre, that any biography of a writer *can only* begin and end with the text. A writer's real life, after all, his or her immortality, is in the text. From that point of view, all readings of Kierkegaard, and they are legion, are 'biographies'. Taken as it were from the top, there are as many biographies, as many lives, as there are readings. The many-lives paradox that this implies is one that many in our age will take in their stride. They will also point to the commonplace that for a writer so concerned about life, Kierkegaard's own life was a conspicuously un-eventful one. So a biographer choosing not to read Kierkegaard's *bios* in his *grafe* is left having to reconstruct any *bios* from hearsay or correspondence about such insignificant remainders as the private person bent over his desk, getting tired, taking a stroll in a city park, looking at the scenery from a carriage, visiting coffee-houses, restaurants, the theatre, baiting his contemporaries, having fleeting thoughts, feelings, and so on.

There is good reason for saying that when looking for the life of the author, in Kierkegaard's case the writings are the place to look. This is sometimes obscured by superficial references to the pseudonymity of the works most likely to provide the source. The fashionable view has always been that the pseudonyms are covers behind which the real Kierkegaard, however large or small, coherent or incoherent a personality himself, lurks. But pseudonymity can just as well be an effective means of exposure, the disguise of a disguise that allows an author to spill more of himself onto his pages than would be prudent or proper if the works were signed. A biographer may be encouraged by this thought to expect to find a good deal of *bios* in the *grafe*. Kierkegaard gives some support to this too, claiming once that he had become as much a product of his writings as they were of him. So if the art of disguise that Kierkegaard is said by so many to have perfected was in fact the art of the disguise of disguise, there would be a distinct possibility that what we find in the pseudonymous works is something very close to the man himself and his inner life.

There are, however, some difficulties with this. Kierkegaard was as much a writer as a thinker. In fact although the description of his mental or spiritual development as 'intellectual' is apt enough, it also had, as we know, its aesthetic (poetic) and religious sides. Not only that, it is unclear that the word 'intellectual' is really all that apt for what he intended even his most convincingly intellectual works both to represent and to convey, just as by the same token it is unclear that he wanted to be thought of as, in any conventional sense, a philosopher. His works, he insisted, were not attempts to put across or defend any set of propositions but were something much closer to poetry – though not exactly that either, because the poetry or literary form had a religious purpose and focus. In one respect you might think this spoke in favour of the view that his works disclose him, insofar as poetry is said to speak from the heart and not (just) the more or less disembodied head. However, this matter of poetic disclosure is not so straightforward, and we should bear in mind W. B. Yeats's observation that the self-images conveyed by the writings of a poet are as a rule the reverse of the truth, even of the truth as the poet sees it. And it does seem plausible to suppose that a main motivation behind the huge effort that writers put into their poetic products stems often from a sense of lacking in themselves the very substance that their works appear to convey.

Besides reasons of this kind for finding the biography in the text, whether that details of the actual life are inessential because trivial compared with the writer's true deed or that a writer's life is somehow taken over by the writings, there are also reasons of a more traditional sort that can be invoked for coming to the same conclusion. A life behind the texts will be just plainly elusive, not just for lack of evidence but by the very nature of evidence itself and the appeal to it. These reasons apply quite generally to anything historical, and even more to the attitudes, beliefs, fears, hopes, and plans of someone long since dead. What could ever confirm or disconfirm hypotheses about what someone was actually thinking when plying pen to paper? And compared to the text in our hands, what would be the use of confirmation in such matters anyway? Does it even make sense to speak of facts of the matter of what the author had in mind? Once again it seems that it is to the text and to the possibilities of interpretation that we must look.

Given the complexities of human psychology and their power to make even autobiographical judgments suspect, there is surely some point to this. There may also be more than a grain of truth in what Barthes and Foucault say in favour of what we have, namely the texts. As for the biography offered here, it 'solves' these more traditional problems simply by riding resolutely, though some may say slipshod, over the disjunction that gives rise to them: either elusive biographical incident or available text. The justification for doing so is simply the commonsense intuition that there is no good reason to suppose that the way to Kierkegaard's life, to the man *of* and to whatever extent *in* the works, is exclusively through the works themselves. An artist's work, fleeting or subsistent, can be linked in many ways with his or her person and life. Not all artists produce themselves in their work, some stand fairly still, or apart, while others go through early, middle, and late periods, even periods of decline, as many claim was the case of Nietzsche, and was widely held regarding Kierkegaard by surviving contemporaries. In their periods of growth they develop their language, their palette, their powers of emotional expression, the range or depth of what it is they try to express. But even in the case of what they bring to expression, the range and depth do not always apply equally to the personality of the creator. In this respect Anton Bruckner's opus is not autobiographical in the way that Gustav Mahler's is. With Kierkegaard the autobiographical aspect is undeniably present in terms both of his own development as an artist and, in a way that seldom applies to composers, of the impact his works had on the environment of which he became a salient part. It is impossible to read Kierkegaard properly without knowing where he stood in relation to his time, its culture, even life in general, and as I anticipate the reader will come to agree, it would be ridiculous to suppose that the life can tell us nothing about how the texts are to be understood. The story told here is one of a struggle, a competition, a combat even, a conflict which Kierkegaard waged with himself and his surroundings.

One main leitmotif of the story as told will be that as the conflict developed Kierkegaard came consciously to present his own life in the form of a drama. Its plot was set primarily in a small city, Copenhagen, and it was only very indirectly that he saw himself as a player in a greater drama unfolding on the European and world-historical stage. But that he saw the significance of his own local drama in terms of its opposition to what was unfolding there is certainly true. If life was his topic, it was primarily his own life that provided the source material, and that life then became a self-written and self-produced stage-piece in which his own writings were the lines, and in the writing of which his own role, as he wrote it, became ever more clearly drawn. That the writings were later to occupy the centre of a European cultural stage with actors playing parts not all of which he himself may have envisaged is another matter. But a work like the present one, by going back to the process of production, can help, among other things, to point out the extent to which, to make them amenable to commentators and stage directors of a later generation, the lines have had to be reworked and their link with the processes of their production to a degree severed.

By publishing his writings, and despite the pseudonyms, Kierkegaard deliberately and in the end provocatively exposed himself to the reactions of his contemporaries, many of whom firmly believed they did indeed see him in his texts. It is as if, somewhere along the way, seeing the inevitability of the dénouement of his own story, Kierkegaard tried to take control of the endgame and assist in the inevitable. The plot, due partly to the sense of drama that went into its making, is not hard to reconstruct. Thanks to the acuity of this very alert and self-aware actor on the local stage, the unities are there for the biographer to see and to reproduce.

Since the biography here is an intellectual one and for reasons discussed its topics do not easily coincide with the biological chronology of the protagonist, I have not felt bound to follow a strictly chronological order. The actual story begins at a moment in the latter's *bios* when the ideas that came to invest his works first made their entry on the public scene. The intellectual story, although already begun, first gets properly going in a youthful speech which seemed carefully crafted to put Kierkegaard in good odour with people whose approval at the time meant much to him. The occasion allows us to sketch in en passant the political and cultural background of the city and of the country in which Kierkegaard was born. The details of the family and *its* life, and of the education that had brought him to the point of making this, his first and only, public speech are presented in the second chapter. Kierkegaard's story ended only twenty years later when, self-cast in the role of martyr, and having it seems deliberately worked himself into a cultural corner from which the only way out was up, and perfectly on cue, he fell ill and died.

There are many interesting perspectives on this. One such sees in it an outcome Kierkegaard would have wanted to avoid, the consequence of his disastrous decision to put to public use a self-image created in the poetic privacy of the pseudonyms. So what we have is another drama, the tragedy of a person who tries fatefully to write himself into a drama and then substitutes it for reality. The drama's plot goes something like this: when at last Kierkegaard strode actively out of his texts and onto the real stage, or when, as some might say, the privately nursed narrative hit the world-historical fan, Kierkegaard lost the power to 'dictate' the continuation, the pages flew apart, and the end was a fiasco. From another perspective, however, it was all carefully considered if not from the start at least well before the end, and the end itself was one that Kierkegaard consistently welcomed. Readers of the following narrative are invited to test these views and any others for themselves. They may also want to test Kierkegaard's own claims, especially the one quite early in his journal that after his death no one would find a single word about what 'filled his life', the 'script' or 'cipher' perhaps, in 'my inmost being that explains everything and which for me often makes into matters of huge moment what people would call trifles, and which I consider of no importance once I remove the secret note that explains it'.[1] Do the subsequent entries, does the later course of the life, does even the aftermath itself betray the secret, if indeed there was one? The author's hope is, in the spirit of one of his subject's pseudonyms, to have provided at least enough biographical and expository material to make the task of arriving at final judgments in all such matters not so much easier as more difficult, and therefore more rewarding.

Although Kierkegaard's own story ended with his death, the story *of* Kierkegaard, naturally enough, still continues. Since our own story must end somewhere it concludes with a short account of the impact, first, of his life and death upon his contemporaries and immediate successors and, second, of his writings when they began to become available in German and then in French translation during the early part of the twentieth century. At the very end I offer some concluding reflections on the reception more generally.

Acknowledgements

THIS WORK is the result of two bouts of concentrated writing and one of detailed revision, all in a period of two and a half years. It would have been impossible without resources available to the Kierkegaard scholar due to those who have devoted infinitely more labour and time to assembling the relevant texts and records. Beyond the Danish biographers mentioned in the references, and not least the editors of Kierkegaard's journals and papers, to say nothing of contributors to the commentaries in the new edition of Kierkegaard's works, the special debt I owe to Bruce Kirmmse will be obvious. Without his *Kierkegaard in Golden Age Denmark*, a detailed account of the broad background to Kierkegaard's writings, and *Encounters with Kierkegaard: A Life Seen by His Contemporaries*, a much-expanded version of Steen Johansen's *Erindringer om Søren Kierkegaard*, my own work could not have begun let alone been completed. Thanks are due, too, to Niels Jørgen Cappelørn, director of the Søren Kierkegaard Research Centre, for putting me on track at the start but also for his own meticulous contributions to the historical records. I owe thanks to Jon Stewart for his encouragement and many helpful comments and corrections, but also for the benefit of his thorough research into the philosophical writings of Kierkegaard's Danish contemporaries. For support, encouragement, and comment I am grateful to Camilla Serck-Hanssen, and to Brit Berggreen for useful references. The period of revision was devoted almost entirely to filling gaps pointed out to me by George Pattison, whose much greater expertise in certain areas of Kierkegaard's background also helped in the filling of them. I acknowledge my gratitude to the editors and publishers of four essays, passages from which are reproduced (slightly revised) and others paraphrased, for allowing me to use that material. The essays are: 'Two Ways of Coming Back to Reality: Kierkegaard and Lukács',

Journal of the History of European Ideas 20 (1995), nos. 1–3; 'Kierke-gaard's Levellings and the *Review*', in Niels Jørgen Cappelørn and Hermann Deuser (eds), *Kierkegaard Studies: Yearbook 1999*, Berlin and New York: Walter de Gruyter, 1999; 'The Judge in the Light of Kier-kegaard's Own Either/Or' and 'Having Lessing on One's Side', in Robert L. Perkins (ed.), *International Kierkegaard Commentary*, Macon, GA: Mercer University Press, vols. 4 and 12 (1995 and 1997 respec-tively). Not least, I must thank the Norwegian Research Council for generously supporting my work with a senior research fellowship.

From Street to Salon: First Blood

THE WORLD FAMILIAR to resident Europeans in the early nineteenth century differed from the one we know today in ways it is easy to lose sight of. The street names after all remain the same and many of the buildings. But we can easily forget that in Kierkegaard's time in the whole world only Paris, London, and Berlin had populations in excess of one million.[1] Copenhagen was even then, by comparison, a small city of less than 150,000, and Denmark itself, or at least that part of it that had a majority of native Danish-speakers, numbered less than a million.[2] In the south of Jutland (Jylland) there was a blend of Danish- and German-speakers in Schleswig (Slesvig), and Holstein (Holsten) was entirely German-speaking. These two 'duchies' were to generate acute political problems and turmoil towards the middle of the nineteenth century.

Formerly almost exclusively agrarian in its economy, and with whatever power not invested in the absolute monarch in the hands of land-owners, during the eighteenth century Denmark prospered greatly as a trading nation, largely helped by an alliance of 'armed neutrality' with Russia and Sweden, later also with Prussia, offering such a strategically situated maritime state great opportunities. Apart from carrying trade to the belligerents in a time of almost incessant war, Denmark also acquired colonies in India and the West Indies, and although it was the first country to banish slave-trading, that too – from a base in Ghana – was among the many sources of its new prosperity.[3] Wealth now came to be concentrated in the cities, and Copenhagen, though small, became a highly prosperous commercial centre. Its architecture still bears the stamp of a period of expansion and wealth that gave a tremendous boost to a city whose name (which translates as 'trading harbour') already betrays its earliest mercantile origins.

The concentration of wealth in a city provides a background for the flourishing of a cultural life independent of commercial interests, and in the first half of the nineteenth century Denmark produced an impressive array of artists, poets, philosophers, and scientists. Among the latter was Hans Christian Ørsted, who in July 1820 issued a four-page announcement in Latin describing the workings of electromagnetism, causing a sensation among European scientists. Technological innovations originating elsewhere, for example the telegraph and the horse-drawn omnibus, and not least the hydraulic press, eventually came in their turn to Denmark. Due to industry's dependence on scientific research, science itself depended to a degree on the continuing success of commercial life. But the collected wealth that allowed an increasingly scientific culture to prosper also generated a level of discussion and debate, worthy of nations with far longer traditions, that permitted that culture to survive commercial disaster and other upheavals. A space was provided in society for the formation of different perspectives upon an uneven course of events typical of unsettled times. Proximity to the German *Länder* as well as the University of Kiel's status as a German-speaking Danish university brought Danish scholars and literati in contact with the latest political, intellectual, and artistic developments in Europe at large. The German connection could even be seen in the Danish infrastructure, where state titles and designations of military ranks were borrowed from neighbours to the south and east. Artists and writers travelled to the south of Italy and even to then-distant Greece, took up residence in Dresden, Paris, and Rome, and knew Europe thoroughly. For the aspiring scholar a visit to the great names abroad was a natural extension to a university education in Copenhagen or Kiel; Danish writers spoke with Goethe, philosophers not only read but met Fichte, Schleiermacher, Schelling, and even Hegel, bringing home with them an enthusiasm born of direct contact with living legends. Nor was the traffic one-way. In the early thirties, in the year before he died, Schleiermacher paid Copenhagen a visit, and several Berlin professors travelled there. Danish philosophers and philosopher-theologians as often as not wrote in German, sometimes with half an eye on a job in Berlin, Tübingen, Jena, or Göttingen. The Norwegian-born *Naturphilosoph* Henrich (also variously Henrik and Heinrich) Steffens (1773–1845), who came under the influence of Fichte, Herder, and particularly Schelling while studying at Kiel, later joined Schlegel in Jena and afterwards became a professor in Berlin.[4]

Economic disaster came in 1807. Napoleon Bonaparte had put an embargo on British trade, closing all ports under French control (including most of Europe's Atlantic coast) to British shipping. Fearing that both France and Britain had an eye on Denmark's serviceable fleet, and with Britain, in response to Napoleon's blockade, now banning trade to and from enemy ports, the king, Frederick VI (at first a fairly liberal-minded monarch, who reigned from 1802 until his death in 1839, and who had agreed even as regent to initiate important peasant reforms) decided to take the part of France. A British naval squadron arrived outside Copenhagen in August 1807 to demand the Danish fleet. The squadron was equipped for the first time in naval history with rocket-fired missiles, under the supervision of their inventor, William Congreve (1772–1828). Rockets by that time had a range of 3,000 yards.[5] Receiving no definite reply (the king was out of the capital), the British began to bombard Copenhagen on 16 August, and the damage and loss of life were heavy. The city was quickly surrounded and taken, and on 6 September the Danish monarch signed away what was left of his fleet. But that was just the beginning. The attack itself and the damage it caused had been expensive enough, but the continuing alliance with Napoleon proved equally so. The next years saw an increasing inflation that led Denmark's State Bank in January 1813 to declare bankruptcy. It took five years and the establishment of the National Bank to stabilize the economy, and it was not until the early thirties that the country began to show significant signs of recovery.[6]

By that time, however, other things were afoot. In July 1830 there had been another revolution in Paris that had sparked off agitation throughout Europe. The 1830 uprising was provoked by Charles X's Charter of 26 July dissolving the Chamber of Deputies and tightening control of the press and universities, as well as disenfranchizing a majority of the then-electorate. In the end, however, the French king was forced to leave and certain significant reforms were made, for instance a nominated rather than hereditary chamber. By 1835 the European governments that had been exposed to similar uprisings sparked off by the French example had for the most part recovered their balance and were now in a position to parry any really radical demands for constitutional reform.

In Denmark itself there had been no such turmoil, nothing to compare to the uprisings in Italy, the German kingdoms, and Poland, all of them largely unsuccessful, or – and for obvious reasons – to Belgium's and Greece's successful bids for independence. On the contrary, back in 1814 Denmark had been forced to cede Norway to a union with Sweden. The most visible though only very recent results of the July Revolution were four geographically separated advisory assemblies, or Regional Parliaments. These were composed of appointed representatives of the several classes and professions, and, if only for his own good, Frederick VI had to consult their opinions. All of these assemblies were situated in provincial towns, and the most important was in Roskilde, quite close to Copenhagen, with representatives from Zealand (Sjælland), on which Copenhagen is situated, and the other Danish islands. The diversification and location of these assemblies, also referred to as Estates, were due partly to complicated relations between Denmark and Germany over Schleswig and Holstein, the latter a member also of the German confederation. Separate Estates were established for these two in the town of Schleswig and in Itzehoe. The fourth assembly covered the rest of mainland Denmark, that is to say Jutland, and was in Viborg. The law establishing the Regional Parliaments was promulgated in 1834. Although precipitated by the July Revolution in Paris, the establishment of an assembly for the entirely German-speaking province of Holstein had already been provided for by the terms of the Congress of Vienna of 1815. But it was not until twenty years later that meetings of the Estates were ever held.

The Roskilde Estates assembly, representing an increasingly articulate middle-class constituency and itself influenced by an increasingly eloquent press, was bound to run foul of a somewhat edgy king and his council.[7] And indeed it was not long before proposals for reform made in the newly founded liberal newspaper *Fædrelandet* (The Fatherland) prompted the king to withdraw the right of judicial appeal from the Press as well as to suspend *Fædrelandet*'s editor, the political economist C. N. David, from his university chair. Still worse for the prospect of a free press, David was prosecuted for violation of the press laws. These events led to the founding in March 1835 of the Free Press Society.

The stage is now set for our story. The date is 28 November 1835, the occasion a meeting of the Student Union at the University of Copenhagen. Universities at this time are of course much smaller than we are accustomed to today. They are dedicated mainly to the education of state functionaries (who include priests, or pastors), teachers, lawyers, and doctors. Instead of thousands, students number only a few hundred.

One of them, a twenty-two-year-old, is about to make his debut as a public speaker. Nothing remarkable about that, but the venue is a special one. In a time of government censorship the Student Union provides, though still within limits not too clearly defined, a unique forum for political debate. Founded fifteen years earlier, its premises have also and by default become the city's main news and gossip centre. As a rule the Union's meetings are occasions for literary and philosophical debate or even just for readings. In 1924 a certain Poul Martin Møller had recited to the Union three chapters of his never-to-be-finished novel, *A Danish Student's Tale* (*En dansk students Eventyr*). But political events have now begun to play a larger part, and the premises afford a meeting place where voices raised against and in defence of the established order can be heard. Because of its new-found functions the Union also has close links with newspaper journalism.

The speaker on this occasion was a slight young man with a shock of light brown hair brushed up rather ridiculously in a crest. With his lively but somewhat sarcastic demeanour he was no stranger to either the Union or his audience. But the location was definitely untypical. 'Usually in the company of somebody and constantly on the street or in public places' was how a former student colleague recalled him.[8] The sight of this peripatetic youth stumbling along half-sideways in eager conversation, sometimes stopping altogether to stress a point, was familiar to all who had come to hear him. But now he was about to stand in front of a public, alone. The young man was Søren Aabye Kierkegaard.

Quite an audience had gathered. According to this same colleague, Johannes Ostermann, then a philology student and senior of the Union, they were looking forward to a debate between Kierkegaard and Ostermann himself. Just two weeks before, Ostermann had defended and applauded the press for its fight against censorship, and the witty young Kierkegaard was known for his disdain of politics. Although eager to see how Ostermann could cope with his junior, they were also curious to see how the well-known street and coffee-shop intellectual himself performed when forced to speak *en face* and to stick to the point for a whole hour.

For it was indeed true that this talk – though following practice, soon to change, talks at the time were papers read before an audience – represented a break in the pattern of Søren's communicational style.

From his early student days in 1831 he had sought contact in conversation, partly perhaps for the human contact, for it wasn't only academics and the learned he liked to pass the time of day with, but also, it seems clear, to exploit his peers as foils for his own thought. These random meetings with friends and acquaintances, on the street or in the Union or cafés, were needed to feed his own typically polemical form of intellect. He needed other minds to sharpen his own, or, just as satisfyingly, to catch the other out or to score a point – perhaps occasionally also for reasons not purely intellectual.

As a senior member of the Student Union, Ostermann understandably had no wish to become the butt of a public display of intellectual virtuosity at the hands of a comparative youngster, especially one known for 'carrying on a witty dialectical game on all fronts'.[9] Himself 'an eager politician', Ostermann was in any case disinclined to take on someone he 'knew only had a slight interest in the substance of the matter'. So he declined to take part.[10] Perhaps it was so that they could remain friends, since there was no personal animosity between them; the two 'often met at the Student Union or at tearooms and frequently went on from there to take walks around the lakes'.[11]

What was it that drove Kierkegaard to the lectern? His eagerness to stand there is evident from the fact that even before borrowing Ostermann's manuscript to prepare his response he had told the Union's leadership of his intention to read a paper. Ready explanations would come to his audience coloured by the young Kierkegaard's reputation for intellectual witticism and mockery. Ostermann himself was inclined to put Kierkegaard's eagerness down to plain rivalry: 'the fact that my defence [of the press] was met with sympathy pushed him into the opposite camp, where he allied himself more or less as a matter of indifference.'[12] That might well be it. Kierkegaard might hope for his reply to be even better received, and he knew that Ostermann's manuscript had immediately been sought by *Fædrelandet*, the newly established liberal newspaper.[13] What better incentive for someone with a growing desire for literary fame than to make a mark in a newspaper belonging to the opposite camp?

Who exactly were this 'opposite camp'? In broad political terms they were the conservative resistance to liberal reform. But conservatism was not at the time, any more than the new radicalism, a single coherent movement or even anything remotely deserving the name 'movement'.

Politically, at least, it was rather the immobility or intransigence of tradition. Conservatism becomes a movement only when reformers become a nuisance enough to spur the authorities and those whose interests lie with them into defensive action. What was mainly causing the Danish establishment unease at the time was an increasingly critical journalism and its effect on the monarchical government. It was when the government took unkindly to a series of newspaper articles calling for liberal reforms that the Free Press Society (or, more correctly, the Society for the Correct Use of the Freedom of the Press) had been founded that March. The society was to become the nucleus of the future Liberal Party. Students were drawn to the cause and to the issues debated in the Union as well as, so far as it dared within the limits of censorship, in the press.

Lack of enthusiasm for reform or downright opposition came as usual from several quarters, and not all of it was focused on the censorship issue. Large property owners would have their special reasons for resisting any undermining of the forms of authority on which their proprietorship depended. Many people with positions in the organs of authority themselves, whether high or low – perhaps even especially low – would know which side their bread was buttered on. And of course among the state officials were the Lutheran clergy, whose livings depended on the established system.

But there was the literary establishment too. Although this did much to colour, and with its publications give voice to, an increasingly erudite and cultured bourgeoisie, it thought of itself as possessing a very special kind of stake in the establishment. At that time, and in the wake of the Romantic movement, artists and literati tended to consider their skills and insights as uniquely qualifying them to be custodians of the human spirit. The great majority of writers were opposed to liberal reform, seeing in the kinds of changes proposed a despiritualization of society, the road to institutionalized philistinism or worse. So while not all estate owners, bureaucrats, or even clergymen may have had scruples about offending the king or have been opposed in principle to the rise of critical journalism, influential men of letters were practically unanimous in their scepticism towards such changes.

Of course, an aspiring writer like Kierkegaard might oppose the reforms simply because his mentors did, since these were the people whose approval he needed if there was to be any chance of becoming one of their successors. In December of the previous year Kierkegaard had already published a brief article which seemed mainly designed to find favour with the influential coterie around one Johan Ludvig Heiberg and his wife, Johanne Luise Heiberg (née Hanne Pätges), Denmark's outstanding actress. But many would expect the young Kierkegaard, with his well-known literary leanings, to take the side of the conservatives anyway. If some people, like Ostermann, thought him likely to do that simply because someone had defended the opposite view, others might think that this aesthetically inclined young man would, if for nothing else, use the opportunity to distance himself from the squalid political fray now building up inside the walls of the Student Union, and help in that way to restore the balance in favour of art and philosophy, that is to say culture rather than politics.

As it turned out, Kierkegaard's maiden speech offered him his own first real entry into journalism, and it was this that opened for him the doors to Copenhagen's literary coteries.

Kierkegaard undoubtedly did have his mentors. One of them was Poul Martin Møller, whose name we have already heard. But among Copenhagen's cultural leaders there were two he held in especially high regard: Heiberg and Bishop Mynster. The influence of Mynster, perhaps Denmark's most impressive cultural figure at the time, went back to Kierkegaard's childhood and is linked with his relationship to his father, to which we will return. But it was Heiberg who dominated the *literary* scene. Even a writer who had misgivings about the salons and their predominantly conservative influence would hope to win Heiberg's professional approval, for Heiberg also edited and owned the most influential literary and philosophical journals.

Both before and after he had access to those coteries, Kierkegaard does appear privately to have despised them. He had recently penned his misgivings about the salon system in a now-famous diary dated the summer previous to the talk in the Union. The diary suggests that the young Kierkegaard had a darker and deeper side that he was unwilling or simply unable to reveal to his contemporaries. In a vein that owes much to the influences of his father and Mynster, he writes in the diary of the need to 'fence his individuality about' and to avoid the 'spiritual laziness' of those who 'live on the crumbs that fall from other people's tables'.[14] The style of the diary, however, whatever the source of the sentiments, is that of an aspiring writer self-consciously flexing his literary muscles, perhaps in the hope of eventually winning the plaudits of a Heiberg.

How did the talk go? Ostermann recalled that it was 'rather heavy going' but nevertheless 'bore the hallmark of [Kierkegaard's] unique intellectual talents'. It was also received 'with great applause'.[15]

What were they applauding? Or, perhaps the first question, who applauded? Were they, conservatives and liberals alike, simply appreciating the anticipated display of wit and erudition? Since, as Ostermann himself points out, only a few trend-setters in the Union at the time 'were seized by the idea',[16] that is to say, the liberal constitutional ideal, was the applause perhaps that of a predominantly conservative majority that felt itself vindicated by Kierkegaard's display on its behalf?

Whatever the case, many who thought Kierkegaard an effete intellectual and aesthete must have been surprised at how down-to-earth his text was. Indeed, it appeared that its main purpose was to bring certain facts to light, facts about the recent journalistic past, facts which indicated how misleading Ostermann's optimistic claims for the liberal press had been a fortnight earlier. This aesthete had done his home-work. He also seems to have had an 'idea' of his own, about facing the facts and not obscuring them by putting them in a false light. Indeed, bringing facts to light, or rather bringing light to the facts, provides both the talk's opening motif and its title: 'Our Journal Literature: A Study of Nature in the Light of Midday.'[17]

The ideals politicians oppose to the established order are, he says, unreal because untried. Not only that, they are also treated as though they were growth points whose unquestioned assistance to progress can be prevented only by external factors, including tradition itself, or complacency. So instead of waiting to see how a new idea actually works, one 'dwells on its first entrance on the world-scene . . . [and] wants people from East and West to come and worship it in its swaddling clothes'. Further anticipating a later habit of scriptural allusion, he says there is wishful thinking in this, a factual grain of mustard seed being made into a 'mighty tree'.[18] It's the same, he says, as the way in which early morning light is preferred by landscape painters because at that time the play of light and shadow picks out nothing in particular and thereby imparts an 'especially favourable overall impression'.[19] To see the facts for what they are, you need to expose them to the light of noon.

In a climate of opinion which sees everything moving inexorably forward Kierkegaard thinks it would be salutary for each person to stop 'the wheel of evolution' long enough to see how much progress has really been made, and to look for any 'grit or whatever' that may have got into the machinery to make it less than we suppose.[20] Two aspects of liberal politics in particular he finds particularly misleading. One is the illusory picture generated by a single party name, since it conceals all the 'innumerable nuances' of opinion really guiding the 'rather hectic' reform effort.[21] And it was of course true in Denmark as elsewhere that the liberal movement, just like the gradually coalescing conservative opposition, embraced a variety of positions. There is also a comment on the unhealthy nature of party programmes: 'rather than a natural and healthy life, [such] ready-made confessions signal one of life's final stages.'[22]

There follows a historical 'recapitulation' of the liberal press's recent activity, Kierkegaard acknowledging in the margin of the manuscript that this was partly written before he received Ostermann's manuscript, as if he had been looking for this opportunity to speak up on the subject.[23] It begins by criticizing Ostermann for identifying the founding of a newspaper in 1831 as the opening of the current campaign. Kierkegaard says this paper did not actually oppose the status quo but was 'on the whole satisfied with the existing constitution'. All that it did was to 'censure alleged illegal conduct on the part of individual state functionaries'. He could recall finding 'in [no] single paper of that kind an attack on any significant organ of the body of state, on the system itself rather than its abuse by some concrete individual'.[24] As for liberal journalism proper, that was of a more recent origin and due to several factors to which Kierkegaard now proceeds to draw his audience's attention, foremost among them the continuing influence of the July Revolution of 1830 in Paris. Comparing it to the bloody events of 1789, Kierkegaard calls it 'a successful operation carried out by an experienced surgeon'.[25] Such recent facts were of course too familiar to his audience for Kierkegaard to have to detail them. But it is interesting for us that the 1834 law establishing the Regional Parliaments both was prompted in part by the precedent of the July Revolution and also set in motion the political events which provided the context for Kierkegaard's talk.

According to Kierkegaard, Ostermann had presented the immediate events that led to the founding of the Free Press Society in a way that made the liberal papers sound as if in the circumstances they had made an effective bid for freedom from censorship. Kierkegaard, for his part, claims this was far from being so: 'The Government and the Liberals . . . stood opposite each other like two institutions which in view of the July Revolution had much to say to each other but didn't quite know how to begin', but it was 'the Government that broke the silence'.[26] According to commentators Kierkegaard was right in this; a wary government had taken precautions to stave off any possible signs of the insurrection it feared. The conflict started with a number of ordinances which had begun to appear even before the July Revolution, indeed as long before as 1789, in the wake of the French Revolution, when an edict had been issued allowing individuals to be sentenced to lifelong censorship.[27]

Kierkegaard points out that the liberal press was not really engaged in an *action* against the government at all but simply reacting seriatim to a well-ordered system of defence.[28] Certainly, the liberal press could be outspoken 'at least in its news pages', but this was 'petty irritation' or 'fuss', a mere 'fitful fumbling'. Real action requires 'calm circumspection'. The way to reach an intended destination is not to wake up en route and try to follow the complicated directions of a local peasant; circumspection requires that 'you first drive to the village nearest and there inquire the way to the next, and so on'. In any 'new development' your eye must be constantly on the compass, and although 'development and progress in other nations can help a lot and teach us many a rule of caution . . . remember it is no good travelling in Zealand with a map of France'.[29]

It was far, however, from Kierkegaard's intention to encourage the liberals to do better – to become more organized, pay attention to detail and so on. Even less was he saying what he himself would do if asked to organize a political defence of the status quo. But what then was the point of the criticism? The question was one that, as we shall see, kept arising in the aftermath. But some inklings appear in a rather curious passage placed at the beginning of the section on the 'fumbling' of the liberal press and prefixed to comments on the newspaper Kierkegaard mainly examines, *Kjøbenhavnsposten* (Copenhagen's Post).[30] His criticism of it is that it lacks unity. To illustrate the point he draws on a favourite metaphor. Physics and higher mathematics had been among Kierkegaard's strongest subjects in the first-year examinations, and he frequently uses astrophysical analogies to delineate relations of unity and disunity. In the diary from the summer, for instance, he had written: 'A person would no more want to decide the externals first and the fundamentals afterwards than a heavenly body about to form itself would decide first of all about its surface, about which bodies it should turn its light side to and to which its dark side, without first letting the harmony of centrifugal and centripetal forces bring it into being and letting the rest develop by itself.'[31]

Heavenly bodies are formed of gaseous clouds, and *Kjøbenhavnsposten*'s 'lack of unity' is referred to as a failure of such to be 'formed through the harmony of centrifugal and centripetal forces combined with the rotation around an axis'.[32]

Kjøbenhavnsposten strikes me as like a fog mass of that kind, but one whose planetary existence a harmony of centrifugal and centripetal forces combined with spin hasn't yet realized. We are not surprised then that, just as earlier on there has been a certain instability in the articles as the centrifugal and centripetal tendencies predominated in turn, so too there has recently been a preponderance of the centrifugal tendency. I need hardly point out that by the axis around which the planet rotates I understand a competent editor, and by the centrifugal and centripetal tendencies what have hitherto been given such appealing popular party names as liberal and conservative tendencies. That *Kjøbenhavnsposten* has lately become somewhat more unified, and that the centre of our political solar system, the Roskilde Estates, has exerted some gravitational force upon it, helping it find its orbit and contributing to the regulation of its course, and that the centrifugal force on the other hand, which was used to having control has now done its best to keep it, is natural enough and surely can't be denied either. But since, as I said, the harmony of the forces has still to come about, as well as the rotation about the axis, it can easily risk being drawn into another solar system, since what to our solar system looks like the centrifugal tendency in another must appear centripetal.[33]

The priority of fundamentals over externals is expressed in another metaphor, this time one which, if they didn't already know, would have betrayed to Kierkegaard's audience his philosophic allegiance. In what to us may seem just a curious insertion, the talk refers suddenly to a 'formal striving'. It is, he says (and the emphasis is his own), '*the whole endeavour in our time*'.

It is what by eschewing the pleasurable led us to stress symmetrical beauty in everyday life, to favour convention instead of cordiality. It is the whole effort well enough described by – to borrow another author's words – Fichte's and the other philosophers' attempts with sharp minds to construct systems and Robespierre's attempt to do the same with the guillotine; it is what we meet in the flowing butterfly-light verses of our poets and in Auber's music; and it is this, finally, which in the world of politics provokes the many revolutions.[34]

Ostensibly these remarks identify Kierkegaard as a late-comer Romantic on the side of those who accused the Enlightenment of deliberately eschewing emotion. Kierkegaard, like Hamann, Burke, and so many others before him, is siding with 'content' over form. But as Kierkegaard explains it, it is not a question of content versus form – he has nothing against this 'whole endeavour to keep hold of form', in fact, he is all for it – it is a question rather of where form comes from. It must not come from outside. In the Hegelian language that had caught on in Copenhagen, form is 'the medium in which we have the idea', and 'the idea decides the form, not form the idea'. The reading is made more complicated by the fact that if, as is plausible, the 'other' author cited here is one of the key Romantic figures Kierkegaard had been assiduously reading, their views on Robespierre had initially been very positive. Just like the Marxists later, Robespierre had argued that since the conditions of rationality did not exist, the obstacles to them must be swept aside. Both Friedrich Schlegel (1772–1829) and Novalis (Friedrich Leopold Freiherr von Hardenberg, 1772–1801) praised Robespierre's passionate and consistent dedication to the ideal of freedom, and both were engrossed in Fichte's idealism, though they later criticized the Terror on the one hand and Fichte's one-sided intellectualism on the other.[35] The conclusion we might draw is that by this time Kierkegaard's own views accorded with these criticisms, and that could well be the result of a Hegelian influence. As those familiar with Hegel realize, the idea that decides the form is something that develops in time. The point would not have been lost on liberal politicians who wanted to impress a form on events rather than let events develop their own form in the crucible of experience.

The jargon of the 'idea' persists in Kierkegaard, and it is as well to remark briefly on its gist and origins. The 'idea' (the term is often capitalized in translation) is the notion of a fulfilment that motivates and guides theoretical and practical activity. In Hegel it is the notion of an autonomous self-generating system, or an ideal of the unity of all cognitive experience, perhaps even a kind of image or conception of the latter, which for Hegelians can be discerned at work, under its own steam as it were, in the course of history.[36] In Kant the 'idea' can be said, roughly speaking, to have been given the limited status of the empty notion of completeness required to make sense of our necessarily incomplete cognitive, moral, and political projects, ideals we cannot help holding before us but can never realize. In Hegel they become something our activities actually embody. Hegel's 'idea' may be thought of as the Platonic Eidos. Instead of remaining invisibly transcendent it actually reveals itself in Logos, materializing in the historical development of thought and of the world towards an absolute unity of the two.

It will be recalled that Ostermann had referred to the 'idea' in saying that in the trend-setting group in the Student Union at that time only a few individuals were 'seized by it'. He would mean the 'idea' in a political guise, some image or conception of a properly democratic and self-sustaining society for instance, or of some other form of social or political unity. But from Kierkegaard's position this application of the 'idea' would involve a twofold distortion. First, instead of being embodied in our activities, it has become a plan or blueprint used consciously to shape those activities. Second, to think of the 'idea' in political terms is to rip it from its true origins, which are not political but aesthetic.

One doesn't forget that the form, for instance in the poetic genius's immediate standpoint, is nothing other than the idea's coming into being in the world, and that reflection's part is no more than to examine whether the idea has also received the appropriate form. One recalls constantly that it isn't through form one receives life but through life receives form.[37]

To anyone in Kierkegaard's audience unaware of his allegiance to the 'opposite camp', these two sentences would instantly place him there. The first sentence says that poetic experience provides access to the 'idea'. The 'immediacy' of the poetic genius's standpoint is the fact that from it things are grasped not in terms of reflective notions, concepts, theories, or principles, or of everyday, scientific, or metaphysical classifications, that is to say, not in terms of what they have or do not have in common with other things, but in terms of the way they strike someone specially equipped to 'shape' experience aesthetically. Being able to shape experience in that way is to have access to the 'idea', but in aesthetic form. Artistic experience (and that is not necessarily just the experience of art or of the artist) is the way in which the 'idea' first manifests itself. The second sentence is a distant anticipation of the existentialist slogan that existence precedes essence, except that for

Hegelians essence is not the free creation of human activity but the sense or coherence that human life can be seen to acquire in retrospect. For the record, although at present he does not develop the thought, Kierkegaard also remarks: 'as for life itself one must remember that it is not something abstract but something extremely individual.'[38]

The main proponent of this kind of view in Copenhagen at the time was Heiberg. A man of prodigious enterprise and ability, he was the son of a well-known dramatic poet and satirist who after incurring the government's wrath was living in permanent exile at this time in Paris. Heiberg's mother, also a writer, had early remarried and brought up her son in close contact with literary circles. Heiberg began his career as an academic, teaching Danish language, literature, and mythology at the University of Kiel, still considered a Danish institution in spite of the fact noted earlier that Holstein, though still a Danish duchy, had since the Vienna Treaty of 1815 been incorporated into the German Confederation. It was during his appointment there that Heiberg travelled one summer to Berlin to assimilate as much as he could of the Hegelian philosophy. He attended Hegel's lectures, was welcomed by the famous man, and at the lectures met several younger thinkers who were later to become influential Hegelians. This was in 1824. Already by December Heiberg had written a treatise 'On Human Freedom on the Occasion of the Latest Disputes on This Subject' (*Om den menneskelige Frihed. I Anledning af de nyeste Stridigheder over denne Gjenstand* [1824]) employing the Hegelian method to resolve a debate on the free will/materialism issue. The following year he wrote 'Elements of a System of Aesthetics as Speculative Science' (*Grundlinien zum System der Ästhetik als speculativer Wissenschaft* [1825]), but dissatisfied with the result withheld it from publication. Unhappy in general with Kiel, Heiberg returned to Copenhagen in 1825 and wrote a second short treatise in German, this time published, on 'Contingency Regarded from the Point of View of Logic' (*Der Zufall aus dem Gesichtspunkte der Logik betrachtet* [1825]). Probably he was angling for a position in Germany, but once his skills both as translator and writer of vaudeville were appreciated he turned professional dramatist and critic in Copenhagen. He also became director of the Royal Danish Theatre, and an editor and publisher. Heiberg later developed an intense interest in astronomy, and among his many accomplishments he was a competent guitar-player. It is a remarkable fact that the unpublished treatise on aesthetics was written six years before the (posthumous) publication of Hegel's *Lectures on Aesthetics*, the first volume of which appeared the very year of Kierkegaard's public debut. Several pieces on aesthetics published in the thirties by Heiberg had attracted the young Kierkegaard's admiring attention. Heiberg, in a way that owed much to Hegel, set genres in order according to a dialectic of immediacy and reflection. Some art forms accentuate immediacy, others reflection. By 'dialectic' is meant, first, the fact that any art form is definable by the degree to which, given two defining factors, the one factor excludes the other, and second, that there is a progression in favour of the degree to which the factor of reflection is not excluded.[39] Music, containing no reflection, is the purest form of immediate sensuous experience, while poetry and written art, including drama, provide progressively successful syntheses of reflection and immediacy. Within drama itself, comedy (though in a wider sense than is commonly adopted today) outstrips tragedy because it puts dialogue before monologue and because the underlying irony in comedy means that the limitations that immediacy and reflection impose on each other in art have finally surfaced (come to reflection) and are seen for what they are.

Two years previous to Kierkegaard's talk Heiberg had also published a monograph entitled *On the Significance of Philosophy for the Present Time* (*Om Philosophiens Betydning for den nuværende Tid* [1833]). Plainly and elegantly written for a wide public, this work presented Hegelian philosophy as alone capable of uniting the disparate factors in modern life and society. It presents what is perhaps the first stereotype of Hegel's philosophy as a general theory of development, with its forward movement provided by successive failures of content (life as it becomes more diversified) to be contained in a current (insufficiently embracing) form which then 'explodes', clearing the way for something richer and more unified. Forms here are expressions of the 'Eternal Idea', and Heiberg reminds his readers that art and religion are only preliminary expressions of the Idea.

Two features of Heiberg's aesthetic views are especially interesting. One of them he would no doubt willingly acknowledge. It is that, on these views and as a consummate writer of vaudeville, Heiberg's own position on the aesthetic spectrum should give him insight into the ultimate inadequacy of artistic expression. For an artist that may seem a disconcerting realization, but to a man of true genius it might be just what qualifies him to speak on behalf of the expressive medium in which the idea can indeed find its adequate expression, namely philosophy. Whatever his views on his own qualifications, and they were hardly modest, that is what Heiberg did. What he said in his book was that the age requires philosophy. Philosophy is 'nothing but knowledge of the eternal or the speculative idea, reason, truth, whose various expressions all designate the same substance'.[40] In a comment that reveals an undercurrent of anxiety in a society in a state of unrest and about to burst the boundaries of its own traditional forms, Heiberg writes:

It is not as one often imagines the growing population, so-called overpopulation, that will be too great for the boundaries of the establishment, since individuals simply as such, i.e. in isolation and not acting *en masse*, are nonentities in the Constitution and have absolutely no place in it. The danger for the established form is overpopulation in the world of ideas, for it is the ideas that found each form, and it is also only they that are able to explode it.[41]

There is an emphatic elitism in Heiberg's thought. Not only is it the case that not everyone can be a philosopher, but also not all philosophies express knowledge of the eternal or speculative idea. The same goes for art and religion. Indeed, in any age, art, religion, and philosophy express only the form of that age's appropriation of the 'idea'. They are that age's idea of itself. For instance, if any work speaks only to the individual and not to the age, that means that it fails to express the age's own conception of itself and is therefore in a way decadent. Art that is true to its age is the age speaking to itself. 'The plastic and literary arts, religion, and philosophy . . . do not add to our property but they open our eyes to what is already there.' There is, however, a progressive alternative. 'Mankind', says Heiberg,

nevertheless has its representatives, namely individuals in whom consciousness is aroused to the higher clarity while in the mass of people it is still more or less slumbering. We call these representatives artists, poets, teachers of religion, philosophers; we also call them teachers and educators of mankind, which is truly what they are, but not in virtue of themselves; what makes them so is their presenting the mirror in which mankind sees itself and becomes conscious of itself as its own object. The spirit is not something they get from themselves but from God, but God's spirit is mankind's. We just had to be Christians, otherwise we would split apart what Christ has united and thereby return to the final crisis of the disintegrated Roman religion.[42]

What Heiberg might not have been so willing to acknowledge about his views on philosophy is how profoundly influenced they are by an aesthetic paradigm. The same applies to the general theory of social and cultural development. The image of ages exploding their forms is one he himself employed as an artist; the artist is someone who finds, through effort, the effortless way to express something. Heiberg was himself a past master of the art that conceals art, a master manipulator of form and content. But it can be tempting to see his pronouncements on philosophy and its unifying role less as insights gained from the self-conscious end of the spectrum of artistic experience and expression – through an access privileged as it were by reflection – than as the typical statements of a person whose cognitive access to the world is inescapably aesthetic. The notion of an ultimate totality may itself be simply an aesthetic notion, equally so the philosophy that is conceived as being knowledge of it. Of course, an idea of such knowledge so closely allied to aesthetic experience makes it all the easier for the artist to cast himself in the role of mankind's special representative.

Our question must be whether, at the time, Kierkegaard thought in this way too. He does seem, like Heiberg, to stress the importance of poetic expression and experience. For Heiberg, however, to say that from the standpoint of the poetic genius form is the idea's entry into the world implies that artistic experience is necessary for any grasp of the way in which the idea, at the level of philosophy, is going to unite mankind. In other words, the poetic genius is responsible to mankind as occupying the vantage-point from which alone the idea can *first* enter human experience. Poetic experience, in the wide sense of *poesis*, pro-vides the person capable of this kind of experience or insight with a form of privileged access to the truth of the Eternal Idea at least under the form of the Aesthetic.[43] Heiberg believed that, having a responsibil-ity to the less-endowed, poetic geniuses also have the right to be sup-ported in the positions from which they can exercise that responsibility.

But Kierkegaard says only that form, 'for instance', in the poetic genius's immediate standpoint, is 'the idea's coming into being in the world'. This could be taken to mean that what anyone at all, poetic genius or not, should look to if they wish to appropriate the idea is first and foremost their ability to cultivate *in their own lives* the unity given by form. To do this they do not have to be poets, but life itself becomes a work of art, the art of developing a form and unity through a harmony of conflicting forces, forces without which there would be no unity and no (human) life. What is interesting here is that the passage indicates that Kierkegaard seems already to have some interest in developing a constructive notion of personal unity based on aesthetic categories, but in a sense of 'aesthetic' that is not the prerogative exclusively of the artist. It is of course relevant in this respect to repeat that the notion of unity can itself be considered in a broad sense to be an aesthetic category. So in referring to 'the individual life' as the point of entry for that form in which the idea provides the unifying shape, Kierkegaard is already departing very radically from the orthodox Heibergian position which says that unity is provided, as one might say, by the 'idea' in the form of Knowledge or Reason. Indeed, the notion that life is the locus of the 'idea', when taken together with the observation that 'life itself is not something abstract but something extremely individual', suggests a point of view the polar opposite of Heiberg's. In the next chapter we shall see in this the influence of two of Kierkegaard's philosophy teachers.

To return, then, to the topic of Kierkegaard's talk, in order to find where in cultural life the 'idea' is actually embodied you will have to look to its 'cordial' rather than to its 'conventional' manifestations, perhaps in dramatic art and religious practices (though in due course Kierkegaard drove an increasingly sharp wedge between these, the church in the end becoming mere theatre) but also in cordial (in the sense of heartfelt but not necessarily conciliatory) human relations. Form, at least, cannot be superimposed but has to be drawn from the resources of life as one finds it. The individual cannot even impose it on himself. Kierkegaard offers the example of someone infatuated with the Greek way of life who then has a house built and kept in the Greek style. Not having tried himself in this lifestyle, or put it to the test as a viable form of development, he may drop it at any time and just as soon prefer something else. '[J]ust as a leap backward is wrong (something the age is inclined on the whole to acknowledge), so also is a leap forward wrong – both of them because a natural development does not proceed by leaps, and life's earnestness will ironize every such experiment, even if for the moment it succeeds.'[44]

In whatever way Kierkegaard's audience took this, today the advice not to leap forward will surprise many in an author now either applauded or castigated almost universally for advocating just that. On the other hand, the leap (*Spring*) is probably one of the least well understood aspects of Kierkegaard's thought. Far from being the irrational appropriation of a life-view already equipped with its 'party programme' or confession of faith, it may prove to be something quite different – more like the resolute choice needed to stay on course when the 'idea' can no longer be seen to embrace life in the form of Thought or Reason. Here, affirming or, better, manifesting the 'idea' would require that the individual reaffirm it from a vantage-point from which (as reflection and its limitations enter reflection, as one might say) it is clear that fulfilment can no longer depend on human cognitive powers or even, ultimately, be measured by human standards. But that is to anticipate.

Ostermann was right in predicting that Kierkegaard would not respond directly to the issue of the press's freedom, though he does mention it. Ending on a relatively conciliatory note, Kierkegaard commends *Fædrelandet* for having survived the crisis, which included the prosecution of its founder-editor for infringing the government's ordinances. Recently, Kierkegaard even allows, this newspaper has proved itself 'strong and sound'. With a good sense of direction under a forceful editor it 'appears to have grasped what I am tempted to call the "myth" of the struggle for freedom of the press in this land'. From which, he concludes, 'one learns among other things to look a little more closely at what press freedom one already has before raising the alarm'.[45]

The central theme of unity informing Kierkegaard's criticism should nevertheless not be lost sight of. It is significant that already at this stage Kierkegaard is judging a corporate entity as he would an individual, including himself. Recall that the passage on 'formal striving' is prefixed to his critical comments on *Kjøbenhavnsposten*, the paper he most liked to ridicule. Achieving form in the proper sense is to manifest however inadequately the unity that belongs to the 'idea', that is, the unity embodied in some goal of self-fulfilment conceived in terms of harmony and a centre. A disunited person, just as a disunited newspaper, or vice versa, by acting only in a piecemeal manner really doesn't act at all, since it merely re-acts to whatever relevant situation it comes upon. It simply copes, assuming a facade that gives the impression it is doing more by having its readers grasp these situations as though they were all of a kind, in this case a struggle for freedom of the press.

Part of Kierkegaard's talk is designed to show that things in Denmark are not as bad as the liberal press has made them appear, and of course very different from the situation in Paris in July 1830. Another, whether or not by design, suggests that the locus of unity in sociopolitical as well as in any other humanly relevant terms is the individual. But we find no direct attack on politics itself. That came later, as the concept of individual self-conscious spirit crystallized in his mind in a later encounter with Hegelians.

With the benefit of hindsight we may nevertheless see in the maiden speech signs of Kierkegaard's maturity. The vision of the individual life as the centre of moral growth, however sketchily presented, seems already firmly rooted. So is the liking for polemic and the eye for an opponent's faults. Kierkegaard's talk must have appeared to many, including Ostermann, to have been unduly aggressive given the balanced nature of the paper it was attacking. Whether or how far their friendship survived the exchange is unclear. What is clear is that, true to form, Kierkegaard had found in Ostermann's measured lecture an opportunity to exercise an uncanny knack for finding, some might say creating, weaknesses in an opponent's text and above all opportunities to score points.[46] Listening as they were to someone they considered a mere aesthete, many in Kierkegaard's audience may have missed the underlying vision concealed in a few oddly inserted remarks. In that case they would have failed to see in what sense Kierkegaard might with better justification be called an 'aesthete'. Not in the sense of the frivolous *flaneur* behind whose mask Kierkegaard even then liked to conceal his more serious thoughts, but in the sense of a person envisaging a conception of human fulfilment based in individual experience and the resources already at one's disposal rather than in 'heady' ideas and new beginnings.

But for Kierkegaard himself at the time, with no sense of what hindsight would later reveal, these notions were of secondary importance. The main thing was that he had successfully seized an opportunity to make himself heard. The response to his talk to the Student Union was clearly to his satisfaction, and it whetted his appetite. One might even say he now tasted blood. The earlier article from just over a year before had no direct relevance for the burning political issue of the time, but in spite of the fact that the talk had avoided it, what Kierkegaard had to say on the liberal press itself placed him squarely in the fray. His real target was not Ostermann but the liberal elite. Chief among these was a seasoned campaigner named Orla Lehmann, the foremost student spokesman for liberalism of the day and a future leader of the Liberal Party.

During the following February and March Kierkegaard published four small articles in one of Heiberg's papers, *Kjøbenhavns flyvende Post* (Copenhagen's Flying Post, or just *Flyveposten* [Flying Post]). The first of these, published early in the new year, on 18 February, was a reply to an article in *Kjøbenhavnsposten* on 12 February. This had resumed some of Ostermann's points but with greater bite and a more skilful rhetoric. If its author had not been present at Kierkegaard's talk it had certainly come to his ears. Speaking directly to Kierkegaard's criticism of the politicians' predilection for dawns, the article wrote enthusiastically of the 'dawn of the people's freedom', of the 'spirit of reform', and of the need of society itself if it is to 'make strides towards a greater fulfilment', as much as of individuals, to recognize its own faults.[47] These faults are identified as an idyllic sentimentalism and a complacent nationalism 'worlds apart from true patriotism'. One must do away with 'philistinism and egoism' and face the hard struggle. Implicitly conceding that he was replying to Kierkegaard's talk, the author admitted that the press had not always done the right or required thing, but then 'everyone makes mistakes', so who should reasonably expect otherwise?[48]

The article, anonymous, was in fact written by Lehmann, who had spent a year in Germany and with his knowledge and incisive, popular style had done much on his return the previous year to strengthen and focus the liberal opposition. Not least in the Student Union, but also because he had been appointed one of *Kjøbenhavnsposten*'s two political editors, Lehmann was able to provide this opposition with a properly public forum.[49]

Replying anonymously on 18 February in *Flyvende Post* under the heading '*Kjøbenhavnposten*'s Dawn Observations in No. 43', Kierkegaard opens by saying that this wasn't the first time the newspaper had proclaimed that 'day was still to dawn'. By painting a black enough background anyone can make the present look alive. For himself, he has never detected the spirit of reform in that particular newspaper's pages, and 'once the sun really does rise' what you will see is the newspaper's entire staff standing there like the guests in Auerbach's cellar in Goethe's *Faust*, holding each other's noses and believing they are dressing vines.[50]

This gives some indication of the sharper tone adopted by Kierke-gaard against his chosen target. There is no attempt here to introduce or defend a view, let alone to take up the issue of censorship – just plain polemics and an exercise in the art of scoring points. Signed 'B', the article was so well written that the author of an unsigned article in another paper (*Statsvennen* [Friend of the State]) assumed that Heiberg himself had written it: 'Heiberg has written plenty of witty pieces but hardly anything better than that article in the *Flyvende Post*.' Kierke-gaard's favourite teacher, the Poul Møller of whom we have heard, made the same assumption and, on seeing Heiberg in the street, started after him to tell him it was the best piece that had been written since the *Flyvende Post* had become political. But before catching up with Heiberg he ran into Kierkegaard's friend and fellow student Emil Boe-sen, who was able to tell him that Kierkegaard had been the author.[51]

There followed three other articles. In March, again in *Flyvende Post*, Kierkegaard wrote a two-part response to an article by Johannes Hage, a cofounder of *Fædrelandet* and now its sole editor, following the pros-ecution of its other cofounder, C. N. David. Anonymity and pseudo-nymity were seldom effective disguises, but there was a convention that one didn't acknowledge another author's real identity until the author in question owned up to his work. Although Kierkegaard had probably known that Hage was the author, he only acknowledged this after Lehmann in a later article, and in an infringement of the practice which indicates something of Lehmann's position, had revealed the fact on Hage's behalf. Hage's article appeared on 4 March in *Fædrelandet* under the title 'On *Flyvende Post*'s Polemic'.[52] It took the conservative paper to task for playing on words and treating the serious issues *Kjøbenshavnsposten* had brought to the fore simply as opportunities for ridicule and parody. Although the article deals with several of *Flyvende Post*'s recent articles it focuses particularly on B's reply to Lehmann's 'dawn' article. It objects particularly to the 'shameless swipe' at *Kjøbenhavnsposten*'s editor, who had been described as 'in some ways too good' for the job, seeing that the staff of that paper would really prefer a 'nonentity'.

Kierkegaard's two-part response, 'On *Fædrelandet*'s Polemic', ap-peared on 12 and 15 March. Again above the signature 'B', it expresses surprise that *Fædrelandet*, which had stayed away from polemics for a time, should now enter the fray, albeit 'stutteringly'.[53] Not only that, its article was a response to an attack directed explicitly at *Kjøbenhavnsposten*, a paper that had always dismissed *Flyvende Post*'s attacks on it as 'shallow and ignorant'. B sets the scene for his reply by portraying the whole article as contrived dramatics. Opening in a 'calmly didactic tone' assisted by some 'passable minor witticisms', it then 'raises itself to the highest pitch of a piteous moralizing's most piercing and heart-rending falsetto', only, and 'as though weakened by this great explosion of energy', to 'calm noticeably down' and 'look down forgivingly' on the author of the pieces 'on the so-called liberal journalists'. It had ended by saying that 'in future it won't bother to reply'. Returning in his comments to *Kjøbenhavnsposten*'s account of the recent past, which he accuses the paper of still holding onto in the face of all (his) attempts to rectify the picture, and to the charge that B is no 'friend of the truth', Kierkegaard ironically admits that it is a tough charge to face given that newspaper's well known partiality for the facts. He accuses *Fædrelandet* of not mentioning the 'confusion' about past events due to *Kjøbenhavnsposten*'s 'squint-eyed' view of things, as had been pointed out in B's first article. Although Lehmann's 'dawn' article to which B had first responded is described by *Fædrelandet* as 'well written', in fact it merely maintained the confusion; anyone could see it was just 'a collection of contradictions all looking up at each other in surprise and wondering what brought them together'. B attacks the liberal account given in *Fædrelandet* as not just 'badly expressed' but 'badly thought'.

Having decided where credit and blame lay with the two main liberal newspapers regarding the pictures they draw of the immediate past and their respective places in it, Kierkegaard then proceeds in the second part to comment on his alleged 'swipe' at *Kjøbenhavnsposten*'s editor, and also on *Fædrelandet*'s defence of the editor. Again the point is made that the undoubted virtues of the man in question make him unsuited as editor for what, in the earlier article, B had already referred to as 'anonymous reformers' who, unlike Moses, Luther, and Daniel O'Connell,[54] need only someone they can have 'hung up in their stead'. In the same article, he recalls, he summarized the whole exchange as an 'annual meeting of postulates' so confused that even 'if we walked blindfold with a stick' we would still 'shatter one china vase of idiocy after another'. Finally, he discusses *Fædrelandet*'s ethics, accusing the liberals, who so pride themselves on their intelligence, of hypocritical moralizing and failing to see that they are guilty of the very sin for which they criticize *Flyvende Post*, namely, ascribing evil motives to opponents. To convey how little he thinks *Fædrelandet*'s objections are worth, B ends by pointing out that one of the two printer's errors *Fædrelandet* had found in his article was in fact not a printing but a linguistic error.

This brought Lehmann into the open. In a 'Reply to *Flyveposten*'s Mr B,' in *Kjøbenhavnsposten* on 31 March and signed by himself, he begins in a patronizing tone by welcoming opposition to the liberal press as a corrective but also as an opportunity for sharpening its own criticism of the government. Lehmann then accuses Heiberg's *Flyveposten* of mere bickering and showing no interest in the facts. He refers again to his previous attempt to characterize the past, rehearsing his account but now extending it backwards to cover the last three decades of the previous century. Lehmann wonders why Mr B thinks his account had been one-sided and unfair. He admits much more might have been said about and in praise of Danish society and culture during the last decades, but that had not been part of his original article's intention. Finding nothing in Mr B's reply to Hage to suggest genuine disagreement, Lehmann proposes that it all boils down to a complaint about the 'form' in which the papers have presented the 'main idea', really just 'a matter of taste'.[55] Also, Lehmann thinks it odd that Mr B, to whom he concedes an 'unmistakable talent for strong words and bold images', should have complained about his own polemical style. It is true that the Danish reform movement, as was pointed out, had found no O'Connell, let alone a Luther or a Moses, but he takes exception to Mr B's identifying the reform effort with actual reformers and these in turn with the editor and staff of a single newspaper. The dawn of the reform movement, admittedly in its infancy, is to be found in the people. Charismatic figures would in any case be in conflict with the whole tendency of the age, with its 'democratizing of everything, wealth, science, yes, even character'. It is unsurprising, therefore, that 'the sum of material welfare, of insight and energy is now greater than ever before' though not, as it once was, 'all squeezed together in exceptional individuals'. Besides, 'the concept of such exceptionality is always relative, and many of those who were previously elevated high above the crowd would nowadays be lost in the mass'. Lehmann had already admitted that the reform movement still lacked strength, so it must be a misunderstanding on Mr B's part to cite that fact in criticism of the

article. He is still unsure whether he has answered the criticism, since
Mr B's point seems hidden beneath a 'very thick skin'. In fact, Mr B's
contribution looks as if it were nothing but a writing exercise 'in the
humorous style' with no intention to cast light on the facts. Indeed, the
distortions are such that if the author's intelligence were not otherwise
so much in evidence there would be reason to doubt it. Since that is
not possible, is it perhaps his good faith that one should question? This,
however, Lehmann cannot bring himself to do, and he supposes Mr B
has simply wanted to amuse, a harmless enough intention in itself.
Finally, Lehmann offers apologies to his 'honoured adversary' for
having taken so long to reply (to B's first piece against *Kjøbenhavnsposten*
on 18 February); he has had more important things to attend to. Signing
the present article with his own name he hopes will be taken as a 'small
token of politeness', for he understands that it pleases Mr B 'to know
who he is dealing with'. He begs Mr B in return not to 'feel bound to
keep his identity secret', since to him, Lehmann, his opponent's name
is of no concern at all.

Kierkegaard's reply in *Flyvende Post* on 10 April was the first occasion
of his signing any piece with his own name. The article bore the title
'To Mr Orla Lehmann'. In an allusion to an earlier reference by Lehmann to the thundery weather from which the press must take shelter
before sunshine returns, he notes that if you counted the seconds between the lightning and the thunder in this case you would think
Lehmann lived at least as far away as Greenland. He takes up Lehmann's remark that how you present things is just a matter of form and
therefore of taste. Surely Lehmann doesn't think the same about forms
of government? And what about his claim that others than Mr Hage
found the remarks on *Kjøbenhavnsposten*'s editor 'shameful'? Does that
mean a majority decision should decide whether or not they were in
fact shameful? Perhaps that is what Lehmann means by a 'democratized
science'?[56] Kierkegaard then notes that by expanding his historical account Lehmann manages to make the more immediate past look like a
temporary setback instead of a straightforward contrast to the present.
Kierkegaard also makes play with the fact that Lehmann is not only
defending Hage's defence of him but also defending himself directly,
while Kierkegaard is trying to respond to the defence of Hage that
Lehmann is directing at Kierkegaard. He voices the hope that what he
says now will not encourage the rest of *Kjøbenhavnsposten*'s staff to take

up their pens. On the question of the reform movement's identity, he says it is difficult to fix in one's mind the idea of a vigorous age whose individual spokesmen lack vigour. He also reminds Lehmann that he has never claimed that the present age lacked vigour, but had reproached the article only for claiming that a present age lacking vigour was better than its predecessor. 'A bad article in a paper that claims it is reformatory, a bad article which is itself an attempt at reform, is surely *eo ipso* a bad reformatory product.'

Responding to Lehmann's thinly concealed irony about Kierkegaard's real purpose lying under a very thick skin, Kierkegaard examines Lehmann's efforts to let him off the moral hook by ascribing to him a desire simply to amuse. In this he sees an attempt on Lehmann's part – in furtherance presumably of Hage's wise words about lovers of truth – to play 'psychologist and heart-searcher'. To the claim that his interest has not been to inform but to entertain, Kierkegaard replies first that the aim to amuse is not inconsistent with the aim to enlighten, and that an exercise of any kind is in any case part of an attempt to acquire an ability, no less so in the case of humour. But second, suppose his aim had indeed been simply to amuse, what then can be made of Lehmann's remark that 'one can deny a love of truth without having to bring in the author's morals'? That would be perfectly in order if the aim were the innocent one of simple amusement. It is only when amusement is bought at the expense of truth that the question of morals enters. But once that assumption is made, there is no side-stepping the moral issue. Indeed, if it were true of the present case it would be Kierkegaard's immorality, not his morality, that Lehmann was side-stepping. Since Lehmann does think Kierkegaard consciously wanted to amuse at the expense of truth, for he uses the word 'distortions' to characterize his account (the more harmless 'palpable but at times quite amusing biasings' might leave his love of truth unimpugned, but distorting the truth is a serious charge), and has done nothing to vindicate that, Kierkegaard reserves the right to postpone his reply until such time as the charge has been substantiated. And as if that didn't deal with the matter he adds another point: Lehmann says either Kierkegaard's intelligence or else his good faith must be drawn in doubt, but then suggests that he may only have wanted to amuse, in which case his good faith need not be drawn in doubt in spite of the allegedly palpable distortions. Kierkegaard asks whether Lehmann has still other explanations up his sleeve

for not questioning Kierkegaard's sincerity, for instance that Kierkegaard has only wanted to bore his readers. In any case, to maintain his
dilemma he must come up with something better than 'amusement at
the expense of truth'. Lehmann stands, like the 'scholastic [Buridan's]
ass',[57] unable to move in either direction. If Lehmann can't help himself,
Kierkegaard can't help him either. It is not surprising, says Kierkegaard,
that both Lehmann and Hage think he only wants to amuse people, for
his own writing is admittedly a 'slight departure from the formal and
unctuous style one generally finds in *Kjøbenhavnsposten*'. As for Lehmann's saying that he 'has put his name to *these* lines to show me a
little politeness, I put mine for the same reason'. But Lehmann implies
that he has written other lines too: 'I couldn't be better pleased at this
change for what I consider the better – I couldn't be better pleased, I
say, at this change, just as I could not congratulate *Kjøbenhavnsposten*
more on the butterfly that has emerged from its chrysalis.'

This was the climax of an exchange that attracted considerable attention in the late winter of 1835 and the spring of 1836. But it was not its
end. A batch of sharply amusing articles appeared anonymously in May
in a journal called *Humoristiske Intelligentsblade*. They were written by
opponents of Heiberg, and it seems clear from their content that Kierkegaard was now considered a member of the Heiberg entourage. They
included a short comedy in six acts including among its dramatis personae one 'K (born B)', described as 'an opponent and genius withal'.
In June, Kierkegaard published a very brief reply, noting in his journals
that such a long time had elapsed since the publication of his own
articles that they were probably forgotten.[58] In fact, only six weeks
separated the last article and the reply, but possibly feeling now be-
holden to Heiberg, Kierkegaard felt he could do no more without his
mentor's consent, and in early June the Heibergs had left by train for
Paris.[59] However, since these new articles displayed a talent for wit
much nearer Kierkegaard's level than that of either of his erstwhile
opponents, he may have thought it wiser to rest on his laurels. Lehmann
himself, who may well have masterminded this later effort, did not
return to the fray himself; no doubt as an aspiring politician he had
'more important things to attend to'.

Who won the day? Some certainly supposed that Kierkegaard had.
Peter Rørdam, a friend of the family, wrote: 'There has also been a
change in the Student Union. Their chieftain and leader, Lehmann, has

fallen, totally beaten. . . . With him has fallen *Kjøbenhavnsposten* for which he had recently been writing. And the victor is the younger Kierkegaard, who now writes in *Flyvende Post* under the label B.'[60]

If sheer firepower is what counts, the younger Kierkegaard did seem to have carried off the victory, but there may be other considerations. No one concerned with the issues themselves would want to take on an opponent so eager to make apparently well-meaning good sense look like a mess of logical confusions. Besides, in the close combat of the exchange itself Kierkegaard had added nothing new to the discussion, appearing only to revel in each new opportunity to put in the logical boot. So it may be that his opponents felt more frustrated than defeated, though there is a kind of short-term victory in that. Of course, Kierkegaard was not alone in writing in this style. It was, as it still is, a form of 'debate' favoured by intelligent young people. Heiberg himself, who was now not so young, was himself still a proficient performer. Perhaps Kierkegaard's main short-term purpose had been to emulate him; he certainly did enough to win his literary mentor's approval. He may have done too well. The experience seems in any case to have been a formative one for Kierkegaard himself. Not only had he made his mark in Copenhagen's cultural coteries, welcomed as he now was in the Heiberg home itself, even accorded the ultimate honour of being allowed to invite himself to its soirées, he had also established a pattern of humorous polemical writing which would be his hallmark and mainstay for the next twenty years and beyond. It would also drive him to the very edge of society. As the pattern unfolded, Kierkegaard was to carry a point he had made that summer day in his diary one step further. There he had said that one should not live from the crumbs that fall from other people's tables. In the not-very-distant future he would prove himself to be the ungrateful guest at the rich man's table who picks up the crumbs to throw them in the rich man's face.

The Matter with Søren

B Y USUAL RECKONINGS Kierkegaard's undergraduate studies should have been over by the time he read his paper to the Student Union. Had he followed his eight-year older brother Peter Christian's example he would already have graduated in the summer of the previous year. Peter, now well established in Danish academic and theological circles, had, like Søren, taken his high school diploma at seventeen but then passed his theology finals less than four years later. With a reputation as one of the university's brightest graduates, Peter had then left in May 1828 for a study tour which included Berlin, Bonn, Göttingen, Utrecht, Leiden, and Louvain. In 1830 he was in Paris at the time of the July Revolution. Søren, apart from four visits to Berlin, a brief trip to his family roots in Jutland, and a day excursion to Sweden, was to spend his life entirely in and around Copenhagen. Peter was big and strong and hiked in northern Sweden; Søren was slight and stooped – he may have damaged his back in a fall at school. Peter's skills as a speaker had earned him in Germany the title of 'devil debater from the North' (*Der Disputierteufel aus dem Norden*). Søren spoke clearly but his voice did not carry, and his talk to the Union was the closest he came to conducting a debate in person. Peter returned home at the end of September 1830 with a doctorate, having successfully defended his dissertation (*De notione atque turpitudine mendacii commentatio* [On the Concept and Wickedness of Lying]) in Göttingen in 1829. When Søren gave his talk on that late November day in 1835, almost five years were to pass before he even took his finals.

What was the matter with Søren? The answer may invite us to revise the question. One not insignificant circumstance was the seemingly innocuous fact that at the time of the talk Kierkegaard was still living in the family home, 2 Nytorv, in the centre of Copenhagen. He shared the house with two older Kierkegaards, the already-successful Peter and their remarkable seventy-nine-year-old father, Michael Pedersen Kierkegaard, the surname an earlier spelling of 'Kirkegaard' (literally 'churchyard', but with 'graveyard' the primary connotation). Except for Peter's tour abroad Søren had shared it with them ever since he was born. Not so long before the spacious home had housed a family of nine. Not only were they alone in the house, these three were the only surviving members of that family. The father's strong and brooding presence had been with Søren since birth, while his brother's celebrated example continued to dog every stage of his life. It was typical that it was as 'the younger Kierkegaard' that Søren first achieved any celebrity of his own.

Søren had in fact been the youngest Kierkegaard of them all, the last of seven children born to Michael and his wife Ane (sometimes spelled Anne). He was born at 2 Nytorv on 5 May 1813, the year the State Bank declared itself bankrupt. But death had been an early visitor. Søren was only six years old when his brother Søren Michael, known as Michael, died at the age of twelve of a brain hæmorrhage after an accident on the school playground. Michael had been born in March of the year 1807, the August of which saw the bombardment of Copenhagen by the British fleet that set in motion the period of economic decline that led to state bankruptcy. Prescient or lucky as usual, Michael Pedersen had just before the crash bought guaranteed gold-convertible bonds and came out of it if anything even better off.[1]

Søren was nine when his eldest sister Maren Kirstine, the apple of her father's eye, died at twenty-five of nephritis. That was in 1822. For the next eleven years things went fairly normally. The two remaining sisters married and had children. The three sons, Peter Christian, the four-year younger Niels Andreas, and Søren Aabye, four years younger still, grew up under the parental roof, well provided for, attending school on weekdays, church on Sunday, taking Communion, studying, succumbing to the usual illnesses and recovering. Peter after returning from his travels in 1830 showed no signs of getting married or moving out, and when he did eventually marry it was his bride who moved in. The only departure was that of Niels in 1832, after squabbling for some time with his father over his future – he preferred books and learning and had no desire to be the son who continued the family's trading tradition, as his father insisted. Peter couldn't be afforded; he was to establish the family's intellectual respectability by grasping all the educational and career opportunities that had been denied to his father. He was already on a path that would lead him one day to be a cabinet minister and later a bishop. As for Søren, whatever his future was to be, there was no indication that he could look after money. His métier was using it. So Niels was the only alternative. After a brief and fruitless reconnaissance in Hamburg, like so many others at that time, Niels had left home to try his luck in the West.

Now, just as the twenty-two-year-old Søren is at long last beginning to make his mark – we are still in the period between the autumn of 1835 and early spring of 1836 – deaths in the family are about all he can remember. His youngest and last surviving sister, Petrea Severine, had died almost a year before. The two had been close, and he had often visited Petrea and her three children. On 13 December 1834, Petrea had given birth to a healthy boy, but then she had died two weeks later. She was thirty-three. Only five months before that their mother had died, in the summer of 1834, of typhoid. And then there had been Niels.

Niels arrived in Boston on 17 November 1832 after a seven-week voyage from Gothenburg, with some money from his father and letters of recommendation. Failing to find opportunities to his liking in Boston he moved first to Providence and then to New York, where he spent from three to five months. Failing to establish himself there too, he followed a possible lead in Paterson, New Jersey. But he was already suffering from galloping consumption and died in a hotel room there on 21 September 1833. From the accounts of his friends and those who looked after him at the close, Niels remained an optimist until near the end. He was going to make his mark in the New World. But once he knew he was dying, he accepted the fact with composure. Niels with his self-dependence may have been the exception in the Kierkegaard family. He had made a break for it and might have succeeded. Niels, more than the others, it is said, took after his mother. A fictitious vignette of him during his stay in New York has him sitting in a bar, eyes shaded by the brim of a hat pulled well down over his eyes, feet resting on the edge of the gaming board. Niels is getting royal straight flushes all the time, and one after another his opponents give up.

'What's your name, stranger?', they ask him. 'Graveyard', answers Niels with a self-ironical grin, pockets his winnings, washes down the whisky and goes out into the sunlight and freedom.[2]

Freedom from his oppressive home had lasted just over a year, and its close was marked by an irony that Niels might not have been the slowest to appreciate. The body of the twenty-four-year-old Mr Grave-yard was the first committed to a newly consecrated burial ground in Paterson.

Niels's death caused dismay at home. Not just the dying, but on his deathbed he had asked to be remembered to his dear mother, failing to make any mention of his father. The thought that it was deliberate caused Michael Pedersen unutterable grief, and it spread throughout the house. Peter wrote to ask for further details of Niels's last words that might put matters right, and some consolation was derived from the possibility that he had believed that his father had died. But correspondence took months, and the affair was never really settled. The event merely served to blacken even further the atmosphere at home, darkened already by Nicolene's death, again following childbirth, on 10 September the previous year – just prior to Niels's departure. Nicolene was thirty-three.[3]

Although alarming even for those times such statistics were not uncommon, and the survivors simply had to learn to live with them. But at what cost? Except in the case of Niels, Søren does not record his own reactions, and there he writes that he felt no real grief over *him* though adds that it would surely awaken eventually.[4] But in one of several long entries recording walks he took on that summer vacation in 1835, away from the pressures of Nytorv, he writes of a favourite spot on the coast just north of Gilleleje, in the silence of which 'the few dear departed rose from the grave before me, or rather it seemed as though they were not dead. I felt so much at ease in their midst, I rested in their embrace, and I felt as though I were outside my body and floated about with them in a higher ether – until the seagull's screech reminded me that I stood alone, and it all vanished before my eyes. . . .'[5] The few dear departed, Nicolene, Ane, Petrea, Niels. It sounds almost as if instead of wishing they could rejoin him, his wish was rather that he could join *them*. Home was now somewhere else. Death had meant more than the departure of the dear, it had also removed the insulation of numbers and left these three disparate survivors too close to each other. We can imagine that, as the youngest, Søren would have suffered most from the internal strains of this unhealthy ménage. He, after all, had been closest to the departed, and unlike the others he had so far lacked an opportunity to get away, to set up his own house or travel abroad, the only effective way of escaping the domination of his father. Deprived of the assuaging influence of his mother, the company of Niels, his nearest brother, and the regular visits an extended family entails, as well as of the recreation of calling on his sisters and their small children, Søren in the company only of his father and brother was virtually homeless. No wonder he sought company in the streets and cafés.

Not that there was anything sinister about either the father or the elder brother, they were both in their different ways admirable persons. Moreover, Søren was quite good at amusing himself, running up extensive bills in the process, bills that his father always seemed happy to pay. The problem was more the inhibiting influence a strong-minded father exerted for so long on both sons – that and the mutual rivalry between these two, a rivalry in which competition for the father's approval also played a part.

Let us briefly follow their careers to this point.

Michael Pedersen Kierkegaard was born in 1756 of peasant stock, formally in bondage at birth, and his childhood was spent on the flat wastes of West Jutland where the family was technically in thrall to the local priest whose land they had once worked – hence the name. But at twelve he had been sent to apprentice himself to an uncle in Copenhagen, who was engaged in the cloth trade. Industrious and extremely astute, at the age of twenty-one and with a career as errand boy and shop assistant already behind him, he was officially released by the priest from his serfdom. Receiving his citizenship, he went into business on his own. Michael prospered, first as a travelling clothier in Danish woollens, then as a wholesale importer of cloth and textiles with a license 'to deal in East Indian and Chinese goods, as well as goods from our West Indian islands such as sugar (refined and unrefined), syrup, and coffee beans, and to sell same at wholesale or retail to all and sundry'.[6]

Through industry, good management, and lucky investments the former serf became a wealthy and respected citizen in Copenhagen. In a town of shopkeepers in the heyday of shopkeeping he was known as Hosier (*Hosekræmmer*) Kierkegaard. By 1785, at the age of twenty-nine, together with a friend Hosier Kierkegaard had made enough to buy a house. In 1796 he inherited his benefactor and uncle, Niels Andersen. Two years previously, at the very peak of his business career, he had married a business partner's sister, Kirstine Røyen, but at the end of those two years she died childless. There was, however, a maid, Ane Sørensdatter Lund, who had been offered the job because she was a distant cousin of Michael's. Not long after the wife's death she became pregnant by Michael, who thereupon offered her a scandalously mean-minded marriage contract. As, it appears, they had not been in any sense lovers, the pregnancy was no doubt due to an unguarded moment of shared loneliness. In the pre-marriage settlement Ane was denied the usual inheritance and became virtually Michael's employee, with a salary and a fixed annual housekeeping budget. There was no provision for her in the event of divorce, not even custody of the child. The officials registering the contract were aghast but could do nothing.

Against all expectation the marriage proved in its way highly successful and lasted thirty-eight years. At about the same time, in 1797, Michael had decided to put his prosperous business in the hands of trustees and live in retirement. Among the several possible reasons was his state of health. He felt suddenly very ill and thought he was about to die. But there were other reasons too. His income as a rentier was enough to maintain his family, and he had never trusted Ane with the day-to-day housekeeping. Also, by staying at home he would avoid public shame at his hasty marriage with a young serving girl who was also his cousin. And, as a deeply religious man, he may also have felt the need to nurture and atone for his private shame at a sexual transgression; but then in any case, if, as was highly likely in those days, there were to be more children, especially boys, Ane could not be entrusted with their upbringing.

Michael Kierkegaard did not die, and there were more children aplenty. But what was the price of his devotion? The eventual insanity of one surviving son, the death in obscurity of a second, and the local notoriety (and totally unanticipated international fame) of the third and youngest.

Still, it cannot be said that their home was a fundamentally unhappy one, though for a child it was certainly unhealthy. It was Michael Kierkegaard's strong but basically guilt-ridden personality and the theocratic regime he chose to impose on the household that did the damage. He managed virtually everything, the shopping too, and with the time now at his disposal he could also devote himself to his own neglected education. On weekdays during the school term a fair proportion of the children (those at least five years old) were out of the house, from before nine in the morning until seven in the evening, though they were free on Saturday afternoons. An impressive autodidact with a taste for philosophy and a talent for argument, Kierkegaard senior was especially interested in the early eighteenth-century German rationalist and Leibnizian, Christian Wolff (1679–1754). The uneducated former shepherd boy preferred reading *Vernünftige Gedanken von Gott, der Welt und der Seele der Menschen, auch allen Dingen überhaupt* (Reflections on God, the World, the Soul of Man, and Things in General [1720]) in the original. He could also take time off to entertain his sons with his rich imagination, though only Søren was temperamentally disposed to gratify his father in this respect. Peter was too pompous and not very imaginative, and Niels less willing to fall in with his father's schemes.

An unpublished work by Kierkegaard from 1842–43 contains the following quasi-biographical passage concerning one Johannes, later to become a pseudonym. Its autobiographical origins are confirmed by several sources:

His home offered few diversions, and since he practically never got out he was from early on used to being occupied with himself and his own thoughts. His father was a very strict man, seemingly dry and prosaic, but beneath this homespun coat he concealed a glowing imagination which not even his advanced age could dim. When Johannes once in a while asked for permission to go out it was usually refused; but the father occasionally made amends, offering to take his hand and walk up and down the floor. This seemed at first a poor substitute, yet like the homespun coat it concealed something quite different. The offer was accepted and it was left entirely to Johannes to decide where they should walk to. They went out of the city gate to a nearby country palace, or to the seashore, or about the streets – always just as Johannes wished, for everything was in his father's power. While they walked up and down the floor the father told him everything they saw; they greeted the passers-by, the carriages clattered past, drowning out the father's voice; the pastry woman's fruits were more tempting than ever. All that was familiar to Johannes his father described so exactly, so vividly, so directly down to the most trifling detail, and whatever was unfamiliar to him so fully and graphically, that after a half-hour's walk with his father he was overwhelmed and weary as if he had been out all day.[7]

Søren later blamed his father for messing up his life by having him raised in Christianity from childhood.[8] Of course the father attended assiduously to his family's religious guidance. He thought Pastor Bull at the Church of the Holy Spirit a suitably intelligent and sincere representative of the Lutheran Church who could give the children a solid start in the State Church. He himself, however, felt closer ties with the Congregation of Moravian Brothers, the *Herrnhuters* (*Herrnhut*, literally, 'the Lord's keeping'),[9] which with its hold among the peasant community he would have known from his childhood. Moravian teaching was almost diametrically opposed to the liberal-rationalist Lutheranism prevailing at the time. It spoke to the feelings rather than to the intellect, was anticlerical and preached inner rebirth and indifference to the trappings of bourgeois life. In Copenhagen the Congregation of Moravian Brothers had grown significantly with the destruction and widespread bankruptcy following the Napoleonic wars. Hosier Kierkegaard's business had miraculously escaped, and when in 1816 the Congregation decided that its meeting house was too small he was chosen as chairman of the building committee for a new house on Stormgade, large enough to seat over 600 brothers.[10]

However, in 1812 a young Lutheran preacher named Mynster appeared on the scene, and the ever astute Michael found in him a useful compromise. Later to become primate of the State Church, Jakob Peter Mynster started his career in heated opposition to the intellectualism of the Lutheran establishment with its university base, and also to the Enlightenment rationalism that rejected many long-standing tenets of Christian faith, including revelation. He came to Copenhagen from a parish in southern Zealand, where he had at first been plagued by doubts about the faith he was supposed to proclaim to his peasant congregation. To preach the Gospel as history, when for him it had an 'almost exclusively poetic value', was a personal trial which threw him into a despair. This nevertheless, following a crisis, seems to have resolved itself happily for all concerned. Mynster said later that he 'had to feel [himself] utterly and painfully abandoned in the world in order to find what is the highest and most blessed of all'.[11] Whatever it was that confirmed him in this discovery, Mynster's new sense of conviction certainly served him well and was to propel him to the top of his 'profession'. In doing that, however, it also proved a blessing for the church itself. Jakob Mynster's sense of the need for a form of devotion that was personal catered nicely to the emotional needs of those growing numbers of the faithful who were becoming disenchanted with the church's aridly intellectual character. Michael Kierkegaard was not slow to see the combined personal and social advantages of a family affiliation with a preacher who, like the Moravians, appealed to the living sense of God but fell short of the anticlericalism which, if allowed to spread, could leave the State Church without a following. By the time the small Søren began attending church it was Mynster's sermons the family were being taken to hear on Sunday mornings, while in the evenings they still attended the Congregation of Brothers.[12]

The girls had escaped – it seems not unhappily – into marriage. A friend and colleague of Michael's was Hosier Hen(d)rik Lund, who had three sons – Johan Christian, who had taken over his father's business and married Nicolene, Peter Wilhelm (known as Wilhelm), who was to be twice a gold-prize winner at the university for dissertations on vivisection and crustaceans and who had a doctorate from Kiel, and Henrik Ferdinand Lund (known as Ferdinand), assistant at the National Bank, who married Petrea. (Two other Lund sons had died of tuberculosis.) The families had known each other for some time, and the Kierkegaards paid frequent visits to a property the Lunds had outside the city walls. It was by no means all work and no play, an impression Søren sometimes later gave. The two daughters, at least, were spared the crushing devotion of their father, since Michael had not regarded learning as a necessary part of their upbringing. Just how far he considered the care of their souls to remain beyond his responsibility is unclear; according to one source, when it was known that Nicolene's life could not be saved after the birth of her new child, Michael rejected the wishes of those who wanted to keep the truth from her, saying, 'My children are not brought up like that'.[13] But, granting that they were not, it would be in keeping with the family ethos, as witnessed also in Niels's case, to prefer the truth in the matter of one's immanent death, so it is overhasty to see this as an unkindness on Michael's part.

What their father expected of the two remaining sons owed partly to age and partly to temperament. For Peter, Michael Kierkegaard could accurately predict a future his own origins had altogether denied him, a degree in theology and a pastorate or a chair at the university. Peter was a prize pupil at the School of Civic Virtue, and it wasn't only that he completed his theology examinations at the university in the shortest possible time, he also did so with the best possible results. Although at the time of Søren's talk to the Union Peter was not yet a theology lecturer, since his German doctorate didn't qualify him for that, he was a much-sought-after private tutor in advanced Latin.

True, two years prior to Søren's talk to the Union a slight hiccough had occurred in Peter's progress. In January of 1833 he had applied for a pastorate on Mors, the largest island in Limfjord in North Jutland. He was appointed and asked his mother to accompany him there to help him set up house. But then Peter wavered and finally withdrew. A strange lapse in an otherwise impeccable career? Not so odd perhaps. The pay was poor compared to what someone of his ability might be entitled to expect, and besides that Mors was quite some distance from Copenhagen, so Peter would be far from his admirers. Perhaps, as Mynster had been, Peter too was unsure in his faith. Anyway, it was a brief lapse. He stayed on in Copenhagen as before, popular as ever, and three years later, in January 1836, in the middle of his younger brother's public polemic, took the Licenciate degree which allowed him as *Privatdocent*, a position payed only by attendance, to teach theology at the university.

But there were other signs that Peter was to prove the less resilient of the two. While Søren was to nurture a lifelong ambivalence towards Christianity which allowed him to hold it at a distance, Peter's relation to it was less articulate, more immediate, and correspondingly more morbid. Christianity had to sustain his zest for life, and if it failed to do so the failure seemed to him to be his own, something he had to make religious penance for. He went through a religious crisis and suffered regular bouts of depression. Søren, on the other hand, though according to Peter's diary given to bouts of acute depression, seems to have been able to protect himself from the worst effects of living so continuously under the same roof with his father. In the journal entry which describes the dread associated with Christianity in his mind due to his father's administrations, Søren adds: 'And then later what I suffered on account of Peter when he was morbidly seized by the religious.'[14] The much younger brother's sympathy for the older suggests a psychological maturity belying their difference in age.

Ever since his undergraduate days Peter had been in close contact with well-known personalities in the growing Grundtvigian movement. Born in 1783, Nicolai Frederik Severin Grundtvig, theologian, politician, pastor, educationist, historian, and philologist, who lived to be eighty-nine, was to become one of Scandinavia's greatest educational influences. He studied theology, but with his strongly poetic imagination Grundtvig found an early outlet in the Romanticism of Goethe, Schiller, Fichte, and Schelling. He began his career working on the *Eddas* and Icelandic sagas as well as writing poems (his later hymns are now among the most familiar in Scandinavia). In 1811, after an inner crisis followed by awakening, he became his father's curate and began a campaign to vitalize not only the State Church but the Christian basis of Danish cultural life in general. Attacking the intellectual straitjacket of liberal rationalist theology, then considered the spearhead of progressive religious thinking, Grundtvig on reading a German author in the tradition once wrote of the 'poisoned plant' that rationalism had placed beneath the 'wizened cross'. During the twenties his by-now exuberant polemics brought him into legal conflict with Henrik Nicolai Clausen, the leading representative of the rationalist tradition, to whose book (*Catholicism and Protestantism: Their Church Constitutions, Doctrines, and Rites*) Grundtvig published an abusive reply. This, *The Church's Retort*, landed him in court faced with a libel charge. For the abuse Grundtvig was sentenced to lifelong censorship. Following his conviction Grundtvig travelled to England, and the ideas he developed of the church were based on a close study of the British liberal market economy. The church's freedom was to be guaranteed by a state constitution that served no other ecclesiastical functions than to guarantee this freedom. By freeing the church and its priests from state interference and allowing people to worship in the parish of their choice, the aim was to bring true Christianity to bear once again on culture.[15]

Grundtvig's *Retort* had included a statement of what he claimed was his recent discovery concerning the unshakable and unchangeable foundation of the Christian Church. The fault with Clausen's Protestantism was that it 'makes the written word everything' and the church into a fellowship of 'bookworms'; even the 'Word of Jesus' is just another text to focus the Christian's attention. What was needed, Grundtvig declared, was that the Christian Church become a 'society of faith with a creed'.[16] The words of Jesus form the basis of what Grundtvig came to call 'The Church View' (*Kirkens Anskuelse*)` as against reliance on scriptural authority as such. This Grundtvig called his 'matchless discovery'. In a biological metaphor suggested by Grundtvig himself, instead of Christian truth being something one deciphers from the biblical texts in a specialist intellectual exercise, then to attach oneself to, it is a continual propagation of Christian life in baptism, the Lord's Prayer, and Holy Communion as people from all stations acquiesce and participate in the living word. Grundtvig also turned critically against the Romanticism of the leading Danish poet, Adam Oehlenschläger, and then against Mynster too, accusing him of formalism and of hedging the main issues of Christian faith, in particular the status of the Holy Scripture. He wrote a much-discussed world history from a Christian point of view.[17]

When Peter Kierkegaard was studying at the University in the early 1820s there was already a group of brilliant young Grundtvigian theologians, some of whom were to become friends with Søren. They spoke to the living faith of Michael Pedersen Kierkegaard but, unlike the Moravians, in a style conveniently suited to an aspiring professor rather than to the son of a peasant. In the general swelling of the ranks of the Grundtvigians, a large section of the Herrnhutian Congregation had gone over to Grundtvig, and the manner of Peter's own induction into the movement in 1832 can probably be seen in this light.[18]

But only in part. Grundtvig was a new father figure with a strong hold on Peter, but he was also someone of whom Peter's own father was openly wary. Thus the move may also have been partly an attempt to escape. However, since no actual physical move was on Peter's mind, his Grundtvigian awakening only created tension at home. Also, in spite of its popularity among young theologians, the Grundtvigian movement by its very nature was still somewhat suspect in academic quarters. So not only at home but also at work the prize pupil, graduate, and feted doctor of philosophy faced a tension, complicating his own clerical and perhaps even political ambitions. There is a tragedy in Peter's situation. With his career cut out for him he was, in terms of the aesthetics of form that Søren referred to in his talk to the Union, someone who, due to his considerable talents plus the fact that they were eminently suited to what was expected of him, could and did assume the 'forms' laid out before him. It is hard not to believe that Søren has Peter in mind when, in a letter written in the summer previous to that talk to the Union, one which seems to have been intended only for himself, he describes two personality types.

First of all . . . a person must stand on the soil to which he really belongs, but that is not always so easy to find. There are, in this respect, fortunate temperaments so decisively inclined in a particular direction that they faithfully follow the path once assigned to them, without being deterred for a moment by the thought that perhaps they should be taking another. There are others who let themselves be so completely directed by their surroundings that they never become clear about what they are

really after. Just as the former has an internal, so has the latter its external categorical imperative. But how few there are in the former class, and to the latter I do not
wish to belong.[19]

Peter's does seem typically a personality obedient to the external categorical imperative. On the one hand he was a collection of talents and
virtues with no sense of direction other than those in which the qualities
his father happily, or unhappily, happened to approve of naturally drove
him. On the other hand, he fell heavily under the influence of another
strong man. Yet he was to prove as vacillating a Grundtvigian as he had
been a job seeker. Perhaps the real reason for the sudden doubt about
burying himself in a remote village was a premonition that deprivation
of his normal surroundings would literally destroy him. Compared to
Grundtvig himself, Peter Kierkegaard was an irresolute man. At the
time when Grundtvig's writings were placed under censorship in 1826
and Grundtvig himself forced to resign his pastorate, Peter was out in
the world improving himself and his options. Later, after 1839, when
Grundtvig was again allowed to receive a living, Peter was to prove only
a very moderate supporter.

Kierkegaard's wish for himself was to be one of those 'fortunate
temperaments' who were decisively inclined in a particular direction.
But clearly he was anything but such a temperament, and as will appear
it is far from certain that Søren, for all his talk about decisions and
decisiveness, was any more resolute than his brother. But with his own
different temperament, and not least due to the rivalry existing between
the two, Søren's path became the opposite of Peter's.

At the School of Civic Virtue, Søren was constantly reminded of
Peter. A testimonial provided by his headmaster when he left the school
typically included the remark that 'once his good intellectual gifts are
given the chance to develop more freely and unencumbered at the
University, he will surely be counted among the able, and in many ways
come to resemble his eldest brother'.[20] Many memories of Søren's
schooldays are recorded, though their reliability is considerably lessened
by the fact that they were provided on demand after Kierkegaard's
death and reflect attitudes towards events that later made him famous.
Still, one may extract from these recollections a fairly vivid portrait.
The image they present is a rather split one, a combination of cheeky
brat and loner. Søren was feared rather than disliked, but there were
some fellow-pupils who recalled him with fondness. One of them re-

membered a 'quaintly dressed fellow, slight, small for his age, pale and freckled'. The unusual clothes in which Hosier Kierkegaard, who had no experience of the closed society of a boys' school, had fitted out his son led to him being called 'Choirboy', though he was also known, due to his father's trade, as 'Søren Sock'.[21] None of his fellow-pupils could later say that they found any indication of the future celebrity. He did only moderately well, though coming usually second or third in the class and without doing much homework. One reason he got by may be, as a colleague reports, that he used a crib under his desk. It is said that he was accused once by a teacher of plagiarizing a Mynster sermon, testimony at least to the effect of his father's devoted care of his soul. The same teacher said that what annoyed him most about Kierkegaard was that he had an answer ready even before getting the question. Some teachers thought he 'lacked diligence' and treated them with 'impudence'. On one occasion his fellow-pupils bound and beat him because they resented his 'all-conquering dialectic', though that expression again probably reflects what had happened between the moment of recollection and the memory the recollector was asked to provide. But there is surely more than a grain of truth in this and other memories. Another ex-pupil said it had been dangerous to quarrel with Søren because he 'knew how to make his opponent appear ridiculous'. We have already seen that trait at work. It is hard to doubt altogether the claim that when Peter came to teach Søren's class, Søren used the situation deliberately to make fun of him.[22]

Such behaviour is easy to dismiss as merely malicious. But there can be more to it than that; it is embarrassing enough having one's brother as teacher, but unbearably so when the brother is a living legend everyone expects you to emulate. His fellow-pupils also refer to Søren's 'otherwise silent and unspeaking existence'. He 'went his own way, almost self-contained, never spoke of his home, and neither brought classmates home with him nor visited them in their homes'. They say that his derision often came unexpectedly. But a pattern was apparently discernible. The outbursts were 'usually directed at big, tall, and strongly built boys'. Whether by choice or compulsion the small, thin Søren 'pounced upon tall fellows who were intellectual midgets'.

In school, oddity must either assert itself or go under. Though used in the first instance for protection, the appearance can often be one of superiority and self-assertion. And even when there is something worth attacking, instead of taking it on in its own terms the weapon of reason may still be used just to pick holes in the opposing view. This, as often as not, is just another way of getting one's own back on the person advancing the view, redressing the balance. It is a weapon one can use to bring down not just intellectual midgets with impressive physiques but also intellectual giants with undeveloped souls.

Søren and Peter drew different lessons from the demonstrations they were given of their father's talent for debate. In the unpublished work quoted earlier, the biography of Johannes contains this account of the father's lesson:

When the father entered into a debate with someone else, Johannes was all ears, all the more because everything went with an almost ritual propriety. The father always let the opponent have his full say, and to be quite sure asked him if he had anything further to say before he began his reply. Johannes had followed the opponent's discourse with wrapt attention, concerned in his own way about the outcome. The pause. Then followed the father's reply, and look! With a flick of the wrist everything was changed. How it was done was a mystery to Johannes, but his soul took delight in this drama. The opponent spoke again. So as to keep it all in mind Johannes was even more attentive. The opponent declaimed at length, Johannes could almost hear his own heart beat, so impatiently was he to see what would happen. – It happened; in a moment everything was turned around, the clear became unclear, the certain doubtful, the contradiction a self-evident truth. When a shark is about to seize its prey it has to throw itself on its back since its mouth is on its belly; it is black on its back, its underbelly silvery white. They say it is a wonderful sight to see this alternation of colour; that sometimes it gleams so strongly as almost to hurt the eye and yet it is a delight to see. Johannes was witness to a similar alternation when he heard his father debate.[23]

Peter took to his father's debating style but in a way that made it a profession. Søren, and his account here is no doubt slanted to bring out the dangers of sophistry which threaten all debate, used the same experience to cast doubt on the pretensions of thought itself, though, for reasons not hard to divine, it was about Søren, not Peter, that it was later said that he 'seemed to live only as a thought'.[24] The account recorded here appears in a philosophical text on the status of scepticism. Indeed, Søren may have had the example of his own brother in mind when he said later that a process of reflection must both begin and be stopped at some point by a decision.

Søren clearly resented Peter. But for all his diligence and the respect he received from teachers and students, Peter probably suffered more than Søren, not just by being exposed to the regime longer but because he had been required to deliver more, as was expected of the eldest son. His diligence and success were nevertheless an undisputed fact, as was Michael Kierkegaard's undoubted pleasure in them. Søren, on the other hand, seems to have been able to count on his father's support whatever he did. Even his failure to show progress in his theology studies was indulged. Not surprisingly, Peter felt the rivalry just as much as Søren. Indeed, he resented Søren in turn for the indulgence he had always received as the younger son, and actively disliked him for not respecting his own dutiful behaviour and sense of family honour. Peter had every reason to be disturbed and depressed by the treatment he received from his younger brother. His puzzlement, as well as the piquant situation in the family, is captured by a letter their father wrote to Peter when he was abroad.

I do not know what the matter is with Søren. I cannot make him write to you. I wonder whether it is intellectual poverty that prevents him thinking of something to write about or childish vanity that keeps him from writing anything except what he will be praised for, and, in so far as he is unsure about it in this case, whether that is why he won't write anything.

Søren had to transcribe this letter in the copybook his father kept of his correspondence, and he added in the letter itself: 'I (Søren) will soon write to you so that I may be able also to gainsay Father.'[25] The idea that Peter's complaint had already been gainsaid by the addition of that sentence is typical of the sharp-minded little mischief-maker.

Part of their rivalry was that Søren despised Grundtvig and sided with Mynster. This placed him on the side of his father's pastor and against his brother's mentor. How much of Kierkegaard's disrespect for Grundtvig, who is often made to appear in the journals as an intellectual midget in the guise of a giant, is sincere or just one more expression of family rivalry is not certain. The somewhat exuberant atmosphere of Grundtviganism was certainly totally alien to his temperament, but there is much in Grundtvig that Kierkegaard seems also to have admired, not least the spontaneity that he found wanting in himself; and as far as being a centre of unified action is concerned Grundtvig was certainly an exemplar. Whatever the underlying feelings and facts, the actual alliances, his own with Mynster and Peter's with Grundtvig, were to have fateful consequences.

As for Søren's own progress or lack of it, we can quote his own words. After three years of study he wrote, 'I am embarked on studies for the theological examination, a pursuit which does not interest me in the least'.[26] Søren had matriculated at the university in October 1830, having turned eighteen the previous May. The testimonial already referred to, provided by his headmaster, Michael Nielsen, whom Søren held in great respect, hinted that progress might not be automatic. It described him as 'a good mind, receptive to everything that requires special application, though for a long time he was exceedingly childish and devoid of all seriousness'.[27] Nielsen's prediction that Søren would come in many ways to resemble his eldest brother proved predictably mistaken. But the chance to develop his gifts more freely was eagerly grasped. Theology was his own choice as well as his father's, but it became clear that as far as he was concerned this was only a convenient platform, chosen because it was quite usual and, due to the special circumstances of his home, already largely in place. With a well-honed talent for intellectual criticism, he was ready for academic excursions in every direction. He entered the university in October with the good grades in all his entry examinations expected of a pupil from the School of Civic Virtue, and with distinction (*laud prae ceteris*) in Greek, history, French, and – to his fellow-pupils' great surprise – Danish composition.[28] His first university examinations (the two-stage propaedeutic second examination [*Anden examen*], which he took in April and October 1831, the first examination being for his school-leaving diploma) embraced science as well as the liberal arts. The first part comprised Latin, Greek, Hebrew, history, and lower mathematics. He received *laud prae caeteris* in mathematics and *laudabilis* in all the others. The second part comprised theoretical philosophy, practical philosophy, physics, and higher mathematics. Here he received *laud prae ceteris* in all subjects.[29] There were military affairs to be put in order. Just a month after matriculation, on 1 November, Herr Student Søren Aabye Kierkegaard enlisted in the King's Lifeguard (*Kongens Livkorps*). Four days later, and without reporting for duty, he was declared unfit for service[30] and removed from the roll.

The lectures in theoretical philosophy and in practical philosophy were given by two sharply contrasting personalities, both of whom became Kierkegaard's personal friends and one of whom came to exert a lasting influence on Kierkegaard's thought. They were Frederick Christian Sibbern (1785–1872) and Poul Martin Møller (1794–1838).

Sibbern was then forty-six. He had travelled in Germany after defending his doctoral dissertation, meeting Fichte, Schleiermacher, and Schelling. Though not by nature a Romantic in the way that, say, Grundtvig was, Sibbern's thoughts and philosophical ambitions lay somewhere within that fairly diverse set of views known as Romanticism. It has been claimed that he also visited Hegel on his journey, but the dates tell against that (Hegel at the time, 1813, was rector of a *Gymnasium* and not yet the famous scholar), and Sibbern makes no mention of such a meeting in his letters from the trip (though Hegel's very lack of fame at the time might explain that).[31] He returned in the year of Kierkegaard's birth to assume a professorship which he held until retirement in 1870. In the winter of 1830–31, Kierkegaard's first winter term, he was lecturing on psychology, and in the summer of 1831 on logic and psychology.[32] Kierkegaard soon struck up a lasting friendship with this serious-minded thinker whose writings make few allowances for readers with ears attuned to a literary style. Sibbern's daughter, born eight years after Søren's first year as a student, wrote as late as 1912 that all her life she remembered Kierkegaard and how, when she was a child, he 'liked to sit in our parlour at dusk, when the fire gleamed in the stove'.[33]

Poul Martin Møller (1794–1838) was a poet as well as a philosopher, with a past and a personality far more colourful than Sibbern's. In fact, he was a bit of an eccentric, wearing his socks, one is told, until they wore out and then throwing them into the gutter outside the shop where he bought replacements. From 1819 he had spent two years as ship's chaplain on a China trader. On returning to Copenhagen he became adjunct at one of Copenhagen's best preparatory schools, the Metropolitan School. It was during his five years there that he began writing that novel, *A Danish Student's Tale*, from which he was to read three chapters to the Student Union in 1824. It was never finished, because, it is said, on being appointed professor of philosophy at the Royal Frederick University in Christiania (now the University of Oslo) Møller felt he had to devote himself full-time to acquiring the competence that position demanded. We know that during his Christiania years (1826–30) he taught Hegel, who was now definitely in fashion. As for the unfinished novel, which in its incomplete form acquired considerable posthumous fame for its author, it is interesting in our context because of the possibility that Møller's intention had been to describe, through the main character, a development towards a form of human maturity, or perhaps better a human form of maturity, that Møller had wrought from his own experience.[34] From 1831 until his death he was Professor Extraordinary at the University of Copenhagen. The lectures Kierkegaard attended were on moral philosophy, but their content can only be surmised. Møller, however, had a great enthusiasm for the Greek and Roman classics, and Kierkegaard's knowledge of antiquity must be due in large measure to Møller, whose draft lectures on The History of Ancient Philosophy (den ældre Philosophiens Historie) show a comprehensive and detailed familiarity with the subject. The fact that Kierkegaard's acquaintance with Aristotle came much later may indicate that these were lectures he didn't attend, though Møller's notes on Aristotle are understandably rather more perfunctory than the rest.[35] Since he became Kierkegaard's first and only true mentor in the university, it is worth noting that Møller's reputation in philosophy rested on a talent for aphorism rather than discursive argument. Smitten though he had been by the recent general enthusiasm for Hegel, Møller had, like Sibbern, already developed his own philosophical focus and style before Hegel's influence made itself felt. As a champion of personal truth, or authenticity as we now say, and a sharp observer of all forms of affectation and mere convention, Møller saw evident limitations in the sheer abstractness of Hegel's speculative philosophy. But he was not a pronounced anti-Hegelian, and when ten years later the pseudonymous author of Concluding Unscientific Postscript wrote a footnote about Møller, it was actively to remind his reader that in his later years Møller had indeed gone against the System: 'Poul Møller, when everything was Hegelian, judged quite differently [and] for some time spoke of Hegel almost with indignation, until the sound good humour in him made him smile especially at Hegelianism.'[36]

Kierkegaard's interests as an undergraduate were not in the first instance philosophical. The meeting with these two philosophers was largely an accident of the curriculum. Probably it was Sibbern's psychology and Møller's critique of social manners that interested Kierkegaard most, but he was clearly also infected by the latter's enthusiasm for classical times. The broadly based propaedeutic exams required of first-year students clearly engaged Kierkegaard's curiosity and intelligence on a wider front. His best results came in physics and mathematics. Through his brother-in-law Peter Wilhelm Lund (1801–1880),[37] the brilliant and later famous paleontologist, he became interested in zoology and botany. Lund had returned in 1829 from a four-year stay in South America, but left again in 1833 to spend the rest of his life in the Brazilian uplands. Kierkegaard was also of course committed to the long haul of theological studies. In the summer ending his first academic year he attended the cultivated but dull Hohlenberg's lectures on the book of Genesis and took private lectures on Isaiah.

As may already have been guessed, the subject he began to take the most lively interest in at the time was aesthetics. That same summer he also took Sibbern's lectures on Aesthetics and Poetry. It was in that autumn that Nicolene died. In his second year (1832–33) Kierkegaard attended Professor H. N. Clausen's Introduction to the New Testament and lectures on the first three Gospels. It was Clausen, regarded as the foremost rationalist theologian, who had been the target of Grundtvig's *Retort*. But Clausen had also been an enthusiastic supporter of Schleiermacher. During Kierkegaard's early student days Clausen became increasingly interested in liberal politics and constitutionalism, and in 1835 he was to be one of the founders of the Free Press Society.[38]

Since not all of Kierkegaard's attendances are recorded, the actual course of his studies during the period remains to a degree uncertain. However, since at the time he was beginning to accumulate a considerable library we may surmise that a good part of his study took the form of reading. We know at least that in the winter term of his third academic year (1833–34) he attended Sibbern's lectures on the Philosophy of Christianity, which included a criticism of Hegel's philosophy of religion for incorporating Christianity within the philosophical System. However, this in no way suggests that the critique of Hegel was already afoot. Sibbern's grounds were Schleiermacherian, that is to say, pre-Hegelian.

Friedrich Daniel Ernst Schleiermacher (1768–1834) was Friedrich von Schlegel's close friend. He was also, though by the same token, the great Romantic interpreter of religion. According to Schleiermacher, religion has its locus in a specific state of mind – in *Über die Religion. Reden an die Gebildeten unter ihren Verächtern* (On Religion: Speeches to Its Cultured Despisers [1799]) a sense of oneness with the world, and in the later *Glaubenslehre* (The Christian Faith [1830]) a mood best described as a sense of absolute dependence. This mood or feeling, for Schleiermacher, is the relation to God. It is in a sense given, though much can get in its way. That very year, the year before his death, Schleiermacher himself had to great celebration visited Copenhagen. Although there are entries in Kierkegaard's journals on Schleiermach-erian themes, none record the visit, which when we come to see the nature of the journals will not seem surprising. Among the Schleier-macherian themes mentioned in the early journal entries is predestina-tion, but it is not until later that we see any antipathy to Schleierma-cher's views on religion. This followed Kierkegaard's first confrontation with the work and personality of Hans Lassen Martensen (1808–1884). The first encounter took place during the summer term of 1834.

Martensen and Kierkegaard seem destined to have become enemies from the start. It began that summer with Kierkegaard's asking Marten-sen to tutor him privately. Martensen was someone who knew German philosophy well, but was also a worthy object for the kind of decon-structive dialectic which Kierkegaard was now getting to be so good at. Martensen came from Flensborg, in the mixed Danish-German district of central Schleswig. His mother was German, and Martensen had spoken German fluently from childhood. He was only twenty-six at the time and had already made a rapid academic career. He may have reminded Søren a little of Peter. He had not asked to have Martensen tutor him on Schleiermacher; the proposal was Martensen's. But it does sound a little as though Kierkegaard was saying, you name it, I'll show you. Martensen recalled that Kierkegaard had no set syllabus; he only wanted Martensen to lecture to him and converse with him.

So I chose to lecture on the main points of Schleiermacher's dogmatics and discuss them with him. I saw immediately that this was no ordinary intellect but also an irresistible urge to sophistry, to hairsplitting games, which surfaced at every oppor-tunity and was often tiresome. I remember it came out particularly when we examined the doctrine of divine election, where there's an open door, so to speak, for sophists.[39]

Was this needling due to Martensen's having taken so much of the limelight during Schleiermacher's visit the previous year? Schleierma-cher had been much feted by the then twenty-five-year-old.[40] Or would it have happened whoever the tutor and whatever the topic? Probably not in the same way, but in any case this tireless and tiresome interrogation by the student may have been a first step towards the position presented by the pseudonym Johannes Climacus in two works published in the 1840s. Kierkegaard was to resume his study of Schleiermacher following Martensen's return from an extended stay in Germany. He was in fact just now about to leave on that trip, with a government travel stipend enabling him to complete his education in Germany.[41] An interesting fact relates to his absence. After Martensen had left during the summer, Kierkegaard frequently visited Martensen's mother to ask for news of her son. Was Kierkegaard genuinely fond of him? Even attracted by this bright young man only five years his senior? Or was he curious about what Martensen was up to, who he was meeting in Germany and so on, and more than a little envious? Of course Kierkegaard may also have been using a merely polite interest as an excuse for the company of a kindly and mature woman. As it happened, it was during the period of these visits that Kierkegaard's own mother died. Ane Kierkegaard had been ill with a fever for some weeks. Kierkegaard was on a two-week holiday at Gilleleje, where according to Peter he had gone on 26 July 'to spend a fortnight for the improvement of his health'. When it was clear their mother was about to succumb, Søren was unable to reach home in time.[42] She died late in the evening of 31 July. Martensen later recalled how his mother repeatedly told him that 'never in her life (and she had no little experience) had she seen a human being so deeply distressed as S. Kierkegaard by the death of his mother'. From which 'she felt she could conclude that he must have an unusually deep sensibility'. There is no other record of Kierkegaard's feelings for his mother; she is never mentioned in his writings or journals, though someone's recollection of being warned once that Kierkegaard, then fifteen years old, was a frightfully spoiled and naughty boy who always hung on his mother's apron strings may intimate a childish dependence.[43] Martensen agreed with his own mother's judgment but not as magnanimously as one might suppose:

The more he developed, the more his life and work became a union of sophistry and a deep though sickly disposition. That as the years passed the sickly nature of his profound sensibility increasingly got the upper hand is something he himself has left the most incontrovertible proof of in the diaries he left behind, which now have tactlessly and without consideration for the deceased been made public.[44]

This comment came after Kierkegaard's death and much that had happened, particularly in connection with Martensen. But Kierkegaard's polemical disposition had not escaped the notice of his philosophy teachers. Sibbern for his part merely humoured it,[45] but when Møller pointed it out to Kierkegaard the latter seems to have taken the criticism to heart.[46] Martensen, however, took offence. He also (and much later Sibbern too) saw something sickly in Kierkegaard's polemical nature. Someone was to say of him that he was a noble instrument with a cracked sound-board.[47] Such remarks nearly all postdate Kierkegaard's later and notorious confrontation with the church and the posthumous publication of his journals. But, as anyone who reads those journals knows, that he was fatally flawed was a possibility that hadn't escaped Kierkegaard himself. Kierkegaard does acknowledge his 'sickness' there, but even the late journals, the ones usually discussed in this respect, are far from evidently those of a sick person, unless of course acknowledging and describing one's own mental condition is, as it was widely at that time, itself considered sickly. Indeed attitudes like those that met the publication of Kierkegaard's journals and some of his writings are also fairly good testimony to the accuracy of Kierkegaard's own diagnosis of his age and *its* maladies. In acknowledging his own states of mind he was initiating a revolution in which delving into the complex movements and relations of a 'deep disposition' provided the opportunity for health. To begin such a revolution it took a man born appropriately, as he himself said, in that 'year they had put so many other bad banknotes into circulation'.[48] And although at the funeral Peter 'confessed' to the unbalanced nature of his brother's mind, it was Peter, consumed by guilt, who ended up in the madhouse.

Madness is one thing, unhappiness, mental suffering, and accentuated vision are another. In April Kierkegaard started keeping notes. His journal entries begin in April 1834, at just about the time he should have been finishing his studies. There are also theological notes from December 1833 and March 1834, in some of which Kierkegaard questions Schleiermacher's notion of religious experience as based on a feeling of absolute dependence (does prayer then become a 'fiction'?).[49] The journals themselves are different, but not because they are records of daily events, of what happened in the home; it is not from the journals, for instance, that we learn that on 21 March 1834, the Friday before Easter week, Søren attended Communion with his father and mother but without Peter. We hear nothing from Søren that might explain Peter's absence on that occasion, for instance that they were not on speaking terms. The fact is that Søren had insulted Peter in some way that Peter was not yet ready to forgive. This was noted in Peter's own diary, where he cites Matthew 5:23–4: 'So if you are offering your gift at the altar, and there remember that your brother has something against you, leave your gift at the altar and go, first be reconciled to your brother, and then come and offer your gift.'[50] Peter's was a diary in the ordinary sense, noting significant events, also in his own life, and adopting the dutiful stance of observer and recorder. He had started keeping it on his return from Germany and was to continue doing so for fifty-three years.[51]

The only comments we have by Kierkegaard on his studies are in a letter to his paleontologist brother-in-law in Brazil, dated 1 June 1835. It was from this that the passage quoted earlier ('I am embarked on studies for the theological examination, a pursuit which does not interest me in the least') is taken; it continues: 'and which therefore is not going specially well.'[52] Nor does Søren mention Peter's typhus in 1835, though it must have directly affected him. He is as silent on these matters as he is about his mother and her death. Not so, however, when his father dies, but then his father was part of the complex relationship to Christianity that Kierkegaard must have felt he had to resolve in his mind if he was to cure his sufferings. By keeping track of the wide variety of themes occupying him in the present, the journals enable him to develop and assemble the parts to give some semblance of a whole, the sort of unity he admired and no doubt found in his own case sadly lacking. The early interest in the notion of form, which we noted in the previous chapter, may thus have a very personal significance. Kierkegaard's eclectic studies and broad literary interests seemed at first to prevent him from acquiring a shape at all of the kind he thought his brother had acquired much too quickly. The early journals take up the matter of a master-thief, the outsider who sees what is wrong with the system, dares to take it on, and accepts the punishment it hands out for doing so. The master-thief, we may note, is loved by a woman and by his mother, and he advises youngsters not to follow in his path. Kierkegaard is toying here with a role he was to try on and test almost if not entirely to destruction, that of the marginalised individual, the person who might today become a gang member, or a satanist, or just go for drugs, but who if he sees some chance of doing society a favour might try to make, or to believe he was making, his marginality educative. We begin to see the outlines of a picture Kierkegaard is forming of himself as a kind of one-man gang.[53]

The theme of unification is a central topic of the first regular journal Kierkegaard kept. It records a summer vacation spent at his father's suggestion, and expense, a year after Ane died. Michael Kierkegaard may have seen in his son a growing despair. At any rate he recommended a spell in North Zealand, at Gilleleje, where Søren had been holidaying the summer before when his mother died. Søren accepted the offer and used it to good advantage. The entries recording this vacation show how distance from those coteries and involvements in Copenhagen, about which he was so ambivalent, allowed him to face and assess his own state of mind. There is a surviving letter from his father which indicates that during the vacation Søren had kept up a correspondence with his family:

My dear son,

    To put your mind at rest regarding your concern at my letting Peter answer your letters rather than writing myself, I send you these few lines from my own hand. There is, thank God, no other reason, internal or external, than the one you know of and surmise: my ever-increasing difficulty in writing, which you are quite familiar with. The past few days I have also been plagued more than usually by my colic.

    Since your letter says nothing about how you are I conclude that you are well, which makes me very happy. Your brother is also in usual good health, as also your brothers-in-law and their children. Please give affectionate and friendly greetings to Mr Metz and his wife from us, and especially from me.

    Your most loving and wholly devoted father,

                 M. P. Kierkegaard

Copenhagen, 4 July 1835
To Student of Theology S. A. Kierkegaard
at the Inn at Gilleleje[54]

    The most famous passage from that summer is the one in which Kierkegaard says that what he needs is 'to be clear about *what I am to do*, not what I must know, except in the way knowledge must precede every action'. 'It is a question of understanding my destiny, of seeing what the Deity really wants *me* to do; the thing is to find a truth that is truth *for me*, to find *the idea for which I am willing to live and die*.'

And what use here would it be if I were to discover a so-called objective truth, or if I worked my way through the philosophers' systems and were able to call them all to account on request, point out inconsistencies in every single circle? And what use here would it be to be able to work out a theory of the state, and put all the pieces from so many places into one whole, construct a world which, again, I myself did not inhabit but merely held up for others to see?[55]

Kierkegaard continues: 'I am like a man who has collected furniture and has rented rooms but still hasn't found the beloved with whom to share life's ups and downs.' To find the idea, 'or more properly to find myself', it is no use 'plunging still further into the world'. He had thought once of 'throwing' himself into jurisprudence, 'to be able to sharpen my mind on life's many complications'. He had thought that 'from the given facts [he] could fashion a totality, an organism of criminal life, pursue it in its darker sides', for 'here, too a certain community spirit is much in evidence'. That is what also made him think of becoming 'an attorney', so that 'by taking on another's role [he] could acquire a sort of surrogate for [his] own life and in this exchanging of externals find some form of diversion'.[56] In the letter, quoted earlier, to Wilhelm Lund, then in Brazil, Kierkegaard admits to being interested in too many things and 'not decisively in anything' and wishes he had something he could passionately investigate like Brazil.[57] A thread here may be traced forward to remarks on *The Concept of Anxiety* saying that, in some way analogous to Lund's Brazilian travels, that work is a domestic journey (*Indenlandsreise*) from his own 'consciousness' to the 'preconditions of original sin in [that] consciousness'.[58] If there is such a thread, it lies in the thought that the solution Kierkegaard finally found was to write a Christian psychology which would rival and over-come the Grundtvigian rewriting of history and culture.

The remaining entries for 1835 (whose order in relation to the journal recording the summer vacation is still to a degree speculative) do not indicate that Kierkegaard saw any solution at the time. But he was clearly disenchanted with Christianity.

When I look at a fair number of individual samples of the Christian life, what strikes me is that instead of bestowing strength on them – yes that, in contrast to the pagan, Christianity deprives such people of their manhood and they are like the gelding in relation to the stallion.[59]

Faust becomes a continuing theme, and on 1 October we read the comment: 'It is also remarkable that Germany has its Faust, Italy and Spain their Don Juan, the Jews (??) The Wandering Jew, Denmark and

North Germany Till Eulenspiegel.'⁶⁰ The folklore of a doubter, a seducer, a man doomed not to die, and a trickster provide the beginnings
of an investigation into the relation between reflection and despair which
was to become an increasingly focal theme. Kierkegaard's own despair
had not diminished as a result of the soul-searching of his summer
diary. One good reason for that may be a conversation with his father,
who on returning from Gilleleje he found in an unusually confessional
mood. What was divulged remains secret, but something of its nature
may be divined from Kierkegaard's later mention of a relationship
between a father and a son where the son finds out things that he
doesn't want to know.

His father is a man of note, God-fearing and strict; only once, when he was drunk,
did he drop a few words that made the son suspect the worst. The son has no other
intimation of it, and never dares ask his father or anyone else.⁶¹

This might be a spur to the remark in October that Christianity weakens
rather than strengthens. Peter, still not reconciled with Søren, also
confesses in his diary to being in a dispirited and irritable mood.⁶² He
too had fallen out with the father, perhaps for the same reason as Søren.

   This then was the state of the Kierkegaard household when the
younger Kierkegaard faced his audience in the Student Union that
November evening in 1835. When in January the three remaining Kierkegaards were to go to Communion together once more, it would be the
last occasion on which they did so. As for the atmosphere in the house
itself, Josiah Thompson has graphically portrayed the scene.

The three of them – Michael Pedersen, melancholy and crotchety; Peter Christian,
stolid and self-righteous; Søren, acerbic and inwardly preoccupied – huddled together in the many rooms of the house that now was too large for them. From his
rooms on the first floor the father could hear Peter's students climbing the stairs
when they came for their tutorials. The two sons had rooms side by side on the
second floor. In Peter's there was a desk by the window where the students sat
while the Doctor (so called because of his Göttingen degree) corrected their Latin
compositions or discussed a point of theology. And off to the side lay Søren,
reading. One of the students later recalled that only once had Søren ever ventured
to interject an opinion.⁶³

Thompson puts Søren's reticence down to insecurity in the presence of
an already so well-thought-of brother. But possibly he also felt that he
no longer belonged there. Søren needed a voice but not at home. The

voice he had was already being exercised assiduously in the innumerable cafes, on the street, and at the Union. But a peripatetic's voice has too piecemeal an employment to make any lasting mark. He heard that a friend 'was to give a paper at the Union on freedom of the press. We don't know, but presumably Kierkegaard went there to hear it even though the subject held little interest for him. Typically enough, however, other people's interest in it did. Replying would in any case be an opportunity to speak for himself, and perhaps he would make a mark and be welcomed in other homes. He informed the seniors in the Union of his intention to read a paper of his own. Ostermann gave him his manuscript and Kierkegaard got down to work.

3

A Faustian Phase

SOME WEEKS after the talk but before the *Kjøbenhavnsposten* piece which prompted his own newspaper articles, Kierkegaard commented that there was 'something rather sad and depressing about wanting to achieve something by talking and seeing that in the end one has achieved nothing and the person in question remains intransigently set in his view'. Both timing and topic could say it was the talk itself that he was referring to. But that had hardly been designed to win people over. That Kierkegaard was thinking of something else emerges in the consolation with which the entry concludes, that it is after all a fine thing that 'the other person, and similarly every individual, is always a world unto himself, has his holy of holies into which no alien hand can reach'.[1]

The pupil of the School of Civic Virtue had gone 'his own way, almost self-contained' and 'never spoke of his home' – perhaps because home was then the holy of holies. But now, though he wouldn't leave the family house for another nine months it was no longer home. Inner sanctuary had to be found elsewhere. The journal entries from the period from January to midsummer reveal a growing instability which in the course of the late winter and spring came near to nervous breakdown.

The development can be traced in early journal entries. There is a harping on themes that had preoccupied him from the months following his return from that soul-searching summer holiday, though also before, and a gradual focusing on the figure of Faust. The early fascination with the master-thief is resumed. The master-thief may 'in some cases resemble an Eulenspiegel'.[2] In what way? The master-thief is a typical boyhood fantasy, the misfit with a superior grasp of society and its ills but ready at personal risk to challenge the system, even if by himself he cannot change it. It is significant that Kierkegaard sees in the master-thief a product of the 'popular class' (*Folkeklasse*). The young Kierke-gaard's fascination with criminality, shared later also by Nietzsche, can be seen as a variation of Hegel's master–slave dialectic. A study of a society's outcasts gives a more faithful picture of the society itself than the society's own official portrait. According to a friend who knew Kierkegaard well and 'often spent up to eight hours at a time with him', once 'eating at his house every day for five weeks', Kierkegaard once confessed to 'an enormous desire to carry out an actual theft, and then live with his bad conscience in fear of discovery'.[3]

Till Eulenspiegel, the hero of a German folktale relating the adven-tures of a wandering cottager, was not a criminal or an outcast but an inveterate trickster. The farce is broad and quite often bawdy. The two aspects are noted in separate entries, one introducing the idea of satire and the other that of the satyr, though with no sense of the pun available also in the Danish. The former reference is a very early hint of Kierke-gaard's notion of the role of humour, more indications of which will follow shortly. This is in an entry dated September 1834. The master-thief's discontent can go along with a 'good measure of humour' because it is general, not piecemeal. He does not contest the idea(l) of the state as such, but only pervasive abuse of it.[4] The humour is possible because the master-thief has, on the side of the idea, distanced himself from its current implementation; he ridicules the court that tries him not be-cause he opposes justice but because he sees *in*justice in the ways justice is currently practised. In Heibergian–Hegelian terms this could be seen either as content overreaching the current form (the master-thief enrich-ing content by forcing us to see anomalies we hadn't seen before) or as the present content (the way things are done now) falling short of an ideal to which lip-service is already given.

The satyr aspect relates to Eulenspiegel's sharing with Kierkegaard's master-thief his lower-class origin. In the second entry we read: 'Eulen-spiegel seems to represent the satyric in the Northerner.'[5] Kierkegaard later complained that he had never had a childhood, a judgment that may be slanted by retrospective embitterment. By all accounts he man-aged both at school and at home to be childish. But that, we may allow, is hardly the same thing and could well be a form of reaction rather than the kind of unfolding to which playfulness is said to contribute. Also, however sympathetic Søren's father seems to have been to his children's imaginative needs, the atmosphere at home discouraged any creative playfulness in the open. Søren resorted to a play with thoughts instead, in the first place other people's. Asked by his sister what he most wanted to be, he had said 'a fork'. The reason? 'Because then I could fork anything I wanted on the dinner table.' 'But what if we came after you?' 'Then I'd stab you.'[6] He thus became known as 'the Fork'.

Adolescence must have been problematic. There was a social or civic side. If Peter was precociously mature, Søren seems to have been given no chance to assume responsibility at all, either for himself or for others.[7] But the theocratic household must also have prevented the boys' undergoing anything like a normal puberty. There were aspects of life that never got spoken of until the elderly Michael told his two embarrassed sons of his misdeed. Or so it has been suggested. It is said that what the God-fearing and strict father had said, and the son had no inkling of and never dared ask him or anyone else about, was that the whole family had been conceived in sin. Not literally, for it was only Maren who had been conceived out of wedlock. But the wedlock inside which the later children were conceived was the very one she had been conceived out of, so in a sense they were all smitten. Speculative as such theories of the inner dynamics of Kierkegaard's life must so often remain, one can see how Søren, who had appropriated his father's pietism without being allowed to see the natural man beneath, would be shocked at this shattering of the presumed holiness of his holy of holies. As if in support, however, the last journal entry Kierkegaard ever made refers to the 'crime' through which he 'came into the world', saying that it was 'against God's will' and that, as befitted the crime, his punishment had been to be 'bereft of all lust for life'.[8]

But at twenty-two, at large in Copenhagen and freed from his 'home', he could savour life. He was making his mark, and new doors hitherto closed were opening. This was to be a Faustian period. The journal entries take up the theme of the legendary German necromancer who sold his soul to the devil in exchange for knowledge and power. Faust's interest in evil, says Kierkegaard, was not like that of the petit bourgeois, to make himself look good by comparison. It was to 'feel all the sluice gates of sin open within his own breast, the whole kingdom of boundless possibilities'.[9]

But it was Faust the thinker in whom Kierkegaard had first been interested, a thinker whose thinking led him to doubt. He represents the intellectual who doubts religion and dares to lift the lid from the world's secrets. Lately Kierkegaard had also been captivated by the image of Don Juan in the shape of the hero of Mozart's *Don Giovanni*. Kierkegaard had attended the performance on 10 November 1835, just before Ostermann's talk at the Student Union, and the opera had made a deep impression on him. He is said to have attended every subsequent performance. Four years later he was to write in his journal:

> In some ways I can say of *Don Giovanni* what Elvira says to the hero: 'You murderer of my happiness'–
> For to tell the truth, it is this piece which has affected me so diabolically that I can never forget it; it was this piece which drove me like Elvira out of the quiet night of the cloister.[10]

The contrast with Faust was apparent. Faust the doubter took a monogamous fancy to the simple and unreflective Gretchen, which then proved an obstacle to his diabolical search for knowledge. Don Juan, on the other hand, was a serial seducer whose search and sex-life were one and unending. His appeal was that of immediacy with no admixture of reflection beyond what was needed to keep things going. Don Juan is not an actual individual, at least in the opera's portrayal, which Kierkegaard came to regard as paradigmatic. In *Either/Or*, Don Giovanni is described as a life force into whose sphere of activities reflection and language do not enter. Faust, however, because he reflects on life, comes nearest to exemplifying a person. There is a third figure, the Wandering Jew, or Ahasuerus, a figure quite topical in Europe at the time (another Dane, Hans Christian Andersen, was to struggle with a play on the theme for seven years [1840–47], and Poul Møller has a small sketch including the comment: 'Ahasuerus wants nothing. He considers himself infinitely superior to those who would do something').[11] The legend had already been the subject of journal entries the previous March after Kierkegaard had come upon or borrowed a book dealing with it. He noted the two main versions in his journal, though without elaborating: Ahasuerus the cobbler (at whose house Jesus stopped to rest the cross, but Ahasuerus pushed him away saying, 'Away with you, away!', and Jesus answered, 'Truly I go away, and quickly, but you are staying until I come') and also Kartaphilos, the doorkeeper of the judgment hall (who struck Jesus as he was led into Pilate, saying, 'Faster, Jesus', to which Jesus said, 'I am going, but you will stay until I return'.).[12] Compared to Faust, the Wandering Jew is a living ghost. In another entry from December, Kierkegaard had rearranged the order in which he originally placed them (Don Juan, Faust, the Wandering Jew), Faust now replacing the Wandering Jew in third place. The happy-go-lucky, lower-class rapscallion Eulenspiegel, with traits of the satyr, had long since yielded his place to an aristocrat, a man whose adventuring seems driven by an uncontrollable urge but might also be interpreted as sustained defiance of the powers that finally overcome him, the very powers which, we note, Faust is prepared to unlock. The reason for the Wandering Jew now coming second is that his refusal is not the outcome of reflection, but his ghostliness also contrasts as ascetic with Don Juan's obsessive lust for life. Faust, who combines this lust and reflection, comes third because, Kierkegaard points out, by embodying aspects of both of the others, he is the 'more mediate'.

The thought and the order are now faithfully Heibergian: 'we shouldn't forget', says Kierkegaard, 'that Don Juan has to be grasped lyrically (therefore with music); the Wandering Jew epically, and Faust dramatically.'[13] As, we recall, the purest form of immediate sensuous experience, music came lowest on Heiberg's scale of aesthetic expressiveness, while drama came highest just because, of all the artistic genres, it is the most successful at synthesizing immediacy and reflection. But 'mediation' here seems no longer to have quite the same force. It is no longer a matter of immediacy impeding reflection's path towards absolute knowledge of the eternal, reason, or the Speculative Idea. Here the dialectic of immediacy and reflection offers, as a whole, a typology of ways of holding religion at arm's length. In Don Juan's case, since religion would interfere with his continual search for erotic pleasure, he simply doesn't want to know about it. Faust, not content with religious faith and eager to know its secrets, when given the chance to gratify this wish by the devil has his wish transformed into a desire to command the mysteries. The Wandering Jew caught the eyes of Jesus but told him to go away.

What do these figures represent? Protected ignorance, doubt that wants to be in on the act, deliberate denial? The answer seems to be that they correspond to an ascending scale of conscious rejection of the meaning of religion. In an earlier entry, naming the three in their original order and written in March 1836 (the month in which Hage's article appeared in *Fædrelandet* and Kierkegaard wrote his two-part

reply), he refers to them as *the* 'three great ideas representing the . . .
distinct directions in which life tends outside religion'.[14] To the Hegelian way of thinking what makes the triad exhaustive is that the third
embodies the features that distinguish the other two. The entry continues: 'It is only when these ideas go over into the individual person and
become mediated that the moral and the religious come into the picture.' Since the legends only portray types, one may speak of the
manner and extent of the exclusion of morality and religion only when
the general descriptions are applied to actual individuals; it is in actual
people and through diverse psychological mechanisms or strategies that
doubt and denial occur. To understand the way these configurations
relate to the morality and religion they variously exclude, one must first
grasp them in the situation of the individual. And the entry ends: 'that's
my view of these three ideas in relation to my dogmatic standpoint.'

Just how innovative that standpoint was in terms of the Christian
dogmatics current at the time is hard to say. We don't yet know what
conclusion Kierkegaard drew at the time when saying that religion is
personal and particular. It could be simply a view close to Schleiermacher's, in which a preestablished unity is available to the individual in a
form of experience acquired by clearing away pretensions of thought
and impediments of worldly feeling that get in its way. It is a view of
religion in which we may see important parallels to what was later to be
called 'religiousness A'. So what Kierkegaard says here may be no more
than a spelling out of the views he had absorbed early on from Sibbern
and Møller.

Yet, in Kierkegaard's incipient Faustianism during this period there
is a distinctly anti-Schleiermacherian element which may mark a first
step away from the potent influence of the great Romantic theologian
and towards the view that Christianity is 'paradoxical', the later 'religiousness B'. In the eyes of a Schleiermacher, Faust fails to see that
divinity, like human freedom, must be something we *cannot* grasp. But
because he cannot grasp religion Faust spurns it and looks for the
sublime in the subterranean instead. How far Kierkegaard was tempted
personally in this direction we cannot say, but certainly this was an idea
that seized him, and at least the time was ripe for his own temptation
at the hands of the devil. The mature but, it is important to add,
pseudonymous view of religion was to be that faith can be sustained
only by a choice against the powers of reflection. Religion, the more we

understand ourselves, becomes no longer a paternal inheritance but increasingly foreign. It can be sustained only in the form of personal dedication to its 'idea'. Christianity, for Kierkegaard, was becoming a choice he would have to make by himself.

Kierkegaard's continuing preoccupation with Faust may be one reason why the conclusion that Faust epitomized despair was not one that he was then ready to draw; it was the Wandering Jew who seemed to him symbolic of the 'despair' of that time.[15] Perhaps that is because the man who looked in God's eyes and said 'go away' is the paradigm of refusal. On the other hand, the legend of the Jew is too abstract to characterize an age. All we know of Ahasuerus or Kartaphilos is that the one was a cobbler, the other a janitor. A Faustian interest in flushing out dark secrets may have seemed to Kierkegaard at this point an indispensable addendum to life, or at least an idea he couldn't avoid.

Kierkegaard had said that though it was depressing to talk to others without being able to affect their views, it did show how people were worlds unto themselves. Later in the same year, or maybe early in the next, he writes that in talking to others the person one leads on is oneself. The entry, dated 2 December (1836), is yet another in the apprentice writer's style and may be another example of a piece intended for possible publication. Kierkegaard the writer is evidently enjoying himself.

I'll talk no longer at all with the world; I will try to forget that I ever did. . . . The trouble is that as soon as one comes up with anything one becomes it oneself. The other day I told you about an idea for a Faust, now I feel *it was myself* I was describing. I have barely to read or think of some illness before having it. Every time I want to say something, at precisely the same time someone else says it. It's as if I were a double thinker and my other *I* was always one step ahead; or while I stand and talk everyone thinks it's someone else. . . . – I will run away from the world, not to the monastery – I still have my vigour – but to find myself (every other gabbler says the same), to forget myself; nor over yonder to where a babbling brook 'picks its way through the meadow of hay'. I have no idea whether that rhyme is some poet's but I wish an inflexible irony would force some sentimental poet or other to write it but make him always read into it something else. Or the echo – yes, Echo, you grand master of irony, you who parody in yourself what is highest and deepest on earth: the word that created the world. Since you give only the network lattice, not the filling – ah yes, Echo, avenge all that sentimental tosh that lurks in woods and meadows, in church and theatre, and which once in a while breaks loose *there* and altogether deafens me. In the forest I don't hear trees telling old legends etc. – no to *me* they whisper about all the nonsense they have for so long been witness to, to *me* they beseech in God's name that I chop them down and free them from these twaddling nature worshippers. – Yes, if only all those twaddle-heads sat on one neck; like Caligula I'd know what to do. I see already you begin to fear I shall end up on the scaffold. No, you see that's where the twaddle-head (I mean the one that embraces them all) would certainly like to have brought me, but you have forgotten no actual harm is done to the world. Yes, Echo – you whom I once heard castigate a nature admirer when he exclaimed: Hark, the solitary flutings of a nightingale in love, how beautiful, and you replied: fool – yes, avenge, avenge – *you* are the man!

No, I won't leave the world – I'll enter an insane asylum and see if the profundity of insanity reveals to me the riddles of life. Idiot, why didn't I do that long ago, why has it taken me so long to understand what it means when the Indians honour the insane and step aside for them. Yes, an insane asylum – don't you think I may end up there? – Still, it's lucky that language has a number of expressions for balderdash and nonsense. If it didn't I'd go mad. For what would that be proof of but that everything people say is nonsense. It's lucky that language is so cultivated in this respect, since that means one can still hope occasionally to hear rational discourse. It's called a tragedy when the hero gives his life to an idea – madness! (So I commend the Christians, they called the days on which the martyrs died their birthdays, and by doing so cursed the happy idea people usually have.) – No, misunderstanding! On the contrary, I grieve when a child is born and wish to God that at least it may not live to experience confirmation! I weep when I see or read Erasmus Montanus;[16] he is right and gives way to the *masses*. Yes, *that's* the trouble. When every confirmed glutton is entitled to vote, when the majority decides the matter – isn't this giving way to the masses, to numskulls? – Yes, the giants, didn't they too give way to the masses? Yet – and this is the only comfort left! – every now and then they terrify the Hottentots who trot over them by drawing in their breath and giving vent to a flaming sigh – not to be pitied – no, all condolences declined – but to frighten.

I want – no I want nothing at all. Amen!

And when at twentieth hand, and much more, one comes across an idea that has sprung fresh and alive from some individual's head – how much truth is left? At most one can say in the words of the proverb: 'Well at least it tastes of fowl', as the old crone said who had made soup out of a branch a crow had sat on.[17]

The hypertension in this humour so clearly laced with despair is clear to see. But it is this very despair which Kierkegaard brings as an innovative amendment to Heiberg's aesthetics. Instead of providing a scale of the ever-more-adequate expression of the idea, the scale of increasing reflection is one of increasingly conscious disenchantment with the immediacies glorified by the poets. The more consciously one excludes morality and religion, the greater the despair, which for Kierkegaard is a matter not of correlation but of definition. For in terms of what is offered for human fulfilment, refusal to accept it is just what despair most paradigmatically is.

It was suggested that for Kierkegaard it was only when the general types are mediated by individual experience that morality and religion come into the picture. But in that context Faust's rejection of religion (faith) in favour of knowledge can be grasped in two ways: as recognition of religion as something apart – something to be rid of since it can't help you in the *human* project, not something to build societies or homes out of as the Moravians and Michael Kierkegaard believed, and certainly not something for a Faust who wants in his own case to extend the human to the superhuman – but also as a 'radical cure' for those who agonize over life and discover that a purely human project is worthless, one which 'like every radical cure one wants to put off as long as possible'.[18] To begin with, the apartness of religion had been something he defended from the vantage-point of religion: 'Philosophy and Christianity can never be united.' Why? Because 'Christianity stipulates the defectiveness of human cognition due to sin, which is then rectified in Christianity'.[19] But Faustian inclinations can lean you in the other direction. Kierkegaard had just found how far his wit could take him, and in the first months of 1836 he had been living on it, in newspaper articles and at parties. The journal entries from January to April 1835 are on several themes. There is the reference to the 'three great ideas' we have already discussed. There is a warm appreciation of Goethe's *Wilhelm Meister* for the way in which Wilhelm personifies the world-view posited by the author at the start, and a caustic aside at metaphysicians 'of a certain kind' who, when they get stuck, 'like Münchhausen take themselves by the scruff of the neck and thereby get something *a priori*'.[20] Many of the entries here are strained and terse: 'Damn and hell, I can abstract from everything but not from myself; I can't even forget myself when I sleep.'[21] One of them takes up a distinction between humour and irony. Both humour and irony depend on 'not coming to terms with the world'.[22] One entry contains just a single phrase, 'the ubiquity of wit';[23] another says: 'I have just come back from a party where I was the life and soul. Witticisms flowed from my lips. Everyone laughed and admired me – but I left, yes, that dash should be as long as the radii of the earth's orbit————and I wanted to shoot myself.'[24]

The brief moment of celebrity had led nowhere. For all his wit – or was it because of it? – he had said nothing really important. Not only that: wit closes as many doors as it opens. All it can do is amuse the converted or the indifferent. His talking seemed to be good for nothing but entertainment after all.

Kierkegaard's final newspaper article, the one signed with his own name and addressed to Lehmann directly, appeared on 10 April. The journals record a meeting just over a week later with a well-known man-about-town and roué. His name was Jürgensen; he was chief clerk in the criminal courthouse but well in with artists and theatre folk, and he knew most of Copenhagen's cultural celebrities. Although twenty or more years older than the undergraduates who frequented it, he was also an habitué of the Union. Kierkegaard, who knew Jürgensen well and probably owed his knowledge of the criminal world to him, describes the meeting.

He was drunk, which you could mainly see by watching the corners of his lips. He thought that poetry was really of minor importance, an outgrowth, and he praised philosophy. He praised memory, envied me my youth, talked of the falling leaves, of the whistling and gusting of the wind. 'Half of life is for living, the other half for regretting, and I am fast entering the latter.' 'In youth one can do much wrong and put it right again.' – 'I have led a very agitated life, been involved in everything that matters nowadays, am on personal terms with all gifted people – just ask me about them.'[25]

On the evidence of later entries one suspects that Kierkegaard did, through Jürgensen's connections, do something 'wrong' which he felt he could never put right again. Later, in 1839 and in connection with a talk he had attended on the benefits a position in life can afford, Kierkegaard says that, as for him, even were his 'whole life devoted to serving God', it would 'hardly suffice to atone for my youthful excesses'.[26] There is a still later note from 1843 in which Kierkegaard weighs up the possibilities of taking up a pastorate as against continuing his career as an author:

There's an ethical requirement. By taking up a definite position in the State as a teacher of religion I am committed to being something I am not. A guilt I bear opens me at every moment to attack from that quarter. Once I am a cleric the confusion will be a sorry one because I kept quiet about something that happened before I entered that estate. As an author the situation is different.[27]

In another note from 1843 we read under the title 'Layout': 'Someone in his early youth has in an overwrought moment succumbed to the temptation to visit a prostitute (*et offentligt fruentimmer*). The whole thing is forgotten. Now he wants to get married. Angst is awakened. The possibility that he is a father, that somewhere in the world there is a living creature who owes him his life, tortures him day and night.'[28] From the title and the rest of the entry (which says it had to be a prostitute, since if it was a love affair or a real seduction the man would know if there was a child) it is clear that Kierkegaard either actually thinks of this as a scenario for a short story or intends the reader to think that. There is also a third possibility, that he intends us to decipher the code and read it as a piece of plain biography.

There is a famous gap in the journals. No entries can be dated after 22 April 1836, which is just four days after his meeting Jürgensen in the street, until 6 June. The reality of the gap cannot of course be proved, since there are many undated loose-leaf notes which may have originated in that period. Nor can one exclude the intriguing possibility that some of the demonstratively dated earlier entries, the Gilleleje entry and the letter to Lund included, in spite of being conspicuously dated from the year before, in fact belong here. The piece quoted above on talking as simply a means of autosuggestion was certainly from about this time. Since demonstrative dating could be just a ruse, Kierkegaard may at this time have been writing these well-executed and soul-searching confessions and the lacunae, again, have been just an illusion. And those who claim that the silence was due to a moral lapse he had no wish, at the time, to publicize could still be right.

We know in any case that it was in June 1836 that Kierkegaard published his very short reply to the satirical pieces in *Humoristiske Intelligentsblade*. We noted his remark in explanation of the brevity of that reply, that such a long time had elapsed since his articles, though in fact only six weeks had gone by. But then six weeks might seem a long time to someone who has in the meantime been thinking and writing about something quite different.

From the summer of 1836 the entries start falling again like hail-stones. Again, of course, there is no mention of what is going on at home. But in fact, the day before the first entry in June, dated 6 June, Peter had announced his engagement to Marie Boisen (sometimes spelled Maria Boiesen), daughter of the late bishop of Lolland. The marriage would take place on 21 October, and the couple would then move into Nytorv. Until then it would be the three of them as usual. Søren did not attend Communion with his brother that summer or autumn, and he was still not on speaking terms with his father. The third anniversary of Niels's death in America fell on 21 September. On 23 September the now seventy-nine-year-old Michael Kierkegaard attended Communion alone. It was a poignant event. That on his deathbed Niels had not mentioned his father had greatly troubled Michael Kierkegaard ever since. There are two entries in Søren's journal about his brother's death,[29] though these uncharacteristically personal references, even if triggered by the occasion, may also have been part of an aborted literary project.

On the social calendar there had been a soirée at the Heibergs on the 4 June, just prior to their departure for Paris on 6 June, the date of the first of the new entries. Both Kierkegaard and Poul Møller were there. It may have been then that Møller, with whom he was still on close terms, complained to Kierkegaard: 'You are so thoroughly polemical it's just awful.'[30] The remark doesn't surface in the journals until much later, in fact the year before Kierkegaard died. Nor does Kierkegaard anywhere comment on a footnote that had appeared on 4 May in one of the *Humoristiske Intelligentsblade* pieces: 'Naturally an author's *literary* physiognomy has nothing to do with his physical physiognomy, which on this occasion is no concern of ours.' The wholly gratuitous reference to his appearance, and the veiled threat that the author could well make it his concern on a later occasion, must have made some impression. If Møller indeed made his complaint on that occasion, then Kierkegaard already had a purely prudential reason for taking the criticism to heart.[31]

What exactly he had to fear from references to his appearance is unclear. It does seem, though, that just as at school, now also as a young man, Kierkegaard struck people as slightly odd. Not now, presumably, just because of his dress, though even at school that was clearly not the whole story. A sixteen-year-old student newly arrived from the provinces, and a later friend and admirer, Hans Brøchner, records that he first saw Kierkegaard at a party. The year was 1836. Not realizing who it was but knowing the family's trading connections, Brøchner took him to be a draper's assistant. There was something 'very irregular in his whole appearance', his hair stood on end in 'a rumpled mass almost six inches over his forehead' and gave him a 'strangely confused look'. The occasion was either Peter's engagement or the wedding itself, and, as seems the rule in the presence of his brother, Kierkegaard said nothing but just watched. When Brøchner, a distant relation, met Kierkegaard again shortly after and began speaking with him he 'soon realized he belonged somewhere else than behind a counter with a measuring tape'.[32] According to Sibbern, Kierkegaard had a 'witty, somewhat sarcastic face and brisk way of walking . . . thin and not large of build'. He also says he was 'bent over as though on the verge of a slight tendency to a hunchback', though this memory of Sibbern's may embrace also a later time.[33] Another memory, from 1837, by Meir Aron Goldschmidt, someone who claimed with good reason to have a 'mental photograph' of Kierkegaard, says that 'at that time he had a fresh complexion but was thin, with his shoulders a little hunched forward, his eyes intelligent, lively, and superior with a mixture of good nature and malice'.[34] The same Brøchner records 'something infinitely loving and gentle in his eye', and in a letter written a month after Kierkegaard's death remembered Kierkegaard as someone who had supported and encouraged him for almost twenty years, a man of 'friendly good will', the 'gentle and loving side' of whose personality 'more and more outweighed the strongly ironic and polemical element that was in him by nature'. But there is more to appearances than looks, as another observation of Brøchner's reminds us:

Because of the irregularity of his movements, which must have been related to his lop-sidedness, it was never possible to keep in a straight line while walking with him; one was always being pushed, successively, either in towards the houses and the cellar stairwells, or out towards the gutter. When in addition, he also gesticulated with his arm and his rattan cane, it became even more of an obstacle course. Once in a while one had to take the opportunity to switch around to his other side to get enough room.[35]

Goldschmidt, who by the time he said so had been largely responsible for the myth of Kierkegaard's deformity, in a later corrective said that he was 'striking in his build, not really ugly, certainly not repulsive, but with something disharmonious, slight and yet also heavy'.[36]

What the journals at the time indicate is that the younger Kierkegaard had returned to his preoccupations with aesthetics. He turns his attention to Heiberg, taking him to task for failing to see the full potential of his own transferral of Hegelianism to aesthetics: the triad of lyric/epic/dramatic (combined lyric and epic) can be applied also *within* the historical periods with which he correlates these.[37] So far he hasn't seen that Heiberg, whose aesthetics anticipated the publication of Hegel's, reverses Hegel's order, making lyric rather than epic the 'immediate' stage. It would not be until 1841, the time of his dissertation, that he read Hegel's lectures in the newly published complete edition of Hegel. As for Heiberg's own speciality, vaudeville, Kierkegaard sketches a 'proof' that its form contains the seeds of its own destruction and that it can therefore have a transitional status only.[38] Other entries show that Kierkegaard has been reading Goethe again; Faust is now a topic rather than a role model, perhaps even the topic of a forthcoming book. There are comments also on Fichte and Hamann, to which we will return.

It looks as if whatever happened in April or May bounced Kierkegaard back firmly into the sanctuary of a religious perspective but in a way that nevertheless gave him an idea to live and die for, namely his own long-term conversion. For conversion, as one entry tells us, is a slow business: one must 'go back the way one came' and be patient, not exploit the fact that it doesn't occur straightaway to postpone it until tomorrow while 'enjoying today'. On the other hand, the eagerness to become a martyr may be due to a fear of backsliding: in order not to be caught out one wants as quick and decisive a trial as possible.[39] But then again one mustn't overdo it. A cryptic reminder, 'It is dangerous to cut oneself off too much, withdraw from the bonds of human society',[40] may be saying: 'too little enjoyment might look like martyrdom.' As if taking his own good advice to heart, Søren continued to run up considerable bills which his father kept paying. Journal entries from towards the end of 1836 noting differences in central figures in *Figaro*, *The Magic Flute*, and *Don Giovanni* indicate frequent visits to the opera. Without knowing it, Kierkegaard had already begun to write *Either/Or*. Already from the spring of 1836, there was material that was later used in that work's first section, 'Diapsalmata'.

Recently Poul Møller had moved into a nearby house on Nytorv. Kierkegaard attended a course he gave that winter term (1836–37) on The Most General Concepts of Metaphysics. Møller's companionship may have been a main factor in bringing Kierkegaard back to his studies. As the sole mentor whose criticism he respected, Møller was probably the only one whose desire to help could have any effect. The precise nature of Møller's benign influence is hard to put a finger on, but according to Hans Brøchner it was the man's character that made the

deepest impression on Kierkegaard. That he was not a naturally happy
person would be a bond between them. But with his enthusiasm for
antiquity and his poetic abilities Møller personified a kind of optimism
and spiritual strength. It is beyond doubt that he also influenced Kierkegaard's views and provided a constructive foil to the latter's own
disposition to split and divide. Møller, who was also a stylist, was able
to capture in clear prose the foibles and 'tendencies' of the age, as we
remember Kierkegaard too attempting in his talk. Under the assumed
designation of 'a young geographer' Møller writes in his Prolegomena
to a (posthumously published) collection of sketches of an imaginary
country house:

It is not without reason that complaints have recently been made over the excessive
number of students occupying themselves with philosophy, theories of art, total
systems, meditations on the spirit of the age and other such things, for which
learning, not least, is required. Even if we admit that philosophy is the soul of the
sciences, a soul can hardly subsist on its own and without a body. Already now
there is little body left. Soon the writers will have nothing to meditate over except
each other's meditations. . . . A remarkable counter-emanation prevails in the republic of learning. All studies are becoming daily less bodily, rarefied and transfigured,
so that it is much to be feared that in the end they will dissolve purely into spirit
and air. In order to counter this unfortunate tendency the author of this work has
sacrificed his powers exclusively to the 'real' sciences. On earth, undeniably, nothing
is more solid than the earth itself. But how imperfect are all descriptions of the
earth! In the largest geographical lexica one searches in vain for towns like Ølseby-
Magle. . . . From two geographies they make a new that is less voluminous than
either and from the three now available they make a fourth, the most compendious
of all. . . . Let us begin from the ground up, let us each undertake a description of
a villa or farmhouse. . . . [41]

The humour and irony are palpable. This dig at current intellectual
tendencies, aimed as much at the writings of a painstaking and honest
Sibbern as at those of an urbane Heiberg, is something Kierkegaard
would clearly have appreciated. Consistent with his own divisive tendency, however, humour was something he began to consider in itself
in distinction from irony. There had been earlier journal entries on
irony and humour, and now Kierkegaard was connecting these with
Christianity. It seems clear from other journal entries of the time that
Kierkegaard was also influenced by a thinker whose style had a more
Faustian accent than Møller's, the German Protestant thinker and Enlightenment critic Johann Georg Hamann (1730–1788). The earliest

Hamann entries from September 1836 are either short comments on remarks of Hamann's or simply quotations. But from the new year references to Hamann in connection with humour become more detailed, though also to a certain degree critical. In the spirit of Møller's stress on the need to begin 'from the ground up', though more trenchantly, Hamann had been typical – if indeed not the paradigm – of those thinkers for whom immediate confrontation with life opened the door to the truths that philosophers thought they could pursue through systematic reflection. His assorted and unsystematic writings on his own life and the nature of man made him a leading influence in the counter-Enlightenment movement (the *Stürm und Drang*) that grew in Germany in the 1770s. Not only do many of the themes anticipate the preoccupations of depth psychology and existentialism, but the manner of Hamann's thought itself is also strikingly modern. Kierkegaard would find in Hamann many themes to his liking – contextualizing reason, saving Lutheranism (with the aid of what Hamann took to be Hume's notion of faith) from the Enlightenment, and insisting on the inappropriateness of rational criticism and proofs in questions of faith. But here it was first and foremost Hamann's humour that Kierkegaard latched onto, as demonstrated in his writings. He acknowledges that Hamann 'could be a good representative of the humour inherent in Christianity', and indeed ends by saying that Hamann is 'the greatest humorist in Christianity, [which is to say] by virtue of being the greatest humorist within the life-view that, in world-historical terms, is itself the most humorous life-view, [he is] the greatest humorist in the world'.[42]

Kierkegaard first compares humour to irony as a total perspective on the world but then contrasts it in ways that link humour specifically with Christianity. Both perspectives involve, roughly, a perception of the world of manners and practices as devoid of the meanings traditionally presumed to attach to these. But where irony, as Kierkegaard says in one entry, says merely *'nil admirari'* (admire nothing), humour's 'diameter' is the greater for embracing the ironist as well. Once the individual sees *himself* in irony's light there is no longer room for irony's 'egoism'. In the same entry Kierkegaard says that 'humour is *lyrical* . . . it is the most profound seriousness of life – deep poesy that cannot form itself as such and therefore crystallizes in the most baroque forms'.[43] For Heiberg, we recall, poetry (lyric) and written art (including drama) provide progressively successful syntheses of reflection and im-

mediacy, and the underlying irony in comedy is a sign that the limitations that immediacy and reflection impose on each other in art have
finally surfaced. The limitations of art as such in relation to rational
thought or philosophy stand thus revealed. In assimilating humour with
a lyricism rooted in something too deep to reveal itself in lyrical form
('Christian humour is like a plant only the root of which is visible,
whose bloom unfolds to a higher sun'), Kierkegaard is saying that the
limitations of art are to be appreciated from a standpoint quite other
than that of rational thought and philosophy.

The *irony* of Christianity is its claim to speak for the whole world
when its message is that the world as a whole, or the world simply as
such, is not to be spoken for: its value is not in itself. A short entry
interjects that for antiquity there could be no irony because, for it, the
divine 'goes into' – in the mathematical sense – the world; though a
later entry from October 1836 takes some of this back, suggesting that
an aspect of what Kierkegaard means by 'irony' can indeed be found in
the Greek notion of nemesis. The *humour* of Christianity is its treating
the whole world as not worth a damn except in relation to a 'supposed
single truth'. The whole world of 'princes, power and glory, philosophers, artists, foes and persecutors, etc.' becomes as nothing.[44] Christianity claims to speak for both sides, except that the other side, where
one must reach to grasp what is needed to bring the world back, is so
very hard to get to. Kierkegaard, who possessed Hamann's *Gedanken
über meinen Lebenslauf* (Thoughts on the Course of My Life [1758–59])
would of course have known, as most did, of Hamann's mystical experience in London in 1758 when, while reading the passage in Deuteronomy that says 'The earth opened the mouth of Cain to receive the
blood of Abel', Hamann realized that he was 'the murderer of God's
only begotten son', and the spirit of God revealed to him 'the mystery
of love' and 'the blessing of faith in Christ'.[45] But no such experience
came Kierkegaard's way or was likely to. No wonder that someone
whose father's religion had 'messed up' his life, and whom Christianity
filled with dread, but who at the same time 'felt strongly drawn to it',[46]
saw in Poul Møller a model to follow, an unhappy man but with warmth
and humour and an ability to create at least aesthetic unities. What
Møller actually spoke about in his lectures that winter we don't know,
and no sign appears in the journals. But it is worth bearing in mind
Møller's attraction to Hegel and the fact that he never explicitly

renounced him. Indeed, it was only in a paper published in 1837, and which he may have been writing at this time, that he noted in passing the inability of speculative philosophy to make room for individual experiences.[47] Being on such close terms with Møller (who in 1837 published *Kunsteren blant Oprørerne* [The Artist among the Rebels]), Kierkegaard may have absorbed this criticism and seen its possible implications.

As we can tell, the journal entries from this period are edging towards philosophy. This is where the explicit criticism of Schleiermacher referred to earlier occurs: 'What Schleiermacher calls "religion" and the Hegelian dogmaticians "faith" is after all nothing but the first immediacy, the prerequisite for everything – the vital fluid – in an emotional-intellectual sense the air we breathe – and which therefore cannot be characterized by these words.'[48] Schleiermacher, for whom religion has its irreducible place in the emotions, says Kierkegaard, is 'Stoicism reborn in Christianity'.[49] We also find a Heibergian or Hegelian justification for contempt for liberal politics.

Since in my view every development first comes to an end in its own parody, it will appear that *politics* is what is parodic in the world's development – first genuine mythology (God's side), next, human mythology (man's side), and then a realization of the world's goal within the world (as the highest), a sort of Chiliasm, which however brings the individual politicians, carried away by abstract ideas, into contradiction with themselves.[50]

This recalls the opening theme of Kierkegaard's talk the previous November: politicians' preference for untried ideas. One entry echoes, or sides with, the young liberals' disgust with the egocentricity and sentimentality of bourgeois life, but talks in a less superior tone than theirs. Kierkegaard refers to 'our' disinterest in trying to 'shape society' or in 'working together in a common cause'. Although 'in fact only interested in ourselves', we are fascinated all the same by forms of life which bind people tightly together ('monks, thieves, robbers, the petit-bourgeois life, the misshapen monsters or parasitical plants of the religious life . . . political life in a time of revolution, chivalry'). And at least 'the associative element manifests itself in our day in external ways', for example in 'fundraising (English Bible societies – associations to support the Greeks – foundations for the morally depraved)'.[51]

Irony? Tongue-in-cheek? Just trying out his pen? Or does Kierkegaard see in such piecemeal manifestations of voluntary association the beginnings of an 'internally' associative society, a society of people associating without having to be members of an association? That at least is what he much later came to propose.

It is hard to know exactly where one is in the journals. But irony, the topic, is a constant beacon. The number of marginal comments on irony indicates that it was a theme about which Kierkegaard was constantly developing his ideas. Often there is a strongly Hegelian slant to these. A note added in the margin (perhaps when Kierkegaard was refreshing his earlier thoughts on irony while working on his dissertation) to an entry from 1837 represents irony in three stages – a period of latency, a period of domination by irony that prevents individuality from coming to the fore, and a 'third position' where through overcoming irony the individual comes to itself, or where irony is 'survived [*overlevet*]'. Kierkegaard develops his ideas of latent irony from a reading of folktales and the naïvely presented exploits of their warrior heroes: 'This is where the development of the concept of irony must have its beginning; the grandiose, fantastic ideas are gratified and reflection has still not disturbed this standpoint's credulity.'[52] The topic of irony again returns, now contrasted with 'resignation', which somehow excludes it. The point is made in terms that we recall from Heibergian aesthetics and the dawning of the sense of some essential limitation.

Irony belongs only to the immediate (where the individual is however not conscious of it as such) and to the dialectical point of view [*Standpunct*], whereas in the third (or character's) point of view the response to the world doesn't have the form of irony since resignation has now developed in the individual, which is precisely consciousness of the limit every striving must come up against if it is to form a world-order, since as striving it is infinite and unlimited. Irony and resignation are the opposite poles, the opposite directions of motion.[53]

Irony, as we have it so far, is the sense of things not having the value generally assumed to reside in them. That you can be an ironist without knowing it must mean that irony takes on forms in which the pretentiousness of worldly values is not consciously envisaged but is nevertheless somehow expressed. From the 'dialectical' point of view you stand consciously at a divide between the world on the one hand, drained of its value, and the source of its value on the other. For a dedicated Hegelian like Heiberg, one still has the Speculative Idea up one's sleeve, in which, as with all oppositions, this one too can be resolved in philosophy. By introducing here the notion of resignation, Kierkegaard is blocking that way. Here Kierkegaard is nearer to Kant than to Hegel.

For Kant, total visions are illusions of finality needed to make sense of human endeavour. To admit they are nothing but illusions is a form of resignation; one no longer hopes to grasp the totality. The concept of resignation that Kierkegaard later develops in *Fear and Trembling*, in which the object of your desire – or what means 'the whole world' to you – is lodged with God when it proves unattainable in the world, may indeed have this Kantian origin. Knowing Møller's doubts about Hegel, it isn't beyond question that the remark itself was prompted by something Møller had said in his winter course on The Most General Concepts of Metaphysics.

It might seem that with his anti-Heibergian utterances Kierkegaard was now adopting a fairly definite anti-Hegelian stance. But that is not at all clear. What Kierkegaard objects to is the facility with which philosophers and others adopt a new style of thinking, or even of just talking, of which Hegelianism is just the current example. 'Great men try in vain to mint new concepts and put them into circulation – it is of no avail; they are used only for a moment, and then only by a few and simply help to make things worse.' In another of those journal entries that look as if intended for literary publication Kierkegaard says that 'one idea seems to have become the *idée fixe* of the age: getting the better of one's predecessor'. Although this, too, could be read as a comment on Hegel's historical approach, the immediate targets are clearly much closer. Here are some excerpts:

If the past is to be blamed for taking a certain indolently complacent pleasure in what it had, we could well accuse the present of the same (the minuet of the past and the gallopade of the present). . . . we see people continually leap-frogging over each other – 'due to the immanent negativity of the concept', I heard an Hegelian say recently as he took me by the hand and made to prepare for his leap. . . . Most systems and life-views also date from yesterday. . . . In [the] wild hunt for ideas it is still very interesting to observe that happy moment when such a system assumes imperial status. Everything is now set in motion, which usually also means making the system popular. . . . it takes hold of everyone. How Kant was treated in his time is well enough known, I need only mention the endless numbers of lexicons, short compendia, popularizations, accounts for Everyman, etc. And how in recent years has Hegel fared, Hegel, that one among modern philosophers whose rigorous form would surely most likely command silence? Hasn't the logical triad been put to the most ludicrous effect? It was no surprise to me that my shoemaker had found it could also be applied to the development of boots, since – as he remarked – even here the dialectic, always the first stage in life, expressed itself in the squeaking, however insignificant it may seem, and which certainly hasn't escaped the attention of some depth psychologist, whereas the unity only comes along later – in which

respect his boots far surpassed all others, which usually fell apart in the dialectic.
. . . As for our modern politicians! By adopting Hegel they have truly given a
striking example of how to serve two masters, pairing their revolutionary exertion
with a life-view which is exactly a remedy for that, a good remedy for removing
part of the illusion needed for putting their fantastical exertion in a good light. And
the reality of the appearance will surely not be denied when one recalls that the
words 'immediate unity' occur just as necessarily in every scholarly treatise as a
brunette and a blonde in any half-respectably equipped romantic household. . . . I
altogether share your disapproval of the way every Christian concept has become so
volatilized, so completely dissolved in a mass of fog as to become unrecognizable.
The concepts of faith, incarnation, tradition, inspiration, which in the Christian
sphere relate to a particular historical fact, the philosophers have taken it upon
themselves to give a quite different and ordinary meaning to, so that faith becomes
immediate consciousness, which is basically just the *vitale fluidum* of mental life, its
atmosphere; tradition has become the sum concept of a certain worldly experience,
while inspiration on the other hand has become nothing more than God's breathing
the life-spirit into man; and incarnation nothing but the presence of some idea or
other in one or more individuals. . . . The invention so characteristic of the time is
to be seen in everything: the [hydraulic] speed-press, even in the queer reflection
the age has entered into, so that by always confining its expression to reflections, it
never actually manages to say anything. This peculiar discursive style has also
supplanted those pithy proverbs that save so much time and talk, and has let a
certain oratorical gabbling obtrude in their place, even taking over our mealtimes.
Only with the introduction of these economies, together with the restoring of
language's prodigal sons, can there be hope for better times. . . . [54]

It was Heiberg who, two years previously, in *On the Significance of
Philosophy for the Present Time*, had been the popularizer of Hegel. It
was also Heiberg who in a lecture introducing a course of lectures in
1834 to the Military School, where he had been appointed lecturer in
1830,[55] was said by critics, friendly as well as oppositional, to have
shown the need to go further than Hegel.[56] The expression 'he took
me by the hand and made to prepare for his leap' has a pre-Hegelian
source and comes from a famous conversation with Lessing recorded
by the German anti-Enlightenment philosopher Friedrich Heinrich Jacobi (1743–1819). It was celebrated for triggering the late nineteenth-
century Pantheism Controversy (*Pantheismusstreit*), which began with a
dispute over whether Lessing was really a Spinozist, and ended with
Spinoza, long regarded as a cautionary example to all who choose the
path of reason alone, being welcomed by the likes of Goethe as the
thinker best able to convey the nature of divinity. The mockery is
directed at Heiberg and his enthusiastic expectations for the Specula-

tive Idea. As for any unified attack on Hegel himself, on Kierkegaard's part, we still have no sign of it. It is significant that Hegel, in Heiberg's version, had already been attacked by others, and although Kierkegaard later made allusions to the debate, he took no part in it at the time.

It would be useful if we could date a remark made later by Sibbern. In a letter written after Kierkegaard's death he says that Kierkegaard, though generally 'preoccupied with what stirred inside him and with expressing that', did once 'during his Hegelian period [meet] me at Gammeltorv and ask me what relation philosophy had to actual life, which surprised me since the whole gist of my own philosophy was the study of life and reality'. But Sibbern 'subsequently realized that the question was a natural one for a Hegelianized thinker, because Hegelians did not study philosophy – to use an expression of Welhaven's when I once discussed philosophy with him – existentially'.[57] It is hard to think of Kierkegaard, in spite of his enthusiasm for Hegelian aesthetics, as having been Hegelianized in just that sense, and one wonders how much Sibbern really understood what stirred inside Kierkegaard. Even as late as 1841, by which time he had read the *Aesthetics*, Kierkegaard seems still to have appreciated Hegel, though he does say that one often grasps Hegel best in his off-the-cuff remarks.[58] But the question Kierkegaard asked Sibbern would make sense even coming from someone not Hegelianized. The relevance of *philosophy* for life was to be a major theme later, and if it had not occurred to him earlier, that might just be because philosophy, as distinct from aesthetics and theology, which must have appeared to him to have a relation to actual life, had not been his primary interest. Besides, the philosophy courses taken in his first year had been given by two independent thinkers both of whom had a basic sympathy with the ambitions of Hegelian philosophy, and though both already nurtured some criticism, neither of them at that time had made any clear stand against Hegel. Kierkegaard had been assimilating the language and background of the prevailing Hegelian modes of thought, now superimposing themselves initially in a fairly benign way on the older thinking stemming from the Romantic era of Schlegel and Schleiermacher. Far from there being reason for him to find in Hegel any obvious target for his polemical bent, Kierkegaard was probably just as taken with the freshness of Hegelian thought as everyone else, and he clearly found very fruitful what he took to be the

Hegelian aesthetics delivered by Heiberg. It is worth noting that Hans Brøchner also refers to Kierkegaard as having been 'apparently overwhelmed' by Hegelian philosophy, until taught to see its errors through his own 'ethical respect for the conditions of existence'.[59] Unfortunately he does not say when it was he thinks that Kierkegaard learned that lesson.

With Martensen, everything changed. First Martensen himself, who the summer he left for Germany, the summer of Kierkegaard's mother's death, had been a Schleiermacherian, had returned two years later a Hegelian. Second, and as a result, the face of local Hegelianism had changed. Kierkegaard was now faced with a professed and popular Hegelian whose views on philosophy he realized he would have to take far more seriously than Heiberg's.

Indeed, it was not Hegel's philosophy that annoyed him so much as Martensen's popularity, though perhaps also the idea of philosophy's becoming a vogue, a craze even, and by implication easy to grasp. This may be what prompted that question on Gammeltorv about philosophy. How could anything like that be important for living? Some years later, when Martensen's popularity had waned and he had just published *Christian Dogmatics*, the visible outcome of his successful lectures, Kierkegaard wrote, under the heading 'Prof. Martensen's Standing', that 'now it is as good as ten years since Prof. Martensen returned from a trip abroad, bringing with him the latest German philosophy, and aroused such a tremendous sensation with this novelty – Martensen who has really been more of a reporter and correspondent than an 'original thinker'. He calls it 'the philosophy of "standpoints" ', which 'fascinated the youth and gave them the idea they could swallow everything in half a year'.[60]

Much had happened to sour relations between them in the ten years and more since Martensen had returned. By itself, then, the return may not have triggered as strong a reaction as that expressed in this entry. Kierkegaard attended the lectures in the winter of 1837–38, and his papers contain some detailed notes not of an obviously critical nature. We also know that when he was at last writing his dissertation Kierkegaard visited Martensen at home and read parts of it to him no doubt hoping for some helpful comment, or was he simply looking for praise? In neither case can there have been open hostility, though in the event Martensen was by his own account decidedly cool, a fact, however, that he himself was inclined to put down to Kierkegaard's hostility. That would put the break between them more than three years ahead.

Martensen says he found the language and style of the section of the dissertation Kierkegaard read to him unpleasant, 'with its intolerable discursiveness and the many tiresome repetitions, the endlessly long sentences and the precious and mannered form of expression' – features which also put him off Kierkegaard's later works. 'He seems not to have forgotten', says Martensen, 'that I failed to show greater enthusiasm for his *opus*.'[61] These comments were made after Kierkegaard's death at a time when Martensen had probably had the opportunity to read remarks in the journals such as the one just quoted about him being only a reporter and a correspondent rather than an original thinker. His own comments, as would be only natural, are infused with a sense of hurt. Kierkegaard, he says, 'tried in every way to discredit me, my abilities and my works, to annihilate and extinguish everything that issued from me'. Yet Kierkegaard never attacked him directly. Martensen has an explanation:

I also assume he was unfitted to engage in a scholarly contest in theology, since the only contest that suited him was in quasi-poetic, humorous contexts in which he could employ a playful and flanking discourse. He had no gift for instructional and dogmatic discourse, which is why he continually polemicizes against 'the docents', whom he detests.[62]

That may turn out to be a somewhat self-serving and less than fair explanation of why Kierkegaard opposed the *Privatdocents*. But Martensen further writes, with undoubted perception, that Kierkegaard's

ambition was unlimited and his demands extremely hard to satisfy if one was not to become a blind admirer and epigone, as is undeniably the case with some of our *literati*. Because he not only claimed incredibly to be one of the world's greatest thinkers, perhaps the greatest, but also – in spite of the fact that he was altogether devoid of immediacy and was pure and simple reflection – to be one of the greatest poets.

'For me', says Martensen, 'he was neither one nor the other . . . he was just a humorist who possessed elements both of the poet and the thinker out of which he develops his humour – which in Kierkegaard has a pessimistic character – the complete opposite of Jean Paul.'[63]

The comment on Jean Paul (pseudonym of the popular German novelist Johann Paul Friedrich Richter [1763–1825], much in favour in the 'sentimentalist' reaction to neo-Classicist formalism) is apt enough. Jean Paul's wit was in the service of an earthy enthusiasm for which, if Martensen's diagnosis is correct, Kierkegaard's overdeveloped powers of reflection left no room. As for what Kierkegaard thought of Jean Paul, whose collected works he owned and with whose treatises on aesthetics he was familiar, in an entry from 1837 he refers to him somewhat disparagingly as 'the greatest humoristic Capitalist'.[64] Something in this idea of investment and gain in the capital of ideas may also lie behind Kierkegaard's disdain for Martensen. He had said that Martensen's lectures gave students the impression that 'they could swallow everything in half a year'. That alone made them immensely popular, and the teacher as much as the students reaped the rewards. We can see how two quite different forms of objection might be stirring in Kierkegaard's heart, or rather one in his heart and the other in his mind. The official Kierkegaard view would be that no important idea can be swallowed in half a year, or swallowed at all for that matter – ideas have to develop in a life and in the fulness of time. On the other hand, Martensen was only five years Kierkegaard's senior and hence a serious competitor for any position in the university that Kierkegaard might at this time have been contemplating. There was also the simpler competition for fame. There must have been a good measure of jealousy in Kierkegaard's attitude towards this astute, serious, and cosmopolitan young man with his German origins and contacts. Matters would become even worse when Martensen later filled the vacancy left by Møller, replacing the sensitively piecemeal style of the latter with the philosophy of what Kierkegaard refers to scornfully as 'standpoints', the Hegelian view we noted in connection with Heiberg in which philosophies are to be arranged, as merely provisional positions, in their relative approximation to the unifying point of view of the Speculative Idea.

Martensen had used his two years abroad to brush up his knowledge of Hegel, visiting Berlin and then Heidelberg, meeting the theologian Karl Daub (1765–1836), who saw the possibility of applying the Hegelian approach to Protestantism. He also met his own exact coeval David Friedrich Strauss (1808–1874) in Tübingen just after the publication of the latter's celebrated *Das Leben Jesu*, attended (Friedrich Wilhelm Joseph von) Schelling's lectures in Münich, and met Franz Xavier von Baader (1765–1841), the ex-physician and ex–mining engineer whose Catholic theology was closely linked to Schelling's notions of spirit and nature. From there Martensen went on to Vienna and finally to Paris and the Heibergs, where by now he must have felt himself more than well qualified to be received as colleague and ally. But Kierkegaard refers caustically to Martensen's having 'taken tea with this or that great man of letters', and to how everyone, as in family gossip, 'spreads tales about Christianity's union with philosophy without properly knowing either party but only at second or third hand from the Magister'.[65] Yet it wasn't until well over a year after his return that Martensen gave his highly successful lectures, and whatever this new alliance with Heiberg meant, it seems for the moment to have given Kierkegaard no reason for a more probing investigation of Hegel. Among the very few references to Hegel that occur in the six months after Martensen's return there is one which shows that Kierkegaard has already seen how he and Hegel differ, but the tenor is more constructive than critical and the focus on his own version of human development as an alternative. Dated 27 January 1837, the entry is headed, interestingly enough for future reference, 'Something on Life's Four Stages, also with Regard to Mythology'.[66]

The first stage is that of the child with (supposedly) as yet no sense of its separation from the environment (the motif of separation from the environment is later applied more generally).[67] Here there is as yet no 'I', but its possibility is present, and the stage is therefore one of 'conflict'. In this childhood stage the unity of the 'I' manifests itself as a host of contiguously placed elements successively ousting each other to make up the 'eternal "I" 's present. Kierkegaard surmises a correspondence here with 'oriental mythologies'. Betraying the classical background that Møller inspired him to acquire, he likens this 'coursing down of divine abundance' to the shower of gold under the guise of which Zeus penetrated both the prison of the immured Danae and then Danae herself, to become the father by her of Perseus.[68] The 'I' is composed here of an 'atomistic multiplicity'. The nearer life, 'through an infinite approximation', approaches self-consciousness, however, the more the conflict comes into the open. But because self-consciousness is not yet achieved – and that would mean 'life having its centre of gravity in itself' (later, in *Either/Or*, the aesthete's definition of the *un*happy man is one who 'has his ideal, the content of his life, the fulness of his consciousness, his real nature in some way or other outside himself')[69] – the multiplicity 'exerts pressure' or oppresses, like the 'heavily decorated ceiling' which corresponds, says Kierkegaard, to the 'heaven of the orientals' as against the 'light drawings and beautiful forms' with which the Greeks produce 'harmony and peace'. Above the strife, however, there is an accompaniment of 'peacefulness', an 'idyllic well-being'. It is the young boy's contentment with family and school (church and state). This is the second stage, and Kierkegaard assimilates it to Greek mythology. Here the divine 'works out' in the world in the mathematical sense, or 'goes into it', as it never did previously and never will again except 'in the development of the individual'. While the Greek's world was one of equilibrium, with Romanticism comes the idea of a 'contentment transcending the world'. Though the entry does not make it clear, this must be the third stage. Now that satisfaction is not to be found within the world, this must also apply in the fourth stage (Christianity) except where the world provides enough for an unassuming person – who resigns – to accept, but also leaves a 'little' still to be hoped for. Christianity answers to that hope and is therefore 'world-historically' the most significant form of life. A marginal note to the entry that may have been added later, even much later (as is typical of the journals), says that Christianity really has 'everything to hope', and it is the philosophers in *their* efforts to grasp the development who talk about that extra as if it were so little.

Kierkegaard notes in conclusion that the Hegelian System has only three stages (the immediate stage, reflection, and unity), while 'life has four'. He sees the unity of Hegel's last stage as a misplaced version of Greek peacefulness, but lacking the previous stage to which, in his own version, it is the appropriate response, namely a state of dissolution (as opposed to mere opposition). As for the conflict, there has to be one to get the whole thing going, but Hegel's first stage, immediacy, is pure abstraction, a 'nothing'. So how can the Hegelian 'retrograde systematic crabwise motion' (the Hegelian three-stage development, at least in the popular understanding of Hegel's methodology) get started? He says that the conflict for Hegel must be between the I and the world, which should be his first stage. In claiming that life itself has four stages, Kierkegaard perhaps means that the unity of world and self that Hegel sees in his third stage, the stage of peacefulness, can only be achieved by Christianity. Otherwise you will have to resign yourself to what little an unassuming person can be content with (though as the marginal note seems to add, you must lose it all before you can hope for the 'everything' that Christianity offers).

The entry is roughly sketched and, as the reader will have realized, hard to elucidate. But it does show that Kierkegaard is already working out a quasi-Hegelian version of cultural development based on mythological types but with stages that also apply ontogenetically, that is to say, they describe the stages through which in the course of a single life any human being achieves consciousness of a self. It may be no accident that the novel Poul Møller never got time to finish, *A Danish Student's Tale*, had been planned as the story of an individual development, or one might say, anticipating a bit, a development towards individuality. In Kierkegaard's sketch the form of the development's actual fulfilment is religion, specifically Christianity. From all this you might think that Kierkegaard would be happy to let Hegel slip into the background. But for an ambitious young intellectual that was to prove impossible. Part of the reason was that in addition to Martensen's lectures in 1837 and 1838, the three years from 1836 to 1838 saw several writings that brought Hegel to the forefront of debate in Copenhagen. In 1836, Martensen, one of the critics who had commented on Heiberg's Introductory Lecture of 1835,[70] had published an article criticizing the subordination of religion to philosophy in Hegel. Martensen finds himself in substantial agreement with Heiberg's view that Hegelian philosophy is essential for the time: it 'contains the most complete and exhaustive development of rational knowledge',[71] but he wanted to retain a personal God, which for him was connected with the concept of personality in a way that clearly also interested Kierkegaard (the concept of personality provides a frame for the second part of *Either/Or*). A second publication by Martensen appeared in 1837, his dissertation, *De autonomia conscientiae sui humanae in theologiam dogmaticam nostri temporis introducta* (The Autonomy of Human Self-Consciousness Introduced into Contemporary Dogmatic Theology).[72] With hindsight we can see that it, too, preempts work that Kierkegaard could have envisaged producing at the time and did in fact come to write but in another style. The dissertation criticizes the modern notion of autonomy, arguing that man is essentially finite and needs divine aid to know the truth, a motif familiar to readers of *Philosophical Fragments*, still seven years away. A comparison of the texts of Schleiermacher and Kant shows how both contribute to

a view of the 'autonomy of human self-consciousness entrusted exclusively to itself' in which 'the dogma of God, *Creator* of heaven and
earth, and the mutual relation which God stands to the creature' are
'totally destroyed'.[73] That could be seen as the seed of *Fear and Trembling*. But although Martensen's arguments are a way of retaining
Schleiermacher's insistence on the 'immunity' of religion from philosophy, it is typical of Martensen's view that the church, culture, and
society are essential to religion – a view Kierkegaard was to state in
Either/Or five years later in order, it later transpired, to distance himself
radically from it. But so far there were no signs of that, and it is
intriguing to see how much Martensen seems, by anticipating Kierkegaardian themes, to have plotted for him the latter's own oppositional
course.

When Martensen's well-attended lectures arrived (Prolegomena to
Speculative Dogmatics in the winter term and Speculative Dogmatics
in the spring), they did even more to bring Hegel's name to people's
lips. In 1838, Sibbern was to add a contentious note by publishing a
critical appraisal of Hegel's thought directed also at Heiberg and Martensen.[74] The criticism was directed primarily at the way in which
Hegelians think philosophy encompasses its own starting-point; Sibbern
criticizes Heiberg and Martensen for likening philosophy's development
to that of a child that finds its strength and origins as life progresses,
starting with no presuppositions. This part of Sibbern's critique coincides with Kierkegaard's early established opposition to the idea that
one can start a life with a clean slate and a plan of action devised a
priori. Was it perhaps Sibbern's attack on Hegel voiced in these terms
that gave him the idea that Heiberg's Hegel could be attacked on the
same principles on which both he and Heiberg opposed liberal politics?
Sometime during this period there may have dawned a plan in his own
mind, to be developed with all due gradualness, to oppose the pretensions of Hegelian philosophy in general. In his critique Sibbern makes
a distinction which he finds also in Fichte, even implicitly in Hegel
himself in spite of what Heiberg and Martensen say, between the merely
preparatory 'explication' a philosophy gives of itself, its description of
its object – Fichte's *die Lehre von den Thatsachen des Bewusstseyns* (Theory of the Facts of Consciousness), and the work of the philosophy
itself, corresponding to Fichte's actual *Wissenschaftslehre* (Science of
Knowledge). Hegelians must first explain what the Speculative Idea is

and then go on to examine the world in expectation of the world's revealing itself in its light. In a second essay Sibbern criticizes Martensen in much the same terms for thinking that it is possible to find a foundation of faith once you are within the Hegelian philosophy, expecting the foundation to be laid bare in the explication of the Idea itself, rather than in the preliminary explication of the idea of the Idea. Sibbern himself, like many others at the time, entertained a notion of the harmony of the universe and a notion of God close to Hegel's Absolute Idea or Absolute Knowing. But unlike Martensen he thinks that, for a Hegelian, the foundation of faith can be found only by seeing how far the actual work of speculative philosophizing is able to 'penetrate' the realm or the life of faith for one who already has it. Sibbern clearly departs here from what was to become Kierkegaard's view as it came to expression in the pseudonyms. Sibbern still wanted to unite Christianity and speculative philosophy.

We see from all this that Hegel was certainly topical, but the idea of a concerted attack on Hegelian philosophy is not yet on Kierkegaard's agenda. If the occasion was still lacking, it may also have been that Kierkegaard felt he would have to know more about Hegel, and that might have been one good reason for attending Martensen's lectures. Apart from that, however, Kierkegaard was in a poor state of mind. A concerted attack on anything would require more concertedness in himself. One can of course bear in mind the psychology of polemics which says that the only way you can pull yourself together may be to collect yourself for a conflict – though not the happy man's way, since for the polemicist the centre of gravity is always elsewhere.

4

The Wild Geese Fly

T HE FACT IS that lately Kierkegaard's self-confidence had taken several severe knocks. One was administered by Martensen. In the journals there is an entry from June 1837, the summer before Martensen's winter lectures. It reads simply: 'Oh how unhappy I am – Martensen has written a treatise on Lenau's *Faust*!'[1] Kierkegaard had been working hard on Faustian themes ever since 1835, and on Goethe, whose version of the legend with the purification and redemption scene in Part Two he thought a travesty of its true meaning. Since that time he had also been preparing his Faustian letters for possible publication. He seems to have acquired from his period of 'perdition' a belief that he had an insider's appreciation of the Faustian mood. The notebooks are filled with comments and detailed references to Goethe. An entry dated 19 March 1837 distinguishes a modern Faust from the old one.

The old Faust was faced with the problem of what to do with his life, and because science then was only in its beginning he believed that what would help him was more knowledge. But today, when science has come so far, it is obvious that knowledge cannot be the way. The new Faust therefore has to retreat to another world – or else just be a cowherd, as Kierkegaard puts it. As a result, the latter-day Faust abandons the practical goal that defined his former version's task, the question of what he was to do with his life. A following but undated entry suggests that Christianity can give Faust some reassurance here; by maximizing the relativity of things it presents an idea so big that 'everything else' disappears beside it. As we noted, Kierkegaard sees in this the Romantic and humorous side of Christianity – it no longer matters what you know and can do.[2]

Nikolaus Lenau's *Faust: Ein Dicht* (1836) focuses on the dangers of the quest for absolute knowledge. Here Faust abandons faith and is tempted by Mephistopheles to rebel against God. But having been saved from drowning by Mephistopheles he realizes his impotence and so kills himself. Martensen wrote his short essay in German while abroad, and Kierkegaard probably read it first after his return. In an undated entry from 1837 he says the suicide makes Faust into too much of a living personality. The story is one that belongs to the level of ideas, and Faust's end should be like Don Juan's – or like the Wandering Jew he should end in despair. Another undated entry says Faust, as the idea hovering over all its actual versions, should complete himself in a new idea.[3] What upset Kierkegaard was that in one of Heiberg's journals Martensen had now published an expanded version in Danish.[4] The resourceful Martensen had beaten him to it. Whatever might come of Kierkegaard's Faust manuscript, it could now never make the impact on the cultural elite its ambitious young author must have been hoping for. Faust could no longer help Kierkegaard to make his mark as an author in the way he had surely been counting on.

That was one setback. There was another. Shortly after that disappointment, death came once more to the Kierkegaard family. In July 1837 Peter's young wife, Maria, died. They had been married less than nine months. In that time she had brought warmth to the household. Peter wrote many years later that Maria's arrival at 2 Nytorv had brought 'a mild sunlight up over our old father'.[5] Maria seems in her turn to have been very fond of the old man.[6] She taught singing and the house was filled, aptly for a bishop's daughter but perhaps irritatingly to her Faustian brother-in-law, with the sound of psalms. But she was a delicate girl and had suffered several bad turns during the winter. At the beginning of January she came down with influenza during an epidemic and after a recovery had a relapse that kept her house-bound until February. It was a cold spring, and not long after the sudden arrival of summer warmth, in mid-June, Maria fell ill once more, with gastric fever. Her condition steadily worsened, and by mid-July she was delirious. She died on 18 July and was buried four days later.

Søren's journal entries, in spite of there being several from the week before Maria died and one from the day after, as usual say nothing directly. But in one from 14 July, when it was clear that Maria would not recover, we read: 'I too have combined the tragic with the comic: make witticisms, people laugh – I cry.' Several entries from July disparage the limited horizons and attitudes of the petit bourgeois, their lack of 'nostalgia for something unknown, something remote', these people have never 'felt the depths of being nothing at all'. Another speaks of an experience of being 'harmonized as in a grand poem' in which the whole world, God's and his own, are 'poetry in which all the various, the fearful disparities of life, indigestible for human thought, are expiated in a misty, dreaming existence'. But then, 'alas, unfortunately I wake up again, and the very same tragic relativity in everything begins worse than ever, the endless questions about *what I am*, about my joys and what other people see in me and in what I am doing, when maybe millions are doing exactly the same thing'.[7]

Peter's diary is predictably more informative: 'Søren these days is perhaps more than ever before weighed down with brooding, almost more than his health can stand but it only makes him unhappy, indecisive, and is close to driving him insane. A recreational trip he began the very day of the funeral had to be cut short towards the end once it went wrong, it didn't help at all.'[8]

This was in the early autumn just before Søren left home, though in fact he was half-way out of Nytorv already, and the holiday was just a preview of the departure. Judging by the size of the bills his father was having to pay, he was already spending most of his time on the town. An overwhelming sense of Peter's occupancy might have been a reason – not just the singing but the constant visitors; although Peter had a heavy teaching load and was away a good deal, he conducted his private tutorials at home. In the circumstances it would be no wonder if Søren himself felt de trop. On top of that there was the sickness, and although Michael Pedersen Kierkegaard had survived the winter in reasonably good health and spirits, he was now clearly ailing. Søren was also on bad terms with him, and both before and after Maria's death Peter's concern and later grief approached the morbid.

There had been something else too, a prospect of being less than de trop. Søren was a frequent visitor to a family by the name of Rørdam. Mrs Rørdam was the widow of a well-known pastor. Her son Peter Rørdam was five years older than Søren, a friend also of Peter Kierkegaard and like him a Grundtvigian, as well as a teacher at the School of Civic Virtue. Søren got on well enough with Peter Rørdam's youngest sister Bolette, then twenty-one, well enough for prospects of a more lasting union to occur, at least to others. But on a visit to the family in May he had been completely bowled over by an enchanting guest they had invited over as company for a young girl staying with them for the weekend. The guest was the fifteen-year-old Regine Olsen.

Kierkegaard had gone to the Rørdams to talk to Bolette. Later that evening, he wrote in his journal that the visit was to see if he could still talk with someone without witticism taking the upper hand ('to make that devil wit of mine stay at home'). He speaks of returning to the world 'to reign there' after being 'dethroned in my own inner realm'. He had gone there to try to 'forget' himself, lay down the protective shield of wit, and converse normally with a friend. But the entry ends with Kierkegaard thanking God for 'not letting [him] instantly lose [his] mind' – 'never have I been more afraid [angst] of doing so; be thanked once more for lending me your ear'.[9]

What had God helped him to prevent? Lapsing as usual into witticism? But the entry includes this quotation from Mark 8:36: 'For what shall it profit a man, if he shall gain the whole world, and lose his own soul?' A quiet conversation with Bolette could hardly count as losing his soul. Quite the contrary, one would suppose, for what better way of confirming one's self than by engaging in open conversation? But wit is here described as 'that angel who with flaming sword interposes himself, as I deserve, between me and the heart of every innocent girlish heart'. The 'as I deserve' gives the clue. It was not wit that was held at bay but wit that, with God's help, held something else at bay, interposing itself between him and an innocent girlish heart. In his inner throne, even if he had fallen from it, Kierkegaard had come to believe he must put that sort of thing out of his mind, and now his wit was actually helping him to do so.

There is no absolutely clear indication, but the date, 8 May 1837, must surely be the day he first saw Regine. More than forty years later the then-widowed Regine Schlegel could recall the event but not the date. She remembered the impression Kierkegaard's lively intellect had made on the others, though she didn't show it herself. He spoke 'unceasingly', his words 'poured forth' in an 'extremely captivating' manner.[10] That doesn't sound quite like devil wit, but who knows? In fact the whole entry is enigmatic. It begins: 'Oh God, how easily one forgets such a resolution!' What resolution? – not to let wit get in the way, or to stay away from the world even, if need be, by the help of wit? If the latter, then it must have been the new acquaintance and not the old friend he was thinking of when thanking God for giving him the wit to keep his natural inclinations in check. But why should it require wit to keep an impressionable young girl at arm's length when wit might be, as it apparently was, just what such a young girl found so fascinating? Or was it wit that kept him from being 'openly' himself and from saying what he felt?

An undated entry from about the same time says:

> Again today, the same performance – still, I managed to get out to R – My God, why should these feelings awaken just now – oh, how alone I feel! – oh, curse that vain self-satisfaction at standing alone – now everyone would despise me – oh, but you, my God, do not let go of me – let me live and improve myself![11]

This, too, is hard to decipher. If, as the wording suggests, the 'performance' preceded the visit, the feelings could be the attraction he felt for the girl from that earlier occasion. Now they are prompting him to question his own motives for thinking it so important to stay out of the world. But then why would people 'despise' him? Surely not because he had shown too obvious an interest in the young girl; Regine's recollections give no hint of his having done that. Maybe he means that people would despise him if he were to give in to his inclinations and actually pursue the girl – after all she was very young. Or was it rather that a well-earned reputation for asceticism would be punctured by any such pursuit?

Given Kierkegaard's dining-out habits and general sociability this seems unlikely. And it does seem more plausible to suppose that the 'resolution' in question was to forswear wit rather than the company of pretty girls. An entry preceding the other two says: 'I will steer clear of those who lie in wait to see if one has made this or that resolution – I shall turn to Him who is happier with one reformed sinner than with the ninety-nine wise men who have no need to reform.'[12] Doesn't that sound as though whatever good intention he might expect to be accused of not fulfilling he didn't care what people thought? But then again, in the last entry he was afraid of being despised. It is hard to keep track.

The 'performance' (*Optrin*) might be something quite different. The perhaps not-too-far-fetched possibility has been aired that Kierkegaard was an epileptic.[13] If so, it would not be unexpected that there had been several attacks of late. An epileptic attack, however, could hardly be described in terms of 'these feelings'. But there might have been any number of other commotions, irritations, or disturbances at Nytorv deserving the word, which would at least leave open the case for Regine's being the occasion for the second but not the first entry.

In any case, at the time, Kierkegaard did not pursue the girl, though he later admitted she had the effect of casting a magic spell on him.[14] Obviously he was in a turmoil, about what others thought of him and about what to do with himself. Beneath the sheen of cleverness and wit he was still somehow just nothing, or only something that – as he says – could be called 'angst'. To become something he would need to get out of the house. Perhaps the meeting with Regine gave added impetus to that idea. It could go in two directions, but one of them was a family home of his own, its centre of gravity his love of his wife.

That was just a few weeks before Martensen's essay on Lenau's *Faust* appeared in its expanded Danish version. One dream gone. Shortly after that his sister-in-law's death must have reminded him of how little time there might be to fulfil dreams at all. Peter's unrestrained grief enveloped the house. Søren went on his unavailing rest-cure, according to Peter in no better shape than himself. Among these tribulations he had also accumulated debts. There are promissory notes from October of the previous year, and in November because of unpaid dues he was warned that he would be excluded from the premises of the Student Union unless he paid up by Monday, 5 December. On 28 July, six days after Maria's funeral, his father's ledger for the first time shows a receipt signed by Søren (for twenty rixdalers, the equivalent today of about two hundred and fifty U.S. dollars),[15] with the remark: 'Since I shall be moving out of my father's house the coming 1 September and will cease being a member of his household, he has promised me until further notice 500 rd. annually for my upkeep.'

On 1 September he moved, with his now quite extensive library, into an apartment at 7 Løvstræde. The new arrangement made Kierkegaard economically independent but also responsible for his own debts – in principle at least, though on 14 January he had to sign again, this time for receipt of over a thousand rixdalers (today about twelve thousand dollars) to cover debts accumulated the previous year to among others a bookbinder, coffee shops, tobacco shops, a draper, bookshops, a shoemaker, and a clothier. Again the signature is accompanied by a comment: 'And thus has my father helped me out of my embarrassment, for which reason I testify to him here my thanks.' In the series of journal entries on humour and irony there is one entry that might well invoke a certain irony in the reader: It points to a 'trait of the Jews when things went wrong for them'. They 'corrupted' the hope for a saviour into an expectation of an earthly Messiah: 'Who doesn't recall the many dreams of money that was to bring health and peace of mind, of a successful marriage, of appointment in a certain position in the state, etc.?' But maybe Kierkegaard saw the irony himself, for there is a short interjection in the margin: 'Every Christian has also had his earthly Messiah.'[16]

That autumn and winter, to ease the financial situation, Kierkegaard taught Latin at his old school to the pre–leaving year pupils. At the university he had joined the many students attending Martensen's lectures. Well before they started, on 15 November, Kierkegaard had for the first time mentioned a doctoral dissertation, thinking a suitable theme would be 'the concept of satire with the ancients' and 'the relation of the various Roman satirists to each other'.[17] Five days earlier he had envisaged a larger topic, perhaps for a longer-term project. It shows him in an optimistically constructive frame of mind.

It would be interesting to follow the development of human nature (in individuals – i.e. the different age groups) by showing what one laughs at at different ages, basing the experiments in part on one and the same author, for example our literary fountainhead, Holberg, and in part on different kinds of comedy. This together with research and experiments concerning the age-level at which tragedy is best appreciated and other psychological observations on the relation between comedy and tragedy (e.g. why one reads tragedy alone and comedy together with others), would contribute to the work I believe ought now to be written – namely, the history of the human soul (as it is in an ordinary human being) in the continuity of mental states (not the concepts) consolidating in particular peaks and nodes (i.e. noteworthy world-historical representatives of life-views).[18]

If the frame of mind is constructive it is still self-referential. Or rather, what might be said of Kierkegaard's 'broodings' in the area of humour and irony at this point is that they are self-referentially constructive. He is fascinated by his own ability to laugh in the presence of continued intimations of life's finitude: 'I am a two-faced Janus, with one face I laugh with the other I cry.' There are many notes written on scraps of paper and inserted later in the notebooks, where the main entries were written with large margins for just such a purpose. Since he continued to frequent cafés many of them may have been written there:

Would to God I was a fiddler – a farmer's woodland dance – O God!, they are after all the happiest class of people, farmers and farm girls. But just now I have no way of expressing all my feelings. If only while out there I had had someone to make myself known to – one of the few who I now more than ever cling to – and be rid of these *petit-bourgeois* and these cadets who don't as many do look on the mote [in their brother's eye] with childish good nature but in their superiority lose sight of the good.[19]

Had he been 'out there'? Yes, on his abortive post-funeral convalescent trip he had been at Hillerød, in the woodlands just north of the city. Ever since his childhood Kierkegaard had visited Hillerød, where his brothers-in-law's family had their country place. There he enjoyed rural activities, including riding, and when Wilhelm Lund had been there, some natural research. But the reference might also be ambiguous and indicate some earlier social event in town. He may in any case have been thinking partly of Regine, there is simply no knowing. The many short entries from this period do, however, bear out Peter's description of a deeply troubled soul. The difference was that while Peter merely observes the depression around him, Søren constantly thematizes it and finds new ways of expressing, if not his feelings, at least the divided mental state that prevented him expressing or perhaps even having any definitely directed feelings. Even the preparations for his Latin classes contribute. 'It's a remarkable transition when one begins to teach the doctrine of indicative and subjunctive, since this is where we first become aware of the fact that everything depends on how it is thought, how in its absoluteness thinking gives rise to a seeming reality.' And just in the way 'the indicative thinks something as actual (the identity of thought and reality)' while 'the subjunctive thinks something as thinkable', his own life is 'unfortunately far too subjunctive'. 'Would to God I had some indicative power!'[20]

The same analogy offers, incidentally, one of the few signs so far of any interest in a critique of philosophy as such:

The grammar of indicative and subjunctive really embraces those concepts of the most aesthetic kind and gives rise to just about the highest form of aesthetic enjoyment (it borders on music, which is the highest). And the hackneyed proposition *cogito ergo sum* holds true of the subjunctive. It is the subjunctive's life-principle (one could therefore really present the whole of modern philosophy in a theory about the indicative and the subjunctive, for it is indeed purely subjunctive).[21]

This is an iconoclastic thought and shows why Kierkegaard finds philosophy uninteresting: it gives rise only to 'seeming' realities. If Descartes's principle were true, the 'I am' (*sum*) that follows from 'I think' (*cogito*) would be unreal. If you are to have any indicative power you will have to either steer clear of philosophy or overcome it. Nevertheless Kierkegaard followed Martensen's lectures and made summarizing notes.[22] There are few comments, but it is not unlikely that the one just quoted follows the fifth lecture, which was on Kant but began by mentioning Descartes. The lectures were given on Wednesdays and Fridays under the title Introduction to Speculative Dogmatics and began on Wednesday, 15 November. The series was in fact a history of modern philosophy reconstructed from the point of view of a Hegelian and beginning with the conventional Hegelian criticism of Kant. It presented earlier views as 'standpoints' in the way that Kierkegaard later referred to so scornfully. But Martensen's main purpose was to arrive at something he called 'speculative dogmatics', a Hegelian position in which religion could trump 'mere' philosophy, reentering at the level of the philosophy of reason, which in the official Hegelian view took over from religion by providing the concepts for truths which religion could only capture in narrative form. The lectures on speculative dogmatics itself were given in the summer. The next winter Martensen repeated his lectures under the revised title Lectures on the History of Modern Philosophy from Kant to Hegel. Kierkegaard attended these too and took fairly extensive notes but without comment.

During early 1838, actually starting from 27 December, there is a long silence in Kierkegaard's journal, though some of the rather hectic and strained loose entries (written on eight separate days from January to February) in fact originate in this period, just as many more may. The first entry in the spring says simply, 'Again such a long time has gone in which I have been unable to rally myself for the least thing – I must now make another little attempt at it – Poul Møller is dead'.[23]

Møller had been ill for some time, and though the entry is marked 'April' he had died on 13 March. He was only forty-four years old and had been Kierkegaard's mainstay, both philosophically and personally, a strong and sound personality with whom Kierkegaard could vicariously share that kind of easy familiarity with life which is born of long experience, a seriousness about life in general but allied to an acute sense of life's detail and of the ridiculous, especially in cases of a seriousness that is misplaced. Hans Brøchner, the young man who on first seeing Kierkegaard took him for a draper's assistant but became a close friend and later taught Greek philosophy at the university, tells how in 1836 Kierkegaard and Møller were present at a dissertation defence, where Møller was an official opponent and Kierkegaard was in the auditorium. Disputations were conducted in Latin, and Møller began each interpolation with the standard '*graviter vituperandum est*' (it must seriously be objected) but then quickly interceded with a friendly '*concedo*' (I concede) as soon as the candidate replied. When it was over he apologized profusely that time didn't permit him to continue 'this interesting conversation'. The session's unusual brevity was due to Møller's, on opening his copy of the dissertation, having lost all the notes he had carefully placed at the appropriate pages. Brøchner remarks that the sight of the large figure crawling about collecting his scraps of paper had 'done not a little to improve the mood of the audience'.[24] On the way out Møller passed Kierkegaard and whispered, 'Let's go down to Pleisch's', a favourite tearoom.

To commemorate Møller an evening entertainment was held at the Royal Theatre on 1 April. Naturally, Kierkegaard attended. He notes in his journal that he went there to 'hear [the actor N. P.] Nielsen recite [Møller's] "Joy over Denmark"', but had been 'so strangely gripped by the words: "remember the far-travelled man." Yes, now he has travelled far – but I for one will certainly remember him'.[25] *The Concept of Anxiety* would be dedicated to Møller. In an unpublished version of the dedication Kierkegaard hailed him as 'the mighty trumpet of my awakening'. Other expressions also omitted from the final dedication were 'inspiration of my youth', 'confidant of my beginning', 'lost friend', and (since at Møller's death Kierkegaard had published nothing) 'missed reader'.[26]

Møller's death left several vacancies, the most obvious being his academic position. Though, due to a lack of suitably qualified candidates, the position would not be filled until April 1841 and then by a professed defender of Kierkegaard, Rasmus Nielsen, it was Martensen who, for the time being, took over Møller's teaching burden. Even if he must have realized the logic in this, the situation must have been hard for Kierkegaard to swallow. Through Martensen, already Heiberg's friend and established in the forefront of Danish intellectual life, Heiberg was now colonizing the university and effectively closing off a main channel for the reception of ideas emanating from writers from the younger generation of German thinkers. After just two years in the temporary lectureship Martensen would, on 1 December 1841, become professor extraordinary of theology at the early age of thirty-two.

Another vacancy Møller's death left in Denmark is less easy to define. Poul Martin Møller was a poet and a philosopher. Although apart from any sense of its inappropriateness Kierkegaard may also have felt some pangs of jealousy at Martensen's succession, he could not have held any realistic hopes of being the successor himself. But on the literary path he was ideally equipped to follow in Møller's footsteps; Møller's death left Kierkegaard an opening if not as a professor at least, or better, as a writer, an ambition more likely to impart the indicative power he so wanted. Møller, in spite of his small production of poems and short stories, was (and is) a Danish classic. His philosophy came out in three posthumous volumes from 1839 to 1843, including the famous 'Strøtanker' (aphorisms, literally 'scattered thoughts'), a form for which Kierkegaard was also admirably suited. There is also little doubt that many of the themes we have traced in the early journals such as the Wandering Jew and the Faust legend are a legacy of Kierkegaard's friendship with Møller.

But then hadn't Martensen himself brought his first plans in this quasi-philosophical literary direction to nothing? Several factors make the view that Martensen rather than Hegel was becoming the next main target seem plausible. First, as noted earlier, feeling that he knew where the weaknesses of Hegelian philosophy lay, Kierkegaard had nothing to fear from Hegel. He was interested in something else, something closer to life. In this he would certainly have been influenced and supported by Poul Møller. An indication of how Møller's early attachment to Hegel's project (in the *Phenomenology of Spirit* and *Encyclopedia*) had not lasted is the view of truth which Møller came to hold, in which 'an expression's presentation of a thought has truth really only at that very moment when the thought is produced' – any other conception of the truth of an expression is abstract. Besides, Hegel himself had been dead since 1831, and so many diverging views now went by the name 'Hegelian' that it would be as futile to address any one of them as it would be impossible to address them all. On top of that, Kierkegaard, in spite of whatever reasons made him feel he could afford to let the great philosopher go by, seems to have maintained a genuine admiration for Hegel, an admiration which Martensen's lectures in the Hegelian style may have done nothing to diminish. And indeed, who could fail to be impressed by the incredible combination of scope and detail characteristic of Hegelianism, the way things, the specifics of human history itself, appear to hang together, or who could fail to have a heady sense of intellectual mastery from the very appearance of their doing so?

It is not beyond the bounds of fantasy to suppose that, in only slightly altered circumstances, Kierkegaard might never have troubled to go to the lengths of his pseudonym Johannes Climacus, or might even have gone to Hegel's defence against Martensen's attempt to assemble a Hegelian Christology, which was polluting once more that clear distinction between philosophy and religion that Schleiermacher, in his own way, had so properly insisted on preserving.

What the circumstances were and how they dictated the actual outcome one of course cannot say for certain. But the possibilities are at least discernible. At a fairly petty level, Kierkegaard's opposition to Martensen may have had something to do with Martensen's being accepted by Heiberg. But there are more interesting sociocultural sides to it. Heibergian pantheism, the official demoting of religion to metaphor in Heiberg's Hegel, as well as the simplistic presentation of Hegelian philosophy in what looks much more like an extension of the aesthetic theory than the view from somewhere above aesthetics, sat comfortably with a cultural elite that felt, if not above the church, at least its equal. Martensen, so long as it was a philosophical career that he was protecting, would also find this extremely congenial. It would suit him admirably if, simply by elaborating the same set of assumptions and without having to go 'primitive', he could bring Christ and a personal God back into the picture; theology and philosophy would be united, the cultural elite would still have its place, and Martensen would have his place among the cultural elite, even a special place.

Whether or not Martensen saw it in this way, it may well have been the way Kierkegaard saw Martensen. He would have a special reason for attacking Martensen on this score, far more fundamental than the disposal of a Hegelian ally of Heiberg or appropriator of Hegel for the church. Far more important for him, too, than merely getting the better of the most influential coterie in Copenhagen: he would be vindicating his father's living religion. Beside the petty rivalries there was the more compelling need to make the people's religion of his father tough enough to withstand speculative philosophy, to be so clearly alien to it that no one should think of the possibility of a speculative dogmatics. This would be a difficult task now that Martensen had learned the Hegelian ropes, but also a necessary one just because he had learned them. It was no longer just a matter of supporting living religion against the vapid intellectualisms of the rationalist theologians. But he would have to distance himself at the same time from the vulgar popularism of that other form of living religion, the Grundtvigianism eschewed by his brother and now gaining a foothold in theological circles. Defending his father's religion – and in the last two years it had kept its fascination for him even if he couldn't enter into it – would require sophistication. The defence would have to be carried out in the terms of the 'opposite camp', his complex allegiance to which Kierkegaard would therefore have to maintain, as a kind of philosopher in their midst who tries to show them, or anyone else for that matter, ourselves included, where the limits of philosophy lie.

What task would be better suited both to his talents and to his indecisiveness about what he should do with his life? If a compulsive tendency towards reflection made him a less convincing adherent of living faith than his father, Kierkegaard's intellectual brilliance could still be employed in the cause of that faith, while the skills of an imaginative writer, which because it was creative rather than destructive was the gift he most prized in himself, could be deployed to ensure that the intellect was being used only ironically in order to show that really, in the case of faith, it should not be used at all.

There was also a kind of built-in insurance in this. If Kierkegaard failed as a writer he might still impress the right people with his dialectic, and if that failed to impress, the efforts of the imaginative writer still might. If both failed, it would still have been in a good cause, of an idea one could really be said to live and perhaps if necessary die for. Poetry, in any case, or writing, seemed to be the place to start. The same day that he noted the passing of Poul Møller, Kierkegaard wrote: 'This morning I saw in the fresh cool air a dozen wild geese fly away, first they were right overhead, then further and further and finally they separated into two flocks and arched themselves like two eyebrows over my eyes, which now gazed into the land of poesy.'[27]

The Dead and the Living:
Debut

Fᴿᴏᴍ ᴛʜᴇ ᴇɴᴅ ᴏꜰ ᴀᴩʀɪʟ 1838 until the beginning of July Kierkegaard puts his journals aside. Twenty-eight entries from April
give way to two for May and June, one from each, before they pick up
again in July. This time there is no doubt what preoccupied him.
Kierkegaard's first publication appeared in the early autumn, on 7
September. The manuscript, published as *Af en endnu Levendes Papirer*
(From the Papers of One Still Living) was ready from his own hand by
mid-July, but he had sent it to Heiberg for possible publication in the
latter's *Perseus, Journal for den speculative Idee*,[1] and Heiberg disliked
the style. In deference Kierkegaard elicited the help of a poet and
former school friend, Hans Peter Holst, who, at any rate on his own
testimony more than thirty years later, rewrote the manuscript,

or rather translated it from Latin into Danish. . . . It was quite natural he should
turn to me in this connection since at the School of Civic Virtue there was a normal
traffic between us, I writing Danish composition for him and he Latin composition
for me. Strange that someone who ended up writing such excellent Danish had no
grasp of it at all in his youth but wrote a Latin-Danish crawling with participials
and the most complicated sentence structures.[2]

When the essay – with its mere forty-five pages hardly more than a
pamphlet – finally did appear, its title announced that it was 'published
by S. Kierkegaard against his will', the latter phrase in bold type. This
bears some interpretation; indeed, in some respects the Preface is as
interesting as the work itself, not least because Kierkegaard suggests
that readers put off by the Preface might as well skip the whole essay.

Kierkegaard cannot have meant that he didn't want to publish it.
Although the Preface makes reference to the 'real author' as an alter
ego, as though confessing that his alter ego had persuaded him to
publish against his better judgment, apart from being pure coquetry,

that would imply that he was really quite pleased with the product –
which can hardly be true if Holst played as large a part as he later
claimed, though that too is of course open to doubt. In any case, since
Heiberg's judgment undoubtedly still mattered to him, the latter's reservations must certainly have left Kierkegaard to some degree dissatisfied with his own work.

It may not have been the publication that occurred against his will
but the fact that he has had to publish it himself, as was indeed the
case. Which, again, was not simply a matter of defraying the costs; for
he could afford that, and indeed the publication made a slight profit.[3]
Much worse was the embarrassment of having to make an authorial
debut under one's own imprint; it is the stamp of approval conveyed by
a process of editorial selection that makes a debut genuine. So it would
have been much better in every way if Heiberg had published it. We
don't know what Heiberg thought of the revised version, since *Perseus*
went through only two numbers, the last that August.[4]

More important than these considerations are the thoughts behind
the publication. Its subtitle is 'On Andersen as Novelist with Constant
Reference to *Only a Fiddler* [*Kun en Spillemand*]'. The Andersen was
the talented and productive Hans Christian (1805–1875), eight years
Kierkegaard's senior and with an already considerable and respected
authorship behind him. According to Andersen himself he and Kierkegaard had met on the street one day and the latter had promised him a
review that would please Andersen more than the others the work had
received. These, according to Kierkegaard, had not properly understood
him.[5]

That could have meant anything. The novel, subtitled *Original Novel
in Two Parts* (*Original Roman i to Dele*) was Andersen's most recently
published. No doubt aware of Kierkegaard's reputation for polemics
Andersen waited with increasing trepidation as time wore on without
Kierkegaard's review appearing. At the end of August, even though the
novel had a few days earlier received a review that well pleased him,
Andersen writes in a diary kept especially for records of visits and states
of his health, 'Suffered mental torments over Kierkegaard's as yet unpublished review'. When it did finally appear, exactly a week later, his
worst fears were realized. 'A disturbing letter from [Christian] Wulff
and immediately afterwards Kierkegaard's criticism. Eduard gave me
cooling powders. Have gone as though in a coma. Dinner with Mrs

Bügel. Wrote to Wulff.' That was on Thursday, 6 September.[6] Whether his close friend Wulff had got wind of the review and it was this that the letter was about, we don't know. But the review itself had become an essay on the importance to literature of a 'view of life', and what it claimed the earlier reviewers had failed to appreciate in Andersen was that his work totally lacked this feature.

Before considering what Kierkegaard was trying to do in or by means of this modestly sized publication, it is worth dwelling a moment on that Preface. Two points in particular are of interest for future reference. One is the mention already noted of an alter ego, and the other is a postscript Kierkegaard appended to the Preface.

At first blush the alter ego might be taken as a reference to the late Poul Møller. That could make the unwillingness to publish genuinely Kierkegaard's, the ideas being Møller's and published in spite of the infelicities remarked by Heiberg. Møller had a fine command of language. There is something to this, since some of the ideas undoubtedly were either derived from or shared with Møller, not least that of a lifeview. Or the unwillingness could be Kierkegaard's presuming to present the aphorist's thoughts in the form of a mini-dissertation. That Møller was much in Kierkegaard's mind as he wrote the work is also certain; he had, after all, died as recently as 13 March, and the journal entry remarking the fact where Kierkegaard talks about trying once more to pull himself together was dated 1 April. Kierkegaard was almost certainly at work from the end of that month on what indeed he called his 'little' dissertation.

These facts do not, however, account for the idea of an alter ego, presented in the Preface as some kind of alien influence working from outside as though the creative work were being done by someone else. The Preface presents the work as if it had fought itself into existence, as though Kierkegaard himself had even fought against it and was at least not directly responsible for what he had penned. Near the close of the Preface he says that, having come so far, he feels now 'bound' by the 'fixed form' that the work has acquired, that of a dissertation. Yet, rather than an apology to the memory of Møller, in context these words seem to be expressing something closer to home, a desire to be free. To 'feel free', he says, he will personally take it all back, back 'into the womb', letting it 'subside once more in the twilight from which it emerged'.

A strange freedom for a creative writer to wish for? This idea of freeing himself from responsibility for what he had written was to recur and even dominate Kierkegaard's writing, at least wherever anything that might be taken for a thesis was offered. Most famously it was to occur in the form of a formal retraction, or revocation, in an appendix (still under the pseudonym) to the final work in the main pseudonymous series, the *Concluding Unscientific Postscript* of 1846. But here, in this first of Kierkegaard's postscripts and appended to a preface, Kierkegaard seems, by withdrawing even before he starts, to vanish from the daylight of serious authorial responsibility even before it has dawned:

Postscript for readers who might possibly be worse off for reading the preface: they could of course skip it, and skip so far that they skipped over the dissertation too, which wouldn't matter.[7]

Take it or leave it, he seems to be saying. One image that springs to mind is of the mischief-maker pressing (or in pre-electric days pulling) the doorbell and dodging out of sight before the owner answers it, taking great enjoyment in the inconvenience caused and even more delight in the thought of not being there to be answerable, thus adding fury to inconvenience, and on top of all that, 'feeling free' in a particularly satisfying because provocative way. But to leave a book on the doorstep without caring whether the occupant reads it is not quite the same thing, and the freedom evoked by not staying to answer for whatever the book says must have some other source than the simple glee of the scamp. Especially, you would think, where the book has the form of a treatise, not caring whether what you have written is read or not, or, if it is, whether the reader agrees or disagrees, looks like a breach of the rules of intellectual life. Just as scientists have to put up with the possibility of being refuted by future empirical evidence, and philosophers expose their views and arguments to scrutiny and possible refutation, so are authors of any work that claims to say something expected to present it as a serious contribution to debate and to wait around long enough to take account of possible objections.

Is this pretence of not being responsible for what he has written simply immature evasiveness on Kierkegaard's part? Or fear of getting embroiled again in a vitriolic debate? Or is it just a literary mannerism typical of the times? Whatever part these explanations might then have played, we may see in this Preface to Kierkegaard's first published work

an expression of an attitude to which he later gives something like the
status of a philosophical position. It is the view that in order to grasp
the truth of what is said you must first share the perspective from which
the words expressing what is said appear compelling to their author. In
the ordinary way of understanding philosophy and philosophical debate
this, for most people, would be a hopeless view to take, destroying as it
does the basis for all rational agreement. Yet not all philosophers would
agree. Some of the exceptions are surprising. Descartes defended his
choice of 'the form of Meditations rather than that of Philosophical
Disputations or the theorems and problems of a geometer' by saying
that he could

> by this very fact testify that I had no dealings except with those who will not shrink
> from joining me in giving the matter attentive care and meditation. For from the
> very fact that anyone girds himself up for an attack upon the truth, he makes
> himself less capable of perceiving the truth itself, since he withdraws his mind from
> the consideration of those reasons that tend to convince him of it, in order to
> discover others that have the opposite effect.[8]

This passage throws interesting light on Kierkegaard's later plan to
emulate Descartes, but the position would be less surprising in a philosopher versed in Hegel. To the Hegelian it makes good sense to say that
the appearance of evident truth depends on replaceable and therefore
not necessarily shared background assumptions, among which are included even the allegedly basic categories of thought and understanding.
Quite apart from Hegel, however, and what Kierkegaard may have
learnt from him, it must be evident to any observer of the philosophical
scene that this self-protective device – a form of relativism – is discernible in anyone whose initial response to criticism is that the reader has
not, indeed cannot have, understood what the author meant to say.
What is astonishing, in a form of discourse where open-minded rational
debate is supposedly of the essence, is how often this defensive response
is evoked, or, from the other side, called for. Although many well-
known contemporary philosophers would be shocked at the accusation
of relativism and vigorously defend the rationality of their positions,
they nevertheless show by their behaviour that they fall squarely into
this bracket. It is a difficult distinction to apply, but there is a crucial
difference between the just accusation that one's critics simply fail to
read one's works closely and the sense, when that suspicion cannot be
seriously upheld, of a total unwillingness to share one's initial point of

view. The serious philosopher who genuinely invites refutation is a very
rare bird. One very famous philosopher, Ludwig Wittgenstein, actually
claimed not to be interested in arguing his points at all, since they
would be clear to anyone who had come to them in the way he had, and
if they had not yet reached that vantage-point then discussion would be
fruitless in any case. Wittgenstein read Kierkegaard, and, as we shall
see, Kierkegaard later adopted a very similar attitude. Perhaps already
in this early work we have an indication of a similar impatience with
discussion and a suspicion, a grounded suspicion even, of the high status
traditionally given to argument. We can of course choose, if we like, to
look at it as Martensen did: Kierkegaard was simply 'unfitted to engage
in a scholarly contest in philosophy'. There are in that vein even deeper
roots to lay bare. The fact that Kierkegaard did not cultivate but came
to scorn such an ability could be a refusal to compete with his famously
disputational brother. But such explanations aside, we can in retrospect
see the kind of reservations concerning scholarly contests that Kierkegaard grew in his own writings to articulate, both directly and indirectly,
as expressions of an innovative view concerning the place of rational
thought in human understanding, a view expressed here briefly and
playfully in the Preface to his first publication.

Whatever the provenance of the treatise's ideas, the main thesis of
the work is one that we recognize as having a special hold on Kierkegaard from the start. It is the view briefly presented in the talk to the
Student Union in which he opposed the fashion of introducing new and
untried ideas into politics. Indeed, the text opens, just as the curious
interpolation in that talk did, with a reference to the way everything
was going. There it had been a 'formal striving'. Now it was the attempt
to subtract the past and pretend that, at last, everything was about to
begin. Kierkegaard cites Hegel's 'great attempt to begin with nothing'
as the 'most respectable' example of this way of thinking, and the
opening pages are replete with Hegelian expressions and allusions. But,
as background for a comparison of recent literature, it is the political
version of the trend that he refers to first. As Kierkegaard puts it, in a
sentence (here much shortened) that also tells us something about what
Holst had to contend with:

Misunderstanding the deeper meaning of a historical evolution, clinging to the
phrase, oddly enough as though life depended on it, that the world always gets
wiser, though grasping it, note, in a way peculiarly fitted though also parodically to
this moment, [the main political tendency of our time] appears [either] in the form

of a youthful arrogance that has too great a confidence in forces untried in life (and this is its best side), or as lacking the patience needed for putting up with the conditions of life, lacking the strength to take on, by filling some position in the State, the rational, light and richly blessed burden of history.

All that politics can offer, in other words, is either a freshness of spirit that lacks the weight of experience, or a weakness of spirit that shuns the rewarding task of sustaining state institutions. In both forms, Kierkegaard says, the political tendency 'is guilty of trying to assassinate actuality'.[9]

The conservatism of the remarks is as evident as their strongly Hegelian tone, and what Kierkegaard says here in his own name clearly anticipates views he was later to pen in the persona of the ethicist, Assessor Wilhelm, in the second part of *Either/Or*. How far their anticipation here is due to the ideas of an alien alter-ego in the shape of Møller is hard to say, but what can be said is that much of *From the Papers of One Still Living* can be seen to be Heibergian, and in at least this respect Kierkegaard is not yet 'free'. But there is a savage little twist in assimilating the liberal politicians' desire to forget history with Hegel's attempt to begin with nothing. Making Hegel's attempt to build an edifice of thought in defence of conservatism appear akin to the formalism which Hegel, Heiberg, and Kierkegaard all deplore in liberal politicians, is to prise out of the Hegel Kierkegaard still admired something that he could attack with the same weapons that all three would agree should be deployed against radical politics. The fact that this something could pass as the quintessential Hegel would make the prospect of separation from Heiberg on the central issue of the role of philosophy even more appealing.

The 'review' Andersen had been promised proved to be a critical assessment of recent literature with Andersen in the role of stalking-horse, allowing Kierkegaard to introduce the notion of a life-view, which he then indirectly explains through enumerating the various ways in which Andersen fails to evince such a thing. Although the themes are not just local, and Kierkegaard is here touching issues that were engaging a new generation of intellectuals in Europe with whose ideas their Danish contemporaries were keenly familiar, the treatise focuses on the local scene. In a brief survey of recent Danish literature he compares, on the one hand, a series of short stories which also 'start with nothing' in the sense that they are concerned with nothing grander than everyday life, but manage to portray in their familiar settings a confidence in life, with, and on the other hand, the work of a lyric poet and pastor who lived in Jutland. The author of the cycle of short stories was in fact Heiberg's mother, Thomasine Gyllembourg-Ehrensvärd (1773–1856), the anonymous author of a feuilleton entitled 'En Hverdagshistorie' (A Story of Everyday Life) published in her son's *Kjøbenhavns flyvende Post*. The cycle that followed this was published in her son's name with the author identified as 'the author of an Everyday Story', emulating in this respect her almost exact contemporary Walter Scott (1771–1832), who famously identified himself as 'the author of Waverley'. Kierkegaard, who certainly knew the identity of the author but always dutifully refers to her as 'he', accepts that these works are aimed at a mature audience whose possession of a life-view is a presupposition of their being written. They in fact demonstrate the way in which a life-view, understood here as a positive attitude towards life, takes shape in the course of life, or indeed of many lives, in the face of whose ups and downs a faith in life is nevertheless sustained.[10] The lyric poet from Jutland, Steen Steensen Blicher (1782–1848), presupposes no such thing. The unity of vision he appeals to is that of a private poetic mood, and it takes more than the 'acuteness of a Cuvier [G. Cuvier (1769–1832), the paleontologist] to make a totality' out of individual 'dramatically pregnant phrases'. Pursuing the analogy, Kierkegaard says that you need, as background, the very depths of nature's own process of becoming. This can also be described as beginning with nothing, for it is after all original and, although it says nothing directly to life, does still 'point in a way to the future' and may have some healthy influence on 'the way in which political questions have up to now been treated'.[11]

Kierkegaard then proceeds to show how Andersen fails to demonstrate this virtue. The biggest criticism is that no life-view emerges from the work under review, and since a life-view is what gives a novel its necessary centre of gravity, Andersen has not really written a novel. That, still being a comparatively young author, he can be excused for not having developed a life-view is really no excuse; rather, it is a reason for not trying to write a novel. And although it is true that a life-view belongs to the end of a life rather than to its beginning, you cannot wait until a person is dead, or even later, for them to have enough of what it takes to get started. A poet, says Kierkegaard, must first gain a personality, and any novel should contain something like an immortal spirit that survives everything; no author should perish with his fallen heroes.

But so closely identified is Andersen with his production that his writing is less a 'production' than an 'amputation'. Also, although the central figure in the story is portrayed as a genius to be counted among the holy, there is no development in the story to make this status convincing, and 'it requires no art' to make a man holy 'with just pen and paper'.[12]

It matters less what justice there is in these criticisms – and Kierkegaard does praise Andersen's abilities and his earlier work – than what sense can be made of the later so crucial notion of a life-view. Since this was to be a key concept in Kierkegaard's later writings, and the way it is introduced here leaves many points unclear, it is worth dwelling for a moment on what he says.

The idea of a life-view (*Livs-Anskuelse*) can strike one as inconsistent with a conservative call to take on the burdens of history. It does so if one thinks of a life-view as something you might put on or adopt deliberately to give shape to your life. However, as Kierkegaard explains it, and we have seen this idea earlier, a life-view is not something you give *to* your experience but something you gain *from* experience, and not just passively. A life-view, says Kierkegaard,

is more than a totality [*Indbegreb*] or a sum of principles maintained in its abstract indeterminacy [*Hverkenhed*]; it is more than experience, which is as such always atomistic; it is in fact the transubstantiation of experience, it is an unshakeable security [*Sikkerhed*] in oneself won from all experience [*Empirie*], whether it has oriented itself purely in all worldly conditions (a purely human standpoint, Stoicism for instance) which remains out of touch with a deeper experiential basis [*en dybere Empirie*] – or, in its orientation towards heaven (the religious), it has found there the central thing, as much for its earthly as its heavenly existence, has won the true Christian conviction [*Forvisning*]: 'that neither death nor life, nor angels, nor principalities, nor powers, nor things present, nor thing to come, nor height, nor depth, nor any other creature shall be able to separate us from the love of God, which is in Christ Jesus our Lord.[13]

If the sense of certainty that a life-view provides has to be won from experience, how can the life-view that does that be available prior to the experiences themselves that the life view comes to 'transubstantiate'? To allow the sense of certainty to stick, one must surely first live in the way that the life-view proposes.

An answer might be found in something like Schleiermacher's 'hermeneutical circle'. Here a preliminary orientation to a field of inquiry raises questions which initiate a movement of circular inference from part to whole and back again. According to Schleiermacher, the reciprocal movement is brought to a sudden close in a moment of enlightenment, or complete illumination, in which everything is understood in its place. Because it is a response to a process of questioning already set in motion, this moment of illumination doesn't come totally unannounced.[14] But even if this idea, designed to explain the process of interpreting texts, could cast light on what Kierkegaard means by a life-view, it cannot have influenced the latter directly, for in his lifetime Schleiermacher published very little on hermeneutics. But also, the unshakeable certainty that Kierkegaard talks about in connection with a life-view often sounds as though it were associated with an element of return, a certainty recaptured. Here, too, however, we have something, the child's certainty (though this would hardly be the right word if, in this state of innocence, no sense of the distinction between safe and unsafe has yet been established) as something that one begins with, and so has a preliminary idea of, and will thus recognize on a sudden if it is regained.

But even if Kierkegaard may be drawing his analogy from the notion of a lost immediacy of this kind, what he discusses is a postlapsarian certainty whose absence it is rather the lot of the adult to feel. In that case, to find what is already grasped before the moment of illumination all we need do may be to look in the culture itself, in life-views that exist but only in the form of words and which need the spark of a moment of illumination to transform them into something that henceforth informs one's life.

Yet another clue to the idea of winning a life-view from experience may be found in Møller's unfinished project, which sees the question of maturity as one of forming a unity out of distinct and initially disparate elements in life. The life-view puts them in their proper order, and that requires giving them an order, not externally by choosing kinds of thing to do or say, but internally by opening oneself to a kind of illumination provided in one's own experience. Kierkegaard says:

If we are asked how such a view of life comes about, we answer that for the person who does not allow his life, to far too great an extent, fizzle out [*futte ud*] but as far as possible seeks to turn its individual expressions inwards again, there must of necessity come a moment in which a strange illumination spreads over life – without his needing in even the remotest manner to understand all possible particulars – for the subsequent understanding of which he now has the key; there must, I say, come a moment when, as Daub observes, life is understood backwards through the idea.[15]

The idea of illumination might seem to repeat the problem. How can a life-view be an illumination that comes to one all of a sudden when it is also won and tested in experience? What must be a wrong interpretation is uncannily suggested in a passage of Heiberg's, where he describes his conversion to Hegelianism fourteen years earlier. Although unpublished at that time, the story was surely already known in Heibergian circles. In the summer of 1824 Heiberg had been in Berlin and had met and talked with Hegel. In his 'Autobiographical Fragments', first published at the end of 1839, just over a year after *From the Papers of One Still Living*, Heiberg recounts that he came away more confused than enlightened. But then:

While resting on my homeward journey in Hamburg, where I stayed for six weeks before returning to Kiel, and during that time pondering constantly over what was still unclear to me, it happened one day that, sitting in my room in the König von England with Hegel on my table and in my thoughts, and listening at the same time to the beautiful psalms which sounded almost unceasingly from the chimes of St Peter's Church, suddenly, and in a way that I have experienced neither before nor since, I was gripped by a momentary inner vision, as if a flash of lightning had suddenly illuminated the whole region for me and awakened in me the hitherto hidden central thought. From this moment the system in its broad outline was clear to me, and I was completely convinced that I had grasped it in its innermost core, however much there might be in the details which I still had not made my own and perhaps will never come to make my own. I can say in truth that that strange moment was just about the most important juncture in my life, for it gave me a peace, a security [*Sikkerhed*], a self-awareness [*Selvbevidsthed*] which I had never known before.[16]

It does sound exactly like an illumination of the kind Kierkegaard says a life-view provides: a key to understanding everything although not in all details, and something very like an unshakeable sense of security. But then Heiberg could have borrowed his wording from the manuscript Kierkegaard had sent him. In a later comment on Heiberg's account in the journals he referred to it caustically as a 'miraculous conversion to a philosophy that does not admit miracles'.[17] When Kierkegaard does speak of Hegelianism as a 'view' it is not as a life-view but as a 'world-view of thought' (*Tænknings Verdens-Anskuelse*).[18] Analogies might be unifying visions of natural phenomena of the kind claimed by Cuvier, or by

Goethe, who while walking in the public gardens of Palermo suddenly saw 'in a flash' the unifying principle of biology which was to 'preoccup[y] me for the rest of my life'.[19] Whatever Kierkegaard means by a life-view, it is not a vision of this kind. He had already confessed some years earlier to his own inability to make sense of the details of nature ('The works of the Deity are too big for me'), claiming a capacity only to see how the particulars in a work of *art* contribute to the whole.[20] A life-view is perhaps best seen, on the model of aesthetic unity, as a way of bringing all significantly discordant elements into a kind of harmony. Probably, if asked, he would have pointed out that Heiberg's illumination was not 'won' in experience in any obvious sense, since it came to him in a flash in the middle of a state of mental confusion, and that whatever unity it brought to parts in a thought system, the illumination did not spread to his life. Or if it did, that was only by providing him with a reason to appreciate his own importance and responsibility as one of an elite to whom the core of the system had been revealed.

It was a time of visions. Later, a pastor named Adler was to enjoy a revelatory vision counter to Heiberg's in which he was commanded by Christ to give up his Hegelianism and to destroy all that he had written on him, which included his doctoral dissertation. At that time, Kierkegaard would be quick to cast doubt on the status of such a vision. But at the time of writing *From the Papers of One Still Living* he may have been less sceptical, perhaps one reason for a tendency to conflate the notion of a life-view won through experience and moments of vision. Not insignificantly with regard to the passages quoted earlier, Kierkegaard while writing this work underwent something similar. In a journal entry precisely timed as well as dated (10:30 A.M. on 9 May), he notes that there is an

indescribable joy that is kindled in us just as inexplicably as the apostle's unmotivated exclamation: 'Rejoice, and again I say, Rejoice.' – Not a joy over this or that, but a full-bodied shout of the soul 'with tongue and mouth, and from the bottom of the heart'; 'I rejoice in my joy, of, with, at, for, through, and with my joy' – a heavenly refrain which suddenly interrupts our other songs, a joy which like a breath of air cools and refreshes, a puff from the trade winds which blow across the plains of Mamre to the eternal mansions.[21]

Although the self-conscious literary style with its allusions might tell us the experience was vicarious, the pinpointing of the time does suggest an actual experience, one that Kierkegaard then conveys in a manner dictated by the current state of his literary art. We don't know whether the entry pre- or antedates the meeting with Andersen, but the euphoria it expresses does lead one to surmise two things: first, that even if Kierkegaard thought that he himself did possess a life-view at this time, it was one that at least so far had failed to provide the sense of security he ascribes to such things, and second, that since the experience was no *more* than an experience, and appears not to have been revelatory of any 'key' to the organization of things, it was inevitably short-lived. Certainly there is no indication that the mood persisted.

How then does a life-view connect with things like epiphany and vision? The remark that 'there must . . . come a moment when . . . life is understood backwards through the idea' does sound remarkably Hegelian: form is given by life, but it takes time, and only towards the end of an epoch is the form raised to the level of consciousness. That, as Heiberg knew and we know from Hegel's own account, is where the inadequacy of the current form becomes apparent and occasions a sense not so much of safety as of despair. Of course, someone who like Heiberg is armed with the Hegelian assurance that despair is merely transitional and preliminary to a new and more encompassing form will not despair. But that is precisely the conceit of Hegelianism. To believe that just because the world outgrows its forms, a ground of the unity of all newly made or newly found differences is already prepared, is still not an assurance one gets *from* experience; it is available only if you can claim to stand above the process rather than simply being a part of it.

The famous journal entry that picks up the saying about life being understood backwards, adding that 'one forgets the other principle, that it must be lived forwards', is from 1843, still five years ahead. This later entry says that it is philosophy that claims to understand life backwards. It also allows that the claim is true but then denies to philosophy an ability to understand life forwards, which is how life has to be understood. Life is moving constantly on and offers no resting place from which any so-called life-view, let alone a 'world-view of thought', can form its *retrospective* understanding of life through the 'idea'. Here, however, in 1838, neither that thought nor the notion that life cannot be grasped backwards through the 'idea' seems to have occurred to Kierkegaard. True, he doesn't say explicitly in this later entry that philosophy can do the job. But the same distinction made in *From the Papers of One Still Living* between a Christian life-view and the kind of life-view exemplified by Stoicism, a 'purely human standpoint' which 'remains out of touch with a deeper experiential basis', was made a year prior to that in the journals but with *philosophy*'s 'purely human view of the world' as the contrasting life-view.[22] So there at least it is allowed that philosophy of a kind can provide a life-view. In talking of philosophy, however, Kierkegaard may well be thinking of philosophies in a wide sense, philosophies of life or ways of thinking about the world that can actually make a difference to a person's practical judgments and ways of seeing things. Even Heiberg's Hegelianism might be admitted to do that. It may indeed be difficult to distinguish between philosophies of life and philosophies in a narrower intellectual sense, at least in a way that leaves Hegelianism on the wrong side. But that, for Kierkegaard, Stoicism counts as both a philosophy and a life-view, however ultimately deficient its experiential basis, does tell us that he allows here that life can indeed be *understood* backwards 'through the idea'. Living it, of course, is another thing. But if Stoicism is both a life-view and a philosophy, then it should be possible for life also to be *lived* according to a philosophy, or some version of the 'idea'.

The Stoics self-consciously applied their view to life, and in whatever flash of vision Stoicism may have occurred to the first Stoic, the Stoic philosophy and way of life were subsequently maintained by being constantly cultivated, and not by the truth of Stoicism recurrently enlightening new generations of Stoics overnight. Is Kierkegaard perhaps confusing two different things here: the Hegelian conception current in his time, that the articulation of a view of life occurs retrospectively, and the quite different matter of a visionary experience, quite fashionable at the time? Examples from the period abound. There was Mynster, whose crisis of despair led him to a new sense of 'what is the highest and most blessed of all'. An example celebrated at that time too was Hamann's seeing the light of true Christianity while on a business trip to London. So there may at this stage be a tension, a latent contradiction even, in Kierkegaard's notion of a life-view. A life-view is supposed to impart the sense of security which, as at least those who do not have it would say, belongs primarily to the unreflective stage of early childhood, but at the same time it has to be applied in a way that brings things satisfactorily together after that early sense of security has been lost. But how do you 'apply' something that, in the form of a revelatory experience, it would be more appropriate to say 'applies itself'? And, second, how can a mood or way of seeing things which comes in a flash apply prospectively unless it really does provide a clue to understanding things in the way that, say, an insight into the cohesiveness of Hegelian thought or a vision of a Primal Plant did? If the flash does not deliver some principle of organization that can guide your thoughts or investigations in the future, how can the vision 'stick'? Many interpreters of Kierkegaard suppose that, in delineating various life-views, Kierkegaard takes them to be chosen *ab initio* by force of a resolute choice which, if constantly renewed, is itself supposed to establish the 'security' he talks of here. But this is hard to square with either of the features of life-views mentioned in *From the Papers of One Still Living*. The Hegelian feature requires that the form taken by a life-view develop in a life that already has that form incipiently, a life that is already at least in part as one makes it become; it cannot be chosen as a way to begin. And this visionary aspect sits equally uneasily with the traditional reading according to which a life-view is precisely something that one takes on, not something that 'comes to one' in a flash.

The solution may be found in another way of looking at life-views also implicit in Kierkegaard's remarks in *From the Papers of One Still Living*. It escapes the visionary problem by simply dropping its revelatory aspect and regarding what are later referred to as 'stages' or 'spheres' of existence as layers of motivation revealed successively as the need for a 'deeper experiential basis' becomes evident. One could say that a Hegelian feature is retained in the way that life-views are held to be incipient in human nature, while the visionary aspect survives in the acknowledgement that the inadequacy of a current way of life in terms of what is fundamentally desired from the point of view of a 'higher' or 'deeper' experience is a matter of intuition, of how it seems to the individual, not of rational persuasion or force of argument, at least not of any decontextualized and so-called objective argument. It may also survive in some sense of having got it right but without recourse to the authority of reason. A life-view, taking this to correspond to a 'stage' or 'sphere' of existence, can be interpreted as a way of life that initially is not consciously ordered by some explicit principle; and its 'key' only comes to mind, whether or not in a flash, at the point where the principle not only becomes articulate but its inadequacy begins to be felt.

In this, his first publication, however, Kierkegaard is concerned less with working out the implications of life-views than in pointing out their absence. And it seems clear that his primary concern is with laying out the notion of a life-view not just as something Andersen lacked and which all authors should possess and give expression to in their works, but as something that he could criticize his peers for having no sense of at all. So just as it was not his friend Ostermann who had been the target of that talk in the Student Union, but the liberal leadership under Lehmann, here the real target was not the unfortunate Andersen, but those 'other' reviewers whose reviews had lacked the basis for the kind of criticism Kierkegaard felt himself called to provide. Kierkegaard was not just jockeying for a position among those he wanted to be able to think of as his literary peers; he was finding a platform, a station even, from which to understand them negatively. What he thought they lacked was a coherent and positive view of life. Not that Kierkegaard possessed such a view himself; he was too 'reflected' for that and too prone to doubt and depression. But it was the Christian view that he had dedicated himself to defending, and it does seem that he was not just using the notion of a life-view as a platform to comment on the conduct of his society and its manners, or to add a Danish voice to a pan-European debate in the declining years of Romanticism. He actually felt called as a writer to defend Christianity *as* a life-view. The extent to which he 'treats' the theme of life-views rather than attempting to convey a life-view, or expressing one in the way he claims authors and their works should, is no doubt the reason for this 'review' being designated a treatise, though equally the form might be seen as providing him with a convenient excuse for not practising what he was preaching. Could it be that he was also nurturing some slender hope of succeeding to Poul Møller's professorship?

Andersen's reaction on receiving the promised 'review' shows that he, at any rate, failed to see in it any expression of the Christian life-view, and if he had been made of sterner stuff he might justly have complained. As it happens he let the incident go by, and whatever resentment he felt at the time, he said later that he had 'better understood this author, who has obliged me along my way with kindness and discernment'.[23]

That Kierkegaard's dedication to the view is nevertheless sincere is supported by the fact that he now appears to have achieved a reconciliation with his father. We read in the journal from 9 July two entries where he thanks God, 'Father in heaven', for having kept the earthly father upon whom he depended alive at a time when he needed him so much, the father, he adds, 'who, as I very much hope, will with your help have greater joy in being my father the second time than he had the first'. On the same day he writes: 'I shall work on coming into a far more intimate relation with Christianity; up to now I have been standing altogether outside it, fighting for its truth. I have borne the cross in a quite external way, like Simon of Cyrene (Luke 23:26).' It is now more than six weeks since the 'indescribable joy' entry. But another entry, just two weeks after that one, had said simply: 'You God have created the world.'[24]

The two main types of life-view – one humanistic, which he says lacks a 'deeper experiential basis', and a Christian life-view in which a person aims at a life centred on 'the religious' – impart a sense of security. No doubt part of the explanation is that to have a life-view is to view life itself and one's participation in it as meaningful and worthwhile. The term he uses for the kind of certainty which the Christian view imparts, '*Forvisning*', translated here as 'conviction', can also be rendered 'assurance'. This term, familiar in evangelical Christianity as denoting the 'sealing' by the Holy Spirit of truths learned and inculcated through catechetical teaching, implies a 'default' state, whether of uncertainty or simply of lack of appropriation.[25] In Kierkegaard's case it is both. The deeper basis of experience also occasions anxiety, a state of global lack of assurance, which the life-view oriented towards the religious is then fitted to correct. You might say that in any case, as a matter of definition, to be 'assured' you must first have felt uneasy. Kierkegaard doesn't say that a humanistic life-view imparts the same assurance, which would not imply there was no anxiety or despair that it too is fitted to correct. If there is a distinction intended here between levels or kinds of assurance, it could have to do with what Kierkegaard means by saying that a humanistic life-view lacks that 'deeper experiential basis'. He had noted the 'reassuring influence' (*beroliginde Kraft*) of Christianity a year previously in connection with Faustian despair. The 'new' Fausts are those who see the dream of a total vision, embracing 'the infinite multiplicity of nature, of life, and of history', as no longer beyond human possibility. For 'much is already unrolled before their eyes, and more is appearing every day'. But beneath 'all this multifarious knowledge' there is a feeling of 'how infinitely little it is', and it is this that 'paralyses their activity'. The 'Faustian element' appears now in a despair of a special kind, a despair not as before at the inability to comprehend everything in a vision but at not being able to 'recognize' everything, every 'nuance', in its 'full, that is, in its absolute worth'. Along with the expanding horizon comes a sense of man's own 'circumscribed position'. Kierkegaard sees the contemporary longing for a 'perfect and true intuition' as inspired by an uneasy sense of 'the relativity of everything'. 'Man longs for a vision which annuls all relativities and shows him the absolute worth of even the most insignificant thing, because for the true (i.e. divine) vision everything is of the same magnitude.'[26]

Two considerations make this a key passage. First, it shows how Kierkegaard fits Christianity into a kind of Hegelian dialectic in which an increase in the knowledge one seeks uncovers a new want, which then calls for something that, if true, makes the previous search unnecessary, except of course as a way of bringing the new need to consciousness. But in showing that the impulse that led to the previous search is unnecessary, the new position also uncovers the hidden motive for the search, which was to seek an assurance, an assurance which that search could not give but which the new position, namely Christianity, does give. Second, the passage indicates a change that has occurred in the intervening year. It is clear from the way Kierkegaard was referring to Christianity in these 1837 entries on the new Faustianism, that he himself was still adopting an outsider's view. In the entry following the one from which we have quoted he says that what is reassuring about Christianity is that it has a 'standard which is definite'. But he gives no indication that he himself is reassured. He speaks of 'the Christian' only as someone with whom it is 'enjoyable to converse' because the Christian has a 'fullness in comparison with which the infinite differences in ability, occupation, etc. are nothing'. He says that one can respect such a 'stance' simply for this reason, 'as long as it does not degenerate into arrogance'.[27] But in May of the following year Kierkegaard writes of that 'full-bodied shout of the soul' which seems to have heralded a reconciliation not only with Christianity but with his father, for whose continued presence on Earth he then thanks God, on the very same day, 9 July, that he rededicates himself to Christianity, saying that he would now 'work at coming into a far closer relation' to it. There are several indications of the change. It was recalled later by Kierkegaard's acquaintances, one of whom said that Peter had done much to bring about the reconciliation with their father. There is also documentary evidence. Ever since leaving his father and brother, Søren had ceased attending Holy Communion, but on 6 July he went to both confession and Communion administered by a Pastor Kolthoff, who according to sources was one of the few clerics the Kierkegaard brothers respected. It has been said that Kierkegaard had actually returned home at this time,[28] but even if that is so, it is significant that he went to Communion without his father and brother and that the only person he felt he could confide in at this time was his friend Emil Boesen, to whom he wrote a letter while on a brief vacation that summer, though it is claimed that it was never sent.[29] Søren was certainly on good enough terms at least to dine with his father and brother, and he may have thought of moving into Nytorv again. He may actually have done so for a period just prior to his father's death.[30] Attending Communion, however, need have no direct connection with the reconciliation with his father. It could have been part of his own independent intention to win the Christian life-view through experience – reconciliation at second-hand, as it were.

A month later 'Old Kierkegaard' died. It was not unexpected. Michael Pedersen was now in his eighty-second year and had been in failing health. The event nevertheless had important repercussions on both the sons' lives. For Søren it meant that he could never show his father any results from his long years at the university. It was still a month, almost exactly, before *From the Papers of One Still Living* was to appear. So apart from his natural grief Søren had the added sorrow of being forever unable to show his father what he could do. Written prior to his father's death, the work of course does not derive its title from that event, though in the circumstances it must have seemed peculiarly apt. There is no clear indication of what the title means. The reference might of course be to Møller, whose death certainly seems to have motivated this burst of energy on Kierkegaard's part, and we have already entertained the thought that Kierkegaard had seen himself as Møller's literary or philosophical heir or both. But the title also appears as part of a proposed alternative title for a play Kierkegaard had sketched about this time, intended as a satire on the Danish Hegelians in a kind of parody of Goethe's *Faust*. The play, *Striden mellem den gamle og den nye Sæbekielder* (The Conflict between the Old and the New Soap-Cellar), may have been intended as another 'paper' from the still-living author, whether or not included with the Andersen review.[31] The entry revealing this is undated, and its preceding the completion of the manuscript on Andersen might affect surmises about what Kierkegaard meant by saying it was published against his will. But the inclusion of the title of the published essay in this context could indicate that in both cases Kierkegaard has in mind a contrast between the culturally dead and those still able to project, even if they cannot yet fully inhabit, a life-view.

Under a cross marked in his journal, and two days after his father's death, Kierkegaard writes:

My father died on Wednesday night at 2:00 a.m. I did so earnestly desire that he should live a few years more, and I regard his death as the last sacrifice his love made for me, because he has not died *from* me but died *for* me, so that something might still come of me. Most precious of all that I have inherited from him is his memory, his transfigured image, transfigured not by my poetic imagination (it has no need of that), but many little single traits I am now learning about, and this I will try to keep most secret from the world. For at this moment I feel there *is* only *one* person (E. Boesen) with whom I can really talk about him. He was a 'faithful friend'.[32]

The burial took place on 14 August at the family burial site in Assistens Graveyard (*Assistenskirkegaarden*), at that time just outside Copenhagen's city boundary. Although in the moment of mourning Kierkegaard writes of what he has gained from his father, later on and as the strain of his destiny, or fate, as a polemical outsider began to tell on him, he was to adopt a much more critical attitude, deploring the fact, as he saw it, that his father had been responsible for depriving him of an ordinary childhood. But the controlled tone of the entry just cited does show that in the months before his father's death, in fact from the time he left home in September of the previous year and set up house in Løvstræde, Kierkegaard had gained enough personal independence to be able to adopt a more detached view towards not only his father but also, as another of the earlier quotations indicated, his father's religion.

It is said that one reason Søren had for leaving Nytorv was an alarming confidence that his father made him concerning his own private life, and that this was the shattering event Kierkegaard refers to in a journal entry from about the period we are discussing. We will return to that in a moment. What is important from a purely psychological point of view is the fact that by his father's becoming more frail Kierkegaard, no longer in the demanding presence even in absentia of his formidable parent, was able even before his father's death to dedicate *himself* to the religion he had inherited. The actual death made no difference to that.

However, the thought that he had nothing to show his father for the years spent at the university must nevertheless have preyed horribly on him once the possibility of ever doing so had been taken from him. In the letter written to Boesen that summer but never sent, he had written, in that playfully literary style he enjoyed:

Can any exiled prince feel more bitterly his subject's faithlessness than a lowly author who has no readers? And what more ridiculous than an *homme de lettres* reading for a university exam? And isn't my whole life so messed up that, unless just *quia absurdum est*, no meaning can possibly come to it, let alone that I should be able to give it one?

In order to give vent to 'what is on my mind, and to shake the viscera of wrath and sympathy', he needed a voice

as penetrating as a Lynceus's glance, terrifying as a giant's sigh, lasting as a sound of nature, with a range from the deepest bass to the most melting chest notes, modulating from the most hallowed whisper to the fire-gushing energy of fury.

Maybe the attack on Andersen was a first attempt and its underlying message that the Christian life-view is wrested from a deep experience of life directed partly at his father, who would have been impressed even though the essay was about literature. According to his brother, Søren's failure to take his theology exam caused their father great suffering. In a letter Peter wrote in 1877, forty years on, he says that their father 'no doubt viewed [Søren's] aesthetic-philosophical studies and his association with poets, etc. as dilettantism and time-wasting'.[33] Whatever independence Søren had won during the previous year, and perhaps especially because it provided the distance that made it possible for the reconciliation to be between equals, his personal sorrow at having disappointed his father must have been immense.

That letter which Peter, by that time bishop of Aalborg, wrote forty years later was in reply to a correspondent interested in hearing the bishop's explanation of some entries found inserted in the form of loose scraps of paper in the journals from this time. There had been considerable discussion about these, sparked off by the eminent Danish literary critic Georg Brandes (1842–1927), who claimed that the 'earth-quake' referred to in one of them was occasioned by Søren's learning of some serious misdemeanour, possibly marital infidelity, on the father's part. Brandes, himself a freethinker, saw in Kierkegaard's later assault on the church an encouragement to convert away from religion, and he therefore had no pious reservations about such a possibility. But the now-bishop of Aalborg's correspondent was appealing to the bishop for an account that would vindicate Michael Pedersen Kierkegaard, and by association also his youngest son, in the name of Christianity. The entries are six in number: two lines from Goethe under the heading 'Childhood', three from the contemporary Danish poet Christian Winther under 'Youth', and a passage from act 5, scene 3 of *King Lear*, above which Kierkegaard has written 'twenty-five years old'. The *Lear* passage, quoted in the German translation by Ernst Ortlepp, is:

> . . . so we'll live,
> And pray, and sing, and tell old tales, and laugh
> At gilded butterflies, and hear poor rogues
> Talk of court news; and we'll talk with them too,
> Who loses and who wins; who's in, who's out,
> And take upon's the mystery of things,
> As if we were God's spies: and we'll wear out
> In a wall'd prison, packs and sects of great ones,
> That ebb and flow by the moon.

Following this, and in apparent reference to it, Kierkegaard writes:

It was then the great earthquake occurred, the terrible upheaval which suddenly pressed on me a new infallible law for the interpretation of all phenomena. It was then I suspected my father's great age was not a divine blessing but rather a curse; that our family's excellent mental abilities existed only for tearing us apart from one another; I felt the stillness of death spreading over me when I saw in my father an unhappy person who would survive us all, a monumental cross on the grave of all his own expectations. A guilt must weigh upon the entire family, God's punishment must be upon it; it was meant to disappear, struck out by God's mighty hand, deleted like an unsuccessful attempt, and I only occasionally found some little solace in the thought that upon my father had fallen the heavy duty of reassuring us with the consolation of religion, administering to us the last sacrament, so that a better world might still stand open for us even if we lost everything in this one, even if that punishment the Jews always called down upon their foes were to fall on us: that all memory of us would be wiped out and no trace found.

After this there is the following apparently appended comment:

Torn apart inwardly as I was, with no prospect of leading a life of earthly happiness ('that I might prosper and live long in the land'), with no hope of a happy and pleasant future – which is part and parcel of the historic continuity of the domestic life of the family – what wonder that, in despairing hopelessness, I seized upon the intellectual side of man alone, clung to that, so that the thought of my considerable mental talents was my only consolation, ideas my only joy, people of no consequence for me.[34]

According to the considered judgment of the now seventy-one-year-old Peter, the three poetic excerpts were most likely written either on or immediately after 5 May (Søren's twenty-fifth birthday but also by Danish law the attainment of his majority), while the 'earthquake' entry, which he observes also has a poetic form but 'unmistakably a mood that is quite otherwise exceedingly distraught', was from the time of their father's death. Peter recites the litany of loss in the family recounted in Chapter 2, recalling how when Peter's first wife came into the household things for a while had nevertheless seemed to go better for the three of them, 'not the least affected' by the lighter atmosphere at home being Søren himself, who 'as can frequently be seen from his writings, had special talents as an uncle'. But then Peter's wife had died. In Søren 'the dark view of things that had affected him with the earlier deaths then took the upper hand'. He believed the family would 'become extinct', that 'father would survive us all', that 'none of us would live to be much more than thirty-three', and that the sons would leave no children who might 'prevent the name dying out.' It dawned on Søren now 'more strongly than ever' how much it would mean to his father if he took his university examinations but also, and not least because he too was to die young, that he should 'be something for and with the father who was to administer the sacraments also to him and bury him'. It was in this 'mood of quiet resignation' that the passage from *King Lear* seemed appropriate: 'As Lear and Cordelia, so too father and Søren, talking together of everything as now bygone.' But just as Søren was hoping to 'become something' for the father whom 'he knew that for several years he had saddened', the father died. This is what caused the violent earthquake. The 'then' that is the third word of the entry refers to that event, and the 'infallibility' of the law was that it was a repetition of the previous quake, a repetition even more violent than the original. The reason why the second occurrence was more violent was that the brothers would now be denied the services of their father at their own funerals, so that Michael Pedersen, instead of at least being able to see them die in the 'hope of salvation', had now gone from them, leaving even his own earthly hopes for them unfulfilled. Since they would never have children (Peter speaks here of his own first marriage as having occurred against everyone's expectations including his own, while in his view Søren himself would see himself disbarred by his breach of the commandment to honour his parent), the family name and its memory would be wiped out.[35]

Peter's account makes sense and sounds plausible up to a point, but the timing he suggests may be questioned, since the entries themselves could well have been written later.[36] Also, the account dwells on the kind of theological points which tended to form the fixed motifs behind Peter's own particular depressions. Still, in the shadow of his father's death it was not unlikely that Søren would take to heart matters which were especially bound up with the faith of a father he was so strongly drawn to but felt he had let down. Some claim that the real occasion underlying the tone and content of the entries here was their father's revelation to Søren that as a boy, tending sheep on the Jutland heath, he had one day cursed God,[37] in return for which God had picked out the Kierkegaard family for special attention, whether to provide it with the dubious privilege of experiencing the blessings of atonement, or just in plain Old Testament wrath. The story may even have helped to give Kierkegaard's depression a kind of dramatic unity of the kind he had a sense for, making it part of something like an ancient Greek tragedy; on the other hand, it doesn't seem enough to cause this depression in someone who, unlike his brother in this respect, was so prone to reflection and general doubt. The same objection applies to the sort of explanation promoted by Brandes, the originator of the psycho-biographical tradition in Kierkegaard biography; marital infidelity just doesn't seem a good enough reason for such an upset in an intellectual aesthete who consorted with poets and actors and was in any case about to cause a scandal by jilting his fiancée. It is questionable how far Søren himself was troubled by thoughts of this kind. And if they did vex him, it seems that he tended rather to let such worries fuel his own intro-spection creatively. As the letter to Boesen shows, Kierkegaard was first and foremost worried about his own future. The fact that he had disappointed his father becomes just an added nail in the coffin of his own happiness, a theme to which he constantly and almost obsessively returns – understandably, given his gloomy prognosis for the future of his family and his belief that he would die sooner rather than later. The main thing was to get something worthwhile done and quickly. To do that, and at whatever personal cost, he had to make the most of his talents, which he was now doing his best to cultivate. This, we saw, is the substance of the second of the autobiographical entries; here he seems to be justifying his sortie into the world of literature and ideas and at the same time recognizing that, instead of his remaining or becoming just part of life's 'ebb and flow', the effort will be rewarded by his being given a mission as one of 'God's spies'.

In the third entry the inward turn is complete. In language that reminds one of Hamlet more than Lear, Kierkegaard says:

What has often caused me suffering was that, for fear that I might fake a result for myself, a reflective *I* has tried as if to impress upon me and preserve what my real *I*, out of doubt, anxiety, disquiet, wanted to forget with regard to forming a view of the world – to preserve it partly because it had to happen, – partly because it was a transitional factor of some consequence. . . . So now, for instance, when my life seems set in such a way that I appear to be assigned in perpetuity to reading for exams and that, no matter how long it lasts, my life will in any case progress no further than where I once wilfully broke it off (just as one occasionally sees mentally deranged people who forget everything that happened in the meantime and can only remember their childhood, or forget everything except some single moment in their lives) – that I should be thus reminded by the thought of being a theology student of that happy time of possibilities (what one might call one's pre-existence) and of my stopping there, in a state of mind rather like that of a child which has been given brandy and prevented from growing more. When my active *I* now tries to forget this in order to act, my reflective *I* would so much rather keep a hold on it because it seems interesting and, as reflection raises itself to the level of a general consciousness, abstract from my own personal consciousness.[38]

Clearly Kierkegaard's serious intention to act upon a life-view is still dogged by the precious doubts that once kept him from doing so in case what was adopted, or the adopting of it, was not authentic. He is almost admitting here that his nature is such as to make inevitable a life of reflection rather than action.

As far as *From the Papers of One Still Living* is concerned, the slim book was much discussed, and Kierkegaard was chosen president of the Student Union at a meeting in December perhaps because of it – but the language came in for criticism. Commenting on the book to Heiberg at the time, the poet, playwright, and aesthetician Henrik Hertz (1797–1870) remarked: 'The Mesopotamian language is a strange language.' Sometime later the same Hertz wrote:

Those who have picked up the German philosophy are completely incapable of practising it in Danish. Their text teems with words of which no Dane knows the meaning. Kirkgrd's work on Andersen shows what language we can expect from philosophy.[39]

Still, Søren was on his way, or at least had set out on a course of his own choosing even if, according to Emil Boesen in a letter written in 1868, it was not until he was writing his dissertation on irony and the period of his engagement that Kierkegaard 'first gained a clear under-standing of what he himself wanted to do and what he was capable of'.[40] Whatever the truth of this, and it will prove quite plausible, before there could be any question of a dissertation there were still those exams to pass.

6

Serious about Irony: The Dissertation

M ETAPHORICALLY, to Peter his father's death meant that he could 'come home': although he had been there all along, he could now move into his father's rooms. Søren, by leaving Løvstræde, and not moving out of Nytorv again until the end of the following year, came home literally. But it was also a homecoming in the sense that he felt himself once more beside 'father', beside rather than under. However, in spite of sharing one roof, both psychologically and careerwise the two brothers had already gone their separate ways. The roof itself they had both bought with their inheritance at the winding-up sale, Søren's share being 33,594 rixdalers, about a quarter of the whole and more than four hundred thousand U.S. dollars today.

Economic independence meant that Kierkegaard could embark on a writing career without having to earn a living from that either. In the event he was able to live quite comfortably for the next ten years, covering the costs of publication of his first nineteen books, only one of which sold out. Really there was no need, either, for him to take his university exams. But the same economic independence also made it possible to think again of Regine, or at least less possible to banish the thought out of hand. The fact that the money was there was no argument against becoming a respectable bread-winner and performing a useful function in society, and for that he would definitely need to complete his education. On the other hand, the idea of setting up a home of his own would be in total conflict with what his darker side told him, that he would die within eight years and that there was 'no hope of a happy and pleasant future', the very kind of future that is 'part and parcel of the historic continuity of the domestic life of the family'.

'In fact it would be good for you if I were dead; you might then still make something of yourself; that won't happen so long as I'm alive.'[1] So Kierkegaard's father once told him, according to Brøchner's account. He couldn't have been thinking of the money, since Kierkegaard would inherit him anyway, but Michael Pedersen Kierkegaard must have had some inkling of the inhibiting effect of his own presence on his children. On Michael Pedersen's death Sibbern, on the other hand, said to Kierkegaard: 'Now you'll never take your theology finals.' Kierkegaard himself knew better. On his own now, it was necessary more than ever to get it over with, and he later wrote that 'if father had stayed alive I'd never have got my degree'. Behind that remark was the panicky thought that he himself might die before he managed to accomplish anything. But he also knew that the money would not allow him to escape: 'With my keen mind and my melancholy, and money on top of that – oh, how propitious for developing all the torments of self-torture in my heart.'[2] There was the point that Kierkegaard could now defend his father's religion without sensing that it was just to please him. Brøchner says that Kierkegaard told him that 'as long as Father was alive, I could still defend my thesis that I didn't have to take the degree [but] after he died, and I also had to take on his side in the debate, I could no longer resist and had to resolve to prepare for my degree'. According to Brøchner, who was in a position to know, since Kierkegaard had chosen a cousin of his father as his 'crammer', he did so 'with great energy'.[3]

As a comment on criticism of the long parenthetical clauses pervading his writing at the time, Kierkegaard said of this time that it was 'the greatest parenthesis in my life'.[4] It was no labour of love. Kierkegaard was getting down at long last to the subject he hated most, theology. Brøchner says he 'worked his way through [this] driest of disciplines, made notes on ecclesiastical history, learned the list of popes by heart, and so on'.[5] From the journals we know that during the winter term (1838–39) he attended Sibbern's lectures on The Philosophy of Christianity.[6]

Through the autumn and winter of 1838–39 the journals show a concern with protecting Christianity from tendencies to debase it, tendencies which Kierkegaard at the time saw mainly in attempts on the part of intellectuals like Martensen and to some extent Sibbern to bring Christianity into line with Hegelian philosophy. There are sixty entries from September to December. We find among them the first mention of Johannes Climacus, the monk in Sinai who wrote *Scala paradisi* and whose name Kierkegaard later adopted as a pseudonym. The entry refers to Hegel as a Climacus who thought he could scale Heaven on a ladder of arguments: 'Hegel is a Johannes Climacus who, unlike the Giants who storm the heavens by heaping mountain upon mountain, boards them by way of his syllogisms.'[7] There is also an early reference to paradox, but couched in what appears to be a fashionably Hegelian idiom: 'Paradox is the intellectual's authentic *pathos*, and just as only great souls are prone to passions, so only great thinkers are prone to what I call paradoxes, which are nothing but grand thoughts still wanting completion.'[8] But in another entry Kierkegaard chides philosophers for thinking that 'all knowledge, indeed even the existence of the Deity, is something man himself produces and that only in a figurative sense can there be talk of revelation'. This may be prompted by a small debate surrounding a short essay by Mynster published in 1839, which Kierkegaard later recalled for another reason. Against the typically Hegelian claim that the issue between supernaturalism and its denials (both rationalism and naturalism) was a thing of the past, Mynster, whom Kierkegaard considered an ally, argued that it was still very much alive – and irresoluble, in fact a matter of *aut/aut* (either/or).[9]

Kierkegaard had not forgotten Regine. Among all these reflections on the difference between true and false Christianity, and between Christianity and philosophy, there intrudes the image of 'my heart's sovereign mistress'.[10] What actual social contact they enjoyed during this period it is hard to say, but later Kierkegaard confessed that the whole time he was reading for the examination Regine's 'existence' had been 'twining itself' around his own, and he even says that he had already set his mind on her before his father died.[11] This added a significant complication to the range of choices Kierkegaard found himself facing. Having experienced the futility of the project of recapturing lost immediacy and dedicated now, in some fairly personal way, to Christianity, perhaps even comfortable with the idea of leading a life of solitary dedication to the Christian ideal – something Kierkegaard was prone to and probably thought himself best equipped for – that choice was now offset by the tempting prospect of marriage and a normal home life. At that time preparing for the theology examination was typically a preliminary to becoming a pastor, a life that would combine Christian dedication with a civic responsibility that also gave room for marriage. The future was becoming complicated. In marked contrast to that 'full-bodied shout of joy' from May 1838 there is now an increasing anxiety. Some of this must be due to doubts about what he was to become, but a good deal can be explained by the sheer drudgery of studying something so dust-dry as theology. Should he continue with a dissertation after the theology examination and then seek a job? If he proposed to Regine and was accepted, what would become of his budding talent as a writer? That work takes time and concentration, and the talent still awaited convincing confirmation. But then again, one cannot be just a writer. Think of Andersen, there must be a life-view. But what if the life-view says you should marry and get a job? What happens *then* to the writing?

Other worries on a more cosmic order or, what paradoxically is often the same, of a deeply personal nature, assailed him – though probably no one noticed. A person as close to him as Sibbern, who had been friendly with Kierkegaard since 1831, later said he 'never knew him to be melancholic'.[12] The diaries give a different impression. Looking back at the time ten years later, Kierkegaard said:

But then my father's death was also a fearfully harrowing experience; how much so I have never told a single soul: My whole past life was in any case so altogether cloaked in the darkest melancholy, and in the most profoundly brooding of misery's fogs, that it is no wonder I was as I was. But all this remains my secret. On someone else it might not have made a deep impression – but there was my imagination, and especially at the beginning when it still had no tasks to apply itself to. A primitive melancholy like that, such a huge dowry of distress, and what was in the profoundest sense the tragedy of being a child brought up by a melancholy father – and then to be able with a native virtuosity to deceive everyone into thinking I was life and joy incarnate. . . . [13]

'How terrible', he said at the time, 'to have to buy each day, each hour – and the price varies so!', and: 'The sad thing with me is that the crumb of joy and reassurance I slowly distil in the painstakingly dyspeptic process of my thought-life I use up straightaway in just one despairing step.' It was a time when there seemed no chance of anything resembling what we call a self-image finding a foothold in him; he was compelled to face his God, as formerly his father, with nothing to show for the talents he had been given: 'God in heaven, let me really feel my nothingness, not to despair over it but to feel all the more intensely the greatness of your goodness', to which he adds in parentheses: 'This is not, as the scoffer in me would say, an Epicureanism, as when the gourmand starves so that the food will taste all the better.'[14]

The sequence of journal entries begun after the death of his father continues for just over a year and then is brought abruptly but with charming ceremony to a halt: 'You, my lucid intervals [*lucida intervalla*], I must now renounce you; and you, my thoughts who sit imprisoned in my head, I can no longer allow you those strolls in the cool of the evening; but don't be downhearted, get to know one another better, and once in a while I may sneak in and have a look at you – Au revoir!' In an apparent allusion to the final scene of Goethe's *Faust*, this mock farewell is signed: 'S. K. – formerly Dr Exstaticus',[15] a name that would return. There is also an entry introducing what was to become the favourite image of an underground river: 'Now for a season, ten miles in time, I will plunge underground like the Guadalquivir.'[16] Since this entry is not precisely dated it is hard to tell whether the plunge is that which preceded the examinations or the later plunge into writing the dissertation. It is also unclear what it was that the plunge would hide him from – acquaintances on the streets and in the cafés, or that gathering company of ideas assembling in the private workshop of his journals? There is no evidence that at the time of reading for his finals he actually disappeared from Copenhagen's streets and cafés; but even if he was less in evidence there, it might still have been the journals he thought of, forced as he was to desert them, and thus also himself, for a time. There was, after all, a sense in which he was taking leave of himself.

The 'silence' continued not just for a season but for nine months, until after the examinations were over. Sometime in the winter of 1839–40 he had moved into an apartment at 11 Kultorvet, which he shared with another student, Peter Hansen. Hansen later wrote to Peter of that period. Allowing for the patina of sentiment and ornament so fashionable in letter-writing at the time, the impression of a deep seriousness pervading the apartment nevertheless comes through:

I beg your most gracious forgiveness for resorting to a letter as a substitute for conversation, and make so bold as to approach you in this just as in the gentleman who was your blessed brother, him – our dear Nathanael (because God gave him to us), the name of an Israelite, indeed of Israel (because he was a true God's warrior!) without guile – with whom I once (1839 and 1840) lived together in a house on Kultorvet, much to my own awakening.[17]

Kierkegaard didn't stay there long, ten months at most, and it is unclear whether he moved into his next apartment, this time at 230A Nørregade (now 38), before or after his finals. In any case Kierkegaard submitted his entry application to the faculty on 2 June 1840, and after the written exam was examined *viva voce* by Professors Scharling, Engelstoft, and Hohlenberg on 3 July and informed that he had passed with the grade of *laudabilis* (commendable) – much to the surprise of his fellow theology students, due less to the grade perhaps than to the fact that they had come to regard him as an eternal student. He was one of twenty-seven of the sixty-three candidates in all to receive that grade, so the result was by no means outstanding. However, the final spurt had been made in record time. Brøchner recounts that soon after Kierkegaard had taken his degree another student, Peter Stilling, approached Kierkegaard's tutor. 'He announced that he thought of finishing in a year and a half, "S. K. studied no longer than that." "Ah, yes," said old Brøchner, who did not excel in courtesy, "Don't fool yourself! S. K. was something else; he knew it all!" . . . At the written exam in theology S. K. was rated fourth by the outside examiners. . . . [These], however, told [the other] three that K.'s essays showed evidence of a far greater maturity and development of thought than any of the others, though their essays held a richer measure of specifically theological material.'[18]

Shortly after learning he had passed his finals Kierkegaard went on a recuperative trip to Sæding, his father's childhood home, hard by the west coast of Jutland. The holiday was not simply to recover from the exertion of his examinations; it was also a pilgrimage to the small community where Michael Pedersen Kierkegaard had grown up and which he had left at twelve to go to Copenhagen, and also to the lonely heath where as a young boy guarding sheep, as he confided to Søren, he had cursed God. He also meant to visit an elder brother of his friend Emil, Pastor Carl Boesen at Knebel, as well as other places in Jutland. Kierkegaard was accompanied by a servant, Anders, probably lent by Peter Christian from Nytorv but later to stay on with him.[19] They set out on Saturday 17 July at 7:00 A.M., arriving at Kalundborg at 10:30 in the evening.[20] From there they took a boat to Aarhus, where Kierkegaard admired the organ in the cathedral. He made excursions to Mols, visited Kalø Castle, and went on to visit Carl Boesen. They continued to Randers, then there was a sailing tour down to Ålbæk and Støvringgaard, where he writes of the fine evening view. The trip was interspersed with moments of boredom and even melancholy: 'no days without tears.'[21] He visited Viborg, the site of one of the Regional

Parliaments, for two days, and Sæding for three, staying with a seventy-two-year-old aunt, Else Pedersdatter, his father's only surviving sibling. She had been married since 1802 to Thomas Nielsen and lived in conditions that Kierkegaard found spartan and not very clean. He had meant to give his first sermon at Sæding, but probably didn't due to arriving too late that Sunday. On 4 August he overnighted at *Them Kro* (Them Tavern), which was filled with counts and barons, company probably more congenial to him than that of his own impoverished antecedents. He was invited by an acquaintance, Elias C. F. Ahlefeldt-Laurvigen, to his estate, Vestergaard in Langeland, where he also met his former fellow (law) student, now *Kammerjunker* (Gentleman of the Bed-chamber) Mathias Hans Rosenørn. Both were Kierkegaard's near-contemporaries. On the return journey Kierkegaard made an observation that in the light of his own intentions may be seen in something of a cautionary light:

On the road to Aarhus I saw the most amusing sight: two cows roped together came cantering past us, the one gadabout and with a jovial swing to its tail, the other, as it appeared, more prosaic and quite in despair at having to take part in the same movements – Isn't that the arrangement in most marriages?[22]

The return trip, first from Aarhus to Kalundborg on board the steamer Christian VIII, then by coach, took six hours, Kierkegaard and Anders arriving back in Copenhagen on the evening of 6 August. Two days after returning – he himself says it was between the ninth and the end of the month – Kierkegaard made his approaches to Regine. Regine was now eighteen years old (Kierkegaard had turned twenty-seven in May), and he proposed to her on 8 September. Recalling the event nine years later, Kierkegaard wrote:

In the summer of '40 I took the finals in theology.

I paid a visit right away to her house. I went to Jutland and maybe angled a little for her even then (e.g. by lending them books in my absence and letting them read some passage in a particular book).

I returned in August. More accurately, it was the period from 9 August to September that I drew closer to her.

On 8 September I left home with the firm intention of settling the whole thing. We met on the street just outside their house. She said there was no one at home. I was rash enough to take this as the invitation I needed. I went in with her. There we stood, the two of us alone in the living room. She was a little flustered. I asked her to play something for me as she usually did. She does so but I don't manage to say anything. Then I suddenly grab the score, close it not without a certain vehemence, throw it onto the piano and say: Oh! What do I care for music, it's you I want, I have wanted you for two years. She kept silent. As it happens, I had taken no steps to captivate her, I had even warned her against me, against my melancholy. And when she mentioned a relationship with [Fritz] Schlegel [a former teacher], I said: Let that relationship be a parenthesis for I have first priority. [In the margin: It must have been on the 10th she first mentioned Schlegel since she said not a word on the 8th.] She mostly kept silent. Finally I left because I was anxious in case someone should come and see the two of us, with her so flustered. I went straightaway to her father. I know I was terribly afraid of having come on too strongly, and also that my visit might somehow occasion a misunderstanding, even damage her reputation.

Her father said neither yes nor no, but it was easy to see he was well enough disposed. I asked for an appointment and got one for the afternoon of the 10th. Not a single word did I say to captivate her – she said yes.[23]

Apart from paying court to Regine on his return from Jutland, Kierkegaard also got to work on his dissertation. That meant that from now on the journals ceased to be the repository for new ideas, at least for a while. The entries following the Jutland impressions are shorter and in a poetic vein similar to those he had made on the tour. But crucially, and with what in hindsight must be seen to have augured badly for his marriage plans, he had formulated some important ideas in a half-dozen longer entries from well before the Jutland trip, in fact from just about the time he had visited Regine after his finals.

Not much more than a month previously, on 25 June, a young theology student, Adolph Peter Adler, had defended his dissertation, 'The Isolated Subject in Its Most Important Forms'. Following a pattern all too familiar to Kierkegaard, in 1837 Adler (1812–1869) had returned from a trip to Germany as a Hegelian. This fact, and also no doubt the thought that a younger man had produced and defended a dissertation before he himself had even begun, prompted Kierkegaard to focus his objections to Hegelian philosophy in a half-dozen remarkable entries, two of which summarize the methodological basis of all his subsequent criticism of the philosophical tradition. These two are worth quoting in full. Here is the first:

Certainly, the abstract and metaphysical should continue more and more to be foreshortened and abbreviated (not only in the sense in which painters foreshorten perspective but also in the stricter sense of a real reduction in length, since the doubt through which the system works its way forward must be increasingly overcome and for that reason less and less talkative). But in so far as metaphysical thought also claims to think historical reality, it gets in a mess. Once the system is complete and attains the category of reality the new doubt appears, the new contradiction, the final and most profound: How to specify metaphysical reality in relation to historical reality? (The Hegelians distinguished between existence and reality: the external phenomenon exists but is real insofar as it is taken up into the Idea. This is quite right, but the Hegelians do not specify the boundary which defines how far each phenomenon can become real in this way, and the reason for this is that they see the phenomenon from the bird's eye perspective of metaphysics and do not see what is metaphysical in the phenomenon from the perspective of the phenomenon.) For the historical is the unity of the metaphysical and the contingent. It is the metaphysical to the extent that this latter is the eternal bond of existence, without which the phenomenological would disintegrate; it is the contingent to the extent that there is the possibility that every event could take place in infinitely many other ways. The unity of these divinely regarded is providence, and humanly regarded the *historical*. The meaning of the historical is not that it is to be annulled, but that the individual is to be free within it and also happy in it. This unity of the metaphysical and the contingent already resides in self-consciousness, which is the point of departure for personality. I become at the same time conscious in my eternal validity, in my divine necessity, so to speak, and in my contingent finitude (that I am this particular being, born in this country, at this time, under the many-faceted influence of all these changing surroundings). This latter aspect must be neither overlooked nor rejected, the true life of the individual is its apotheosis. And that does not mean that this empty, contentless *I* steals, as it were, out of this finitude to become volatilized and evaporated on its heavenly emigration, but rather that the divine inhabits the finite and finds its way in it.

The objection to Adler's assumption that metaphysics 'thinks reality'[24] anticipates the later claim in Chapter 2 of Part Two of *Concluding Unscientific Postscript* that, although a logical system is possible, there can be no system of existence. Besides his dissertation, Kierkegaard had almost certainly read Adler's discussion that year of Heiberg's 'Det logiske System' (The System of Logic), from 1838, concerning the place of 'becoming' in relation to 'being' and 'nothing' in Hegel's scheme.[25] The issue raised is internal to Hegelianism, and Kierkegaard in effect takes issue with both authors, though at this point fairly cautiously, saying only that Hegelians have no way of showing, from the point of view of time, how far any phenomenon can become 'real', or 'actual', in the sense in which it is said to do so by being comprehended by the Speculative Idea. By adopting the point of view of the Speculative Idea in the first place, you abstract from historical time and disallow at the outset the very element in history, considered as the unity of metaphysics and the contingent, that makes it appropriate to call that unity 'history'. As a good Hegelian, Adler believes that in becoming real the individual 'overcomes' the contingencies of time and environment that make up its identity in time, proving any initial sense of its 'isolation' to be illusory. Kierkegaard suggests that, on the contrary, these contingencies are ineluctable givens that have to be grasped for what they are. In place of the Hegelian picture of human fulfilment (becoming 'real' or actual as opposed to what the human being is only potentially) as a kind of evaporation of the finite, Kierkegaard proposes the idea of a 'divine inhabitation' of the finite. The centrality of this idea for the later Kierkegaard will become apparent, as will also its connection with 'personality' and the notion of a person's 'eternal validity'. These, in the not-so-distant future, will be central themes in Part Two of *Either/Or*.

The other passage seems to be opening the way to a new kind of philosophizing, a kind which has its roots in the German Idealist tradition but which takes over where that leaves off:

All in all, one must say that modern philosophy, even in its most grandiose form, is still really just an introduction to making philosophizing possible. Certainly, Hegel is a conclusion, but only of the development that began with Kant and was directed at cognition. We have arrived through Hegel, in a deeper form, at the result which previous philosophers took as their immediate point of departure, i.e. that there is any substance to thinking at all. But all the thinking which from this immediate point of departure (or, as now, happy in this result) enters into a properly anthropological contemplation, that is something that has not been begun.[26]

Another of the entries introduces a possible topic for this form of contemplation. It raises the question of the place of natural language in Hegelian philosophy, for it is the medium in which Hegelian philosophy has to unfold, while at the same time that philosophy is supposed to begin without presuppositions. Against the tendency to think of language as something we give to ourselves, Kierkegaard says, why not look at it as something freely given and which we learn to appropriate?[27] Three ideas from another of these entries also help us, as it seems likely that they were helping Kierkegaard, to bring the outlines of his thought into sharper focus. One idea is the attractiveness of the Platonic view of knowledge as recollection, in contrast to any view that places the point at which a human being 'could really find rest' somewhere beyond the range of human possibility. This has a strongly Schleiermacherian flavour, for it says that the point from which knowledge, in Plato's sense, as recollection of eternal truths lost to view when born into this world, is possible must be one of rest, but also within one's compass. The rest cannot consist, however, in some special form of cognition, speculative philosophy for instance. Far from 'all philosophizing [being] a calling to mind of what is already given to consciousness', as he says modern philosophy explicitly assumes, the one Kierkegaard advocates is at once 'more pious' and 'even a little mystical'. It generates a 'polemic . . . aimed at subjugating knowledge of the external world in order to bring about the stillness in which these recollections become audible'. Finally, there is the all-important idea that, although the point of rest is not one in which one remains 'stationary', marking time as it were, this doesn't mean that in moving on one then finds out or determines what it is one is to become; the point is rather that the individual, through a development, 'take possession of what it has'.[28] This, again, will be a theme in *Either/Or*, Part Two.

The dating of these entries from before the pilgrimage to the Jutland Heath, and therefore prior also to Kierkegaard's proposal to Regine, when seen alongside the fact that reading Adler focused his mind on topics that were to become themes in his first publication after breaking with Regine, is highly significant. Kierkegaard had already formulated a philosophical future for himself, a future that might even allow him to fulfil his long-entertained hopes to be a writer, not just a philosopher in the more traditional and pedestrian sense – nor just a writer in the general literary sense, for the role he might have as a writer would also be religious. He would be writing on matters of life and death. Better still, in doing so he would be be acting as custodian of an idea that was worth living and dying for. It was not a future it would be easy to fit Regine into.

First of all, however, the dissertation had to be written. So long as that occupied him the choice need not be made or even clearly formulated. To all outward appearances Kierkegaard and Regine behaved as any ordinary happy couple would; he visited her daily, often twice, and they went out frequently on walks and coach rides, chaperoned often by Sibbern, whom Kierkegaard also took along on visits to her home. Sibbern, it seems the couple's only confidant in respect of the varying fortunes of their relationship, said later that he detected the note of discord that crept into the relationship.[29] It was Regine who needed Sibbern's kindly support most; Kierkegaard could confide his tribulations to his journals, where they could also be assuaged by the literary challenge or even pleasure of transmuting them into literature. Some entries were to find their way into the first part of *Either/Or* and specifically on the theme, to marry or not. The message there was to be that you will regret it either way. Besides this, or in spite of it, and even though he saw her almost every day, Kierkegaard kept up a correspondence with Regine. His own letters are undated. They are playful and artful rather than emotional and a little affected in their expressions of attachment, as if were again exercising his literary muscles rather than giving expression to his love. The onslaught of doubt penetrates the artifice all the same, as the letters also become less frequent. What Regine wrote we do not know; she later asked to have her letters returned and burnt them.

But Kierkegaard still seemed firmly on course for a pastorate, or perhaps a chair, a life in which in either case there would be room for a wife. He was duly enrolled in the Royal Pastoral Seminary, though we note that even here his mind fastened on ideas that were to find their way into *Either/Or*.[30] Early in the new year (12 January 1841), in Holmen's Church, and as part of the seminary's homiletic and catechetic exercises prior to ordination, he gave his first sermon. The commentators noted that it had been 'very well memorized', 'the voice was clear', the tone 'dignified and forceful'. The sermon had also been written 'with much thought and sharp logic'. They added that although admittedly the thought was 'consistent', its 'wealth of ideas' put it beyond the reach of the average person. One commentator remarked that Kierkegaard had represented 'the struggles of the soul' as being far too difficult to have any 'appeal' to average people 'to whom such matters are unfamiliar'. The language, however, won 'great' praise.[31] Kierkegaard had prepared several drafts for sermons in connection with the Pastoral Seminary; one of them is a freely rendered version of the story of Abraham and Isaac. Here too he was on course, but not in the direction that his attendance at the seminary would have led people at the time to believe.

From Chapter 4 we recall that already in 1837 Kierkegaard had thought of writing a dissertation on 'the concept of satire with the ancients' and 'the relation of the various Roman satirists to each other'. This topic appeared to grow out of a larger one noted a few days earlier, in which Kierkegaard envisaged a 'history of the human soul (as it is in an ordinary human being) in the continuity of mental states (not the concepts) consolidating in particular peaks and nodes (i.e. noteworthy world-historical representatives of life-views)'.[32] In the event, however, Kierkegaard chose to focus on the concept of irony and, fittingly enough, picked out Socrates as the crucial historical representative of a life-view in which irony played a central role. Thus it was the Greeks rather than the Romans who were to populate the discussion, as well as the Romantics. A reason for choosing the theme may be that he had already formed some notion of how to treat it, while the larger topics would take him further afield. But a more compelling reason could be the current topicality of the theme. In Germany, interest in Schlegel's novel *Lucinde* had been reawakened in recent years by the Young Germany movement, which read it against the background of their own interest in a return to the bodily and the sensual,[33] something that would have appealed also to Møller, whose little manifesto against what he called the 'counter-emanation' evident in the republic of learning has been quoted here. As early as October 1835, just before that talk to the Union, Kierkegaard had referred to *Lucinde*.[34] Another, and more than cosmetic, link with Møller may be found in the fact that one of Møller's 'Aphorisms' (*Strøtanker*) bears the very title Kierkegaard chose for his dissertation, *Om Begrebet ironi* (On the Concept of Irony). Although not published until well after Kierkegaard's dissertation period, given the closeness of their relationship the passage could easily be one that Møller had shown to Kierkegaard. Møller, too, was criticizing Romantic irony.[35]

The earliest recorded remark on irony occurs in the famous letter from Gilleleje dated 1 August 1835. Irony is referred to, in connection with Socrates, as an 'irksome travelling companion' that one must be 'free of' if life is to acquire 'repose and meaning'.[36] Earlier we saw how freeing oneself of irony, or 'surviving' it, was presented as a third stage in a typically Hegelian triad: first a period of latency, followed by one in which individuality is dominated by irony, and then an overcoming of irony in which the individual as such emerges. There is talk of the 'self-conquest of irony', and of the individual in this way finding 'its true height'.[37]

In the dissertation itself, mastery of irony is a topic that appears only in the final section, and in connection with literature. The poet (read: writer of literary texts), we are told, besides mastering irony in his writing, faces the task of mastering it 'in the reality [*Virkelighed*] to which he belongs'.[38] In order to see how this topic emerges in the dissertation we can note, first of all, the crucial place given to reflection. It will be recalled that, in Heiberg's version of Hegelian aesthetics, art forms are arranged in order of increasing awareness of the distinction between their immediate and reflective aspects, the highest forms being those in which the limitations that immediacy and reflection impose on each other are visible. It is because the irony in comedy means that the limitations that immediacy and reflection impose on each other are visible for what they are, that this form is accorded a high status. In Kierkegaard's dissertation irony itself is now treated as something that assumes increasingly reflective forms. Romantic irony is its most reflective form. In it, the individual is too abstract to engage the world of morals or ethics, a world that should appear in the 'twofold form' of a 'gift that refuses to be rejected . . . and a task that wants to be fulfilled'.[39]

The thrust of the dissertation is, however, that irony is nevertheless a good thing. Even if one must be free of 'life's irony', it must first be allowed to establish itself and run its course; otherwise there will be no spiritual development. That irony should be cultivated is already suggested in an early journal entry, from 1836. It implies that there are other and less admirable ways of being rid of life's irony than mastering it. Indeed, you may fail to discover it simply because you are too busily engrossed in life.

Life's irony must of necessity belong most to childhood, in the age of imagination, which is why it is so marked in the Middle Ages, why present in the Romantic school. Manhood, being more merged with the world, hasn't so much of it.[40]

Irony distances you from the world at the same time that it allows the world to reappear in more vivid but also more elusive and, as the Gilleleje reference indicates, more disturbing guises than it does for a person preoccupied with the everyday. It is this distancing that, in typically Hegelian fashion, prepares you for a better return to the gift and task of the world. At this time, the idea that the return should take on the ethical form later described in *Either/Or* has not firmly established itself in Kierkegaard's mind. That had to await a difficult personal choice of his own just ahead: to marry or not to marry. At this point, marriage was crystallizing itself in his mind as a step which the very writing of the dissertation was allowing him, or conveniently forcing him, to postpone.

Roughly speaking, the dissertation has two main manifest concerns. One of these is to vindicate Socratic irony in the face of Hegel's dismissal of it as merely a rhetorical device. This dismissal was part of Hegel's criticism of the Romantics; Hegel reproached the Romantics for mistakenly taking Socrates' irony to have some world-historical point and then embracing him as one of their own. For Hegel, however, the 'world-historical' importance of Socrates lies not in his irony, in the form of feigned ignorance, but in his personifying an emergent 'freedom of self-consciousness'. Through this freedom, the inherent subjectivity of thought found its place in the human spirit; for thought, though universal, in the sense that thoughts employ general concepts and can be shared, is always at bottom the thought of a particular thinker. In the dissertation, in place of the Socrates whose irony was nothing but a rhetorical strategy, Kierkegaard presents a Socrates whose world-historical significance is exactly his mastery of irony.

The second manifest concern of the dissertation is to rescue Romantic irony from Hegel's dismissal of it as a dead-end. After putting them right on Socratic irony, Hegel had turned to the Romantics themselves to point out how their own irony lacked any dialectical potential. That meant that it contained no inner tension out of which something positive could be derived and allowed to emerge. Early journal entries testify to Kierkegaard's belief that Romantic irony had just such a dialectical role to play. One such entry, from 1837, likens the romantic 'standpoint' to a 'see-saw whose ends designate irony and humour'. Thus Romanticism swings between 'the most heaven-defying humour' and 'the most despairing surrender to irony', and yet it finds a certain 'rest and equilibrium' in this movement to and fro. The same entry talks of the individual 'surviving' irony, though only when 'raised up above everything and looking down, he is at last elevated above himself and from that height has seen himself in his nothingness'. This is what enables him to find his 'true height'. And it says that irony 'kills itself' when, 'with humour [it has] scorned everything including itself'.[41]

We must note, however, that humour by itself will not stop the descent again into despairing irony. Finding one's true height means leaping off the see-saw at the humorous top of its swing onto something else – or perhaps 'nothing', or an absolute one knows nothing about. Another entry from the end of that same year gave what seems a conventionally Hegelian account of this something else.

When the dialectical (the romantic) has lived out its world historical time (a period I could very appropriately call the period of individuality – something which can also easily be shown historically), sociality must most decidedly come to play its role again, and ideas such as the state (e.g. as the Greeks knew it, the Church in the older Catholic meaning of the word) must of necessity return enriched and rounder – that is, with all the content that the surviving distinction of individuality can give to the idea, so that the individual as such means nothing but all are as links in the chain. This is why the concept of the Church is increasingly making its claim, the concept of a fixed objective faith, etc., just as the propensity to found societies is a precursor, though up to now a bad one, of this development.[42]

What did Kierkegaard mean here by the 'dialectical' in Romanticism? Its unsteady fluctuation between irony and humour? In the dissertation Romantic irony is contained in another polarity, a given world of 'paltry philistinism' on the one hand, and on the other 'dimly emerging shapes' that fail to reach eternal life.[43] Or is it the transfer to a more stable, even eternally 'valid', place that resolves the to-and-fro movement? Whichever is meant, this journal passage appears to attribute to Romanticism a world-historical role regarding *individuality* quite analogous to the one the dissertation has Hegel attributing to Socrates regarding subjectivity. Just as the inherent subjectivity of thought, introduced by Socrates, opened the way to what was general, objective, and substantial in the form of thought, so also the individuality cultivated in Romanticism will provide essential input for a sociality enriched with the true form of eternal life. That is a very Hegelian way of thinking, and there are indications that it survives in the dissertation. In 1850, nine years after the dissertation, Kierkegaard was to write:

Influenced as I was by Hegel and by everything modern, lacking the maturity really to comprehend greatness, I was unable to resist pointing out somewhere in the dissertation that it was a shortcoming in Socrates that he had no eye for the totality but only looked, numerically, to the individuals. . . . Oh, what a Hegelian fool I was! This is precisely the big proof of how great an ethicist Socrates was.[44]

At the end of Part One of the dissertation, in a section entitled 'Hegel's View of Socrates', Kierkegaard cites Hegel's reference to Socrates as the founder of morality, and he reminds the reader that, in the terminology of Hegel's *Philosophy of Right*, the moral person, as opposed to the ethical one, is the 'negatively free individual' for whom 'nothing is a matter of earnest', while

true earnest is possible only in a totality to which the subject no longer arbitrarily decides at every moment to continue his imaginary constructions but feels the task to be something that he has not assigned himself but has had assigned to him.[45]

If this is the passage Kierkegaard later regretted, it is not its concluding thought that he would want to retract. That the world is a task assigned to us, and not something established in poetic representation, continues to be a motif of his thought. What on Kierkegaard's maturer view would be wrong in the passage is the suggestion that Socrates was someone for whom what should emerge positively from negative freedom could do so only if the task assigned were conceived in terms of the individual's membership in a totality. As it is, the first part of the dissertation ends by according to Socrates the status of a 'divine missionary' who ushers people individually out of reality.

> Just as Charon took people across from the fullness of life to the shadowy land of the underworld . . . so Socrates also shipped individuals from reality [*Realitet*] to ideality; and the ideal infinity as the infinite negativity was the nothing into which he had the entire multiplicity of reality disappear.[46]

Later on, Kierkegaard could be more enthusiastic about such Charon-like activity. The 'nothing' into which negative freedom led would be the first step towards an individual God-relationship. Ethics would be built out of such relationships. The ethical totality would then be a feature of the individual's will, not a collective matter in which individuals surrender their individuality to a group, a nation, or a state. The individual conscience, instead of merely feeding into ethics, as Hegel had it, would be what ethics, once seen to be mediated by a God-relationship, ultimately consisted in.

The accolade of 'divine missionary' is nevertheless enough to give Socrates a stature that the Romantics fail to measure up to. A focus on freedom helps us to see this. Although the ironical stance towards the world raises one above it, in principle there need be no clear sense of occupying some better, or lasting, alternative. Indeed, if ironists were honest they would turn their irony upon themselves, and then they would have no place to stand. Usually, however, the very freedom of irony seems its own justification. As Kierkegaard himself says, the 'dissimulation' in irony has a 'purpose [namely] to feel free. . . .'[47] Now freedom is also at the heart of Socratic irony, but in the denouement of Socrates's own life it acquires a special format. Socratic freedom has the form of ignorance (that 'not-knowing' with which irony 'bids true knowing begin', as we recall from the Gilleleje letter of 1835).[48] Hegel argued that because Socrates took his ignorance seriously, Socratic ignorance could not be irony.[49] Kierkegaard defends Socrates by pointing out that although in its simulation of ignorance Socratic irony is playful, the application of that unserious ignorance can be serious enough.

[Socrates] is ignorant of what death is and of what there is after death, he is ignorant about whether there is anything or nothing at all. But he does not take this ignorance to heart; on the contrary, he feels genuinely quite liberated in this ignorance. The ignorance isn't therefore serious for him, and yet he is deadly serious about being ignorant.[50]

Socratic seriousness lies in the extremes to which Socrates was willing to take his playful ignorance. Introducing another Hegelian notion to be made much of in later writings, that of the tragic hero, Kierkegaard says that, while the tragic hero's death is 'truly the final battle and the final suffering' in which 'the age he wanted to destroy can . . . satisfy its fury for revenge', in the case of Socrates the (Greek) state was deprived of this satisfaction, 'since by his ignorance Socrates had frustrated any more meaningful communication with the thought of death'.[51] Seriousness, or 'true earnest', is the attitude of someone who faces the world as a task to be fulfilled, a gift that cannot be refused. Socrates employed the unserious device of irony in the service of such earnest.

How is it then with the Romantics? Although irony for them was not a precise notion, in cultivating it they sought a kind of 'true knowing' in irony itself. Friedrich Schlegel, for whom literature as far back as Boccaccio had been inspired by irony's 'divine breath',[52] tried to establish irony as a literary or quasi-philosophical category. He sought its basis in Kant's focus on the 'transcendental', a focus, that is to say, not directly on objects themselves but on ways that we have of experiencing them.[53] Kant had drawn attention to considerations that made it no longer possible to conceive a clear separation of the knowing subject from the object known. For Romanticism, with its cultivation of poetic experience, this impossibility invited the thought that the subject in a wide, existential sense could invest 'mere' or mundane reality with the ideality that made it really real. To Kant was then added the Fichtean idea that the relation of subject to object is a reflective one, initiated by the subject. There thus arose the idea of a reflective form of poetry, which Schlegel himself proposed should 'by analogy to philosophical jargon be called transcendental poetry'.[54] It became easy for the Romantics to assume that in poetic expression they had found a more adequate way of gaining access to truth, of being true to the world, than any in traditional philosophy, including Kant's Schleiermacher's 'feeling of absolute dependence' was a religious variation on the same theme, and although there was no definite notion of what it meant to unify the finite and infinite in experience, or – and to be more faithful to the insight that the Romantic vision assumed it had gained – precisely because there was no one such notion, or even no such *notion*, the Romantic tradition felt it had grounds for claiming a superior grasp of that goal.

Kierkegaard, who owned *Decameron*, had read the Romantics widely. Brøchner says he even recited the Romantic poets; he could recall 'with what expression and force' he did so.[55] Is there perhaps an autobiographical reference in that claim about childhood and the 'age of imagination' being where irony belongs? Recall those early 'broodings' in the area of humour and irony in connection with his own ability to laugh in the presence of continued intimations of life's finitude. The same notion is found in Schlegel's utterance, shortly before his death: 'True irony . . . is the irony of love. It arises from the feeling of finitude and one's own limitation and the apparent contradiction of these feelings with the concept of infinity inherent in all true love.'[56] The real world's finitude is focused and brought into relief against the background of human aspiration that remains unsatisfied with mere finitude, an aspiration that may have been merely implicit but which is uncovered, or brought to awareness, in the 'discovery' of the temporal limitation of any human endeavour.

Kierkegaard agreed with the Romantics in their criticism of that 'whole Idealist development' that 'in Fichte certainly found an "I", an immortality, but without fullness [*Fylde*]'. But according to Kierkegaard, Fichte 'capsized' because he 'threw the empirical ballast overboard'. A notion that he connects with what was jettisoned is that of 'personality', one which Novalis helped to introduce into the philosophical arena even though Kierkegaard dismissed what Novalis himself hauled on-board again as nothing but the 'opiate fumes of soulfulness [*Sjelsfylde*]'.[57] As we hinted earlier, a more full-bodied notion of personality would become central in Kierkegaard's thinking. What may be surprising is how close his views on it are to Hegel's. In a journal entry from about the time of the dissertation Kierkegaard notes that

[i]n one place Hegel himself seems to hint at the incompleteness of mere thought, that philosophy by itself is after all an inadequate expression of human life, or that

the personal accordingly does not fulfil itself in thinking on its own but in a totality of existential modes [*Arter*] and ways of expression.[58]

Kierkegaard recognized in the Hegel of the lectures on fine art someone who had insight into the structure of personality, and who appreciated the role of imagination in any living thought. That he was also the author of the *Science of Logic*, which maintained that reality and ideality are ultimately united in reason, was another thing, though Kierkegaard had also shown that work some respect.[59]

Kierkegaard's criticism of Romantic irony comes late in the dissertation, in a section in the second and concluding part, under the title 'Irony after Fichte'.[60] In this concluding part, it is suggested that, to whatever extremes Socrates took it, Greek irony is still really only an undeveloped version of what first comes to fruition in the Romantics. As a kind of *undisturbed* subjectivity, 'not 'combatted' but 'pacified' by a subjectivity still in its uncritical phase, Greek irony is typical of someone for the first time 'obtaining [his] rights'. Romantic irony, for its part, is a further development of this, in fact a form of the subjectivity *of subjectivity*. In what Kierkegaard refers to in a journal entry, already cited, as a 'crisis of the higher life of the spirit',[61] it allows the positive side of the dialectic to which irony contributes to come more forcefully to the fore as its opposite. Kierkegaard discusses three writers criticized by Hegel: Solger, Schlegel, and Tieck. Wilhelm Ferdinand Solger (1780–1819) was a German Romantic philosopher who made much of the polarities to be grasped in an otherwise fragmented existence, seeing the possibility of reconciliation only in the infinite Idea. To define the 'depths' to which Solger was willing to take the 'philosophical Idea' in order to bring off this reconciliation – 'so negating itself as infinite and universal as to become finitude and particularity, and in nevertheless cancelling this negation in turn and so re-establishing the universal and infinite, the finite and particular' – Hegel used the expression 'infinite absolute negativity'.[62] In discussing Romantic irony, Kierkegaard adopts the term too, but it is important to observe that it was not infinite absolute negativity in itself that meant, for Hegel, that there was no dialectical potential in Romantic irony. The point is that this negativity is just 'one element' in the Speculative Idea. What was wrong was to 'interpret' it as a 'purely dialectical unrest and dissolution of both infinite and finite'.[63] Hegel's criticism of Solger, as of Schlegel and Johann Ludwig Tieck (1773–853), is that the Idea is reduced, without remainder or the possibility of dialectical development, to a pendulum state of unrest, what Kierkegaard referred to as the see-saw of irony and humour. Of course, the Romantic ironists themselves would not have put it in that way; they would have said that they sought the positivity inherent in irony in irony itself. But, and as Kierkegaard himself had already seen, irony is not a 'position': once irony is applied to itself, there is nothing left to stand on, there is no longer any room for irony's 'egoism'.[64]

The question is where to go from there. As we noted, the notion of reflective irony had, due to Fichte, given Romantic irony the appearance of being in direct descent from Kant, thus allowing the Romantics to suppose that the proper contemplation of being lay in the cultivation of modes of experience. This is where the Romantics went wrong. The state expressed in the ironic stance is one of unreality; carried to its logical conclusion it involves a radical breakdown of the subject's sense of being present to its world. In a purely negative account of irony, 'the whole of existence has become alien to the ironic subject and the ironic subject in turn alien to existence', and 'as actuality has lost its validity for the ironic subject, he himself has [also] to a certain degree become unactual'.[65] This idea was to be pursued in works to follow. In particular, what came to be labelled the 'aesthetic' mode of life, or life-view, is precisely one in which, by going through that mode's various infra-stages, as Kierkegaard later presents them, the aesthete is left with no reality and therefore faces the problem of creating his own. However, since the aesthete is nothing but an aesthete, the only landscape he can envision is a satisfyingly aesthetic one. That the attempt thus proves unsuccessful and that persistence in it has the character of despair is something Kierkegaard would develop in the second part of *Either/Or*. Here, in the dissertation, irony is presented as a levelling process, creating a clearing in which the world can reappear as a gift and a task, and with it the possibility of a reconciliation between subject and object. Romantic irony, because it actually destroys the distinction, cannot in its own terms conceive the task it is its function to propose. To its own final question, whether irony has an eternal validity, the dissertation ends by saying that the answer can only be given – we could say, irony's task only conceived – in theanthropic rather than humanistic terms. But then our topic will have become the more embracing one of humour.

On 3 June 1841 Kierkegaard delivered *Om Begrebet Ironi med Stadigt Hensyn paa Socrates* (On the Concept of Irony with Constant Reference to Socrates) in person to Sibbern, then dean of the faculty of philosophy. The royal dispensation to present his dissertation in Danish rather than in Latin was sought and duly granted, for which we may be grateful. The official faculty appointees gave their assent to the dissertation as worthy of defending, though not without criticism. One of them was Martensen, asked because the first choice, Rasmus Nielsen, had begged off. Kierkegaard had shown Martensen some of the dissertation previously, and Martensen later wrote that he found the style mannered and intolerably discursive. His approval was not unexpectedly curt. The other appointees, though admitting that the dissertation showed considerable intellectual talent, expressed similar reservations: too verbose and too much affectation, also 'various excesses of the sarcastic or mocking sort' which have no place in academic writing, as well as 'vulgar exaggeration'. Sibbern himself wished 'our author's idea were carried through with more precision' and hoped, and the others concurred, that in a revision certain things 'appropriate to a lower sort of genre' would be removed. Largely through Sibbern's intercession and insistence, the university's highest executive committee recommended, on 29 July 1841, that Kierkegaard be allowed to obtain the degree of *Magister* with a dissertation in Danish, though by then it had been insisted that, in addition to the dissertation, a set of theses in Latin be presented, which would be topics of the public defence. The king signed the necessary resolution on the following day, though for some reason the decision itself was not conveyed to the faculty or the candidate until 28 August.[66]

The successful defence took place on 29 September 1841, the disputation itself being carried out as tradition demanded in Latin. The fifteen theses Kierkegaard had himself formulated in summary of its substance were printed after the dissertation's title page in Latin. Sibbern, as dean, was formally in charge but also an official opponent, the other being *Etatsraad* (cabinet minister) Peder Oluf Brøndsted, who was also professor of Greek.[67] The session lasted for seven and a half hours and included exchanges instigated *ex auditorio*. Among those who added their comments in this way were Peter Kierkegaard and Heiberg. It would be nice to think that Peter was bringing his expertise in both Latin and disputation to lend his brother a hand. In April, under the strain of indecision about Regine and the sheer pressure of completing the dissertation, Søren had been ill and spitting blood.[68] The more typical concern on Peter's side, however, would be with upholding the family's reputation. Heiberg must have spoken for quite other reasons. Whatever other points he took up, he must have been provoked by a passage towards the dissertation's close comparing him disadvantageously to Goethe. The session was concluded and the long ordeal over. On 14 October the king signed the required authorization conferring upon Kierkegaard the title of *magister artium*.[69] The diploma was dated 20 October 1841.[70]

So much for the course of events. So, too, one might think, for the dissertation. But some questions wait to be asked. What if the dissertation on irony is itself ironical, as some have claimed? And even if it isn't, is there not some hidden agenda, for instance a critique not just of Hegel's views on Socrates and the Romantics, but of Hegel himself? One reason for suspecting the latter is that irony is, by Kierkegaard's own admission, not a position of any kind, to be described, placed, and defended, but more like an attitude towards the world. Irony, by providing a form of synoptic reflection that gives insight into the limitations of a life dedicated to what is 'immediate', leads you to a view of the world as a limited whole: 'It isn't this or that phenomenon, but the whole of existence [*Tilværelsens Totale*] that is viewed *sub specie ironiae*.'[71] If so, what point can there be in bringing irony 'to the concept', as Hegelians would say, or in talking of its 'truth', as the last section claims to do. Surely, rather than formulating and defending theses about irony, Kierkegaard is really giving us an elaborate example of it and, in doing so, cocking a snook at the academic procedure he is outwardly engaged in. In that case, since irony is to say something other than what you mean, the dissertation cannot be saying what Kierkegaard really means. Or, if there is nothing Kierkegaard *could* really mean about irony, then the irony on display is simply that anything is said on the subject at all.[72]

Familiarity with Kierkegaard's immediate past as an author should certainly make one wary about taking the dissertation at its face value. We remember that the 'little treatise' on Andersen was offered in a take-it-or-leave-it spirit that clearly broke with intellectual etiquette. Are we to assume that, in the case of this much longer treatise, whatever considerations weighed so heavily three years previously no longer apply? Is the dissertation an exception to Kierkegaard's own rules? Is it simply an academic treatise to be read as such, something Kierkegaard wrote out of respect for the memory of his father, or to refute Sib-

bern's prophecy ('Now you'll never take your theology finals'), or just
to keep open the possibility of a job?

Even if some of these suspicions may appear plausible, none seems
necessary. The Andersen review had life-views as its topic. Kierkegaard
was complaining that Andersen's novel lacked one. What the little
treatise required of the reader was an interest in life-views and therefore
at least some inkling of what such a view is. A reader lacking these
might as well leave the text alone. But the same might just as well be
said of the dissertation. It is about irony, and a reader who has no idea
of what irony is, or of how literature can be brought within its compass,
might just as well leave it alone too. Except, of course, that Kierkegaard
would hope that, for any one of the faculty appointees who had little
idea of these things, there would still be enough erudition and intellectual acumen on display in the rest to show that he deserved the title of
Magister.

In this respect, Kierkegaard's dissertation need be considered no
different from any other on an elusive topic such as irony. This, however, does not exclude the possibility that, in addition to the two manifest concerns outlined here, there is a third, less developed but underlying theme.

In the dissertation's final section ('Irony as a Controlled Element.
The Truth of Irony'), Kierkegaard says that irony in writing should
pervade the whole work and not just part of it. Resorting to a favourite
metaphor, he says that irony must be the work's centre of gravity, just
as in the treatise on Andersen he had said a life-view should be that. If
the work has its own centre of gravity, then it has in a sense released
itself from its creator. Not, however, in the sense that we recall Kierkegaard intended when he called Andersen's work an amputation rather
than a production; when the work has its own centre of gravity it is the
author *himself* who has been released from the work, just as much as the
work has released itself from him. This mutual release of work and
author occurs when the author is 'master' over the irony in his work:
'irony simultaneously makes the poem and the poet free.' From the
writer's side the freedom is, however, in respect *only* of his work; so far
it says nothing about his own personal mastery of irony in life itself. In
what seems a direct reference to the earlier essay, Kierkegaard says: 'the
more the writer has abandoned the standpoint of one who is engulfed
in his genius [*det Geniales umiddelbare Standpunkt*]', the more significant

any discrepancy one may find between what he writes and who he is, and also 'the more necessary [it is] for him to have a total view of the world, and in this way to be master over irony in his individual existence', for which reason all the more important it is that he be, and we note the qualification (here emphasized), '*to some extent* a philosopher'. We therefore have to direct attention at the actual life of the poet and consider details that 'don't usually concern us'. The point of that is to see how far a writer's works have become 'moments', as Kierkegaard says, in his own 'development'.[73] But, and here perhaps lies the possibility of a third, underlying theme in the dissertation, there is also another question: how can a writer, whether immediate genius or one who has had to resort to philosophy, impart such moments in his own life to his reader?

The hyper-reflective Kierkegaard was far from the position of immediate genius, but he was certainly on the way to being a poet in the wide sense of the word then current, a writer of literary texts. As a writer he was also already an ironist, displaying all the characteristic features of irony. But was he able, or did he ever intend, to produce works in which the irony was pervasive, works with their own ironical centres of gravity?

Some will say that the future pseudonymous works do have their own centres of gravity, and that their very pseudonymity underlines the fact. They may say this whether or not they would also say that the centres of gravity are ironical. Others will disagree; they will say that none of the pseudonymous works has a centre of gravity; on the contrary, it is characteristic of the pseudonymous works, indeed their genius, to suggest that their centres of gravity are somewhere else. This indeed is their irony, and it is pervasive. The irony is, moreover, something the author is being serious about. It is his edifying intention that the bottoms fall out of them, leaving readers lurching in yet another unreality and clutching for another (way of experiencing) reality that might help them to regain balance. In fact, Kierkegaard suggests that irony itself puts us on the right path.

As soon as irony is controlled, it moves in a direction opposite to that in which uncontrolled irony proclaims its life. Irony limits, finitizes, and circumscribes and thereby yields truth, actuality, and consistence. . . . Anyone who does not understand irony at all, who has no ear for its whispering, lacks precisely thereby what could be called the absolute beginning of personal life. . . .

So the unrealities into which, Charon-like, the ironical author leads the reader are clearances that open the way for reality to return undistorted by literary representation, to be faced as a gift and a task. But the return is not a simple return. Due to irony it occurs at a higher level. 'Just as scientists maintain that there is no true science without doubt, so it may be maintained with the same right that no genuinely human life is possible without irony.'[74]

If Kierkegaard has indeed achieved the kind of mastery he talks about, thereby releasing himself from his works, and them from him, then that release is of a special kind. He is bound to these works in ways that other authors seldom are. If the products of his irony are indeed moments in his own actuality, that is not by his floating above as a ghostly presence that is totally *free* of them. It seems more accurate to say that Kierkegaard haunts his works like a ghost *unable* to free itself, which some would agree was the very essence of ghostliness. That may be his and the works' great strength, and the reason why his art is so radical. If to master one's irony is to retain what one has written as a 'moment' in one's own development, then in order to share that development with the reader one must tip the reader continually forward, or backward, to as-yet indeterminate centres of gravity that converge on the author's own. If this is how it is with the pseudonymous works, then they form a new kind of literature, even a new kind of literary irony. The dissertation only hints at these things, but we may see it as tipping *us* in a direction that, if we see it, makes it no surprise that *Either/Or* and its sequels will soon be on their way.

The dissertation itself, whatever its thematic unity, conspicuously lacks a centre of gravity. But that is due to its being a work on irony, and not a work of irony. If it were intended to be the latter, it would certainly fail its own test; its author has signally failed to let irony pervade the text. But there is every reason to suppose that it should not do so. The dissertation is serious in what it says about irony, and also in what it proposes about irony's *truth*. Its seriousness may not be on the Socratic scale. No life is at stake, nor the meaning of death. Kierkegaard is just a writer. But Socratic seriousness is certainly his theme, and one may choose to read the dissertation in part as a prolegomenon to embarking on the personal life which is possible when irony has been lived and then 'outlived'.

We recall the letter from Emil Boesen cited earlier, saying that it was not until Kierkegaard was writing his dissertation and the period of his engagement that he 'first gained a clear understanding of what he himself wanted to do and what he was capable of'.[75] Kierkegaard's own grasp of what the remarks at the end of the dissertation meant for the kind of writing that irony, and the implementation of its truth, called for may have been what led him to resist Sibbern's suggestion that he apply for a position at the university. He told Sibbern that he would need a couple of years to prepare himself. When Sibbern objected that they'd never hire him on those conditions, Kierkegaard asked Sibbern snidely whether he meant that he should, like Rasmus Nielsen, 'let them hire me unprepared'. Sibbern was angry, accusing Kierkegaard of always 'picking on' Nielsen, who had succeeded to Møller's chair in philosophy.[76] To Sibbern's repeated urging that he have *On the Concept of Irony* translated into German, Kierkegaard sent persistently non-committal replies. Was the reason his realization that the dissertation didn't belong to the kind of literature he now saw it as his task to produce? He must have known, in any case, that he could do better in another style and genre, and in another place.

7

The Breach and Berlin:
Either/Or

I N JUST UNDER A MONTH after the disputation Kierkegaard had boarded ship for Stralsund en route to Berlin. Already before the disputation, some weeks after the dissertation itself had been approved, Kierkegaard had returned Regine's ring. The engagement had lasted thirteen months. He said later that the day after he had proposed he knew it was a mistake.[1] It wasn't that he didn't care for her, on the contrary he was totally captivated and once said it would have been impossible to live without her had he not been so sure that his own 'melancholy and sadness' were bound to get in the way. Not, however, *just* because it would be unrealistic to suppose that he could get rid of them. In fact, in his complicated state he saw them as a blessing in disguise.[2]

Not just as an excuse to get away from Regine – the melancholy and sadness now seemed inextricably bound up with what was most 'him'. Rather than leave himself behind, he was determined that something good should come of it, that is, of him. Besides, for Kierkegaard any sense of love in an erotic form making 'infinite' claims, in the way Friedrich Schlegel had suggested, seems to have been out of the question. For that he would actually have to fall in love, and whatever fondness or fascination entered into his side of the relationship, here as elsewhere and always before, Kierkegaard was too full of reflection and preoccupation for anything so spontaneous to occur. Helplessly pinned down under the weight of melancholy and sadness, it was in these that he had to find anything infinite in his life, not in the yea-saying, world-affirming experience of love. Of the relationship between himself and Regine he says in one place that while she perhaps admired rather than loved him, he had not so much loved her in any erotic sense as been touched so much by the child in her. In another he says:

I cannot quite place her impact on me in a purely erotic sense. It is true that the fact that she yielded almost adoringly to me, pleaded with me to love her, had so touched me that I would have risked anything for her. But the fact that I always wanted to hide from myself the degree to which she touched me is also evidence of the extent to which I did love her, though this really has nothing to do with the erotic.[3]

Exactly: Regine certainly aroused in Kierkegaard feelings of love, but in saying what he senses as the truth in that love the word he uses is 'responsibility' rather than any expression of tenderness, and what makes him tender is to 'see her enchantment in being in love'.[4] From the start there was a sense that one of them would have to lose. If he was to lose, then his privacy, his secrets, and his melancholy, in fact all that his own life up to then had become, would have to be surrendered.[5] This was a life he had not revealed to others, so its only custodian was himself, he had a sole and also inalienable responsibility for it – a way of thinking that he would later come to call a form of despair. If he did what was right for himself, however, then Regine would lose everything *she* had – her happiness, the life a spontaneous and lively young girl should with luck be entitled to look forward to. 'This girl had to be very costly to me, or I had to make myself very costly for her religiously.'[6] In the marriage ceremony he would have to make vows of openness, but there was so much he would have to keep from her that the whole thing would 'be based on a lie'.[7] Also, in Kierkegaard's sense Regine was not even religious,[8] so whatever he might do to help her along they would be walking different paths. Perhaps he saw that a not insignificant portion of the fascination she had for him was that she was the child he had never been.

On 11 August he sent the ring back with a letter saying, 'So as not to go through more rehearsals of what must happen in any case, something that when it does happen will surely give strength, let it be done. Above all forget the one who writes this: forgive someone who whatever else he was capable of could not make a girl happy.' The letter was later reproduced in *Stages on Life's Way*.

The strength Kierkegaard's letter produced in Regine was not of the kind he hoped. Instead of inspiring stoic fortitude it energized her into a frenzied defence of the engagement. On receiving the letter she went immediately to Kierkegaard's apartment, but finding him away sat down there and wrote him what was, according to Kierkegaard, an 'altogether despairing letter' in which she begged him 'with tears and prayers (for the sake of Jesus Christ, in memory of my dead father)' not to desert her. He could do 'anything with her, absolutely anything' and she would 'still thank [him] all her life for the greatest of blessings'.[9]

There was nothing for it but to pretend he no longer cared. Better still if somehow he could turn the tables and get her to lose interest in him, get *her* to want to be rid of *him*.[10]

The two months to come before the final break he called a period of 'deceit'. The deception was not in failing to tell her that he was going to bring it to an end; he deceived Regine by putting on a show of indifference that he hoped would induce her to end it herself, or at least to agree that they should go their separate ways. Apart from provoking Regine into doing the opposite, the result was also in a strange way to bind her to him forever. Paradoxically, by the time Kierkegaard recorded these thoughts Regine had become engaged to someone else – as it happened to a man named Schlegel. Appropriately and with a double irony, a journal entry brings to mind the more famous Schlegel's claim that true love is infinite. In his own case Kierkegaard found that the infinite in love was possible only in the pain of recollection and regret. Here he says that even though they were now parted, his thought had been – 'and it was love' – 'either I become yours or you will be allowed to wound me so deeply, wound me in my melancholy and my relation to God, so deeply that, although parted from you, I will yet remain yours'.[11] The sense in which he will remain hers is that his life will be forever dedicated to the memory of their failed association. If she took that sense to imply that she remained his as well, then he had not freed her from her ties to him, which would of course bespeak the failure of his strategy. But what he in fact ensured by having her wound him with the arrow he says he himself placed in her bow was that *he* could never forget *her*. That too can be thought of as a way of making one's love infinite. In *Fear and Trembling*, the knight of infinite resignation 'keeps' his unattainable love by promoting her to the level of an ideal:

His love of the princess would take on for him the expression of an eternal love, would acquire a religious character, be transfigured into a love of the eternal being which, although it denied fulfilment, still reconciled him once more in the eternal consciousness of his love's validity in an eternal form that no reality can take from him.[12]

As for the prospects of actual marriage, Kierkegaard saw things realistically.

In the course of half a year or less she would have gone to pieces. There is – and this is both the good and the bad in me – something spectral about me, something that makes it impossible for people to put up with me every day and have a real relationship with me. Yes, in the light-weight cloak in which I usually appear, it is another matter. But at home it will be evident that basically I live in a spirit world. I had been engaged to her for one year and yet she really did not know me.[13]

Kierkegaard says that Regine saw in his desire to break off the relationship just a symptom of the depression he was prone to, his 'madness, a melancholy bordering on craziness'. What Kierkegaard thought she failed to see was that underlying it all was a 'religious collision'. This word 'collision', which occurred increasingly in Kierkegaard, was used by Hegel in his lectures on art, which Kierkegaard had read and admired, to refer to the kind of conflicts of interest or motivation that are the stuff of tragedy and a requirement of drama.[14] It seems clear that Kierkegaard looked at his own situation, at least in retrospect, as a tragic one. In fact Kierkegaard came increasingly to regard the actual events in his life in the light of dramatic categories that he had learnt from Hegel. Whether he did so at the time of the events he records, or only later made the dramatic interpretations, in the recording, is not easy to see. But as it becomes increasingly difficult to separate the record from what is recorded, the suspicion becomes all the stronger that Kierkegaard had begun to write himself into a real-life drama.

One thing was certain. Regine would be unable to see herself as part of the play. When Kierkegaard realized that she would not draw the tragic conclusion, he tried to put her off. But to his further melancholy and dismay she fought a woman's fight to keep him at all costs. Tragedy, for Kierkegaard as for Hegel, was due not to fate but to the consequences of fatefully disastrous decisions. Regine's spirited resistance to his attempt to be rid of her aroused his respect and admiration; she ceased to be the child he had never been and became an adult demanding her due and right. The strength she showed in her antagonism was the beginning of a process of maturation to which Kierkegaard even hoped his own writings might contribute – thus allowing his love to become infinite all the same.

He talks of the time as having been 'fearfully painful – having to be so cruel, and loving her as I did. She fought like a lioness: if I had not believed there was divine opposition she would have won'. He writes: 'During those two months of deceit I took the precaution at intervals of telling her straight out: Give up, let me go, you won't stand it. To which she replied passionately that she would rather stand anything than let me go.' When he suggested directly to Regine that she break the engagement, 'so that I could share all her humiliation',

[s]he would have none of it, she answered that if she could bear the rest she could probably bear that too, and she added, not un-Socratically, that probably no one would make her feel it in her presence, and what they said about her when she was absent would make no difference.[15]

On 11 October, Kierkegaard went to Regine to say that the break was final. There followed a wrought conversation sadly reminiscent of television soap-opera, after which Kierkegaard 'went straight to the theatre',

where I was to meet Emil Boesen (this is the basis of the story around town that I was supposed to have told the family, as I took out my watch, that if they had anything more to say they had better hurry, for I was going to the theatre). The act was over. As I was leaving the back stalls, the Counsellor [Regine's father] came to me from the front stalls and said: May I speak with you? I accompanied him home. She is in despair, he said, it will be the death of her, she is in utter despair. I said: I will try to calm her but the matter is settled. He said: I am a proud man, this is hard, but I beg you not to break with her. He was truly magnanimous; he jolted me. But I stuck to my guns. I ate supper with the family, spoke with her when I left. The next morning I received a letter from him saying that she had not slept that night, that I must come and see her. I went and made her see reason. She asked me: Will you never marry? I answered: Yes, in ten years time, when I have had my fling, I will need a lusty girl to rejuvenate me. It was a necessary cruelty. Then she said to me: Forgive me for what I have done to you. I answered: I'm the one, after all, who should be asking that. She said: Promise to think of me. I did. She said: Kiss me. I did – but without passion – Merciful God!

Kierkegaard also recalled that Regine 'took out a small note on which there was something written by me which she was accustomed to carrying in her breast; she took it out and quietly tore it into small pieces and said: So after all, you have also played a terrible game with me.'[16]

Others thought so too, including Regine's elder brother Jonas, who sent Kierkegaard a note saying that 'what had happened had taught him to hate as no one had hated before'. Her elder sister, Cornelia, however, whose 'rare and genuine womanliness' Kierkegaard much appreciated, said to her friends that she didn't understand *Magister* Kierkegaard but still believed he was a good man. To Kierkegaard's own brother, Peter, for whom respectability meant so much, the breach must have been a severe disappointment. Already on speaking terms with Mynster, Sibbern, and the famous physicist Hans Christian Ørsted, as well as with the newly acclaimed philosopher Rasmus Nielsen, Heiberg, and the respected theologian Andreas Gottlob Rudelbach, all Søren as *Magister* needed now to find an important niche in Danish culture and society, and thus add lustre to the Kierkegaard name, was a well-connected marriage. Peter said to Søren, 'Now you are done for', but to the rest of the family he would make it clear that Søren wasn't a scoundrel. To this Søren replied: 'If you do that I'll blow your brains out.' The news was not spread. Henriette Lund, Kierkegaard's niece, said later that she had no inkling of the broken engagement when the family was invited over to Nytorv, where Kierkegaard was now once more staying with his recently remarried brother. They had all just returned from the country, where most well-off people spent the summers.

When we children from Gammeltorv and those from Kjøbmagergade, who were also sent for, arrived there that evening, she [Aunt Henriette Glahn Kierkegaard, Peter's second wife] received us in a very kindly fashion, happy that we had come to visit her of our own accord; but she was soon made wise to her mistake when Uncle Søren immediately arrived to take us up to his apartment. He appeared much moved, and instead of his usual playfulness he kissed my hair so gently that I was quite touched. After a moment, he wanted to speak to us, but instead broke into a violent fit of weeping, and without really knowing what there was to cry about – at least this was the case for me – but simply in the grip of his suffering, we were soon all sobbing as if burdened with a heavy sorrow. Uncle Søren quickly pulled himself together, however, and he told us that one day soon he would be leaving for Berlin, perhaps to stay for quite a while. So we had to promise to write to him often, because he was anxious to hear how each of us was doing. With many tears, we promised.[17]

Kierkegaard says himself that he 'spent the nights crying in his bed' but during the day was his usual self, indeed 'far more flippant and witty than need be'. He went round to Regine's to fetch a few belongings and sent her father a letter which was returned unopened.[18] When, on 25 October, Emil Boesen and Peter accompanied him to the Swedish steamer bound for Stralsund, he had told them he planned to be away for a year and a half.

In the event he stayed no more than the rest of the autumn and winter, but by the end of that time in Berlin, he would predict in a letter to Boesen that the months spent there would prove to have been of 'great and lasting importance'.[19] The ostensible motive for the trip had been to hear Schelling's lectures on the Philosophy of Revelation. Kierkegaard, like many others, had been excited by the talk of a 'positive philosophy' which promised to sweep Hegelianism and all the newer 'negativity' aside. Friedrich Wilhelm Joseph Schelling (1775–1854), younger than Hegel but an early inspirer of his philosophy, and in earlier days along with the poet Hölderlin a sharer of the same student residence in Tübingen, was now the foremost exponent of philosophical Romanticism. He had been called from Munich by the authorities to counteract the politically disruptive influence of the 'Left' Hegelians. The lectures had been widely announced, and listeners came from all Europe. They included Friedrich Engels, according to some indications also Karl Marx, the Swiss cultural historian Jakob Burckhardt, and possibly also the anarchist writer and revolutionary Michael Bakunin, who was at any rate in Berlin at the time.[20] They were all in their twenties. Whether it was with any genuine expectation of finding something new in Schelling is hard to say. As far as Kierkegaard was concerned, what may have intrigued him was the possibility of some philosophical advance that gave room for a life-view and not just a world-view of thought, something that went beyond Romantic irony but still preserved a place for the depth of individual concern and feeling that had been Romanticism's answer to Fichte. Fichte's strong sense that reality is self-conscious ethical activity, and that what is not posited as belonging to the self is nevertheless posited *by* the self, and negatively as simply what is not the self, left no room at all for the idea of a reality that was genuinely 'other' than it. The question was how this reality could break into the circle of human ideas. If it was a world posited by God rather than the self, perhaps it could be revealed by God too. It would not be too far from that thought to the further notion that 'self-positing' selves, however compelled to conceive themselves as creatures of their own spontaneous powers of reflection, are really and in the final resort posited by God. This would reverse the Romantic view that made poetic experience a kind of world-making in the realm of human sensibility. Kierkegaard had just finished saying that the ironical stance of the Romantics left the experiencing subjects out of touch with all reality, including their own. What had Schelling to offer in defence of reality?

In his earlier work, *System des transzendentalen Idealismus* (System of Transcendental Idealism),[21] dating from 1800, quite a lot. Reality is captured in concepts that themselves have no reality except in the objects they conceptualize; sensation and feeling intimate limits, forces working on us, or the impact of other intelligences on ourselves; and the feeling of intensity is derived from the sense that we have of our own activity pressing forward in time. This was a kind of naturalization of Kant's *Ding-an-sich* but also a contextualization of Fichte's self-positing self. In the nature of things there was also a place for Nature; in Schelling's philosophy of nature from 1797, nature itself is just as real as the world of the ego. In his more recent work Schelling, although nothing new had been published since 1803 (*Vorlesungen über die Methode des academischen Studiums* [Lectures on the Method of Academic Study],[22] a copy of which Kierkegaard owned in addition to the first of the volumes of collected writings, published in 1809), had turned his mind to existence, and his final phase is often referred to as existentialist. Schelling was led to think of human history in terms of a kind of philosophical anthropology based on what, for Schelling, were the deepest forms of human activity, namely myth-making and religion. This would provide an account of human essence, of what it is to be a human being; the account would be a structured one, since mythology for Schelling was a kind of symbolic system of ideas with its own a priori structure, just as much as Kant's a priori conditions of the understanding. But apart from the essence of being, Schelling was also concerned with the very fact of being, the 'that' of existence as against the 'what'.

There are notes from Martensen's lectures on The History of Recent Philosophy from Kant to Hegel in which 'the main outlines' of Schelling's system are sketched. These notes are not in Kierkegaard's hand, so we don't know if they pick out the points that chiefly interested him, but he did at least place them among his journals. The notion of limitation appears here too. To experience the mere massiveness of nature is to intuit it at the lowest level. Here there is no sense of the other being identical with an Absolute that is also the 'truth' of the self, rather exactly the opposite. Higher positions accord conceptions of nature on the one hand and history on the other, in both of which God is wholly present, even though, to our way of seeing these, they divide into, respectively, the real and the ideal. The unity of these is revealed to an 'intellectual intuition' which is a 'unity of rational and aesthetic intuition'. Nature and history increasingly reveal the essence of their media, that is to say physical and human nature. The higher up we go in the natural ascent the nearer we are to the truth. Schelling sees inorganic nature as somehow a derivative of organic nature rather than the reverse. Geophysical nature is analogous in some way to the skeleton left when the parts making up the living body have decayed. Increasing self-consciousness correlates with theology and affords the highest and most comprehensive intuition, and Christianity finds its place as a revelation of the fundamental relationship between God and the world.[23]

In his later period Schelling had come to refer to what he called positive philosophy. Earlier he had argued that you cannot get the whole truth simply by putting a philosophy of nature and a philosophy of knowledge together; the identity of nature and knowledge still has to be vindicated, and for this one needs a philosophy of reason, or rather of reason understood in Schelling's typically idealist way. Since it is one and infinite, reason is the nonpartisan source both of nature and of knowledge. But this he now regarded as only a negative result. It provided merely the crucible into which a positive understanding of existence itself still had to be poured. It was in eager anticipation of what Schelling had to say on this score that intellectuals from all over Europe arrived in Berlin to hear Schelling lecture.

Kierkegaard, if indeed he ever really put his trust in Schelling's 'promise to assist science',[24] was in any case quickly disenchanted, both by the lectures and by Schelling himself, 'a most insignificant man to look at . . . like a tax collector'. In a letter to Emil Boesen, he wrote:

Schelling is lecturing to an extraordinary audience. He claims to have discovered that there are two philosophies, one negative and one positive. Hegel is neither of these, his is a refined Spinozism. The negative philosophy is given in the philosophy of identity, and he is now about to present the positive and thereby help bring science to its true heights. As you see, there will be promotions for all those with degrees in philosophy. In the future it won't just be the lawyers who are *doctores juris utriusque* [doctors of both civil and canon law], we magisters are now *magistri philosophiae utriusque* [masters of both negative and positive philosophy], now, but not quite yet, for he has not yet presented the positive philosophy.[25]

Writing to Sibbern, Kierkegaard describes the audience as 'select, numerous, and diverse [*undique conflatum*: blown together from all quarters]'.[26] Although he attended Schelling's full course of lectures (his notes are preserved along with his journals and other papers),[27] at the end and just before returning to Copenhagen, he wrote to Peter that 'Schelling talks quite insufferable nonsense', and said that just as he himself was 'too old to attend lectures' so was Schelling 'too old to give them'.[28] Kierkegaard recounts how he expected Schelling to comment on the second volume of Hegel's *Encyclopedia*, which had just come out with a Preface by the editor (Michelet) severely criticizing Schelling. But for all that Schelling was, according to Kierkegaard, very polemical in his lectures, he made no mention of it. Still, Schelling was in an awkward position:

He had got involved in Court interests, and that makes people rather despise his appearing, and is of course harmful as is every external consideration. The Hegelians are fanning the flames, Schelling looks as sour as a vinegar brewer. To get some idea of his personal resentment you only have to hear him say, '*Ich werde morgen fortfahren* [I shall continue tomorrow]'. Unlike Berliners . . . he pronounces the 'g' as a very hard 'k'. . . . The other day he was half an hour late . . . [and] . . . vented his anger in a number of attacks upon the arrangements in Berlin, that there are no public clocks. To make up for it he wanted to lecture a little past the hour. That isn't tolerated in Berlin, and there was scraping and hissing. Schelling became furious and exclaimed, 'If, gentlemen, you object to my lecturing, I can just as well stop. *Ich werde morken fortfahren*'.[29]

Kierkegaard kept up a punishing schedule, absorbing the philosophical atmosphere by also attending several other lecture series, though not in their entirety as with Schelling's. He heard Schleiermacher's opponent, Hegel's pupil, speculative theology's founder as well as an initiator of the Hegelian 'Right', Philipp Konrad Marheineke (1780–1846), and Henrich Steffens, whom we met earlier in Chapter 1. On Steffens, Kierkegaard wrote to Sibbern: 'I paid my fee to hear him but strangely enough he doesn't appeal to me at all. And I who have read with such great enthusiasm much of what he has written, *Carikaturen des Heiligsten* [Caricatures of the Most Holy], to mention just one example . . . I am utterly disappointed', though to another correspondent he wrote, 'The streets are too broad for my liking and so are Steffens's lectures. . . . but of course the passers-by are exceedingly interesting, just as Steffens's lectures'.[30] He also attended the lectures of the Hegelian Karl W. Werder (1806–1893). Again to Sibbern:

. . . a virtuoso; that's all one can say about him. I suspect he must be a Jew, for baptized Jews always distinguish themselves by their virtuosity and of course take part in all fields these days. He can play and frolic like a juggler with the most abstract categories and with never so much as a slip of the tongue in spite of talking as fast as a horse can gallop. He is a scholastic in the old sense who has found in Hegel, just as they did in Thomas Aquinas, not only the *summa* and the *summa summae* but the *summa summarum*. For me he is, in this respect, almost a psychological phenomenon. It's as though his life, his thought, everything the outside world has to offer has meaning for him only with reference to Hegel's *Logik*. On the other hand, it is a great advantage for the young people studying at the University that there is someone like that.

To another friend he wrote: 'Werder juggles with the categories just as the strong man in Dyrehaven juggles with balls weighing twenty, thirty, forty pounds. It's terrifying to watch, and just as in Dyrehaven one is sometimes tempted to believe they are balls of paper.'[31]

He also read copiously and kept up a correspondence not only with Boesen, Peter, and Peter Johannes Spang, a pastor at the Church of the Holy Spirit in Copenhagen, but also with his niece and nephews Henriette, Michael, and Carl Lund. At the same time, as he divulged to Boesen in a letter just quoted, he was 'furiously writing'. Kierkegaard describes this writing as not 'expository' but 'purely literary', and to do it he had to be 'in the right mood'. At the time he disclosed this activity to Boesen he was engaged in writing 'one part of a treatise'. This was later to become the second of two long 'letters' comprising the 'Or' of *Either/Or*, famous for its notion of the choice of oneself.[32] The work's title itself is referred to frequently in his correspondence with Boesen, though with no one else, and as an intimation of the pseudonymity that was to be a feature of his most successful work in this period, he tells Boesen to keep this writing a 'deep secret'.[33] Kierkegaard said later that *Either/Or*, a work of well over seven hundred pages, took just eleven months to write.[34] On returning to Copenhagen he had serviceable drafts of several sections of both parts. The writing had begun in fact as soon as he arrived in Berlin, which suggests that Schelling was not the real point of the journey. 'When I left "her" ', he says, 'I begged to God for one thing: that I might succeed in writing and finishing *Either/ Or*.'[35] A special point to this remark will emerge later.

The letters to Boesen harp continually on 'her', though never by name. Kierkegaard asks after 'her' but also asks that his interest remain altogether a secret.[36] Except to Boesen, Kierkegaard wished to maintain a facade of selfish indifference to Regine's fate, an impression he says he had been careful to convey during the two weeks prior to his departure for Berlin. To Boesen's suggestion that it would be better if he received no information about Regine, he writes:

So you would leave me to my daydreams! In this you are mistaken. I am not dreaming, I am awake. I do not turn her into poetry, I do not call her to mind, but I call myself to account. This is as far as I can go: I think I am able to turn anything into poetry, but when it comes to duty, obligation, responsibility, guilt, etc., I cannot and will not turn those into topics of poetry. If she had broken our engagement, my soul would soon have driven the plough of forgetfulness over her, and she would have served me as others have done before her – but now, now I serve her. If it were in her power to surround me with vigilant scouts who were always putting me in mind of her, she could still not be so clearly remembered as she is now in all her righteousness, all her beauty, all her pain. So just keep me informed. In the course of these recent events my soul has received a needed baptism, but that baptism was certainly not by sprinkling, for I have descended into the waters, all has gone black before my eyes, but I rise to the surface again. Nothing, after all, so develops a human being as adhering to a plan in defiance of the whole world. Even if it were something evil, it would still serve to a high degree to develop a person. So just write, and if I may say so, a little more clearly whenever you receive any intelligence. I don't shy away from the thought of her, but whenever I think of the poor girl – and yet she's too good to give – to call a poor girl – and yet she is a poor girl – and yet my strength of mind has been guilty of breaking the proudest girl – as you see I am in a treadmill and all I need is to tread for an hour a day like this, and then let my hypochondria be a surly coachman who shouts Giddyap all the time and hits the most sensitive places with his whip, and that's exercise enough for that day, then I need all possible strength of mind to say, Stop, I will now think of other things. And yet my soul is sound, sounder than ever before.[37]

Mostly, however, Kierkegaard's references to Regine's fate are dispassionate. He describes the way in which the engagement was broken as 'subtly planned'.[38] In Berlin there is even a Demoiselle Schulze from Vienna, singing the part of Elvira in Mozart's *Don Giovanni*, who Kierkegaard says 'bears a striking resemblance to a certain young lady' and who he can think of approaching not precisely with the 'purest of intentions'.[39] Clearly, however, the events of 1841, very far from being forgotten, were stirring in his imagination if not to turn Regine herself into a poetic topic, at least to fire his inventive writer's mind in generating imaginative reconstructions of the dilemma in which the events themselves had placed him.

Of the sections that were to appear in the 'Either' of *Either/Or*, at least 'Ancient Tragedy's Reflection in the Modern', 'Crop Rotation', and part of 'The Seducer's Diary' were written by the time Kierkegaard returned to Copenhagen. The task he got down to as soon as he arrived in Copenhagen was the first of the two treatises of the 'Or'. This was an aesthetic defence of marriage ('Marriage's Aesthetic Validity'), a provocative theme in the context of Romanticism, since it was part of the Romantic ethos to disparage the arrangement. In fact marriage was claimed by some to be on its own terms impossible, not just as an institution supposed to combine love and propagation, but as a way of 'developing' the subjectivity to which Romanticism was so attached. The problem of combining nature and duty in the cases of love and marriage had been addressed by Kant and Fichte. The former made marriage merely legal, while the latter argued that the law should in this case be made to conform with nature. Marriage's seemingly irreducible dual nature, and its consequent lack of any grounding or 'validity', became the themes of writers such as Beaumarchais and Goethe, in *Figaro* and *Wahlverwandtschaften* (Elective Affinities).[40] In the treatise that he told Boesen he was writing in Berlin, Kierkegaard was attempting a kind of Hegelian reconciliation of the notions of nature and duty in which nature is enriched by duty. It was a defence of the 'validity' of marriage, but in aesthetic terms. Marriage deepens love by giving it the dimension of time, making it possible for love to have a history.

What was the point of this and why did the theme appear so urgent? After what he had just done you might think Kierkegaard would attack rather then defend the institution of marriage, or at least leave it alone and think about something else. That, however, would presuppose that *Either/Or* was a project born of the immediate past, something he had thought of on the spot when finally released from a future that would deprive him of the conditions he needed in order to write. The indications, including his own words, are that quite the reverse was true. This was a project he had kept in mind all the time he was collecting his experiences and encapsulating them in his journals. Cruel though the thought is, what had just happened, and what he had done to Regine, had merely given him more of that experiential basis he once wrote of in connection with Hans Christian Andersen, and which confirmed him in his predilection for a religious life-view. Far from escaping the thought of marriage, marriage was now something he could think rather than endure. No longer having it in prospect, he could do the Hegelian thing and look at in retrospect, but not exactly in the Hegelian way, since he had no real reason to suppose that marriage itself was not 'valid' and could be surpassed; it was simply that it would not do for him, and so there must be some way of seeing that marriage is a task for which not all are fitted, not because they are too immature but because they are overmature, or too *little* natural. He was later to say that it was due to Regine, his melancholy, and his money that he could become a writer. They were all in a good cause. He even speaks, without a trace of irony, of Regine as having helped him with his relation to God and, in this way, to become 'myself'. Marriage was a good thing but had to be sacrificed. Kierkegaard himself says why even at that time (or is it especially at that time?) it seemed to him such a good thing. The reason why the 'second part [of *Either/Or*] begins with marriage' is that it 'is the most profound form of the revelation of life'.[41] Kierkegaard's problem, and he seems to have been determined to make it into, if not some kind of gift or advantage, then at least a trial or test of character of a kind that most married couples do not have to endure, was that he was incapable of having life reveal itself through him in that way. But it was this very inability that now engrossed him – not to overcome it, but to see what it really amounted to. So he wrote two long treatises on the subject, one on the meaning of the wedding ceremony and the aesthetic grounds for marriage, and the other on the opportunity marriage offered for becoming oneself, in fact for becoming a self at all.

Either/Or is therefore in many respects a resumption of the Faustian project that Kierkegaard gave up after Martensen published his treatise on Lenau. He had said that the modern Faustian problem was how knowledge, instead of empowering the one who seeks it, leaves the knower feeling increasingly insignificant and impotent. The vast explosion of knowledge in the modern age leaves no place for the knower, not least because the kind of knowledge in question, natural science, takes no account of individual knowers. We saw how the theme of the self's disappearance, or rather dissolution, had also been the outcome of Kierkegaard's study of the Romantics, the study that led to the dissertation. Since irony is the mood of the first part of *Either/Or*, and the recovery of selfhood the theme of the second, the work can also be seen, as was suggested earlier, as a development of *On the Concept of Irony*, while in its appeal to the notion of a life-view it also harks back to *From the Papers of One Still Living*.

The crux is that selves need histories, and Romanticism can only come up with isolated moods,[42] dislocated moments of truth in which nothing happens between the moments that allows or counts for personal growth. Nothing in the series of moments amounts to or can become a subject, a self. Without a subject or self there is no world – it is a Fichtean scenario, except that both the world and the self will, for Kierkegaard, in the end be posited by God and not by the self – that is to say, no reality. What that means is not just that there is no world out there, indeed it does not mean that at all; it means that nothing out there (the world) or in here (the self) is allowed to become what it is. It is surely not insignificant, in identifying the nature of the project Kierkegaard had entered upon, to learn that the eleven-month period during which he wrote and assembled *Either/Or* began with just 'a few *diapsalmata*'.[43]

There are two interesting sides to this. One is the word '*diapsalm*' itself, the other is Kierkegaard's claim to have made a start quite as clean as he claims. Consider the first. '*Diapsalmata*' is the plural Greek form for the Hebrew *sela*, a word that in the Psalms of David recurs at the end of verses. It can easily put one in mind of a refrain, as seems to be intended, that is to say of something, a mood for instance, that is repeated over and over again, getting nowhere. Writing in his journals of a central topic of the second treatise in 'Or', namely that it is 'every man's duty to become revealed', he says this is 'in fact the opposite to the whole first part [of *Either/Or*]. . . . The aesthetic is always hidden: if it expresses itself at all it is flirtation'.[44] The *diapsalmata* themselves are expressions of Romantic irony, of the kind he had garnered on the long way to the dissertation, and linked especially for him personally with the period of his break with his father and 'home' in general. To readers of the journals many of the passages appear strongly autobiographical. But for those who have learned how to read the journals they are also the products of an incorrigible poetizer disposed to render his own thoughts and feelings in ways designed to appeal to literary sensibilities. But we must remember that this was also what the Romantics thought was the proper form of experience, just the way to have the world revealed, the way to transform the raw material of feeling into the specifically Romantic *Logos*. Looking at *Either/Or* as the culmination of a long process of gestation, one could also say, without departing from that idea, that Kierkegaard had for many years been planning to write a work in which the raw material of his own experience would, quite rightly for one self-educated in the Romantic tradition, be the principal resource. In that case, putting his personal pains into acceptable literary form would be a deliberate policy, and practising the art of the Romantic's *Logos* would be one of the main motivations for writing his journals. The very first *diapsalm* puts the point and also captures the state of Kierkegaard's art at the time.

What is a poet? An unhappy man who hides deep anguish in his heart, but whose lips are so formed that when the sigh and cry pass through them, it sounds like lovely music. His fate is like that of those unfortunates who were slowly tortured by a gentle fire in Phalaris's bull;[45] their cries could not reach the tyrant's ears to cause him dismay, to him they sounded like sweet music. And people flock around the poet and say, 'Sing again soon' – that is, 'May new sufferings torment your soul but your lips be fashioned as before, for the cry would only frighten us, but the music, that is blissful'. And the critics come forward and say: 'That's the way, that's how the rules of aesthetics say it should be done.' Of course, a critic resembles a poet to a hair, except he has no anguish in his heart, no music on his lips. So I tell you, I would rather be a swineheard at Amagerbro and be understood by a swine than a poet a misunderstood by people.[46]

Of this particular *diapsalm* Kierkegaard says that it is really 'the problem of the whole work'. It assumes an 'enormous dissonance' and then says: 'Explain it.' The lines 'posit' a 'total break with actuality', a break grounded not in 'vanity' but in 'melancholy and its ascendancy over actuality'.[47] The dissertation had also noted the break with 'actuality': as existence becomes alien to the ironic subject, so does the subject itself become correspondingly 'unactual'. This, however, was to look at irony only negatively. Positively, it cleared the way for the self to emerge, to become 'actual'. The second part of *Either/Or* vividly portrays the possibility of its doing so in the form of the ethical.

But just how bare was Kierkegaard's desk when he began? Were there just those few *diapsalmata* on hand? According to one comment by Kierkegaard the work contained no old material at all, though he did say that there was plenty he could have drawn on if he had wanted to.[48] It depends perhaps on whether recasting old material counts or doesn't count as starting afresh, and on how much of what seems new is in fact memory retrieval. We noted early on where Kierkegaard could be said to have begun writing *Either/Or* without realizing that is what he was doing. Textual research indicates that quite a lot of what went into *Either/Or* existed well beforehand. That is especially true of the opening section.[49] Several of the *diapsalmata* are drawn from the journals, and over twenty of them are at least *based* on material that dates from as far back as June 1836. That, we may recall, was just after the bitter newspaper polemic from which some thought Kierkegaard had emerged the victor, but it was also the point at which he saw that although he had paid his dues to the cultural elite, this polemical style of writing was not the way to change anyone's point of view.[50] Some may have been written as recently as the period just prior to the final break with Regine, while others stem from a rich assortment of appropriate material to be found in the spring and early summer of 1839.[51] That had been a period rich in Romantic irony but also in thoughts later to develop into themes for books that had to be postponed as Kierkegaard buckled down to his studies. The whole period includes Kierkegaard's preoccupation with the Wandering Jew and Faust, as well as with Don Juan, or more particularly the performances of Mozart's *Don Giovanni* which had 'driven' him 'out of the quiet night of the cloister'. So much so, we recall, that he could say of the piece, just as Elvira said to her hero, and in the same spirit: 'You murderer of my happiness.'[52] There was the famous gap in the journals when nostalgic thoughts of quiet nights in the cloister may have mingled with other unhappier thoughts about the way a hyper-reflective mind gets in the way of a capacity for joie de vivre – a theme Kierkegaard was already prepared to follow up in the second main section of 'Either', 'The Immediate Erotic Stages or the Musical Erotic', which he did on his return to Copenhagen, making use of at least five journal entries and other notes as well as a piece he had written on Faust. What he was to write there was also to be an amalgam of his studies in Heiberg's Hegelian aesthetics and the comparisons he had made between central figures in Mozart's operas, both stemming from 1836.

Given the diversity of the origins of its parts, as well as the apparent heterogeneity of the parts themselves – a set of aphorisms, a treatise on the aesthetics of the erotic, two papers and a talk delivered to a group calling themselves something like 'the fellowship of buried lives' (*Symparanekromenoi*), a review of a French play, a short dissertation presenting an ironic theory of social prudence ('Crop Rotation'), a seducer's diary, then two long treatises on marriage followed by a sermon – you might wonder whether *Either/Or* exhibits any sort of unity at all or isn't just, as Kierkegaard found that people thought, 'a collection of loose papers I had lying on my desk.'[53] That would be a grotesque result for someone so consistently obsessed with imparting unity to things, centres of gravity. The title does, however, indicate that a certain disunity is intended. The fact that the first part is assigned to someone who signs himself 'A' and the second bears the heading 'Containing the Paper of B: Letters to A' seems to indicate that the whole point is that there are at least two centres of gravity here, and a choice to be made between them; or is there a third centre of gravity not visibly present in either of the two parts but somewhere ahead (or behind), available upon proper appreciation of the comparative merits, but also the irresoluble demerits as centres of gravity, of the two on offer?

On the subject of the Preface, which he wrote last, Kierkegaard gives the impression that whatever unity the work has grew upon him rather than being imposed by him from the start. That sounds familiar; it is the same sort of impression as that conveyed in the Preface to *From the Papers of One Still Living*. The Preface's explanation of the title begins by saying that 'after familiarizing myself with all the parts, I let the whole thing come together in my mind in a moment of contemplation'. That sounds as if he had to realize the unity in the assorted texts himself. Although there may be some half-truth in this, it is clear that already when working on the earliest drafts he was noting down what would have to be put into the Preface. But there may still be an element of truth to the remark, associated with his hope that the idea behind the work as a whole would, since there was no other way, come to view for a reader in the way he particularly prized, namely in a momentary intuition embracing all the parts. This, though the editor's emphatic 'the reader should do the same' puts the reader in the driving seat, is clearly something that could be said on the author's behalf too. Either way, to apprehend the work's unity requires looking back on the same kind of past and gathering the pieces into the same kind of collective present.

[T]he whole thing was to be like a point, separating disjunctively. But here the reader would enter into a relation of self-activity to the book, as I wanted and had striven to contribute to by abstaining completely from saying anything about the plan of the work, since in any case I was in no position to have any more definite view on this than any other reader, should there be one. The plan was a task for self-activity, and to impose my own understanding on the reader seemed to me an offensive and impertinent meddling. Every person experiences an either/or in his life. . . .That is the essential thing, sentence-length and the number of middle terms are contingent. But the grasp of the plan will differ according to the degree of the individual's development. . . . [54]

So there is a plan, though Kierkegaard says – both seriously and jokingly – that no one sees it, since the Preface 'makes a joke of it' and 'makes no mention of the Speculative Idea'.[55] It is to have readers read their own experience into the work as well as they can. Since writing his little treatise on Andersen, Kierkegaard's own experience had widened, or deepened, considerably. At that time his personal either/or had been between a 'humanistic' and a 'properly' religious life-view, where both – Stoicism and Christianity – involved distancing oneself from the world. But now there had been Regine, and the world had made its claims. Now the dilemma presented was more complex. One might say it is this dilemma that forms the surface 'unity' of *Either/Or*, in the disjunctive form of a choice. Ostensibly, it offers the reader a choice between an aesthetic life and an ethical way of life, a hidden life or a life of self-revelation, revelation by the same token both to oneself and to others. As the protagonist of the ethical way of life, Assessor Wilhelm, puts it, it is a matter of choosing between a life that eschews the categories of good and evil and one that appropriates them. The positive option in the original either/or has thus been replaced with the kind of life Kierkegaard envisages dedication to the Christian God would imply if it took the form of civic virtue. He himself, however, had failed in that respect. But this too is provided for. There is a third option lurking not just behind the production of *Either/Or* but in its very pages: choosing and being able to write such a remarkable work as *Either/Or*, and also being justified in taking the course of action which made that possible. Naturally, for someone of Kierkegaard's religious scruples, it would not be enough simply to have produced a remarkable work of literature, which is what it turned out to be, a work that by the standards of the day became an instant best-seller in Copenhagen. That would be no more than an aesthetic justification; some more fundamental justification must be found than that it was an estimable, even a conspicuously innovative work of art, since creative writing could not be an adequate excuse in itself for leaving Regine in the lurch. In fact *Either/Or* contains several messages to Regine. One (as Kierkegaard himself stresses)[56] is to repel her, through 'The Seducer's Diary'. Another is to show her how creative he can be if left to his own and unhampered by marital and civic ties. But a third, and the outcome of the second of the two long treatises (in the form of letters) defending marriage, probably written in the autumn following Kierkegaard's return from Berlin, is that a case might well be made for certain exceptions to the rule that one should pursue the positive option, that is, that in some cases the right thing to do will be the second-best thing, namely to live a life of dedication outside the conventions of marital and civic virtue.

In a sense, then, Kierkegaard does here side with the Romantics. Marriage can be sacrificed to the needs of subjectivity, though the question of what those needs amount to still has to be asked – fortunately enough for Kierkegaard, since his own 'life' depended on the answer not being a conventional one.

Kierkegaard had been impatient to return to Copenhagen. Betraying the hold the motto 'Either/Or' had taken on him, he announced with engaging flippancy: 'It is absolutely imperative that I return to Copenhagen this spring. For either I shall finish *Either/Or*'s 'Either' by spring, or I shall never finish it [*Either/Or*].'[57] He needed his library at Nørregade. He returned on 6 March 1842. The first job was to finish the 'Seducer's Diary'; he managed that by the middle of April. Then came the long essay on the 'Immediate Erotic Stages', which was to go at the beginning once the *diapsalmata* had set the tone. The draft of the essay was ready by mid-June. Then followed the three portrayals of abandoned women, 'Shadowgraphs'. It was ready just over a month later, after which he may have written the review of the French playwright Scribe's *First Love,* though the published version of this appears to be based on an original review written in the mid-thirties but not then published. As for 'Diapsalmata', since this section borrows so extensively from earlier work, we may assume that these aphorisms too were put together at that time. They may even have been assembled in conjunction with the editor's Preface, the draft of which dates from November, the last of the manuscripts to be completed, though, as mentioned earlier, there are hints to be found in the earliest written drafts as to what it would have to contain.

The editor was not Søren Kierkegaard but one Victor Eremita. When, later, Kierkegaard planned a second edition, he wondered about adding a postscript to *Either/Or*: 'I hereby retract this book. It was a necessary deception for deceiving people, if possible, into the religious, as has been my constant task all along. Maieutically, it certainly had its impact. Still, I don't need to retract it, for I have never claimed to be its author.'[58]

Perhaps that is true. Not only in the sense that he didn't *publish* it under his own name, but in the sense that he never once owned up, publicly or even privately, to having written it. The conventions of the time would allow for that, even if everyone knew quite well that he was the author. As we saw earlier in connection with the newspaper polemic, there was an etiquette to be followed in the case of a publication not signed with the author's own name. Whatever the gossip, one would respect the suspected author's intentions by not posing the question directly to the author or presuming that one knew the answer in conversation with him. More important than what Kierkegaard may or may not have omitted saying in this respect is the question of in what sense it might still have been true for him to claim positively that he was *not* the work's author, or that *he* was not its author.

The pseudonymity of *Either/Or* is elaborate, with the two main parts assigned to fictitious authors, the first containing a diary by a third author and the second a sermon by a fourth. To cap it all, the work starts off with a Preface telling how the manuscripts came to be found. Why such subterfuge? Well, anybody could see that the alleged editor's explanation was just a good story. It tells how an impatient blow with an axe on a newly acquired second-hand escritoire, instead of freeing a recalcitrant drawer in which the owner had placed the housekeeping money he needed to pay the postilion waiting outside, released a catch and revealed a hidden recess in which the manuscripts lay.

Still, why this facade of secrecy or distance? Presumably it had to do with the reasons Kierkegaard had for telling Boesen to keep this writing a 'deep secret', some other ground than the usual author's concern not to arouse in his anticipated public too many or the wrong kind of expectations. Not wanting to infringe on the 'freedom' he had given Regine, he would not want to have rumours of any kind spread about what he was doing. The conventions would dampen talk of it, even if word got out.

The editor's pseudonym, however, is not just a means of concealment. 'Victor Eremita' translates literally as 'Triumphant Recluse' or

'Solitary Victor'. There is a clear religious connotation; of *Either/Or*, Kierkegaard later wrote that when writing the work he was 'already in a cloister' and that this was the 'thought hidden in the pseudonym'.[59] What does that tell us? Kierkegaard says in the same passage that at the time of writing the book he had long before given up the thought of a comfortingly marital solution to life. How long? Perhaps from the day after he had proposed, but certainly from two months before the final break. He doesn't say whether he means life in general or his own, but the fact that he personally was not prepared to follow Wilhelm's advice hardly justifies the inference that Kierkegaard himself thought the advice should not be followed. Nor does it justify our saying of Victor Eremita, as does one commentator, that *he* is 'no more taken in by the aesthete's paean to enjoyment than he is by the Judge's vision of marriage'.[60]

That would imply an aloofness and control to which neither the texts nor the facts of Kierkegaard's life at the time testify. But that 'neither/nor' is the conclusion to which the reader is being drawn, as already suggested, is surely an interesting possibility. It gets support in the sermon that Wilhelm attaches to his final letter, a sermon sent to him by a former student colleague, now a pastor in lonely Jutland, and its theme: 'before God we are always in the wrong.' That text stems from Kierkegaard's seminary training in 1840–41, before he presented his dissertation.[61] We don't have to assume that Kierkegaard actually inhabited a religious life-view to suppose that he wanted his readers to see that such a life-view was the one his writings were trying to drive them towards.

Whether we place Eremita above, below, or behind his two protagonists, we can still see that we are one layer away from Kierkegaard himself. The role of recluse is an adopted one – and the solitariness primarily a writer's. The question of what a writer can do to earn occupancy of a religious life-view, in the way Kierkegaard would require, that is, by actually living it, remained to be seen or worked out. He was now returning deliberately to the reclusive life of a writer that he had earlier been seduced out of: was it not *Don Giovanni* that had once brought him, just like Elvira, out of the cloister? Meanwhile the pseudonymity kept the question 'on hold'. Or, in another telephonic metaphor, the pseudonymity 'scrambles' the author–reader link in a way that allows the writings to enjoy a genuinely independent existence, letting them become considerations in the mind of the reader, to do

there whatever work they have it *in themselves* to do.[62] This for Kierkegaard was by no means a new idea; in fact as early as 1835 he had
written a note on the Gutzkow re-edition of Schleiermacher's *Confidential Letters on Schlegel's* Lucinde. There had been doubt as to whether
the novel really had been written by Schlegel, though as Kierkegaard
says, the 'internal evidence' was overwhelmingly in favour. But then
Kierkegaard goes on to say of the collection itself:

It is probably a model review and also an example of how highly effective such a
thing can be, in that he constructs a host of personalities out of the book and
through these illuminates the work and also their individualities, so that instead of
the review confronting us with various positions, what we have instead are a whole
lot of personalities who represent these various standpoints. But they do so as
complete beings, so that it is possible to get a glimpse of the single individual's
individuality and through numerous but merely relatively true judgments to draw
up our own *ultimatum.* Thus it is a true work of art.[63]

The title 'ultimatum' is given by Victor Eremita to the last section,
which is the sermon with Assessor Wilhelm's covering note to the
aesthete. There its force is rather different. Here it means something
like 'final judgment,' and the portrayals are to help the reader make up
his or her own mind with no appeal to abstract points of view or
knowledge of the author's identity or position.

In a comment on *Either/Or* 'leaked' under a later pseudonym, Kierkegaard gives us to understand that the work's special purpose was to
'exhibit the existential relationship between the aesthetic and the ethical
in an existing individual', the motive behind this being the need to
remind people 'what it means to *exist,* and what *inwardness* signifies',
something that 'because of the great increase of knowledge' his age had
forgotten.[64] The modern Faust despairs because too much is known.
Whatever the ethical view of life has to offer, it can direct its appeal
only to individual sensibility. But that of course means directing it to
where the aesthetic view of life also makes its appeal. So aesthetics is
where one inevitably has to begin, and that applies equally to the
religious view of life, not portrayed in *Either/Or* but heralded in the
sermon provided by the magistrate under the heading 'Ultimatum'.
This is an ultimatum neither in the sense of terms to be complied with
'or else', nor in exactly the sense referred to just above, a final judgment
up to the reader. This 'final word' is put into the hands of Wilhelm,
who then passes it on to the aesthete, and that fact is then presented to

the reader by Victor Eremita. What is clearly not meant is that responsibility for the final judgment has been taken away from the reader and retained by either Eremita or one of his dramatis personae. Rather, it is being hinted that even if we were to decide in favour of Wilhelm, there is some background that both he and we do not yet share and which may upset the choice or cause us to see it in an entirely new light. Wilhelm's horizon may still be too narrow; from within it the ultimatum comes from another world. It is someone else's final word, and all that readers of *Either/Or* can do with it, since it is not their final judgment – nor does it provide a portrayal that might help them towards making it so – is take note that not everything relevant for *their* final judgment has been provided. The same later pseudonymous author comments on the absence of a distinctively religious perspective in *Either/Or* but says that the fact that his age had forgotten what it is to exist religiously implied also that people had first of all forgotten what it was to exist as human beings. *Either/Or* is the required reminder, a necessary prolegomenon to the later reminders about what it is to lead, first, a religious existence and then, second, a specifically Christian existence.

Some people, reading Kierkegaard from within the perspective of modern existentialism, interpret *Either/Or* as presenting its reader with a 'radical choice'. The word 'criterionless' is sometimes used. Yet, however radically the views presented differ, it is hard not to see the work as having the character of a dialogue. Part One contains implicit arguments against the ethical life-view, which are then rebutted in Part Two. There are also such arguments in Part Two, in the form of objections to ethical ideals which Wilhelm recalls his young friend having voiced and to which he replies. Further, it is hard to read the two main sections in Part Two otherwise than as a sustained argument in favour of the ethical life-view, which is also continually underpinned by arguments against the aesthetic life-view.

Typically, however, dialogues aim at agreement, if only on some position that turns out to be neither of the original alternatives, and such agreement requires some kind of choice on the part of at least one of the participants. There are a number of quite different ways in which a choice might be made at the conclusion of a dialogue. One would be where one party convinces the other by making him see how his argument 'stands to reason'. Here there would be no appeal to what Kierkegaard calls inwardness. Another way, that does appeal to inwardness and sensibility, would be where the convinced party simply goes over to the new position as a matter of course, in the light of certain appeals to which he or she was already attuned but without being clear about their relevance to the case in hand. The function of the dialogue would be to bring about that clarity and the result might still, though only just, be called a kind of choice. But neither of these captures the sense of choice required by Wilhelm of his young friend's entering upon the ethical life. That choice, as the reader discovers, is said to be 'of oneself'; and part of what that means is precisely that one no longer regards oneself as a being who, as in the second case, moves from one position to another simply from the weight or pressure of argument or circumstance. The ethical life involves rejecting any idea of oneself as just a passive accumulator, or in the case of the mature aesthete also as imaginative manipulator, of life's contingent blessings; it requires acceptance of the quite different idea that one is a responsible agent. The choice of oneself is therefore one that cuts short the passivity and imaginative manipulation. It requires, first, that one acknowledge a peculiarly human ability, indeed a need, to ask what it is essentially to be a human being. Second, it requires that one take this ability at its face value, as a genuine freedom to stake out one's own future according to a view of life; and, third, it requires that the view of life one adopts be one in which one is revealed in a context of familial and social responsibilities. This is not revelation of a self previously hidden. A hidden 'self' is precisely not (yet) a self in Wilhelm's sense. The choice of oneself is the choice of a visible selfhood, choosing the area of public morality for one's projects, and making of oneself a self that is amenable to the ethical categories of good and bad, praise and blame.

The choice is still in a sense radical. Its radicalness still lies in an overall redefining of the values of a human life. It is important to realize the compass of the redefinition. It isn't a matter simply of turning over a new leaf; the choice of oneself means rewriting the whole book. In choosing oneself, as Wilhelm says, one takes responsibility for one's past and 'repents' for not having taken on this responsibility earlier. The ethicist's task, as Wilhelm sees it then, is to persuade the aesthete of the urgency of the choice. But this task is made the easier by the fact that the mature aesthete's life has already taken a form which an ethical redefinition of values can be seen to fit, as easily in principle as a glove fits a hand, the actual practice requiring only the will to put it on. His aestheticism is driving him out of the world in which his pleasure is sought; it has driven him into a corner from where he has to rely on his ingenuity and imagination to keep things going, on his ability to enjoy things in reflection, to enjoy the idea of things rather than the things themselves. He should be well disposed, in principle at least, then, to seeing what Wilhelm is getting at when he describes the aesthete's life as a life of despair. Wilhelm does not mean that the life of the aesthete is especially exposed to disappointment, frustration, and in the end despair; he means that the aesthete is already in despair because he makes so much depend on the moments that life can offer. The aesthete's life is one of despair even when, by the aesthete's lights, everything is going swimmingly. Wilhelm advises his friend to 'choose despair'. That is to say, he advises him to give up the world as one does in total irony, rather than undertaking some occupation, even marrying, if that is undertaken just for the kinds of reasons that an aesthete must give. In that case, then, it might be possible for him, or for someone, perhaps the reader, to see how both getting a job and marrying might be radically reconceived as vehicles of human fulfilment instead of as ways of putting off despair.

Faith and Tragic Heroism

Bᴀᴄᴋ ɪɴ ᴄᴏᴘᴇɴʜᴀɢᴇɴ Kierkegaard's cloister needed walls. Regine would notice his earlier-than-expected return: 'True enough, she looked for me after Mynster's sermon at Easter. I avoided her to put her off, in case she got the idea that I had thought about her while I was abroad.'[1] Regine had told Sibbern she wouldn't be able to bear the sight of him. But in any case he didn't want others to know that he was spending so much time writing, and even had articles published in *Fædrelandet* to put people on the wrong track. When the time came to publish *Either/Or*, Kierkegaard did all he could to preserve the secrecy of its authorship. As with his first book and the dissertation, this too was being published privately, which in this case meant he needed a go-between to make payments and collect whatever was due from sales. This role was performed by *Fædrelandet*'s managing editor and business manager, Jens Finsteen Giødwad (1811–1891).[2]

The reason for entrusting Giødwad with this task is allegedly that Kierkegaard had heard that Giødwad steadfastly refused to reveal to a reader the identity of the writer of an anonymous article in his paper.[3] The two had not met before Kierkegaard came to ask Giødwad to take care of *Either/Or*'s publication. Considering *Fædrelandet*'s liberal policies, the choice might otherwise seem a strange one, though we may remember that in that early exchange Kierkegaard had let *Fædrelandet* off fairly lightly. Perhaps it was the manner of the paper's leadership under its editor, the nationalist poet Carl Ploug, that attracted him, more than its politics. Also Giødwad, according to Ploug's son, Hother, had made the newspaper's office into a kind of club for his friends, and Kierkegaard may have liked the idea at this time of being able to indulge his addiction to talk in a place off the street but conveniently close at hand (Købmagergade 35). At any rate, once admitted to the Giødwad club, or rather having announced his membership, Kierkegaard attended almost daily, according to Hother, talked and held forth quite oblivious of the inconvenience he was causing, while the managing editor 'sat listening reverently at the master's feet'. One imagines, due not least to the hold Kierkegaard had on the two-year older Giødwad, with whom he apparently came to be on good enough terms to be seen walking with him in the street arm in arm, that the pieces he published in *Fædrelandet* during the completion of *Either/Or* heralded a long association with that newspaper. That Kierkegaard also visited and partied at Giødwad's is testified to by reports of his collapsing there on more than one occasion, adding credence to the view that he suffered from some form of epilepsy.[4]

Giødwad duly delivered the manuscript to the printer, the final copy (the 'editor's' Preface) in November (1842), and from late December to the middle of February he copy-read furiously, receiving and disposing of the proofs at the rate of four signatures (thirty-two pages) a day.[5] The fact that the two-volume work appeared in Reitzel's bookshop on 20 February 1843 indicates the speed with which it finally came from the press.

That same November, Peter was ordained by Mynster, at Vor Frue (the Church of Our Lady), having received an appointment to an out-of-town parish (Pedersborg-Kindertofte). From Peter's diary we learn that there had been an increase in the family: three weeks after Søren's return from Berlin, 'where Schelling had not at all satisfied him', Peter records that his wife had given birth to a boy. He was to be baptised Paskal Michael Poul Egede Kierkegaard.[6] Whether Peter knew of the more satisfying outcome of Søren's Berlin stay, we don't know. Could he have no inkling at the time of the identity of *Either/Or*'s author? The brothers appear to have been on reasonably good terms, discussing the possible sale of their family home. Søren confided to Peter his ambivalence about the place: on the one hand it might be the death of him, just as it had been of his father, on the other hand just as it had kept his father going in time of need, it might save him too.[7] Did he mean he could have had a home there with Regine? Søren even had Peter's wife and son over to stay with him in his apartment on Nørregade when Peter had to go on ahead to take up his new post. It seems most unlikely, on the publication of *Either/Or*, when in spite of all his precautions, as Weltzer puts it, Søren Kierkegaard became 'the great unknown everyone-knew-who-it-was',[8] that Peter was the only one not in the know. Bröchner, of course, knew the moment he set eye on the 'Diapsalmata'.[9]

But Kierkegaard did manage to keep up an effective facade of frivolity, was out on the streets all day, and in the evenings allegedly visited the theatre between acts to give the impression that he never worked then either. At least some were deceived, though the first review, in a broadsheet called *Dagen* (The Day), was quite likely tongue-in-cheek when it wondered whether several authors weren't behind this huge book, not only in view of the variety of its contents but also because of what it must have cost to produce. The review came just two days after publication, so unless the reviewer had access to the printer, who had the copies ready five days before publication, his favourable comments must have been based on a very cursory reading. The next day *Den Frisindede* (The Liberal) devoted much of its space to a review with excerpts from *Either/Or*, with an episode from the 'Seducer's Diary' a special feature. The reviewer chose to defer comment on the author's occasionally impenetrable German terminology, but says that although one may 'feel tempted to summon the moral custodians of the Free Press Society to anathematize the author, or ask the moral police to confiscate the work and burn the unknown [author] in effigy', one has 'instantly and unreservedly to concede' that no one is likely to 'come to any harm from reading the book'.[10]

Kierkegaard, touchy as any author can be on such occasions, relapsed into the aggressive sarcasm of the earlier polemics: 'Yes, we could wish that *Den Frisindede* which, not having had time to read the book, has nevertheless found time to review it, may never have time to read it, in order to remove the only conceivable possibility that any one at all might be harmed from reading it.' But on this occasion, curbed by the need to preserve his pseudonymity, his remarks had to be confined to the journals. He also strongly objected, understandably enough, to the review actually being entitled 'Episode from the Seducer's Diary'.[11]

The review Kierkegaard most anxiously awaited was Heiberg's should he deign to write one; Kierkegaard had arranged for copies to be sent to him and to other luminaries. Heiberg did indeed comment on the book in his own *Intelligensblade* on 1 March, in an article entitled 'Litterær Vintersæd' (Literary Winter Seed). He began by expressing the fears of those who might be put off by the book's sheer size – 'One thinks, "Have I the time to read such a book?" ' – and he wrote of the impatience that the 'Either' induces 'in one', because 'there the author's exceptional brilliance, learning and stylistic accomplishments are not combined with an organizing capacity' which would 'enable the thoughts to leap out in plastic form'. The whole thing becomes 'dreamy, indeterminate and evanescent'. The author has given Scribe's play (a review of which is included in the 'Either') a status it doesn't merit, and as for the 'Diary', 'one is disgusted, one is sickened, one is enraged, and one asks oneself, not if it is possible for a man to be like this Seducer, but if it is possible that a writer can be so formed as to find pleasure in studying such a character and working at perfecting him in his quiet thoughts'. But Heiberg, after commiserating with the reader who might want to stop there and go no further, had high praise for the 'Or'. He says readers would 'stumble' there 'on such lightning thoughts which suddenly light up whole spheres of existence, that they sense that there must be an organizing power here which makes every-thing into a genuine whole'. People who went through the whole thing again having read the 'Or' may be 'so entranced by the book, that they can scarcely put it down, feeling themselves continually under the influence of a rare and highly gifted spirit, which brings before their eyes the most beautiful aesthetic vision as though from a deep specula-tive spring, and which seasons its presentation with a stream of the most piquant wit and humour'.[12]

Kierkegaard, sensing condescension in these token expressions of praise, reacted with fury and was provoked into making comments as unkind as those he had once used against the press when trying to curry favour with Heiberg:

Prof. H may, for all I care . . . throw both volumes at the head of the unknown authors, he has my word for that; and so he should, since otherwise, after all, he might have scruples, especially since he seems so extraordinarily upset by the thought of the book's size. The effect will be awful if it hits them. . . . It says in the psalm that all the world's princes could not create a straw – yet the most miserable chatterbrain can create a 'one'. . . . We now know how 'one' to our knowledge has treated this work – Prof. Heiberg is too important a capacity to come in any way under the category of 'one'. . . . I am really happy that Prof. [H] has with unusual courtesy had the goodness, in a prophetic vision, to enlighten the reading public, and also me for that matter, on how 'one' does and will treat *Either/Or*. So far as I know, Prof. H has not indeed tried his hand at prophecy, but one gets older and Prof H. is eminently perfectible. It must be getting on for two years since the Herr

Professor, from being the witty, playful, frolicsome writer of reviews, at times apparently a little wayward in his faith, the victorious polemicist, the measured aesthetician, became Denmark's Dante, the troubled genius who, in his apocalyptic poetry, gazed into the eternal secrets of life, became the Church's obedient son, of whom the diocese's most reverend clergyman expected everything to the betterment of 'the congregation'. If it hadn't happened, who would have believed that it could, but since it has happened, who cannot believe Prof. H. capable of everything. . . . [13]

Some of his bitterness Kierkegaard vented in an article in *Fædrelandet* under the pseudonym Victor Eremita. Eremita thanks Heiberg for tips on how 'one' is to deal with *Either/Or*.[14] In one of several unpublishable remarks Heiberg is likened to a prostitute: 'Prof. Heiberg has been sitting there painted for some years now at the window of literature, beckoning to the passers-by, especially if it was a fancy fellow and he heard a little hurrah from the next street.'[15]

There were other reviews which showed greater appreciation of the work's overall design. One paper, *Forposten* (Outpost), its ears better tuned to the reverberations of a Europe in dissolution and to which Heiberg's talk of visions drawn from a deep speculative spring would appear hopelessly old-fashioned, gave a four-part review presenting *Either/Or* as a work that manages to put across what is really needed to form any life-view worthy of the name. The anonymous reviewer enjoyed the 'Either' but saw it in an importantly expressive rather than salacious light.[16] *Fædrelandet*, in a three-part review by Johan Frederik Hagen, brought to its readers' attention the connection between *Either/Or* and literary trends in Germany which highlighted eroticism, suicide, and despair. Hagen asks: 'Who has not perceived the rending and dissolution which, like a stream of screaming dissonances, is heard from our age's most gifted children?'[17] The most comprehensive and perceptive review came from a young theologian who took the church to task for not appreciating the dimensions of the struggle for a life-view at a time like the present, when authority had disappeared on all sides and the individual was faced with making the choice between egotism and humanity entirely alone. The reviewer praises 'Either' for its subtly varied and rich portrayal of the aesthetic life-view, according its author a high place in literature, but finds the 'Or' equally subtle in its undermining of the appeal of the aesthetic life-view for the aesthete. But the reviewer also praises the sermon, and he praises it precisely because it does have an appeal for the aesthete. Of this sermon he says that it 'will make a much deeper impression on an aesthetic personality than most of those we have heard up till now'.[18]

That remark was to bring a rebuke from Mynster, now bishop of Zealand and thereby primate of the Danish Church. But Mynster's comments would not appear until 1 January 1844, and then they included a reference to another recent publication entitled *Fear and Trembling*.

In May 1843, about two months after the publication of *Either/Or* and even before the longer reviews had appeared, Kierkegaard revisited Berlin, though this time staying for only a few weeks. But they were put to good use. In a letter to Boesen from Berlin dated 25 May 1843, he wrote:

I have finished a work important to me; I am in full spate with a new one, and I cannot do without my library, also a printer. In the beginning I was ill but am now to all intents and purposes well, that is, my spirit swells and will probably do my body to death. I have never worked so hard as now. In the morning I go out for a little, then come home and sit in my room without interruption until about three o'clock. My eyes can hardly see. Then I sneak off with my walking stick to the restaurant, but am so weak that I think if anyone called out my name I would keel over and die. Then I go home and begin again. The past months I had in my indolence pumped up a proper shower-bath and now I have pulled the string and the ideas are cascading down upon me: healthy, happy, thriving, gay, blessed children, born with ease and yet all of them with the birthmark of my personality. Otherwise, as I said, I am weak, my legs shake, my knees ache, etc. . . . Unless I die on the way I believe you will find me happier than ever before. It is a new crisis, whether it means that I now begin living or that I am to die. There would be one more way out: that I lost my mind. God knows it. But wherever I end up, I shall never forget to employ the passion of irony in its justified defiance of any non-human half-philosophers who understand neither this nor that, and whose whole skill consists in scribbling down German compendia and thus defiling what has a worthier origin by making nonsense of it.[19]

The thriving, blessed children were to find their place in an impressively diverse series of pseudonymous publications. But what was the pressure of ideas that had been building up and was now finding shape in the confident hands of a tried author with a considerable literary work to his credit?

It seems clear that, whether or not Kierkegaard had read it by then, the point made in the last review, namely that the sermon at the end of *Either/Or* should appeal to the aesthete more than typical sermons did, was one that he felt a pressing need to elaborate. To see why, we can compare two ways of reading the relations among the aesthetic, the ethical, and the religious, both in that work and in the ensuing pseudonymous production. To do this we must suspend chronological constraints for a moment and consider things in the round.

Kierkegaard later claimed that the 'nerve' of his production was religious all along and that he had been 'religiously committed' even when writing *Either/Or*.[20] But in spite of some of the reviewers' relating the work directly to what was generally seen at the time to be a religious crisis, it requires a considerable stretch of hermeneutic imagination for a reader not embroiled in that crisis to read *Either/Or* as a work designed to uncover the distinctively religious. The direction of its manifest message is onward from the aesthetic to the ethical, upon which the religious as such as yet indistinctly, and even indistinguishably, supervenes. Except for the appended sermon with its arresting assertion that we are always in the wrong against God, there is nothing in *Either/Or* that tends to reveal any cracks in the ethical position as such. The sermon is not a portrayal of a life-view in the way that the two main parts are. Rather than being offered in a Socratic spirit, it is more like an afterthought, an insert even, or an advertiser's flyer, promising a new point of view but not putting the reader in a position to grasp its point existentially.

Against this, it is clear that at least Assessor Wilhelm himself regards the message of the sermon as a development from within his own universe, and that might indicate at least the possibility of expanding it Socratically into something religious. He recommends the sermon to A for saying what he himself has tried to say to A but saying it 'more felicitously'. But here there is an extremely important point. The terms in which Wilhelm annexes the sermon to his own point of view argue sharply against its representing, for him at least, what Kierkegaard himself was coming to see that *he* would have to mean by a specifically religious point of view. In asking the aesthete not to 'sneeze at' the sermon just because the priest 'is confident that he will make every farmer understand it', Wilhelm observes that the 'beauty of the universal consists precisely in everyone being able to understand it'.[21] But then it is clear that, at least in Wilhelm's eyes, the sermon does not introduce what a future pseudonym was to refer to as the 'doubly reflected religious categories in the paradox'.[22] The pastor is not presented as being in the position of being *denied* the possibility of being understood by the farmers, nor are they portrayed as being in the position of not being able to understand one another. The idea that religion may be based on something unthinkable plays no part in *their* way of being religious.

In the work that Kierkegaard was now writing, however, he would say of Abraham, whose faith was being tested by God, that he could not make himself understood. The 'relief of speech', says the new pseudonym Johannes *de silentio*, is that it 'translates me into the universal'.[23] Abraham is denied that relief – or rather he chooses to go without it and 'suspends' the ethical. A later Johannes, Johannes Climacus, philosopher enough to know how to distinguish the religious from the ethical, tells us unequivocally that *Either/Or* is 'ethically' and not 'religiously planned' and that its categories are those of immanence.[24]

The same can of course be said of Socrates; if you follow a procedure properly called Socratic you will never exceed the categories of immanence, for immanence is what human existence is confined to, and to be clear about that was part of what it meant to be Socratic. You can also say, quite rightly, that in *Either/Or* there is no Socratic advance beyond the ethical. For that, you would need a maieutic advance out of the categories of immanence and into those of the paradox. But nothing of the kind is to be found in *Either/Or*. We still have no inkling of the 'leap'.

The idea that the life-views Kierkegaard's pseudonyms are now busy elaborating succeed one another in a simple linear progression seems wrong.[25] In the work which would complete the first period of pseudonymity, aptly entitled 'Postscript', there is a section called 'A Contemporary Effort in Danish Literature' where the author presents a survey of the pseudonymous authorship to date. Assessor Wilhelm's creator is taken to task for assuming that in order for Wilhelm to choose himself 'in his eternal validity', it was enough for him to despair out and out, as if that provided platform enough for his making that choice all on his own; whereas properly to despair is to give up the idea of there being any human platform at all from which, or any procedure at all whereby, to establish one's kinship in thought and action with God.[26] In another work from this period, entitled 'Stages on Life's Way', we see quite clearly that the linear reading is wrong. What is offered there is not a development of the ethical point of view in Part Two of *Either/Or* but rather a reversion to the problem out of which the ethical was offered there as a solution, but *prematurely*. This throws new light on

Either/Or's sermon. We might simply read it as an admission of failure on the part of Wilhelm and a noble offer from his side to leave the matter in the hands of the aesthete. Where Wilhelm has failed, his young friend, or some new version of him, may do better, not necessarily at being religious but at seeing what being religious requires. At any rate, as we see later, what emerges in *Stages* is that the ethical proves to be an inadequately prepared anticipation of the task of 'realizing the universal' exactly because it fails to give that task a properly religious dimension. A proper preparation requires one to go back to a development within and out of the aesthetic. Whatever meaning we get out of the pseudonymous works subsequent to *Either/Or*, and to whatever extent we are willing to read them in the light of Kierkegaard's own dramatic sense of his situation, the works themselves deliberately undermine the suggestion presented in *Either/Or* that life confronts us with a radical and exhaustive choice between an aesthetic and an ethical view of life. The ethical view is now presented as a limitation, as a kind of recourse, something one might even feel tempted to adopt in order to escape the rigours of true individuality, a comforting and self-satisfying reduction of life to what is intelligible, grasping at the relief of translatability into a common and transparent moral discourse.

Some might claim that the lack of linearity shown by what came after *Either/Or* marks a personal rejection on Kierkegaard's part of the goal of 'realizing the universal'. This seems a mistake. What is new is not that some new goal is posited but that it is looked at again in the light of those who have exceptional difficulties in realizing it. The reader may often feel that the difficulties, which are formulated precisely in the categories and concepts that give meaning to being religious, would be removed if the categories and concepts themselves were left out of account. But that would be counter to the whole tenor of Kierkegaard's effort in those productive weeks in Berlin in the spring of 1843.

There it was precisely the problem of exceptionality and its costs that energized him, and out of that preoccupation came two remarkable books, one of which, he later said, would alone 'be enough to immortalize my name as an author'.[27] Its theme was one he had considered for a sermon when preparing for his finals in 1841 – Abraham's willingness to sacrifice Isaac at God's command. The book was *Frygt og Bæven* (Fear and Trembling). Kierkegaard wrote down a summary of the main theme of *Fear and Trembling* in a journal entry from late March or early

April 1843,[28] not long after *Either/Or*'s publication. It is interesting for
its identification of the role that he was seeking to make for himself as a
writer, a special role which none of his contemporaries could fill. Most
readers of *Fear and Trembling* would say that its theme is Abraham's
willingness to sacrifice Isaac, that the gist of its argument is to suggest
that Abraham can only be justified if morality as we ordinarily understand it can be suspended by an overriding authority whose edicts
demand blind obedience. It is easy to conclude that since there is no
direct argument to the effect that morality can or even should be
suspended, the work is in effect yet another either/or, leaving its 'ultimatum' to the reader: the human world without Abraham or the divine
world with Abraham. The shock of the idea that these are mutually
exclusive worlds should be enough to make fledgling Hegelians of
us all.

In surmising that *Fear and Trembling* would bring him fame, Kierkegaard said 'and *then* it will be read and also translated into foreign
languages'. Given the innumerable traditional and modern philosophical
disputes into which commentators have tried to plug the manifest content of *Fear and Trembling*, he could have said 'philosophical languages'.[29] But since the work clearly does have a more personal reference, it is on this that an intellectual biography must focus. As
Kierkegaard also said in that retrospective entry from 1849, the book
'draws attention to the difference between the poet and the hero'. This
difference is also the topic of that 1843 entry which this later one refers
back to.[30] What then is the difference, and what is there about it that
makes such a drastic illustration appropriate?

Kierkegaard sees himself as potentially both poet and hero. As a poet
or writer he should be in a position to grasp and portray the noblest of
all tragedies, and this he finds exemplified in a version of the story of
Abraham and Isaac. The epic story of sacrifice puts in sharp focus the
situation of a choice where the outcome, whatever you choose, is to be
regretted. In what is entitled an 'enthusiastic lecture' in 'Diapsalmata',
we are told: 'If you marry, you will regret it; if you do not marry, you
will also regret it; if you marry or if you do not marry, you will regret
both. . . .'[31] It seems evident enough that the task the works following
Either/Or take up, beginning with *Fear and Trembling* and *Repetition*, is
to try to grasp what deeper justification there might be that could
mitigate or, if only it could be grasped and shared by both parties, even

abrogate the regret of parting and sacrifice. For Kierkegaard everything depended on there being some objective and not purely selfish basis for breaking off his engagement with Regine. Otherwise what his brother had said would be true – he was 'done for'. If he was to avoid that fate, there would have to be some way out of the tragic either/or, a way of losing that was really a gain.

Kierkegaard uses the term 'collision' to describe this kind of predicament. As we already know, the term occurs in Hegel's account of dramatic poetry, of which Kierkegaard had been an avid reader. There, collisions occurring 'in human experience . . . between characters and between their aims' form the central motif of drama. Formally, they result from the 'ideality' of the ethical life having to be enacted or pursued under the imperfect conditions of human life, or the 'mundane sphere'. In true tragedy the suffering due to such collisions is not simply owing to that general circumstance but is also a consequence of the individual agent's own action. The tragic action is demanded by the ideals of the ethical life but is also blameworthy on account of the suffering it is bound to incur. The tragic hero's own suffering is his knowledge that there is this collision. The only alleviation on hand is the thought that there is a perfect order of things from which the legitimacy of the action occasioning the tragedy can be derived. Hegel speaks of this higher order as a kind of higher harmony. Above the fear and tragic sympathy that we feel with regard to such figures, says Hegel, 'there stands that sense of reconciliation which the tragedy affords by the glimpse of eternal justice'.

In its absolute sway this justice overrides the relative justification of one-sided aims and passions because it cannot allow victory and permanence, in truth and actuality, to the conflict and contradiction of naturally harmonious ethical powers.[32]

The 1843 journal entry introducing the plot of *Fear and Trembling* is entitled 'Set-up' (*Anlæg*). It includes a variation, perhaps a first sketch, of the first of four cameo versions of the Abraham and Isaac story, all given in the short opening section of *Fear and Trembling* called 'Attunement' (*Stemning*). These are versions which the pseudonymous author understands, as against the version he is about to tell. The connection between the four intelligible and the one unintelligible version becomes clear when we see that what the pseudonymous author assumes but cannot convey is exactly what Hegel would call the reconciliation; and the special point with regard to Hegel becomes clear when we bear in mind that in the Hegelian philosophy such reconciliations occur in the realm of thought and are therefore in principle intelligible.

The first of the four intelligible versions assumes something that, as Kierkegaard points out in the entry, is not to be found in either the Old Testament or the Koran, namely that Isaac *knew* that Abraham intended to sacrifice him. What then, asks Kierkegaard, would they say to each other? It might have gone as follows:

At first Abraham looked upon him with all his fatherliness, with his venerable countenance; his crushed heart has made his speech more affecting, he has be-seeched Isaac to bear his fate with patience, he has let him obscurely understand that, as his father, his own suffering was even greater. – But it didn't help. I can then imagine Abraham turning away from Isaac for a moment and when he turned to him again he was unrecognizable, his gaze wild, his mien icy, the venerable locks risen like Furies above his head. He grabbed Isaac by the chest, drew the knife and said: 'You thought I was doing it for God's sake; you were wrong, I am an idolator, this desire has reawakened in my soul, I want to murder you, it is my pleasure, I am worse than any man-eater, despair, you poor boy who imagined I was your father; I am your murderer, and it is my wish.' And Isaac fell on his knees and cried to heaven: 'Merciful God, have mercy on me.' But then, under his breath, Abraham said to himself: 'That's how it has to be, for it is better after all that he believes I am a monster, that he curses me for being his father, and still prays to God, than that he should know that it was God who imposed the temptation, for then he would lose his mind and perhaps curse God.'[33]

The autobiographical connection is obvious. If he can make Regine believe he is the sort of scoundrel you would expect to break off an engagement, Kierkegaard can save her from losing faith in the world – or even from losing her mind, since there would be no sense in a world where such behaviour was acceptable. Of course in one way, just by disencumbering her future of a husband whose God-relationship would overwhelm both her and her own God-relationship, he is setting her free to develop her own God-relationship. But that would be too little, it would be to disregard her pride and his failure to show himself to her in his true light; after all, he had left her, not died. To keep her faith, Regine would have to revise her view of him and see him as having been all along a scoundrel. Still poor psychology on Kierkegaard's part no doubt, indeed so poor for someone so feted for his psychological insight as to tempt one to doubt the honesty of the intention – or, failing that, the honesty of Kierkegaard's claim actually to have had it.

But it does make a kind of *poetic* sense and is just the sort of thing a poet or a dramatist would readily grasp and exploit on page or stage.

What a poet or a dramatist, or indeed anyone with a fair knowledge of human behaviour, would be quite unable to grasp, however, is the Abraham described in the story actually considered in *Fear and Trembling*. That, at least, is what the work says to us. Subtitled 'dialectical lyric', the work extols Abraham 'lyrically' but then subjects him to a 'dialectical' comparison to classical figures, mere 'tragic heroes' and 'knights of resignation', not 'knights of faith'. The difference is that in their case an intelligible justification is available. As consul, Brutus was charged with enforcement of the law and had to condemn his son to death. The success of the invasion of Troy depended on Agamemnon's sacrificing his daughter, Iphigenia. If Jephtha, leader of Israel to victory over the Amorites, had not kept his promise to sacrifice the first to greet him on his return, who happened to be his daughter, the victory would have been taken away from him. The sense of a tragic justice is due to accidents of circumstance, position, and so on, which produce collisions when one shoulders the burden of social, political, or national responsibility. Abraham, however, can appeal to no wider responsibilities that would make his sacrifice intelligible; indeed, as far as that goes, considering the promise 'that all nations of the earth should be blessed in his seed',[34] keeping Isaac was the widest responsibility anyone could have.

In the version of the story *Fear and Trembling* adopts, Abraham proceeds with no doubts or scruples, and father and son travel to the mountain as if nothing in their relationship was or would be disturbed. Abraham acts as though, and in the belief that, the solution to his collision is a fact. He does that even though the collision that would be evident to everyone, including himself, the actual sacrifice, is something he himself is still to perform and could refrain from. What Abraham believes, says the author, is that even if he carries out God's command he will keep Isaac 'in this life', not that 'he should be happy sometime in the hereafter'. In Hegel's terms, he believes the ideals of the ethical life will be preserved even if he carries out an act in direct contravention of those ideals. Hegel said that tragedy affords a glimpse of eternal justice, the state of things in which the tragic action is vindicated. But Abraham acts as if that state of things were already true here on Earth. He does so 'on the strength of the absurd', believing that 'for God all things are possible'.[35] In Hegel's terms, because he ignores the imperfections of the 'mundane sphere' out of which tragedy emerges, Abraham's action is testimony to his belief in eternal justice. Abraham keeps going as though the outcome of what he is about to do, murder the son he loves, will not be tragic; at the end of the day he will still have his son and his son him. As for the suffering, it is Abraham's alone, since Isaac is not in the know. He has therefore not had to blacken himself in the way the author both compares to and contrasts with the mother's blackening of the breast to wean the child (in Abraham's case it is the entire father who is blackened, for to blacken the breast is not to blacken the mother, though the accuracy of that claim from the child's point of view may of course be questioned).[36] The suffering lies in the 'passion' with which Abraham holds steadfastly to the belief that what God has commanded means that the point of view of an eternal justice applies here and now. It is this belief that earns him his title 'Knight of Faith'. The story of Abraham and Isaac is not that of the tragic outcome of an act of visible justice, an act that affords us a glimpse of an eternal justice in which the tragedy is resolved; it is the story of someone who takes it upon himself to put the notion of an eternal justice into practice *without* the benefit of an act of visible justice. And not only is there no act of visible justice to afford that glimpse, Abraham's way of putting the notion of an eternal justice into practice is to perform an act of visible injustice.

Kierkegaard had tried to blacken himself. Although *Either/Or* was not faked in any way, he did rather hope this product of his complex nature and diverse talent would make him 'hated' and 'loathed', by either Regine or the reading public. But to his no doubt qualified dismay it was a 'brilliant success', so much so that perhaps only other members of Regine's own family reacted as he had hoped she would.[37] In other words the attempt, if genuine, had been a fiasco; Kierkegaard had become a respected author on the basis of a book he believed his readers quite misunderstood, and even the repellent 'Diary' was being received 'jubilantly'. His project, 'to arouse everybody's indignation against me', had 'misfired completely'.[38] So it was natural enough that he should be interested in the story of Abraham as someone who instead of blackening himself acted resolutely as if eternal justice already reigned. And natural enough, too, that he should seek to draw consequences from the story for what must have seemed both to others and to himself a case of visible injustice in his behaviour towards Regine.

Thus *Fear and Trembling* assumes that Abraham is a hero and argues that if Abraham is to remain a hero, then the individual must take priority over the general or universal. This has devastating implications for philosophy and not just for ethics, but the most obvious implications, as well as the most relevant contextually, have to do with ethics. Ethical principles apply equally to everyone, there is no such thing as an individual morality. If something is right for me, then it has to be right for anyone else in relevantly similar circumstances. Kantian and Hegelian philosophy are both explicit about their acceptance of the principle, though in slightly different ways. For Kant the content of morality is embodied in a law that holds universally and absolutely, while for Hegel its embodiment is historically and culturally local and provisional; the Good for Kant is the morally good will, while for Hegel it is the ethos that prevails in an historical society. But in both cases the universal (the more appropriate word in the case of Kant) or the general (for Hegel) takes precedence over the particular.

Kierkegaard may well have known Kant's reaction to the biblical story. Kant criticized Abraham for irrationality in taking it for granted that it was God who commanded him to sacrifice Isaac.[39] Hegel, on the other hand, saw in the narrow identification of the God of Abraham with the Jewish people merely a hint of the properly religious notion of a Lord of Heaven and Earth.[40] As for the faith of which Abraham was hailed as the father, that was nothing but a primitive promise of what would later come to bear the stamp of Reason. Hegel wrote:

[T]he principle of the Christian religion should be worked out for thought, and be taken up into thinking knowledge, and realized in this . . . and it should attain to reconciliation . . . and the riches of thought and culture belonging to the philosophic Idea should become united to the Christian principle. For the philosophic Idea is the Idea of God, and thought has the absolute right of reconciliation, or the right to claim that the Christian principle should correspond with thought.[41]

Abraham is of course not a Christian, but *Fear and Trembling* is concerned with ethics and in a quite radical way. The collision that Abraham's faith is presented as a way of averting is not an ethical collision in the sense of a tragic conflict of duties, or a conflict between duty and feeling, but rather a collision with ethics as such. It raises the question of what it means to talk about the ethical life. Abraham is conflicted whatever he does – whether he disobeys or obeys God, he will regret it either way. In Kantian and Hegelian terms his actions make him a moral pariah. But in the 'Set-up' journal entry Kierkegaard describes Abraham's conduct as 'genuinely poetic' and 'more noble-minded than anything I have read about in tragedies'. He then says that none of his contemporaries would be able to understand this, but that anyone who could explain this 'puzzle' would also have 'explained my life'.

Was Kierkegaard's feverish activity as a writer at this time energized by a wish to explain how Abraham might have been noble all the same and thus, by analogy, how some eternal justice might justify (also in something like the printer's sense) his own ethical lapse? Or was he motivated by a wish to subvert Hegelian ethics and the idea, common to Kant and Hegel, that God is Reason incarnate? This would be in line with the one single theme that continues throughout Kierkegaard's intellectual life, namely his concern to protect religion from philosophy. A particularly glaring example of what he considered the misappropriation of religion by philosophy would be Kant's belief that the essence of Christianity is captured in what we know as morality. This can be called 'immanentism'. For philosophers such as Kant and Hegel (indeed for most philosophers, with Spinoza as a shining example) what counts as good can only be that which can be determined as so by powers of reasoning. According to these ways of determining goodness, whether ours or God's, there is no room for the thought that 'against God we are always in the wrong', no point in appealing to God independent of the moral code. Mankind is, by virtue of reason alone, adequately equipped with regard to all that relates to God and to goodness. In which case, as Kierkegaard's pseudonym puts it, 'the whole of human existence is entirely self-enclosed, as a sphere, and the ethical is at once the limit and completion'.[42] By positing Abraham's nobility at the outset, *Fear and Trembling* is able to 'deduce' that this is not the case. Abraham fails to be ethical on all three of the successive counts specified (as *Fear and Trembling* defines it, ethics is universal [there are no exceptions], divine [there is nothing more to God's goodness, i.e., ethics is immanent], and disclosed [others can judge the moral worth of your actions, you can reveal your moral purposes to others]).[43] So defenders of Abraham must leave ethics behind, at least thus understood. The pseudonymous author says that in order for Abraham to be understood as other than a criminal or insane, a new 'category' is required. He doesn't say what it is; the benefits and costs of breaking with the ethical are left for the reader to ponder, though again, be it noted, not of simply

infringing the basic requirements of the ethical – universality, immanence, and disclosure – but of actually breaking with them as requirements. The choice of pseudonym (*de silentio*) indicates that in pondering
this second-level break the reader is poised at the very edge of communicability. *Fear and Trembling* takes poetry, or literature, as a way of
presenting Abraham heroically, to the edge of religion as what cannot
be grasped in philosophical terms, the 'philosophy' here being only
negative, clarifying the logical distance between what can and what
cannot be understood.

Although the work rises above Kierkegaard's own personal circumstances by questioning the whole idea of the 'self-enclosure' of human
existence, or what Kierkegaard had from early on called a 'humanist' or
a 'philosophical' life-view, the spur for the exercise seems clearly to
have been an interest in resolving a tragic collision in his own life. In
this way Kierkegaard was bringing the categories of Hegel's *Aesthetics*
to bear on himself. But just as clearly, his personal collision has struck
a rich vein of anti-Hegelian, and indeed antiphilosophical, ideas. These
now allow him for the first time to place himself in relation to the
debates that Heiberg's introduction of Hegel to the world of Danish
letters had sparked off. In bringing the categories of the *Aesthetics* to
bear on his own life, Kierkegaard was able to add an important footnote
to Hegel, indeed a footnote capable of subverting the whole Hegelian
opus. There is, after all, a wonderfully seditious touch in the addition
of Abraham's name to the list of 'firm and consistent characters' Hegel
so admired in tragic poetry but whose ruin Hegel attributed to their
lack of 'ethical justification'.[44] True, in Hegel's terms, Abraham too
lacks ethical justification. But according to *Fear and Trembling*, that is
exactly what makes him a hero. The observer of Kierkegaard's life may
look with an admiration not unmixed perhaps with a little suspicion at
the ease with which an attempt to justify his own actions defines a place
for himself outside the Hegelian encampment in his midst.

Alongside his 'dialectic lyric' Kierkegaard was writing another work.
This was subtitled 'An Experiment [*Forsøg* – literally, a shot or venture
at something] in Experimental [*den experimenterende*] Psychology'.
There is no philosophical component in *Repetition* corresponding to the
three '*problemata*' in which Johannes *de silentio* spells out Abraham's
failure to be ethical. Here we meet a young man, evidently a version of
Either/Or's A, but the idle luxury of whose irony has given way to real-

life tribulations due to involvement with a girl. For this reason, as
Kierkegaard remarks in a journal entry, 'feeling and irony are kept apart,
each in its representative: the young man and Constantin'.[45] Constantin
Constantius, the pseudonymous author, is presented as a worldly-wise
and even cynical person who has interested himself in the mental state
of a young man he has befriended in Copenhagen coffee-house circles.
Typically concerned with others only from the point of view of an
observer, Constantin's interest in the younger man is initially a form of
aesthetic fascination. But this very detachment proves to be an advantage, since it enables him to uncover his young friend's deeper motives.
The latter are in a state of what Constantin describes as a form of
spiritual puberty in which things are not yet under the kind of control
that comes with age and experience. He is engaged to a girl with whom
he professes to be deeply in love but to whom at the same time he feels
obligated. On the other hand, he feels unable to consummate the relationship in marriage, as his obligation dictates. The reason he gives is
his melancholy, which has deprived him of the spontaneity that marriage requires. Constantin, from his more detached point of view, can
see that his young friend is really through with the relationship. With
his irony he is able to observe that the girl is not really the object of the
young man's love but only 'the occasion that awakened the poetic in
him'. He adds that by making him into a poet she has 'signed her own
death warrant'. As the poetic melancholy – something that the knowing
Constantin observes can make him even more attractive in the girl's
eyes – becomes compounded by guilt and takes the upper hand, his
love now turned to longing, the young man is strengthened in his
resolve to sever the relationship. Constantin, to help him out, devises a
well-thought-out scheme for making the young man appear 'contemptible'. He is to make regular visits to another girl whom Constantin sets
up in an apartment which has doors onto two streets, so that no one
need find out how short a time he actually spends there. However,
having first approved of the idea, the young man finds he can't go
through with it and leaves town. Constantin never sees him again.[46]

Constantin's role is Socratic. He presents the young man with ways
of looking at and dealing with his situation, so as to find out how much
he really loves the girl, whether it is his own or his sense of the girl's
pride that effectively prevents an open break. He also has a Hegelian
background. Impressed by the strength of the young man's love for the

girl, he calls it a case of the idea in motion, something he says you never encounter in the novel or short story but can – 'God be praised!' – in real life. 'When erotic love is in the idea, every agitation, even every fleeting flurry, is not without meaning, because the most important thing is always present: the poetic collision.'[47] The poetic collision is the conflict that arises when love and the loved one are 'poetized', that is to say when real people are made creatures of the lover's imagination. As the Romantic ironist, following Schlegel, would say: love is a contradiction because it purports to be – indeed has the sense of being – an experience of the infinite in what is merely finite. The finite can assert its oppositional rights not only by being inescapably short-lived but also in the obligations that a lover can, and in the nature of true love ought to, feel with regard to that real and other person.

Constantin then enters upon a reflection on alternative ways of looking at a love that has failed a test of time of this latter kind, as in the young man's case. One way is the young man's own way; he sees himself as a 'sorrowful knight of recollection'. The other way is that of what Constantin calls 'repetition', a notion which Kierkegaard had discussed in an aborted philosophical project written about the time *Either/Or* was in press, and to be entitled 'Johannes Climacus eller De Omnibus Dubitandum est' (Johannes Climacus or Everything Is to Be Doubted). That unfinished work had concluded, so far, that since a meeting of 'ideal' and actual' repetition was impossible both in time and in eternity, it could occur only in consciousness. One place where it might be supposed to occur there is in recollection, but the ideality repeated is in that case not the one that was sought. One might try literally to recollect by actually doing again what one has done before, but that fails because impressions cannot be deliberately recreated. So repetition has to be a way of moving on, recreating the ideal perhaps, bringing it into being.[48]

That you cannot literally repeat the same experience is something Constantin has himself confirmed.[49] He tells how, after the young man's departure, he had gone to Berlin in order to relive what had happened there on a previous stay. The attempt failed, as it was bound to, since to repeat things only in externals leads only to boredom. To repeat his love, the young man would have to move forward, not try to recapture the past; he would have to consummate both himself and his love, that is, keep his love, which means not deceiving her, or himself, which means not engaging in self-deception. But to do so, he would have to look at his love from another and higher point of view, his occupation of which would then be a repetition of himself.

To the proposal that philosophy might be that higher point of view, Constantius says,

He is right not to seek clarification in philosophy, either Greek or modern, for the Greeks make the opposite movement, and here a Greek would choose to recollect without this tormenting his conscience. Modern philosophy makes no movement at all; as a rule it makes only annulments [*Ophœvelser* – Hegel's *Aufgehebungen*, though Kierkegaard's expression, 'den gjør kun Ophœvelser', would suggest to a Danish reader a colloquialism meaning 'making a fuss'], and, if it makes any movement at all, it is always within immanence, whereas repetition is and remains a transcendence.[50]

Repetition's second part contains letters that Constantin, on returning to Copenhagen, has received from the young man. But Constantin's remarks are directed to the reader, not the young man, a device justified by the young man's having left no return address for Constantin to write to – though in a letter with which Constantin concludes the work, we read to our surprise that the young man, 'who I have let come into existence', is really just Constantin's own fabrication.[51] In the letters, however, the young man also talks of repetition. In comparing his own suffering to that of Job, who like Abraham made the 'movement' of faith but only after losing everything *in fact*, he says: 'Job is blessed and has got everything *double* – this is called a *repetition*.'[52] But Job's repetition is, so to speak, immaculate, for he has done no wrong: Job 'knows he is innocent and pure in the very core of his being', indeed he is 'in the right'.[53] Here, however, in ordinary life, in the mundane sphere where against God we are always in the wrong, our repetitions must take account of guilt. Constantin indicates what kind of stance would be required, but he himself as an ironist is incapable of adopting it. In the concluding letter, now addressed directly to the reader, Constantin, just before signing off in a way that suggests that even he is not a real person but only represents a point of view ('I am a vanishing person, just like a midwife in relation to the child she has delivered'), sketches a framework in which the possibility of a 'religious' exception is envisaged.

Had he possessed a deeper religious background, he would not have become a poet. Then everything would have had a religious meaning. The situation he was ensnared in would then no doubt have had meaning for him, but the hindrance in that case would have come from higher places, and he would also have had a quite other authority, even if bought with a still more painful suffering. He would then have acted with an entirely different iron consistency and imperturbability, he would have won a fact of consciousness to which he could constantly hold, which would never become ambivalent for him but be pure earnest because it was posited by him on the basis of a God-relationship. Simultaneously, the whole question of finitude would become a matter of indifference; actuality itself would in the more profound sense be neither here nor there. He would then have religiously emptied that situation of all its frightful consistency. If actuality should put on another face, essentially he would change not at all, as little as if the worst should happen, that would horrify him more than it had done already. With religious fear and trembling, but also with faith and trust, he would understand what he had done from the very beginning and what in consequence he was obligated to do later, even though this obligation would have strange results.[54]

That is very unlike the cynical Constantius whom we know from the beginning of *Repetition*. He too has journeyed and is in danger of losing his grip on the irony he represented so well at the start. But just like the sermon at the end of *Either/Or*, his letter to his 'dear reader' seems designed to indicate the height from which the true author hoped to be able to justify his own poetic activity.

The 'dear reader' then turns out to be none other than Regine herself. Kierkegaard began the manuscript in May in Berlin. It has been suggested that a first version, consisting of the present first part, was completed between 11 and 25 May and that it was for this that Kierkegaard so urgently needed 'a printer'. In this version the young man commits suicide, which leaves us and Constantin with the thought that repetition is an impossible ideal and can indeed occur only in consciousness, or in imagination. This would be consistent with the view that irony is a negative precursor to faith; as an ironist Constantin is no better able to assure anyone of the possibility of a repetition than Johannes *de silentio* is able to explain to anyone what it means to have faith. The first few notes, dated in May, suggest alternative subtitles – 'Fruitless Experiment', 'An Attempted Discovery' – and the term 'philosophy' is introduced only to be discarded along with a more elaborate pseudonym: 'Victorinus Constantinus de bona speranza.' That sounds as though Kierkegaard was indeed hoping for the best, that a higher unity would bring him and Regine together in a new kind of understanding and love. But in *Repetition* the hope that Constantin entertains on behalf of the young man is in the end dashed, and if the original version did end with the latter's suicide, the original hope may have been a different one, a forlorn hope when entertained by a worldly-wise man, and dashed designedly.

If *Repetition* really was the work Kierkegaard had just finished when he wrote to Boesen on 25 May, that fact seems the more likely for the manuscript's not yet containing the young man's eight letters. So we may presume these to have been written on Kierkegaard's own return from Berlin, during June perhaps, at the same time that he was finishing the other work for which he said he needed his library. *Fear and Trembling* contains many allusions, classical references, and quotations from the Bible. And though that work too may have been 'important for him', of the two *Repetition* is clearly the more directly personal.

Whether or not it was the reason for reviving the young man, it remains the case that sometime between his return from Berlin and the end of July Kierkegaard had learnt of Regine's engagement to Johan Frederik (Fritz) Schlegel, the former teacher with whom she was on friendly terms even before she met Kierkegaard (who was aware of that fact).[55] The published ending has the young man rejoice at having 'this "self" that nobody else would pick up off the street' returned to him through her 'generosity' in marrying someone else.

In having the young man say this, it is suggested that Kierkegaard was giving his blessing to the betrothal even at the expense of some consistency in the account given of what it takes to bring off a repetition. The inconsistency would be that Regine, not God, had picked him up off the street and given him back his self. But to anyone who wants to see it, there is heavy irony in this use of the term 'generosity', and Kierkegaard may well just be putting the words into the incorrigibly poetic young man's mouth, knowing full well that Regine would recognize that Kierkegaard himself was not so naïve. As for his own repetition, although he had given up the idea of receiving back his self entire with its love of Regine, at least in the way such things can happen in the ordinary world, he seems still to have thought of his own repetition as a common project in which Regine and he would both pursue their God-relationships in parallel and in some higher union. It was still important for him and his love that he be the one who helped her with her God-relationship. Whether the enormity of that assumption struck him at the time – the idea is radically examined in a later work on the topic of love – his immediate reaction to the news was far from loving.

The original revision of the manuscript directed a harsh rebuke to the lady who saved the young man. And a sole journal entry from the time on this topic provides a piece of otherwise unmotivated gallows humour, under the heading 'Lines'.

Someone with a sense of humour runs across a girl who once had assured him she would die if he left her; on the occasion of their meeting she is engaged. He greets her and says, 'May I thank you for the kindness you have shown me; perhaps you will allow me to show my appreciation (he takes two marks and eight shillings from his waistcoat pocket and hands it to her. She is speechless with indignation but stands her ground and tries to wither him with her glance; and he continues): don't mention it, it's to help with the trousseau and the day you [the polite form – *De*] hold the wedding and put the final crown on your kindness – I swear by all that is holy, for God's sake and your eternal salvation, that I shall send you another two marks and eight shillings'.[56]

The bitterness is plain, and the entry probes closer to the heart of this couple's past than any other document, not least in the sense it gives, to Regine's great credit, of a fight between equals.

As a personal document *Repetition* is an attempted explanation, both to himself and to Regine, of what strange results Kierkegaard's views on what his own obligations to her might lead to. But Regine's re-engagement meant they could not be brought to fruition anyway. On the other hand, as a psychological experiment, as the early notes suggest, the result of *Repetition* was that repetition will in actual fact be impossible anyway. It fails at every level, from the banal attempt to repeat the events of a previous visit to a city, through Constantin's failure to persuade the young man to get his girl back by a ruse, to the failure that such a ruse would have led to in any case even if the young man had gone along with the plan. But the work seems also designed to show why these are and must be failures. The only possible solution, given the circumstances, is in fact an *im*possible one. The only hope lies in the young man's not being a poet, but that is what he is. The standpoint of the solution is that of religion, but if he had stood there Kierkegaard would not have become a writer, and he could have married Regine. Writing, however, was now where Kierkegaard's 'gift' was obviously taking him. And he was no ordinary writer. By displaying his Constantinian insights he could also show his reader what no other contemporary writer was able to, namely the nature of the 'poetic' collision in which he himself was involved and what it would take to overcome it or avoid it. As for himself, and whatever his special talents, he was of course, like Johannes *de silentio*, still just a writer. He was what the young man in *Repetition* would not have become had the young man been religious. And despite his somewhat effusive advertisement for what 'making the religious movement' would do for the young man, Constantin makes it clear that he himself cannot execute it. 'It is', he says, 'contrary to my nature.' For Constantin Constantius repetition 'remains a transcendence' also in the sense that it is 'beyond' him.[57]

The later Kierkegaard, more convinced that he had been a truly religious writer from the start, might interpret this strategically: it was not beyond the writer as a person, but it was beyond him, or any other writer as such, to convey what it means, in any individual case, to achieve what is referred to as a repetition. Besides, once you allow that the moral behaviour stemming from the higher point of view of a repetition may be nontransparent, you cease to be able to talk on behalf of others; for someone else there is no way of predicting what the right thing to do will be.

What Kierkegaard's own religious standpoint was at the time is unclear, even if one takes into account work of a quite different genre in which he had also been busily engaged. When *Repetition* and *Fear and Trembling* both appeared in Reitzel's bookshop on 16 October 1843, it had been only eight months since *Either/Or* had done the same. As it happened, this was the very same day on which the longer and more penetrating of the reviews of *Either/Or*, the one by the young theologian, had appeared. The two works had been ready earlier, but Kierkegaard had postponed their publication because he wanted to publish, at the same time and under his own name, three 'Edifying Discourses'. Two such discourses had already been published in the middle of May while he was in Berlin working on *Repetition*. The two sets of discourses were dedicated, as were those to follow in the course of just over a year, to 'my father, the late Michael Pedersen Kierkegaard, formerly hosier in this city'.

The combination of poetic intensity and high seriousness typifying these discourses indicates Søren's dedication to the 'part' of his father's religion. But there are questions to raise and facts to note. One particular question is, was the religion keeping its hold on him or was he keeping his hold on it? He might have been writing these pieces under his own name just to show that he could shine in this area too. And if that was the reason, might that not too be simply in a spirit of competition, showing that here he could do just as well as, if not better than, others? Or was it to redress the balance in favour of what he would see as a more just picture of his own relation to life than the one that had grown out of his reputation as the presumptive author of *Either/Or*?

All six sets of the (in all) eighteen discourses are preceded by prefaces expressing, in subtly appreciative and self-deprecatory, even mock-modest language, the hope that they may find their way to '*my* reader, that single individual'. In a journal entry from 1849, from which we have already quoted several extracts, Kierkegaard notes how the early focus of his work seems to have had a potentially broader relevance, which only later became clear to him, and which gave his work a far wider significance. He says that he had already realized this at the time he wrote the first of the discourses, and that 'from early on' he knew that there was some wider, philosophical, perhaps also political significance in the notion of 'that single individual'. But in that same entry he says that 'when I first wrote [this about his reader being that single individual] I was thinking of my reader in particular, for that book [the first two edifying discourses, published in May 1843] contained a little hint to her, and then for the time being it was especially true for me that I only sought that one single reader'.[58]

Back in March 1842 Kierkegaard had been anxious in case Regine misinterpreted his early return to Copenhagen. So he 'avoided her' when she looked for him after Mynster's sermon that Easter – in case she had got it into her head that he 'had thought about her' while in Berlin. The avoidance persisted a whole year or more, in spite of punctual attendance at Vor Frue, until at Evensong on Easter Sunday the following year, 16 April 1843, three weeks before Kierkegaard left on that second visit to Berlin, Regine turned in Kierkegaard's direction after Mynster's sermon and nodded.

I do not know if it was pleadingly or forgivingly, but in any case so affectionately. I had taken a seat at a remote spot but she discovered it. Would to God she hadn't. Now a year and a half of suffering are wasted and all the enormous pains I took; she does not believe I am a deceiver, she has faith in me.[59]

The role of cad not having worked, Kierkegaard had wondered whether he should try that of hypocrite – that one professing such high principles should behave as he did. However, she would see through that too.

He no longer felt he could devote his life just to her. He says that at this time Regine, knowing 'the road I usually take', contrived that their paths would cross every Monday between nine and ten in the morning. A page has been torn from the journal, but the entry goes on to say that although he has done everything to shield her from any sense of guilt for what happened and kept his own reactions to himself, she has, by failing to take his melancholy seriously and by provoking his pride, made matters worse for them both.

In setting out for Berlin that second time, then, Kierkegaard now assumed that in spite of his tactics Regine still 'believed in' him. He wasn't the heartless Don Juan others took him to be.[60] The motivation for writing *Repetition* then becomes clearer. He was no longer thinking only of her, and with the success of *Either/Or* behind him he could explain both to her and to himself the kind of humanly insoluble dilemmas that can arise when the everyday and religion conflict. That Regine was nevertheless his intended 'reader' is readily understood. If she couldn't be repelled she could still be helped, and if they could both have faith, then the unhappy events could in the end acquire, for each of them, a 'repetition', even if the exact nature of the solution would in the nature of repetition be impossible to predict. We may assume that the first two edifying discourses were written in the week following that Easter. In any case they came out two days before Kierkegaard left for Berlin. That Regine read them we know because Sibbern made sure she received them. This is reflected in a journal entry, though written nine years later. It says that it was in connection with these discourses that Regine gained 'her first religious impression of me'.[61]

It was sometime in July, several weeks after his return, and with the manuscript for *Repetition* completed, that Kierkegaard heard of Regine's engagement to her former admirer. He was forced to reconstrue the Evensong episode and the subsequent crossings of their paths. It was not an expression of forgiveness and understanding on her part, or her saying that she had seen through the deception and appreciated the motive behind it so that now he need not worry: Regine's two nods meant, 'You must give me up'. Kierkegaard now saw it as presumably it was, a request for his approval of the engagement. What caused her friendliness when they saw each other on the street had been her thinking she had received it, when in fact we know that on discovering the engagement Kierkegaard was thrown into a bitter and sarcastic mood. It revealed an assumption on Kierkegaard's part that Regine's future was to be one in the development of which Kierkegaard himself would be involved, and the successful development of which would somehow not only compensate for but justify their broken engagement. Schlegel got in the way, and Regine too, laughably enough. Schlegel, furthermore, was a teacher, which may be why Kierkegaard so insists in the prefaces to the discourses that this is exactly what he is not.

The prefaces nevertheless continued to express the wish that they would reach that single reader whom 'with pleasure and in gratitude' he called *his*.[62] Since the reader is also referred to in the prefaces as 'him' there was no reason to change the address. Kierkegaard was able under this cover to communicate to Regine his continued regard even after her new engagement, something that seems clearly to have been necessary for him in order to keep his side of a 'bargain' that the unfortunate Regine was part of but had no part in making.

There was something else as well. The discourses were also a preparation for the future he had at least to plan for in case he failed to die at the appointed age of thirty-three. If he lived on there would still be an end to the writing, since as conceived at present it was not an entirely open-ended project. At some point he would be looking for a job. The discourses helped him to keep that option open. In the midst of all this Kierkegaard held a qualifying sermon (on a set text: 1 Cor. 2:6–9) at the Trinitatis Church on 24 February 1844.[63]

For the present, however, the ideas were still in full flow. Indeed, the cascade had only just begun. By the time the sixth set of edifying discourses appeared on 31 August 1844 Kierkegaard had published three more works, two of which were to have an impact well beyond the boundaries of Denmark's own culture and one just as great as that of the first two sequels to *Either/Or*.

More to Being

THE NEW WORKS, all pseudonymous, came hard on the heels of the June publication of 'Three Edifying Discourses'. They were *Philosophiske Smuler: eller en Smule Philosophi* (Philosophical Crumbs or Just a Crumb of Philosophy), by Johannes Climacus, and then – just four days later – both *Begrebet Angest: En simpel psychologisk-paapegende Overveielse (i retning af det dogmatiske Problem om Arvesynden)* (The Concept of Anxiety: A Plain Psychologically Oriented Deliberation [in the Direction of the Dogmatic Problem of Hereditary Sin]), by Vigilius Haufniensis, and *Forord: Morskabslæsning for enkelte Stænder efter Tid og Leilighed* (Prefaces: Light Reading for Various Stations of Life as Time and Opportunity Permit), by Nicolaus Notabene.

Although they appeared almost simultaneously, so that towards their completion Kierkegaard was attending to several manuscripts at once, these oddly titled works published in June were begun at different times and with distinct aims in mind. The first was *The Concept of Anxiety*, which Kierkegaard began writing towards the end of 1843.[1] But already the following March, with that project still unfinished, he was on the way with *Philosophical Crumbs* (henceforth referred to for convenience by its usual but rather staid and potentially misleading English title, *Philosophical Fragments*). In the light of what was said at the close of the previous chapter it is worth looking in the cultural setting for the 'cues' that triggered this intense activity, whatever it was that reawakened, now that the Regine episode had been exploited and its ethical implications grafted into Kierkegaard's thought, reflection on matters that had preoccupied him from the start. It is worth noting that at first Kierkegaard intended neither of these works to be pseudonymous. Does that mean that whatever reasons finally decided him to make them so were not the same as those that had led him to pseudonymity in the previous works? An answer may be found in the cues themselves. Where better to begin an account of this fertile year than on New Year's Day?

On 1 January, Bishop Mynster published an article in Heiberg's *Intelligensblade*, under the pseudonym Kts. It was in sharp response to the anonymous review of *Either/Or* by the young theologian (H. P. Koefoed-Hansen) who had noted the loss of authority in modern society. *Either/Or* was a book for the times: not only did the public's enthusiasm for the first part confirm that their lives were far more infected with aesthetic attitudes than most of them would like to think, but also for such a public the full-bodied arguments brought by the Assessor in the second part made a far more effective appeal to their moral instincts than the usual pronouncements of the importance of a moral attitude. And the reviewer had claimed that the closing sermon would make a much deeper impression on an aesthetic personality than most of what they heard on Sundays.[2]

In his New Year's Day article Mynster, a primate famed for his own sermons, attacked the suggestion that the aesthetic point of view provided a better intellectual basis for the appreciation of the meaning of Christianity. In so doing he referred to ironic aesthetes as 'the half-educated, the lopsidedly educated, the miseducated'. He mentioned in support the recent pseudonymously published *Fear and Trembling*, a work that offered no comfort to those who think they have access to religious life by way of the aesthetic point of view. But he also referred to Kierkegaard directly, drawing attention to the author's dedication of the edifying discourses to his father, a man of no formal education, and to the acknowledgement in this way by a person of undoubted intellectual brilliance of faith's independence of any intellectualism of the kind encouraged by exponents of the aesthetic point of view.[3]

For Kierkegaard, having Mynster thus publicly identify Michael Pedersen Kierkegaard as a man of simple faith must have been a source of great annoyance. (Mynster's reference here to his father's personality had another effect on Kierkegaard that was to come to light only in one of the very last journal entries, and we will return to that later.) Although his dead father's unwavering belief was something he privately respected and held before (or above or ahead of) him as an example to keep hold of, such a public reference to his father's faith must have sounded not only patronizing but also embarrassing, since in the public eye it placed him, as author of the discourses, in a region of the cultural landscape to which he had no wish to be seen to belong.

As for that landscape itself, the very fact of Mynster's article casts light on the salient players. Both Koefoed-Hansen and the authors of the two previous longer reviews of *Either/Or* represented an active aestheticist movement in Denmark at the time. There was then, as perhaps always and certainly still now, a split between those who saw traditional academic studies as necessary for upholding the human spirit and those who saw them instead as imposing outdated constraints on spiritual progress, a progress whose proper path was in literature. The latter formed a radical and influential minority opinion centred at Sorø Academy in central Zealand, southwest of Copenhagen, which also happened to be where Kierkegaard's brother had his pastorate. As an institution of higher learning the academy had been founded in 1820 with royal support,[4] subsequently acquiring a reputation, among some, for *avant-gardisme* and among others, led by Heiberg, who in 1830 had conducted a campaign against the 'Sorø men', for dilettantism. Heiberg's own Hegel-inspired theory of poetry had played an important part in this cultural conflict. We don't know how Michael Pedersen Kierkegaard would have reacted to this defence of his religion, except that to have it associated thus publicly with institutionalized authority might have annoyed someone so theocratically minded and nonconformist. To the son, who in those prefaces made a point of not speaking with a preacher's authority, the support would seem to be in danger of giving quite the wrong message. Kierkegaard can hardly have intended the dedication to be regarded as a pointer to his own religious attitudes; it was a symbolic gesture in memory of his father. But quite apart from that, a defence by someone openly opposed, as Mynster was, to Sorø's self-consciously 'aesthetic' belletrists and intellectuals would mislead readers into assuming that Kierkegaard would oppose them too, or oppose them for the same reasons. All in all, not least because of his father's connection with Mynster, but also because he nevertheless really agreed with Mynster on several basic issues of religion, Kierkegaard would be especially ambivalent about Mynster's support. Personally it would please him, just as Heiberg's praise meant something in the literary field. But publicly he would not like to be defended at the expense of people, conspicuous among them the avant-garde, still able to appreciate the more comprehensive experience to which religion should respond.

Some days after Mynster's article *Kjøbenshavnsposten* published a piece called 'Gross Lie' (*Plump Usandhed*) by 'a priest'. It rejected Kts's claim that the churches were full on Sundays. It went on to say that Kts had done nothing to respond to well-known criticisms of religion.[5] It mentioned in particular Bruno Bauer (1809–1882), a German theologian and originally a follower of Marheinecke on the Hegelian right, who on moving from Berlin to Bonn had become radically left-wing. Bauer espoused David Friedrich Strauss's *Das Leben Jesu kritisch bearbeitet* (The Life of Jesus Critically Examined) (1835–36) but went even further than Strauss, exposing the texts of the Gospel stories to standard literary criticism, thus calling in question the entire historical basis of Christianity.

Kierkegaard had kept abreast of these developments and for three years (1835–38) had subscribed to *Zeitschrift für spekulative Theologie*, which Bauer edited. He also possessed a later work of Strauss's, in Hans Brøchner's translation, and although there is no record of him owning *Das Leben Jesu*, the work was famous, or notorious, and he refers to it several times in connection with Martensen's lectures.[6] He also possessed a copy of Franz Xavier von Baader's *Über das Leben Jesu von Strauss*, published in 1836, as well as works by other writers mentioned by 'the priest', notably Heine and Feuerbach. On the one hand, Kierkegaard must have applauded what, in a summary of Martensen's lectures, is referred to as a 'driving [of] the theologians from their purely historical defences'.[7] This in itself would not be something over which, at the time, he could have said he differed from Martensen, for Martensen aimed at erecting his dogmatics not on history but on faith. Still, as far as 'a priest''s criticism of Mynster's position was concerned, Kierkegaard would certainly not want the merits of left-wing theology to count in favour either of a fashionable atheism or of any 'half-educated' aesthetic acceptance of Christianity, as if the truth of Christianity lent itself to presentation *within* the horizon of Romantic irony.

Mynster too had earlier touched on these themes. In an article, 'Rationalism and Supernaturalism', published in July 1839 and already referred to in Chapter 6 (see note 9), he had responded to a claim on behalf of 'the more recent rationalism' that the issue between the two positions of the title was now passé. If that were true, then since he himself had long ago decided in favour of the latter position, his own standing, Mynster had pointed out, would now be that of an historical curiosity, which of course he denied. Mynster made no attempt to support his own supernaturalist position, he only wanted to show that the issue was still alive. He claimed to find the essentials of a 'more recent rationalism' in Strauss's *Das Leben Jesu*, whose basic proposition he takes to be God's becoming human, thus bestowing divinity on human life. The view, Mynster thinks, can be set alongside a Christian naturalism that sees all finite life as dependent upon God, so that no religious fact need be seen in terms other than those in which facts of nature determine it. Mynster understandably associates the idea of the absolute dependence of nature on God with Schleiermacher. Opposed to both of these is Mynster's own supernaturalist position, in which God is still a living presence 'lending an ear to our prayers, observing humanity's misery and hearing its sigh, and sending immediate salvation'. The article, written before Schelling's Berlin lectures, asks its readers to see how things are unresolved even in the Hegelian world in this respect. An ultrasupernatural branch had formed in opposition to the Straussians, and there were reports that Schelling had some new insight to offer that went beyond Hegel, a place for religion in his philosophy, though what it was he had so far kept a closely guarded secret. Mynster ended his article by suggesting that, far from being antiquated, the tension between rationalism and supernaturalism was a feature of spiritual life itself, an either/or, in other words a contradiction that cannot be resolved or overridden in terms available to a more comprehensive view of things, a contradiction between whose terms 'people divide themselves according to their mental disposition'.[8]

Apart from echoing Kierkegaard's own hopes for Schelling's lectures at the time, Mynster's essay, if it didn't set the agenda for Kierkegaard's later thoughts and writings, at least contains many of their main ingredients – not just the either/or between a humanistic and a 'deeper' religious experience but also the status of historical truth and the notion of the God-man, both also specifically mentioned by Mynster.[9] This would be the main focus of *Fragments* and ultimately of its huge 'Postscript'. Kierkegaard would in effect be exploring the implications of supernaturalism, though with several twists. He would make the division, which Mynster takes in his conciliatory style to distinguish people according to their dispositions, into a division within each individual.

Second, as with so many other apparently negative outcomes, Kierkegaard with his Hegelian eye could see that the theologians' loss of
history could be turned to true religiosity's advantage by depriving
people of a form of support that a truly religious person shouldn't need.
At the same time it put out of play an issue about historical facts that
could so easily be decided to the advantage of those already predisposed
to atheism. Third, and strengthening further the impression that he was
a better Hegelian than Mynster, Kierkegaard would take from the 'new
rationalism' the motif of 'becoming' which Mynster's focus on devotion
had led the primate to ignore. The idea that Being is still to be achieved,
a fulfilment of human being to be brought about by every human being,
is already discernible in *The Concept of Anxiety*.

Kierkegaard had been working on *Anxiety* already for more than two
months when Mynster's New Year's Day article in response to the
review of *Either/Or* appeared. He continued apace with that project
while the shape of the later work gradually formed in his mind. Not
surprisingly, the works cross-fertilized and share several themes. Their
points of view are, however, very different. The one is (although only a
mite, a scrap, a particle of) 'philosophy', the other 'psychologically
oriented'. But it is clear that they have a common aim, an elucidation
of the properly religious frame of mind. Let us briefly recount the main
themes of each.

Anxiety (*Angest*) was no new concept. In his reading of the Romantics, 'Angst' was a term Kierkegaard would have come across often
enough. The final page of *The Concept of Anxiety* refers to Hamann's
characterization of *Angst* as an 'impertinent unquiet' and 'holy hypochondria'.[10] In describing anxiety as 'holy' Hamann's thought was rather
like Kierkegaard's own, namely that anxiety was fundamental to human
being but could be turned to spiritual advantage, was indeed a kind of
privilege. Along with other familiar psychological terms, 'anxiety' was
also part of the vocabulary of the German Idealists, not least of Hegel's
but also of Schelling's. Even Hegel, who despised the cult of the morbid
and melancholic, uses it in his portrayal of the trials of spirit. A passage
from the *Phenomenology* replete with motifs now considered peculiarly
Kierkegaardian goes:

in positing . . . a single particular . . . [consciousness establishes] the beyond . . .
[and in this way] suffers . . . violence at its own hands, [spoiling] its own limited
satisfaction. When consciousness feels this violence, its anxiety [*Angst*] may well
make it retreat from the truth, and strive to hold on to what it is in danger of

losing. But it can find no peace. If it wishes to remain in a state of unthinking inertia, then thought troubles its thoughtlessness, and its own unrest disturbs its inertia. Or, if it entrenches itself in sentimentality . . . [etc.]¹¹

Sentimentality, including the 'sighs and prayers' of religion, for Hegel simply indicated that consciousness had so far failed to see the 'true identity of inner and outer'.¹² For Kierkegaard the failure to do that is inevitable and should be accepted. One way of reading not just *Anxiety* but the succeeding pseudonymous authorship as a whole is as an attempt to replace the still dominant Romantic view of religion with another that acknowledges the strain religious belief puts on the understanding, presenting the whole area as an unknown to which the natural response is to recoil in the way the psychologically perceptive Hegel remarks.

Whether as an acute sense of impending but unspecified disaster or a vague and undirected feeling of unease with no immediate cause, what Kierkegaard calls '*Angest*' is something that most people will have experienced. Were it not for the fact that the now acceptable English word 'angst' has acquired a fairly specific clinical use in connection with neurosis and certain exaggerated forms of fear or remorse, Kierkegaard's '*Angest*' might nowadays be straightforwardly translated by that term. The word 'anguish' is perhaps too easily associated with a culturally local, hair-tearing Romanticism. Although 'dread' has the advantage of a weight and richness that 'anxiety' lacks and that lends it to the metaphysical use to which Kierkegaard puts it, 'anxiety' is, I think, the better because more neutral term. All of them can be applied to a more diffuse and also more familiar range of phenomena than those Kierkegaard is interested in: I can be anxious about my children's meeting with the youth culture, about the outcome of an interview, about a meeting with my psychiatrist. These are all forms of apprehensiveness, a fear of a possible and definite but as yet undecided outcome. Fear or even dread itself, as we use these terms, is even more focused; we are afraid not just 'in case' something will happen, but *that* it will happen. '*Angest*' in Kierkegaard's sense is a generalized apprehensiveness with no particular 'in case' in view, one might call it a state of global uneasiness. Zoobiologists have some familiarity with this application when they induce frantically undirected behaviour in animals by depriving them of their natural frames of reference. Anxiety is the humanly equivalent state in which the world *as such* presents itself as no longer our home. Kierkegaard formulates it in a telling metaphor: '[A]nxiety can be compared with dizziness. The person whose eye happens to [*kommer til at*] look down into the yawning abyss becomes dizzy.' The dizziness is said to be 'freedom's'.[13] Once we see what this means, it will appear how naturally the topic of anxiety follows upon that of irony. In other words, Kierkegaard's thoughts are returning now, three years later, to themes that had found their first clear articulation in his dissertation. We know that the themes themselves go back even further, to those seminal journal entries Kierkegaard made in reaction to Adler's dissertation, but *Anxiety* rehearses even more of Kierkegaard's intellectual development; it goes back to classical themes that animated him in his first student years. It is no merely nostalgic gesture that the work is dedicated to Poul Martin Møller, that 'happy lover of Greek culture'.

Irony too, we noted, is global: 'not this or that phenomenon, but the whole of existence . . . is viewed *sub specie ironiae*.'[14] To distance oneself ironically from the world is to deprive oneself of the familiar. The ability to do so is peculiarly human, an advantage, as Kierkegaard seemed to say in the dissertation, rather than a fatal flaw. Such distancing is not necessarily ironical, but in having it in them to put themselves apart from the world in any way, humans as such are capable of inducing in themselves a condition in their own lives quite analogous to that which produces the frantic restlessness of animals when taken from their natural (and not merely customary) surroundings.

But anxiety in humans does not exhibit itself in this popularly paradigmatic and behavioural fashion. Certain modes of behaviour may be regarded as typical expressions of anxiety, but there is no specific behaviour that can be said to be essentially characteristic of it; anxiety can manifest itself in innumerable ways. It is what Kierkegaard, within the conceptual framework of his time, would call a spiritual phenomenon, and the fundamental modes of dread are linked with corresponding stages in the growth of human powers of reflection, including reflection on oneself. In turning in *The Concept of Anxiety* to the general phenomenon and tabulating its main forms, Kierkegaard seems to be embarking on an undertaking of the kind he had, in those entries on Adler's dissertation, called 'anthropological'. He had said there that all Hegel had managed to do was to establish that thinking works, but that this brings us only to the point where the anthropological undertaking starts, and so far it had not even 'been begun'.[15]

If this is the task Kierkegaard undertakes, it is clear that he sees it from a religious perspective. So we might want to say that his interest here is in religious psychology. In a comment on the title of the first chapter of *The Concept of Anxiety* ('Anxiety as the Presupposition of Hereditary Sin and as Explaining Hereditary Sin Backwards [*Retrogradt*] in the Direction of its Origin'), Kierkegaard as we saw in Chapter 2 offers the metaphor of an 'inland journey' (*Indenlandsreise*). Although the entry is grammatically incomplete and says '. . . has only taken, and is taking, an inland journey from his own consciousness to what is presupposed by hereditary sin in his own consciousness',[16] we can take it that the missing pronoun refers to the author, the point being that the chapter limits itself to identifying the psychological conditions under which the notion of hereditary sin can take effect. But that limitation is also intended to indicate the journey's importance precisely for what it leaves out. We might gauge its importance in Kierkegaard's eyes by presuming the metaphor of an inland journey to be a deliberate comparison with the travels abroad he refers to so often, and with so much admiration, by Peter Wilhelm Lund, the famous paleontologist and much-respected friend of his youth.

Equally important, as it appears from this first chapter, is the need to distinguish between what belongs to psychology or science and what belongs to dogmatics and ethics. Not the least of *Anxiety*'s targets, as is clear from the Introduction, is what it sees as the bad habit of obliterating disciplinary boundaries. It is as though holding a Hegelian ticket allowed you to ride anywhere. What is less clear from the Introduction is exactly where among the academic flora *Anxiety* is supposed to belong. It seems that however much it touches on topics appropriate to such enterprises, this is neither a theological nor a philosophical treatise. Yet the Introduction is, in its dozen or so pages, so burdened with references to classical and local thinkers, from Plato to Martensen, and several to Hegel that are probably aimed more directly at Adler, who had paraphrased two parts of Hegel's *Logic*, that it is hard not to see some serious intellectual intent or at least targets in the chapters that follow.

Nevertheless, and although the work is dressed up as a treatise with academically correct section-headings employing the current jargon, and as with *On the Concept of Irony* bears its theme on its sleeve, the author's credentials and expertise and thus also his intentions are not easy to place.

The opening chapter suggests one answer. It is at pains to make clear just how far psychology can help in the task at hand but insists at the same time that going that distance is vital for understanding the impact of theology and ethics on our lives. The answer then would be that there is an anthropological and psychological gap in the literature dealing with the topic of hereditary sin, and Kierkegaard in the guise of his pseudonym Vigilius Haufniensis (the wide-awake Copenhager) is out to fill it. Evidence that *Anxiety* is part of this project is found in a remark in Kierkegaard's papers in connection with this work to the effect that '[p]sychology is what we need and above all adequate knowledge of human life, and sympathy for its interests . . . [for without them] there can be no question of completing a Christian view of life'.[17]

Still the work itself, for all that it is tricked out as a treatise, hardly seems intended as a treatise in psychology as such. Indeed, early on in the second chapter the author disclaims that he is writing a treatise at all, or a 'learned' book. At the same time he disparages those 'solitary stiff-necks' who try to *construct* rules on the basis of individual experience. Grasping psychology is a matter of possessing a 'psychological-poetic authority', also called a 'poetic originariness' (*Oprindelighed*). But once you have that kind of authority you have no need of even the best of the stiff-necks, since you are able (in a by now quite familiar motif) to 'create at once the whole and law-like out of what in the individual is always only partially and irregularly present'.[18] In other words, an account based on actual cases will never be sufficient, but having what would be sufficient renders any such account unnecessary in any case. So there is no point in *elaborating* the psychology, the knowledge of human life, we need in order to complete a Christian view of life. What we need is an ability to grasp the unity of experience poetically, and then it will be impossible, or at least serve no useful communicative purpose, to assemble in the form of a treatise the words you need to express what you know.

The absence in the text of the stylistic homogeneity and strict inner organization one expects of a book presenting itself in treatise form, along with the occasional levity and a use of metaphor to make what appear to be the most important points, understandably have led some to question the seriousness of Kierkegaard's intentions in writing *The Concept of Anxiety* at all. The issues are similar to those raised earlier concerning the dissertation. Isn't the whole thing just another exercise in irony and the textbook format intended simply as parody? Evidence for this is a lack of congruence that gradually emerges between what is being said on the topic of anxiety and the form in which it is being presented, as if part of what was being said was that if what the book says about anxiety is right, then what anxiety is cannot be expressed in this way. It has been alleged that what the book actually says about anxiety is deliberately at variance with the kind of phenomenon the work, if read literally, claims it to be.[19]

But what does the book, read literally, say about anxiety? Looking at the chapters individually and successively we find a number of what appear to be strategically placed and well-stated theses. The first chapter, tracing hereditary (or original) sin to its origin, says that the categories and concepts used to characterize the human spirit are essential for grasping the phenomenon of anxiety in the transition from innocence to sin. That transition, as the book describes it, is the gradual loss of the human being's sense, when in an initial state of 'peace and repose', of being simply what, quite naturally, it is. But instead of the state of innocence being a condition out of which spirit emerges, we are to understand it as one in which spirit is so far 'outside'. The crucial thesis of *Anxiety*, to which Kierkegaard repeatedly returns, is that human being has the structure of a synthesis. It is a composition of mind and body, but any interrelationship between these is unthinkable without a 'third factor' uniting them. 'This third factor is the spirit.' Admittedly this is an extremely abstract formula, but for that very reason it allows Kierkegaard to place anxiety where he wants it in respect of his 'psychologically oriented' deliberation. The state of innocence too is a state of the synthesis, but one in which the synthesis is not yet aware of itself as such. However, since the other factor must nevertheless be accounted for even in this state of rest, there is a sense even in innocence of there being some other state than the one it is. There is no inkling as to what that state might be, or perhaps even of whatever it is that exceeds the present state being itself another state. As yet totally unspecified, it takes the form of 'nothing', and it is this nothing that even in a state of innocence 'begets anxiety'. But in the story of the Fall, Adam is told not to eat of the fruit of knowledge, and this prohibition creates, as it were, a scenario. Though it still leaves him in a state of anxiety in the face of nothing, this nothing now has something to do with his own future and activity. It is the 'nothing' of the 'alarming possibility of being able'.

Considering anxiety backwards towards its origin, the first chapter says the following: (1) the conditions under which the Fall occurred include anxiety and in general do not differ from those in which all later humans acquire the sense of sin; (2) not being a science of the human spirit (since there can be no such), psychology cannot account for postlapsarian repetitions of the Fall (that requires a 'qualitative leap');[20] but (3) the concept of human being as a synthesis sustained by spirit allows one to make unscientific (in Hegelian terms, unsystematic), 'plain' or unfancy psychological observations which help to fill in the picture of a Christian view of life, including, for instance, as the first chapter makes clear, the role played in Christianity by the notion of sexuality, which is central to the idea of original sin. That is the way 'backwards'. The state of innocence in which we all begin is one of ignorance, a state of 'immediate unity' in which spirit is 'dreaming' in man. The metaphor of dreaming spirit was not uncommon at the time and is found in Karl Rosenkranz's *Psychologie oder die Wissenschaft vom subjectiven Geist* (Psychology or the Science of Subjective Spirit), a work Kierkegaard had been reading and whose title strongly suggests a role in the forming of *Anxiety*'s demarcational agenda.[21] It is found also in Schelling, the fact of Rosenkranz's interest in whom is acknowledged in *Anxiety* in a footnote.[22] *Anxiety*, by applying to this notion the Hegelian idea that 'being' as such or in general is opposed to 'nothing', portrays the inner peace of innocence as one in which there is nothing to strive with, but it strives with it all the same as a 'nothing' outside it, and this 'begets anxiety'.[23]

The second chapter, entitled 'Anxiety as Hereditary Sin Forwards [*Progressivt*]', a no less tightly packed repository of 'unsystematic' observations, says that the sin that anxiety let in from the beginning, once let in, brings with it its own anxiety, which then becomes a background feature of the world into which later generations are born. The psychology that extends to the positing of sin applies in each subsequent case too, as the discipline accounting for the individual's ambivalent attitude towards freedom and for how the human 'synthesis' resists taking up a personal relationship to sin in the mood appropriate to it, a mood which already in the Introduction we have been told is seriousness.[24] The dizziness metaphor is introduced to capture the phenomenology of the involuntary vision of the 'yawning abyss' which opens up for the individual when first realizing that its 'naturalness' is not enough and that the world in general does not present itself to human being simply as such as its 'home'. The *natural* reaction is to hang on to the familiar:

Thus anxiety is the dizziness of freedom which arises when the spirit would posit the synthesis, and freedom now gazes down into its own possibility and then grabs hold of finiteness to save itself [*at holde sig ved*]. In this dizziness freedom collapses.[25]

In other words, in the very act of grabbing hold of the finite world to stay upright, freedom, by failing to support *itself*, falls down. It is important to see what freedom means here. The sentence quoted earlier said that the person whose eye 'happens' to look into the abyss becomes dizzy, and goes on to say that 'the reason is just as much his eye as the abyss, for what if he didn't look down?' That could sound as if freedom in Kierkegaard's sense is already being exercised in the gaze that causes the involuntary reaction, or at least as if the reaction itself is not involuntary. But to say that the reason is as much in the eye as in the abyss is not to say that there is a free will already at work prior to that first glance down into the abyss, a will that is perhaps even at work trying to avert its owner's gaze. It is the general structure of human being as schematized in the idea of a synthesis that causes the dizziness, the very 'naturalness' of the psychosomatic synthesis that resists the radical unfamiliarity of the notion of actually being spirit and not just another piece of nature. Freedom, in this context (and it is not to deny that there is also freedom of action or of will in some ordinary sense), is the area of possibilities that open up when the synthesis posits itself as a synthesis sustained by spirit.

The same passage continues: 'Further than this psychology cannot go and will not. That very instant everything is changed, and when freedom gets up again it sees that it is guilty. Between these instants lies the leap which no science has explained or can explain.'[26] The language is as unscientific as that of the 'scientific' Hegel's own *Phenomenology of Spirit*, and *Anxiety* is in one sense written in the 'spirit' of that work though decidedly not in its letter. What the word 'leap' here implies is that there is no explanatory path that you can follow that begins with psychology and ends with truths about spirit and selfhood. In speaking of psychology, Hegel was of course not thinking of an empirical discipline but of part of an all-embracing science of man as emerging self-conscious spirit. Psychology, along with phenomenology

and anthropology (though also in his senses of these terms), was a
science of 'subjective' spirit (also Rosenkranz's topic) – as against 'objective spirit', or the public expression and historical forms of emerging
self-conscious spirit, including legal institutions and social morality,
though also the social aspects of the individual conscience. Kierkegaard,
for his part, does indeed talk of psychology as an empirical science, or
at least of an 'experimental' psychology (recall the subtitle of *Repetition*).
But by that he means that the portrayals, however imaginative rather
than documentary, are drawn from life, and in a double sense, since a
good psychological description will draw in something in addition to
what it draws from, making connections from the drawer's own experience but also enlarging it. Good experimental psychologists in this sense
will be in possession of the key to the totality from which all individual
variations can be deduced. But it is not an intellectual key, a thought,
not an idea in Hegel's sense; it is what Kierkegaard refers to as 'knowledge of human life, and sympathy for its interests'. Knowledge of this
kind requires a profound grasp of everything that slows or prevents the
emergence of self-conscious spirit, not least among the hindrances being
the forces that incline people to the view that self-conscious spirit can
be the subject of a science. The point is put succinctly towards the end
of *Anxiety*'s second chapter in a comment on what it means to say that
sin is selfishness:

[S]elf signifies precisely the contradiction of positing the general as the particular
[*det Enkelte*]. Only when the concept of the particular is given can there be any talk
of what is selfish. But regardless of there having lived countless millions of such
'selves', no science can say what the selfish is, without again stating it in perfectly
general terms. And this is the wonderful thing about life, that every human being
who gives heed to himself knows what no science knows, since he knows who he
himself is.

Here, says Haufniensis, lies the profound truth of the Greek saying
gnothi seauton, 'which for too long has been understood in the German
manner as pure self-consciousness, the airiness of idealism'.[27] Calling
into question the 'modern' principle that thought and being are one, an
accompanying footnote puts it even more sharply:

It is only the general that *is* just by being thought and by being thinkable (and not
only in imagination [*experimenterende*], for what can't be thought!), and *is* just *as* it
can be thought. The point in the particular is exactly its negative, repellent self-

relation to the general. But as soon as this is thought away it is annulled, and as soon as it is thought it is transformed, so that either one doesn't think it but only imagines one does, or does think it and simply imagines that it is included in the process of thought.

In its third chapter *Anxiety* then proceeds, still in a psychologically orienting way, to examine the forms that anxiety takes in the human synthesis's failure to reach that point where sin as something particular and individual is admitted to consciousness. Here Vigilius Haufniensis draws both on classical Greek philosophy and on a distinction which applies readily to the idea of subject–world alienation we encountered in Kierkegaard's dissertation. The distinction, familiar from Plato's *Parmenides*, is between Being and non-Being. In the dissertation on irony Kierkegaard spoke of the 'whole of existence' becoming alien to the ironic subject and the ironic subject in turn alien to existence'.[28] It isn't difficult to see how this can be made a description of man after the Fall. In a footnote we read:

The Christian view takes the position that the non-Being is present everywhere as nothing from which things are created, as semblance and vanity, as sin, as sensuousness removed from spirit, as the temporal forgotten by the eternal; consequently the task is to do away with it in order to bring forth Being.[29]

The Greek and the modern philosophical view sees the task as that of bringing what is not (or is not yet) into being; but the properly Christian view sees non-Being all around and seeks to replace it with actuality. The presence of non-Being in the shape of nothing may sound odd, but Haufniensis takes the case of the absent self, the nothing that is the particular which vanishes when you try to think it, insofar as to think is always to think in general terms which then fail to grasp the particular in its particularity. The chapter focuses on the ways in which the human 'synthesis', lacking the self or spirit that sustains it, anxiously projects its intimations of itself, as one might say, upon the world. According to Haufniensis it does so in ways that progressively acknowledge guilt, that is to say, the possibilities in respect of which the 'synthesis' glimpses its 'nonnatural' possibilities, and which its freedom swoons at the sight of, but which eventually, when freedom manages to raise itself up again, it sees as a matter of personal responsibility. Before coming that far, however, the nothingness that the synthesis for lack of a self projects its freedom onto is fate. Haufniensis sees this form of anxiety in paganism but also in corrupted forms of Christianity. He also discusses the case of the genius as an apparently anomalous example of someone whose freedom is to be understood as related to fate rather than guilt. The genius, however, does not appear to be afraid of fate. But that is because he feels it is his friend and that he has a pact with it. 'Genius', says Haufniensis, 'cannot grasp itself religiously, and so does not come to sin or providence, and that is why it comes under anxiety's relation to fate.'[30]

If the progression towards sin and Providence in which an omnipresent non-Being (semblance, vanity, sin, etc.) is to be replaced by reality itself, or Being, is to be a matter of *freedom*'s failures and eventual success, then however much psychology has to say in the matter, it must be allowed that the movements in that direction occur freely. The chapter in fact opens with a polemic against Hegel's notion of the transition as a logical one and appeals to Plato's notion of the 'instant' as the category in which the transition can be thought of as freely occurring. But Plato's view of the transition from non-Being to Being was the Greek one to which, along with that of modern philosophy, Haufniensis opposes the Christian view. Kierkegaard returns to the problem in the Interlude section of *Philosophical Fragments*, but here, in an untitled section on time and change which introduces the above discussion, Haufniensis brings the instant down to earth by refurbishing Plato's account of it. For Plato the instant is an abstraction, something that you cannot fit into the process of change, which is unremittingly successive. It lies outside time and is in that sense the eternal. But Haufniensis wants to say, as he does in concluding another tightly written footnote, that 'it is only with Christianity that sensuousness, the temporal, the instant, are to be understood, precisely because it is only with it that the eternal becomes essential'.[31]

This again has to do with the Christian view that non-Being is already here and not in some limbo waiting to be transformed into Being. The abstract notion of the instant is a consequence of the ordinary spatial or linear view of time as succession. According to this the instant can only be something altogether abstract, a limiting concept. By acquiring a sense of the instant as 'now', and not abstracted from a spatialized continuum but as containing both past and future, we synthesize the temporal and eternal by incorporating the latter into the former. The eternal is then no longer the 'future' (as it is for innocence), or the 'past' (as it is for the Greeks), but the present. It is the 'instant' (*Øieblik* – literally, glance of the eye), that 'ambiguity' in which 'time and eternity touch one another'. The instant defines the present *as* a present, and not as a vanishing and abstract time-slice cut out of a time-continuum. Instead of being defined in relation to past and future, the present becomes (in some sense) identical with past and future. Since nature and sensate life belong essentially to time and history, they have to be defined in relation to both past and future. Their 'imperfection' is that they can have no eternal qualification in which their past and future can be incorporated, brought home to bear, in a 'now'. Thus, and this is the point, it is only by positing the instant that the past and future (*Tilkommende* – literally, what is to come) can be grasped as they are – as dimensions of the individual's existence. Otherwise, as Haufniensis also notes, the central Christian concepts of conversion, atonement, and redemption are lost sight of; they become merely dimensions of individual and world-historical evolution. In short, the instant is not really an atom of time but of eternity; it is 'the first reflection of eternity in time, its first attempt as it were at bringing time to a stop'.[32]

In whatever way the revised notion of the instant makes it possible to grasp the movement towards a sense of guilt and sin as freely occurring (and this is essential if the guilt is to be or to include a sense of responsibility for holding onto one's 'naturalness'), it cannot be Haufniensis's intention that the mere occupancy of 'now' betokens the presence of freedom, spirit, and therefore of anxiety. In fact the first of the sections of the third chapter to be given a heading accounts for the case of 'spiritlessness' (*Aandløshed*) in which there is no anxiety, or at least – since even here Haufniensis must insist that the schema of the synthesis applies – it is there but 'hidden and masked'. Not only that, he equates the spectacle of such a spiritless person with the horror we would feel at the idea of the Grim Reaper making a professional appearance in the guise of a courteous entertainer.[33]

When spirit, guilt, and sin are 'posited' (i.e., acknowledged by the individual, now a self, as part of its world) the object of anxiety ceases to be nothing and is 'something' instead. It is in fact sin, and *Anxiety*'s fourth chapter offers a typology in which we are introduced to the Kierkegaardian notion of the 'demonic'. Armed with the concepts of good and evil, the individual is first anxious about not measuring up to the requirements of the good, an anxiety that implies the self's Christian possibilities (the good) are still targeted. But then the next development, by making the individual conscious of the separation from its world that has to take place if the Christian possibilities are to be realized (since they do not straightforwardly reconcile the individual with its world), is one in which the individual instead of respecting the good, fears or even hates it. This anxiety in the face of good rather than evil is 'the demonic'.[34]

This, then, with the addition of a short and, by general agreement, hastily written final chapter on the spiritually educative possibilities of anxiety, or Hamann's holy hypochondria, is the work about which it has been claimed that it was written in jest as a parody of the learned treatise. Given the extent of the text's departure from the norms of the genre, and knowing what we do of Kierkegaard's polemical bent, that claim may have some initial plausibility. But the text itself gives no direct indication that it is not making an appeal to our understanding, so it would be unwise to accept the claim as it stands and merely en passant. It is nevertheless worth teasing out certain claims that can underlie the allegation of parody.

What might strike some as deliberately odd about *Anxiety* is the presentation of its topic in the form of a kind of Hegelian 'phenomenology'. It is absurd, surely, to suppose that a psychological topic such as anxiety can lend itself to the same treatment as the topic of spirit as emerging self-consciousness. Doesn't self-consciousness precisely break out of the psychological context in which it is enmeshed? Who would ever think of providing a special itinerary in a 'world-historical' account of spiritual growth for a mere state of mind? But the answer is surely that the enmeshing psychology that dogs the emergence of self-conscious spirit makes the historical approach altogether appropriate. This particular state of mind follows self-conscious spirit all the way and provides the increasingly evident background against which it must battle all the more, whether in an active or an actively self-deceptive way. This topic is one for which the Hegelian format is admirably suited. That the direction in which emerging self-consciousness takes us here is the exact opposite of that intended in Hegel's *Phenomenology* or in the *Aesthetics* doesn't render inappropriate the historical form employed by those works. On the contrary, as the gap between subject and object increases, the intellectual and psychological risks of reconciliation become at once more apparent and more critical, setting the scene for a properly human struggle, the real form of any 'history', and more real from the human point of view than anything Hegel offers. True, what *Anxiety* describes is also a development within the *individual* self-consciousness, not only of spirit in Hegel's historical and collective sense; but Haufniensis's section on 'objective' anxiety could well find its place there.

Among *Anxiety*'s Hegelian readers there could be a perceived irony in the thought that the grasp a treatise of this kind customarily imparts is one that assists the reader towards enjoyment of an intellectual unity with the world. Here, if we believe what we are told, the more we know, the more distant we should feel from the world. More than that, among the things we are to grasp in this case is the total irrelevance, in respect of what it really takes for self-confirmation, of a merely intellectual exercise of this kind. But given what has just been said, even that would not show that the treatise form is so glaringly inappropriate as to force us to conclude that the choice of it was deliberately ironical on Kierkegaard's part.

What is true, if *Anxiety* is right about what is required, is that the work itself cannot claim to touch the heart of the matter it discusses. To understand anxiety requires an imaginative ability to see how the things discussed hang together in a life, and a treatise could never accomplish that purpose. But if we now ask what job this treatise-like work is nevertheless intended to perform and why Kierkegaard chose this form, we find the obvious answer to the first of these two questions in the subtitle. It is pointing *from* a psychological perspective towards that general topic, much discussed at the time (recall the title of Martensen's dissertation), of self-consciousness or consciousness of self. The perspective calls for a repositioning of the topic in the developmental framework with which Kierkegaard's readers were familiar from their first- or (typically) second-hand acquaintance with Hegel. In a way, the repositioning and the emphasis given to psychology (in Kierkegaard's sense) take the whole topic out of the hands of those who had written and would go on writing learned treatises on it. Even if the topic (along with the psychological phenomena inextricably bound up with it) has a historical dimension, it does not lend itself to a systematic treatment that marks a preordained conceptual progression. That is why we read in a footnote that although Rosenkranz's *Psychology* (which Haufniensis says he assumes his readers have read) makes a good deal of sense, it would have been better if the author had eschewed 'his rhapsodic superstition for an empty [and highfalutin] schema'.[35] But given the theological and philosophical framework that Kierkegaard shared with his erudite readers, it was certainly appropriate to show in what way philosophical and theological concepts should be rearranged to correct the wrong impression given of the nature of anxiety and other relevant psychological states by Rosenkranz and others, including Schelling,[36] to say nothing of those who, like Heiberg, regarded psychology as in principle irrelevant.

As for the choice of the treatise form, even if the author claims not to be writing a learned book he is at least addressing the learned. It is, you might say, the right kind of envelope on which to write that address. There could be an element of mischief in this: the addressees might take *Anxiety*, with its style unsuited to the form, as a deliberate demonstration of Heiberg's much-touted Hegelian principle that present developments can no longer be contained in forms inherited from the past. There would indeed be a wonderful irony in this, since the example would be an application of the principle to Heiberg himself. But since Kierkegaard was to use the treatise form in a recognizably Hegelian format at least twice again, in *Postscript* and *The Sickness unto Death*, the latter when any polemic directed at either Hegel or Heiberg had long since lost any point, it is unlikely that this subtle dig is what lay behind the choice of form. The answer may be a purely practical one. The well-established treatise form provided a mould into which his rapidly reassembled and not easily organized thoughts could conveniently fall. And besides, even if he had entertained no iconoclastic intentions, Kierkegaard would have been quite happy to show that he could produce writings with a properly academic look about them. If there was also the thought that in adopting the form he was presenting a parody of the academic genre, so much the better. His main interest, however, was the admittedly polemical but nevertheless respectable one of presenting to his learned readers the thought that what arises in the dawning of self-consciousness is awareness of the omnipresence not of Being but of non-Being, and also an awareness of what it takes to attain to Being, that is to say, to be a real individual in a real world. There is another thought, perhaps not uppermost at the time but surfacing, and that is that having an intellectual interest of this kind must be provisional. Thinking forward to *Postscript* we might see already in this earlier work some hint of the 'humour' in which Kierkegaard had so long been interested in connection with Christianity, and which he finds in the 'objective' treatment of topics the appropriate mood for which is 'seriousness'. Humour in this sense is not dismissive, it is the ability (though if exercised beyond its role it becomes a culpable disability) to view ethically significant questions dispassionately from a distance.

In sum, it makes more sense to read Kierkegaard's *Anxiety* – and it was only at the last minute that he decided to publish it under a pseudonym – as an attempt to make serious capital out of a long apprenticeship in philosophy and theology, and among other things to demonstrate an academic ability to those whose colleague he would like (also them) to think he might have been, not least because he knew they had always suspected that he was not serious, than as a deliberate attempt to tease them or to flout before their very eyes the fatal limitations of their cherished medium – the learned treatise.

Reading *Anxiety* seriously also allows certain aspects to surface that might otherwise be lost to view, for instance its resumption of reflections from the journals, even as early as 1834. These, on predestination, are related to others, from 1837, on freedom, evil, and hereditary sin,[37] all relevant to the case in hand. Indeed, *Anxiety* is readable as offering its readership a totally novel conception of sin. No longer something collective that we just find ourselves in, brought about once and for all by the original Fall, and not linked directly to sensuality, sin is rather the result of the latter being seen in a peculiarly acute way as in opposition to man's spiritual side. Sin, far from being our divinely sealed fate, is 'posited' when the individual becomes aware of itself as having the structure that Kierkegaard calls a 'synthesis', that tension of opposites. Sin is the inherent tendency, in one's increasing clarity over the cost of not benefiting from the advantages of being 'spirit', to be willing, as it were, nevertheless to pay that price.

The work which Kierkegaard began in March, *Philosophical Fragments*, presents a curious (some might say 'paradoxical', others 'ironical') contrast. Here the subject-matter seems to dictate the treatise form. Yet what we get is a five-act play, even an opera, one might think even a comic one, since the author is a 'humorist', with an 'intermezzo' (*Mellemspil*) between the fourth and fifth acts. The rather complicated system of sections and subsections does suggest, however, more an attempt to let the content find its own form than a precast mould which might

betoken a deliberate demonstration of the inability of a traditional form
to cope with new material. The evidence is that *Fragments* acquired its
present shape in the final revision. Originally Kierkegaard planned a
work consisting of independent parts under the title 'Philosophical
Pieces [*Piecer* – in the literary sense] or Just a Tiny Bit of Philosophy
[*eller en Smule Philosophi*] by S. Kierkegaard'.[38] In spite of the reorganization and last-minute changes, compared to *Anxiety* the impression
Fragments gives is of a less hectically compiled work. Its language is
concise and often, fittingly for its artistic form, has the pregnance of
poetry. It is, like *Anxiety*, based on a theological theme, in this case the
Incarnation. Here, similarly, there is no attempt to exploit either rhetorically or in the content itself the humour of the contrast between worldly
preoccupation and the Christian reduction of it to worthlessness.

But *Fragments* is, in this too like *Anxiety*, concerned with the relation
between non-Being and Being. However, whereas *Anxiety*'s dogmatic
theme, hereditary sin, concerns the loss of Being reexperienced by every
dawning self-conscious life, *Fragments* focuses on the Incarnation as the
Christian's remedy for the retrieval of Being, though it couches the
problem in what looks at least on the surface like traditionally philosophical terms. The opening sentence of the first chapter asks, 'How far
does the truth admit of being learned?'

This theme is more sharply focused on the title page, on which
appears the following threefold question: 'Can there be a historical point
of departure for an eternal consciousness; how can such a thing be of
more than historical interest; can one build an eternal happiness on a
piece of historical knowledge [*en historisk Viden*]?' The earlier version
had a first-personal focus (emphases added): 'Can there be a historical
point of departure for *my* eternal consciousness; how can such a thing
interest *me* more than historically; how can *I* build *my* blessedness on a
piece of historical knowledge?' In its published form the topic was given
the appearance of being raised from an impersonal, objective viewpoint.
To signal this more objective viewpoint Kierkegaard disclaims formal
authorship of the work, assigning it to Johannes Climacus, though
retaining his own name on the title page as publisher-editor.

We recall that the name Johannes Climacus had actually appeared in
the title of the manuscript of a philosophical project written during
1842–43, about the time *Either/Or* was in press. 'Johannes Climacus
eller De Omnibus Dubitandum est' (Johannes Climacus or Everything

Is to Be Doubted) was never completed. Subtitled 'A Tale' (*Fortælling*), it was the story of a young student, Johannes Climacus, whose ambition was to reach an eternal consciousness not, as it happens, by way of history but in the accepted manner of the philosopher. Whatever the autobiographical element (we took its authenticity for granted in Chapter 3 in drawing on two passages, one of which illuminated Kierkegaard's imaginative childhood experiences with his father and another, later, his meeting through his father with the thrilling world of dialectics and disputation), the Johannes in the story is not straightforwardly the Kierkegaard who had once thought of publishing 'De Omnibus'. Johannes Climacus is less the real Kierkegaard in disguise than a name given to a fictive character with a point of view which someone might genuinely adopt, though that would not of course have prevented Kierkegaard's own name from appearing on the title page as author. In the work itself Kierkegaard shows that he is perfectly capable of adopting the philosophical stance himself, and in a journal entry he even describes it as an exercise in the Hegelian manner: 'my first attempt to develop a little speculation.'[39]

In fact the drift of the speculation is to undermine the philosophical ambitions of speculative philosophy itself. It is an attempt to restate questions that the 'newer' philosophy took itself to have found better ways of posing, but without satisfactorily solving or dissolving them. This could still be called philosophy, and, as the above remark indicates, there was a time when Kierkegaard seems to have been on the point of publishing a piece of philosophy under his own name. The impression is strengthened by an earlier journal entry from the winter of 1842–43: 'Cartesius [Descartes] has put a major part of his system into the first six Meditations. So one doesn't always have to write systems. I shall publish "Philosophical Meditations" [*Betragtninger*] in pamphlets and can come out with my provisional views in these. It might not be such a bad thing to write in Latin.'[40] But as time passed Kierkegaard had got caught up with the questions that preoccupied him in *Fear and Trembling* and *Repetition*, and when he returned to the philosophical themes of the would-be meditations, his mind was focused once more on the question that had occupied him from his earliest student years, the relation between Christianity and philosophy. That, too, would no doubt have been a subject for the philosophical meditations, but Kierkegaard was now consciously adopting the point of view of Christianity.

In *Fragments*, the 'piece' of philosophy (now 'just a bit' of philosophy) that finally emerged, philosophy as any kind of investigation into the truth, whether the piecemeal system of a Descartes or the comprehensive enterprise of a Hegel, is contrasted with what Mynster had referred to as a 'supernatural' point of view. It was presumably when it came to the final reorganization of the work and he realized that it had after all the form of a philosophical meditation, raising the question of an eternal consciousness and blessedness in general, that is to say in impersonal terms, that Kierkegaard decided at the last moment to remove the first-personal references in the title and make his former philosophical persona, Johannes Climacus, its author.

The original Climacus, a monk who flourished in the seventh century in a Sinai monastery and later as a hermit, was so called as author of a book informing monks *gradatim* how, and against what obstacles, to achieve the perfect life, *Scala paradisi* (or in the original Greek *Klimaks tou paradeísou*, published in English as St Johannes's *The Ladder of Divine Ascent*).[41] We noted earlier, in Chapter 6, Kierkegaard's reference in a 1839 journal entry to Hegel as a 'Johannes *Climacus*' who does not storm the heavens, like the giants, by setting mountain upon mountain, but 'climbs aboard them by way of his syllogisms'.[42] 'De Omnibus' concludes with a brief quasi-Hegelian account of the origin of doubt and correspondingly of the place of faith. The account in fact turns Hegel's own thought upside down: faith for Hegel belongs to the initial stage of immediacy, doubt arising through the inner separations that occur in one's grasp of the world when it is exposed to distinctions of understanding through reflection. Unity is then regained at a higher level through the cognizing subject's ability to resolve all the oppositions in a unifying conceptual grasp of itself. This was the drift and itinerary of Martensen's lectures, lectures that in the winter of 1838–39 aroused Kierkegaard to reflect philosophically on his own account. Martensen had acknowledged Descartes as the first to pronounce the principles of 'Protestant Philosophy' but claimed that it was only through the German philosophers that these principles had first been put fully into effect. Martensen distinguished Protestant from Catholic philosophy as having a subjective as against an objective principle. Its main idea was the familiar one that after the confusion of the scholastics one had to 'make an entirely fresh start' (*begynde heelt forfra*), which meant doubting everything. 'De Omnibus' takes its theme from the point of departure Martensen chose for his lectures, but the motivation was in Martensen's later elaboration of what he had said in those popular lectures. In 1841 he had published *Grundrids til Moralphilosophiens System* (Outline for a System of Moral Philosophy), in which it was made clear that, and how, Hegel's largely theoretical philosophy could be given an ethical and religious supplement.[43] 'De Omnibus' goes to the root of the whole project by examining the notion of doubt and its overcoming on which philosophy is supposed to rest. It sets out, as a kind of Cartesian project in reverse, to demonstrate the impossibility of philosophy. It is an investigation into the claims that philosophizing must begin with doubt, that doubt is what actually prompts one to philosophize, and that modern philosophy really does begin with doubt,[44] and read in one way it appears to be a reductio of these claims. In the tale, Johannes is put through his paces as a cautionary example to the philosophers, or to anyone who would take these claims seriously. Its own philosophy, particularly towards the end, verges in its telegrammatic brevity on the impenetrable, but the outcome is easy enough to see. Doubt is not a task one sets oneself at the beginning, then to be overcome by dialectical and speculative thought; rather it is something first made possible by positing an ideal in relation to what is actual. As the scope of the ideality increases, so too does the doubt, until it is overwhelming. The question arises whether, when the doubt is not merely intellectual, it is indeed possible to doubt to that degree.

The text contains several anticipations of views and thoughts Kierkegaard was to exploit later. One of these is that doubt is an attitude we actively adopt, or try to adopt, rather than something we succumb to in the face of uncertainty. Uncertainty is distinguished from ignorance, in which doubt is absent, and Kierkegaard suggests that doubt is that 'higher moment' in uncertainty where I settle for a negative attitude towards a claim – for instance, 'that ghosts exist' – an attitude that amounts to less, of course, than straightforward denial.[45] Like irony and anxiety, doubt proper is not just doubt about this or that, for instance ghosts, but about everything.[46] Kierkegaard also makes the point that he was to have Climacus make later in criticism of the author of *Either/Or*'s treatment of Assessor Wilhelm's despair, namely that really to doubt everything leaves you with no purchase on anything, no foothold or handhold that will help to bring you back, or for that matter – since the doubt is total – to recover reality or Being; for in doubting *everything* you must use every resource you have ('*all* your strength').[47]

Another thought crucial for later is that one may get rid of doubt, or again try to do so, by eliminating the ideality that generates the interest in respect of which doubt first arises. Thus, genuine doubt arises only in connection with what interests the individual. Christianity (in particular its Protestant version) has given man, or rather it has revealed, a specific interest in being a 'self'. One may think of this in terms of Martensen's distinction as a 'subjective' version of the goal of the original Climacus's *Scala paradisi*, the achievement of the perfect life. But the focus on selfhood doesn't just add to the difficulties in the way of achieving that life, it threatens in some ways to undermine the very basis for trying to achieve it. If fulfilment has to be conceived in these terms, then we may be tempted to abandon the whole project – something Kierkegaard was later to call 'despair' – and of course with it, conveniently, the doubt to which positing this particular ideality can give rise.

Another important point is the 'disinterested' nature of reflection. Reflection is concerned with the 'possibility' of particular reality-to-ideality relations, treating them as a 'dichotomy' (terms that match or don't) in which nothing else is involved. By 'possibility' Kierkegaard means thoughts, whether taken for true or not, that are entertained from a point of view which does not engage one personally. This includes all 'knowledge' (*Viden* – literally, knowing). Kierkegaard mentions mathematical, aesthetic, and metaphysical knowledge.[48] But reflection is not the same as consciousness.[49] Unlike reflection, whose topics are posed 'dichotomously' – 'such as ideality and reality, soul and body, knowing – the truth, willing – the good, loving – beauty, God, the world etc.' – consciousness is 'trichotomous', an actual working instance of such a relation. More than just a relation, it is a rela*ting*. Thus in the ascent from ignorance to uncertainty that gives room for the act of doubting, we see how in cases of personal concern, or concern over one's person or self, genuine doubt occurs against a background of what might be called strained reality/ideality relations. According to 'De Omnibus' consciousness would never arise if ideality and reality 'in all innocence got along with each other'.[50] The task of consciousness is to synthesize wherever gaps appear causing doubt, not on the mere cognitive level but where what causes the gaps are the special problems of Protestant selfhood.

In a metaphor suited to its form, the scene is now set for *Fragments*. The cases of doubt that Kierkegaard is concerned with are not cognitive or theoretical (what he calls bringing reality [*Realitet*] into relation with ideality), nor those concerned with prudent practice or rational decision, but those in which idealities defining the perfection of the *self* are brought into relation with a given human reality, so the question of knowledge that *Fragments* raises is that of knowledge of how to be a fulfilled self. How far does the truth in *this* matter 'admit of being learned?'

The questions that appear on the title page concern historical knowledge. Christian knowledge is supposed to stem from certain facts recorded by the apostles. The authenticity of the reports and of the texts embodying them should thus be essential to learning the Christian truth. The point was not a new one for Kierkegaard. Already in some of his very earliest journal entries he had criticized Grundtvig's reliance on the authenticity of original texts as revelations of the truths claimed by Christianity.[51] On the contrary, notes Kierkegaard, the words have become enriched through time, acquiring greater and deeper meaning. On Grundtvig he had said:

It occurs to me that Grundtvig looks on the development of Christian understanding not as progress down a difficult road but like a steam conveyance running on a railway, with steam fired up by the apostles, so that Christian understanding is prepared in closed machines.[52]

In notes preparatory to *Fragments* Kierkegaard returns to Grundtvig but to make another point, namely that even though Grundtvigians were right to claim that the church existed, since existence is not to be proved, their claim that the church was apostolic introduced a historical element that did call for proof. An essential point made in *Fragments*, though without mentioning Christianity until the last pages, is the anti-Grundtvigian one that truths of history are contingent and are all that Christians have to go on. The case with the apostolic church which claims to preserve the living word in the sacraments is exactly the same, says Kierkegaard, as with the Bible.[53] It makes no difference, either, whether you were an apostle or are a contemporary believer. Just as in *Anxiety* the notion of hereditary sin is presented as a repeatable discov-

ery that can dawn in each individual, in *Fragments* Christian understanding is made available to everyone on the same basis, however close
to or far from the alleged historical facts. Indeed, the facts are, in a way,
neither here nor there. Referring to the disputes over the Bible's historical accuracy, Kierkegaard says, 'This is just delusion since the very
moment one has defended the whole Bible one can have lost everything,
and the very moment one has lost the Bible one can have won everything'.[54]

In his reading of Brøchner's translation of Strauss's *Die Christliche
Glaubenslehre* Kierkegaard would have come across a reference to Lessing's assertion that accidental historical events can never prove necessary truths of reason. Strauss gives a full account of Lessing's use of the
notion of a leap in the latter's *Über den Beweis des Geistes und der Kraft*.[55]
Questioning the assumption that if Christ's words could be authenti-
cated, his claim to be the Son of God would be more than just historically certain, since the recorders of these facts were inspired and
therefore infallible, Lessing says in respect of his vantage-point with
regard to the truth of such a claim that here there is a wide and
'repugnant' chasm which he cannot cross. Lessing had used Leibniz's
distinction between truths of fact and truths of reason to argue that no
such consequences can be derived from merely historical truths. Even
if everything said in the Bible were true, all the claims made on behalf
of Christianity could still be false. Conversely, even if what the Bible
said were false, the latter claims might still be true. As Lessing says:
'The letter is not the spirit, and the Bible is not religion, so that
objections against the letter, or against the Bible, are not *ipso facto*
objections against religion.'[56]

Kierkegaard planned an expression of gratitude to Lessing in *Fragments*, but along with a good deal of other material originally intended
for that work, he kept his comments on Lessing for the later *Postscript*.
Originally, *Fragments* (then 'Pieces') was to have had three parts, but in
the end it contained only the first, the other two becoming, by comparison, its much larger 'Postscript'. Heading the first chapter of the
published version is a '*propositio*', a statement of the stance assumed by
the author. It reads: 'The question is asked in ignorance, by someone
who doesn't even know what made him ask such a thing.' What question? It is the question already cited: 'How far does the truth admit of
being learned?'[57] The *propositio* was originally the first of two 'positions',

the second being: 'the one in ignorance who though knowing historically what he is asking about, seeks the answer.'[58] A third part was to provide both the question and the manner of seeking the answer with its historical identity. But the author failed to come that far. He talks at the end of the published version of a 'next section of this piece' which would 'call the matter by its real name and . . . clothe the problem in its historical costume'. That would turn out to be the brief first part of *Postscript*. Just following this comment in the published version there appears a passage originally intended for the beginning of the work. As originally intended it reads:

As we know, Christianity is the only historical phenomenon which, in spite of the historical, yes precisely by means of the historical, has wanted to be the point of departure for the individual's eternal consciousness, has wanted to interest him otherwise than just historically, has wanted to base his blessedness on his relation to something purely historical. No philosophy, no mythology, no historical knowledge has had that idea, of which it then may be said – is that a recommendation or the opposite? – that it did not arise in the heart of any man. For these three areas would have to produce analogies for this self-contradictory duplicity, if such are to be found. But we will forget this, and have done so as though Christianity had never existed; on the contrary, we will make use of the unlimited discretion of a hypothesis, assuming that that question was an idea we had come by, and which we will now not give up until the answer is given. . . . [59]

Appearing at the end of the published work, the phrase 'we will forget this' has been changed to 'this I have to some extent wished to forget'.[60]

That *Fragments* could appear as an exploitation of the 'unlimited discretion of a hypothesis' had several significant implications. It meant that specific questions of historical fact could be altogether ignored, so that the questioner was free to consider the idea of an historical basis for an eternal consciousness in its own right, as a 'thought-experiment,' as the title of the first chapter has it. But being able to assume that he has thought up the whole idea by himself, the questioner is also released from the personal hold that the question in its actual 'historical costume' has on him. His discussion of it will therefore be general, and it will not only be appropriate but right to present the questions in the more objective versions that Kierkegaard gave them in the revised version of the title page. This also meant it was possible to present the whole questioning not as his own but in the style of one who has seriously tried the philosophical approach, namely the Johannes Climacus of 'De

Omnibus Dubitandum Est'. Who better to prepare the way to showing
the requirements of faith than one who has grasped the true scope of
its opposite, doubt?

Still, as the passage above indicates, Climacus is not a philosopher in
the sense of a thinker who aims to establish the answer to his question
in the medium of thought. In the published version the phrase 'for that
is only for thought' is inserted parenthetically after 'philosophy' (similarly 'only for imagination' after 'mythology', and 'for memory' after
'historical knowledge'). So *Fragments* is written from a point of view
from which the criticism that something doesn't stand to reason is not
allowed to be decisive. In fact the core of *Fragments*, what it gives the
impression of urging most insistently and seriously, is the illusory nature of the shock one feels when something fundamental proves to be
unintelligible. One should not be shocked that the truth is neither
communicable in propositions nor able to be validated by reason, nor
even that it is, by rational standards, absurd.

After indicating that a succeeding 'section' will provide the historical
costume, Climacus adds: 'if I ever do write a next section – an author
of pieces as I am has no serious intent, as you will doubtless hear said
of me; why, then, should I now end up by pretending a seriousness in
order to please people by making what is maybe a large promise? For
writing a piece is frivolity but to promise the System, that's a serious
matter and it has made many a man serious in his own and in others'
eyes'.

The multilayered irony is worth unpacking. Kierkegaard appears
under the flimsy disguise of his pseudonym first of all to be having a
dig at his rivals quite independent of his views on their System-
mongering. There may even be a touch of envy and sour-grapes. He
was also no doubt prepared for accusations of frivolity; they were something he had grown accustomed to, and by playing on that experience
he was arming himself against a repetition. At a deeper level, however,
Climacus is accusing their own seriousness of being baseless. In other
words it is they who are frivolous. If the truth that matters depends on
an historical event which for all a human intellect can tell will never be
more than historical and therefore contingent, then a superior intellect
is not going to put you in a better position to find it. Serious promises
in this respect from an intellectual elite will therefore be ludicrous, and
no one should take them seriously. A more than just personal bite is

being added here to the irony; readers are being asked to see that what Kierkegaard fails to provide is not anything that anyone could provide – assuming, that is, that an historical point of departure is the only one we have. A serious point is being made against Hegelian apologists and any others, not least the Grundtvigians, who obscure the radical implications of a purely historical point of departure. There might even here be a personal factor. In presenting a position that is (as we are to guess) Christianity's, but purified on the one side of the right-wing Hegelian absorption of the articles of Christian belief into a universe of philosophical discourse that purportedly leaves the 'merely' contingent and historical behind, and on the other of the new left-wing controversies that focused only on the historical, Kierkegaard is saving a place for the religion of his father, a religion of 'personality' and of resolute faith, open to anyone – except for intellectuals for whom the term has lost all meaning. A certain anti-intellectualism is being asserted here, too, except that it is put into the learned hands of Climacus, a would-be philosopher. That means into the hands of someone not yet asking how his *own* eternal happiness can be reached but interested enough in the idea to pursue a thought-experiment. What that thought-experiment does is to compare the demands made by a Christian promise based on an historical event to a traditional and what Climacus calls 'Socratic' position regarding truths that matter.

The five chapters of *Fragments*, a work of less than a hundred pages in the new edition, divide into two parts separated by an 'Interlude' representing the eighteen hundred years or so that separate the time of Christ from Kierkegaard's time. There are five chapters in all, together with the intermezzo or interlude. The first part (comprising four chapters, one with an appendix) presents the 'thought-experiment'. It opposes to a position called Socratic (or A), in which every person is in possession of the conditions for learning the truth (as in the famous example of the slave-boy in Plato's *Meno*) and only needs to have the truth drawn from him by appropriate prompting, another (called B) in which the conditions for learning the truth must be given by the teacher. There follows a 'literary attempt' (or 'essay' [*Forsøg*]) conveying in imagery the kind of relationship 'the' God (the eternal God become a particular being in time) must have to the learner of truth if there is to be no deception. The parable of the king who woos a humble maiden and cannot raise her up to his own level or impress her with his magnificence without destroying, and thus not giving, the condition of truth, leaves us with the idea that the one who imparts the conditions for learning the truth (the 'teacher' and 'saviour') must do so freely and in the guise of a servant – out of love, since God is not forced by any necessity to incarnate. But unlike any human fiction, the idea thus conveyed, namely that God *needs* the learner, is unintelligible and miraculous. The third chapter ('The Absolute Paradox: A Metaphysical Fancy') reverts to the contrast between A and B and suggests that thinking, by its very nature, provided the reader takes himself to be more than just his thinkings ('forsaavidt han jo tænkende er ikke blot sig selv'), passionately invites its own undoing.[61] For the thinker, to allow that he is more than his thinkings is to admit to ignorance about what he is, which is to say that he lacks and needs to be given the condition for knowing what human Being is. What, however, if the notion of these conditions being given is an absolute paradox, as it is if the point of departure is exclusively historical? The ideality involved requires a 'leap' which occurs in an 'instant', that is to say *outside* time.[62] There is an argument to the effect that those who try to establish the ideality's intellectual credentials by proving God's existence already assume it and therefore also assume they have successfully taken the leap. Climacus speaks as though the ideality is really a background assumption in our ordinary lives, so that any attempt to prove God's existence involves an attempt to forget one's own. As soon as I leave off my attempt to prove God's existence, God's existence springs back and 'is there'. This leaving off and letting go are what one must do, for to let reason decide the fate of the paradox is to assume that you know what man is. A short appendix suggests that the reader should reorient himself or herself outside thought and into a way of thinking in which the sense of outrage provoked by the paradox proves to be only an 'acoustic illusion'. The fourth chapter ('The Case of the Contemporary Disciple') says that there is no advantage, as far as what has been said so far, in being the teacher's contemporary.

The interlude then simulates the period from the time of the teacher to the present, and the main text resumes with the concluding fifth chapter ('The Disciple at Second Hand'). As for the interlude itself, the points made there appear not to be part of the thought-experiment introduced at the beginning but philosophical notions that would be required were the B-position outlined there true. We are given a glimpse, as it were, of the philosophical machinery behind the scenes, or offered a short visit to the sorcerer's kitchen. It may well be a device in subtle jest to allow Kierkegaard – in what in a real drama or opera would be light entertainment between acts (an *entracte*) – to speak his own philosophical mind. Or is he just demonstrating to his colleagues that he has one? Whatever the personal motive, the interlude is still an integral part of the overall 'argument', and its few pages present the most concentrated set of philosophical thoughts to be found in all of Kierkegaard. In brief summary of what is already a masterpiece of conciseness, the gist of this intermezzo which its author presents in 'a spirit of jest and earnest', is as follows.[63]

To come into being is a change but not in what comes into being, for otherwise what existed would not be what had not yet done so. A plan, if implemented, must be the same plan after implementation as before, otherwise *it* would not have been implemented. If there was a plan in the nature of things that was *self*-implementing, then that implementation would not be a change even in that sense – because the plan's coming into being would have been part of the original plan, and we would have determinism. Coming into being happens freely, and that is why its movement (*kinesis*) differs from that (*alloiosis*) of the transformations (including ceasing to exist) that occur in things that have already come into being. The change that is coming into being is future-oriented and takes place freely. It is in every case caused but not in the sense that causes are thought by some to be the same as logical grounds, for even if natural laws allow deductions of their consequences, the natural objects they are about have still come into existence freely. Space is the category of nature which, by being God's creation, has that much history. But within it lies another history whose category is time and in which Being has still, as it were, to be 'come into'. With regard to certainty, its not having yet done so does not differentiate it from the historical past, for no necessity is bestowed upon historical events post mortem simply because they are 'there'. The past too has come about freely. Therefore, with whatever justified certainty we believe what historians and others tell us, in respect of its origin the past is as uncertain as the future. And this must be the same even for those who were contemporary with the events. In general, it makes no difference how close to the events you are, for their coming into existence – and that *is* their historicity – remains forever cognitively elusive. To believe, either as contemporary or on the basis of testimony, is to give one's assent, otherwise it is to treat what you believe as though it were unhistorical.

The interlude demonstrates, just as reading it requires, considerable erudition but also a close knowledge of Kierkegaard's sources. These include Parmenides, Aristotle, Epicurus, the Stoics, Megarians, Cicero, Boethius, Spinoza, Leibniz, and Lessing, as well as ideas from Møller and Sibbern.[64] But its role is clear even to the uninitiated. And the fact that it has one is signalled by the brief appendix following it called 'Application' (*Anvendelse*).[65] With regard to the transition from non-Being to Being, which is a movement from the possible to the actual brought about by a freely acting cause, it puts us all in the same boat both epistemically and practically. Epistemically we are excluded from the action of Creation but as free agents we are able, by taking on the conditions for learning given in the teacher's example, to participate in it by actively transforming our lives. Once we realize in the light of this truth that the characteristics we possess are negative, we see that Being is a possibility still left open for us to actualize by our own free action. Just as the past is to be looked upon not as necessary just because past and immoveable, but as the freely caused coming into Being of what was possible but not yet, so too is that movement open to us now insofar as there are possibilities so far unfulfilled and which, so long as they remain so, mean that we are still in a state of non-Being.

Fragments ends with a 'moral':

This project goes indisputably further than the Socratic one, as is apparent at every point. Whether it is therefore more true than the Socratic is quite another question, which cannot be decided in the same breath, since here a new organ has been assumed: Faith; and a new presupposition: the consciousness of sin; a new decision: the instant, and a new teacher, the God in time, without which I would certainly never have dared present myself for inspection before that ironist admired through the centuries, whom I approach with a palpitating enthusiasm that yields to none. But to make an advance upon Socrates and yet say essentially the same things as he, only not quite so well – that at least is not Socratic.[66]

Recall that in his dissertation Kierkegaard had given Socrates a central place by having him represent the capacity for irony that precedes the self's properly individual constitution. He had nevertheless criticized Socrates for focusing only on individuals 'numerically' and failing to grasp the importance of the social whole for the ethics of substantial selfhood. In the second part of *Either/Or*, Kierkegaard had come to place the individual in the centre of ethics, as the 'concrete' set of abilities and opportunities that each individual must grasp in its situation, and in grasping which it is serving God's purpose. That was rather less Hegelian. But by the time of *Fragments* the starting-point for the project of substantializing the subject had moved to a more desolate position than that envisaged by the Assessor. It was in the understanding of *that* that the truth in Socrates's focus on individuals 'numerically' emerges, showing that he is a religious thinker for whom a relationship with the absolute is a presupposition for any return to the world. Nevertheless, and it is something that it shares with the history of philosophy subsequent to Socrates, the crux of the A-position is its assumption that the individual possesses the condition of truth. The individual has it in the form, not of reason certainly – after all Socrates is ignorant – but of the ability to expunge personal projects in favour of those enacted on behalf of the absolute source of the value of all things. What the thought-experiment in *Fragments* asks us to consider is the possibility of going further than that. It envisages the need to disabuse ourselves of the belief that we have the condition. Not having it, and having no other recourse than to history, we must suppose that the condition is given, to the one who believes, in an historical example. Which implies that notion of the God-man much discussed in debates surrounding what Mynster had called the 'new rationalism'. As Mynster said, 'When rationalism thinks that reason can help itself, and naturalism that nature can help itself, then in supernaturalism is recognized man's drive to another and higher help'. The God-man may signify several things: man's ideal of himself (Feuerbach), man's divinity (maybe Strauss), or God's humanity. The first two imply that Being is within our grasp, but the latter raises the stakes; it says there is more to Being than we can grasp. That idea is already implicit in the concept of repetition; in a journal entry from this same period Kierkegaard talks of 'the presuppositional basis of consciousness, or as it were, the [musical] key' being 'continually raised, but within each key the same [being] repeated'. Correspondingly, everything rational or natural has been lowered.[67] That is to say, the standard for what we assume is in our grasp if we do not already have it is raised so that we do not really have it, and to get it we must repeat it at a higher level.

Fragments has a motto: 'Better well hanged than ill-wed', a rendition

via the German translation of the clown's 'Many a good hanging prevents a bad marriage' from *Twelfth Night* (act 1, scene 5). It sounds as
though Kierkegaard were afraid that his thought-experiment might be
taken in the wrong way, perhaps by Hegelians who would soon find
where in their System to place it. But although we can safely assume
that Hegel is in his sights, that is not his immediate aim (indeed, the
thought that it was might be just that bad marriage to which he would
prefer a hanging). The A-position, and its later development, what will
be called religiousness A, is already an advance upon Hegel – or at least
upon the general tenor of Hegelian philosophy. In a journal entry
already drawn from, Kierkegaard talks of the 'accursed mendacity that
entered philosophy with Hegel'. To recapture an honest view of things,
he appears to say, we need to start again in antiquity, of whose philosophy modern thought is merely a distortion. He speaks of the 'endless
insinuation and betrayal, and the parading and spinning-out of one or
another single passage in Greek philosophy', and says that 'the Greeks
will remain my consolation'.

It is in the same passage that he admits to 'De Omnibus' having been
an attempt 'to develop a little speculation'. He also admits that 1844,
this year of *Anxiety* and *Fragments*, was the one in which he read
Aristotle for the first time, his interest aroused by reading Adolf Trendelenburg.[68] The entry ends: 'Praise be to Trendelenburg, one of the
most sober philosophical philologists I know.' His reading of Trendelenburg's *Elementa logices* (1842), *Logische Untersuchungen* (1840), and
Erläuterungen zu den Elementen der aristotelischen Logik (1842) equipped
him with a conceptual apparatus that allowed *Postscript* to provide much
more than the historical costume, which was, after all, as Climacus
himself says, something that could be done by uttering just one word:
'Christianity.' In addition to specifying its historical costume, *Postscript*
would also offer a 'new approach' to the problem of *Fragments*, though
'in the same direction'.[69]

It is interesting to surmise whether Kierkegaard might have said all
this under his own name, as at the start he had clearly intended. What
was it that prevented him? That the work is too 'aesthetic' to count as
an extension of that original attempt, in 'De Omnibus', to engage in
philosophical speculation? Is *Fragments* a mere intimation of what one
might say in a genuine piece of dialectics designed to bring out the true
dimensions of doubt, and the correspondingly heightened demands

made on faith? Or was it because, since the outcome of that earlier speculative attempt would in any case have been not truth itself but only an appreciation of how far we are from it, the speculative manner was inappropriate in any case? The real reason may lie in what *Fragments* adds to 'De Omnibus' and not in whatever the two have in common in the way of philosophy, or anti-philosophy. If the truth requires a new 'organ', namely faith, then we are left on our own. And of course the author too must keep to himself, there being no organ of truth that he shares with the reader, for to treat faith as a shared organ would be to revert to some version of the A-position. And there is a further consideration: the concluding motto says that it is quite another matter whether the B-position is indeed true. *Fragments* makes no claims of validity, so it is not a contribution to a discussion, scholarly or unscholarly; it aims only to spell out what would have to be true if one assumed that an eternal consciousness has to build on contingent historical fact. Whether Kierkegaard himself believed it was true would be immaterial. Even if he did, he would hardly want to let on. Think what people would say if he claimed to have succeeded where Lessing had failed, in crossing that wide and repugnant chasm. But there would be no harm in pointing out that it is there, how wide and repugnant it is, and what it would take to find oneself on the other side. It may not be entirely irrelevant that some years before, in 1839, in response to Mynster's claim that any resolution of the dispute over whether Christianity was supernatural or not could only diminish Christianity, Martensen had observed that Christianity's central doctrine, the Incarnation, was precisely that 'the supernatural has become nature'.[70]

Notabene's Meditation

THE THIRD pseudonymous work published in June 1844, *Prefaces*, was an approximately sixty-page collection of eight prefaces, itself prefaced and under the authorship of Nicolaus Notabene (Nicholas Mark Well). With the exception of the seventh chapter (preface), originally intended for *Anxiety*, none of the others was written to preface an actual publication, though the final chapter might have been intended as an unprefaced publication in its own right. What did Kierkegaard aim to achieve with this series of unaccompanied prefaces? Who were its addressees? The better question will prove to be, who were they aimed at?

Most of the materials existed in some form before Kierkegaard thought of compiling them under one cover. Whatever the original intentions, and however diverse, in their revision the texts were provided with a common though never directly named target, Heiberg. It was by all accounts the publication on 15 December 1843 of the 1844 edition of Heiberg's ornately bound 'yearbook', *Urania*, that prompted Kierkegaard to edit the existing material for inclusion in a single volume of essays.[1] For publishers the traditional exchange of gifts during the Christmas and new year season was a high point for sales. Authors, naturally, were not unwilling to lend a hand. Kierkegaard would no doubt have disdained to participate in this practice, but there is no evidence that he had any strong feelings about it. Before now, that is.

What provoked him was a brief remark by Heiberg in a long article he had written in *Urania* called 'The Astronomical Year'. There Heiberg criticized in passing the recently pseudonymously published *Repetition* for failing to distinguish between repetitions in nature and repetitions in the social world. Kierkegaard prepared a reply ('Open Letter to Professor Heiberg, Knight of Dannebrog, from Constantin Constantius') which he did not publish. Just as in the case of Heiberg's comments on *Either/Or*, which rankled still, the turns of phrase Kierkegaard resorted to here were unpublishable.[2] Among his papers are notes for a satirical piece, 'New Year Present by Nicolaus Notabene, Published for the Benefit of Charity Children, Dedicated to Every Purchaser – and the Charity Children'. Dated 1844, but since *Urania* came out on 19 December probably begun just before the end of 1843 and in anticipation of the boom season, perhaps even as a seditious contribution to it, it was a mischievously conceived attack on Heiberg for overcoming 'the age of distinctions' as he had overcome so much else. The notes include anti-Hegelian asides, for instance on how philosophers don't just conclude their books but feel the need to 'bring their conclusions to consciousness' by adding a blank page with 'conclusion' written on it. The ritual admission that there may still be some misprints in the work is exploited by Notabene to deliver himself of the philosophers' pet expression: 'But here is not the place to go into the matter.'[3]

However, under pressure of working on the draft of *Anxiety* nothing came of the initial project. It was not until several months later, in April or May, that Kierkegaard collected and revised the material that became *Prefaces*. From Notabene's own projected new year present, if that is what it was, he extracted a passage which forms the first preface, short but still heavily satirical in tone. It introduces a 'new year present' made specially for the 'marriage of convenience' between publisher and reading public. It was conceived in the combined light of a publisher's interests and 'the demands of the time', a phrase of Heiberg's out of which Kierkegaard constantly made his own kind of capital.[4] The second preface, slightly longer, again with Heiberg in its sights, humorously considers the literary critic's usual role (not, as one might suppose, 'sergeants of police in the service of good taste' but 'co-conspirators' [with the 'mob of readers'], 'worthy members of the Intemperance Society'),[5] and ends by suggesting seriously that the critic's role should be that of a 'ministering spirit'.[6] The comments were originally meant to introduce an actual example of criticism which Kierkegaard never completed. Then, next, a single page masquerading as a preface to a second edition of the 'new-year present' parodies a 'Postscript [*Eftertale*] to *Urania*' which Heiberg had published in February in his own *Intelligensblade*,[7] and promises well-disposed readers, as Heiberg had done, not to disappoint them the following December with another edition, which will 'lack nothing in elegance and taste'.[8] The fourth preface, three pages long, returns to the theme of the first, ridiculing the idea that the literary high season should consist in the ritual exchange of gifts. The fifth, also short, is an address written to the general assembly of the Society for Total Abstinence (*Total Afholdenheds-Selskabet*). It floats the idea that the writer's moral responsibility to his readers is just like that of members of the society itself, who feel called upon to 'spread the word about wine'. It closes abruptly when the author becomes so intoxicated by this thought ('more than the poet by Bacchus') that he goes out to do just that.[9] The equally short sixth preface lampoons the idea, by ironically appearing to promote it, that what literature lacks is an edifying work designed especially for 'the cultured' (*de Dannede*). The author writes as if he were prefacing a collection of twenty-four sermons which demonstrate a 'continuous line of thought, a systematic tendency', in other words just what the cultured were looking for but had failed to find in the most widely read edifying work of the time, Bishop Mynster's *Sermons*.[10]

The cue for this latter preface was no doubt the anonymous review of *Either/Or* that had complained about the church's taking too little notice of recent developments among the intelligentsia. It had said that the church had so far been unable to 'win over [*at bemægtige sig*] the more cultured [*de mere Dannede*]' and that the contemporary intelligent-sia could 'no longer be satisfied with old-fashioned Christianity or the old faith' but wanted it presented in a 'new and fresh form' which only a 'philosophical bath' could give it.[11] This, we recall, was the review to which Mynster reacted in his New Year's Day article. Under cover of his pseudonym's irony Kierkegaard clearly takes Mynster's side here. The twenty-four sermons to which this is the preface are tailored to the age's demands for something more systematic.

The seventh preface, a left-over from *Anxiety* no doubt because inappropriately polemical for that work in its references to local au-thors,[12] criticizes writers who merely add one more volume to the literature on a given theme but advertise it as more significant than all previous contributions put together.[13] Of the book (*Anxiety*) to follow, the author of its preface says that he has thought a great deal on this topic, and is not unfamiliar with what has previously been written on it, but that instead of trying to understand 'all men' he has chosen what people may regard as a 'narrow and foolish aim', namely to understand *himself*, a task in which progress is likely to be much more slow.[14] And focusing a point made indirectly in the previous prefaces, he says that he has no intention of trying to attract a readership for what he is about to write before he writes it.[15]

Much the longest and most significant preface is the last of the eight. Unlike the others it is in (three) sections and equipped with a motto (Horace's *Satires*, Book II, 50.59): 'What I foresee will either happen or not happen; / for Apollo has granted me the gift of prophecy.' The words are those of the ubiquitous blind Theban soothsayer of Greek myth, Tiresias, who even in the underworld retained his powers of prophecy. The preface announces a new journal of philosophy to be edited, of course, by Nicolaus Notabene himself and can be traced to an entry in Kierkegaard's journal from 1842–43 already commented on in the previous chapter. Noting that Descartes had managed to incorporate a large portion of his system into the first six *Meditations*, Kierkegaard writes that he had thought of presenting his own 'provisional views' in the form of brief meditations,[16] emulating Descartes even to the extent of writing in Latin. He seems seriously to have considered this course; there is a plan (presumably from early 1844) for the first two meditations, each divided into three sections under Latin headings. The first manuscript page of the preface appears to be that also of the planned meditation, the heading for the first section of the first issue (*Praemonenda* [preliminary remarks]) being simply crossed out in the revision. The motto also looks as if it had belonged to the original but survives to do service in this final 'preface'.[17]

Kierkegaard's own name ('Mag. Kierkegaard') had also survived the revision, suggesting that perhaps the eighth preface had at one point been intended for some philosophical work in the spirit if not the letter of Descartes and direct from the *Magister*'s hand. Now, however, that possibility had been fictionalized into the thought of a journal, the first journal of metaphilosophy or, behind the cover of its irony, the first antiphilosophical journal of philosophy. The *Magister* erased his own name and replaced it with 'N. N.' (*Nescio nomen* – I do not know the name, i.e., anyone), this then, in order to lend the appearance of a more local habitation, expanded to the name 'Nicolaus Notabene', an optimistic would-be philosophy journal editor who sticks to his plan even when he has tested its possibility to destruction.

Nicolaus Notabene launches straightaway into the difficulties at-

tached to publishing a philosophy journal, and we quickly learn that
this is to be a rather special philosophy journal, designed for those who
like Nicolaus himself have difficulty understanding the subject. In allusions that, if Heiberg hadn't known from the start, would alert him
immediately to the fact that Nicolaus was Kierkegaard's invention, the
author recalls his youthful excitement at the thought of having a first
piece accepted – as Kierkegaard's was in Heiberg's *Flyvepost* in 1833.
But as Nicolaus points out, Heiberg's own philosophy journal (*Perseus*)
hadn't lasted long (in fact only two issues). What success then can the
insignificant and commercially innocent Nicolaus hope for? True, interest in philosophy has greatly increased since then, but he is not Professor Heiberg, indeed 'even less than not being Prof. Heiberg', he is only
N. N.[18]

The journal is to have a very important aim. Philosophy now becoming accessible to everyone, there is a need to help those among that
multiplying number now encountering it who nevertheless have difficulty understanding it. To raise these difficulties with a view to solving
them must certainly be to take philosophy's side, just as surely as a
journal that helps those in these difficulties must be a journal of philosophy. It is no good for philosophers to say that philosophy conquers all
doubt – and who isn't interested in that claim? – until you understand
what philosophy is. Moreover, and with Heiberg in mind once again,
since philosophy is said to be what the age demands[19] and theologians
too are now said to have to be philosophers, it should be possible not
just for eminent theologians (such as Martensen) but for all who, like
Nicolaus Notabene, have passed their exams so that they too can satisfy
the demands of the age, to grasp it. In the universal acclaim for philosophy, now echoed by all academic disciplines ('like a tutti sounding
from all mouths'), Nicolaus speaks for those for whom there is still a
'residuum of doubt'.[20] The worthy purpose of his journal is to extinguish that doubt. Like Descartes, Nicolaus himself wants to be convinced. He and his journal want to win by being vanquished, their
worries put to rest.[21]

A lover of the discipline from early youth, Nicolaus Notabene holds
philosophy in too great esteem to bend it to his will; rather he is
prepared for philosophy to reveal itself to his deferential and loving
gaze in all its true splendour. He has both commercial (external) and
scholarly (internal) expectations of his journal. Commercially, not want-

ing to convince others of something in the way typical of philosophy editors such as that of *Perseus*, but himself wanting to be convinced, he cannot claim to command the kind of support given by people who feel they are being offered something for which they should feel indebted to the editor. Accordingly, he cannot ask for subscriptions but must appeal to their charity, in return for which all he can offer is a receipt. As for contributions, the situation is slightly paradoxical: if he received a large number that would be a 'dangerous argument against any philosophy, especially one that wants to be understood by everyone'.[22] It would only show how widespread were the editor's own doubts. On the other hand, getting no contributions at all would mean that the probability approached certainty of his internal, scholarly interest in understanding philosophy being satisfied. Since he is optimistic on this score, Nicolaus feels sure that apart from receiving no subscriptions he will receive no contributions either.

His internal interest is in having 'good people' succeed in making him 'wise to philosophy'[23] – wise, that is, to what philosophical activity amounts to, what its point is. As for why such good people should pay any attention specifically to him, Notabene says that the very question must be an abomination to a philosophy that aims to be popular and intelligible to 'everyone', a category that makes no 'petty distinctions'.[24] Indeed, the less his significance, the greater the triumph of philosophy should it succeed in overcoming his doubts. Alluding to Hippocrates' aphorism, *vita brevis, ars longa*,[25] he replies to those who tell him that understanding will come in the end if only he will 'keep quiet and listen', that there is the 'deepest contradiction' in a philosophy whose art is too long for a short life, as when it 'costs an entire lifetime to understand Hegel'.[26] As for Hegel, the thought that Denmark has taken him so warmly to its heart comforts him. Now perhaps, since Hegel has reputedly explained everything, someone will explain Hegel's explanation, this time in a way that he, Nicolaus, will understand. The chances should be good, since one philosopher – again a reference to Heiberg – even claims to have gone beyond Hegel.[27] But perhaps that only adds to the difficulty. After all, the treatises one reads are so Hegelian in their thoughts and expressions – a reference here to Martensen as well as to Heiberg[28] – that one would think they were written by dependable secretaries, and yet here we have a dependable secretary, although writing what is 'to a hair'[29] indistinguishable from Hegel, adding a final paragraph to what was supposed to be the culmination of all previous thought.

But what, Nicolaus then asks, if he is simply too stupid to grasp explanations of Hegel's explanation? In that case won't 'everything be lost' and the journal 'have to be dropped'?[30] The deft and tongue-in-cheek Hegelian dialectics in which Nicolaus now immediately engages to defend his project demonstratively belie the allegation of stupidity. That itself can be seen as part of the argument in what might justifiably be called Notabene's 'Meditation'. For in suggesting reasons for his inability to understand philosophy Notabene confronts philosophy's claim to be a universal discipline. His inability to reap the reward of philosophical knowledge would deprive him of the possibility of human fulfilment and disqualify him as a human being. The argument, however, is Hegelian, not Cartesian. Since his own inability to fathom Hegelians must be mirrored by their inability to fathom his stupidity, both parties must share in a higher stupidity, each admitting that something escapes them. Since, according to philosophy's own principle, any limitation on its understanding is a finitization of itself, philosophy must accept that Nicolaus represents a genuine problem; philosophy has to define itself in continuity with its 'other', so Nicolaus is included whether philosophy likes it or not. But how included? As its limitation. As a tiny little piece of a philosopher, part of that 'chaotic mass' over which the cultured ('as points of intelligence and souls') exercise their organizing activity.[31] But what does that mean when the little piece of a philosopher is too stupid to grasp what they are doing? Doesn't it mean that the only way he can be part of it is to be the part that *mis*understands it?

Suppose, Nicolaus then wonders, that his stupidity with regard to understanding why he cannot understand philosophy's explanation is just the same stupidity that prevents his understanding philosophy in the first place. Maybe it means he lacks some essentially human quality. That would mean in turn that he cannot be saved as others can. In which case, if he is indeed to be saved it won't be by philosophy, indeed it will be a sheer accident if anyone at all is saved by philosophy. However, since the benefits of philosophy will be reserved for those who just happen to be properly equipped, one is entitled to revise one's notion of what it is to be essentially human so that whatever is required for saving someone qua essentially human is something higher than philosophy. But then one will no longer be inclined to regard philosophy as 'absolute'.[32]

In spite of this apparently devastating argument against philosophy Nicolaus perseveres with his project on its behalf; being 'somewhat dull-witted' there is 'much [for him] to learn' in this matter of philosophy. Suppose, for instance, he were accused not so much of stupidity as of harbouring a 'narrow-minded spite', refusing to see what philosophy is. Still, you would expect philosophy, seeing that it possesses the truth, to get the better of this spite, unless of course the spiteful person – 'with an almost demonic power'[33] – were against philosophy and truth from the very start. Knowing that Nicolaus's intentions are good, we can discount that in his case, but in something like Descartes' assumed doubt in the service of a not-so-dissimilar project, Nicolaus makes its ability to resist spite the test of its claim to possess truth.

What Nicolaus elicits from his meditation is the fact that if wisdom is to be anyone's in the way philosophy is said to be for everyone, a claim of which Notabene claims to be a living refutation, then the truth that philosophy claims to control must be in the hands of a power higher than itself, a power with a 'necessity' higher than knowledge, high enough to resist 'the will's spite'. Spite must give way to wisdom, for that is what philosophy itself offers. At the least, then, the spite had better not increase with wisdom – the thought that it might was to surface again later in the work of another pseudonym concerned with despair, one form of which would actually be named 'spite', the deliberate rejection of the hope of salvation. Now, asking whether in spite of spite he can still attain wisdom, or whether in spite of wisdom he would continue to be spiteful, he claims to be too dim to see which of these is true. But still giving his project the benefit of the doubt, Notabene feels entitled to stick to his guns.

The power higher than knowledge he now relies on, to be relevant to his project, must somehow be 'related to knowledge [*Erkjendelsen*]':

[O]ne [then] asks whether this power might be the subject of scholarly treatment; what the name of the discipline [*Videnskab*] dealing with it; the relation of the latter to theory of knowledge [*Erkjendelsens Videnskab*]; whether in becoming a scholarly discipline [*Videnskab*] it doesn't become an object of knowledge; one asks what relation knowledge then has to that power which turned out to be higher than knowledge; whether the power itself might assist knowledge in its ability to understand it; whether knowledge needs its assistance only in this case, or whether it is always thus; whether there might not after all be an exception, and if so what; whether knowing it might not be important before one begins to know something else; what kind of an exception this is, and what follows from this fact with respect to the nature of that knowing [*Erkjenden*]; what knowing it is, then, that spite cannot resist; whether all knowing is necessary knowing; or whether all knowing is to the same degree both free and necessary; if so, then this power is able to exclude me from all knowing, but if not, then it can exclude me only from a certain kind of knowing; [one must then ask] whether the kind of knowing it is able to exclude me from is for this reason higher, or whether [and] for the opposite reason the other kind of knowing is higher; if the latter, then philosophy is not the highest but only even at its highest, namely in the last kind of knowing, a knowledge [*Viden*] *of* the highest.[34]

Although the latter part of the passage sounds rather like Hegel in the mouth of a Helfgott, if paraphrased in terms very close to its own the point is clear enough. Talk of a power higher than knowledge must mean that knowledge is not autonomous. In that case, the question arises, of what knowledge it is true to say that it is not autonomous? All or just some? And does it include knowledge of the power? If the power can exclude him from a certain kind of knowledge, by making him stupid or spiteful for instance, then that knowledge had better be lower than wisdom rather than higher.

The result of this reasoning is that, on the assumption that there is such a power, one can at best conclude on behalf of philosophy that it provides knowledge *of* the highest but that this knowledge *is* neither the highest nor a requirement for grasping what is. Although, if based simply on that assumption, the conclusion looks in no way conclusive, and is indeed circular once we are given two other premises underlying Nicolaus's whole discussion – the first adopted in order to show its falsity, namely that philosophy according to its own lights should be intelligible to everyone, and the second to show that his disability is not human – it does seem possible to present a conclusion to the effect that philosophy is only for some people and therefore (on the further assumption, in extension of the former premise, that the highest is for everyone) not itself the highest.

Resigned now to his inability to understand philosophy but in the embrace of a power higher than knowledge, Nicolaus makes one last attempt to keep his project afloat. Since he cannot communicate with philosophy, in a kind of revelation it must communicate with him.

Nicolaus imagines it speaking to him as a disembodied (and ungendered) voice from the clouds but as though from 'inside him'. It is a divine yet mild voice, for philosophy itself is not unfriendly, 'it is only philosophers who are *böse* [German – angry, or bad-tempered]'.[35] Philosophy tells him that he is not alone in his misunderstanding, there are others to whom 'it is not given to understand me'. Indeed, that is true of the 'majority of mankind'.

I am only for the chosen, for those who were marked out early in their cradles; and in order for these people to belong to me, time, industry, and occasion are required, enthusiastic love, magnanimity to dare to love hopelessly, renunciation of much that other people consider beautiful, and which also is thus. He in whom I find this I reward also with the kiss of the idea. I make the embrace of the concept fruitful for him; I show him what the earthly eye wishes to see, to see the grass growing. I show him this in a far higher world; there I let him understand and see how the thoughts grow within each other more and more perfectly; what is dissolved in the multiplicity of languages, what is everywhere present in the speech both of the most simple person and of the most clever, is collected here and waxes in its silent growth. To you I cannot show myself, by you I cannot be loved; don't think that it is because I am too proud. No! But my essence makes it necessary. Farewell! Do not demand the impossible; praise the gods that I exist; for even if you yourself do not grasp my essence, there are yet those who do; be glad then that the happy ones become happy; do so and you will not regret it.[36]

In his imagined reply, Nicolaus now says that here at last he has an explanation every word of which he understands. Not of philosophy, nor a philosophical explanation of why he cannot understand philosophy, but a nonphilosophical explanation by philosophy itself, in deference to the power it acknowledges to be higher than it, of why not everyone, or the age, needs to have or to understand philosophical explanations. Not only does it explain why he and others should be excluded, it also shows why those on whom the reward of philosophy is bestowed are not fully of this world and so not really part of the age. Thus, listening to philosophy's words, Nicolaus feels the urge they impress on him to contribute to 'the protection of philosophy's tranquil dwelling', that 'lonely place to which you always call your devotees', undisturbed by the 'noise and pain of the world'. But why then, asks Nicolaus, doesn't philosophy send out one of its lovers, one with 'anger in his nostrils' as well as 'thoughts in his head', to 'consume [those] most hypocritical worshippers' who 'desecrate your pure being; who frighten us weak ones, by wanting to make it necessary to understand you'. To clear away the confusion in which people like Nicolaus are pressured into philosophy when it and its practitioners advertise themselves as what the age demands, the chosen should be separated from the 'rest of us'. But this idea of separation once again provokes a thought Nicolaus will have heard from the philosophers: 'difference in existence has its deepest ground in a unity in the absolute.' 'For I'd think, wouldn't you', he asks philosophy,

> that the possibility of letting this unity come to perception is denied to no one, that precisely with this possibility this existence points towards a more perfect one where the unity will perfectly penetrate everyone, and not as in this world be conditioned by the difference. . . . I don't see how the difference can be existence's perfection. I'd think, wouldn't you, that the perfect existence will make everyone into everything and all into just as much. This you can't deny, you though of divine origin, are yet so human; and is being human anything else than to believe this? This you can't deny, in order not to make mankind unhappy – your lovers because they alone were happy, us others since we do not become your lovers.[37]

The outcome of the eighth preface is interesting. You would think the project had to be dropped. Nicolaus, who had already give up any claims to *being* a philosopher, now sees as a result of his explorations in thought why also he should not *become* one, along, furthermore, with the majority of human beings. But that doesn't mean, he says, that there aren't 'a great many things to meditate over that might interest them'. His journal was to be called *Philosophical Meditations*, but he can still 'indulge in meditations without being a philosopher', and he might even be able to call his meditations 'philosophical', since there 'must always be a *confinium* between philosophy and the doctrine in which we others seek sanctuary [*søge Tilhold*], and in this respect philosophy could indeed be useful to us if by nothing else than by holding us at arm's length [*ved at Støde fra*]'.[38] One situation in which Nicolaus thinks he might be able to sustain his increasingly forlorn hopes of being a philosopher would be where, instead of in its 'sublime simplicity' offering an explanation of the kind he suggested, or one that was even better, philosophy continued as now in pursuit of its beautiful goal of being understood by everyone, namely by becoming more and more abstruse and mysterious. In a closing sigh (ironic from Kierkegaard's hand but fully in keeping with the worthy Notabene's good intentions), Nicolaus Notabene says what a terrible contradiction it would be if there were no certainty to be got from at least some part of the System; and, as for himself, his ambition to be included in it would be satisfied if only there could be an originally Danish System, a 'perfect domestic product' rather than an imported one, even if the only part he could play in it would be as its express messenger. In a parting wish he hopes people will stop quoting authorities at him, and he recalls for his readers an explanation he was once given of something in Aristotle, an explanation he found very intelligible but nowhere in Aristotle. Irrespective of it coming from Aristotle or a serving girl, the explanation itself was enough. There is a concluding note saying that in the journal itself he will forswear personal references of the kind he had found it expedient to include in the preface.

> I have endeavoured in the above as best I could to recommend my undertaking. I have not let it lack for *captatio benevolentiae* [in rhetoric, expressions designed to predispose the audience to lend a favourable ear what is to come] both to right and left. I have done what stood in my power to turn every sensitive person into my benefactor: my subscriber, my teacher, my mentor. I have no more to add except that I hope I have done the necessary. In the journal itself I dare not give my heartfelt outpourings place; there I continue to jog with my crooked gait along the way of thought.[39]

Its subtitle, as we noted at the beginning of the previous chapter, describes *Prefaces* as 'light reading for various stations of life as time and opportunity permit'. The Danish term translated 'light reading' (*Morskabslæsning*) is contained in the title of a book in Kierkegaard's possession, a three-volume collection of traditional stories published in a new edition over the years 1828–30.[40] '*Morskab*' means amusement as well as diversion. Five years earlier, in a journal entry, Kierkegaard had expressed his delight in the preface form, where he can 'give up all objective thinking' and 'simply spend himself in wishes, hopes, and a private whisper in the reader's ear, a Horatian *sussuratio* in the evening, for the preface should always be construed in an evening light, which is also undeniably the most beautiful. . . .'[41] The prefaces to his own works tended to be amusing and self-deprecatory, as we saw in *From the Papers of One Still Living*, where he does not insist that the reader read either the preface or the book to follow, though the suggestion there was that one should at least read the preface, to hear the author say that the book was not all that important.

Here, however, was Heiberg using prefaces to announce the importance of his own books, the same Heiberg who could tell people how to read Hegel, or even how to go beyond Hegel, and who could explain to the whole age the importance of objective thinking. It is hard not to believe that the eighth preface is the crucial one. In it, far from giving up objective thinking, Kierkegaard has his author actually engage in it, along of course with the *captatio benevolentiae* proper to the genre, in order to suggest the limitations of such thinking, in particular the claims made for it and not least for the claimants themselves by those who believe that a facility with the Speculative Idea has been especially bestowed upon them. The amusement that was typically an author's becomes in this preface a polemical tool in which the amusement persists but now at the expense of those who use prefaces for self-advertisement. A certain malice may be fused with the glee Kierkegaard seems obviously to have felt in assembling this collection. Its own preface, almost as long as each of the two longer prefaces it precedes, is about prefaces. It gives, as an appropriate illustration of the genre, an amusing explanation of the publication itself. It was a writer's compromise designed to ease Notabene's marriage or even to save it. Adept enough in the art of thought to be able 'to dispute with the devil himself' (perhaps a reference to his brother), at home Notabene can never get beyond the preface because every time he says something with which his wife disagrees she exclaims, affectionately but categorically, 'it's just splitting hairs [*Drilleri* – teasing, perhaps with some basis in the original sense of 'tease' as teasing apart fibres, but maybe just an empty exercise, as in drilling]'. She also says that for a married man to be an author is to be 'unfaithful'. So the happily married Nicolaus decides to publish only his prefaces.[42]

Whether well enough married in another sense, that is to say, to a readership able to understand *him* sufficiently for a thoroughly good hanging not to have been preferred, is another matter. In a journal entry he voices the fear that Nicolaus Notabene will provide Heiberg with just another opportunity to raise uncalled-for objections (*gjøre Vrøvl*).[43] It is clear that by this time Kierkegaard, with a considerable authorship in progress, though no longer worried about his standing as such, was becoming acutely sensitive about *where* he was seen to stand. Although he no longer required Heiberg's praise, the effect on the attitudes of his own readers of casual words dropped by someone of Heiberg's magisterial authority mattered a great deal. This may not even have been because Kierkegaard himself knew what to make of his own authorship.

It was just that if anything was to be made of it, it was imperative that he was the one to decide what that was. Indeed, far from fearing Heiberg's praise, he might have felt applause from that quarter to be an even greater danger.

Then there was the reception of *Either/Or*. The kind and extent of interest it had aroused, and still did, gave its author a fashionably avant-garde image which made it difficult for him to be appreciated as a religious writer. The pseudonymity made little difference. Whatever came later, whether under the same or other pseudonyms, would be seen in the light of the reputation earned by that celebrated predecessor, Victor Eremita. Something would have to be done.

Completing the Stages

E VER SINCE *Either/Or* had come out Kierkegaard had contemplated some sort of supplement to that work. Now, in light of the notions and views for which he had found expression in the interim, he felt even more urgently the need to revise the impression made by his early authorship. Adding a further section to *Either/Or* was one possibility that crossed his mind – a section on his own tribulations to conclude the second part, balancing the seducer's diary concluding the first. The idea would be to make Wilhelm's solution look too easy. But by this time Kierkegaard had realized that doing justice to what *Either/Or* failed to bring to light would require a separate publication.

If it was still uncertain in Kierkegaard's mind where his authorship was heading, part of that uncertainty must have been due to the complexity of the motivations driving him to write. Since what was vitally important to him personally was that he should be the one to decide in the end what role the writings should be seen to have in the longer term, not unnaturally the extent and nature of *Either/Or*'s reception made him extra wary. Not least because of the 'Diary', Victor Eremita's accidental compilation had achieved a celebrity which quite overlooked ethics and religion. Indeed, the very name had acquired a standing in literary circles and was in danger of upstaging any that Kierkegaard, whose authorial intentions became increasingly inscrutable as the pseudonyms and genres proliferated, might have intended for himself.

So Victor Eremita had to be retired. Kierkegaard hit upon the expedient of having Eremita, in a 'Post-Scriptum to *Either/Or* by Victor Eremita' dated 1 March 1844 and probably written in late February when he had delivered his qualifying sermon, retire himself.

If this was before the idea of assembling and publishing *Prefaces* had formed itself in his mind, the polemic motivating the latter was clearly in place. The pseudonym wants to avoid the misleading impression that his name is a trade-mark or imprint, a 'firm' called 'Victor Eremita' whose stock could rise and fall, whose future publications a 'friend' could 'announce' ('We can expect at New Year a new work by V. E., editor/publisher of *Either/Or*'), or of an author about whom people might ask, 'Isn't it about time we heard something from Victor Eremita?'[1] Kierkegaard needed to isolate *Either/Or*, letting it stand alone so that supplements that would embrace it in a new light could appear as independent perspectives whose destiny Kierkegaard could control. He therefore has his pseudonym 'wind up the firm' (*ophæve Firma*). Eremita reminds us that *Either/Or* has no author; the title was one the book gave to itself (the title 'looks in on the book, not out from it') or to any reader to whom it imparted a sense of either/or, as it did to him – and for all he had known at the time he might be the only reader. He acknowledges that the work might well be read in other ways, in different circumstances he might have read it differently himself: so there is nothing essential in it to himself, Victor Eremita. As for that name, it too was just an honest expression of his own reaction to what he had read. He supposed that any reader who got as far as seeing an either/or would come to the point when 'in a instant' he would feel 'Eremita' was an apt name, since 'contemplation of a more serious kind often makes one lonely'. There might follow another instant too in which 'Victor' seemed apt as well – 'however he grasped this victory'.[2] To allow himself to be seen to 'go further' than Victor Eremita, the latter is made to say that if one ever comes across the name in any other guise than as '*Either/Or*'s natural guardian', then he, Eremita, is not the writer.[3]

In fact the name reappears in the first part of *Stages on Life's Way*, though not as a contributing writer's. Now he is a character under the care of another guardian, William Afham, and participating along with several other familiar figures, Johannes the Seducer along with the pseudonym responsible for *Repetition*, Constantin Constantius, in something called 'In Vino Veritas', a version of Plato's *Symposium*. Originally planned as two separate publications, *Stages* combined them and, as then had to happen, under the yet-more-embracing guardianship of a pseudonym appropriately dubbed 'Hilarius Bogbinder' (Hilary Bookbinder).

But this lengthy work would not appear for almost a year. *Stages* cost Kierkegaard much effort and some despair. In the same August he made a short 'report' to himself:

I just can't get on with 'In Vino Veritas'. I keep writing parts over and over again but it doesn't satisfy me. Basically I feel I've given far too much thought to this matter, and that has made my mood rather unproductive. It can't be written here in town, so I must travel. On the other hand perhaps it isn't really worth finishing. The idea of the comic as the erotic is hinted at in *The Concept of Anxiety*. The fashion designer is a very good figure, but the question is whether I'm not putting off more important things with all this. Anyway it has to be written in a hurry. If the opportunity for doing so doesn't come I won't do it. Just now the productivity has failed me and keeps me all the time writing more than I want to.[4]

Kierkegaard didn't travel, not this year. But in July and August, following the publication of *Anxiety*, *Fragments*, and *Prefaces*, he took frequent carriage rides north of Copenhagen, to the woods and to his favourite hostelries, in particular to the mail-coach inn at Hørsholm, where he would sometimes spend the whole day eating well and talking with locals. These excursions had begun at the end of January, at that time of feverish activity on several manuscripts, and continued through the year. Sometimes he was accompanied by the philologist and linguist Israel Levin,[5] whom he employed as a copyist and proofreader. There was another excursion just four days after the 'report', on the day yet another set of discourses was published, the third that year. These regular outings seem to have provided a kind of punctuation to his writing; in September and October they were commas – even dashes – rather than full stops or periods, as he came up for air in the struggle with 'In Vino Veritas'. He moved back, on 16 October 1844, into rooms at 2 Nytorv, an apartment on the first (not ground) floor at the back of the building. Why Kierkegaard did that is not clear, since he had by all accounts been quite happy with his arrangements in the apartment at Nørregade. True, when Peter had left in September 1842 to take up that appointment in Pedersborg, Søren had been left with the administrative responsibilities for the family property. But that wouldn't be a reason for moving in there. More than a year had elapsed since, in May 1843, Søren had bought out his brother's share.

Had it anything to do with Kierkegaard's difficulties with his writing, was the move itself an attempt to clear the decks and start afresh? We don't know, but there are other reasons why he might in any case have found writing 'In Vino Veritas' so hard. Up to now he had been writing forwards, one might say, bringing into focus ideas half formed from quite early on. That can be a wonderfully self-confirming creative experience. In the opening pages of 'In Vino Veritas', which serve as its preface, the author William Afham remarks that so long as one remains a child one has the fantasy of keeping 'one's soul at its extremity, even for an hour in the dark'. As one gets older one's fantasy works in the opposite direction, and is 'liable to make one tired of the Christmas tree before one has even set eyes on it'.[6] Instead of writing a supplement to *Either/Or* that would allow that work to be reread from a new point of view, Kierkegaard was now trying to create an entirely new version which would embrace the key personae from the previous pseudonymous production. It was an attempt at 'repetition'. No longer tapping the accumulated store of thoughts, those 'dear blessed children' that had rained down on him on that earlier trip to Berlin and after, Kierkegaard was now striving to reclothe ready-made figures in the light of considerations that those same figures had already been used to bring to the reader's mind – even if without representing in themselves, so to speak, the consequences. Kierkegaard was now having to look back and deal with the consequences, and the task was clearly a painful one. No wonder the fashion designer pleased him most, the only newcomer to the gallery of personae attending the 'drinking party' (*Gjæstebud* – literally, feast, banquet), or 'symposium' in the original sense of the word (*symposion* – from *symposia* – literally, drinking together) reported in 'In Vino Veritas'.

The original plan had been to publish 'In Vino Veritas' along with what is now its sequel in the first part of *Stages* as a separate volume under the title 'The Wrong and the Right' (*Vrangen og Retten* – in Danish conveying a sense of something being the wrong or the right way around, as when you wear a sweater inside or 'right' side out). Both the original preface to that volume and the final version, called a 'pre-remembrance' (*Forerindring*), which serves to introduce 'In Vino Veritas', stress the creative role of memory, or remembrance (*Erindring*), as against simple recall (*Hukommelse*). What you remember you cannot contrive to forget, or if you try to do so it will return 'like Thor's hammer' or with a 'yearning' like the homing instinct of 'a pigeon that, however many times it is sold, never becomes another's'. What you remember is something 'essential' to yourself. Afham even puts it by saying that if you have 'broken with the idea' you will be unable to act 'essentially' or 'undertake anything essential'. To remember things in the ordinary sense is simply to succeed in not forgetting them, something people can 'join in helping one another' with, as with 'banquets, birthday presents, pledges of love, and costly commemorations'. Such *aides-mémoires* belong to the same category as 'turn[ing] down the corner of the page to remind one where one left off'. Not so with remembrances, however; here there is no helping one another. Remembrance has to do with 'moods, situations, surrounding conflicts', and the 'wine-press of remembrance is one which each must tread on his own'. There is 'no curse in this', however, for 'in so far as one is always alone with a memory, every memory is a secret' anyway and any 'appearance of publicity', due to the fact that more than one person is interested in the same object of a memory, is 'just illusion'.

But the festive gathering recounted by Afham is no kind of reminder, neither for the participants nor for Afham. For him it is a situation, a mood, a conflict in some sense, that homes in on his memory, though strangely he seems to have had no part in the party himself. He is in relation to what he presents almost another Eremita, except that what he has at his disposal – as pure remembrance – is what has been said by some people rather than written. Given what he remembers, he is now able to recreate the mood, the situation, the conflicts for the reader. Some not-very-serious attempt is made at characterization. Constantius is the level-headed master of ceremonies, Eremita effusive and whimsical, Johannes as we would expect him, and the fashion designer modishly dressed and with the latest hairstyle, always polite but occasionally venomous in his remarks, while the young man is a tender-minded twenty-two-year-old and somewhat withdrawn.

Obviously it isn't a case of remembrance proper, the whole account is fictitious. Nor does it even try to be realistic – or it does, but this is where Kierkegaard's creative grip loosens. Reading 'In Vino Veritas' is like listening to a tape-recording of speeches given by a series of spokesmen for distinct points of view, ones in which Kierkegaard was well versed, in fantasy if not also in remembrance. (That these two are closely connected is a point carefully prepared by Afham in his pre-remembrance Preface.) Kierkegaard himself, alluding to the title of the book by Steffens he once told Emil Boesen had aroused such enthusiasm in him, describes the spokesmen as caricatures, less in the modern sense of exaggerated distortion than as deliberately one-dimensional.

The purpose of the five speakers in 'In Vino Veritas', all of whom are *Caricaturen des Heiligsten*,[7] is to throw essential yet false light on women. The Young Man understands women solely from the point of view of gender. Constantin Constantius considers the psychological factor: faithlessness – that is, frivolousness. Victor Eremita conceives of the female sex psychologically as gender, her significance for the male, i.e. that it has none. The fashion designer considers that sensual element outside the essentially erotic, in the vanity which has more to do with a woman's relationship to women, for as an author has said,[8] women do not adorn themselves for men but for each other. Johannes the Seducer considers the purely sensual factor in regard to the erotic.[9]

The light thrown on woman is variously but generally false. What emerges from the long and quite elaborate speeches 'In Vino Veritas' is the 'wrong' way, in contrast to which the second part, entitled 'Quite a Lot about Marriage in the Face of Objections, by a Married Man' was originally to be the 'right' way. We note that Constantin Constantius, whose cynicism in *Repetition* helped to pry the young man from a naive interpretation of his problem, and whose irony then enabled him to project a religious justification for being an 'exception' to normal morality in respect of his beloved, is now clearly presented as having too limited a view of what his own suggestion implies. Moreover, where in *Repetition* Constantius admits that the young man is his own fabrication, here the latter has an existence independent of Constantius. And Eremita, whose function in *Either/Or*, at least as his own latest explanation has it, was no more than to register the impression made on him by the work (as its first and possibly only reader), is here given the floor. The attitude he expresses is one of enthusiastic resignation: given woman's nature there is no hope of a solution within normal morality. He does insist, however, that he is not, as his name might imply, 'preaching the monastery', which he has the insight to see is 'just an immediate expression of spirit'. Once you realize that 'spirit does not lend itself to immediate expression', you also see that, as far as protection against threats to spirituality is concerned, it is 'safer' to remain an Eremita on the outside 'even if he travels all day and night in an omnibus'.[10] But then, whether on the inside or the outside, to be an Eremita is still to resign from the problem.

Of the five participants, it is to the first speaker, the young man, with antecedents in *Either/Or* and *Repetition*, that Kierkegaard gives the best promise of coming further. Here, however, or for that very reason, he appears in a more innocent version than his forerunners (in *Either/Or* we are even allowed to suspect that the young aesthete and Johannes the Seducer are identical). Not only has he not fallen in love, he hasn't even ever tried to 'eye' a woman. Yet he does have irony enough to see (the topic Kierkegaard remarked that he had already touched on in *Anxiety*) something comical in the very idea that everyone 'loves and wants to love'.[11]

It is noticeable how the better-placed participant appears to be the least experienced while the last speaker looks more like a lost cause. This is true also in *Either/Or*. Who could ever conceive the Johannes whose 'Diary' concludes the first part progressing to the ethical life promoted by Wilhelm in the second part? Here, in what proved to be just the first of two parts of *Stages*, Johannes again has the last word and is the least likely of the drinking companions to be swayed by what immediately follows. It is as though greater experience and self-consciousness, as in Hegel, make the qualitative changes and corresponding choices increasingly abrupt.

The sequel to the account of the drinking party, 'Quite a Lot about Marriage against Objections', is by 'A Married Man'. The man in question, we are led to understand in the closing pages of William Afham's account of the 'banquet', is an assessor, or junior magistrate, just as Wilhelm was in *Either/Or*. Whether this is indeed Wilhelm is left to us. The well-oiled party-goers, instead of accepting Constantin's offer of five separate carriages to take them home, have decided to take a stroll together in the early morning sun. On their way they pass a pavilion in a garden close by, where a woman is pouring her husband's morning tea. Even if, for all they know, the couple have been married for some time, she does it with the 'childlike sincerity [*Inderlighed*] of a newly wed'. Perhaps, reflects Afham in the spirit of the banquet speeches, she is still at the stage of not knowing whether marriage is 'in earnest or a joke', whether being a housewife is 'life's work, a game, or a pastime'. For the husband's part, as they could overhear from a short exchange, beneath his devotion runs an undercurrent of not-so-gentle irony. On being reminded of a conversation which had been interrupted the previous day and in which she had remarked on how much better he would have succeeded in the world had he not married, he now replies, in a serious tone, that he forgave her that earlier foolishness which she seemed 'to have so quickly forgotten' and asks her, it seems accusingly, 'What sort of success is it you think I should be in the world?' At first nonplussed she quickly collects herself and delivers him a lecture 'with a woman's eloquence' while he looks away drumming his fingers on the table. When she is finished, he remarks that it is legal in Denmark to beat one's wife, to which she smilingly replies: 'How can I ever get you to talk seriously?' We might easily suspect we were in the presence of the happily married Nicolaus Notabene.

While the other party-goers are witnessing this little marital drama, Victor Eremita has on some pretext gone to the house itself and entered it through the open French window. As his companions go by, he jumps out triumphantly waving a manuscript which he says is 'by the Assessor'. No doubt his behaviour is due to the excessive amount of alcohol consumed at the party, but Afham, who now materializes, compounds the felony further by removing the manuscript from Eremita's grasp as the latter fumbles with it while trying to put it into his pocket. This, then, is the manuscript that he now publishes under the title, 'Quite a Lot about Marriage against Objections'.

To the reader who has long wondered how Afham can remember so much about events to which he himself shows no indication, apart from his remembrance of them, of having been witness, he gives the assurance, like so many pseudonyms before him, that he is a nobody, a nothing, in fact 'pure being' and therefore 'practically less than nothing', since, as Hegelians say, pure being is 'constantly being annulled'. There is thus no sense in which sneaking the manuscript out of Eremita's hands and publishing it can be 'his' idea. The manuscript is 'the Assessor's' and is published under the pretext that it has been borrowed from Victor, who must have felt he had acquired the right to publish it, and for whom Afham, in his 'nothingness', is simply a nemesis.[12]

Although the magistrate's case bears some resemblance to Wilhelm's in *Either/Or*, its mood is much lighter, particularly in the beginning, and the argument throughout more compact. The opening passage is removed from the draft of Notabene's preface to the *Prefaces*,[13] where in order to save his marriage Notabene agreed to write prefaces instead of books. Here the author begins by jokingly urging marriage as 'the most important voyage of discovery a person can undertake' upon those who don't want to spend their lives in exploration or cosmological research.[14] He claims, however, as a husband to make no new discoveries, they are what every married man knows.[15] The essay is in fact a return to themes from both of Wilhelm's letters in *Either/Or*. The husband, in what is in effect a continuation of the discussion begun by Kant and Fichte, resumes the defence of 'Marriage's Aesthetic Validity' against the typical Romantic objections. The immediacy or naturalness of erotic love and of being 'in love' is contrasted to the decision in which marriage begins. A union in which a couple decide to live together as long as it works differs from one based on a resolution to create a bond come what may. It is not just that, while in the case of the former, since it depends always on something not happening, the happiness can occur only after it hasn't – which since it always may happen means 'after I am dead' – a love placed decisively in the 'universal' allows one's joy to be anticipatory as well as present.[16] In the concluding half of his advertisement for marriage the author does not focus on choice of self, as Wilhelm did in 'Equilibrium', but takes up Wilhelm's closing queries about possible exceptions to the rule that one should marry. The author warns, however, against those seeking exemption. He admits that marriage is not 'the most sublime [*høieste*] life', for he knows a higher. But, assuming the role of one who stands at 'this narrow pass' in order to examine the credentials of those who would skip marital service, he describes cases that typically disqualify a person from gaining exemption. He opposes a 'feint' of the kind in which, in the name or even cause of spirituality, a person forgets that he is a human being and not, like God, 'spirit alone'.[17] In comments obviously straight from the hand of the pseudonym's mentor and directed at Heiberg and Grundtvig, he warns against intellectualized forms of religiosity which disparage the merely physical side of life, a new version of the medieval monastery, and also against revivalist religion. For the true religious exception – and clearly none of the speakers in 'In Vino Veritas' qualifies – 'something must happen'.[18] And it must happen in the context of genuine love, a breach for instance. If not parading Kierkegaard's own problem the author is at least reverting to the kind of situation it exemplified.

'Quite a Lot about Marriage' is addressed to 'My dear reader'. That was the form also used by Constantius in the pages concluding *Repetition* and clearly intended for Regine. It is therefore not unlikely that the

choice of this form here, as distinct from the 'My friend' with which
Wilhelm opens his long 'letters' to the aesthete, indicates the special
reference of this particular, or apparent, either/or. Kierkegaard is en-
couraging his reader to suppose that the defence of marriage is genuine
on his part. That does not mean that it was indeed genuine, only that
he wished his reader to take it to be so. However, if we are seeking a
rationale for Kierkegaard's decision at the last moment to publish what
was to have been 'The Wrong and the Right' under the umbrella of an
either/or, when that work despite its title's grammatical form has the
appearance of being an either/or in its own right, we can see that there
are just as good reasons for taking the defence to be genuine as for
treating it as merely provisional, the expression of a position to be won
only in order to provide a platform for jumping to something higher.
Adopting the former alternative, we could put the overall theme of
Stages in a nutshell by saying, in the now-familiar manner, that marriage
is the standard or 'default' position in respect of which any exception
needs to be satisfactorily explained.

The succeeding part of *Stages*, originally conceived as the supplement
Kierkegaard had all along thought of adding to *Either/Or*, is a probing
examination of the conditions that can exempt one from the norm. Its
title from the start, ' "Guilty?" – "Not Guilty?" ', is in the form of yet
another either/or. The question is whether the work as a whole is to be
read as presenting two pairs of either/ors, to be read in linear fashion,
the second 'either' confronting the first 'or', or whether these two
either/ors form options (ways of seeing the choice) in a more embracing
either/or.

If the order of composition may reasonably indicate an author's
priorities, the question of exceptionality would seem to be uppermost
in Kierkegaard's mind. It was after all his own problem. He was even
inclined to see it as *the* problem of the pseudonymous authorship. Just
a few years later he wrote that the way in which this 'matter' of 'the
single individual' appears in the pseudonymous works – and it appears
in 'every one' of them – is as the hinge on which an ordering of the
notions of 'the universal [*det Almene* – the general or generality], the
single individual [*den Enkelte*], the exceptional individual [*den særlige
Enkelte*], the exception [*Undtagelsen*] turns'. The object of the exercise
is 'to make out the exceptional individual in his suffering and in his
extraordinariness'.[19] At the time of that entry, in 1849, the notion of the

single individual had acquired a more 'public' meaning for him, including a political aspect, and he was able to add that 'the pseudonyms, as books, also put the notion of the single individual into effect in relation to the reading public'. But now, in 1844, still in the midst of the pseudonyms, it is very probable that Kierkegaard was still trying to explain to himself as well as to others his own justification for the authorship, looking for some good reason for being an unmarried writer of books, even books defending marriage, rather than a married preface-monger.

In this light, the second part of *Stages*, ' "Guilty? – Not Guilty?" – A Story of Suffering. Psychological Experiment by Frater Taciturnus', addresses both the 'either' and the 'or' of its first part. The suffering is a case of what must 'happen' before a religious exception can be allowed through the 'narrow pass'. So, as an indication that the either/or in *Stages*, if there is one, hinges on the opposition of 'In Vino Veritas' to whatever emerges as an alternative in the remainder, this second part picks up where the married man leaves off. It accedes to his case for marriage but also accepts his requirement for the possibility of a religious exception. Going on from there, it then examines that very possibility. As for 'In Vino Veritas', we note that none of its participants qualify, not even the young man, since in this version he has not given himself the chance to fall in love and therefore for any happening of the kind required – though nothing prevents that from occurring in his future. As for the rest of them, their very attitudes deprive them of such a possibility, even Eremita, who has given up hope of meeting his own fulfilment with a woman. In one way or another, all five are clinging helplessly to the finite in the vertigo of anxiety, if not also jubilantly defying their spiritual possibilities.

Seen in this light, what ' "Guilty?" – "Not Guilty?" ' in a hopeful but critical spirit examines are up-graded, spiritual versions of the 'excuses' tried out by the various figures in 'In Vino Veritas'. That would help to explain why Kierkegaard found the figures hard to form. His thoughts had from well before this time been focused on his own excusability; and the direction in which they had already led really required occupation with those 'more important things' he was putting off. By all accounts Kierkegaard was at this time planning a set of discourses appropriate for church rituals (confession, the wedding ceremony, and burial),[20] occasions closer than were memories of a drunken party to his sombre view of his own situation. That he had nevertheless felt the need to bring his old characters along to reshape them in the light of what they themselves had helped him to see, was also understandable. There is also the possibility that writing a new version of Plato's *Symposium* would have appealed to his vanity as well as to his loyalty to Poul Møller.

That a renewed defence of marriage ('the right') would have to accompany the now ever-wider negative consensus on marriage ('the wrong') is also plain enough. Since we know that a passage praising marriage was removed by Kierkegaard from the draft of that preface by Notabene to form the beginning of 'Quite a Lot about Marriage', such a defence was already in progress. After repeating the special demands marriage makes for the benefits it bestows, but at a pitch high enough to make justified exceptionality a matter critical enough to take the question over into that of one's own guilt, Kierkegaard now had the platform he needed for dealing with the matter of repentance, and of how guilt can ever be assuaged.

" 'Guilty?" – "Not Guilty?" ' opens like *Either/Or* with an account by its pseudonymous editor/publisher, on this occasion also a contributor, of how he came across the work's key-text, a diary. Trying his luck with borrowed tackle at one end of a boat as his friend, a naturalist, dredges a lake for interesting flora from the other, Frater Taciturnus accidentally fishes up a rosewood casket. Besides the diary, the casket proves to hold various valuables. Frater Taciturnus tells us that he advertised their discovery, asking anyone interested to contact him through Reitzel's bookshop. A bound volume, as in the case of *Either/Or*'s diary, this diary was the record of one man's dialogue with himself. The entries are dated (according to an expert Frater Taciturnus has consulted, the year must have been 1751) and divided into two mostly alternating sets, morning and midnight. The morning entries are recollections of the writer's engagement, a year before, and his breaking it off. The midnight entries confront that recorded 'reality' with the writer's 'ideality'.[21] After the final entry ('on this occasion') of Quidam's diary,[22] Frater Taciturnus provides a 'communication' for the reader, in the form of a redescription of Quidam's own account of the way in which his own conflict develops. Less of a second opinion, Taciturnus's account is more in the nature of an incorporation of Quidam's self-portrayal into the universe of discourse created by the pseudonymous

authorship to date. The fact that it also includes terms such as 'deception' familiar to us – though not to readers at the time – from Kierkegaard's own story of suffering to be related later, only adds further
whimsy to the tale of Taciturnus's catch.

The relationship between Frater Taciturnus (Silent Brother) and
Quidam (the man in question) resembles that between Constantius
Constantin and his young letter-writing friend; he is a guiding spirit
who turns out to be creator (for the purposes of experiment) rather than
accidental discoverer – which reveals the story of the fishing trip as a
device for establishing the initial separation without which 'guidance'
would not be an appropriate notion (and makes one wonder why the
same might not have been admitted in the case of Victor Eremita). The
guidance here is of another kind, however, since with the time-lag built
into the story, Frater Taciturnus can address only the reader.

As in *Repetition*, where Constantius left his protégé at the juncture
where he himself could go no further, ironist as he was, and the possibility of a religious form of exemption lying beyond his imaginative
scope, Taciturnus leaves Quidam at the point where he cannot further
enlighten *us* on him – except that where *he* leaves off no further 'communication' is possible in any case. The young man in *Repetition*, a
poet, lacked the religious sensibility that would have made into a practical possibility Constantin's suggestion that there might be a religious
solution to his 'collision'. As an ironist, of course, Constantin too lacked
religious sensibility. But in " 'Guilty?' – "Not Guilty?" ' both parties
differ correspondingly. According to Frater Taciturnus, the Quidam of
the diary is 'demonic in a religious direction from the start'.[23] The word
'demonic' in Kierkegaard's vocabulary describes, as we saw in *Anxiety*,
fear of what is nevertheless acknowledged to be good. Demonic behaviour is behaviour that can be explained as a more or less, and even
unconscious, shunning of some ideal which nevertheless cannot lose its
hold. The demonic person differs, therefore, from someone whose fear
is not of the good itself but of not being able to measure up to it – that
is a case of fear of evil or of what is bad. The fact that Quidam,
according to Frater Taciturnus, is demonic in the direction of the
religious means that he possesses the religious sensibility Constantius's
young man lacked; but there is more than enough in that sensibility to
evoke fear, for instance the prospect of having to repent.[24] As for Frater
Taciturnus, he is a 'humorist', which means among other things, but

especially, that he is 'preoccupied' with the religious 'as a phenomenon'. Not only that, it is the phenomenon that he is 'most preoccupied with'.[25] So Quidam, who Taciturnus tells us at the outset is a figure he has 'conjured forth' (while Constantius, we recall, only at the end admits to being merely a midwife, just as he proceeds to tell his reader that he too is someone merely conjured forth), is delivered to us as someone who grasps the point of what it means to be a religious exception. What it means to say that Frater Taciturnus is a humorist, then, is that although he too grasps the point, since it is only a preoccupation it is something from which he himself is still personally detached. His interest is one of keen curiosity and needs to be fed by interesting cases, like the one he has fished up from the lake. But given that the story of suffering is basically Kierkegaard's own, we can also see the fishing episode interestingly in reverse. By the 'happy chance' of its being brought into the hands of a Taciturnus, his tale of woe can now be offered to the 'dear reader' as one in which the ingredients leading one to ask whether one can be a religious exception were there from the start.

This throws an interesting light on the pseudonyms. It is as if the detached attitudes they represent are detached also from any self that could be their own topic; they need to latch onto a case history instead. And it also seems as if the case that has that history would escape adumbration of any kind were it not for the sympathetic detachment of a pseudonym able to provide the appropriate 'spiritual' diagnosis. This is not true with all of the pseudonyms. Johannes Climacus, who although he makes a token pretence of being interested personally in his own adumbrations of what it means to be a Christian, remains consistently humorous, admitting that his own preoccupation is with very general questions, indeed very general ones such as What is the difference between *asking* a general question like 'Are we guilty?' and a personal one such as Quidam's 'Am I guilty?'.[26] The point may be that the latter question is one that no adumbration or reflection of a general nature will help you to escape or answer. The pseudonym's expertise, at best, assists you in seeing when it is that you are really asking. It delivers you, as it were, to the question, but in so doing makes it quite clear that there is no expert answer.

The separation in time characteristic of the relation between case history and pseudonym suggests that the case history is not real but an example for the reader. It cannot be Kierkegaard's intention that the diagnosis provide the answers that the person's whose case it is wants answered. That would be just the position he is attacking. It is not even clear that what the pseudonym says about the case history, whether the young letter-writer's in *Repetition* or Quidam's in ' "Guilty?" – "Not Guilty?" ', says anything directly to us on the crucial issue of exceptionality and its justification. It is just that the case histories and their publicized exposure to the ironical influences of the pseudonyms offer demonstrations of the way in which the hold of immediacy may be loosened and poetic possibilities opened up in preparation for a proper grasp of what is something quite different, namely a religious solution. But for that you must already be religiously sensitive, and things must 'happen' that give rise to the question of guilt. Under those conditions a case history might go the full distance without outside help.

Frater Taciturnus is a 'silent brother' but he is also a humorist, which means that in the end he must let go of what he has 'conjured up'. Unlike Constantius's midwifery, which helps to deliver the young man into the reader's presence, Taciturnus's version can only usher his own young man out of the reader's presence, delivering Quidam to himself. In writing Quidam out of his 'communication' with the reader, Frater Taciturnus has to use, and admits to using, a language that Quidam himself, if it is true that he goes further, will not use. Frater Taciturnus says that Quidam, when he reaches faith, will not regard, as he himself does, the passionate hold that he keeps on God in faith, and his personal self-annihilation, as the 'negative unity of the comic and the tragic'. Frater Taciturnus sees tragedy in a soul suffering when it is immortal (a concept he possesses by virtue of his overriding preoccupation with religion), but also comedy in the bathos of its being just a matter of two persons.[27] But to a Quidam who holds fast in his faith, there is neither tragedy nor comedy. It is after all he, in spite of his self-annihilation, who holds fast, and that is the kind of fact that matters in a religious setting, however tragic, laughable, or unintelligible it appears even, or especially, to someone who grasps the way religion proposes to come to terms with the reality that a Quidam finds he cannot otherwise come to terms with. Long before, in 1836, before he had come upon the idea of separating human attitudes into pseudonyms that represent them in isolation, Kierkegaard wrote that irony and humour 'may well unite in one individual'. But why shouldn't irony and humour unite in someone,

like Quidam, who reaches the point of faith? Perhaps further light can
be thrown on the pseudonyms if one sees that there is no such thing as
a humorist who never comes to the point of 'feel[ing] moments when
the world makes fun of him'.[28] If he were a real person, Frater Taciturnus might well have followed Quidam into faith, just as Quidam, even
in his faith, would be able constantly to see himself in the eyes of a
humorist.

So Quidam is not a humorist in the way Frater Taciturnus is, that is
to say he is not a professional. But it is still a question whether humour
in Kierkegaard's sense is not supposed to be a necessary ingredient in
his or any ascent to faith. If so, and if it appears that Quidam himself
shows none of it, we could conclude that there is a more integral
symbiosis in the relationship between him and Taciturnus than we have
assumed. But that could only be because Quidam is as abstractly conjured forth by Taciturnus as Taciturnus is by Kierkegaard.

Whatever conclusions one comes to here, Quidam and Taciturnus
between them complete the itinerary which began in *Either/Or* with
portrayals of the aesthetic and ethical life-views. Indeed, Quidam's diary
with Taciturnus's commentary provides all the material the account
requires. Despite the demonic fear of repentance, Quidam tends always
in the direction of the religious. The presence of the tendency from the
start explains his reserve, that very fact which prevents his responding
spontaneously to love but is also an intimation of a 'higher life'.[29] Even
when Quidam tries to tackle the matter ethically, the 'religious possibility lies deepest in his soul' as it already did in his first life-view.[30]
Having followed Quidam so far, Frater Taciturnus sums up the progress of his 'experiment' to date by saying: 'This is how the stages are
arranged: an aesthetic-ethical life-view in illusion, with the dawning of
the religious possibility; an ethical life-view that condemns him; he sinks
back into himself', and now, says Frater Taciturnus, 'I have him where
I want him'.[31]

What Taciturnus means is that here is where humour can finally
sever Quidams's lingering worries over what kind of noble deed to be
done, or what undeserved hurt in the past, will excuse him for his
failure to conform to the demands of the universal or 'generality' (*det
Almene*). Beyond tragic heroism, with its anchoring still in historical
achievement, and now with the thought that if something is really worth
achieving then it is laughable to suppose that there is any call for the

person doing it to be oneself, Quidam must face the possibility that
when it comes to religion no excuses will work. The long and the short
of it is that Quidam, who began 'demonically' opposing the prospect of
a possibility he really hankers after, ends up accepting a condition
without which a religious basis for exemption from ethical norms is
impossible. He takes upon himself the guilt for what he has done,
including, or as one might also put it, discounting, whatever might be
explained and excused by pointing to background factors – social, en-
vironmental, or psychological. Even if he might find explanations there
for the hurt he has done (as Job had no need to, since like Abraham he
was sinless, though the latter was prepared to do it for God), he takes
personal responsibility for all that he has done. Then and only then can
he ask about repentance.

Frater Taciturnus summarizes by saying:

There are three spheres of existence [*Existents-Sphærer*]: the aesthetic, the ethical,
the religious. Metaphysics is an abstraction, and no human being lives metaphysically. Metaphysics, ontology, exists, but not in existence [*det er ikke til*], for
when it arises in existence it does so in the aesthetic, in the ethical, and in the
religious, and when it is there, it is as an abstraction from or a presupposition of [*et
Prius for*] the aesthetic, the ethical, the religious. The ethical is a transitional sphere
and consequently its highest expression is repentance as negative action. The aesthetic sphere is that of immediacy, the ethical that of debt (and that debt is so
infinite that the individual always goes bankrupt), the religious is that of fulfilment,
but, be it noted, not in the way one fills a walking stick or a bag with gold, for
repentance has made the room for itself infinite, and hence the religious contradiction: to rest upon the seventy thousand fathoms deep and yet be joyful.[32]

Philosophically literate readers at the time would be reminded of
Hegel in the *Phenomenology*. Hegel writes of 'the way of the soul which
journeys through the series of its own configurations as though they
were stations appointed for it by its own nature, so that it may purify
itself for the life of the Spirit'.[33] This, for Hegel, was also 'the way of
despair'. That is because for the traveller 'press[ing] forward to true
knowledge' every new station has to be reconstructed in the aftermath
of the doubt which each previous station gives rise to, when tested to
destruction. The difference in Kierkegaard's version is so radical as to
make the comparison itself ironical. Where Hegel talks of the pursuit of
objective (self-)knowledge, Quidam's journey can only be described in
a personal diary whose import is available only to a person wise enough
to the limits of 'communication' to realize where the diary has to stop.

The stations on this journey, a 'Story of Suffering' (the subtitle of Taciturnus's publication), are in a private world, and the significance of their names can only be conveyed in a relationship to 'a reader'.[34]

If the anti-Hegelian side is for local consumption what was the main purpose of *Stages*? Is Kierkegaard here still working through his own problems, or does *Stages* perform a role in some larger context? With its focus from start to finish on the 'woman', and considering that Taciturnus's descriptions of 'the experiment's *quædam* [the lady in question]' follow Kierkegaard's of Regine, while many of the diary entries are taken verbatim from Kierkegaard's own records of his broken engagement,[35] *Stages* for all (perhaps because of) its paraphernalia of pseudonymity does undoubtedly read as a deeply personal work. All of it, that is, except 'In Vino Veritas,' the part that proved so hard to write. There is little evidence in the work of any attempt by Kierkegaard to rise above the difficult situation he had shared with Regine. Quidam is even allowed to say, in his final midnight entry: 'I would have been more fulfilled if I could have remained faithful to her, and my spiritual life put to daily employment in a marriage . . . such are the priorities.'[36]

One can think of several reasons why Kierkegaard would want to keep the ideal of marriage in place. One was personal. He had broken his word to Regine and made her suffer. He could hardly repair that damage by claiming to satisfy some overriding condition of human fulfilment which, for those lucky enough to have access to it, justifies the breaking of vows. To do so would also deprive him of the possibilities both of restitution and, if only it could come to the same, of justifying his exceptionality. If you are to be an exception to a norm, the norm itself from which you seek exemption must stay in place. But Kierkegaard seems genuinely to have approved of the norm in any case. The fact that the author of 'Quite a Lot about Marriage' says that marriage is the individual life's (*Tilværelsens* – the word is often translated 'existence' but like the related German term *Dasein* refers to living or specifically human existence) 'highest telos' doesn't of course prove anything. But, as we saw, Kierkegaard does say in his papers, of *Either/Or*, that 'the second part begins with marriage because it is the deepest form of the revelation of life [*Livets Aabenbarelse*]'.[37]

Not altogether accidentally, perhaps, both passages include a reference to Jupiter and Juno (or Hera) as *teleios* and *teleia*, or in Latin, *adultus* and *adulta*, meaning 'complete' or 'consummated'. In 'Quite a Lot' the point made is that in pagan, that is to say pre-Christian, times, even though there was no god of marriage but only of love, marriage – a 'higher expression' of love – nevertheless had its protectors.[38] The additional point is that in pre-Christian times the protection was conceived as given from outside, while what the author especially recommends about marriage is that it protects itself from inside, by a decision or conclusion that owes nothing to chance, as in pre-Christian days was still the case, notoriously so, even with divine protection.

What then are we to make of the 'stages on life's way' or 'spheres of existence'? Is this a theory of human development, an alternative to Hegel, or are the stages simply 'stations' along the way that one particular single soul despairingly wandered in its search for forgiveness and the opportunity to purify itself for the life of the Spirit? Taciturnus's closing letter suggests a much wider and more forward-looking perspective than either concern can provide, the locally Hegelian or the privately personal. Recall that *Stages* was written while the project of which *Fragments* was only a partial result remained unfinished. Things of more importance were still to be done. It would be implausible to suppose that they were not forcing themselves on Kierkegaard's mind as the manuscript grew, and the third part of *Stages* reads easily as a text in which the *Fragments* project was already being resumed, so that what we have here is a prelude to its completion. All that was said earlier about the relationships of the pseudonyms to the case histories, to which they themselves in a manner of speaking owe their very existence as ministering spirits, can be reread in the wider context of poetry's or fiction's relation to history. The case histories are themselves poetic, but that is what allows them to present themselves to the reader as possibilities, of what can be rather than of just what plainly is. Among copious other classical and literary allusions, Taciturnus refers in his letter to Aristotle and Lessing. Owning Lessing's collected works, Kierkegaard would be familiar with Lessing's frequent references in *Hamburgische Dramaturgie* (1767–68) to Aristotle's discussion of the relation of poetry to history.[39] The point made earlier, that for one who holds fast in his faith there is neither tragedy nor comedy, is in fact one that Taciturnus relates directly to the issue. Poetry is still commensurable with the outer, while faith is not. This gives us a hint that the completion of the *Fragments* project that now follows is not simply a return to that project but a new look at it in the light of all that has been learned from Quidam's example.

Concluding Business

For all the effort Kierkegaard had put into *Stages on Life's Way: Studies of an Assorted Assemblage* [*Forskjellige Sammenbragte*], the work once 'brought to print and published by Hilarius Bogbinder' (on 30 April 1845) had nothing like the success of its model, *Either/Or*. It was little noticed and sold badly. Bitter satisfaction rather than dismay at this failure to win the audience that would permit the new work to replace the old was Kierkegaard's official response in the (designedly only pre-posthumous) privacy of his journals. 'That's fine', he wrote, 'that way I'm quit the gawking rabble that wants to be on hand wherever it thinks something's astir.'

He also says he knew this would happen and had even said as much, in 'my [please note the use of the first-person pronoun] epilogue to " "Guilty?" – "Not-Guilty"?', and perhaps because Kierkegaard feared the worst, the epilogue does indeed adopt a mock-defensive tone.[1] The underlying frustration and real disappointment came out in Kierkegaard's subsequent efforts to drum up interest in these latest pseudonyms. Those efforts and the dramatic turn they took belong to the next chapter.

True to form, almost simultaneously with *Stages* Kierkegaard had managed to publish the signed *Three Discourses for Imagined Occasions*. These were completed after several drafts and changes of plan between mid-February and late April 1845.[2] More discourses were soon to follow. But there was still that much larger job to complete, the *Fragments* project. It still lacked its 'historical costume', and Kierkegaard began to conceive the 'Postscript' to *Fragments* as the final completion of the task he now saw himself as having begun in 1841 in Berlin. Time might be short. The nemesis of the Kierkegaard family beckoned. In May 1846 he would be thirty-three, the age at which he later told Brøchner he was firmly convinced he would die. (Brøchner's surmise was that this was because that was the age at which Christ was crucified, but we recall that two of Kierkegaard's sisters also died at the same age – though even their deaths might have been linked to the former in Kierkegaard's mind.)[3] This June, not long after *Stages* came out and directly following a three-day stay with Peter and his family at Pedersborg, the journal records a visit to his father's grave, 'prompted by a special need'.[4] The move back to Nytorv may have prompted the visit. Sometime between the end of 1844 and the spring of 1846 Kierkegaard wrote instructions for the repair, that spring, of the family burial site, leaving room on one of the stones for '*Søren Aabye*, born 5 May 1813, died ——'.[5]

Much of the plan and some of the material for the unfinished *Fragments* project lay to hand. But it was to prove a far larger task than Kierkegaard had anticipated. The text of *Concluding Unscientific Postscript*, especially towards the end, leaves the impression of a writer making use of a last chance to commit himself and his ideas to print. The character of the work tends increasingly towards that of a container into which all of the important ideas he has ever had must be crammed. But true to form, Kierkegaard managed to have the mammoth manuscript of *Concluding Unscientific Postscript to* Philosophical Fragments: *A Mimic-Pathetic-Dialectical Compilation: An Existential Contribution*, 'by Johannes Climacus, Edited by S. Kierkegaard', delivered to the printer by 30 December 1845, just eight months after the publication of *Stages*.

The problem raised in *Fragments* was posed against the background of the thought-experiment that human beings lack the ability to recognize the truth about human being. The problem itself took the form of a question: how can an eternal happiness be built on an historical event? The connection between this and the background hypothesis was the thought that, with regard to the truth of human being, either we have it in our power to discover, or in a sense recover, that truth on our own given the appropriate Socratic prompting, or else it has to be disclosed or demonstrated to us in an historical setting that can never be known to be otherwise than merely historical. Being in possession of the truth is spoken of in terms of having an 'eternal consciousness', and the difference between the two positions is that, while the Socratic position assumes that we are somehow already embedded in that consciousness and can be made to become aware of being so, the other position takes it that we can come to possess such a consciousness only in the form of faith, a deliberate choice in favour of the unthinkable, namely that something historical can both be eternal and demonstrate what possession of an eternal consciousness amounts to. As promised, *Postscript* gives the problem, at least from the point of view of the latter alternative, its historical costume. In one sense it can do that very briefly, simply by saying 'Christianity'. But it involves something else too, something that we have learned from Quidam and Frater Taciturnus, namely that there is a process of development and that it occurs, or has to be produced, in the individual, each individual. That is what allows Johannes Climacus, who resumes his *Fragments* project, now to ask in a personal way the questions formerly posed impersonally: 'How may I, Johannes Climacus, participate in the happiness promised by Christianity?' It is, he says, a question that 'concerns myself alone', though 'if properly posed it will also concern everyone else in the same manner'.[6]

We said earlier that *Fragments* aims to make us think differently about thinking. That aim is even made a principal objective of its 'Postscript', a basic theme of which is something called 'subjective thinking'. The suggestion is that this thinking is appropriate for questions and answers concerning the truth of human being.

Maybe so, but will what Climacus says about subjective thinking apply equally and in the same manner to a person who declines Christianity's offer, or who cannot come to believe that anything enjoys the position Christianity claims to be in to offer such a thing? The question is really whether, whatever subjective thinking turns out to be, it applies just as much to any truths at all of human being, or truths about what can be true of human being, including nihilism or the view that there is no eternal consciousness and that finite facts of nature and history are all there is. Is it implied, for example, that if nihilism were true there would be no use for subjective thinking, so that objective thinking would be appropriate in all questions of truth?

Since Climacus is not directly concerned with that question it is hard for us to say how he should answer it. He does say introductorily, however, that it is impossible for anyone who has 'lost the sense' of an eternal happiness ever to enjoy it.[7] If subjective thinking were needed to acquire that sense, and that sense were in part the idea (from the outside, as Climacus admits, the quite comical idea) of 'such a weight' being laid on one's 'little self', then maybe there is a correspondingly opposite sense (perhaps comical too from the outside, though tragic also from the inside) of an absence of any weight at all being laid there. If that could be called a sense of nihilism, then that too might be said to be a proper topic of what Climacus calls subjective thinking. It is at least clear that it is only in the light of such thinking that the individual appreciates what is at stake in grasping the promise extended by Christianity.

There is a further question. What if the needs that the Christian promise addresses, and to which subjective thinking makes the individual peculiarly sensitive, are ideological? That is, what if the needs are felt only because Christianity has already persuaded us that without the benefit of what it promises, we will remain forever and even in all eternity incomplete? Again, this is not a question Climacus directly addresses. Were he to do so, he would have to ask whether Quidam's story were a case-history of another kind, that of a deviant. One would then point to circumstances, for instance that he was suffering from false consciousness, for which he need not, indeed should not, accept guilt and feel that he had to repent. But that would be to adopt a quite different point of entry to the problems that *Postscript* raises and deals with.

These questions aside, we can note that Climacus, situating himself outside Christianity but equipped 'with my infinite interest, with the problem, and with the possibility',[8] confines himself to asking what is required of the individual's relationship to Christianity. He begins by addressing and dismissing two ways which would make the reflection required objective rather than subjective. The targets are familiar, Grundtvig's historical and Heiberg's Hegelian accounts, nor are the observations new; indeed, as noted earlier in connection with *Fragments*, Climacus's remarks on Grundtvig make use of material from the earliest journals. The general point made is the inappropriateness of thinking of Christianity as something 'out there', to which one assures oneself one will relate once the facts of what exactly it is out there that one is to relate to are clear. Climacus reviews three such approaches, one focusing on the Bible, another on the Church, and a third called 'the proof of time'.

There are some not-so-very-clearly separated strands in the argument. The case against resorting to the Holy Word to decide Christian doctrine is that it runs afoul of the problem of historical uncertainty, so that however honourable a discipline historical philology may be, its results, excellent in themselves, can still at best always only approximate the truth of what was written, and when, and can therefore never provide the basis for an eternal happiness. The problem here appears to be the inaccessibility of the basis of one's belief, but Climacus keeps on interjecting that this whole way of relating to Christianity as something 'out there' is wrong in any case. Approximation is a quantitative affair, a matter of accumulation (of evidence) or removal (of reasons for doubt) as if in the end the facts, ideally at least, could lie bare before us. Nor is what is inappropriate about this simply that waiting for someone else's expert judgment on such things takes away the opportunity to make faith one's own; even if the facts were delivered on a plate they still would not suffice as a basis for an eternal happiness.[9] The same applies to Grundtvig's proposal, in apparent reversal of the characteristically Protestant move away from Catholicism, to substitute the church for the Bible. His 'matchless discovery', as we recall, was to substitute the *living* word for Clausen's form of Protestantism, which 'makes the written word everything' and the church into a fellowship of 'bookworms'. What Grundtvig said was needed was a 'society of faith with a creed'.[10] The words of Jesus thus came to form the basis of what Grundtvig called 'The Church View'. The advantage of the idea, as Grundtvig saw it, was that it eliminated all those difficulties about reaching back to the past. The Christian truth could be made a living presence. Climacus says again, praise be to those to whom praise is due, particularly Magister Jacob Christian Lindberg, who has developed this point 'with competent juristic precision'.[11] But, as noted earlier in connection with *Fragments*, it is one thing to claim that the church exists, quite another to claim that the existing church is the apostolic church. The latter claim relies just as much on historical accuracy as do claims for the authenticity of the Bible. Similarly with the third approach, or the alleged principle that the longer a hypothesis stands the test of time, the more reliable it becomes. As far as that goes, 'eighteen centuries have no greater demonstrative force than a single day in relation to an eternal truth that is to be decisive for an eternal happiness'. Indeed, everything that has been said about it in the course of the centuries can just as well serve to 'take one's mind off it'.[12]

A relationship to Christianity is not one that people acquire by adapting themselves to a set of truths discoverable in the world, by acquiesc-

ing in certain facts whether in the form of scripture or of devotional
practice. To believe so, as the 'old' Grundtvig does, praising it as a sign
of 'youthfulness', says Climacus, is to have

no idea of the subtle little Socratic secret: that the nub of it is precisely the subject's
relationship. If the truth is spirit, it is an internalization and not an immediate and
highly artless relationship of an immediate *Geist* to a sum of propositions, even if to
compound the confusion, this relation is given the name of the most decisive
expression for subjectivity, faith.[13]

The latter aside seems clearly intended also for the Hegelians, whose
view of faith as prereflective and 'immediate' Kierkegaard has constantly
criticized. That the 'nub' is to *establish* the relationship in the subject
says that faith proper is a post- and not a prereflective attitude. It
requires 'self-activity', in connection with which notion it is interesting
to observe what was said in the motto that concludes *Fragments*, namely
that even if the B-position outlined there were an advance on Socrates,
it says essentially the same thing that Socrates did. In advancing to the
B-position one does not leave the achievements of the A-position behind, and it will appear that the A-position is exactly the one in which
self-activity (though paradoxically in the form of self-annihilation) becomes focal in the cultivation of a religious attitude. Without it no
occupancy of the B-position would be possible. The A-position is the
way in which the individual transforms *itself* in order then to relate
appropriately to Christianity, the B-position.

The 'speculative' approach is dealt with swiftly: '[It] takes Christianity to be a historical phenomenon; the question of its truth therefore
becomes a matter of so interpenetrating it with thought that in the end
Christianity itself is the eternal thought.'[14] 'But suppose', says Climacus,
'that Christianity is nothing of the kind?'[15] If it were, it would have to
be 'given'. If it were given, how would one distinguish it from anything
else? Once, says Climacus, it was dangerous to declare oneself a Christian; today it dangerous to deny it. Christians are everywhere, and so
by the same token is Christianity. So objective have we become that not
just civil servants but 'even their wives' are now 'arguing from the
whole, from the state, from the idea of society, from the science of
geography, to the single individual'. But what if the whole project of
interpenetrating Christianity with thought were 'chimerical', an impossibility because Christianity

is precisely subjectivity, an internalization, and . . . only two classes of people can
know something about it: those who with an infinitely passionate interest in an
eternal happiness base this on their believing relationship to Christianity, and those
who with an opposite passion (but in passion) reject it – the happy and the unhappy
lovers. What if an objective indifference could learn nothing at all?[16]

That goes some way towards answering our earlier question about
nihilism. But Climacus is more concerned with those who adopt an
objective attitude and at the same time claim to be believers. The
speculating philosopher need not of course be a believer; nor is there
anything inherently wrong with speculative philosophy: 'All praise to
anyone who truly occupies himself with it.' For him, Climacus, to deny
its worth would be, he says, to 'prostitute himself', and 'particularly
foolish' in someone 'most of whose life has in its small way been
consecrated to its service', and indeed the more foolish in an admirer of
the Greeks such as he is, who would know that Aristotle, mindful that
thinking was 'the blessed pastime of the eternal gods', 'identifies the
highest happiness with the joys of thought'. Besides, he, Climacus,
should have 'some conception of, and respect for, the dauntless enthusiasm of the scholar, his persistent devotion to the service of the idea'.
But, he says, 'for the speculator, the question of his eternal happiness
simply cannot arise, exactly because his task consists in coming ever
further away from himself and becoming objective, and thus vanishing
from his own view and becoming the power of speculative gazing'.[17]

These comments sound autobiographical. Kierkegaard – as one senses
even in the comical example of the would-be philosophy journal editor,
Nicolaus Notabene – not only respected philosophy and those who
devoted their lives to the idea, but also in his own 'small way' had given
quite a lot of his own life to it. Whether the 'small way' is confined to
the works of Johannes Climacus, or included there at all, and if not
what else can be included, is an interesting question. We can keep it on
hold as we follow *Postscript*'s further course.

We noted in Chapter 9 that among the undeveloped material Kierkegaard had originally assembled for *Fragments* were some comments
on Gotthold Ephraim Lessing (1729–1781), the famous dramatist and
critic and a central figure in the German Enlightenment. These had
appeared under the heading, 'The Apologetic Presuppositions for
Christian Dogmatics or Approximations to Faith, Section 1: An Expression of Gratitude to Lessing'.[18] What was all this about, and why does

Kierkegaard have Climacus now devote two whole chapters of *Postscript* to a long-dead littérateur?

Not to seek respectable sponsorship for unfashionable ideas; if there is one general thesis in *Postscript*, it is that authority has no place in matters of faith. Indeed in the very first sentence of the second of these chapters on Lessing, Climacus assures us that he is not invoking Lessing to have someone to 'appeal' to.[19] Nor can it be a simple matter of giving credit to sources; the two chapters form far too elaborate an expression of gratitude for that. We have already seen that Kierkegaard had come across Lessing's use of the notion of a 'leap'. It was in connection with the topic we have just seen discussed: the impossibility of extracting eternal truths from contingent historical data. The chapters on Lessing embed his reference to a leap in a portrayal of Lessing as a paradigmatic subjective thinker, and it is at the end of the second chapter on Lessing, just prior to what follows on what it means to 'become subjective', that we are presented with Climacus's famous twofold thesis that a logical system is possible but not an existential one. Lessing commends himself first and foremost as a thinker who does not lose himself to become the power of pure thought, but also as one whose notion of the leap compares favourably to other versions that in Kierkegaard's time were familiar to students of recent philosophy. Lessing provides just the basis Climacus needs to go on to discuss, in apparently objective terms, the nature of subjective thought.

As an able apprentice of Lessing's ironic style, Kierkegaard/Climacus may also have hoped that favourable comparison would allow some of the great man's literary prestige to rub off on his own efforts. Ostensibly Climacus presents his tribute to Lessing as an independent thinker's call for outside help. A poor lodger, Climacus looks down wonderingly from the heights of his garret and sees all that is being done to expand the building and improve the facade, but cannot help worrying about the foundations. Commentators often identify the building with Hegel's System, but the entrepreneurs are closer to home. Heiberg was not only a professed Hegelian but also, as it happens, in light of his eclectic reputation as poet, dramatist, and critic, Copenhagen's best-qualified candidate for the position of local Lessing. The real Lessing, of course, was not a Hegelian. Nor indeed, though famously professing himself a Spinozist, had Lessing articulated any consistent or systematic philosophical position. Indeed, so eclectic had been the real Lessing's contribution to late eighteenth-century German culture, and so piecemeal his expressed views on philosophical matters, that all attempts to place him in the philosophical landscape would be in vain. In a comment whose style would lend some support to his own claims to be a local Lessing, Climacus says:

> Lessing, of course, has long since been left behind, a vanishing little way-station on the systematic railway of world-history. To rely on him is to stand self-condemned, to confirm every contemporary in the objective judgment that you cannot keep up with the times, now that one travels by train – and the whole art is to jump into the first and best carriage and leave it to world-history.[20]

The advantage of Lessing is that he is a writer whose work the Hegelian edifice that Martensen and Heiberg were so keen on expanding has been unable, or has not even sought fit, to get around. Deference to *Fragments*' motto, 'Better well hanged than ill-wed', would of course always lead Kierkegaard to prevent having his work interpreted and judged by the System. But in his polemic against the System it would serve his purpose well if he could find an ally in someone the System itself had been unable to assimilate. Better well hanged than ill-wed to an objective thinker, but better still to be well-wed to a subjective thinker. Yet how is such an affiliation to be conveyed?

Well, at least there would be no harm in a marriage to someone so passé as Lessing. However, such high-profile weddings need some more solid tie than the mere ability to escape the clutches of the System. What might that be? We note how carefully prepared is Climacus's portrait of Lessing. First everything upon which Lessing's fame rests is stripped off; we are told to disregard the scholar, the legendary librarian, the poet, the turner of phrases, the aesthetician, the sage, and so forth.[21] These are the externals which have been duly flagged on the map of eighteenth-century German culture, but fortunately too scattered to be collected under a single rubric suited to the System. The question is, once out of the way, how can they be replaced by a plausible portrait of a subjective thinker?

In the second, and longer, of the two chapters Climacus begins by attributing to Lessing two theses which are not textually attributable to the historical Lessing but are his own. One of these clarifies the difference between objective and subjective thinking and introduces the notion of 'double reflection' as characteristic of the subjective thinker. The subjective thinker has to find the right way of expressing a personal interest in something, over and above the conventions for describing whatever it is he is interested in. The other thesis ties comedy and pathos to one and the same subjective thought, so that what sounds like a joke can nevertheless be meant and grasped as deep earnest. The plan clearly is to present Lessing as someone whose famously ironical remarks can be interpreted as expressions of subjectively reflected thought. Lessing and Socrates are being made to form an alliance which makes the marriage even more acceptable. By linking these theses, crucial to Climacus's exposition, to Lessing's name in this way, Kierkegaard can use them as markers to define the hermeneutic horizon within which to interpret the remaining theses which are actually attributable to Lessing.

Chief of these is the use, noted earlier, Lessing makes of Leibniz's distinction between contingent truths and truths of reason in order to declare that eternal truths of reason cannot be inferred from accidental truths of history. This was made the background thesis to the problem in *Fragments*: how to base an eternal happiness on something historical. Now, in *Postscript*, Leibniz's distinction is used to define what Climacus following Lessing calls the leap, something which in turn is central to Climacus's notion of faith. Since faith is the principal topic of *Postscript*, we can see how under Climacus's astute direction Lessing has been brought out of world-historical obscurity and placed polemically at centre stage.

The Lessing brought to life in these two chapters is not the historical Lessing. But given the nature of subjective thinking, or what it means to say that a thinker is subjective, why should that prevent his being the actual Lessing all the same? History can get it wrong. Equally, of course, this may be nowhere near the actual Lessing – we simply cannot tell. But that is just what the position to be outlined should lead you to expect. Whether or not the portrayal is true, there is a sense worth noting in which any portrait of a subjective thinker cannot help but be a fiction. You may nevertheless guess that the picture Climacus presents is on all accounts far from incredible, especially in light of the fourth thesis, in which Lessing confesses to being a searcher rather than a finder. Lessing says that, offered the choice by God, he would prefer the lifelong pursuit of truth to truth itself.[22] This underpins Climacus's admiring observation that Lessing has no 'result'. Certainly by no means

all of the actual Lessing's views would appeal to Kierkegaard,[23] but
there is something in Lessing's attitude towards Christianity which
would surely attract him; as one commentator nicely puts it: 'Lessing
spent his life hoping that Christianity was true and arguing that it was
not.'[24]

The kinship Climacus seeks with Lessing, then, and in the ironic
spirit of Lessing himself, lies at the level of subjective thinking, which
apart from other things is the thinking of someone in continual development and never resting on a 'result'. It is almost as though Climacus
were saying that Lessing's grasp of subjective thinking was good enough
for him to have been able to write the *Postscript* himself, though historically, of course, he could not have done that. World-history, as Climacus himself might have said, was still awaiting Hegel's arrival; what he
does remark is that Lessing never had to contend with the principle of
mediation.[25] But something more is still needed. If kinship at the level
of subjective thought were enough to provide a basis for Kierkegaard's
alliance with Lessing, he might have settled straightaway for Socrates.
The extra needed is to be found in the indications provided by scattered
remarks to the effect that Lessing had a better grasp than his contemporaries of the notion of a leap of faith and, connected with this, as a
journal entry from 1848 says, a considerably clearer notion of the true
problem concerning the relation between Christianity and philosophy
than 'the common herd of modern philosophers'. The problem is of
course the threefold question of *Fragments*: how to reach a historical
point of departure for an eternal consciousness, how such a point of
departure can be of more than historical interest, and how to build a
personal happiness on a piece of historical knowledge. Kierkegaard adds:
'Lessing uses the word *Sprung* [leap] as if its being an expression or a
thought didn't matter. I take it as a thought. . . .'[26]

Exactly what distinction Kierkegaard had in mind here is not clear,
especially since Climacus will later tell us that the leap is not a thought
but a decision. But Climacus does tend to think that when he talks
about a leap, Lessing plays with words and images rather than with
concepts. To try to grasp what it is that Lessing has understood better
than the common run of philosophers, let us by way of a comparison
Climacus himself intends look at the two contrasted thinkers mentioned
in the chapters on Lessing: Johann Georg Hamann and Friedrich Heinrich Jacobi (1743–1819). It is significant that both are well-known for

their contributions to what is called the spirit of the counter-Enlightenment. One question we shall have to face, then, is why Kierkegaard, the alleged irrationalist, should cast in his lot with Lessing, the great Enlightener himself, rather than with these two renegades and potential existentialists.

Answering that question requires uncovering some of the anatomy of the period during which the currently somewhat glibly named Enlightenment Project had lost much of its impetus. What was undermining it was the apparent inability of the programme of free inquiry and criticism to achieve its anticipated political goals. As in any time when culture divides, parties form, and thinkers jockey for position on one side or the other, it was also a time of creeds.[27] The Enlightenment's own official creed had been reason, but in the movements constituting the counter-Enlightenment it was exactly faith in reason that had begun to crumble, due as much as anything to the transparency reason had been able to bring upon itself, above all in the critical philosophy of Kant. Kant remained a rationalist, but in some quarters the faith in reason gave way to – in a manner of speaking to be made a little clearer later – a faith in faith. In others even the grounds for a faith in faith appeared to crumble as the conspicuous successes of natural scientific reasoning appeared to destroy the very humanist assumptions upon which the original Enlightenment goals had been based. This, we saw, was the basis for Kierkegaard's thoughts on the modern Faust.

The two thinkers we are considering remained unaffected by this deeper crisis. This meant that their break with the Enlightenment was a correspondingly ambiguous affair. Often the Enlightenment is in retrospect spoken of as if it were based on a narrow conception of human rationality, reason in a 'thin' sense. It is not only more accurate but also more revealing to regard the Enlightenment as a movement of thought based on a basic trust in the human being's capacity to secure its own basis for the traditional supports of human life (morality, religion, and the state); Enlightenment was to replace a capricious tradition and unsupported appeals to revelation, scriptural authority, and the like. But then any nascent doubt about the ability of human powers of systematic reasoning to perform this role need not in the first instance lead to an abandonment of the high aims of Enlightenment itself. One may suppose rather that the first natural reaction within the Enlightenment horizon will be to appeal to some other human capacity, or perhaps to review the account currently given of what human capacity amounts to. Such a review may lead in the end to revision of even such a key notion as that of reason itself, as happened in the cases of both Kant and Hegel. That is to say, one need not abandon the project of reconstituting human values and practices on a human basis simply because human reason as currently conceived proves inadequate to the task.

An example of this was the new liberalism which appeared late in the eighteenth century in such figures as Schiller, Humboldt, and Forster, though Lessing and Jacobi were also involved. Here we find the diminishment of reason compensated for by an attribution to individuals of a native ability to take care of their own welfare, religion, and morality. The new liberalism urged characteristically that states should protect human rights but not actively intervene in promoting stability and welfare. That would be to inhibit, and thus in the end to destroy, an innate human capacity to promote them. Seen in this light, even the extreme form of liberalism – anarchism – is simply a projection of Enlightenment thought. It assumes a human talent to produce organization at the level of the individual from below. A romantic dream no doubt, but still within the terms of the project.

The same, however, can be said of Romanticism itself and of the *Sturm und Drang*. Here too we have an extension of Enlightenment faith, even if the typical interpretation of Romanticism sees it, as did Hamann himself, as a polemic against the Enlightenment. Hamann, who we saw was an early hero of Kierkegaard's, proposed the life of artistic feeling and expression, or indeed of lived experience in general, as the proper source of the truths humanity needed and to which reason had been inappropriately applied. One can of course also say that Hamann saw in lived experience the locus or source of truths that would lead to a radical revision of the humanizing project of the Enlightenment, so that in effect through Hamann that project acquired a nature and dimension it had previously lacked, and that therefore this is indeed a polemic against the Enlightenment. But by looking at the Enlightenment in terms of its goals rather than its chosen method, we may see both the liberal and the Romantic developments as attempts to save the project itself. Both developments involve typically 'immanent' points of view, pushing reason aside to make room for a power of appreciation and apprehension which had been unnecessarily ignored and suppressed. That this is not the normal way of looking at the Enlightenment project, least of all the way for those like Hamann who began to criticize it, is due mainly to the project's being identified with those philosophers who despite these criticisms continued to believe that the crucial human truths could be established by reason, as they conceived that capacity, alone.

Hamann called his new sense of life and artistic feeling 'faith'. But there is no invocation here to look or leap *beyond* reason. Hamann, for whom the rational horizon merely defines the limits of a shallow, debilitating intellectuality, proposes instead a return *to* experience, not a leap beyond it. As has often been pointed out, there is a strong 'existentialist' strain in Hamann to which Kierkegaard early responded.[28] Not only does the appeal to lived experience as the place to which to address significant human questions, as well as the place from which to ask them, have its clear counterpart in the writings of Climacus, but what Hamann himself wrote based on his own lived experience provides an important source for just those psychological concepts Kierkegaard had already exploited in his own 'experimental' writings – for example, anxiety, as we saw earlier, where Hamann sees '*Angst*' as a 'holy hypochondria'. Kierkegaard is also clearly influenced by the way Hamann reappropriated the Enlightenment's hero, Socrates, to turn the tables on the Enlightenment by focusing on Socratic ignorance: 'The greatest humorist (Hamann) has said concerning the greatest ironist (Socrates), that what made Socrates great was that he distinguished between what he knew and what he did not know.'[29]

But Hamann's thought lacks dialectic. Although for Hamann 'faith is not the work of reason, and therefore cannot succumb to its attacks', he has no thought of faith as being antagonistic to reason. And even if faith 'happens as little for reasons as do tasting and sensing',[30] it still happens in much the same way as do these latter. Hamannian faith is an immediate trust in one's sense of things; indeed, he saw Hume as the precursor of his brand of faith in faith. Although Kierkegaard acknowledges Hamann's position on how the common understanding of religion errs, he does not see Hamann as occupying the point of view of religion developed by Climacus in the *Postscript*. And, whether due to inadequacy of perspective or to his own failure to do the perspective justice, Hamann's criticism had not in fact survived in a way that would have made him a suitable ally.

What about Jacobi? In spite of his zealous criticism of current exponents of Enlightenment thought, Jacobi still held onto the 'humane' goals of the Enlightenment. Since he was also satisfied that he had identified the limits of reason, for him the choice was obvious. If you cannot prove the existence of God and the immortality of the soul in the way that a philosopher such as Moses Mendelssohn (1729–1786) thought one could,[31] you must accept these vital truths on faith. For Jacobi, reason's cognizance of its own limits leads the *rationalist* to atheism, but in his uncritical refusal to countenance that conclusion he, too, is a proper heir of the Enlightenment, and his faith is merely a change of horses in midstream – from the faith in reason to a faith in faith itself. Anticipating one side in the recent debate between Popper and his critics as to whether rationalism is inherently irrational because itself the result of a basic choice, which therefore cannot itself be rational, Jacobi saw faith as a basic human attitude to which even the rationalist must resort in order to choose reason.[32] This and a continued belief in revelation, and also his 'leap [*salto mortalis*] of faith', earned for Jacobi an anti-Enlightenment and irrationalist label. But exactly as with Hamann's so-called irrationalism, Jacobi's was merely a concern to keep reason within its own bounds – bounds that do not define the limits of human understanding in a large sense but, when they are defined, allow room for another mode of human understanding.

Later on in *Postscript*, at the conclusion of his chapter on subjective truth, Climacus acknowledges the contributions of both Hamann and Jacobi. But neither is suited to his project. Typical of the tone of high irony preserved throughout the two chapters on Lessing, Climacus's manifest reason for not allying himself with either of these thinkers is the inherent or simply de facto inability of their work to resist Hegelian compartmentalization.

> . . . I won't hide the fact that I admire Hamann, though freely admitting that the pliancy of his thought lacks proportion and that his extraordinary vitality lacks the self-control needed for working in any coherent way. But his aphorisms have the originality of genius, and the pithiness of the form is entirely suited to the casual throwing off of a thought. Life and soul, and to the last drop of his blood, he is captured in a single phrase: a highly gifted genius's passionate protest against an existential system. But the System is hospitable, poor Hamann! you have been reduced by Michelet[33] to a §. Whether some stone marks your grave I do not know; whether it is now trodden under I do not know; but this I do know, that with the devil's might and main you have been pressed into the §-uniform and pushed into the ranks.[34]

For someone protesting vigorously against enrollment in a system, such treatment is no better than being brought into a bad marriage with the system itself. In fact it is worse, for as the metaphor implies, it means being forced to continue fighting all the same but on the wrong side. But Kierkegaard's real criticism of Hamann is that the appeal to lived experience is still the expression of an aesthetic point of view. This is made all the clearer by noting that, in Hamann's case, reason and faith are not in conflict with each other, they simply have different roles, lived experience now being given the due of which the Enlightenment's 'thin' reason had unfairly deprived it. In this respect, Hamann's understanding of the roles of faith and reason is not unlike that commonly ascribed to Wittgenstein, a language-game view in which reason and faith each have an independent part in the complex structure of our language-based practices, so that it would be wrong to apply the standards of one language-game to the practices of the other. But if reason is not in conflict with faith, then faith neither is nor requires a leap beyond reason; one merely switches from one game to the other, simply making sure not to confuse the standards appropriate to each.

Jacobi too is dismissed for having survived merely as an entry in the System's encyclopedia.

Poor Jacobi! Whether anyone visits your grave I do not know, but I know that the §-plough overturns all your eloquence, all your inwardness, while a few scant words are registered as what you amount to in the System. There it is said of him that he represents feeling with enthusiasm. . . .

As Climacus says, 'a reference like that makes sport both of feeling and of enthusiasm, whose secret is precisely that they cannot be reported second-hand. . . .'[35]

But (to quote Climacus himself) 'now to Lessing'.[36] If Jacobi's weakness was to have said too much, clearly Lessing's merit is to have said very little and, in respect of what he did say, to have 'remained a riddle'. His strength, as Climacus says, is that 'it was quite impossible to have Lessing killed and world-historically jointed and salted in a §'.[37] That could be said to be the ironical explanation, to be read as evasive humour by those able to grasp only second-hand explanations. The serious point, to be picked up first-hand by subjective thinkers, has to do with the leap and what it means to have faith. It is here that Climacus turns the 'riddle' of Lessing to his own, and he would assume Lessing's, advantage.

The third thesis, as we know an actual thesis of Lessing's in this case, is that 'accidental truths of history can never serve as proof for eternal truths of reason, and the transition by which one would base an eternal truth upon historical testimony is a leap'.[38] According to Climacus, what Lessing 'constantly' opposes is the 'direct transition from the historically reliable to the eternal decision', or any attempt to 'quantify oneself into a qualitative decision'.[39] Lessing uses the distinction between historical contingency and necessary truths of reason to mark the illegitimacy of any attempt to convert the purely historical facts on which Christianity is based into the eternal facts constitutive of Christian faith. As historical contingencies they cannot amount to the eternal truths embodied in Christian belief. As Lessing says, 'The letter is not the spirit, and the Bible is not religion, so that objections against the letter, or against the Bible, are not ipso facto objections against religion'.[40] Climacus reminds us that Lessing describes the unbridgeable gap between letter and spirit as a 'ditch' that is both 'repugnant' and 'wide',[41] and also that Lessing says he has tried, 'often and earnestly' but without success, to leap over.

There are, he thinks, two glaring mistakes in Lessing's account. First, the 'leap' is a decision ('the category of decision'), which means that you either do it or don't do it. There can be nothing called trying or failing to do it. The idea of 'having been quite close to doing something' has in itself something of the comical about it, but 'to have been very close to making the leap is nothing whatever'. Second, if there can be no trying to leap, then there can be no 'earnest' in doing so either, and Climacus's next comment is that the notions of trying and earnest can only apply here to the attempt 'with the utmost earnest to make the ditch wide', indeed 'infinitely wide', as infinitely as the 'bloodstain that Lady Macbeth makes so monstrously large that the ocean cannot expunge it' (Kierkegaard conflates Macbeth's 'Will all great Neptune's ocean wash this blood clean from my hand?' [II.3] and Lady Macbeth's 'all the perfumes of Arabia will not sweeten this little hand' [V.1]).[42]

Consider what we ordinarily mean by leaping over a distance. Usually a leap is an attempt to minimize some inconveniently great distance, treating the gap as much as possible as if it were nothing. Leaping is an effort to take that distance in our stride – make nothing of it, as the expert leaper might say. But Climacus suggests we should be making everything of it, not trying to ignore the distance but making it 'infinitely' large. What he would convey is not a bound from one foothold to another; outwardly the leaper just keeps going; it is the leaper who changes, not the location, and if there is anything corresponding to a space or a void, it is in the thought that what one takes to be one's normal, easy stride is in fact infinitely difficult. For all the normal strider knows, this ground on which he walks is not the space of his own and of God's possibilities, but what Kant once referred to as the 'black abyss' of a world without Providence.[43] The leaper of faith (though the expression never occurs in that form in Kierkegaard's writings) dares to assume, without ground, one might say, that the gap realized in his understanding is not such an abyss. The leaper's trick, as Johannes *de silentio* says in *Fear and Trembling*, is 'to transform the leap in life to a gait, to express the sublime in the pedestrian absolutely'.[44]

Climacus presents Lessing's words about the leap as essentially comical. Their comical nature is presented as the visible aspect of that Socratic combination of comedy and pathos which characterizes the existing thinker. He describes Lessing's whole account as that of a 'wag' (*Skjelm*),[45] as indeed it would have to be if Lessing's earnest is that of a subjective thinker. In conclusion Climacus subtly brings Lessing's humour to bear on Hegel by introducing a 'more popular' way of poking fun at the leap: 'you shut your eyes, you seize yourself by the scruff of the neck *à la* Münchhausen, and then – then you stand on the other side, on the other side of sound common sense, in the promised land of the System.'[46] But if the presentation is a subtle mix of irony and polemical strategy, the argument underlying it is no less subtle. Climacus admits that Lessing has 'very little to say' about the leap and that therefore there is little to be said about 'Lessing's relation to the leap'. Nor is it 'altogether dialectically clear what Lessing has wanted to make of it'.[47] Yet on the way he has been careful to bestow on Lessing just those features which would indeed lead one to expect him to say very little. His words have acquired a Socratic 'complexion',[48] and we have been told earlier that in addition to 'poetic imagination' he has the 'sceptical ataraxy and religious sensibility needed to become aware of the category of the religious'.[49] Lessing's evasive facetiousness can, in short, be read as Socratic jest, just as the brevity of his comments can be taken to demonstrate his constant ability 'cleverly to exempt himself, his dialectical insight, and inside that his subjectivity, from every express delivery service to the bearer'[50] – all of which, again, is consistent with the thesis that Lessing is a subjective thinker. Climacus's argument in a nutshell is this: Lessing says little about the leap, but the little he does say is consistent with a genuine understanding of the leap, which will then explain why he says so little.

The clearest picture we are given of Lessing as someone able to avoid answering in ways which would betray his grasp of what the question asked occurs in Climacus's rendition of part of the famous conversation between Jacobi and Lessing, which according to Jacobi took place in July 1780 at Wolfenbüttel, a few months before Lessing died, and a report of which Jacobi published after Lessing's death.[51] Jacobi claimed that Lessing had told him he had left Leibnizian metaphysics behind and now fully embraced Spinoza's pantheism with all its determinism, finding no difficulty in renouncing the freedom of the will. Jacobi's shocking disclosure sparked off the *Pantheismusstreit*. It is at the end of this conversation, says Climacus, that we have Lessing's 'last word' on the leap. The exchange follows Lessing's famous confession and Jacobi's suggestion that a *salto mortale* can get you to where reason cannot reach. After Jacobi has outlined the researcher's task as being that of 'disclosing existence' (*Dasein zu enthüllen*) but with 'explanation' as just 'the first goal', the last being 'what cannot be explained: the irresolvable, immediate and simple', Lessing remarks: 'Generally speaking, your *salto mortale* does not displease me; and I can see how a man with a head like that will want to stand on it to get somewhere. Take me with you if it works.' Jacobi then invites Lessing to '[j]ust step on the elastic spot which catapulted me out and it will go of its own accord.' To which Lessing replies: 'That already requires a leap that I can no longer ask of my old legs and heavy head.'[52]

Of course Lessing may just have slipped away on his old legs simply to avoid further badgering by the persistent Jacobi. But just as Jacobi exploited Lessing's last word for his own ends, so Climacus does the same for his, pointing out that faith for Jacobi is a cheap surrender of his human gift of understanding. Lessing just humours Jacobi, 'realiz[ing] very well that the leap, or the crux, is qualitatively dialectical and allows no approximating transition'. What Jacobi egregiously lacked, in Climacus's language, is that 'passionate dialectical abhorrence [*Avsky*] for a leap' which makes that 'so infinitely wide' ditch 'repugnant'.[53]

Whatever Lessing may have meant by that phrase, it is undeniable that the commitment to reason and the acceptance of Spinozistic conclusions – and it was these that for Jacobi were repugnant – bring Lessing within reach of the existential dialectic expounded in the two Lessing chapters. The moral seems to be that precisely because faith in Climacus's sense involves a clear break with the Enlightenment, the Enlightenment itself is a better background against which to grasp it than the various moves made to save it in the so-called counter-Enlightenment.

In a subtle twist of counterfactual reasoning Climacus contrives to enlist Lessing's support even though, in matters of faith, support (*pace* Jacobi) is just what you cannot have. He appeals to Lessing as someone who would agree that if he could be appealed to, then the project that calls for his support would not be the right one. There can be no direct acknowledgement, but at least you know for certain that if there were, then someone had got it wrong. Attachment on that point should be beyond reproach.

You see, that's how hard it is to approach Lessing in religious matters. If I were to present the individual ideas, ascribing them to him directly and in parrot fashion, if I were to enfold him politely, obligingly, in my admiring embrace, as the one to whom I owed everything, then he might smilingly disengage, leaving me in the lurch, an object of ridicule. If I were to keep his name quiet, come out bawling joyously over this matchless discovery of mine, which no one before me had made, then that *polymetis Odysseus* [wily Odysseus], if I imagined him there, would no doubt, with a look of ambivalent admiration on his face, thump me on the shoulder and say: 'Darin haben Sie Recht, wenn ich das gewusst hätte [You are right there, if only I'd known].' And then I, if no one else, would understand that he had the better of me.[54]

Suppose now that the outcome of these chapters on Lessing is that, to one who understands religious discourse (and therefore its relation to experience), *if* another writer were to embrace him as a colleague, then the right thing to do would be to look at one's watch and plead another appointment. What then are we, the readers, supposed to make of the fact that in the remainder (Part Two) of *Postscript* there are still more than four hundred and thirty pages to go?

There are many proposed reasons why Climacus, once affirming the incommunicability of subjective thought, continues for so long, or at all, in seeming communication with his reader. Some, pointing to the humour that surfaces so often in the work, have taken *Postscript* to be no more than a witty exposé of the speculative genre; all that we are intended to grasp is the caricature itself, while (unless we are Hegelians) savouring the ironic humour that conveys it. Others, locating the humour not in any simple parody of the Hegelian style, but in what is seen to be the deliberate illogicality of the argument designed to poke fun at Hegelians in that more subtle way, see *Postscript* as seditious but in a way that only professionals will detect. At the other extreme are those who attach either less or no importance to the humour, perhaps because (excusably, if dependent on some standard translations) they simply fail to see it. In many people's eyes *Postscript* is just a piece of bad philosophy, a flawed attempt to perform some standard philosophical task – anything from the provision of an alternative, anti-idealist science of spirit, unloading the heavy burdens borne by Hegel's *Geist* onto the 'single individual', to a prolegomenon to any future radical theology, or more narrowly still, the basis for an existentially correct Christian apologetics. There are even attempts to read *Postscript* as some kind of amendment to a Fichtean theory of subjectivity, a theological adaptation even, while others have looked at it with the wisdom of hindsight as an attempt to turn the Kant–Fichte self-consciousness tradition in the direction that was to end in Husserl, Heidegger, and Sartre.

All of which speaks, if not for the clarity of the work's intentions, at least for the richness of its text. But is there perhaps some less spectacular and more systematic explanation of what Kierkegaard thought he was doing in that latter half of 1845 as he struggled to complete this huge project in a language that only two million Europeans spoke and in a style and terminology that only a handful of these could be expected to appreciate? In his own attempt to sort out the confusion of understandings that *Postscript* and its humour had then evoked even in this little group, Kierkegaard wrote some years later:

The reason why *Concluding Postscript* is made to appear comical is precisely that it is serious – and people think they can better the cause by taking separate theses and translating them into pieces of dogma, the whole thing no doubt ending in a new confusion where I myself am treated as a cause, everything being translated into the objective, so that what is new is that here we have a new doctrine, and not that here we have personality [*Personlighed*].[55]

That passage could be quoted with advantage to those commentators today who, in telling us what Kierkegaard 'means', find causes for him to defend and oppose whose names and locations have been invented only very recently. Identifying what Kierkegaard's texts stand for and what cultural causes and trends they represent would be deeply misleading if, for example, it turned out that part of what Kierkegaard meant to convey in *Postscript* was that to represent a cause was antithetical to becoming a subjective thinker.

The other extreme is to take some totally parochial view. A version of what was uppermost in Kierkegaard's mind could go something like this: 'I must at all costs avoid being allied with Mynster against the Sorø people, or with them against Mynster, or with either against Grundtvig; not because of disagreement with any of them, though in fact I do tend to disagree with them all, but just because I find myself wanting to disagree with anyone; you name it, I'll oppose it – unfortunately Poul Møller was right, I am thoroughly polemical by nature.'

That isn't entirely fanciful; at least it probes the psychological dynamics of Kierkegaard's production, which is just what the large-scale accounts fail to do. The view might even be tested by seeing whether, whenever Kierkegaard became convinced that someone agreed with him, he revised his position to ensure sole occupancy. That he was attracted to the role of lone-wolf we know already from those earliest journal entries on his favourite topic: the master-thief. 'Single-mindedly single-handed' might not be an unsuitable a motto for a powerful strain in the complex of motivations guiding Kierkegaard's hand as he wrote, and that Kierkegaard was a writer who systematically reserved his position, aligning himself neither with locally represented 'causes' nor with what he himself had already written, at times not even with what he was actually writing at the time, would be one view that the quotation just cited on the seriousness of *Postscript* might be read as supporting.

There are, on the other hand, more constructive alternatives which make sense both of what Kierkegaard says in the quotation and of what *Postscript* says following its effusive presentation of Lessing as a subjective thinker – a thinker, one might say, precisely *without* a cause in the narrow, cultural-political sense that Kierkegaard opposed. A clue here is the word which ends the quotation: 'personality.' For us, today, the topic of personality is not high on the philosophical agenda. But already in Chapter 6 we noted the important place it had in the prehistory of the philosophy of Kierkegaard's time. It happened to be Hegel's philosophy that provided him with the philosophical scenario best suited to his concerns. It enabled him to formulate the question of unity from the urgent viewpoint of separation where, to use the current terms, 'ideality' and 'reality' seem to be forever separated. And as we noted earlier, not long before starting on *Postscript* Kierkegaard had written: 'In one place Hegel himself seems to hint at the incompleteness of mere thought, that philosophy by itself is after all an inadequate expression of human life, or that the personal accordingly does not fulfil itself in thinking on its own but in a totality of existential modes [*Arter*] and ways of expression.'[56] Familiar as he had now become with the original Hegelian aesthetics, as opposed to Heiberg's impressive but more superficial anticipation, Kierkegaard will have noted Hegel's appreciation of the 'firm and consistent characters' portrayed in Shakespearean tragedy.[57] With their total engagement these characters epitomize the type of active life that Kierkegaard from his earliest student days prized as engaging the whole personality, even whole newspapers, as we recall from Chapter 1. He will also have noted, as Hegel did, how these figures 'come to ruin simply because of this decisive adherence to themselves and their aims'. It was a form of this adherence that generated the tragic heroism of antiquity, something that Kierkegaard also owes to Hegel. Because for the Greeks, as for Hegel, and as, in Frater Taciturnus's scornful words, now 'even the wives of civil servants' were wont to say, the 'argument' goes from 'the whole, from the state, from the idea of society' to the single individual, it is Antigone who is 'shattered' in the 'collision' between the individual's and the ruler's 'one-sided pathos'.[58] To the question 'guilty or not guilty?' one has to answer in the case of tragic heroes that they 'are just as much innocent as guilty'.[59] The outcome of a decisive, one-sided, pathos-driven adherence to one's own 'cause' is inevitably tragic. In order to avoid it, one must, at whatever personal and intellectual cost, accept total guilt and give oneself up to God. In a signed work written a year later, Kierkegaard says that only the eternal can be willed in a unified, that is to say personally unifying, way.[60]

If we follow Kierkegaard's own pointer, then, *Postscript* can be read as offering a nonphilosophical notion of the unified and 'concrete' personality. This was a topic raised earlier in *The Concept of Anxiety*, in a comment on Rosenkranz in the section on anxiety in the face of the good (the demonic), where Haufniensis talks of seriousness as an acquired 'originariness' of disposition and refers back to claims made by Constantius about seriousness in respect of repetition.[61] Personality was a concept very much in the air, and Kierkegaard's contribution was to give it a new twist by making his controversial notion of faith the unifying factor. What *Postscript* provides is an itinerary for the path to 'personality'.

That is one interpretation. Another reads the work negatively, as showing how large the scope for despair increasingly becomes. Actually the text incorporates the ambiguity in a way that suggests that this itself, the very ambiguity, might be the main theme, that is, for those readers able to grasp what it says about that other topic, subjective thinking. The plausibility of such readings is something we may judge for ourselves once we have seen what the rest of *Postscript* contains.

Part Two opens by stressing that the 'task of becoming subjective' is not part of some objective problem, it is actually to *become* subjective, and in the course of a lengthy, wide-ranging, and not-very-tightly argued discussion, Climacus points to the infrequency with which one finds 'individualities'. These are people who not so much 'preserve' but 'ethically speaking . . . gain . . . the virgin purity of ethical passion, in comparison with which the purity of childhood is but an amiable jest'.[62] That the task of becoming subjective is 'the highest proposed to a human being' is not stated as an axiom, nor is it argued positively. It is only pointed out how 'beautifully arranged' everything is if it is indeed true. World history, from whose perspective the task doesn't even appear, can be 'left to the poet laureate'.[63] The discussion ends with a list of some of the 'simple' subjective questions that, if pursued persistently, become difficult enough to make choosing 'astronomy or the veterinary sciences and the like'[64] seem facile options and not worthy choices for someone wanting a task for a lifetime. The examples given are: what it means to die, to be immortal, to thank God, to get married. Then, as a final touch, he tells how, sitting one Sunday afternoon outside the café in Frederiksberg Garden, smoking his cigar, and wondering what contribution he could make to mankind after ten years of 'splendid inactivity' as a student, it suddenly struck him that since with 'his limited abilities' he was unable to make things easier than they had already become, he might 'with the same humanitarian enthusiasm as the others' take it upon himself to 'make something more difficult'. He decided on the spot, and 'out of love of mankind', that his own task was to 'make difficulties everywhere'.[65]

That might tell us how to read what follows. The immediate sequel is a more closely argued chapter on truth, in which Climacus says that for a 'subjective reflection' truth is a matter of appropriation, a matter of *how* one believes something, not of whether some proposition adhered to is true or not. In contrast to objective reflection, in which, as already noted, subjectivity vanishes along with its task, in the case of subjective reflection it is subjectivity that is left over and objectivity 'the vanishing factor'. So it doesn't really matter whether the 'what' of the belief corresponds to facts 'out there'. Indeed, as Climacus notoriously adds, 'if only the how of [the] relationship is in the truth, the individual is in the truth even if he should happen to be related thus to untruth'.[66] The highest truth available to an existing individual is 'an objective uncertainty held fast in a most passionately inward appropriation'.[67] That statement has been read as carte-blanche legitimation of any zealously held point of view. But we should not forget that *Postscript* is a postscript to *Fragments*. Whatever the form of reflection that aims at it, the truth can always surprise one and is only seldom what is wanted. More importantly, wanting the *truth* is a special kind of wanting; it is wanting something even if it turns out to be something you would prefer *not* to have. The test of your truthfulness – of the consistency with which you act on this realization – is whether you maintain your belief even when, to you personally, what is evidently true is totally repugnant. Socratic ignorance gives us one case. In the quest for knowledge of human nature and self-understanding one confesses ignorance but at the same time, as if in partial mitigation of the way in which truth may be repugnant, assumes an ability to recognize the truth all the same, once, so to speak, it is on show – in effect a denial of ignorance. The B-position gives another. It drops the assumption that the truth can be recognized – at least in any authorizable way – for here it is the truth itself that is paradoxical. The eternal, the timeless, has to become historical, the position specifically of Christianity. If the truth here is repugnant we are not even compelled to put up with it all the same because we see that it is true, for here it is entirely up to ourselves to admit to its truth.

The paradoxical nature of the truth, against the A-position's placing the paradox in the existing subject's relation to a nonparadoxical truth, plays only a small part in *Postscript*. Absurdity enters the definition of truth as subjectivity at the last minute to indicate that highest possible inner tension of inwardness that constitutes faith. The bulk of Part Two is concerned with the finite subjective thinker's relation to an eternal truth independent of that truth having to manifest itself absurdly in an historical event.

In an appendix to the chapter on truth as subjectivity Climacus proceeds, by an amusing device, to show how *Postscript* both presupposes and upstages the works of the earlier pseudonyms. Entitled 'A Glance at a Contemporary Effort in Danish Literature', the appendix gives an extensive account of how Climacus, before he managed to write his own works, *Fragments* and *Postscript*, and in attempted execution of his brilliant plan to help people by making things more difficult for them, found each of his successive authorial intentions systematically anticipated by someone else's publication. The device appears to have a serious purpose all the same. It positions *Fragments* and then *Postscript* in relation to the other works in preparation for, at the very conclusion of what Kierkegaard planned as a 'concluding' postscript, his final word, a recantation as it turns out, and his farewell to his readers.

There follows a chapter that serves a purpose similar to that of the 'Interlude' in *Fragments*, providing what, apart from the extensive footnotes that appear towards the end of *Postscript*, is the most conventionally philosophical part of its text, though interspersed with humorous analogies and asides. The philosophy is, in fact, as in the 'Interlude', philosophically subversive; standard philosophical terminology is used to revise the philosophical landscape, and although the explicit, because closest, target is Hegelianism, the revisions go far beyond a critique specifically of Hegel. After some opening remarks about the language of abstract thought abstracting from the very reality to which a subjective thinker must try to attach thought, the chapter ('The Real, or Ethical Subjectivity: The Subjective Thinker') goes on to remake a previous point, saying that abstract thought removes the difficulty from all 'existential questions' (*Existents-Spørgsmaal*) simply by failing to let them arise.[68] Existence is what reality, or actuality (*Virkeligheden*), is; it is where choices have been and have to be made, and constantly renewed, and where passion belongs; for we who exist there is just one reality, our own ethical reality – another person's, including ours from their

point of view, is not actual but only possible, that is to say a thought
we have but not our own reality, the continuity sustaining the instanta-
neous impulse that keeps this movement of making and renewing
choices going is the eternal factor (though a footnote says that worldly
as opposed to 'idealizing' passion turns existence *into* the 'instantane-
ous').[69] You cannot conclude from thought to existence (*Tilvær*), for
thought goes in the opposite direction, away from the real, and annuls
it.[70] But neither is thinkability a condition of relating to something, you
can still relate to it in your life, and grasp it in that way, paradoxically
and with the passion of inwardness.[71]

The next section elaborates the latter point into a distinction between
'the aesthetic and the intellectual principle' that no reality is grasped
until it has been turned into a thought – what Climacus calls a possibility – and, on the other hand, the 'ethical principle' that you first grasp
what is, or was, possible when you realize it in your life.[72] That says
something like: your life will never be made to conform to a preconsti-
tuted thought, because the forward impulse in life transforms what you
thought into a reality of which the thought was not the possibility. But
also, we must bear in mind, the forward movement acquires a special
passion when driven by something that cannot be constituted at all as a
thought. In a comment on Hegel's criticism of Kant, Climacus says that
the questionableness of Hegel's 'Method' already appears in his use of
thought to rescue us from the scepticism Kant's philosophy leaves us in
with regard to what things are in themselves, in their independence of
our thought-constructed view of them. How can the 'fantastic shadow-
play of pure thought' halt a scepticism that is itself about thought? But
Climacus attacks Kant too. The critical philosophy is itself criticized for
the 'deviation' (as in a compass that points the wrong way) whereby it
brings actuality into relation with thought. As for the *an-sich*, the only
thing-in-itself that cannot be thought is 'to exist' (*at existere*).[73]

In the chapter's third section, science's identification of thought as
man's highest and species-specific attribute is said to be a 'confusion' in
which science departs more and more from the 'primitive impression of
life', treating the imaginative and emotional sides as surpassed. Love,
faith, and action are not things that one does or performs but that one
knows about.[74] In existence the bodily, psychological, and spiritual
'stages' confront us all at once. The final section defines the subjective
thinker's task as that of 'understanding oneself in existence', and life is

said to be not a science but an art.[75] 'The subjective thinker's form, the form of his communication, is his style', and that is 'as manifold as the opposites he must keep together'.[76] When told some pages later that the task is to 'transform' oneself into 'an instrument that clearly and definitely expresses the essentially human in existence',[77] we realize that (as is obvious in the Danish) the instrument is a musical one, not a means or a tool. Each one of us can be that instrument, since (echoing a principle exploited by Notabene) 'everyone must be assumed to possess what it takes to be essentially human'.[78] That sounds Socratic as against Christian, but Climacus has told us of his 'infinite interest' in the truth of Christianity, and since he is still working his way up to the B-position the reference must be to what the A- and B-positions have in common, and therefore not yet to what is specific to the Christian's acceptance of the condition for recognizing truth.

What follows is a revamping of the thought-project of *Fragments* – how is an eternal happiness to be built on historical knowledge? – with the A- and B-positions now clearly identified as forms of religiousness.

A natural question is, has Climacus been offering us, as this summary certainly suggests, a philosophy of subjective thought? If so, isn't that fatal? For what then prevents an encyclopedist from doing to him, and to Lessing, what Michelet did to Hamann and Jacobi? The irony on Lessing's admiring face as he thumps Climacus on the shoulder and says, 'Darin haben Sie Recht, wenn ich das gewusst hätte', speaks volumes.

But if this *is* philosophy, Kierkegaard has certainly done his best to remove all traces of the heavy seriousness associated with the discipline. The light tone, of which the bare inventory of theses recited here offers no indication, gives the chapter a literary and rhetorical feel quite inappropriate to the genre to which the terminology nevertheless belongs. If this is philosophy, it is philosophy in some form of disguise.

That might be to look at it from the wrong end. What if the light tone, the humour, is the serious thing and the philosophy the disguise? Recall Kierkegaard's remark that 'the reason why *Concluding Postscript* is made to appear comical is precisely that it is serious'. Socrates was serious, too, about his irony.

Postscript's own comments on humour come in the course of Climacus's new treatment of the *Fragments* question. In spite of being told that the subjective thinker communicates through his style and not his words, Climacus there proceeds to give a very full verbal account of the 'existential pathos' that the style must express if it is to be that of a Christian. Since pathos is essentially something one feels rather than conveys, even by one's style, this implies that Climacus knows something about it. And yet *Postscript* just as surely cannot itself be a piece or a result of subjective thinking. How could such a vast compilation of words, ideas, arguments, and scholarly footnotes, part intellectual challenge and, with its acute and ironic observations, part entertainment, express a subjective reflection, let alone that reflection's 'truth'?

But what if humour *belongs* to the subjective thinker's style, is a necessary part of it, and *Postscript*'s humour is its way of betraying an origin in the area of subjective thought? Of course, Climacus would object to our calling humour, just as he objects to our calling irony, merely a 'style' (*Tale-Form*).[79] Yet the suggestion is not that humour is *added* to *Postscript* to signal something or other, for instance that what it says is not meant seriously. It is that the text as a whole has its origin in what Climacus in the same passage calls a quality of life (*Existents-Bestemmelse*).

Is there such a quality deserving the name 'humour'? A few pages earlier Climacus has added to Frater Taciturnus's list, in *Stages*, of three spheres of existence, two borderlines (*Confinier*) between the spheres: 'irony is the boundary between the aesthetic and the ethical; humour the boundary between the ethical and the religious.'[80]

Both boundaries are connected with tensions in life that first appear to subjective reflection and then become increasingly 'difficult' in subjective thinking. The would-be ethicist, says Climacus, grasps the 'contradiction' between the way he exists in his innermost soul and his failure to express this outwardly. By ironizing the finite and 'all the world's relativities' he avoids the comical misunderstanding that he is actually fulfilling the requirements – irony becomes his 'incognito'. To keep pure the ideals that he nurtures in his innermost life, he pooh-poohs the world's relativities.[81] For the ironist the irony, accordingly, is a cover, a veneer of superiority which guarantees that he will never be mistaken for someone with sheerly immediate enthusiasms. Among ironists, however, the irony will be an indication of the inwardness that is being protected.

Similarly with humour: insofar as the religious person is incompletely religious, he protects what religiousness he has (or aspires to inwardly) against the confusion that his outward behaviour might come from something less. In this case the something less is not just something aesthetic or immediate, but also what would be motivated ethically, that is to say, inspired by the thought that the important thing is to be him*self*, or reveal *a* self, a socially motivated self, in the face of the world. The religious person certainly has to *do* with the world, as much as the ethical person, but only in the light of a focus first *away* from the relativities to an absolute, or eternity. In religiosity it is one's relationship to God that now bestows the value that the ethical bestowed on relativities through collecting and transfiguring them under the 'continuities' engendered by one's own socially expressive self. In a footnote attacking the portrayal of tragic heroism in *Fear and Trembling* as 'illusory', as a 'foolhardy anticipation' that makes religiosity look like an 'accomplishment' instead of the continual striving in the 'medium of existence' that it is, Climacus even appears to say that a religious person will *always* adopt the incognito of humour. That may be because there is no such person as one who is purely religious. In reply to the suggestion that the religious person's real incognito is that nothing at all reveals the 'hidden inwardness', he says that, 'so long as the struggle . . . in inwardness continues, [the religious person] will be unable to conceal his inwardness completely'. Not wanting to 'express it straightforwardly', he will hold it back 'with the help of the humorous'.[82]

Both irony and humour are thus inhibitions to the proper expression of inwardness in the world of relativities. They are at once impediments to its full development and ways of protecting what inwardness there is. They are also indications of that inwardness to those in the know. Climacus stresses, however, that if you are looking for a religious person, then you should be on the lookout for humour. But if the person does happen to be religious, you would be quite wrong to suppose that the *person* in question is humorous: 'strictly speaking the religious person is infinitely higher than the humorist', and the religious person will be essentially serious. That is why the humour is an incognito. If not just a style, it is still a facade. To the one who is essentially humorous, that is to say, a humorist through and through, the humour would be more than a facade, it would betoken occupancy of a place, or at least a boundary position, in the hierarchy of stages. The humorist stands between the ethical and the religious.

But can there be such a person? Or, partly the same question, can a boundary be an area? Perhaps the humorist straddles the boundary, having a foot on either side. But Climacus claims that he is a humorist 'purely and simply'. The implications are unclear, and the matter bears some comment. In one place Climacus says that an 'existing' humorist 'presents the closest approximation to the religious person'.[83] If approximation means 'on the way but not yet', then Climacus can very well be (represented by Kierkegaard as being) an existing humorist. But what would a humorist 'purely and simply' be? Are we to take it that Climacus is no more than a personification of a trait? 'Someone' who was purely and simply a humorist, and not at all religious, would lack that inner way of existing that contrasted with the humorous exterior. In the pure and simple humorist's own stance there would, in short, be nothing for the humorist to laugh at. The absurdity of that result suggests another interpretation.

Generally, Kierkegaard does not talk of the humorist as merely a personification of some *Existents-Bestemmelse* abstracted from life. On the contrary, he typically speaks of the humorist as someone who, compared to the systematizing philosopher, is particularly aware of what it is to live. Early on he had written:

[T]he humorist can't really ever become a systematizer, for he regards every system as a renewed attempt . . . to burst the world open with one single syllogism . . . whereas [the humorist himself] has precisely come alive to the the incommensurable which the philosopher can never account for [*beregne*] and must therefore despise. He lives in the fullness of things [*i Fylden*] and is therefore sensitive to how much is always left over, even if he has expressed himself with all felicity. . . .

After which he interjects: 'therefore this disinclination to write.' As we confront *Postscript*'s nigh six hundred pages, that comment is itself comical. Surely at least one humorist has been signally able to overcome his disinclination.

But has he? There is another reading. *Postscript* conspicuously emulates, perhaps mimics (the word is one of the predicates in the work's subtitle), the systematizer in accounting for all that can be accounted for, but differs totally by holding in the highest respect what is left out. That early journal entry ends: 'The systematizer believes that he can say everything and that whatever cannot be said is erroneous and secondary.'[84] For the humorist, on the contrary, it is what cannot be said that is true and primary.

Climacus describes humour as a capacity to detect the comedy 'present in all stages of life'.[85] Irony and humour both 'level' everything. But while irony does so 'on the basis of humanity in the abstract', the humorist does so 'on the basis of the abstract God-relationship'. The humorist remains on the outside in the sense that he reaches the point at which the God-relationship makes sense but turns away at the last moment. He 'parries with his jest'.[86] But that is because humour is the incognito that protects him from entering into what he knows is needed. At this point the humorist now sees that he himself is comical. Of course, if Climacus is simply an illustration of the humorous stance, and his insight into suffering is not into his own (that not being included in the fiction of the pseudonym), then he himself is *not* an existing humorist, or rather he is not an *existing* humorist. He is, in fact, and like those existentially amputated diagnosticians before him, Constantius and Taciturnus, some-'one' who helps others to understand *their* suffering. Aware of the challenges that exist, the pure and simple humorist treats them in the way physicians treat matters of health while not worrying about their own. As Climacus says, reverting to the topic of Taciturnus's concern with Quidam, the humorist can grasp that 'we are all guilty', can understand that sentence but at the same time ignore the implication, indeed not see what it means to say, that he himself is guilty.[87] But in grasping also this latter fact, that he is not in a position to see what it means, he realizes his own limitations.

By uncovering the comedy of his own position Climacus sees that he has come to that position's own epistemological limits – they are indeed the limits of epistemology, at least with regard to the truth that *Fragments* and *Postscript* are concerned with. The limit is reached because, as soon as one turns inward and away from the world, as in religiousness A, which is a 'dying from the world', one offers no comical contrasts. The religiousness of 'hidden' inwardness prescinds from earthly goals and therefore leaves nothing for humour to catch hold of. The end of the privileged access Climacus has to the comedy of life comes when he sees, both in and by virtue of his humorous detachment, that he has disclosed the 'ultimate' contradiction – between his own detachment and (provided it exists) the seriousness it conceals.

But we still haven't identified *Postscript*'s serious purpose. Can we say that it is simply to point out that one should *not* theorize when action is called for? That would leave us wondering what the purpose of all the theorizing has been. Does *Postscript* merely pretend to be theorizing? Is it a parody with no underlying argument of its own? Are we supposed to laugh at Hegelians and others as representatives of the huge comedy of thinking at all in regard to faith? But then, surely, since normally any practice at all can benefit from theorizing, why should that not be true in the matter of faith as well?

Recall Climacus's faulting Hegel for attacking what he calls Kantian scepticism using the very means that Kant was sceptical about, namely thinking. Kant was of course not sceptical about thinking as such, but only about just the kind of claims Hegelians later came to make on its behalf. But some have argued that *Postscript* makes the same mistake, only in its case deliberately and as a subtle joke: Kierkegaard with his partiality for paradox is sporting with the idea that reason can be used to destroy reason. They note Climacus's reference to the need to crucify reason if you are to have faith, and ask, how can you use reasoning, as Climacus does, to crucify reason?

The answer must be, surely, to use just enough reason to make sure that reason in its improper application is properly crucified. There is no paradox in that. Kierkegaard himself makes the point on behalf of Climacus.

When . . . I believe this or that on the strength of everything's being possible for God, what is the absurd? The absurd is the negative property which ensures that I have not overlooked some possibility still within the human range. The absurd is an expression of despair: humanly it is impossible – but despair is [just] the negative mark of faith.[88]

These remarks can be set alongside others in which recognition of the absurdity of Christian doctrine is presented as essential to having faith:

Hence the unholy confusion about faith. The believer is not dialectically consoli- dated [*dialektisk consolideret*] as 'the single individual', and cannot put up with this double vision – that the content of faith, seen from the other side, is the negative, the absurd. This, in the life of faith, is the tension in which one must hold oneself. But the tendency everywhere is to construe faith in the straightforward manner. Such an attempt is the science which wants to comprehend faith.[89]

Dialectical consolidation seems a good enough goal for reason to con- tribute to, and just what we would expect of an author who stresses the need for focused action. The elaborate dialectic in *Postscript*, often taken as parody, would be peculiarly apt for *Postscript*'s addressees: those disposed to believe that faith can be comprehended.

What then are we to say to those who caution us as follows: 'It has to be borne in mind that Johannes's magnificent writings are no more Kierkegaard's than are the productions of the other pseudonyms. The reader becomes so entangled in the elaborate joke that the whole production is seen and talked about as if it were completely "serious".'[90]

Not completely serious, that we grant. But serious enough to be saying something, and not saying it just to take it away again, as the same author, in agreement with many others, suggests: *Postscript* 'defines a problem, how to exist in the modern world, and claims there is an answer, to become a Christian; then annuls the answer by demonstrating that it cannot be reached'.[91] But *Postscript* itself nowhere poses a problem to which becoming a Christian is an answer; it asks not what requirements Christianity must fulfil but what becoming a Christian requires. Nor does it ask the latter question from some point of view from which Christianity is not yet in focus, and then through some peculiarly subjective method proceed uniquely but mysteriously, even 'misologistically', to locate that truth as the most 'repulsive form of nonsense'.[92] *Postscript* explicitly (though is that too a subtle joke?) assumes the focus and then asks what must be done to appropriate it truly. That to do so requires one, in a sense, to traverse Hegel's path of despair backwards does indeed add an ironical touch, but it is a bonus due to the requirement. Considering the lengths to which Climacus goes to explain the requirement it would be absurd to see that as itself just a means to the bonus.

It is essential to note that no comedy is implied by the 'absurdity' *Postscript* employs in its definition of 'faith'. Absurdity here is a logical notion. The relatively brief space assigned in *Postscript* to religiousness B is a final twist to the achievement of religious inwardness in A. Religiousness B is said to preserve the inwardness of religiousness A (B 'presupposes' A – just as A presupposes humour).[93] It is by facing the 'unthinkable' thought that the eternal can be part of history that inwardness is taken to the limit. If there is comedy here, it is in Climacus, who by his very persistence becomes the more 'absurd' by continuing his objective account, not in the believer the conditions of whose faith he persists in negatively defining.

An elaborate joke? Hardly. Why should Kierkegaard spend eight months of what he feared might be the last year of his life preparing a party trick he might never enjoy, and an untopical jest at that, since Hegel's star had long been in decline? Surely Johannes's magnificent writings are the culmination of an authorship whose continuing theme bears comparison to that of other great authors. Faust comes to mind. One might even see *Postscript* as the completion of the Faustian project commentators claim Kierkegaard began but later abandoned. Think of it. Lessing left an unfinished play ennobling Faust's quest for knowledge and allowing reconciliation with God (so much for the subjective thinker);[94] Goethe, in the second part of his poem/play, has Faust purified and redeemed, a travesty of the myth according to Kierkegaard. He himself had toyed with the idea of a modern Faust, a Faust who realized that knowledge can no longer be the way. Kierkegaard had even wondered whether Christianity might not give Faust some reassurance, with its 'levelling' on behalf of an idea so big that all others disappear beside it. We recall that Kierkegaard saw in this the Romantic and humorous side of Christianity – it no longer matters what you know or can do.[95] Kierkegaard had agreed with Lenau, with his focus on the dangers of the quest for absolute knowledge, but thought the ending of his version of the legend unsatisfactory. By taking his own life from a sense of impotence Faust becomes a person and not an idea; the myth should be saved by having Faust rise above all previous versions and complete himself in a new idea.

Perhaps the journey from 'Either' in *Either/Or*, through *Repetition*'s young letter-writer to his more untried version in 'In Vino Veritas', and finally to the Quidam who vanishes from the zone of communicability at the end of ' "Guilty?" – "Not Guilty?" ', should be seen as that of a Faustian figure turned anti-Faust, someone who instead of selling his soul in return for knowledge, receives his soul by renouncing knowledge. The Faroese author William Heinesen has a wonderful description.

As a spiritual type, in a wide sense, Kierkegaard belongs to the Mephistopheles category. Like that devil's chargé d'affaires in Goethe, he is possessed of a superior intellect which he deploys with the same supple facility and tirelessness. They are both, in their at once witty, impudent, and dazzling ways, irresistible. In fact, Kierkegaard goes one better than the devil, being without rival in the art of attacking reason with its own weapons. He is not just Mephistopheles, he is at the same time Mephistopheles's victim, man, Faust. It is not only against others that he turns his weapons, in the end he turns them without mercy on himself.[96]

Kierkegaard's anti-Faust is also a man, not just an idea, or if that, then the idea of a single individual, a very special 'idea' in view of its total contextuality, exemplified by a Quidam who in the end ascends to a privacy and inwardness to be encompassed neither by ideas nor by causes. To be or to become the single individual, to prepare oneself in the only possible way for purification and redemption, by standing alone in a God-relationship – that at least can stand as a not implausible corrective to the 'parody' reading. Later, looking back at his pseudonymous work, Kierkegaard wrote:

My whole activity and existence as an author is like a challenge: I have covered the terrain, exciting curiosity [*æggende*] and spying to see whether that single individual might turn up – in which case I would have immediately appointed myself his master of ceremonies, pointing out the configuration as the pseudonyms always do: that the older is at the service of the younger who points out the highest, while the older is nevertheless the maieuticist.

Since in real life Kierkegaard never found his Quidam, his 'cause' had to remain in the text. He hoped he had found a candidate. But

[t]hat has not happened. If [Professor] R[asmus] Nielsen, without any personal help from me, had been able straightaway to say what he stood for [*tage en Position*], I at least would have been very attentive to him, even if it were doubtful to what extent he could be the single individual. But now he has himself decided his situation by seeking my personal support. In terms of the Idea he is now, if you will, a disciple.[97]

In some newspaper articles Nielsen had shown appreciation of Kierkegaard's writings. But Kierkegaard, who had always spoken rather scornfully of Nielsen,[98] felt embarrassed by his attentions, as he imagines Lessing would have been by his own. However, for want of a genuinely singular individual he was drawn to the idea that in the role of literary executor Nielsen might be the person to convey his thoughts after his death to those who persisted in misunderstanding him. But this was to be at a later date, when Kierkegaard had survived his 'deadline'.

In the effort to complete *Postscript* in time, far from it being a 'supreme effort' to 'outwit melancholy' as has been suggested, a melancholy that after all was now serving some good purpose, the likelier assumption is surely, as indicated earlier, that Kierkegaard was doing his utmost to put his intellectual estate in order. The sheer comprehensiveness of the work says as much, with its comments on subjects as diverse as science (in relation to subjective thinking) and the medieval monastic movement (as too abstract a way of 'dying from the world') and so much else. There are other signs too: the inclusion of the twin theses on the possibility of a logical system and the impossibility of an existential system, in the second chapter on Lessing, is Kierkegaard's long-delayed settlement with Heiberg and his commentators in the debate that followed the publication in 1838 of Heiberg's 'The System of Logic'.[99] The long and often tightly written sections towards the end of *Postscript* give the impression of a writer trying hard to get down, in straightforward prose, all that he has to say to his immediate philosophical contemporaries – what he would have said if he had engaged in their debates.

And yet, Climacus recants the entire book. Indeed, in a postscript (*Tillæg*) to *Postscript* ('for an understanding with the reader') he not only 'revokes' the work but announces its 'superfluousness'.[100] Echoing that postscript to the Preface of *From the Papers of One Still Living*, but with a curious twist, he says that he doesn't wish 'by any manner or means to obligate any single *real* person to be the reader'.[101] What is behind that remark? A note scribbled in preparing the manuscript doesn't help much. If readers should put themselves to the trouble to acclaim him, they will have 'misunderstood him', while since he himself doesn't want to be 'put to any trouble for something that he did just for amusement', if taken to task he would rather retract the whole thing, and similarly 'if it should occur to the censor to strike out the least thing'.[102] The text itself says simply that Climacus is not 'foisting' the book on a public, but just appealing to anyone who would look at the work sympathetically. Wanting to be understood and not to be misunderstood, he addresses an 'imagined reader', one who both reads the book and, we may guess, once apprised of the real comedy as opposed to the humorous rhetoric, would know to put it aside. This ideal reader will read it 'piece by piece', 'hold out as long as the author', and 'understand that understanding *is* a revocation' – but also appreciate that to revoke a book 'is not the same as not to write it'. Respect due to such a reader, one who bends to the author and never resists, is far greater than that due to the 'noisy contradictions of an entire lecture hall'.[103] The book is superfluous because it has no life beyond the orbit of a reader who understands where it leads, and because the life it has only begins if the reader has the right kind of interest.

Having had Climacus come to an understanding of sorts with his ideal reader, Kierkegaard then adds, in his own name, a brief and (to make the transition clear) unpaginated 'First and Last Explanation' (*Forklaring*). The Danish word can also have the senses of 'deposition', a binding testimony, and an 'accounting' as of oneself. In it he assumes responsibility for all the pseudonymous works, and also for the newspaper articles written under the same pseudonyms, saying that the 'pseudonymity and polyonymity' has no 'accidental' basis of a personal nature but is due to something 'essential . . . in the production itself'. Though every word is written by him, not a single word is his, he has been merely a 'prompter'. Accordingly, he has 'no opinion about them except as a third party, no knowledge of their meaning except as a reader, not the remotest private relation to them, since it is impossible to have that to a doubly reflected communication'.[104]

So are Johannes's writings no more Kierkegaard's than the productions of the other pseudonyms? Well, that is what Kierkegaard's own words in his explanation undeniably say. But does that mean that the texts are to be read in total independence of some project or aim of the author of the 'authorship'? Can't we find some 'essential' reason for the polypseudonymity that doesn't leave the texts just floating about for anyone to do what they will with them? An alternative may lie in the notion of doubly reflected communication. Double reflection was that theme introduced in connection with Lessing and subjective thinking. It is what distinguishes an immediate communication, 'indifferent' to subjectivity,[105] from a communication that tries to express it, or as we have seen, betrays it to the alerted in its attempts to hide it behind a facade, an ironic or humorous incognito. It is easy enough to see how Kierkegaard's explanation can lead one to think that the whole authorship is itself a mere facade, or that in claiming that not a word of it was his own, he is disclaiming any personal involvement in what is said, and that the whole production is simply let loose on the world to mean, at any time and in any circumstance, what it may – 'to whom it may concern'. But what if their concerns are not his? Might not Kierkegaard's denial that the words are his own be better explained by his realization of the inextricability of his involvement than by any desire to sever the texts from their origin?

If Kierkegaard was himself a subjective thinker, then irony and humour would be his own incognitos, personally. In the pseudonyms the incognitos become 'persons', or at least figures: Constantius, Taciturnus, and Climacus. What these pseudonyms write *cannot* be Kierkegaard's own words; not only would they, if we thought of them as cardboard cut-outs, have no inner existence which their words could doubly reflect, but even if they had, they would not be the words that doubly reflected Kierkegaard's own innermost existence. But for all the evident fiction of the cast of characters representing the aesthetic and ethical life-views, their close connection with Kierkegaard's own innermost life is obvious enough. If Kierkegaard wished his writing to be seen as a contribution to 'self-understanding' and to have its place as such in the cultural heritage, also in the future, then it would be natural and politic for him to write as he does in his 'First and Last Explanation'. By the same token we could read Climacus's attempt at an understanding with his reader as a wish for cooperation on the part of the reader, not as the refusal of the actual writer to bring his own 'innermost existence' into play in this literary extension of the arts and strategies of indirect communication.

But then again, there is also the thought that we touched on before: Kierkegaard's jealously guarded freedom to decide for himself what to make of his 'authorship'. Perhaps, whether from despair or from a sense of destiny, which might bring its own despair, he hoped it would amount to something, and he was damned if he was going to let others decide what that was. Paradoxically, letting the words float freely might also be a way of letting them be re-collected in a satisfying light, satisfying in terms of his own intentions on behalf of singularity and subjective thinking – even if he would soon be dead and it would have to be done by later generations.

But he lived for another ten years. The experience of writing this vast and complex but well-organized work may even have inspired him to think there was more to do. *Concluding Unscientific Postscript to Philosophical Fragments* (the Danish title might be more accurately translated 'Concluding Unscholarly Addendum to Philosophical Crumbs') was nevertheless the fulfilment of the 'secret writing' he had written to Boesen about back in 1841, from Berlin. On 7 February 1846, just five weeks after the 'entire manuscript was delivered bag and baggage to the printer', Kierkegaard wrote:

My idea is now to qualify for the priesthood. For several months I have prayed to God to help me further, for it has long been clear to me that I ought not to continue as an author, which is something I want to be totally or not at all. That's also why I haven't begun anything new while doing the proof-reading, except for the little review of *Two Ages* which is, once more, concluding.[106]

The not-so-very-'little' review, a signed work that he had been busy with while *Postscript* was at the compositor, was to be the first occasion since *From the Papers of One Still Living* that Kierkegaard would speak directly about life and his times, without constant reference to his own 'tale of suffering'. It does, however, contain a reference to a new chapter of suffering which was about to begin.

Reviewing the Age

In Josiah Thompson's biography, Kierkegaard, with the manuscript of *Postscript* now off his hands and four years of uninterrupted writing behind him, was at loose ends. With nothing to sustain the momentum generated by the break with Regine he looked up from his desk and, fatefully, his eye fell upon a slim volume, just recently published, of literary criticism. Confirming that '[i]dleness is a dangerous condition for small boys and writers', that idle glance led to the notorious *Corsair* affair. 'Just as he had teased bigger boys twenty years earlier in the school playground', the incorrigible polemicist and inveterate tease now began to bait that satiric weekly.[1]

Certainly Kierkegaard's polemical instincts had not deserted him, but there was more to his reaction to what he read on that occasion than just the desire to make trouble. Or, better, there was more to the desire to make trouble than a mere compulsion to tease. The result, by design it seems, was to begin a new chapter of self-induced torment with which, now that Regine had dropped into the background, to keep his mind and pen busy – though from now on largely in the privacy of his journals. For although the exchange was brief, its effect was long-lasting and the pillorying which Kierkegaard provoked from *The Corsair* made him a social outsider on a scale that he could scarcely have anticipated. It was to fix his image in the minds of generations to come and, for himself, it ushered in a period of self-questioning and, the trait he had always scorned in others, indecision.

What made this more than a case of gratuitous provocation? Kierkegaard had already armed himself in December for an attack on *The Corsair*, which had first appeared six years earlier, in October 1840. Its editor since then had been Meïr Aron Goldschmidt, who, only twenty-one years old at the time of its founding, had sought and received

Kierkegaard's blessing. Politically it was to the left of the official liberal
opposition whose politics Kierkegaard had always opposed, but in its
constant ridiculing of local celebrities it was too disreputable to gain the
status of an official organ of political opposition. Although Kierkegaard
had some respect for Goldschmidt's talents and in his turn Goldschmidt
was a decided admirer of Kierkegaard, to have his pseudonyms praised
by a liberal-oriented journal that also went out of its way to satirize the
establishment would once more, as Kierkegaard saw it, be to misrepre-
sent the aims of his authorship. Goldschmidt had already in 1843
praised *Either/Or* in the pages of *The Corsair*, and now in 1845 he had
declared that the name of its editor/author, Victor Eremita, would
survive when all other Danish writers were forgotten.

In a response never published Kierkegaard wrote, using that same
name, a 'Prayer to *The Corsair*'. It went:

Sing sang resches Tubalkain – which interpreted means: Cruel and bloodthirsty
corsair, high and mighty sultan, you who hold men's lives like a silly device in your
powerful hands and like an irritant in the wrath of your nose, be still moved to
compassion, cut short these sufferings, kill me, but do not make me immortal! Most
high and mighty Sultan, reflect in your swift wisdom what the paltriest of all those
you have slain would soon be able to see, think what it means to be immortal, and
especially to be certified as such by *The Corsair*! Oh, what cruel mercy and forbear-
ing to be branded for all eternity as an inhuman monster because *The Corsair*
inhumanly spared one! But above all, do not say I shall never die. What an idea!
Such a life sentence is unheard of. [In the margin: Kill me so that I may live with
all the others you have slain, but do not kill me by making me immortal.] I became
so weary of life just from reading it. What cruel distinction, that none shall be
moved by my complaint when put so effeminately [text uncertain] as to say it will
be the death of me – but everyone laughs and says 'he cannot die'. Oh! be moved
by pity, stay your exalted, cruel grace, and kill me like the rest.

Victor Eremita[2]

In parentheses Kierkegaard adds: 'Perhaps add here the words at the
end of the postscript to *Either/Or* which are in the narrow tall-boy
closet nearest the window.' These words, in German, Kierkegaard had
included at the end of that unpublished Postscript to *Either/Or* in which
we remember Eremita 'winds up' his 'firm'. In a new version in Danish
added to the 'prayer' it goes:

Be not afraid – why spare me? I have no wife to sigh at you or grieve . . . [unclear
text] for the husband you put to death, no loved one who feels the chop more
devastatingly, no children whose sensitivity makes the blow heavier for them than

for the father – I have no official mark of distinction in our civil society which it might be bitter at the time to see forfeited, I have no famous name so that a whole family would suffer an attack on just one member – spare, rather, anyone who has a third party unable to avoid feeling offence even when the injured party scorns the attack. . . .[3]

It seems that even before *Postscript* was completed Kierkegaard was playing with the idea of martyring himself in the relatively minor and petty cause of rescuing himself and his work from inappropriate affiliation.

But it was not *The Corsair* his eye fell on sometime after 20 December but before the manuscript of *Postscript* was handed to the compositor on 30 December. It was *Gæa, Aesthetic Yearbook*, yet another of those new year publications Notabene had poured scorn on. The editor was Peder Ludvig Møller (1814 – 1865), a writer, poet, and literary critic with academic ambitions. The nineteen contributions included one by Møller himself, called 'A Visit to Sorø'. It was a review of the year's literature based on conversations with several writers living in Sorø and included an account of an evening party, a miniature 'In Vino Veritas', in which three people discuss the year's literature. Not unnaturally the work of Hilarius Bogbinder comes up. One interlocutor says sourly that reading *Stages* is like running the gauntlet, but with such bright and refreshing oases on the way as memories of Latin school to help the reader survive the torture. Another says that just as you begin to appreciate a pseudonym, the author has to butt in with his unwanted questions about ethical and religious development. The third contrasts the nonpareil dialectics demonstrated by the author to such extremes as, on the one hand, an abstract aesthetics ('nothing but decorated Epicureanism') and, on the other, contrary to all poetry, an ethics of marital bliss that borders on philistinism. The author of *Stages* must be old and tired, or else highly intelligent but with a morbid imagination. A good writer but cynical, an ironist of irony, and he writes too much, out of some physical compulsion it seems, or else as therapy.[4]

Møller, the author of these caustic but quite penetrating remarks, was reputedly the model for the seducer of the 'Diary', who was also one of the speakers in 'In Vino Veritas'. That he should engage himself in *Stages* seems natural enough. On the day his volume was published Møller sent Kierkegaard an invitation to respond, addressed to 'Victor Eremita'. Kierkegaard replied:

Esteemed Sir!

I have received today, at the hand of Mr Giødwad, your highly esteemed and confidential message. My answer to you as to any other who proposes or has proposed such a thing: I have nothing prepared and never bind myself to a promise. Respectfully yours,
Victor Eremita.[5]

Møller had a connection with *The Corsair* which he wished to keep secret for fear of spoiling his prospects for a professorship in aesthetics at the university. Kierkegaard, who suspected Møller of being Goldschmidt's right-hand, knew of this. Now, in a newspaper article published on 27 December ('An Itinerant Aesthetician's Activity and How He Still Came to Pay for the Dinner'), under the pseudonym Frater Taciturnus attacked by Møller, he disclosed the connection. Wondering rhetorically why ('supposing that we pseudonyms are one [author]') he had been singled out for the dubious distinction of being spared *The Corsair*'s abuse, he wrote,

If only I could soon get into *The Corsair*. . . My superior, Hilarius Bogbinder, has been flattered in *The Corsair*, if I remember correctly; Victor Eremita has even had to undergo the humiliation of being made immortal – in *The Corsair*. Still, I have been there already, for *Ubi spiritus, ibi ecclesia: Ubi P. L. Møller, ibi the Corsair*.[6]

On the day before the *Postscript* manuscript was handed over, Møller replied in the same paper, 'To Mr Frater Taciturnus, Chief for the Third Part of *Stages on Life's Way*'.[7] There was no special acerbity in his remarks, and when, on 2 January, *The Corsair* itself carried an article entitled 'How the Itinerant Philosopher Found the Itinerant Real Editor of *The Corsair*', the tone here too, in keeping with the respect in which Kierkegaard was held by the really real editor, was playful rather than malicious. But now, with *Postscript* out of the way, Kierkegaard used this response from *The Corsair* to needle the periodical directly. In an article that appeared on 10 January entitled 'The Dialectical Result of a Literary Police-Function', again in the guise of Frater Taciturnus, he wrote:

One can engage *The Corsair* to throw abuse at people just as one can engage an organ grinder to make music . . . *The Corsair*'s faded brilliance ought to be ignored from a literary standpoint, along with its hidden helpers, the professional traders in vulgar witticisms, as are prostitutes in ordinary life. Anyone insulted by being praised in this paper, if it should happen to come to his notice . . . can retort: 'Please throw abuse at me, for it is really too much to be made immortal by *The Corsair*'.

Then, mindful of Climacus's professed desire to help people by making things more difficult, Kierkegaard says, 'I can do no more for others than to request that abuse be thrown at me too'.[8]

The Corsair did so with a vengeance. The 2 January issue carried drawings caricaturing Kierkegaard himself, his crabwise gait, his hunched shoulder, the thin legs and apparently uneven trouser legs, the cane or umbrella always in hand. Not only had *The Corsair* broken the unwritten code that protected pseudonymity even when an author's real identity was known, its coverage in the months that followed made Kierkegaard a household name and fair game for the mockery of any 'butcher's boy'. In an attempt to place this period in a wider perspective Kierkegaard sums it up in a long 'Report' dated 9 March 1846:

Concluding Postscript is out; responsibility for the pseudonyms acknowledged; one of these days the printing of the *Literary Review* will begin. Everything is in order; all I have to do now is keep calm and say nothing, relying on *The Corsair* to support the whole enterprise negatively, just as I want it. At this moment, from the point of view of the idea, I am as correctly situated in the literature as possible, and in a way that makes being an author a deed. It was a most fortunate idea in itself to break with *The Corsair* in order to prevent any direct approach, just as I was through with my authorship and, by assuming responsibility for the pseudonyms, ran the risk of becoming some kind of authority. . . . In addition, just when I am coming out polemically against the age, I owe it to the idea and to irony to prevent any confusion with the ironical rot-gut served up in the dance halls of contemptibleness by *The Corsair*. Besides, as frequently happens to me, for all my deliberation, an increment emerges due not to me but to Guidance. It seems always that I understand far better afterwards whatever I had given most thought to, both what it means ideally and that it's just what I should do.

But it is an exhausting existence. I am convinced not a single person understands me. The most anyone, even an admirer, might allow is that I endure all this nonsense with a certain poise; but that I should actually wish it so – well naturally no one dreams of that. But again, it would be facile human thoughtlessness which took it that a double reflection might, after all, let me wish it so and then concluded: ergo he is not suffering at all, he is impervious to all these manifestations of rudeness and brazen lies. As though one couldn't freely decide to take all tribulations upon oneself should the idea demand it. The article against P. L. Møller was written in much fear and trembling; I did it on days of religious observance, but for the sake of a regulatory constraint I neglected neither my church-going nor reading my sermon. So, too, with the article against *The Corsair*. Yet they were written with all propriety, for if I had given expression to feeling, someone would have used that as the occasion for a direct relationship to me. It was amusing and psychologically superb to see how quickly P. L. Møller took the hint about retiring from *The Corsair*. He came on, bowed politely, and then went off to where he belongs.

What pains me most, however, is not the loutishness of the mob but the way the better people secretly participate in it. I, too, could wish to make myself understood to one single person, to my reader. But I dare not, for then I betray the idea. It is just when I have triumphed, when the rudeness reaches its most shameless, that I dare not say it. In short it is my responsibility – so long as I do not contribute to too many being totally misled by my consistently not giving in. I can't help that. I must be silent.

The last two months have been very rich in observations. What my dissertation says about irony making phenomena stand revealed is so true. My ironic leap into *The Corsair* helps, first, to make it perfectly clear that *The Corsair* has no idea. In ideal terms it is dead, even if it got a few thousand subscribers. It wants to be ironical and doesn't even understand irony. It would have been an epigram over my existence were it ever said, 'There existed contemporary with him a slap-dash ironic journal which praised him; no, wait – he was abused, and he asked for it himself'. Secondly, my ironic leap into *The Corsair* reveals the surrounding world in all its self-contradiction. Everyone has been going about saying, 'It's nothing, who cares about *The Corsair?*, etc.'. What happens? When someone does care he is accused of irresponsibility; they say he has deserved all this (now it's 'all this') because he brought it on himself; they scarcely dare walk with me in the street – for fear they too will come in *The Corsair*. Moreover, the self-contradiction has a deeper basis; they half wish in their Christian envy that the paper will continue, each hoping *he* will not be attacked. They now say of the paper that it is contemptible and nothing; they inveigh upon those attacked not to risk becoming angry or make a rebuttal, ergo may the paper flourish. And the public has, first, the titillation of envy and then the shameless pleasure of seeing whether the victim reacts. . . . And this phenomenon in such a little country as Denmark – this phenomenon the only currently topical one, and it is supposed to be nothing! How well cowardice and contemptibility suit each other in league with dishonour! And when the whole thing one day bursts, Goldschmidt will be the one to suffer; and it is absolutely the same public – and then what a fine place the world has become!

Further, my observations confirm in abundance that when someone expresses an idea consistently, every objection to him reveals something about the speaker [in the margin: who thus talks not about him but about himself]. They say it is I who am concerned about *The Corsair*. What happens? The *Concluding Postscript* was delivered in its entirety to Luno before I wrote against P. L. Møller. Admittedly, particularly in the preface (which incidentally was written in May of 1845), there was something which might seem to point to the latter (this, among other things, shows how early I was aware of it). If I had been worried about *The Corsair* I would have made some changes there, just to avoid the appearance. I know how I fought with myself about doing that anyway, because it pained me to think of, e.g., Bishop Mynster saying, 'That Kierkegaard should bother with a thing like that even in a book'. But I remained true to myself in not troubling with *The Corsair* – and what happens? Well, just as you would expect – in everything I write one sees allusions to *The Corsair*. Here is the self-disclosure, for it must be 'one' who himself has *The Corsair* in mind, since he finds it even in what was written before that episode.

Two things in particular occupy me: (1) that I remain true in the Greek sense to my existence-idea whatever the cost; (2) that for me it becomes in the religious sense as ennobling as possible. I pray God for the latter. Solitary I have always been; now I have a real chance again to practice. And note, my solitary secret is not my sorrow but precisely that I have the upper hand, that I turn what is hostile into something that serves my idea without giving any suspicion of my doing so. Yes, certainly this life is satisfying, but it is also terribly strenuous. And what a sad side one learns to know people from, and how sad that what looks so good at a distance is always misunderstood at the time! But again, it is religiosity that redeems; in that there is sympathy with all, not a garrulous sympathy with party-colleagues and followers, but infinite sympathy with each – in silence.

But certainly it is educational to be placed, as I am, in such a small city as Copenhagen. To work to the limits of one's abilities to the point of despair, with profound mental agony and much inner suffering; to put money into publishing books – and then, literally, not to have ten people read through them properly, while students and other authors for their part almost find it proper to ridicule writing a large book. And then have a paper which everyone reads, which also has contemptibility's privilege of daring to say anything, the most lying distortions – and it is 'nothing', but everybody reads it; and then the whole pack of enviers who lend a hand by saying just the opposite, to belittle it in that way. Being perpetually the object of everyone's conversation and attention, day after day, and then the pay-off is to defend me against one attack – if they make one – just to launch an even worse. Every journeyman butcher feels he can insult me on *The Corsair*'s orders; the young students simper and giggle and are happy to see a prominent person trampled upon; the professors are jealous and secretly sympathize with the attacks, and spread them, of course with the proviso that it is a shame. The least thing I do, even just visit someone, is distorted into lies and told everywhere. If *The Corsair* finds out, it is printed and read by the whole population. The man I have visited is embarrassed, gets almost angry with me, and one can't blame him for that. In the end I shall have to withdraw and associate only with people I cannot suffer; it does after all amount almost to doing wrong by others. So it goes on, and once I'm dead men's eyes will be opened; they will admire what I wanted to do, and at the same time they will treat some contemporary, who is probably the only one who understands me, in just the same way. God in heaven! If there were no interior in man where all this can be forgotten in communion with you, who could endure it?

But my activity as an author, God be praised, is now over. That has been granted me – and next to publishing *Either/Or* this is what I thank God for – to conclude it myself, to understand myself when to stop. I know very well and could prove it in two words that people will once again not see it in this way; I know that quite well and find it quite in order. It has pained me. I thought I could still have aspired to that recognition. Let it be.

If only I can manage to become a pastor. Out there, quietly active, allowing myself a little writing in my free time, I shall breathe more easily after all, however much my present life has gratified me.[9]

Apart from giving Kierkegaard's own interpretation of the events described, the report is significant in another way. It comprises the first two entries in the first journal belonging to a series of thirty-six in all dating from 9 March 1846 to 13 December 1854. These differ from previous ones in not being theme-focused or devoted to the working out of ideas, or recording impressions given by other writers. They are the repository of reflections of a more personal kind, attempts at tying things together, at bringing his own life and work into perspective. They also record what Kierkegaard called the 'collisions' unfolding between him and his contemporaries. The thirty-six journals, all labelled 'NB' and carefully numbered as if to ensure their textual integrity, and no doubt also their publication posthumously, might well be thought to form a further, signed addition to the authorship. The entries would disclose too much that was 'inner' for such a work to have appeared in his lifetime. Indeed, the intense self-preoccupation typical of the entries in these later journals leads one to suppose that they played a large part in creating Kierkegaard's own image of what his life and work amounted to.

The report's date, 9 March, is at its head, indicating when Kierkegaard began it. That was just ten days after *Postscript* had come out on 27 February. The review now completed, its printing being what Kierkegaard was now awaiting, would appear on the second last day of March. Drafts had already been written shortly after the work reviewed first appeared. *Two Ages* was published in October 1845, but the later sections of the review may have been written after the diversion caused by Møller's discussion of *Stages*. The review itself, however, was not in infringement of Kierkegaard's decision to give up writing. It was more like the fulfilment of a promise he had made himself, a promise to return to its author, that very same 'author of *A Story of Everyday Life*' whose work he had praised in his first publication. One might of course see in the start of the NB journals heralded by the 'Report' a new burst of activity, but the first NB journal may not have been marked as such, and the report ends: 'If only I can manage to become a priest.' Not very convincing perhaps, but it does sound as though the report itself was supposed to be, like the 'little review' and *Postscript* before it, and as the entry quoted at the end of the previous chapter has it, definitely 'concluding'.

Two Ages, as we can now guess, was the latest novel from the hand of Thomasine Gyllembourg, the unnamed author Kierkegaard in his publishing debut had picked out for favourable comparison to the poetry of Blicher. Instead of mere moods this author portrayed everyday life in its ups and downs and in its demonstration of positive attitudes towards life. The work he discussed at that time by Gyllembourg, who as we know was Heiberg's mother, *A Story from Everyday Life*, was a feuilleton that in the manner of Balzac she had published serially in her son's literary journal, *Kjøbenhavns flyvende Post*. Madame Gyllembourg, energetic and talented, had made her own authorial debut the year before, at the age of fifty-three, when Heiberg, with space in *Flyvende Post* badly needing to be filled, had asked his mother for help. This she provided in the form of a fictitious letter to the editor that caused a considerable stir, not least among those curious to know who the writer was. And she wrote more, the letters taking the form of installments in a developing story. Later, in 1837, these were published in a collection as *The Family Polonius*. Madame Gyllembourg's works appeared under the imprint 'The author of *A Story of Everyday Life*' (in the same way as her almost exact contemporary Walter Scott signed his works, the so-called Waverley Novels, 'The author of Waverley').

Before the turn of the century Thomasine Christine Buntzen, daughter of a bourgeois Copenhagen family, had married the radical poet P. A. Heiberg, twenty years her senior. He was exiled in 1799 for his political activities. On forming her attachment to the man who became her second husband, Carl Frederick Ehrensvärd Gyllembourg, a wealthy Swede who was also a political exile, Thomasine divorced Heiberg. Out of resentment he made his then nine-year-old son a ward of court, though he later relented. After her second husband's death in 1815 Thomasine moved in with her son, who was already establishing a name for himself as a writer. These two, later joined by the leading lady of the Danish stage, the half-German actress Johanne Luise Pätges, whom Heiberg married in 1831 when he was approaching forty, enriched Danish cultural life with that much-sought-after salon whose welcome the young Søren had so eagerly solicited. Madame Gyllembourg herself, in spite of an exceptionally late start, was able with her own talent and the help of her entrepreneurially and artistically gifted son, to establish for herself a reputation as a significant writer and pioneer of the Danish novel.

Her special talent lay in an ability to portray the ties of family life as a medium in which were reflected the larger currents of life at the time. *Two Ages* (*To Tidsaldre*), which was to be Madame Gyllembourg's last work, tells the story of a family whose fortunes span the immediate post-revolutionary age, the age of honour, loyalty, and passion, and the advent of modernity, the age of prudent choices, calculation, and reflection. With her own connections and Denmark's place in Napoleonic politics, the author's familiarity with both ages enabled her to portray them in miniature in the local setting of Copenhagen. The age of revolution is reflected in the youth and love story of Claudine, who falls for a young Frenchman, Charles Lusard, a member of the newly arrived French legation in Copenhagen. Various connections are associated with the idea of revolution, and Claudine's loyalty to the memory of Lusard, who has left to join the army, is rewarded after many complications by a reunion after she discovers that he now lives in an inherited estate in Jutland, in the firm belief that Claudine had married and was living in Germany. The centre of the story reflecting the later age, 'The Present Age', is the return to Copenhagen in 1844, after a long period abroad in both Europe and America, of their now fifty-year-old son, also named Charles. What he finds, as Kierkegaard puts it in his résumé, is a Copenhagen without legations or any other intimations of 'world-historical catastrophes' in the offing, but a life that is

undisturbed by the energetic passion whose form is in its very energy – yes, even in its vehemence – and isn't hiding the power of a secret and forbidden passion. On the contrary, everything is manifestly nondescript, and thus trivial, formless, knowing, coquettish, and openly so. Here there is no great revelation and no deep secret, but superficiality all the more.[10]

This Lusard, living alone with his recollections of personal loyalties and reunion, seeks a worthy heir, someone close whom he can make happy, and the story ends in a form of 'repetition' in which, following further vicissitudes, another faithful woman is reunited with her lover.

Repetition, as his introduction shows, is a leitmotif for Kierkegaard's own interest in the work. Preceded, typically, by a preface saying that his review is written only for those with the time and patience to read a little book, though even they needn't actually do so – except that those 'whose aesthetic and critical education comes from reading newspapers' are exempted – the introduction itself reminds the 'unknown' author of Kierkegaard's earlier review of 'his' work (in *From the Papers of One Still Living*). At the end of a lengthy appreciation, he hopes that the 'author of *A Story of Everyday Life*' will find him

unchanged or, if possible, changed in the repetition: a little more clarity in presentation, a slightly lighter and more flowing style, in recognition of the difficulty of the task a little less hurried, a little more inwardness in the discernment: in other words, changed in the repetition.[11]

We recall that the unknown author's son had found the manuscript of the earlier treatment of his mother's work stylistically deficient and hadn't found a place for it in his journal. Besides that, Heiberg, as we also remember, had made uncomprehending remarks about *Repetition*, not grasping that repetition meant a kind of inner revision of the motivation with which one approaches the same life-situations. In praising Madame Gyllembourg for her even-handedness in her treatment of the two ages and allowing his résumé to conclude with Lusard's 'Amen' to a declaration of faith in human progress, he is preparing the way for a much more pessimistic account of the present age, an account that would follow naturally from the work he was still writing when Madame Gyllembourg's book appeared, namely the *Postscript*. Indeed, the declaration that Lusard says 'Amen' to is paradigmatically Heibergian:

I am happy to live in an age that despite its deficiencies makes such great advances in so many directions. I subscribe to the faith that the human race, no doubt through many fluctuations, will with steady stride nevertheless approach the goal of that perfection that can be imagined for an earthly existence.[12]

Neither of the reunions that end both parts (both ages) are repetitions in the proper sense. They are due to a matching of a certain kind of constancy, not yet ethical, with a fortuitous fate. Nor is the reunion that ends the second part properly a repetition of the one that ends the first. Instead of being the product of a resolute will to risk everything, typical of the revolutionary age, it is formed nostalgically in the light of recollection. The younger Lusard, after his long travels now no longer young, having 'let the time of love pass by, having turned off at the point where a person's future really begins, has beautifully installed himself in remembrance and chosen the past, wanting only to secure a memory for himself in making one member of his family happy'.[13]

The last part of *A Literary Review* to be recognizably a review is a section called 'An Aesthetic Reading of the Novel and Its Details'. Here Kierkegaard notes that in spite of the author's sense of the greatness of that earlier and passionate age, the characterizations are shallower there than in the second part. Whether directly caught up in these events or affected by them more peripherally, the characters 'in a state of passion . . . stand out less sharply' as persons.[14] In the present, reflective age people are related to local events more directly, and even 'the most insignificant minor character . . . comes alive to the reader'.[15] What Kierkegaard particularly admires in the author, and what makes it possible for the novel to reflect the character of an age in (what Hegelians would call) the private sphere, is an ability to present personally motivated actions and the guiding spirit of the age in a kind of mutually illuminating interplay. The character of the age is reflected in the way the persons see and respond to their local and personal conflicts. Lusard, the Frenchman of the first part who comes with the legation, is able to call Claudine his 'little wife' even though they are together only briefly and not married. In the romanticism of the revolutionary age the 'natural side' of marriage is 'emancipated' from the 'ethically binding one'. Claudine, for her part, a local girl led astray 'by her love rather than by the influence of modern ideas', conceives the relationship in the light of a reversion to an earlier form of romanticism, the 'pastoral-idyllic'.[16] Both of these differ from the way in which the characters act in the present, reflective age. Here Mariane's lover thinks that the prospect of financial difficulty is a good enough reason to break off an engagement (he hopes that the rich Lusard of the second part, known to be looking for someone to make happy, will propose to her). In general, in the absence of embracing visions, the situational focus of the second part allows the author more freedom to develop a talent for dramatic narration, and Kierkegaard (preserving the formality of ignorance of the author's identity) writes: 'The author's possible preference for the revolutionary age's more animated life is balanced by the actual preference he has shown for the present age through his greater artistry in depicting it.'[17]

But what did the Lusard of Part Two find when he returned to

Copenhagen from his travels? A city typified by what it no longer possessed, 'undisturbed by the energetic passion that has its form [visibly] in its very energy . . . in its vehemence', a city that was openly 'nondescript, trivial, and formless'. What is it about a characterless society that provides the author with an opportunity to exploit a gift for characterization? Surely the fact that in such a society people will be left more to their own devices, so that their characters have a chance to emerge or be formed in particular situations. Or at least that will be true of characters worth writing novels about, characters who find the times *lacking* in character. It may also be that a characterless society, through its own formlessness and heterogeneity, throws up a plethora of 'characters', like those of Charles Dickens, that mirrors its actual lack of form. Given that analogy, one wonders what preference Madame Gyllembourg 'actually' had for the present age apart from her interest in characterization. It also makes us aware that, as Kierkegaard points out, it was on the basis of a fortuitous reunion, a happy ending preestablished by fate to the dramatic complications that converged on it, that Lusard was able to say 'Amen' to a confession of faith in human progress and the prospect of mankind's earthly perfection.

Form, formlessness, formalism – these are notions that we remember Kierkegaard has used about his own society from the start. There was that reference to a 'formal striving' in his first and only public address. It drew attention to a general tendency to attach importance to form at the expense of content. But although this attachment to form was the age's 'error', rather than denying the importance of form, Kierkegaard was then asserting the essentially Hegelian view that life generates form and not vice versa. There was something of Heibergian aesthetics in Kierkegaard's talking at that time of the idea's 'coming into being in the world' from the immediate standpoint of the poet. By 'idea', we recall, is meant an ideal of perfected being, a form of earthly existence in which shared humanity plays an essential and indeed primary part. The Hegelian version was known as the 'Speculative Idea'. Now, in partial deference to Heiberg's mother's appreciation of the lost age of revolutionary fervour, Kierkegaard in the long third part of *A Literary Review* ('The Results of Observing the Two Ages') has the idea first appearing in a more active context, in the form of an 'inner drive' that 'propels the individual on'. The comment comes towards the end of the long and much-discussed section on 'the present age' and is made in connection with what it really means to act from principle. In the usual sense, to act from principle means to apply some rule that one has inherited or internalized or that in some other way one unquestioningly subscribes to. In its proper sense, however, a 'principle' is what comes first, and that for Kierkegaard (and we note how unresistingly both Hegelian ideas and terminology are employed by an author still putting the final touches to reputedly one of the most radical criticisms of Hegel's philosophy) is 'the substance, the idea, in the unopened form of feeling and enthusiasm'.[18]

A formless society such as the second Lusard found on returning from his travels is one in which the 'passionate' distinction between form and content has been (in yet another Hegelian term) 'annulled'. What does that mean? Not that by removing form there is no longer any meaning or content, as in 'madness and stupidity'. There can still be meaning and content, even truth, but if so it is a truth that is spread 'extensively', in an 'all-inclusive' or 'all-intrusive' manner, but that can never be what is 'essentially true'. Essential meaning, whatever might seem the 'limitation' of its origin, has the 'intensiveness' of a 'self-deepening'.[19]

The reason why Kierkegaard's deference to Madame Gyllembourg's appreciation of the revolutionary age is only partial is that sheer enthusiasm is the idea in its substantial but as yet unopened form. The age Lusard was still able to recall was one which bore its enthusiasm for the idea on its face, in the 'energetic passion' that has its form in its very energy, 'yes, even in its vehemence'. Unlike the more recent post-1830 political movements Kierkegaard had earlier criticized for trying to impose forms on life, the revolutionary age had at least been seized passionately by the idea, so that its inspiration among the 'inspired' still had 'truth' in it. At that time inwardness was not done away with. Compared to the present, the age of revolution was a *kind* of opening, a revelation as well one might say, but still only half-way,[20] an expression of human immaturity. The idea had unfolded indeed, but not opened fully. Kierkegaard refers to the 'reactionary immediacy' reflected in the domestic life portrayed in Part One of *Two Ages*. He means that rather than being self-determined, the actions of the persons involved are reactions to events and therefore lack constancy.[21] Resorting again to his cherished astrophysical analogy Kierkegaard says that 'the harmony of the spheres' is the unity of every planet relating to itself and to the whole. Take one of these relations away and you get chaos. But in the human case there is an additional factor to take into account, namely the idea: 'Remove the relation to oneself, and we have the mass's tumultuous relating to an idea; but remove this too, and we have rawness.'[22] There is a sketch of a typology of concerted activity. At the bottom of the scale is the raw and unformed behaviour of the mob. Here the multitude, far from its members being individually inspired, is itself not even informed collectively by an idea. Because a mob lacks a centre of gravity or indeed any internal structure at all, it is at the mercy of suggestion and governed by primitively holistic psychological reactions. But if a group or crowd is inspired by a revolutionary ideal it acquires a structure. However, its members are related *en masse* to the ideal and still not separated out as individually enthusiastic for the ideals inspiring the revolution. In contrast to cold formalism there is passion indeed, but it is due to the mutual encouragement of numbers and can result in the violence of a reign of terror. What is needed is the individual's own relation to the idea.

The remainder of the *Review* focuses on this relationship to give a pessimistic account of an age that comprehensively contradicts Lusard's 'Amen'. The nondescript, trivial world he met on his return, being reflective rather than passionate, far from being at a point where progress to human perfection begins, offers no opening at all for the idea's unfolding, let alone in some immature and immediate form. There is neither room here for the idea here nor any avenue that can lead to it. The 'idea-passage is barred' and individuals merely 'put spokes' in their own and each others's wheels, while a 'selfish and mutual other-regarding opposition' forms a 'quagmire' in which 'one then sits'. Where individuals fail to 'turn away inwardly from one another or outwardly [towards one another] in unanimity for an idea . . . gossip and rumour and specious importance and apathetic envy become a surrogate both for the former and for the latter'. Typical of an age of this kind is a 'crippling and disheartened, tactless, levelling reciprocity'.[23] Kierkegaard takes 'levelling' to be the nemesis of his age, a catastrophe for the idea in its proper unfolding, a blocking off of the only viable path to human completion. It is also able, if carried to its extreme, to produce a crisis that reawakens individuals to their possibilities.

The metaphor of levelling has many applications. Most historical examples are, in a very literal way, down to earth. In Irish history the levellers were agrarian agitators who tore down hedges enclosing common ground. They were preceded in English history by a group so called for removing park palings as well as hedges, in this case from crown lands. But both groups had an underlying political motive which is what, in a more abstract sense, really gave them their name. That sense became quite explicit with certain radicals during the time of Charles I and the Commonwealth; they were 'levellers' because they insisted that everyone should have equal eligibility to hold public office. In his first reference to levelling in the *Review* Kierkegaard speaks of levelling in what seems to be an even more abstract sense. He describes it as a 'quiet, mathematically abstract affair,' one that 'avoids all fuss [*Ophævelse*]',[24] which means that it cannot be a political one, at least not in the way usually associated with egalitarian ideals being framed and fought for by removing physical and other kinds of barriers to free association and opportunity, forcibly if need be.

The first occurrence in Kierkegaard's published works of the verb 'to level' (*at nivellere*) is in the dissertation. There in connection with irony, too, it is described as abstract: what 'typifies irony is the abstract measure through which it levels everything'.[25] But then he had been an 'Hegelian fool' for taking Socrates to task for looking 'only numerically' at the individuals and having 'no eye for the totality', when that was 'precisely the great proof of how great an ethicist Socrates was'.[26] Kierkegaard's criticism of *Two Ages* is that *its* 'totality', the life-view that defines the frame of its main characters' responses, is not ethical but aesthetic. He notes the aesthetic limitations of the viewpoints of the characters, the women in particular. Claudine, whose story provides the main thread of Part One, though faced with the disappearance of her loved one to the wars, with looking after herself and her child, sees her own situation in an openly romantic light, constant in her love but also fixed in her picture of herself and Lusard. But the corresponding figure in Part Two, Mariane, with no illusions and made to work as a servant, develops, in the face of the humiliations to which she is subjected, the makings of a Kierkegaardian version of the slave's vantage-point in the Hegelian master–slave relation: a 'quiet inwardness'.[27] But if ethics is to find its place in the world, this tenuous foothold on the 'singling out' (*Udsondring* or *den individuelle inadvendte Udsondring*, but sometimes just *indre Sondring*) that the proper unfolding of the idea requires, needs encouragement from the age at large.[28] It is precisely this that levelling prevents. In the dissertation, irony's levelling is a preparation for spiritual ascent, and nothing is said to suggest that it might get in the way. It can, after all, be 'controlled'. Here, in the *Review*, levelling is an unstoppable process of spiritual stultification. Were it not for the fact, according to Kierkegaard, that it had come to the point where nothing could stop it, it might even look like a deliberate attempt to flee the thought that 'singling out' needs to be cultivated at all. Yet the levelling is not deliberate in any literal sense, since no one actually chooses this stultifying path, and in any case everyone is to some extent on it, as though on an escalator: it is, as Kierkegaard says, a 'quiet, mathematically abstract affair' which 'avoids all fuss'.

Readers of *Being and Time* and the lectures preceding that work will recognize here the model for what Heidegger calls *Einebnung*. Heidegger writes of a culture which people assimilate and in which choice is no longer required, one in which *Dasein* is 'deprive[d] . . . of its choice, its formation of judgments, and its estimation of value' and which 'relieves *Dasein* of the task . . . to be itself by way of itself.'[29] But although Heidegger's remarks, so close to Kierkegaard's that we all but see the well-thumbed copy of the *Review*'s German translation lying there *zu-handen*, provide a paradigm of levelling which invites careful comparison to Kierkegaard's, it becomes clear that the accounts have significantly different foci. Heidegger's *Einebnung* is one element in an account of the way in which *Dasein* can be dominated by its own *das Man* mode. Heidegger pinpoints a 'phenomenon' labelled '*Abständigkeit*' (distantiality) that is a deeply embedded concern with difference, so deeply embedded that even the concern to get rid of difference is evidence of it: 'this concern constantly lives in the concern [*Sorge*] over being different from them, *even if only to equalize that difference.*'[30] But there is no sense in Heidegger's notion of distantiality of a distance being created away from one's true self – losing in extensity what belongs to one in intensity. Had Kierkegaard wanted to put the word '*Abständigkeit*' or some suitably coined Danish equivalent to use, he would have had it designate exactly the distance such concern with difference creates between levelled individuals and individuals in their singularity. The significance of this distantiality would then be, in Heideggerian terms, that it prevented *Dasein* from becoming a place, locus, or location for the disclosure of truth about what it is to be with

others and to share a world. The thought here would be that in order
to become close to others *as* others, one must be in relation to them at
the level of selves, of disclosed, singled-out selves; whereas the absorption in *das Man*, although from a certain point of view it may seem an
excellent way of getting or acting together, working cooperatively, a
selfless way of being about things, in actual fact removes us from each
other just as, and because, it removes us from ourselves.[31]

What Kierkegaard in the *Review* finds entirely negative about levelling is, in short, that it abstracts from and ideally eradicates the unique
locus of human fulfilment, the only place where the ideal can arise in
the way it must, in the form of sustained concern on the part of the
individual. In a reflective age enthusiasm is marginalized and manifests
itself in brief eruptions,[32] last-ditch and in their very nature inconstant
protests at the gradual disappearance of 'personality', merely futile attempts to revert to spontaneous immediacy. Lacking any grip in personal continuity they are followed typically by ennui and indolence.
One might think, not inappropriately in the light of the Hegelian
thought that 'reduction' to the rank and file and rescue from mere
abstract individuality are the way to spiritual *ascent*, that the *Review* is
a criticism of Hegelian political theory.[33] But by now the Hegelian rage
was over, and if it addresses politics at all, the *Review* speaks to the
exaggerated concern shown by liberal politicians for what Kierkegaard
considers mere externals – not symbolic externals such as palings and
hedges, but the institutional conditions that externalize what belongs to
inwardness. The proper flowering of the idea in the individual had been
brought to a stop by an externalizing of its goals. The way in which
politicians aim to introduce equality is one in which, as Kierkegaard
says in a passage deleted from the final draft of the *Review*, 'the dialectic
turns away from inwardness and wants to render equality in the negative; so that those who are not essentially individuals constitute an
equality in external association'. Levelling, he adds, is 'the faked anticipation of eternal life, which people have done away with as a "beyond"
and now want to realize here *in abstracto*'.[34]

But the criticism clearly seems much wider than that, embracing
indeed the whole of culture, the ways in which people interrelate at all
levels. The target is one that, in his papers, Kierkegaard encapsulates in
the notion of envy, a 'self-establishing envy': 'one wants to drag down

the great.'[35] So deeply embedded is it in the collective consciousness, or so far in the background, that nobody sees it for what it is. Superiority in others is treated as hubris, but the concealed motivation is obvious on reflection, since in order to envy someone you must in fact admit their superiority.[36] When it is *one* that wants to drag down, however, the acknowledgement of the other's superiority vanishes into thin air. Who is this One? Heidegger would say that it was *Dasein* in its *das Man* mode, not envious individuals, at least not singled-out individuals. In fact, if you were to look for someone responsible for levelling, worse than there being no one at home when you knocked on the door, there would be no door to knock on. What has done the levelling in such a case is 'the public'.[37]

The public, says Kierkegaard, is levelling's 'spirit', a 'monstrous abstraction, an all-encompassing something that is nothing, a mirage, a phantom'. More particularly it is a phantom brought about by the press. Although the remarks about 'one' wanting to 'drag down the great' bear the heading, '*The Corsair*'s Standpoint', these words about an abstraction are addressed not to *The Corsair*, which could hardly claim to represent Copenhagen's journalistic establishment, but to journalism in general and to the liberal press in particular. Still, in Kierkegaard's eyes, that periodical was certainly an instrument of the levelling he writes about in the *Review* and whose spirit was the public. Moreover, an allegory Kierkegaard uses to illustrate the sinister side of levelling with its seat in the anonymous public closely anticipates his own fate at the hand of *The Corsair*, so closely that it may have been inserted at the last moment when those events had begun to unroll. We will see, though, how Kierkegaard came to regard this not as fate but as something he brought upon himself deliberately. We recall that unpublished prayer when he was toying with inviting *The Corsair*'s attentions.

In the allegory the public is personified by a bored Roman emperor who has a dog (identified as 'literary vilification') let loose on someone just for amusement, the emperor knowing that he can then blame the dog (by common consent a mere cur for whose savagings no one need take responsibility) for whatever harm is done.[38] In the event, Kierkegaard's colleagues were to go public, so to speak, in just this negative sense when they refrained from defending him when he was exposed to scurrilous attacks in a journal that they could all pretend they would never stoop to reading. As Heidegger neatly puts it: 'The public is involved in everything but in such a way that it has already always absolved itself of it all.'[39]

The section called 'The Result of Observing the Two Ages' returns, in another sense, to those features of Copenhagen life in 1844 noted by Lusard on *his* return: triviality, formlessness, a 'know-it-all' attitude, flirtatiousness, and superficiality. Adding some items, or specifying some already included, Kierkegaard asks: What is it to chat? What is formlessness? What is superficiality? What is flirtation? What is it to reason? In each case the answer is some variation on the theme that the 'passionate' distinction between inner and outer, between the extensive and the intensive, has been done away with. Thus to chat is no longer to observe a distinction between keeping quiet and talking, while to argue, like abstract thinking, lacks the 'dialectical depth' for 'full-blooded individuality'. These all represent a 'suspension of the principle of contradiction', the consequence of which is to place the existing individual in 'contradiction with himself'. As noted earlier, formlessness is the failure to let form emerge from individual inspiration and consequently leaves all that has to do with form in externals, in formalities that even suspend the virtue of decorum, by removing the immediacy that decorum presupposes in order to be what it is, namely the ability to overcome it. Superficiality is the failure to observe a distinction between concealment and revelation, while flirtation fails to distinguish love from debauchery.[40]

One reason why the individual can be said to be in self-contradiction when these distinctions have collapsed is that the distinctions are needed for there to be any foothold for the cultivation of individuality. With nowhere for inwardness to develop, an *individual*'s existence will never be shaped by the appeal of an idea. Where enthusiasms never acquire the constancy upon which personality is built, there simply cannot be individual existences; and the ideals of equality and freedom which fired the revolutionary age, deprived of an inner dimension in which to unfold, simply wither and take on the form of an all-consuming envy. Another reason is that when people have eyes only for how they differ from one another, in prosecuting the ideal of equality in this new 'form' they are depriving themselves of the only sense they now retain of being themselves and not another. Although Kierkegaard warns that the result will be catastrophic for the individual thus laid bare, he also says that this result may be just what is needed.

There is a parallel here to the role played earlier by irony in Kierkegaard's thought. Just as irony levelled all finite interests, forcing a space in which an 'infinite' self could be grasped, so now envy contrives a levelling of all 'external' distinctions, forcing a space in which selfhood's only possibility is to flourish 'inwardly'. To measure one's worth in a way in which nothing external counts leaves you with no distinguishing marks at all. The merciless logic of levelling as Kierkegaard presents it betokens the 'ascendancy of the category of the generation over that of individuality'.[41] Carried to the limit it leads to a pure abstraction, for once all external measures of distinction have been eliminated all you are left with is a totally empty way of defining selfhood and the self. At its extreme, therefore, levelling leaves you with a clear choice: either you really are nothing in worldly terms and you are left to make your own self – rather than be the self given to you by God – or you are what you are in those terms, the finitely given self, but these terms are to be grasped as given to you by God.

It might be tempting to add, as the 'equipment' you have been provided with to do God's work to the best of your ability. But readers of the discourses Kierkegaard continued to write throughout his career will doubt the aptness of this pragmatic metaphor. Kierkegaard seems to some to be urging a nonutilitarian conception of the divine 'purpose'. We are not meant, for example, to interpret the Incarnation as 'a tallying up of guilt and sin'.[42] To be carrying out the divine purpose is to *be* in a certain way, not to be trying to do or achieve certain things, for example seeking a reward or avoiding a punishment, let alone bringing about Heaven on Earth. This was the theme of 'Purity of Heart Is to Will One Thing', written in 1846 and published the following year in a volume of signed discourses, *Edifying Discourses in Another Spirit*.

Kierkegaard regards the 'principle of sociality' that is 'deified' in his time as 'demoralizing'. In 'thrall' to reflection, it is what makes the virtues into the pagan's 'glittering vices'. Seeking comfort in company is simply a way of dodging the threat of being singled out or separated.[43] Whether or not by being in thrall to reflection he means that association builds on concepts and generalizations, thus losing sight of the particular, which would be a continuation of Kierkegaard's criticism of Hegel, he does imply that collectivities or groupings, and the cult of them, are an attempt to stave off the inevitable. However, where levelling has become the order of the day there is no escape. No authority, either individual or corporate, can stem its progress:

No single man – the eminent person in terms of superiority and of the dialectic of fate – will be able to halt levelling's abstraction, for the single man's is a negative elevation and the age of heroes is over. No congregation will be in a position to halt levelling's abstraction, because in the context of reflection the congregation is itself in the service of levelling. Not even the individualities of nations will be able to halt it, for the abstraction of levelling reflects on a higher negativity, namely that of pure humanity.[44]

In extension, then, of the earlier thought of irony's potentially edifying levelling being in the service of spirit by making room for it, this levelling that has also arisen from the cult of reflection and is now being driven by its own momentum, has one benefit in prospect. Though initially motivated by a fear of individuality, the very process through which people prone to reflection efface their individuality by seeking identity through group membership will, if carried to the limit (forcing them to identify themselves only as members of the group of all groups), force them to face the very thing they are trying to escape. They will see that they must either 'be lost' in the 'dizziness of abstract infinity' or be 'infinitely saved' in the 'essentiality of religiousness'.[45]

But if levelling has an unstoppable momentum, what is left for the would-be cultural critic, educator, or enlightener? Towards the end of the 'Result' section Kierkegaard assigns a role to 'the unrecognizables' (*de Ukjendelige*).[46] These are people who have grasped levelling's 'meaning'. And what is that? The answer, oracular in its brevity and Hegelian in its expansiveness, is in reality a reapplication of Kierkegaard's thoughts on tragic drama, as becomes even clearer in a journal entry repeating it four years later where he introduces the 'chorus'. Antiquity's guiding thought was excellence, eminence, or distinction, as against the insignificant crowd. The eminent (those who 'dared to consider everything permissible') were exposed to (what is described in the later entry as an 'envious') fate (also called in the later entry 'the principle of nature'). In the Christian era fate is replaced by an inscrutable but benevolent providence, and the guiding thought is 'representation', in the church, even by a monarch, and even perhaps by the kind of representation by the Estates that was the typical political system of the time. Individuals are represented but not yet as genuinely individual; it is only in a kind of 'consciousness of self' that they are freed from mass insignificance. The guiding thought in the present age is equality, or perhaps better, equal- or fair-mindedness (*Ligelighed*), and, says Kierkegaard, its most consistent but abortive 'implementation' is levelling ('the negative unity of the negative mutual reciprocity of individuals'). Here it is not fate or providence that is the unknown force carrying one along but the act of levelling itself: a 'reflection-game in the hands of an abstract power' that takes the leveller along with it.

Just as one calculates the diagonal in a parallelogram of forces, so too can one calculate the law of levelling. For the individual who himself levels a few is carried along too, and so it goes on.[47]

In antiquity, when fate crushed the hero, the chorus was 'oblivious to its blows'. The modern analogy of this 'negative principle' is 'the concept of the universal, an abstraction, the public and the like'. The corporate personality of the chorus has gone, but its anonymous successor inherits its imperviousness to the hero's suffering. 'The insignificant individual lives on happily in the public, while this abstraction levels the eminent individual.'[48]

To grasp the meaning of levelling is to see its inevitability and then willingly to go along with it. Doing that is 'maximally' to have learnt its lesson. Excellence, heroism, eminence won't help. 'Levelling, consistent to the last, prevents that.' Its proper pupil is the person who sees that he cannot prevent it. No hero, all (but it is not so little) that he can be is 'an essential human being in the fullest sense of equality'. He will level himself and by example, or other forms of indirect influence, seek to awaken in others a sense of what is positive, namely the weight of moral and social responsibility that lies on each individual. Exerting an influence in this hidden way requires sacrifice and suffering. Later, in summarizing his experience in both the *Corsair* affair and its aftermath, but also his position in Copenhagen in general, Kierkegaard says:

I posed . . . the problem the whole generation understands: equality between man and man. I posed it executively in Copenhagen. That's more than writing a few words about it; I expressed it approximately in my life. I have levelled in a *Christian* sense, but not in the rebellious sense against power and worth which with all my might I have upheld.[49]

This had not yet happened. Here Kierkegaard is merely suggesting how levelling, once the work of irony, now of an age of reflection and understanding, can be transformed into a properly Christian world in which no outer distinction counts for your true worth. Living as though that were true would be what it means to answer as well as pose the problem of equality between man and man in practice, the problem Kierkegaard says he expressed 'approximately' in his life. This idea was to be the theme of his next major work, and the question of how far he himself approximated to this ideal itself was to trouble him during the next few years.

As usual Kierkegaard signs off with a disclaimer. He has not tried, any more than has the author of *Two Ages*, to judge or compare the merits of the ages portrayed. All he has done is to describe them. That is a little disingenuous, since he has approached the events described in the book from another point of view. That, apart from being a kind of judgment on the book itself, implies a radical corrective to the optimism shown in Madame Gyllembourg's 'even-handedness' regarding the respective merits of the two ages. But Kierkegaard, again taking quite a lot back, ends by being even-handed himself, though with a Hegelian twist that to a Hegelian would nevertheless appear quite un-Hegelian. He asks the reader (anyone, Madame Gyllembourg, or Heiberg?) to balance the advantages of the present age's 'extensity' against the 'intensity' that it is increasingly losing and offers in the name of Socrates a Hegelian *tertium*: first, the spontaneity of an immediate inspiration; second, the growth of understanding and ingenuity in the service of prudence; and then third, the highest and most intensive inspiration of a Socrates who sees very well what the prudent thing to do is and does the opposite.[50]

The suggestion is of course in any obvious sense outrageous as a rule for the maintenance of life. Perhaps less so as a proposal about how to grasp the character of life as seen from some point of view beyond utilitarian considerations of its maintenance. Did Kierkegaard see himself as writing in the 'cause' of such a proposal, or perhaps just from the point of view of such a perspective? Did he really think such a proposal might be able through the medium of politics to affect the very manner of life's maintenance, the sociopolitical structure, replacing its inherent utilitarianism for instance? Or was the Socratic image merely a fanciful projection of his own 'outsider's' position vis-à-vis the circles on which he hoped his writings would have some impact? All this remains unclear. The same is true of how far the apocalyptic vision of a purely levelled world was for him a genuine fear. And if it was, did he regard his remarks in 'Results' as prophecy? Were he alive today, would he see his prognosis realized in *our* present age? Should we regard him as truly a prophet? What in fact would confirm such fears, genuine or not? Marxism, modern nihilism, drug addiction, the internet?[51] One thing that is clear, however, is that Kierkegaard was now occupied obsessively with the question of how to interpret his writer's role. What was the status of these insights that had appeared on his pages? Were they torn out of him or vouchsafed to him by his circumstances, by his own gifts and not least by his oddly peripheral yet central position in his own society? Was that perhaps too a gift?

14

Refashioning the Exterior

FOUR WEEKS after the *Review* appeared Kierkegaard left again for a brief visit to Berlin. Brøchner was there at the time, his first visit, and they met unexpectedly in a restaurant which had been a meeting place for Danes that Kierkegaard had found on *his* first visit. On being invited to dine at Kierkegaard's hotel the following day, Brøchner noted how 'ingeniously' Kierkegaard had arranged his rooms 'in order to encourage the mood' for his work. What he was working on we cannot tell but it might have been Adler – but we shall return to that.[1] There are many journal entries from 1846. These may also stem from that visit; some were on his situation at home but many on wider themes related to what he had written in *Postscript*, one on the place of science: 'Most of what flourishes best of all under the name of scientific research (especially the natural sciences) is not science at all but curiosity.'[2] He appears to have enjoyed the amenities in Berlin, and frequented a park in the zoo 'surrounded by flower beds', a substitute for Copenhagen's Frederiksberg Gardens. According to Brøchner, Kierkegaard had a predilection for *Liebfraumilch* because its name suggested 'something mild and light', neither realizing nor apparently noticing, as at least Brøchner thought, that 'it was in fact one of the stronger Rhine wines'.[3] The trip was short and Kierkegaard was back in Copenhagen on 16 May, just two weeks after he had left.

The text of that 'First and Last Explanation' had been 'dashed off on a piece of paper' which, instead of including it with the rest of the manuscript for *Postscript*, Kierkegaard had kept aside 'to be worked on'. He also wanted to delay handing it in 'as late as possible so as not to have it lying around at the printers'. Was he afraid someone might leak it? It was a touchy time for his pseudonymity, but *The Corsair*'s unflatteringly illustrated response appeared only three days after the manuscript was delivered, while the official acknowledgement of his responsibility for the pseudonyms is dated 7 February, just three weeks before *Postscript* was published. What kept the piece of paper back for those five weeks?

Naturally, Kierkegaard would be anxious about the final formulation, but also about openly acknowledging what – apart from that irresponsible periodical's breach of etiquette – was still officially no more than a universally known secret. Other things were also on his mind. The seventh of February was also the date of the Preface to the *Review*, which must have been receiving its final touches at the time; it appeared only seven weeks later. Among other things he was probably adding those parts about the emperor and the stray dog.

But then Kierkegaard adds: 'The lies, gossip, and vulgarity that surround one make one's position fairly difficult at times, perhaps make me all too extravagantly anxious to have the truth on my side, down to the least thread – what's the use?' This is a different worry, but what exactly is it? A comment in the margin tells us. To accept that the truth is not up to him, or anyone, but is in God's hands, is itself a hard truth to stomach. 'I was momentarily in two minds as to whether, in consideration of the circumstances (the *Corsair* nonsense and town gossip), to leave out the acknowledgment of my authorship and just indicate that the whole thing was older than all this babble by giving the dates in the printed material. But, no! I owe it to the truth to ignore this kind of thing and do everything as decided, leaving the outcome to God's will and accepting everything from his hand as a good and perfect gift, scorning to act from prudence, putting my hopes in his giving me a firm and wise spirit.'[4]

Kierkegaard was prevaricating about whether he really was that most un-Hegelian, Socratic *tertium*: a Socrates who sees what the prudent thing to do is but then does the opposite. During those five weeks he may have been asking himself questions at two levels: what was prudent and whether, having found that out, he should dare the imprudent thing. Why? So that, like Socrates, he could act consistently with what his readers would have been led to believe he stood for. But did he really stand for it? If so, it would have to be translated into personal action. Perhaps it was less easy to tell, now that the pseudonyms and the writer were officially to converge in one person. Of course, to be a Socrates it is not enough to find out what the prudent thing to do is

and then, as if it were a simple rule, just do the opposite. The imprudent alternative is not chosen *because* it is not the prudent thing to do –
that would be a kind of defiance and mean that one was still bound,
though negatively, to considerations of what it was prudent or imprudent (for him) to do. The anxious grip on the truth would still not have
been loosened. One must rise above such considerations altogether, or
'level' downwards in the sense of erasing all signs of one's personal
preferences in the landscape of truth.

As for the prudent thing, Kierkegaard implies that life in Copenhagen
would be easier for him if people could be made to see that the pseudonymous authorship was now well and truly behind him. There could
also be more private reasons. Since the impetus was gone, the best thing
in any case might be just to retire. He could still afford to. If he still
felt any urge to write, it could be in the form of reviews such as the one
he had just written.

> To now I have served by helping the pseudonyms become authors. What if I
> decided from now to do what little writing I can indulge in in the form of criticism,
> putting what I had to say in reviews which developed my thoughts out of some
> book or other? So they could also be found in the book. Then at least I'd avoid
> being an author.[5]

Having his own thoughts look as if they emerged from the work of
another author would relieve him of the inconvenience of inventing
pseudonyms for them. That suggests again, as we found right at the
beginning, that Kierkegaard had difficulty thinking of the thoughts that
came to him as being his own. They were blessed children from above,
perhaps even divinely inspired – what a responsibility! How important
then not to attach one's own name to them as 'responsible'.

The entry is dated 9 February, just a month before the 'Report'
opening the first NB journal announcing Kierkegaard's now-firm resolve to 'remain true in the Greek sense to [his] existence-idea', and in
such a way that the idea should become, for himself, 'in the religious
sense, as ennobling as possible'.[6] The resolve was firmed by the thought
again of his father: 'How dreadful, the thought of that man who as a
small boy tending sheep on the Jutland heath, in much suffering, starving, and exhausted, once stood up on a hill and cursed God! – And that
man was unable to forget it when he was eighty-two years old.'[7]

In May Kierkegaard would be thirty-three. He had survived the four-year ordeal, though readers must be struck just as much by the unfailing energy and humour of Kierkegaard's pseudonymous writings as by their combined originality and (sometimes too quickly and inaccurately tapped) learning. It was a physical and in one sense mental ordeal, but not a spiritual one; he was solving, not making problems. It had also been written against the 'deadline', or in Heideggerian terms, the writer – and during the time he was not much else – had been living 'towards death'. But now that the impetus was gone and he wasn't dead, what was he to make of it all, and not least do next, for as long as 'next' was to last? It seems not unlikely that when it was all over, the thought that struck him most forcibly was not, 'See, I did it!', but, 'What have I done?' Given his obsession with centres of gravity, and the harmony of forces, and keys to understanding details, he must have begun, if he hadn't started long ago, to wonder what the underlying meaning of his activity to date was. The answer would determine what he should make of his future. In the event Kierkegaard took no steps towards retirement or a living and continued to write, just as copiously, though from now on the larger part was to be confined to the journals.

The reasons why Kierkegaard had originally intended to let *Postscript* conclude his authorship were of his own choosing, though he may have thought of them as also being God's. But as the *Corsair* affair developed in the spring and summer of 1846, matters became more complicated. At first, he may have thought of it as simply pushing him more effectively into retirement – to continue his good work in a more conventional way. But then it struck him that to stop now would be to leave the impression that it was *The Corsair* that had brought him to a stop, not his or God's idea of what formed the logical closure of a completed project. There was also an element no doubt of pride. Retiring to a country parsonage would look like dodging for cover.

But what if he had misread God's plan? Maybe this was not the logical closure. Wasn't it God after all who had put it into his head that he should have *The Corsair* 'level' him in the cause of truth? If so, to try to stop the train of events now set in motion would be to frustrate God's plan for him. By going along with the public's levelling at the hands of 'literary vilification' Kierkegaard would be performing that edifying role he had just defined in the closing pages of the *Review*, doing what he could do, the only kind of thing that in the circumstances could be done, on the side of truth, more or less unrecognizably.

Some wonder whether the *Corsair* fracas really had the effect on Kierkegaard's life that he claims it did. A contemporary thought his complaints about being taunted by young boys in the street was 'a rather small martyr's crown'.[8] If we suspect paranoia, as Thompson is inclined to, we would expect exaggeration. He wonders whether the 'looks and insults [Kierkegaard] claimed to see were really there'. Should we, as many suspect, begin now to doubt the balance of Kierkegaard's mind? If so, we should also cast doubt on his ability to define the significance of his own work without succumbing to the perils of self-deception and plain delusion.

Thompson supports his suspicion with an event that Kierkegaard himself describes as 'just one but typical illustration' of the treatment he received as a result of the *Corsair* business.[9] Kierkegaard records a meeting on the street with Lieutenant S. C. Barth, adjutant of the Hussars, and Barth's young son.

He approached with his little son. The father greeted me with his usual almost exaggerated courtesy; he stepped aside to allow me the pavement – if the lad hadn't known who I was he might have suspected I was something special – but he obviously knew me, he was a reader of *The Corsair*. What a state of affairs! Mustn't it cause any child serious harm to see someone treated in print in a way that all but amounts to an invitation for every schoolboy to hiss at him on the streets – and the next moment see him treated thus by his father, or read excerpts from his writing in the school's Danish readers.[10]

True enough, Kierkegaard's works were by then excerpted in school readers. But then the exaggerated courtesy would surely be in place, a demonstration by the father of his respect for one of his son's literary models. Besides, doesn't Kierkegaard say that Lieutenant Barth's approach was his 'usual' one? Clearly it is the son Kierkegaard suspects of belonging to the 'rabble' that had destroyed his world. In the entry in question, part of yet another 'Report', Kierkegaard writes of how 'extraordinarily gratifying for my soul, and for my powers of ironic observation . . . [it had been] to roam about in the streets and be nothing while thoughts and ideas worked within me, being a loafer in this way while I was decidedly the most industrious of all the younger ones, irresponsible and "unserious" while the others' seriousness could as well be jest beside my deep concern'. But now this was 'all ruined'. The rabble had been roused, 'the apprentices, the butcher boys, pupils, and all such'. It was the lad's generation – he was twenty years Kierkegaard's junior – that had poisoned the atmosphere for him, the small children running up and staring at his legs, or the 'couple of louts' who in church 'had the cheek to sit down beside me constantly staring at one's trousers and making mocking remarks to each other in voices high enough for every word to be overheard'.[11] However, as Thompson points out, Kierkegaard seems to have been mistaken about this particular lad. He adds: 'Some years later Georg Brandes asked Barth's son about the encounter. The boy could not recall it but told Brandes that both he and his father had been earnest admirers of Kierkegaard, and that neither had ever laid eyes on *The Corsair*.'[12]

That Kierkegaard's sense of persecution was nevertheless not groundless can be seen from Brandes's own 'earliest recollection of Kierkegaard'.

[W]hen, as a child, I failed to pull my trousers down carefully and evenly over my, what were in those days serviceably long, boots, the nanny would admonish me, saying: 'Søren Kierkegaard!' This is how I first heard mention of the name that at the time also echoed so strongly in the ears of the grown-ups. The caricature drawings in *The Corsair* had made Kierkegaard's legs known in circles where his genius had not penetrated. His trousers had achieved a fame with us that parallelled that achieved by Théophile Gautier's red vest ten years earlier in France.[13]

The *Corsair* affair clearly had long-lasting effects. For Kierkegaard himself they lasted all his lifetime – the event of the sniggering youths in church came a whole year later than the original exchange – but, in terms of his later reception, much longer. We may trace its effects in the dismissive tone typical of some descriptions of Kierkegaard even today. Thompson quotes Stephen Crites's portrait: that 'hypochondriacal young man born old, with his eccentricities, his love affair that we are sick of hearing about, his abysmal melancholia'. Typically, Crites's description begins with that ineradicable image of 'the spindly figure with the umbrella', which subtly sets the tone for the rest, more subtly than Walter Kaufmann, who straightforwardly offers his account of Kierkegaard's works as 'the desperate attempts of a misshapen man . . . for whom . . . the desire not to know the truth was an important element in . . . his faith'.[14]

Crites, by saying we see the spindly figure 'on every page', is suggesting that we may doubt Kierkegaard's claim in that 'First and Last Explanation' that not one word by the pseudonyms is his own. But if we do doubt it, might that not too be due simply to the fact that *The*

Corsair's caricatures are the only full-length portraits we have? It is indeed true that Kierkegaard is unmistakably present in almost all of his writings, even including according to one report a letter of recommendation he had written for a trusted servant who wanted to join the police,[15] but it is their liveliness and bite that the unspoiled reader 'sees', not the persecuted man's legs. In short, there is little real doubt that the effect of *The Corsair* was and continues to be devastating for Kierkegaard's reputation. To this, in the proximity of a reference to the uneven trouser-legs to what, by apparently gratuitous analogy, he calls Kierkegaard's 'twisted life', Thompson's own book bears testimony.[16]

Amusingly, in later years the younger Barth confirmed the deep respect in which he actually held Kierkegaard. Like so many younger people at the time, Barth was an enthusiastic reader of *Either/Or* and took it therefore as a stroke of 'the greatest possible good fortune' when the opportunity offered itself to see and talk with his 'idol'.

My knees shook under me as I rang the bell, and when the little man stood before me I was on the point of fainting. With difficulty I stammered out the purpose of my visit. K. naturally took in the whole situation immediately. But he was wrong about one thing, and that was when he assumed I was a 'student' [at the University]. I am in fact a 'Polytechnician' [graduate of the Polytechnic Academy] and therefore really a 'beggar at the temple door' in relation to him. Despite the fact that during the fifteen minutes my audience lasted I did nothing but stare at him, all I can recall of his personality is that enormously demonic look with which he seemed to read one's very soul. We went through some very uncomfortable rooms and came to a room in which, true enough, there stood a desk with drawers in it! It's the one he bought from the pawnbroker, I thought: Oh, if only one dared ask if I might see the compartment in which *E/O* was found. He asked me to sit down and did so himself. Now comes my real story. 'I was pleased to see that the government of Saxony has rewarded your father for his honourable activities by giving him the Order of Albrecht; but tell me, wouldn't he rather have money?' You have to admit that the question was an extremely delicate one, designed to sound me out a bit. But you have to hear also how the innocent can walk unharmed amid serpents. I replied: 'I don't know, but it seems to me that a government cannot very well offer an officer money on such an occasion.' 'No, of course not', K. answered, as much as to say he had posed a rather silly question. And he began talking about other things, about Plato, Mrs Gyllembourg, etc. I sat there, and from nervousness (and not because I couldn't have understood him) was 'so dumm / als ging mir ein Mühlrad im Kopf herum [as stupid as if a mill-wheel were going round in my head]'.[17]

The teasing provocation shows some friendliness on Kierkegaard's part and little if any sign of patronage. By now the younger Barth was in his early twenties and it was a time, the early fifties, when Kierkegaard had long established a pattern of not receiving visitors whom he suspected of being motivated mainly by curiosity. When the Norwegian author and women's rights campaigner Camilla Collett rang the bell, with naïve enthusiasm in her case rather than quaking knees, she was told that Kierkegaard was not at home. On reaching the street again, however, and glancing up, she saw Kierkegaard standing at the window. Their eyes met and they 'involuntarily nodded to each other in surprise'. As the narrator of the story nicely puts it: 'Unaccustomed to visits by ladies, he none the less wanted to have a look at this pushy person.'[18] Brøchner amusingly recalls another episode, recounted to him by Kierkegaard himself, about a German scholar whom Kierkegaard thought must have come to see him because someone had tipped him off about this local curiosity. Kierkegaard received his visitor politely but said he must have made a mistake: 'My brother, the doctor, is an exceedingly learned man, whose acquaintance I'm sure you would be interested to make, but I am a beer-seller.'[19]

That was sometime in the winter or spring of 1852–53, by which time Kierkegaard had for long, and as the conclusion of the long entry recalling the encounter with Barth and his son has it, 'refashioned [his] exterior'. The inveterate peripatetic was a figure of the past. Kierkegaard now kept mostly to himself. Conscious of his public image, he had, as in the same entry he now thought, put on 'a weightier look'. The entry concludes tellingly: 'People in some quarters will say I have changed for the better. Alas!, and yet they fail precisely to serve my idea as they did then.'

Kierkegaard is saying that by becoming 'the' public his former public were no longer able to contribute the part he had assigned to them: to be able to see him as an expression of his own idea, the anti-Hegelian idea that Spirit is born in inspiration and feeling and develops and unfolds from the heart, or rather from the passionate will of individuals, who then single themselves out from one another, not by excelling or even by manifesting solidarity among themselves, but by fostering the idea individually within themselves, in ways not immediately recognizable except to those in a position to appreciate what it is for the spiritual in a person to adopt an incognito. Since his colleagues now ignored him and the riff-raff that did pay attention lacked the background to appreciate or react positively to his own performance, his was an act without an audience.

In a note dated 7 September 1846, when *The Corsair*, as opposed to its first- and second-hand readers, had stopped victimizing him, Kierkegaard wrote that 'to live on the streets and alleys while writing the pseudonyms' had been the 'ironically correct' thing to do. The irony was directed at 'the intellectually affected Hegelian forces we have, or rather had, here at home' and depended on Kierkegaard's maintaining an appearance of irresponsibility at odds with what he was writing. But by making it look 'as though the street was where he really belonged', the 'literary hooligans' of the Left had removed the very ground on which any such ironic tension depended. And as 'the irony quite rightly disappears, so I take my leave.'[20] '[M]y days of writing, too,', he said, 'are now over.'[21]

But not so. By January of the following year, 1847, Kierkegaard was able to say that the plan to retire had been due to depression.

God be praised that all the rabble's barbaric attacks have landed on me. I have had time really to learn inwardly and convince myself that it was after all a melancholy idea to want to live out in a country parsonage and do penance in seclusion and oblivion. Now I am ready to go on, and determined as never before. If I hadn't received that drubbing of insults and mockery I would have been pursued for ever by this melancholy thought, for there is a certain way of things going well that fosters ideas precisely of a melancholy kind; if, for instance, I had not had private means, with all my disposition to melancholy I would never have reached the grade I sometimes have.[22]

There is another question. How is Kierkegaard able to avoid the suspicion, not only in others but also in himself, that in defining his work as he was about to do, he is not just revising the play to suit his role? First co-opting the literary establishment in his plan as he now conceives it and, when that doesn't work, seeing the very causes of that as indicative of an even greater participation of his society in his plan, this whole project of defining his life in terms of his lifework begins to look like a desperate retreat from one barricade to the next. Aren't we simply witnessing a frenzied ad hoc effort to keep the show going, with himself in the main part?

Not the least fascinating part of this period in Kierkegaard's life is the difficulty one has in distinguishing the life from the writings. The latter begin to be confirmations of the self-image and thus also contributions to it. Kierkegaard saw this himself, and the remainder of his life and work is virtually an attempt to escape accusations of this kind. Not by special pleading, which he would be the first to see through, but by becoming the living and dying answer to the regressive questions that requirements of honesty and clear-mindedness endlessly pose. Kierkegaard hung on desperately to the idea that he was 'in the truth'. As for paranoia or madness, although that was the verdict of many contemporaries as well as others, the story as it unfolds presents a far more nuanced picture.

If the riff-raff made the streets unfriendly, Kierkegaard's colleagues made no attempt to offer him shelter. He could imagine why. Why pay attention to a scurrilous periodical the more celebrated of them had their own excellent reasons to ignore? Besides, didn't they all know, some of them all too well, how capable the (still) young Kierkegaard was of defending himself? The more philistine among them would say, 'What harm a little amusement?', while the élite will ask whether any *serious* littérateur should stoop to mention, let alone read, *The Corsair*. Kierkegaard had already put this into words in a single page of the *Review*. By having the stray dog of literary vilification level the great, the emperor-public subtly rechannels sympathy for the victim into something less strenuous: a complacent vilification of vilification. But he had added that even to offer sympathy would just be another way of consolidating complacency. It assumes a kind of self-importance. One should realize that it is always the sufferer who is 'the stronger'.[23]

In terms of a sheer trial of strength, of the kind even those with quite conventional ideas of the idea, or even no idea at all, would appreciate, Kierkegaard might seem to have won this contest, as many once thought he had triumphed over the liberal politician and journalist Lehmann, whose star had fallen so dramatically after that earlier exchange. Already in the report dated 9 March 1846 we saw that 'P. L. Møller [having] taken the hint and retired from *The Corsair* . . . [had gone] where he belongs'. His chances for a professorship had been ruined, and he later died in poverty and obscurity abroad.[24] In the autumn Goldschmidt resigned as editor of *The Corsair* and only five days later was on his way to Germany and Italy, though in his case to return. Kierkegaard, perhaps prone in his own case to the hazard of self-importance manifested more in the withholding of sympathy than in the offering of it, wrote:

Look at little Goldschmidt; he played the hypocrite to himself in the fond belief that he was called upon by God to be a scourge for us poor wretches – then he gets a chance to abuse what he himself had immortalized! He seizes it. In him there was accordingly no truth; his divine wrath was hypocrisy, otherwise he would have been faithful to the truth and persecuted the wicked, not what he himself admires – just because it won't admire him.[25]

Goldschmidt later claimed that it was *The Corsair* that 'triumphed'. The reason he gave up the periodical was precisely because of the bad taste victory had left in his mouth. For Kierkegaard, of course, with his defensive moves so well prepared, that explanation could only have meant victory for himself but on a higher level. In confessing, even boasting, that he had resigned because, as he said, he did not want to be a person 'to be looked down upon', Goldschmidt virtually admitted to having been an instrument of the anonymous power of levelling, an ownerless dog let loose to savage the great in the 'name' of an anonymous public.

There is a pregnant irony in the relation between Kierkegaard and Goldschmidt. The two had first met at the Rørdams' in 1837, and since then Kierkegaard, seven years the senior, having recognized Goldschmidt's talent, had continually tried to persuade the younger man to take up comic composition in the well-intended, even faithfully Heibergian belief that to do so would take him nearer the truth. That would be a constructive alternative to the destructive, visionless path he had begun to plough in *The Corsair*. According to Goldschmidt, Kierkegaard became very angry when he as much as mentioned that, as editor, he had received anonymous information disclosing secrets of celebrities' private lives, even after Goldschmidt's own assurance that such material was never used and that everything he published was based only on what he had read in the newspapers. The two nevertheless enjoyed good relations and were even walking arm in arm in the street when Kierkegaard first brought up the subject of the recent publication of *Gœa*. On their last encounter, however, Goldschmidt later wrote, Kierkegaard 'walked by me with an extremely embittered look, not wanting to greet me or be greeted'. The irony of it, at least according to Goldschmidt, was that he believed that in his taunting of Kierkegaard he was at last succeeding in doing what Kierkegaard had always wanted him to do, to write something genuinely comic. To him Kierkegaard's exaggerated reaction was incomprehensible – all that about being a martyr to *The Corsair* and having intended it from the start. As for that final meeting on Myntergade:

In the bitterness of that look, as in Kierkegaard's entire personal presence, there was something that touched on the comic. But this slipped aside and gave way to something elevated and ideal that his personality also contained. There was something in that intense, wild look that in a way drew the curtain aside from the higher court on which Kierkegaard had until then prided himself, and which I had been unable, but also unwilling, to see in spite of certainly sensing its presence.[26]

Sometime in 1846, before early November, Kierkegaard had talked to Bishop Mynster about taking up a rural living. Although representing opposite poles of the world of Danish letters, for Kierkegaard the main difference between Goldschmidt and Mynster lay in Goldschmidt's representing nothing at all. Although *The Corsair* was 'liberal and took its whip to Christian VIII, officialdom, etc.', its editor 'lacked vision' and its activity was nothing but 'an offshoot of the opposition',[27] something we have heard before. It wasn't that Kierkegaard had nothing in common with the younger writers who set themselves up against the conservatism of Heiberg and others. Far from it; but Kierkegaard seems to have been sharply divided between his aesthetic and religious 'selves'. This was a cause of his unending dispute with himself, not least over his sincerity, and surely a mainspring of his life as a writer or, as was by now virtually the same thing, his life. It was always as a matter of either/or, as the counter-Faustian journey in his pseudonymous works testifies, that any search for a life-view would inevitably end in 'the religious'.

Mynster was both conservative *and* a visionary. His attitude towards religion was not so far removed from Kierkegaard's own and, unlike the predominantly Hegelian thinkers whose influence had been so widely felt during Kierkegaard's student days and after, Mynster believed that religion and faith were natural drives that could not be incorporated into a logically consistent system. His own relationship to religion, born of a moment of conversion in his younger days mentioned earlier, focused on the need for 'quiet hours' and for people to come together away from the 'noise of the world and from all worldly affairs',[28] this distinguishing him, favourably in Kierkegaard's eyes, from the more extrovert congregationalism of the populist Grundtvig. We recall an article by Mynster from 1839 entitled 'Rationalism and Supernaturalism' that may well have given Kierkegaard the motif for *Either/Or*, and may even be a source of the Socratic and more-than-Socratic positions, A and B, so important for the Climacus pseudonym. Since Kierkegaard also strongly identified Mynster with his own father, it seemed natural in this hour of public oppression to turn to him for support.

But he also describes Mynster as one of those who thought he had it coming to him when he 'threw himself before the rabble'. Mynster even said that it might 'do him good'.[29] When Kierkegaard visited him that November in 1846, still thinking of becoming a rural pastor ('an integral part of the small circle around me'), Mynster actually advised him to do that. But Kierkegaard immediately assumed that it was for the wrong reasons: 'Bishop Mynster evidently does not understand me'; the two had 'entirely different premisses'.

He assumes that I want in some way or other to make a career of it [like Peter, his brother], that I aspire to *be* somebody after all, but just there is the rub: I aspire to be as little as possible; that is precisely my melancholy's idea. For that very reason I have been content to be regarded as half-mad, though this was simply a negative form of being something out of the ordinary. Quite possibly this may remain the essential form of my life, so that I shall never attain the beautiful, quiet, calm existence of being something very small.

Talking with the bishop, his last resort, made Kierkegaard realize there was a general as well as genuine problem of communication here. 'What I have always privately known, and why I have never spoken with anyone about what really concerns me . . . is [that] it leads nowhere, for as I cannot and dare not talk about what totally and essentially and inwardly forms my existence, the conversation on my side amounts almost to deception. In relation to a man like Mynster I really feel the pain of this, because I revere him so highly.'[30]

This reverence, even 'fondness', for someone who 'expresses the purely human with a mastery' the like of which he 'had never seen',[31] however genuine, was nevertheless mixed with suspicion, a suspicion Kierkegaard thought was mutual: 'Although Mynster harbours certain feelings of benevolence for me, in his quiet moments perhaps even more than he admits, he clearly regards me as a suspicious and even dangerous person.' He thought Mynster's real reason for advising him to take up a rural living was to get him out of harm's way – not his own of course, but Mynster's.[32] Succeeding visits the next November and later in June 1849 proved more chilly. Indeed, on the first of those occasions Mynster said that he was busy and Kierkegaard left after only a very brief exchange, while on the second the bishop simply refused to see him. Had he become too great a nuisance? Or was it that Mynster, now that Kierkegaard was tarred with the brush of *The Corsair*'s special brand of 'levelling', though a friend of his father and the very cleric who had officiated at Søren's confirmation, now found it an indignity to have to help him?[33]

What seems true is that Mynster had begun to feel, rightly as it turns out, that Kierkegaard's writings were now being aimed at him, or rather at the church, which in Kierkegaard's eyes, due to Mynster's great ability and charisma, was virtually the same thing. A clash here appears to have been inevitable, since Kierkegaard now found himself following a route which that conclusively 'concluding' *Review* had opened up for him. It was not an entirely new route, or so Kierkegaard thought. He began to see that it was the one he had been following all along. The signpost said 'The Single Individual', a notion, indeed more than that, a 'category', to which he believed 'any historical importance' he might later acquire would be 'unconditionally linked'. As he began reviewing his own authorship to date, Kierkegaard found that the category had been at work from the start: 'It's what the pseudonyms' computations concerning the universal, the single individual, the special individual, the exception, turn on, so as to bring out the special individual in his suffering and extraordinariness.' Thus Assessor Wilhelm's questions about exemption from marriage are about the single individual. *Fear and Trembling* and *Repetition* are both 'commentaries' on it. To begin with, and continuing through the *Discourses*, the original of the single individual had been 'my reader', undisputably a reference to Regine. In *Either/Or* the direction is reversed as the topic of exceptionality, Kierkegaard's own case, becomes salient. Later discourses were dedicated to a generalized readership picked out 'distributively', as logicians would say, rather than collectively, each as 'that single individual'. And looking back, Kierkegaard now sees the whole production to date as homing in on that individual. 'The movement described by the whole authorship is *from* the public *to* the single individual', the very movement that the understanding reader who is also able to read the present age aright will take. 'As an aesthetic author', Kierkegaard writes, 'I have gone out, as it were, to get hold of the public – and the same thing was given expression in my personal way of life [*Existeren*] by living in streets and lanes – that is how the movement is described: from the public to the single individual.' Now, three years after that earlier and friendlier meeting with Mynster and with three major manuscripts on or around the theme of the single individual completed, and one of them published, Kierkegaard was again thinking of rural retirement. It was all to end 'consistently in me', he says, 'myself the single individual, living in solitude in a country parsonage. . . .'[34]

It was this category of the single individual that Mynster seems to have become increasingly unable to come to terms with. To any Lutheran, at least of any Pietistic leanings, it should present no difficulties, at least at first. And even if Mynster's own concern for the individual focused primarily on the protection the church gives for undisturbed devotion, he too could hardly have seen anything seditious in the notion of the single individual as such. But the more the implications of Kierkegaard's own conception unfolded – this category through which, as he now says, 'in a religious respect, this age, history, the human race must pass' – the less a Mynster, or any cleric, will seem at home in it. That 'as "the single individual" one is alone, in the whole world alone, alone face to face with God' is not a characterization it is easy to associate with those whose profession it is to tend the souls of others. Conversely, in Kierkegaard's eyes, Mynster through his behaviour proved increasingly the disparity between his own position and that of this category with which 'the cause of Christianity stands or falls'. Either he could not or just would not see that practising this category 'is always dangerous and at times may claim its practitioner's life'. But then if no one else could demonstrate its truth, not even the primate of the Danish Church, perhaps he, Kierkegaard, would have to do so. Could it also be that practising that dangerous art, even unto death, might be just the proof he was looking for, to convince not just others but himself too, that it had not all been vanity, indulgence, an excuse?[35]

Works of Love

K IERKEGAARD'S category of the single individual had two roles, one for times of peace ('without altering anything externally, to awaken inwardness to a heightened life in the established') and the other for times of rebellion ('to draw attention away from the external, to guide the individual towards an indifference to external change and to strengthen the individual in inwardness').[1] A theme common to all three major manuscripts completed by the end of 1848 is this matter of indifference to the external. The first was *Works of Love*. It was this work, published at the end of September 1847, that had made his meeting with Mynster that November so short and chilly.[2]

Obsessed now with the idea that his whole authorship should demonstrate the unity whose lack he had always criticized in others and had long worried about in his own person, Kierkegaard had begun revising some of his older journals. In one from 1839, which held otherwise nothing 'really felicitous or accomplished', was a brief entry on marriage not being true love. He notes that he might well have used that in *Works of Love*,[3] the work whose completion is announced in an entry in his current journal dated 2 August 1847. The time of that earlier entry had been one of personal agonizing, loss of religious motivation, and doubts about the future complicated by the image of his 'heart's sovereign mistress'.[4] He had said then that marriage was a unity 'in sensate form', not 'in spirit and truth' – hence the Genesis expression about 'becoming one flesh'. The impossibility of becoming one *spirit*, not focused in that entry, is now Kierkegaard's central concern, and its relevance for *Works of Love* is clear enough when one sees that true or Christian love has the form of a loving relationship between 'single individuals'. Prone as ever to pronouncement on the 'tendency of the age', Kierkegaard in a journal entry from this period now saw 'the evolution of the whole world' tending 'in the direction of the absolute significance of the category of the particular . . . precisely the principle of Christianity'. Hitherto this has only been recognized '*in abstracto*', which 'explains why it still strikes people as presumptuously and over-weeningly arrogant to speak of the single individual, instead of realizing that absolute humanity is precisely that everyone is a single individual'. To be one requires 'ethical [and] religious courage'.[5]

According to an accompanying entry, *Works of Love* is written 'to arouse and vex', not to 'assuage and comfort'. Its subtitle is 'Some Christian Deliberations in the Form of Discourses', and the term 'delib-eration' (*Overveielse*), as the same entry (on 'the difference between an edifying discourse and a deliberation') makes clear, is chosen precisely to stress that the work is a provocative one.

The time for deliberation is before action and is a question, therefore, of putting all the factors properly in motion. The deliberation should be a 'gadfly', its palette therefore quite different from that of the edifying discourse, which rests on mood, whereas the deliberation's own mood should be, in a good sense, impatient and spirited. Here irony is needed and a good portion of the comical. One may even laugh a little now and then, if that helps make the thought clearer and more striking. An edifying discourse on love presupposes that people really know what love is and then seeks to win them for it, to move them. But that, indeed, is not the case. So the 'deliberation' must first fetch them up the narrow cellar stairs, call on them and with truth's dialectic turn their convenient ways of thought upside down.[6]

The discourses form two series, each with its Preface, the first em-phasizing that the work's topic is not love but *works* of love. What the book sets out to 'vex' the reader into seeing is just how much our ideas of what love means in practice *are* turned upside down once the notion is conceived in the category of the single individual. That applies equally, indeed especially, to Christian love. Ten years earlier Kierke-gaard had commented on what petit-bourgeois parents believed the Christian injunction to 'love thy neighbour' meant with regard to their children's upbringing ('these well brought-up children, now useful members of the state . . . highly susceptible to every passing influenza of emotion' but trained to say things like 'have the goodness to . . .' and 'with great pleasure').[7] In the second of the two series of discourses in *Works of Love*, itself a work of more than three hundred and fifty pages, and for some the centrepiece of Kierkegaard's production, it becomes clear that works of love undertaken according to the Christian ideal would not only outrage bourgeois sensibilities but by ordinary worldly standards make the Christian look a fool. The Christian must presuppose love's possibility in the other's heart, for love's work is to build love in another,[8] but that work is *of love* only if it is prepared to build love in *any* other, including those in whom to the loving person no trace of love is visible. Not only people known for their wicked deeds can be your 'neighbour' but also those by whom one is 'repelled by a natural and unconquerable aversion', as Kant said when arguing against the possibility of implementing any literal interpretation of the Christian commandment to 'love one's neighbour as oneself'.[9] True Christians will be, like Dostoevsky's Prince Myshkin, stigmatized as idiots for their blindness to wickedness and their irresponsible optimism. As is clear from the last discourse in the first series, Christians must even expect to be persecuted and vilified, for where ordinary, 'purely human' standards bring to acts of self-denial the reward of 'esteem' and 'honour', and make one 'loved as righteous and wise', the 'Christian idea of self-denial is: give up your self-loving desires and cravings, give up your self-seeking schemes and purposes so that you truly work unselfishly for the good – and then, for that very reason, put up with being abominated almost as a criminal, insulted and ridiculed'.[10]

Since Christian love is presented in the Gospels as a duty and therefore subject to command, we are faced with an 'apparent contradiction'. It was one noted by Kant, who in the Preface to his *Metaphysical Elements of Ethics* had written that '[l]ove is a matter of feeling, not of will or volition, and I cannot love because I *will* to do so, still less because I ought'.[11] Kant contrived to preserve some at least of the letter of the scripture by taking the first commandment, to love God with all one's heart and soul and mind, and one's neighbour as oneself,[12] to be our duty to 'like to do [God's] commandments'.[13] God, not being an object of the senses, could not be loved 'pathologically', to use Kant's expression, so the pathological element in the commandment must (and fortunately for Kant, with some stretch of linguistic imagination can) be reassigned to the frame of mind in which one carries out one's duties to God.

Works of Love, though much more, can be seen as a refutation of Kant's assumption that because love belongs to the feelings it cannot be willed, or alternatively as a refutation of the assumption that love must be a form of feeling. Which of these two captures the 'argument' best is hard to say, but Kierkegaard's two discourses on Christian love provide an extraordinarily rich array of distinctions and insights that make the question both far more interesting and also far more complicated than it appeared to Kant. The first and main distinction is between 'self-denial's love', or Christian love, and 'love [*Elskov*] and friendship', which are 'predilection and predilection's passion'.[14] Because self-denial means a transformation in our selves, it makes sense to say that a self-denying love can be 'commanded', we have to cultivate that indifference to externality. The title of the first section of the second discourse, devoted to the commandment to love one's neighbour as oneself, says 'You "shall" love'.[15] The effort required for this love to be fulfilled is conveyed both by the absolute character of the love, its making no exceptions, and by what it really means for your love to be fully addressed to your neighbour. What, for example, if the one you love suffers a transformation, a disfiguration perhaps, plus some significant personality change as in Alzheimer's disease, perhaps acquiring characteristics by which, in Kant's words, you are no longer attracted but 'repelled by a natural and unconquerable aversion'? That, for Kant, would mean that love, as a matter of attraction, would be out of the question.[16] But Christian love requires that none of this makes any difference; for if it did, your love would be shown to be conditional. By the same token it would be preferential, because, given the same susceptibilities, you would prefer another with the preferred characteristics to the one who had once had them but, having now lost them, has lost also the ability to attract you.[17] All such love is really a form of self-love; it is not, as a Christian love must be, an unqualified devotion to the interests of the other quite independent of your own interests and preferences. Fully to address the other, one's love must find a way through and beyond such things.

Whether, once it does so, what survives the journey and reaches that address is still anything we would still want to call love is another matter. But then we have been warned that our concepts may be upset once we are in the sphere of singular individuality. So let us first look more closely at the notion of struggle that a commanded love clearly implies.

Although the struggle is one that bears comparison with the kind implied in Kantian morals between inclination and duty (and where, in terms of Kierkegaard's idea of a Christian levelling, we could say that

the categorical imperative was designed to guarantee motivation by the
idea of membership in the association of all human associations), a more
enlightening comparison is available in the parallel notion of *agon* in
Nietzsche. The struggle there, at least on an optimistic reading, is one
in which Dionysian chaos is channelled into creative order; conflicting
and mutually destructive forces are converted into constructive activity,
and energies which otherwise work divisively, and to the ends of power,
are harnessed into socially creative ends.[18] In Kierkegaard this motif
appeared in the ontogenesis of the ethical agent, first in *Either/Or*,
where the destructive aesthetic forces which 'poetize' the other out of
reality are brought under the stabilizing influence of selfhood,[19] and
then later when motivations that split the self are brought together
under the unifying ideal of the eternal. Just as, in Nietzsche, the power
play of politics is favoured because the social politics of pity serves
merely to conceal lack of the strength and dignity to stand alone, so in
the struggle out of which Kierkegaard's individual emerges there is, as
we saw, a hardening against the pity one is disposed to feel for human
suffering, and the emergence of an ethics in which suffering is accepted
as an inescapable challenge. Pain and suffering then become part of the
struggle out of which alone true individuality and ethical excellence can
be sustained. Kierkegaard, also just like Nietzsche, opposes prudential-
ism, as we may presume he would all social programmes which presuppose fear, insecurity, and self-interest in their beneficiaries.[20] This attitude is also evident in a section of *Works of Love* that Kierkegaard says
elsewhere is an attack on communism (in its pre-Marxist form; the
Marx–Engels *Manifesto* was still a year away). It includes the contention
that if all human suffering were remedied but without mercifulness,
then this, the latter's absence, 'would be a greater misery than all
temporal need'.[21]

Unlike Nietzsche's, however, Kierkegaard's *agon* is, like Kant's, decidedly moral. Its *telos*, or 'excellence', or the 'fulfilment of the law' is
the formation of a genuinely social intention called 'love'.[22] Others must
be treated as autonomous generators of value, and this requires the
would-be moral agent to struggle free of attachments to the other, as
well as unattachments, since these reduce the metaphysically incontrovertible otherness of the other to a feature of the would-be moral agent's
own world. Similarly, morality is not the immersion of individuality in
common projects, but a devotion to being or becoming the kind of being

a human being is, a being capable of individual and autonomous ethical
reflection. This devotion is expressed in situ, in daily dealings with
one's fellows, the neighbour or the one close by. 'Neighbour' means
anyone with whom one stands in relations of responsibility. Nowadays,
of course, 'close by' can mean anything from visibly across the garden
fence to invisibly at the receiving end of a ballistic missile.

Have we lost sight here of anything or perhaps all that is recognizable
as love? We note that what is said to be love is not the struggle towards
fulfilment of the law but the actual fulfilment. Perhaps, however, along
with Kant, one can say that an action motivated by a will to fulfil the
law, however mixed with other considerations, is to an extent a loving
act, a work of love. As for its being appropriately so called, ample basis
does emerge in the text for describing the aim itself as motivated by a
form of love, a respect for individuality and in the end for the world
itself as God's creation. Christian love implies a form of openness. To
love one's neighbour is to love every man according to (i.e., not in spite
of or regardless of) his peculiarity. Thus indifference to the external
does *not* mean turning a blind eye. It is flesh-and-blood persons that
Christian love addresses, not their immortal souls if these are considered something tucked away out of view. Two kinds of peculiarity
(*Eiendommelighed*) or ways of being 'oneself' are distinguished, one
valuable and one not. The latter can be brought (along with something
that looks at first sight like its opposite, a hunger for power) under the
heading of 'pettiness' (*Smaalighed*). Pettiness is not worthy of love
because it is a trait acquired by the person himself; 'the created being's
own impoverished invention'.

The petty-minded person has seized hold of a quite definite guise and form which
he calls his own. It is only this that he seeks, only this he can love. If [he] comes
upon it he loves. In this way pettiness cleaves to pettiness, [and] this petty solidarity
is then prized as the highest form of love, as true friendship, as the truly faithful,
honest form of unity [*Samdrægtighed*] . . . [It] is equally petty in both directions;
just as petty in idolizing . . . one of pettiness's 'own' . . . as in wanting to suppress
everything else. Precisely because pettiness is an acquired nature, and thus false,
[and] precisely because it has not, in its inmost depths and never open-heartedly,
had anything to do with God, but has crippled itself and falsified God, precisely for
that reason it has a bad conscience. For him who has [his own] peculiarity, no
foreign peculiarity is a disconfirmation; rather it is a confirmation, or one more
proof; since what he believes, that each has his peculiarity, proves to be the case, it

cannot disturb him. But for pettiness every peculiarity is disconfirmation; it therefore experiences a clammy, uncomfortable anxiety at the sight of an alien peculiarity, and nothing is more important than to get rid of it.[23]

The real opposite of pettiness is not to think big but to be open to peculiarity, it is an optimistic willingness to accept human diversity as an intrinsic good so long as the peculiarity is God-given and not something you are trying to give to yourself. If such open-mindedness were also a way of conquering initial aversions, then there would be a foothold here for the notion of love from the start. It would be to allow the other to show his or her God-given peculiarity. In recognizing in the other the possibility also of *their* fulfilling the law, one can be said to be on the way to fulfilling it oneself. It is in compliance with a command, the command to get on with the struggle, but at the same time a way of obeying a command to 'love'.

The opposite of neighbour-love would be to love mankind but no one in particular. For Kierkegaard the only way in which mankind can be loved is by each individual loving just anyone. To do that, the individual must disengage from the network of preference and become a 'single' individual. Until we have *this* 'I' we cannot have a 'we', for what 'we' expresses is not some characteristic innate to humankind but an active attitude of love adopted by individuals towards one another. Thus, contrary to Hegel, any ethical import attached to 'we' is by virtue not of any feature of our social forms and institutions but of the individual will, which may or may not be expressed in such forms. The primordial sense of 'we' is embodied not in society but in the will to society that is implicit in any exchange or interaction between individuals, and must be cultivated and then maintained. Therefore not least among those aspects of the network of preferences that the individual must disengage from are those that offer the blandishments, subterfuges, and protective devices of association. One has to become an individual *apart from* other individuals before one can establish a relation *with* those other individuals, who in terms of their 'actualizable' selves are also individuals apart and faced with the same task of realizing those selves so as to be able to will society. The 'we' aspect of *Works of Love* needs accentuating. After critics of the recent *Edifying Discourses in Different Spirits* had complained that the discourses showed little understanding of the social, Kierkegaard responded by saying that they

were 'fools' but then admitted that there was something a fool might
easily be fooled by. For one side of something has to be 'clearly and
distinctly brought out' before the 'relevance of the other side comes
correspondingly to the fore'. The theme of *Works of Love*, his 'next
book', he said would be that other side: 'sociality.'[24]

The two sets of discourses comprising *Works of Love* divide roughly
into one series that brings out the crucial features of Christian love and
another that presents works of love in a light that by ordinary secular
standards is paradoxical. The first series also makes a point of stressing
what implications are *not* intended to follow from what is said, for
instance that Christian love replaces other forms of love, when what is
claimed for it is that in an ethical perspective it is *it* rather than they
that should stand as the paradigm. The second series, on the other
hand, presses home unremittingly the actually intended implications, in
so doing making many morally significant observations of the kind
quoted earlier concerning each person's peculiarity. There is a discourse, too, on the way that love can hide the 'multiplicity of sins', just
as the attempt to understand evil is always an attempt to come to terms
with it.[25] And we have already mentioned the section on mercifulness.
The penultimate discourse includes love of the departed among works
of love, and the final discourse adds for good measure 'extolling love'.

Whatever fate Kierkegaard thought awaited him as its author, *Works
of Love*, a signed work as in the case of all of the *Discourses*, presents
itself vividly as a work (of love perhaps) by a writer at the peak not only
of his literary and intellectual powers but of what might be called a
power of moral psychological insight. Apart from containing a wealth
of apt metaphor, it has a force and energy that can captivate even the
sceptical reader. Among its well-chosen similes are some designed to
convey the way in which an obsession with how we differ in externals
prevents our seeing what we have in common, invisibly to an eye
clouded by concern for social distances, what Heidegger calls *Abständigkeit* (a widespread instance of which would be what Kierkegaard calls
'pettiness'). The differences are garments we wrap too tightly around
us, so that we fail to pick out the inner likeness inside them. We should
try to see our difference as a travelling cloak that can be loosened or
unwound when we come to the inn, or, in the favourite image of the
theatrical stage, as a disguise we take off when the curtain falls. The
beggar and the king are then both actors, equal human beings, just as

at death it will not be our various stations that count for who we are. Similarly when facing God today, alone. In the Christian view of things 'dissimilarity hangs loosely', allowing us a glimpse of that 'inner glory' in whose terms we are all equal.[26] God is an element in Christian love too, a love which not being as 'worldly wisdom takes love to be', that is to say, at cloak level, has God as the 'middle term'.[27] God is the focus of a Christianly loving person who sees in each and every person, friend or foe, whom life in any context at all brings 'nearest' (the literal translation of the word for 'neighbour' [*Næste*]) that inner glory on which depends the possibility of building love in that other.

Works of Love has links with Kierkegaard's own neighbours and with how he saw the neighbourhood. Its version of a Christian ethics fits very well with the polemical role of the 'unrecognizable' assigned at the end of the *Review* to people like himself. It clearly fits Mynster far less. A work of love is not open and aboveboard, nor does it aspire to be mutual in the way worldly wisdom would expect. It belongs in a context of polemics and awakening. In a kingdom of singular individuality, just as in the Kantian kingdom of ends, there would be no more works of 'true' love to perform. But that need be no criticism, since the conditions under which awakening is needed may be permanent. Also, there is in the notion of Christian equality a mutuality of sorts in the prior requirement that the loving person's work be motivated not by distinctions but by a sense of equality due to disregarding, that is to say, neither seeing nor making, distinctions.[28]

So while on the surface *Works of Love* should have appealed to Mynster and his church – it would be hard for them to find fault with what Kierkegaard says about Christian love – Mynster was nevertheless quick to see the work's seditious side. As the most recognizable of all 'teachers' he would feel keenly that the visible church that was the medium of his teaching was being taken to task by an upstart writer, a rentier who chose to shoulder no social responsibilities and seemed intent only on making trouble – a writer who had furthermore taken it upon himself to criticize the church and dared even to present himself as a model of what should replace it. Evidently trying to upstage both the primate and by the same token his church, an amateur with no heavy burdens of responsibility of his own was almost literally stealing Mynster's thunder. Nor would Mynster have forgotten how, in the closing pages of *Postscript*, Johannes Climacus looked in vain, and not very reverently, for that teacher 'of the ambiguous art of thinking about existence and existing' which among all his poetic and linguistic skills he cannot find in the 'Right Reverend Sir'.[29] So when Kierkegaard payed a visit to Mynster that second November, and in the meantime the primate had been received, like Heiberg, into an order according him the highest public mark of distinction, it was perhaps not just because he was too busy to see him that Mynster sent Kierkegaard packing. Of the episode Kierkegaard himself said that although he had never actually courted Mynster's support 'it would have pleased me indescribably to have him agree with me'.[30]

The naïveté of this hope that Mynster might actually agree that he, Kierkegaard, knew better than the primate of the Danish Church both how and what to teach, is truly staggering – that is, unless one looks at the matter from Kierkegaard's own unorthodox point of view. Granting that Kierkegaard sincerely believed what he said about the need for teachers of the living truth to be unrecognizable as teachers, he faced an insuperable problem when it came to giving his own written views any authority. The only authority his words could acquire was their possible acceptance by larger numbers of readers, but gaining acceptance in that way would be a very slow process indeed, and it might never make the difference that would be needed. How convenient in that case if Mynster, an actual authority, in fact the greatest in the land in matters of faith and religion at the time, and a person whose views Kierkegaard had always felt were not really so very far from his own, were himself to become such a reader. By virtue of his position and personality an authority incarnate, Kierkegaard's own father's favourite among the Danish state clergy, and a family friend to boot, Mynster could be the key that turned the tide of opinion in Kierkegaard's favour, so that people would see the point of his vexing and harrying instead of just feeling vexed and harried, as Mynster did, or else simply amused or indifferent.

Lacking Mynster's support, the real nature of Kierkegaard's problem became acutely apparent. What possible weight could his words carry? He was, after all, only a writer. No ordinary writer certainly, he had made that clear often enough, think only of Nicolaus Notabene! But then again, there was no getting away from the fact that he *was* a writer, and a very good one who had also demonstrated his talent when using it directly in the service of religion. But there was the rub, or one of several rubs. With what right does a mere writer presume to attack the authority of the church? And when the attack ends by saying that what is said is said 'without authority', should it not be made clear that all that has been said is one single individual's point of view? In that case, why not leave it at that, and others to their points of view? If that is all the category of the single individual means, well and good.

But clearly there is more to it than that. The category of the single individual is both ethical and religious. More still, according to Kierkegaard Christianity stands and falls with it. He has even spoken up for it on behalf of the human race.[31] While he writes Kierkegaard is not thinking, 'This is just my point of view', or even, 'How else would you expect someone like me to think?' What Kierkegaard found himself actually saying was, 'My life, if not my hand, has been steered by God, or Guidance.' But here we have a third and the largest rub of all. With what right can one claim to speak for God?

The question of authority arose not just because Kierkegaard had now begun to appear openly in the guise of a rebel trespassing on the church's own domain. For him there was the more pressing danger, as usual, of having himself and his work wrongly assessed. The reason is to be found in the story of the unfortunate Adolph Peter Adler, the very Adler whose Hegelian dissertation, just before that summer trip to Jutland more than seven years earlier, had elicited from Kierkegaard the first clear formulations of his later critique of Hegelianism. In 1843 Adler, by then a pastor on the island of Bornholm and highly thought of by Mynster himself, began publishing several controversial tracts in which he claimed to have received divine revelation directly from Christ. In the preface to *Nogle Prædikener* (Some Sermons) he told of how on just completing a book on Hegel, he had as if in a gleam of light realized that 'it was not thought but spirit that everything depended on, and that there was an evil spirit'. The same night 'a hideous sound came down to us in our room' and then 'the Saviour asked me to get up and go in and write down these words'. After which there follow some lines on how evil has arisen through 'man's thought becoming absorbed in itself'. Among the sermons to follow were several 'written with the participatory grace of Jesus' in which 'I have only been the voice [*Organ*]'.[32]

Once the authorities read this Adler was suspended, in January 1844, while his case was investigated. After a hearing, the following year he was forcibly retired (with a pension) for heresy and insanity.[33] Adler already in 1843, on a visit to Copenhagen to propagate his vision, had paid Kierkegaard a visit. Kierkegaard told his brother of this in passing in a letter dated 29 June. He praises Adler's intelligence but thought him at the moment to be 'a trifle ecstatic [*exalteret*]'.[34] On what must have been a later visit, Adler told Kierkegaard that he thought of him as 'a sort of John the Baptist in relation to himself, who, since he had received the direct revelation, was the genuine Messiah'. The report this time comes from Brøchner, who adds that Adler had brought with him a work he had just published and read it, some of it aloud and the rest in a whisper. When Kierkegaard remarked that he could see no new revelation in the work, Adler said he would return later that evening and read it all in a whisper. We don't know whether he did. Kierkegaard was apparently amused, telling Brøchner that having no ambition to be a Messiah he found the role of John the Baptist perfectly respectable.[35]

Not yet ordained, Kierkegaard could not be laicized or unfrocked or even pensioned off, but that would hardly have mattered. The difficulty was that under *The Corsair*'s long shadow the public might put him and Adler, about whom the general belief was that he was unbalanced, in the same boat. Worse, people might begin to think that his vexing and harrying were based on what Kierkegaard would come to claim was some revelatory experience of his own. Deeper still than either of these was perhaps a personal worry: how to convince *himself* that this was not so, how to be sure that his new conviction that his work was under divine guidance was a matter of faith and not revelation. Indeed, in spite of Adler's confused state of mind, Kierkegaard had some sympathy for the unfortunate man and expended considerable effort once again on disentangling his own anti-Hegelianism from the Hegelianism that Adler, in the visions he claimed to have had, had been commanded by Christ to disown.[36]

The Liberal politician
and historian Henrik Ni-
kolai Clausen (1793–
1877), by C. A. Jensen,
1836 (The Royal Li-
brary, Copenhagen)

Journalist and politician
Orla Lehmann (1810–
1870), by Elisabeth Jeri-
chau Baumann, 1848
(Det nationalhistoriske
Museum, Frederiksborg)

Johan Ludvig Heiberg
(1791–1860) (The Royal
Library, Copenhagen)

Johanne Louise Heiberg
(Pätges) (The Royal Li-
brary, Copenhagen)

Kierkegaard's father, Michael
Pedersen Kierkegaard (1756–1838)
(Bymuseum, Copenhagen)

His mother, Ane Lund
Sørensdatter Kierkegaard (1768–
1834) (Det nationalhistoriske Museum, Frederiksborg)

Nytorv in 1839 (Det nationalhistoriske Museum, Frederiksborg)

The theologian, historian, poet, and educationist N. F. S. Grundtvig (1783–1872), by P. C. Skovgaard, 1847 (Det nationalhistoriske Museum, Frederiksborg)

Hans Lassen Martensen (1808–1884) by J. V. Gertner, 1854 (Det nationalhistoriske Museum, Frederiksborg)

Kierkegaard's teacher
and mentor Professor
Poul Martin Møller on
his deathbed

Kierkegaard's friend and
teacher Professor F. C.
Sibbern (The Royal Li-
brary, Copenhagen)

Regine Olsen at the time of her engagement to Kierkegaard, an oil portrait by E. D. Baerentzen (Bymuseum, Copenhagen)

Kierkegaard's lifelong friend Emil Boesen (1812–1881) (The Royal Library, Copenhagen)

Søren Kierkegaard (1813–1855), by Luplau Janssen, 1902. A plausible likeness by an artist who never actually saw Kierkegaard. (Det nationalhistoriske Museum, Frederiksborg)

The primate of Denmark, Jacob P. Mynster (1775–1854), photograph from 1850 (The Royal Library, Copenhagen)

Kierkegaard's elder brother Peter Christian Kierkegaard (1805–1888). Picture from 1871. (The Royal Library, Copenhagen)

Defining the Deed

KIERKEGAARD had acquired copies of Adler's works in the summer of 1846, immediately on their publication.[1] The statement from the bookseller is dated 12 June, almost a month after his return from that short trip to Berlin. Were it not for the fact that Adler had already presented Kierkegaard in 1843 with a dedicatory copy of the *Sermons* with that revealing Preface, that could weaken the surmise that it was Adler he was writing on when Brøchner visited him there. In any case, with *Works of Love* behind him, Kierkegaard now began to draft a large-scale work on Adler. By 1 December 1847, after many drafts and partial expositions, he had written and 'rearranged' two hundred pages. But then, on the pretext of avoiding a 'cockfight' between himself and the defenceless Adler on this 'minor' affair, just for the amusement of 'an inquisitive public',[2] he chose in the end to publish – though not until 1849 – a mere summary with all references to Adler expunged, 'On the Difference Between a Genius and an Apostle' (*Om Forskjellen mellem et Genie og en Apostel*). There he says that apostles are not born, but are called by God to 'proclaim the doctrine and use authority'.[3] Kierkegaard is quite sure he is not that: 'Good God, instead of helping to honour Christianity I would have ruined it.' As a genius he might, however, try to exemplify it. But then again, '[a]s an author I am a rather odd kind of genius – neither more nor less, with no authority at all and therefore constantly under instructions to annihilate himself so as not to become an authority for anyone'.[4] And although, 'I am', he says, 'a genius who might be martyred for the truth, I am not capable of being a martyr for Christianity, for I cannot call myself a Christian to that degree'.[5] By that later time when he published this essay along with a companion piece, 'Has a Human Being the Right to Let Himself Be Put to Death for the Truth?' (*Har et Menneske Lov til at lade sig ihjelslaae for Sandheden?*), Kierkegaard was arming himself for a fight.

Geniuses can still live and even die for what the apostle teaches, but not with the authority that makes martyrdom possible for an apostle. But how can a life be judged good enough for the taking of it to count in any case – whether a martyrdom for the truth, a sacrifice in return for genius, or the unrecognized end of anyone chosen to be a tool of Guidance? If it is to work, any kind of martyrdom demands a constituency that can appreciate the gesture. But what if there were no constituency, or if those who would appreciate it did so for the wrong reasons? Kierkegaard was to be plagued until the end by the thought that his death was what the truth required, that Guidance was writing the plot in which the 'collisions' produced by his pen created both the truth in whose cause a martyrdom was called for and the conditions of the martyrdom itself, but that he lacked the authority a martyrdom requires. Did the sense of being guided mean he had authority after all and might die for the truth? If, on the other hand, he was a genius, then he would have to let that fact run its own course, perhaps also unto death but not the death of a martyr.

These thoughts, his own private ones to begin with, and provoked by the case of Adler, began, as time proceeded, to define an issue that could be given a public setting. The very suggestion of martyrdom for the truth, as well as the fate of the genius, the extraordinary one, would 'raise the key' considerably in terms of the attitudes of the various echelons in current Danish Church life. The bourgeois or populist Pietists (Mynster and Grundtvig) and the elite intellectuals (now mainly Martensen) would all be provoked by this annoying reminder of Christianity's link with martyrdom. It is easy to see that the motivation behind the pseudonymous publication of these essays in 1849 was part of a strategy on Kierkegaard's part to upstage them all with, though the question was to be whether also *in*, a role retrieved from the Christian past.[6]

As *Works of Love* was nearing completion sheer fatigue turned Kierkegaard's mind increasingly to travel. Both Berlin and Stettin are mentioned, also the possibility of a longer stay abroad. However, besides his obsession with Adler, a number of practical affairs had kept him at home. He became involved in negotiations with his publisher over the remainders of his works, and there was the sale, finally, of the family home on Nytorv. There were abortive negotiations over a new edition of *Either/Or* (the publisher could not agree to Kierkegaard's price). All this put an end to further plans of travel in the autumn of 1847, for which Kierkegaard says he was thankful since it would have broken his mood and *Works of Love* might not have been completed.[7] However, during this time Kierkegaard paid two visits to the ailing king, Christian VIII, in July and October. Their conversations are recorded in the journals and snidely commented on by Kierkegaard's amanuensis, Levin.[8] (The king died on 20 January the following year.) In the following months he contrived plans for several new publications, writing chapters which would become parts of *Practice in Christianity*, which, when it eventually appeared three years later, proved to be the last of Kierkegaard's major works. Regine and Fritz Schlegel were married the day before that unavailing visit to Mynster in November 1847. In December Kierkegaard sold his family home but with a clause allowing him to stay on in a part of it until Easter 1848. The journal ends the year with a reference to an idea that was to be the theme of *The Sickness unto Death*.[9]

January 1848 ushered in a year that Kierkegaard later described as a crucial one for him. The following year he was able to say: 'God be praised, I understand myself now; and it's just as well I didn't travel last spring . . .' and 'what I have suffered, however frightfully, the past year, has been an indescribable benefit.' Several years later he recalled: 'I was granted a perspective on my life that almost overwhelmed me. The way I saw it, I felt Guidance had directed me, that I had really been granted the extraordinary.'[10] But at the time the same thought had made him think he must be willing to 'act in character'. That would mean being 'willing to live in poverty, suffer in a way other than he had imagined'. He adds that he had 'never really been robust', and in 1848 'there were a few occasions when the nearness of death was brought home to me'. It was not the events in Europe that brought the thought of death near. There was the February revolution in France with its repercussions throughout Europe, including the Dano-Prussian war over Schleswig-Holstein. It is customary to remark that for Kierkegaard the most immediate impact of the conflict so near home was that it deprived him of the services of his man-servant, Anders, who was drafted for military service. For Kierkegaard the time was one of deep anxiety about the fate of his project. He even thought of looking for someone to speak his cause if he died. One could say, with regard to the wider conflict, that Kierkegaard was practising what his journals of the year preached regarding the single individual, namely that in time of rebellion that category should be used 'to guide the individual towards an indifference to external change and to strengthen the individual in inwardness'.

Not that Kierkegaard was insensitive to the political events of 1848. But to him they merely demonstrated the pernicious tendency to ascribe action and initiative to groups rather than to individuals.[11] Kierkegaard would see them as part of a vain flight from the individualizing tendency of the age, the tendency his category of 'the single individual' was supposed to exploit and to bring to proper fulfilment. As it was to prove, however, the constitutional monarchy and people's church established in the aftermath of the 1848 uprisings, which Kierkegaard saw as merely finite institutions catastrophically usurping the true role of religion, provided him with a political target for ideas which had been taking ever-clearer shape since that time, in 1841, when he had had to face the moral dimensions of his own situation on his first visit to Berlin.

The year 1848 year proved a personal trial in outward respects too, not least financially. There was a matter of the income tax levied for the war. In April he moved into a newly built apartment in Rosenborggade, which he had long had his eye on. In order to offset his living expenses he took in a lodger. As the summer came he was disturbed by the stench from the nearby tanner from whom he rented the apartment and in the end found the apartment quite unsuitable.[12] A host of other practical matters added to the moral decisions plaguing him, threw him into a state of anxiety, and produced alternating moods of optimism and depression as clear visions of what he could do gave way to obstacles in the way of doing it. That April he announces (to himself) that his whole being has changed and that he is now resolved to 'speak' (instead of what, just write? Or is he resolved to write now exclusively in his own name and voice?);[13] just five days later, however, he is saying it is too soon.[14] In general, the entries for this period are full of an uneasy succession of resoluteness and self-doubt. Those on the look-out for neurosis and self-pity will find plenty to pore over here. But the introspection is itself continually introspected from a more dispassionate and self-critical vantage-point, and many journal entries seem clearly to be Kierkegaard's own working through of these moods in order to wrestle

out his future plans against a background of practical and moral difficulties.

The political events did nevertheless provide Kierkegaard with a new
sense of a more general and immediate purpose. The commotion and
changes in Denmark helped to confirm in his mind the direct relevance
to culture and political life of this concept or category of the 'single
individual'. More could be written, and in 1848 Kierkegaard wrote
much, including material that was not to appear for another two years,
in *Practice in Christianity*. But *The Sickness unto Death*, which was
written 'in mid-year', some of it before the Schleswig-Holstein crisis,
was the main work in progress.[15] The work would be published in the
summer of 1849. There was also the manuscript for the posthumously
published *The Point of View for My Work as an Author*. The only actual
publication in 1848 was the *Christian Discourses* in April. But to provide
much-needed capital for financing the further production, Kierkegaard
was also occupied with bringing out a second edition of *Either/Or*. The
manuscript for *The Point of View* must be seen in that context.

To justify the republication of *Either/Or*, he decided now to announce that his intentions as an author had been religious all along. The
second (and unrevised) edition of *Either/Or* was to be published along
with some nonpseudonymous religious work which would indicate the
true author's religious credentials. But, as the entries for this period and
some of the next indicate, there were strategic and other difficulties
with the idea. So Kierkegaard hit on the idea of publishing the second
edition along with an explanation (*The Point of View*) of the relation of
that and the subsequent pseudonymous works to the Christian themes
of his nonpseudonymous production. The manuscript was 'as good as
completed' in November, by which time, although 'quite exhausted', he
felt 'nearly at [his] goal', namely of 'justify[ing] my productivity existentially'. Of this time he says that he has been 'only a writer', but the
effort is taking its toll: 'My spirit is strong enough but regrettably all
too strong for my body. It is, in one way, my spirit that helps me
endure such a sickly state of health, in another it is my spirit that
overwhelms my body.'[16]

The explanation describes the early pseudonymous works as 'decep-
tions' because they adopted a position lower than the one they were
designed to lead the reader 'back' to, though later in the book Kierkegaard admits that 'deception' is rather too strong a word, suggesting as

it does that the works were deliberately planned in that way. It would be nearer the truth to say, as we noted in the Preface, that the productivity had been his 'education' and that it was this education that the productivity 'reflected'. *Postscript* had represented a 'turning-point' by posing the problem of what it is to be a Christian, a problem that his present activity was now tackling directly and without deception. It also talks of his 'compulsion' to write, of his God-given talent, and of the way Guidance has from the start given his work the character not of anything an apostle or conveyer of revealed truth would write, but rather of a living example of what it is to be brought up to be a Christian.[17] This public explanation was withheld, to be published only after his death by his brother (in 1859). When the second edition of *Either/Or* appeared in May (now in one volume), it was accompanied by a signed religious work (*The Lily of the Field and the Bird of the Air*), as originally planned, but not by those others he had thought of issuing under his own name. Instead, he assigned these to a new pseudonym, Anti-Climacus.

Both the withholding of the explanation and the renewed resort at this stage to pseudonymity are explained in detail in the journals. Although Kierkegaard wished to indicate that the intention behind the whole pseudonymous authorship had been religious from the start, resolved as he now was to depict for people the high spiritual standards which religious faith and observance required, he nevertheless felt unable to present himself in his own person as someone able to exemplify those standards and to judge others. He must not appear to presume to have become a Christian of the kind he was now describing. In other words, he could not claim personally to 'act in character' to the extent required by the implications that his writings were now drawing from this category of the single individual. To avoid the risk of a deception of a quite different kind – appearing higher than he was, rather than lower as in the early pseudonyms – this could not be the way in which he spoke personally to his contemporaries. Journal entries from the time bear vivid witness to the inner debate leading to the Anti-Climacus pseudonym.[18]

Instead of publishing *The Point of View*, and also partly to underline the fact or impression that he was not claiming extraordinary status as a Christian, Kierkegaard made steps via Mynster and the minister of culture to appear to be trying to get a position in the church, initially at the Pastoral Seminary. Whether that itself was a deceit or not, the effort was half-hearted and in any case came to nothing. In late June the manuscript of *The Sickness unto Death* was delivered, and this work, which Kierkegaard himself thought the best he had done ('it was granted me to illuminate Christianity on a scale greater than I had ever dared hope; crucial categories are plainly brought to light there'),[19] appeared on 30 July. Its treatise form, which the author admits in his Preface may strike the reader as 'too rigorous to be edifying', while the content on the other hand will seem 'too edifying to have the rigour of scholarship', was facilitated by an application of philosophical categories that enabled him to collect a wide spectrum of ideas into a fairly narrow compass. The terminology was due to his enthusiastic reading of a new work by Adolf Trendelenburg, the one philosopher he says he now regrets not having 'bothered with' when he was in Berlin – because he had heard 'that he was a Kantian'.[20]

The Sickness unto Death, the idea for which first appeared in that journal entry from December 1847, identifies two forms of despair, one of them weakness and the other defiance. Despair is the sickness of the title, and it is specified in the second of the work's two parts as sin. In view of the advantage many commentators take of the fact that sin is introduced as a specification of despair only in the second part to draw the conclusion that the first part can be read as a general, pre-theological account of despair, it is interesting to note that Kierkegaard at one time planned to publish the work as the first part of a volume also containing essays of an unmistakably 'vexing' character, such as 'An Attempt to Introduce Christianity into Christendom'. Also interesting is that the journal note conveying this sees such a volume, once more, as ending his work as a writer: 'And that should conclude it.'[21]

Despair plays a part as early as *Either/Or*, but later it surfaces only occasionally, as in *Postscript*, where Johannes Climacus says 'despair is despair because it does not know the way out'.[22] But this is a telling quotation, as it makes despair sound as though it were (as the word's etymology suggests) a sense of hopelessness in the face of a task that has proved impossible – hopelessness and helplessness. That would be the normal notion, one would think, but more to the point also Hegel's, or at least the first part of Hegel's concept. The point is that the concept of despair in *Sickness* is crucially not Hegel's.

Hegel's idea is roughly this: consciousness is on course for knowledge of the truth about itself, the truth that it itself *is* knowledge. On the way to that destination, however (and to adopt the characteristically Hegelian manner of speech), consciousness makes a succession of progressively better stabs at what real knowledge is, and therefore, by prior assumption, at what it itself is. For instance consciousness identifies itself with 'phenomenal knowledge', knowledge of the world as it appears. But this identification proves inadequate, and the recognition that it is so is experienced as 'loss of its own self'. Hegel actually says that the road can therefore be regarded as the pathway of doubt (*Zweifel*), or more precisely as the way of despair (*Verzweiflung*), despair being distinguished from doubt – mere 'shilly-shallying about this or that presumed truth, followed by a return to that truth again, after the doubt has been appropriately dispelled' – as the 'conscious insight into the untruth of phenomenal knowledge'. But then in Hegel despair resolves itself into a healthy scepticism, in the case in question, about 'all the so-called natural ideas, thoughts, and opinions' that have 'hampered' progress so far; it leaves the way open to examine further 'what truth is'.[23]

It isn't hard to transfer this idea to Kierkegaard, particularly since the stages offer a plausible parallel both to the 'road' along which Hegel has consciousness travel and to the 'series of configurations which he has it go through in its 'education . . . to the standpoint of Science'.[24] In *Either/Or* Assessor Wilhelm tries to persuade his young friend the aesthete that any aesthetic life-view 'is despair'. Of his friend's mature aesthetic life-view Wilhelm remarks that 'it has to an extent admitted to itself a consciousness of the nothingness of such a life-view'. What was entered upon as *the* way to become, or to be, oneself proves unviable. Wilhelm's otherwise rather enigmatic injunction to his friend to *choose* 'despair' as the way to choose himself is like saying to him that he should see the scepticism of his way of life for what it is and thus prepare for the new 'way' that he himself represents. Choosing despair is the choice of 'my self' because the new way is opened by the very fact that the choice encompasses the whole of one's finite being and so must be taken from an 'absolute' point of view outside or above it.[25] In this way despair is a kind of solvent-cum-propellent needed for keeping the journey going.[26]

This notion of despair as a solvent is certainly present in Kierkegaard's earlier pseudonymous works. But in *Sickness* despair is presented as something much closer to a retardant. This comes out in a comparison between *Either/Or* and *Sickness*, the alpha and (apart from *Practice in Christianity*) omega of Kierkegaard's pseudonymous production. The works define 'self' in almost identical terms, but the latter makes an important distinction not found in the former. In *Either/Or* we are told that the self is a 'diversely determined concretion', and that to choose oneself 'concretely' is to be 'aware of this self as this definite individual, with these aptitudes, these tendencies, these instincts, these passions, influenced by these definite surroundings, as this definite product of a definite outside world'.[27] It's almost as if the self one is to choose, from the absolute vantage-point, is the one that is already there in its setting. In *Sickness* we are also told that the self is 'this quite definite thing [*dette ganske Bestemte*], with these aptitudes, predispositions, etc.' or 'aptitudes and talents'.[28] But the passage where this definition occurs clearly distinguishes the self that a person 'takes possession' of in a merely 'outward direction' ('what he calls his self') from the self in a 'deeper sense', which one can possess only by taking an 'inward direction'. We see here the influence of the category of the single individual. It doesn't mean of course that, while we are to look for an inner direction in the selfhood that *Sickness* talks about, the self corresponding to Assessor Wilhelm's ideal is defined merely in terms of civil status and the like. Wilhelm does talk, after all, of an inner history that begins with the choice of oneself. What is true, rather, is that in the meantime the notion of 'inner' has acquired those additional and partly revisionary characteristics charted in the progress leading to Quidam's disappearance into the privacy of faith. It is on the basis of this new distinction between inner and outer that Kierkegaard is now able to draw up a typology that collects and distinguishes between the innumerable facades that individuals adopt to escape the prospect or vision of their bare or naked singularity. Kierkegaard's 'path of despair' is in Anti-Climacus's hands one in which people become progressively aware of a tendency, first unconsciously, then willingly, and in the end defiantly, to wrap the cloak of their outward identities tightly around them. Whether, and if so where, Wilhelm's proposals would fit in is an interesting question.

The book is in two parts, and in the first, at the beginning of his account of the development of the consciousness of despair, Anti-Climacus pegs the development's end with a limiting case, the devil, a 'pure' spirit, in whom or which there is no 'obscurity which might serve as a mitigating excuse'. The devil's defiance is 'absolute'; standing before God, and knowing exactly that this is what he is doing, the devil turns his back on God. But human beings are not pure spirit, their self-knowledge is never pure, they are exposed always to that ambivalence and special pleading with which despair exploits the fatal gap between 'understanding' what is to be done and 'doing' it. So even when they understand that the task of becoming themselves requires that they are 'conscious of themselves before God as spirit', and that only when selfhood is conceived in that way can they free themselves from despair, they still face the prior 'task' of mastering their own susceptibility to self-deception.[29]

Quite generally, one might say that despair in Kierkegaard is unwillingness to live up to an expectation of selfhood. The difference between the early and the late pseudonyms is in the standard set. In the opening pages of Part Two of *Sickness* we read: 'Everything is qualitatively what it is measured by', and, applied to the self, its 'standard . . . is always that directly in the face of which it is a self'. The child, who first has its parents' standard, 'becomes a self through acquiring, as an adult, the State as its standard', but then an 'infinite accent is laid upon the self when it acquires God as its standard'. The notion of self is linked with that of a goal or *telos* which is the 'measure' of what it means to become a self, the self that one, according to whichever standard is being applied, potentially is and would 'in truth' be if the possibility were actualized. This is the sense in which selfhood might be called a project: '[t]he self is the conscious synthesis of infinitude and finitude, which relates to itself, whose task is to become itself, which can only be done in the relationship to God.'[30]

Self-deception has a clear autobiographical reference. It is a remarkable feature of *Sickness* that while bringing Kierkegaard's own personal dilemma into focus, it tries to see it against a background which brings his problem conceptually into continuity with what Kierkegaard saw as the malaise of Danish (and of any other relevantly similar) society. The problem facing Kierkegaard himself was that even when the 'measure' is God, one still does not *know* whether one is in despair or not. Such knowledge is always suspect. The 'calling' that requires one to be 'extraordinary' (and not just odd, like Adler) may, from the perspective of this elevated standard, simply be just one more easy way out, a way of avoiding the truth rather than witnessing to it. One treats 'the thorn

in the flesh' as if it had been specially implanted by eternity to equip
one for some divine purpose. But if God is the standard, perhaps the
thorn in the flesh should be accepted as part of the 'definite thing'
which is oneself? If so, one should 'humble oneself under this weakness'
before God, for whom after all everything is possible. Maybe the only
convincing proof that one has done that, and is not still in despair,
would be martyrdom, for to lose everything, even life itself, would *show*
to the world that the so-called calling was not an easy way out, and
therefore not despair. Perhaps from the point of view of the theological
self losing one's life in the cause of the universal might be a way of
realizing it (something which according to the 'human' standard would
be quite unintelligible). But conceivably, even this thought might be a
despairing one, still an example of 'before God in despair not wanting
to be oneself'.[31]

Seemingly quite far from these personal dilemmas we have the claim
in Part One of *Sickness* that the most common forms of despair 'in the
world' are those in which people are still not conscious of themselves
'as spirit'. A person lacking 'consciousness of an infinite self' cannot yet
see the task of selfhood for what it is. This is the case with his own
society, thinks Kierkegaard, and the most widespread form of despair.
The point is that flight and evasion take many forms, and society itself
is a rich provider of ready-made identities for those too weak to be
spirit, as well as of opportunities for those stronger ones bent on being
their own selves rather than the selves they are when the measure is
God.[32]

The crux in the analysis in *Sickness* then is the idea of a weakness
that might be described as addiction to the world. The analysis unfolds
the strategies with which despair deals with the dawning conscious of
this weakness, and of the fact that to be addicted to the world is indeed
a weakness. In brief outline, it goes as follows: despair as 'weakness' is
anything that counts as failure to adopt the position of one's singularity.
This might be because it has not yet occurred to one that one is singular
in this way, but the analysis focuses on the thought that much of human
behaviour is an attempt to escape this position or to obscure the thought
that it is there to be claimed. At the level of experience, this despair is
experienced as loss of earthly things or of the earthly as such. What
underlies this response, however, on Anti-Climacus's account, is the
opposite: an attempt to 'lose' the 'eternal', which amounts on this

account to wanting to be rid of oneself, the 'formula for all despair'. But in the transitional case the individual recognizes its concern for the earthly (its touchiness about finite losses) as the weakness it is. In the first instance, however, there is an attempt to cancel this unwelcome recognition of weakness by repressing the very notion of what it is an unwillingness to appropriate. After all, the less salient some prospect one is too weak to face, the less topical the idea that one is too weak to face it. Because this form of despair, which goes by the name of 'reserve' (*Indesluttethed*),[33] still expresses resistance to the appropriation of singularity, it still counts as 'weakness'. Defiant despair, which comes in two forms, active and passive in that order, ensues when the idea that one is singular can no longer be held at bay. Active despair exploits the consciousness of being singular – Anti-Climacus, drawing directly on Hegel's *Aesthetics*,[34] calls it the abstract and negative form of the self – 'experimentally'. Despair here takes the form of making one's own mark on the world, putting one's talents to one's own use, totally turning one's back on the idea that dedication to the world can be a weakness. This is correct in a way, the world is indeed where personality belongs, but it is not how a self 'transparently grounded in the power that established it' is dedicated to the world, and the latter is Anti-Climacus's formula for the uprooting of despair. Here the relation to that power is put aside and the negative form of the infinite self treated as though it were an absolute beginning from which selves can be fashioned perpetually de novo.[35]

It is crucial to understanding Kierkegaard here that any such exploitation of the negative form of the self is a form of weakness rather than of (e.g., Nietzschean) strength. It is the weakness of a conveniently presumed inability to free oneself from the pull of the world when we know that what we really aim for cannot find its fulfilment there. The subtlety of the analysis appears when we see that despair is now not the weakness itself but trying not to see the weakness, because that is what it is seen to be. Instead of eliminating it and going on to faith, or hope ('humbling himself before God under his weakness'), which would be the progressive development and what it means to accept or want oneself, the person despairing is one who backs off from the notion that there is anything eternal to measure up to. The passively defiant despairer, instead of putting the weakness out of mind, makes a point of being weak. He parades weakness as a decisive reason for claiming that the project of selfhood in any nonimmanent sense is not worth the candle, at least for him, and in the extreme case as proof that there is no such project.

Apart from its general reference to Kierkegaard's society, *Sickness* conceals some more specific addressees. The first, the Grundtvigians, can be found indirectly in the text itself. We noted that the task being accomplished in 'the relationship to God' is that of 'becoming oneself'. The expression used to describe the self that has the task included 'synthesis'. The self is 'the conscious synthesis of infinitude and finitude', a conscious synthesis that 'relates to itself'.[36] Although Kierkegaard's notion of a synthesis is never explicated in depth, it is at least clear that by 'synthesis' Kierkegaard does not mean anything Hegelian, a successful 'mediation' between thesis and antithesis, or here infinite and finite. If that were so, becoming oneself would be successfully grounding oneself in God, and repeating the success in one's allotted time and place, not being engaged in the struggle to *be* doing that. It seems equally clear that the synthesis is the position from which the task is presented, not completed. Human beings, when conscious of their special nature, or the special nature of their consciousness, are already this synthesis, and that is, or that is what sets, the problem. Negatively, the synthesis can be understood therefore simply as a juxtaposition of opposites, the task being to get them together *as* opposites. What the reader is being expressly told is that the task can only be successfully carried out with God's help. The development towards self-consciousness which Kierkegaard has Anti-Climacus trace is one in which the opposition becomes ever clearer, assuming on the moral and practical plane a status analogous to what Hegel called an 'either/or' of the understanding. The opposition is not metaphysical dualism, mind – body dualism, or the like. The idea of a synthesis in this negative sense has to do with what Kierkegaard refers to in his journals as the human being's 'double nature' and is to be understood in an ethical context. Kierkegaard is here criticizing those including in particular the Grundtvigians who do not admit this double nature. They believe human fulfilment to be the fruition of a natural development. Anti-Climacus's 'theological self'[37] is in direct rebuttal of this (in more than one sense) popular conception. By making the relationship to God the sense of the 'eternal' in oneself and the unthinkable God-man the model to follow, Kierkegaard pushes fulfilment beyond the reach of our natural capacities. Some would agree but deny that this can be the measure; ought implies can, and it is simply cheating to say that everything is possible for God. For Anti-Climacus, however, a veritable Christian, such denial is the ultimate sin. To despair is to give up the hope of this good. But then on these terms, the Grundtvigians too, who included Kierkegaard's brother, would be sinners.

Another addressee can be found in the very title 'The Sickness unto Death' (*Sygdommen til Døden*). One of the *New Poems* Heiberg had published in 1840 was entitled 'A Soul after Death'. In this comedy in verse, the main character, Soul, personifies the petit-bourgeois populace. The poem records his conversation with Mephistopheles in Hell, which is much like the place he has left, though true to type he takes exception to its name.[38] Heiberg's description of his society coincides pretty well with Kierkegaard's, but the point of the allusion is not to be missed: in Heiberg's case the malady is diagnosed post mortem because he sees it as due to a failure in the course of life to rise above philistinism; while for Kierkegaard, since the malady is (continually) self-inflicted, it can be diagnosed ante mortem with a view to its remedy. Crucially, where Heiberg's comedy is a caustic comment on an age that has refused to listen to its cultural elite, Kierkegaard's 'treatise' (though he says this is not really what it is) is an invitation to a salvation open to everyone, though one which the well-adjusted elite (due to what Climacus calls the sin of intellect, a halfheartedness [*Halvhed*] in the man of culture's predominantly intellectual and objective orientation) would find it particularly hard to accept.[39]

'Heiberg' had been Kierkegaard's addressee in another connection. Almost exactly a year before *Sickness* appeared, in July 1849, and while both it and its successor *Practice in Christianity* were in progress, he had written a *feuilleton* article, 'The Crisis (and a Crisis) in the Life of an Actress'.[40] Madame Heiberg, Johanne Luise Heiberg, had to great acclaim performed in the part of Juliet again nineteen years after her breakthrough in the role. In a journal entry he makes it clear that, apart from discharging what he saw as a debt to Madame Heiberg and humouring Giødwad, the editor who had asked him to write it, and not least 'having another dig' at Heiberg himself, Kierkegaard saw it as an opportunity to correct his public image. Now that his writing was taking a decidedly religious turn, he was worried that people thought he was going 'saintly' under the pressure of criticism; but in particular he saw it as 'vitally important' to oppose the 'heresy' that his own religiousness 'was the sort of thing one turns to in old age'. He had been religious all along. 'The nerve in all my activity as a writer', he says, 'is really to be found in the fact that I was essentially religious when I wrote *Either/ Or*.' The claim is repeated in the posthumously published *Point of View*: in writing *Either/Or*, having dropped the idea of marriage he was 'already in the cloister', as the very pseudonym Eremita conveys (he says 'conceals'). It was the understanding of the interests of 'vanity and worldliness' and 'the point of view from which people look patronizingly down upon the religious as something for run-down subjects' that had always been his task.[41]

It is interesting that Kierkegaard adds that only a world inattentive to religion could suppose that a person who proclaims religion must be 'incapable of the aesthetic'. It means that the 'deception' of the early pseudonyms was not that of a religious person masquerading as an aesthete; the aestheticism was genuine, and by writing this article, and also by arranging for a second edition of *Either/Or*, he was showing his readers that it still was. The point is that any religiousness worthy of the name must sustain itself in a constant communication with the aesthetic while resisting the tendency to stay beneath the aesthetic's ceiling. Climacus said the subjective thinker had to be 'aesthetic enough for his life to have aesthetic content, ethical enough to regulate it, and dialectical enough to master it in thought', and that his form is *concretely* dialectical, 'having the categories of poetry, ethics, dialectic, and religion at his disposal'.[42]

The primary reason for republishing the successful *Either/Or*, however, had been to finance the publication of all that he was now writing. Doing so with a suitable accompaniment nevertheless allowed him to stress that the full subjective thinker's repertoire was still at his disposal, though also, as he now wished everyone including himself to believe, that this had been the case from the very beginning.

A significant fact about *The Sickness unto Death*, which appeared one year after the article on Madame Heiberg, is that as so often previously, right up to the time of delivering the manuscript, Kierkegaard was of two minds about publishing under a pseudonym. In the event his name appears, as with the Climacus pseudonym, as that of the legally account-able editor. This shows once again how difficult it is to swallow the assurance of the 'Final Explanation' that no accidental circumstance lies behind the pseudonyms. Even granting that Anti-Climacus is post-Climacian, which might exempt him from the claim, Kierkegaard's constant indecision in these matters even before the 'Explanation' belies the widely held view that the use of pseudonymity in itself is the implementing of some deep strategy, the application of a coherent theory of indirect communication, or the launching of a new form of philosophical literature. In the case of Anti-Climacus and *Sickness*, the decision seems to be in fact due to last-minute scruples about the immodesty and plain unrealism of supposing himself to qualify, from just his own suffering, to speak on such an elevated level on behalf of Christianity. For the benefit of future readers of his journals, Kierke-gaard apologizes 'for attempts to elevate myself in much of what I have noted down previously in this journal, for which God forgive me'. It would be a deception of the wrong kind: 'When the claims of ideality are set at maximum one should above all take care not to be mistaken for them, as though one were oneself the ideality . . . awakening is the last, but it is too high for me personally – I'm too much of a writer.' He had said much the same when deciding not to publish the *The Point of View* with its claims for his religious intentions (a work which it was of course impossible to delegate to a pseudonym). 'I can't', he said, 'it's too high for me.'[43]

Publication of *Sickness* put 'an end to all that terrible torment of promising myself too big a task' by publishing all he had been writing in one go; 'lighting the fuse for established Christianity' would be a 'despairing step', and 'for now there is no question of the force of one single jolt'.[44] That would have to wait.

Was this prudence nevertheless? Apart from the worry that people might think age had made him religious, there was the real danger of being cast as a Dr Ecstaticus along with the likes of Adler. In October, in an extemporized address to the Roskilde Convention, Peter Kierke-gaard had praised Martensen's work at the expense of Søren's as a model of composure, compared to the latter's, which was representative of, yes, 'ecstasy'. The talk was published. Søren was indignant and wounded. Peter had taken St Paul as a reference point from which to contrast Martensen's direction with his own. Søren remarks bitterly in a journal entry that compared to Martensen, St Paul himself, even with his sobriety, would be pure ecstasy, and talks of the 'Martensen-Petrine concept of sober-mindedness' as 'to an extent an irreligious concept of philistinism and complacency'.[45] It rankled so much that he was to remark five years later on the label 'ecstatic', that 'for most people that word means the same as mad and is also classified in medical works as a kind of insanity'.[46] At the time he wrote:

Dear Peter,

I have now read your article in *Kirketidende*. To be honest, it has pained me in more ways than one. But it would go too far afield to enter into that here. Let me thank you, on the other hand, for the article inasmuch as you meant well by it.

Incidentally, if I am to be compared as an author with Martensen, I think in fairness it should have been said that only one side of me was considered, that I am after all an author with a different orientation from Martensen's and on a different scale. However, that isn't so important. But if I am to be compared with Martensen *qua* author, it does seem to me that you should have pointed out the essential difference that I have made unusual sacrifices while he has gained unusual profit. Perhaps it should also be remembered that Martensen really has no primality but lets himself take over, without further ado, all of German scholarship as his own.

Finally, I think for your own sake and mine that you should modify your utterances about me. If what you say is apposite at all, it may apply to one or two of my pseudonyms. As author of edifying discourses (my authentic, signed writings, which are already quite voluminous) it doesn't really quite fit me. I have myself begged in print that this distinction be observed. It is important for me, and in conclusion I could have wished that you of all people should not in any way contribute to authorize a negligence I have to suffer under often enough.[47]

That 'First and Final Explanation' that he had been so careful about had long before proved in vain, and people seeking an audience with the now celebrated author still addressed their correspondence to Victor Eremita.[48] Now his brother was only making things worse. It is uncertain whether the letter, from December 1849, was written before or after Peter's election on 29 December to the upper house of the Danish parliament. In either event that fact cannot have helped to improve Kierkegaard's attitude. Martensen's own recent elevation may also have contributed to the pain of Peter's comparison. Martensen was now professor of theology and in July had published *Christian Dogmatics*. Kierkegaard began reading it in August, making notes. In the broad margins that he always left for additional comments he wrote:

While all existence is falling apart, while anyone with eyes must see that all this stuff about millions of Christians is humbug, that if anything, Christianity has vanished from the face of the earth, Martensen sits and puts together a dogmatic system. Now what does this mean, his undertaking such a thing? It means that as far as faith is concerned, everything is as it should be in this country, we are all Christians, no dangers are afoot, we can safely indulge in scholarship. Since everything else is in order, the most important thing now is to determine where to put the angels in the system, and the like.

As for the scholarship:

Really it's ridiculous! People have been talking now about system, scholarship, scholarliness, etc. – then finally the system arrives. Gentle Father of Jesus!, my own most popular work is more rigorous in its conceptual definitions, and my pseudonym Joh. Climacus is seven times more rigorous in his. In fact Martensen's *Dogmatics* is the kind of popular affair that lacks any great imagination or the likes that could give it that kind of value; and the only scholarliness I have come across is that it is divided into sections. He has no more categories than Mynster. And curiously enough Mynster is about the most cited source, as – a propounder of doctrine [*Dogmatiker*]. And it was Mynster once upon a time 'the System' was meant to overthrow.[49]

A pattern had been set. Mynster, once the inspiration of Kierkegaard's own antisystem theology and fiercely opposed by Martensen, was now an object of Martensen's systematic respect. That could say as much about Mynster as about Martensen, but it was Martensen's further elevation to Mynster's own position as primate that was to provide the occasion for a much more comprehensive falling out, this time with the church itself. Then there really would be a question of the force of one single jolt.

Mischievous Martyr

'COLLISION' was the dramatic category under which Kierkegaard liked to grasp the meaning of his life. Regine gave him his 'erotic' collision. Collision with 'the crowd' had been triggered by *The Corsair*. Course was now set for Mynster. Each collision served a purpose, or so Kierkegaard now believed. Not his own purpose, for if only these clashes could be allowed to play out their possibilities in a space beyond prudence and imprudence, bringing them under Guidance (*Styrelsen*), they would be in the service of God. Should we not then say 'God's purpose'?

Surely not. The very idea of God transcends purpose, and thus prudence and imprudence too. In putting ourselves under Guidance we are already acting in the light of eternal justice, not working on God's behalf towards it. That at least is the spirit of much of Kierkegaard's *Discourses*. However, in looking back on his life as having been favoured by these collisions, Kierkegaard can't help seeing that there was some purpose in it; perhaps the purpose of coming to see and bear witness to the truth that living under Guidance is the form of human fulfilment and serves no further purpose.

'Guidance knows well how to relate every man's collision to his capacities', and because Kierkegaard has been 'granted unusual capacities', his own collisions with their 'potential for expansion' have been particularly fruitful. If it had been Regine who had broken with him instead of vice versa, or if the rift had been cancelled by something outside, for instance death, then it could not have been himself who was 'obliged to demolish an authentic love'. But neither was this obligation forced on him from outside. There was his 'melancholy' and the fact that he had 'repented' his 'earlier life'. He himself had been the obstacle to their marrying, not some external factor that would excuse him. But the collisions had begun even earlier. That matter of trousers. Although even now people still stared to see if they really were so short, his fellow pupils had laughed at his trousers. Quite aptly Kierkegaard points out that it was quite normal for older men (he was now thirty-seven) to prefer trouser-legs shorter than those favoured by fashionable youth. That was why his fellow pupils laughed at him in school; he had been dressed by his father, who he 'never knew otherwise' than as 'an old man', to look like one too. Already old at the age of eight Søren had his first meeting with the crowd. Of the second meeting he says that what they were really attacking was his dead father. Now, towards the end of the course, this final collision, the 'essentially Christian' one, was already on the way. And although it was his own collision, even here his father was implicated.[1]

The rift with Regine was one he now wanted to repair. Not 'wanted', exactly, because at least in his own mind the reasons were religious; prudence would have said, *don't* do it. He thought 'she would go out of her mind if she found out how things really were', in the belief that her marriage with Schlegel worked only because she could dismiss Kierkegaard as a scoundrel, or as excessively ambitious. Had Kierkegaard only known, even during their engagement Fritz and Regine had read his works aloud to each other. They continued reading him (Kierkegaard did send her all his religious discourses) when married, and Schlegel immediately on publication bought a copy of the first *Nachlass*.[2] In August of the previous year, during that time of acute indecision (publishing the attack on 'Christendom' would end that 'distant possibility' of a pastorate) and poor health (he might die before he had finished his task),[3] Kierkegaard had driven to Fredensborg, where the Olsen family had a summer residence, with a hopeful premonition of meeting the family there. Sure enough, he ran into Counsellor Olsen on the street. However, though with 'tears in his eyes' and in a voice 'of stifled passion', Regine's father said he did not wish to speak to him. When Kierkegaard persisted, the older man turned and ran off, with such agility indeed that 'even if I'd wanted, it would have been impossible for me to catch up'. Kierkegaard shouted after him, saying that now the blame for not listening to him would be his.[4]

But then, the following summer, belying the counsellor's apparently good form, and just two days before Kierkegaard was to give the printer the go-ahead for printing *The Sickness unto Death*, Regine's father died.

That this might be another excuse to delay publication was a thought Kierkegaard quickly put aside as a prevarication that would put him in as bad a light with the printer as with himself.[5] The occasion did, however, present itself as an opportunity to attempt once more a reconciliation with Regine. Hoping he was right in thinking that Regine's father had been the main obstacle, he composed a letter to her (after many drafts). It was dated 19 November 1849, and he sent it under cover of a note to Schlegel in which he said his reason for approaching Regine was a religious obligation.[6] Schlegel returned the letter to Regine unopened. Kierkegaard writes: 'Now the matter is decided. For one thing is certain – without Schlegel's consent not one word. And he has explained as definitively as possible. Now it's up to him.' Regine is recorded as having said in an interview she later gave that Schlegel had written 'a very polite but firm refusal', but the fact that it was Schlegel who took the initiative was partly due to the husband's being at that time 'still the woman's boss'. The real motive had been less a matter of manners or custom than an earnest desire to 'avoid having this intellectual trouble-maker in his home'.[7]

This one collision remained unresolved then, at least in Kierkegaard's eyes. But it was the collision that had made him a writer, and that in turn had led to another collision, with the crowd. It, again, had propelled the writer into privacy and reduced him, in a sense, to a product of the writing, his own writing certainly, but writing that bore the mark increasingly of the category of the single individual he claimed it had uncovered. The third collision would be a trial of strength in which the self-renunciation that Kierkegaard saw as essential to that category would have to prevail. That collision had just begun.

Though in a way it had not, at least not visibly. People still mostly thought of Kierkegaard and Mynster as allies against the System, at least when that was still the thing. Now that it was a thing of the past they were considered allies against avant-garde aestheticism. But Mynster represented Christendom, and in his journals Kierkegaard refers to *The Sickness unto Death* as an 'attack upon Christendom', even calling the latter 'an altogether un-Christian concept'.[8] Just before sending the manuscript to the printer Kierkegaard had visited Mynster again, but once more Mynster had pleaded lack of time, though this time saying so frankly and putting on a show of friendship, saying repeatedly 'dear friend' and even 'come another time'. Kierkegaard has two entries recording the event, the first a jittery one from the time which tells us that Kierkegaard may have seemed to Mynster to be in far too nervous a state to talk, so that Mynster might genuinely have wished that he would come back later, and the other from three years later recalling how 'impatient' he had felt with Mynster and 'the friendly way in which he had really been working against me', so that when he sent the manuscript to the printer just afterwards he had said to himself: 'Let him have it!'[9]

Sickness therefore has still one more addressee, indeed probably its main one. The work is an attack on Christendom laid at, if not nailed to, the door of the Danish primate. But Kierkegaard's grudge against Mynster may go further back, as far back as his father's death. In one of his last journal entries and shortly before his own death, Kierkegaard wrote: 'Then father died. It was I who brought the news to Mynster. What he said at the time is in curious contrast with the fact that he later [changed to: six years later], even in print, to please me, could recall father so well.' It appears that Mynster, always regarded at least in Søren's time as the family's pastor, could form no clear impression of Michael Pedersen Kierkegaard when his son came to inform him of his death.[10] And yet, six years later, in that New Year's Day article in 1845, which had triggered off *Fragments*, Mynster had referred to Michael Pedersen Kierkegaard as that man of simple faith. On that earlier occasion Mynster of course may just have been distracted, later to recall the not-very-forgettable older Kierkegaard. But clearly the son didn't think so. He assumed that it was from his own dedications to the *Discourses* that Mynster had picked up for his own purposes the idea of a man of simple faith. In 1855 that had been all of eleven years earlier, and seventeen had passed since his father died. A long time for a grudge to fester.[11] Or was the entry, with the heading 'Some Historical Data Concerning My Relation to Bishop Mynster', no more than a useful reminder of the salient episodes in that relation for the benefit of a confidant-to-come? He had said that he would have to make posterity his confidant now that, as one might imagine him putting it, the public was no longer qualified to act as his Greek chorus (one good reason for committing his thoughts to the journals).[12] In the light of what preceded that entry the presence of a distinctly personal edge is hard to miss there, and the watchful reader may detect in these later texts only thinly disguised expressions of Kierkegaard's bitterness towards Mynster, a resentment for which there may be more than one reason.[13] But the list simply ends: 'How I came to hear of his [Mynster's] death.'

A fearful symmetry? The public attacks on Mynster that 'lay ready' and were later delivered certainly look like the wreaking of an awful revenge. But then, was it not Guidance that placed Mynster in his path, just as his father, Regine, and Goldschmidt had all been placed there too? To say nothing of the deaths of all those dear departed?

Just under a month after *Practice in Christianity* appeared on 27 September 1850, Kierkegaard again talked to Mynster, who had by then read the book, a copy of which Kierkegaard had earlier delivered in person . Although it nowhere mentions him, Mynster told Kierkegaard that clearly he himself was the target. The expression he used (*at vilde ham tillivs*) was a colloquialism that can mean 'have it in for' or 'get the better of' but even has overtones of a fight to the death. According to Kierkegaard, on giving Mynster the copy he had mentioned expressly that he really wanted it published *after* one or the other of them was dead. So if it was Mynster who died, the *book* could hardly be wishing him dead. He didn't add, as he might have done, that it is the author's privilege as well as his occupational hazard to kill and be killed posthumously, though in that kind of death resurrection is not uncommon. Kierkegaard had also explained to Mynster that there were things he wished to change in proof. That would have meant writing it all over again, while *Practice in Christianity* had in fact been written two years earlier and had waited long enough. This, the second of the Anti-Climacus books, was to be positively the end. If not a pastorate, a position at the Pastoral Seminary would be a useful solution, something Kierkegaard had also suggested in a meeting with Mynster in March of the previous year.[14] This thought and the visit to Mynster now were not unconnected. Working 'extensively' for a living, as Kierkegaard puts it, instead of intensively and at an expense he could no longer afford, would allow him some further activity whether or not in the form of writing. That Mynster didn't offer to help him left Kierkegaard thinking on this occasion that it was really the other way around: Mynster had it in for him.[15]

So *Practice in Christianity* had been written in 1848. Whatever the truth of Mynster's claim that a third of the book was also an attack on Martensen, it was unlikely to be the Martensen of *Dogmatics*, which came out fairly late the following year. Kierkegaard had said on finishing

Practice that the work was 'of great personal importance' and its 'potent remedy' one that perhaps he personally was 'one of the few' in need of. If that were so, what a false impression it would give if he published it before trying to benefit from the remedy himself! He should first become a Christian in earnest. In that regard, then, there was 'no hurry' for its publication. But what if he died before becoming a Christian in earnest? That thought seems to have given way to the more modest one we mentioned earlier; he saw his limitations – his 'weakness', as *Sickness*, written at the same time, would have it. It is indeed rather hard to imagine Kierkegaard accepting the 'humiliation of having to receive unconditional help', 'humbling himself under his weakness before God', as that work's text has it. Either way, we have one more addressee for that multipolemical text: Kierkegaard himself. The solution had come when he hit upon the Anti-Climacus pseudonym. But why was *Practice* kept back longer?[16] Was it *just* because its publication would spoil Kierkegaard's chances of getting a job?

'Sin' came into *Sickness* in Part Two. That part told us that the task of selfhood as Part One has described it is only from the human point of view, with 'man' the measure. Part Two presents another measure: God, and towards the end of *Sickness* this measure becomes more concretely Christ, through whom God has revealed 'what stupendous reality a self has'.[17] The potent remedy provided in *Practice in Christianity* is a strict interpretation of what imitation of Christ practically implies. The word translated 'practice' (*Indøvelse*) is used of practising artists, musicians, or actors, for the way they work up their roles or performances. Here it means more than just rehearsal, or the process of 'taking on' a part, or in the case of the musician, practising (scales or whatever) in the way that makes perfect. The emphasis is on *Ind* ('in'). We might think rather of the kind of internalizing that 'Method' acting requires, letting the original take over, or coming as close as one can to replicating the original by taking on the original's inner form: 'Christ's life here on earth is the paradigm; I and every Christian are to strive to model our lives in likeness to it', and 'to be an imitator means that your life has as much similarity to his as is possible for a human being to have'.[18] That last clause is vital. However much you succeed, you are still human and not divine. The logic of imitation always holds, one cannot both imitate and be what is imitated. That is what human being as a 'synthesis' of infinite and finite signified, a notion addressed to the

Grundtvigians and other 'perfectibilists' who believed the two categories could merge.[19] It means that no human practice makes perfect, that salvation cannot be reached by any extension of natural religion, or for that matter in any 'extensive' way at all. What truth means in practice, as was already said in *Anxiety*, must be the topic of a 'second' ethics, an ethics that leaves room for repetition and transcendence, and thus goes beyond Aristotelian naturalism to recognize the reality of sin.[20]

Just as *Sickness* goes back to themes in *Anxiety*, *Practice* returns to those of *Anxiety*'s companion piece, *Fragments*, to contemporaneity and offence, though as also with *Sickness*, with the potency of the required remedy now significantly increased. As Kierkegaard says in his brief ('editor's') preface: 'the requirement for being a Christian is forced up by the pseudonymous author to a supreme ideality.'[21] Take the first. In regard to what Christianity essentially is, the history that falls between our time and Christ is of no consequence But it does pay a vital publicity role, for without it we would have no grip on the promise of a Christian salvation; without his apostles and the church and the rise of Christendom, the lowliness and abasement of the life of the God-man would be lost to view, and its point would not be available. And, of course, if Christ himself had taken care of the publicity by appearing in his glory, we would never think of trying to imitate him, we could only admire him. Anti-Climacus doesn't put it this way, but the history, which includes the church, functions rather like the figurative narrative that religion is in the Hegelian philosophy – indeed, they are much the same thing. Once again Hegel, so far, has got it right. And as in Hegel it has to be forgotten. But not in the Hegel–Heiberg way, that is to say by translating the narrative into a superior intellectual insight. That is the very self-absorption of human thought that Adler's vision told him was the root of evil. Instead we must get back to the beginning, with lowliness and abasement. Which brings us to a possibility one must face before one can choose faith, namely 'the possibility of offence'. Do Copenhagen's good citizens and its cultural elite satisfy this condition? Suppose they were transported back to the time of Christ. The prudent and sensible would ask how someone who makes himself out to be so extraordinary should be so 'foolish, so weak-minded, so altogether lacking in knowledge of human nature, or so good-naturedly vain, or whatever one wants to call it, as to go about as though almost forcing his charity upon us'. The clergy would dismiss him as 'an impostor and rabble-rouser', as no true Messiah would be a revolutionary; he would talk of evolution, appeal to the established, and of course 'call all the clergy to a convention'. The philosopher would complain that Jesus had no system, only 'a few aphorisms, some maxims, and a couple of parables, which he keeps on repeating or revising thus blinding the masses'. These, and along with them the wise statesman, the solid citizen, the people's iconoclast, would all in their own ways have found themselves in confrontation with Christ at the 'parting of the ways' (*Skilleveien*) where the choice between faith and offence must be made.[22] But are they, through the looking glass of history and the images of Christianity it produces, offended today?

What then, in the physical and temporal absence of Christ, have we to focus on if we choose faith? It can't be the thought of the God-man, because properly grasped that is 'the absolute paradox',[23] offensive to thought. But improperly grasped it will fail to offend. The object of faith is, says Anti-Climacus, the God-man himself, 'just because the God-man is the possibility of offence'.[24] The God-man must be able to draw our attention qua paradox, because faith is not the ability to *overcome* the paradox in thought, or even to overcome thought, for then it would not be faith. The contradiction must stare you in the face and you must accept it. What we must focus on, then, is symbolism or imagery. The image of the crucified Christ is an example, as is the Cross itself.[25] These are pictures, even pictures of pictures, since even to see the actual cross with Christ on it would only give you an image or symbol of the truth; but approached in the right frame of mind such foci give you the God-man and the nature of the inner form that it is the believers' belief to imitate to the best of their ability. What is certain is that the appropriate imagery is not that of the robes and rituals of the church, the theatricals that in the course of history have led people to lose sight of the offence and the ability to have faith.

Practice in Christianity, in short, answers Lessing's question, that question that gave rise to *Fragments*: how is an eternal happiness to be based on something merely historical? More to the point it answers the thought-experiment's opening question, how far can the truth be learned? It gives the B-position answer but no longer in hypothetical form. Its point of view is well ahead of Socrates, and its answer is a wound-up version of the notion of imitation current in Lutheran theology[26] but with origins in the influential (though insecurely attributed)

De imitatione Christi (1702) of Thomas à Kempis (1380–1471). Kierke-gaard had possessed a copy of this work for some time, and the full Danish translation appeared the very year *Practice* was written. Thomas à Kempis's *Of the Imitation of Christ and of Contempt for All Worldly Vanities* was intended, as its full title indicates, as a guide for followers of the monastic life, but its focus on the figure of Jesus provided a general insight into the ways in which religious and natural practices are to be distinguished. Not least of its appeals to Kierkegaard must have been the lightness of Thomas's theology, for like Kierkegaard he too seems to have been reacting to the academic theology of the day. Together with *Works of Love*, written in the previous year, *Practice in Christianity* provides that second ethics that Vigilius Haufniensis had referred to in *Anxiety*, an ethics with sin which therefore preserves the logic of imitation: however successful an imitation, it is never 'as good as' the original.

That Kierkegaard 'had it in' for the church is clear enough, but Mynster? Well, Mynster *was* the church, and the fact that Kierkegaard personally handed him a copy of *Practice* must have struck Mynster as pointed to say the least. At least in Kierkegaard's mind, the collision was on course. No one except the protagonists themselves seems to have had any inkling of a rift, and the visits to Mynster, though less frequent, did not stop. Why did Kierkegaard persist in their apparent alliance? Just to keep up the appearance? One of the subjects of a conversation that took place on 2 May 1851 was a recent reference by Mynster to Kierkegaard and Goldschmidt as birds of a feather, or rather 'talents' of a kind. Kierkegaard thought Mynster's defence was lame. He said that Goldschmidt had 'talent' but that Kierkegaard was 'gifted'.[27] It is clear from journal entries made subsequent to the meeting that Kierkegaard was incensed by the comparison because he saw it as an attempt not to restore Goldschmidt's reputation but to spoil his own. Otherwise the conversation had been long and on Mynster's side affable ('Dear friend', talk of his daughter's forthcoming marriage, etc.). As for Kierkegaard, as his record of the conversation has it, the friendliness with which he himself nevertheless reciprocated was inspired by the respect in which Mynster had always been held by his father.[28]

This was a period during which, as we noted earlier, Kierkegaard now kept more to himself. In May 1849, again through the good offices of Jens Giødwad, he had sent to the printer those two essays, one of which was a distillation from the unpublished book on Adler. That was on the fifth, his birthday, and a journal entry from that day ends: 'Things look dark but I am nevertheless so calm. For me this, my birthday, will be unforgettable!'[29] It seems Kierkegaard thought some crucial turn of events had occurred. The second edition of *Either/Or* had appeared just over a week later, followed five days later by the 'Two Minor Ethico-Religious Essays', as they were called. There had been those fruitless visits to Mynster, and also to the minister of culture. Counsellor Olsen had died. From when *The Sickness unto Death* was published in July it was over a year until *Practice in Christianity* came out, in August 1850. Then there had been that October meeting with Mynster after the latter had read the work. That was to be about all for some time to come. There began that period from January 1850 to May 1852 sometimes referred to as 'the silent years'. But not unoccupied years, for Kierkegaard was busily engaged in his journals.

In April 1850 he had moved from the apartment in Rosenborggade, where in spite of its inconveniences he had still managed to produce some remarkable writing, and moved to 43 (now 35) Nørregade, the street he had lived on following his father's death but at another number. Apart from some correspondence and accidental encounters on the street, he does not appear to have kept up many personal connections. Even contact with Emil Boesen had become desultory, no doubt partly because Boesen was by now a priest and engaged. In a letter from 12 April 1850, Kierkegaard suggests another reason: Boesen's failure to settle down had made the relationship less rewarding, at least for Boesen. But the light tone of the letter shows that they were still on good terms:

Dear friend,

First a reminder: if you want to write to me please write so I can read it. This wasn't writing at all, but small pinpricks on monstrously thin paper. I could have used a microscope to read it.

Iam ad alia.[30] So finally I got a letter from you. And what do I read in it? I read that 'when you used to visit me, I was usually the one who did most of the talking, so I ought to do most of the writing as well'. Excellent! There's gratitude for you! But enough of that.

You have three wishes. The first two concern your father and your fiancée, both of whom I am supposed to visit. Answer: can't be done. That you could have forgotten me so completely in such a short time! I happened to run into your fiancée on the street and told her that you had asked me to visit her, and also what I had decided to reply to you on the subject, using the opportunity there and then to say it to her. As for your father, you know how fond I am of him, not to mention how dear the memories are that the sight of him brings to mind, but I have been away from it all for so long that it would take some accident to get it started again.

Finally, you want to learn the art of constructing themata.[31] Now there you see, you have given me one. Besides, in my view there's nothing more foolish than to sit down and try to come up with a theme. For that you must arrange your life sensibly. See to it that every day you have at least half an hour to incidental reading in the New Testament, or a devotional work. When you go for a walk you must let your thoughts flutter randomly, sniffing here and there, letting them have a go now here, now there. That is how to arrange one's housekeeping. Themata are the accidents that the week should deliver to you in abundance. But the more you see to it that the dividends are uncertain, the freer, better, richer they will become, and the more striking, surprising, penetrating.

I am happy, further, to note that you are pleased with your new position. I had expected as much. In a sense, you have a lot coming to you, but also a lot to catch up with, for, as I've always said, you took far too long before taking orders. But of course that will soon pass. Your relationship with me eventually stopped being truly beneficial for you, precisely because you were not quite sure what you wanted. As soon as you have consolidated yourself a little as a clergyman, ditto as a married man, you will see that, from this firmer basis, you will view me with a new equanimity and gain more pleasure and satisfaction as a result.

As for me, everything is as usual. As you know, I am reluctant to discuss this further in a letter.

Live well, be hale and healthy, happy and confident! Before you lies, I hope, a smiling summer, which I suppose you are looking forward to and which will also bring you both encouragement and smiles. So be happy, and let me have the happiness of being happy with someone who is happy, and let that happy someone be you.

Your S. K.[32]

What Kierkegaard wished for Boesen he could no doubt have wished for himself, though not realistically. During this time he became ever more preoccupied with grasping what in one journal entry from 1853 he was to refer to as his 'task' and in another from 1853 as his 'life's operation'.[33] The specific mode, under the general ethical category of the single individual, in which he sees his own life is that of 'heterogeneity', the apartness that prevented him from 'realizing the universal' in the way he was happy to see Boesen realizing it, a fact which he now increasingly traces back to his childhood. The historical significance of his heterogeneity is with regard to 'Christendom', to combat what history has made Christianity into, a naturalization and therefore a gross distortion of the true Christian message which he now sees it is his task to champion. There is the problem of how to champion Christianity when what Christianity requires is not teachers or writers but witnesses. But the thought of his own death as a move in his life's operation becomes ever more insistent, and the topic of martyrdom, originating in his treatment by the 'rabble' during the *Corsair* affair, constantly recurs. By now his creative work was done. What else could he do but force the rift that he had been designed to create and exploit?

There were still publications. In September 1851 a work appeared entitled *For Self-Examination, Recommended to the Present Age* (*Til Selvprøvelse, Samtiden Anbefalt*), in which Kierkegaard portrayed a society in which a king's command, instead of being conveyed to his functionaries and subjects, becomes the topic of endless interpretation to which all the members of the executive branch themselves contribute. An earthly king dependent on his functionaries and subjects, says Kierkegaard, would reward the more intelligent interpreters with higher office, but then let us

[i]magine that this king was omnipotent and never feels the pinch even when all functionaries and subjects deceive him. What do you suppose this omnipotent king would think about such a thing? Surely he would say: The fact that they do not comply with the edict is something I still might forgive; furthermore, if they got together and made a petition to me to be patient with them, or perhaps to exempt them from this edict altogether . . . that I could forgive. But what I cannot forgive is that people even displace the standpoint for what counts as seriousness.[34]

Seriousness is taking whatever you can directly grasp as a divine commandment as the assignment of a task to get down to straightaway rather than to put off until all are agreed on the right interpretation. Earlier in this short work Kierkegaard defines his own nonconformism in relation to Mynster and Grundtvig. On the one hand there was that 'Right Reverend old-timer' whose sermons Kierkegaard still assiduously attended, but to which, though agreeing with what they said, he would add that 'stronger accent' born of what he firmly believed was his own personal 'distinctness'. On the other hand there were the Grundtvigians, who claimed actually to be Christians of the 'strictest' kind. Mynster aimed too low, while the Grundtvigians failed all too conspicuously to attain the high level they claimed for themselves. As for himself, the more important reason for not joining them was that he felt 'too little Christian' to be part of anything so ambitious.[35] Irony, false modesty, or privately sincere? In another work, *Judge for Yourself*, written shortly afterwards but not published, several of the themes later to appear in the attack on the church make their first appearance. These include what it is truly to be a witness to the truth, and the idea that Christianity is something to be proclaimed, not to live off. Already in *Practice in Christianity* and much to Mynster's annoyance, Kierkegaard had introduced the idea of the need to 'introduce Christianity into Christendom'.

By then Kierkegaard had moved again, this time outside the old city walls to 108A Østerbro, where Willemoesgade meets Østerbrogade. The building, since demolished, was a villa at the end of Sortedamssøen (Sortedam Lake). Maybe Kierkegaard was making himself less accessible to visitors, but he still took regular morning walks into the city. Emil Boesen, one of his few visitors, reported to his wife that Kierkegaard was living well;[36] there seems to have been little outward sign of the poverty and unimagined suffering he had spoken of three years earlier as what would be required of him if he were to 'act in character'. A curious incident nevertheless hints at an inner tension. A pastor, journalist, and author, A. F. Schiødte, who was almost Kierkegaard's contemporary, recorded that after he had moved to Østerbro,

[Kierkegaard] associated with a carpenter who had been a childhood acquaintance, whose family were most likely keeping house for him and his servant. A daughter of the family was confirmed, and K. presented her with a beautiful outfit, shawl, other accessories, etc., and probably some gold ornaments as well. In the afternoon he sees her walking in the garden, flaunting all that finery and putting herself on display with obvious delight. He was horrified by all this, perhaps also fearing what people would say, and instantly decided that the carpenter family should move away and rent rooms elsewhere at his expense. This decision was put into effect immediately, but it made K. the object of much anger on the part of the family – especially the somewhat crazy carpenter who naturally couldn't understand it.[37]

That Kierkegaard was by now obsessively repelled by finery is unlikely, since he had himself chosen the gift. More likely he feared his criticism of the church might suffer if he seemed to be condoning it in connection with a confirmation. That would show he was still on course. And in a journal entry from 1852, under the heading 'The Possible Collision with Mynster', Kierkegaard reaffirms that he himself represents 'a more authentic conception of Christianity than Mynster'. He also says, however, that to make the collision still possible 'I must take a still higher view of Christianity'.[38] Just how high it had already become since the time of Victor Eremita can be judged by the following assessment of his own either/or:

What a range of ways I have gone through of specifying what my Or means!

I marked out marriage as Or but marriage was not my own life's Or; I am further still from that Either.

For that Either means gratification in the most licentious sense. Then there are all the in-between positions: gratification but with a touch of ethics added. But that's not where my Or is. Then comes gratification with a touch of the ethico-religious added; but this is still not my Or.

So there's just one Or left: Suffering, renunciation, the religious, becoming less than nothing in this world.

If I am a dialectician by origin, a dialectician by nature, then I can rest only in the last Or, not in any intermediate Or; for only when one comes to rest in the last Or is the Either-Or exhausted.[39]

As if the Or of suffering and renunciation did not already put the feted primate in a bad enough light, Kierkegaard was able to find more human faults. He sensed weakness of character in Mynster's failure to make his criticism of Kierkegaard public. Kierkegaard seems determined to find fault in Mynster, and many journal entries give the impression that he is trying hard to convince himself that this considerable personality indeed has feet of clay. Though Mynster's church was the official target, since the church and the man had become inextricably linked even unto identity in Kierkegaard's mind, while outwardly it was the church he attacked, in the privacy of his journals Mynster was being depicted as a more and more discreditable character. The journals also became a repository for remarks of a kind he still felt it inappropriate to make in public. Closer to the time of the final collision, there is the remark that in Denmark calling oneself a Christian had become so much part and parcel of getting on in the world that probably you couldn't get a license to run a brothel without a birth certificate, but that then again, that was all you needed to prove you were a Christian.[40] It was in this spirit that the journals had now become a forge for the honing of his weapons for the conflict to come. Kierkegaard's late encounter with Schopenhauer's *The World as Will and Idea* (1818), *On the Will in Nature* (1836), and *The Basis of Morality* (1841) was an encouragement: 'despite total dis-agreement' he found in the German philosopher a kindred spirit, not only 'charming' and 'superbly unparalleled in well-aimed abuse' but

also full of sympathetic insight into the misery of life. His disagreement
with Schopenhauer was over the proposal for ascetic withdrawal. What
would be equally sympathetic and less elitist was a return to the world
in order to 'help people out to where he is'. But then Schopenhauer,
after all, was 'not a Greek philosopher living his philosophy', only 'a
German thinker, bent on recognition' and with an 'unethical view of
the ethical' that makes ethics a matter of 'genius'. On the other hand,
the 'incomparable coarseness' of Schopenhauer's remarks on the professors 'who live off philosophy under the guise of teaching it' was something Kierkegaard could appreciate. It was the very kind of invective he
needed in his own campaign against the 'priests of religion', where
'Christendom is everywhere in such a state of degradation and demor-
alization that by comparison paganism is divine elevation'.[41] That remark is from 1854.

By then Kierkegaard had moved yet again. Now he lived very cen-
trally, at Klæderboderne 5–6 (now 38 Skindergade and 5 Dyrkøb), with
a view of Vor Frues Kirke. This was to be his final residence.

The 'silent years' before the storm was the time during which Kierkegaard committed to his journals many reflections about himself, his
'task' and project, and his past, and about his relationship to Regine,
many of them quoted earlier. When the storm arrived outside factors
also helped to set the stage for the conflict. In the late summer of 1854
a cholera epidemic hit Copenhagen. It revealed scandalous deficiencies
in the city's hygiene and welfare apparatus, and thousands among the
lower classes died. The summer was when the better-off spent their
summer vacations out of town. The fact that with few exceptions the
clergy had found it convenient to be on vacation at the time aroused
deep indignation and scorn among the poorer people as well as among
those concerned with their welfare. When Kierkegaard's attack was
launched on the church, the mood in many quarters was receptive.

Mynster died on 30 January 1854. There was a memorial service in
the Royal Chapel. Martensen, now court chaplain, gave the address, to
be published almost immediately afterwards. In it he referred to the late
bishop as a 'witness to the truth'. The time had come for the final
collision to bear fruit. That phrase was all that was needed, coming
from Martensen, in that setting, and on an occasion like this, one in
which religion, even more evidently than usual, takes on the form of
theatre. One might say either of two things: it was too much for

Kierkegaard, or it was just what he was waiting for, the moment for decisive action. Kierkegaard immediately wrote an article, 'Was Bishop Mynster a "Witness to the Truth", One of the "Proper Witnesses to the Truth" – Is *This the Truth?*'. In it he said that least of all was Mynster such a witness. Not only did Mynster suppress the fact that to take Christianity seriously always involves suffering, but also his own life in no way represented the true challenge of Christianity.

Yet, as so often before in Kierkegaard's life, here too there was delay. Although the article was for all intents and purposes ready for publication by the end of February, Kierkegaard did not publish it until the end of the year.[42] The reason in this case, however, was less indecision than a keen sensitivity to the political situation and the requirements of what he now surely did look upon as his cause. Martensen had for long seen himself as Mynster's successor. His candidature was supported by the conservative circles controlling the government at the time. But there was also opposition on several sides. Had Kierkegaard simply wanted to prevent Martensen from becoming primate, he could easily have exploited this opposition by adding its weight to his own, or his to its. But a scrupulous devotion to the terms of his own point of view prevented him, not only from doing that but also from acting in any way that might be interpreted as lending support to some change that in his view was merely political in character. Kierkegaard would also want to distinguish his own reasons for opposing Martensen from those of people whose opposition stemmed from a criticism of the church already being generated from within the church itself, in particular by the Grundtvigians.[43] Also, although in his own criticism of the church there was clearly a personal element directed at both Mynster and Martensen, Kierkegaard never quite lost his respect for Mynster. The fact that he had already delayed his attack until Mynster's death was mirrored in his scruples about engaging in a polemic that might interfere with a campaign to finance a monument to the late primate. Kierkegaard's scrupulousness in keeping the issues that concerned him clearly in mind is evident in a letter from 1854 which he wrote to Mynster's son, who had sent Kierkegaard a book written by his father:

Thank you, dear Pastor Mynster, for remembering me with such affection! I found it, in all sincerity, most touching, and that is also why I shall keep your little note that accompanied the book you sent me.

But I cannot accept the book itself. My relationship with your late father was of a quite special kind. I told him privately the first time I spoke with him, and in as solemn terms as possible, how much I disagreed with him. Privately I have told him again and again – and I shall not forget that he had the good will to listen to me with sympathy – that my principal concern was the memory of my late father.

Now that he is dead, I must stop. I must and intend now to have the freedom to be able to speak out, whether or not I want to, without having to take any such things into consideration. And for that reason I ought to avoid everything that might bring about any kind of misunderstanding that might be binding on me, such as for example now accepting this book. For, as your sending it to me says (and that was nice of you!) that everything is as it used to be – well, but that is not the way it is.

Dear Pastor M., if this should have such an unpleasant and disturbing effect that you do not think you can maintain your affection for me, please be assured of one thing: I remain

Your affectionate S. K.[44]

The date of this letter is not recorded, but it could postdate a long journal entry dated 1 March 1854, two months after Mynster's death, written while Kierkegaard was still biding his time, and which would have made any reader (had there been one) suspect gross naïveté, disingenuousness, or incipient megalomania. Headed 'Bishop Mynster', and as complex in the intertwining of the contraposed attitudes it expresses as any text can be, it reads:

Now he is dead.

If he could have been moved to end his life with a confession to Christianity that what he had represented was not really Christianity but leniency, it would have been much to be desired, for he sustained a whole age.

That was why the possibility of such a confession had to be kept open to the last, yes to the last, in case he wanted to make it on his deathbed. That is why it was not possible to attack him; that is what obliged me to put up with everything, even when he went to such desperate lengths as with that matter with Goldschmidt [we recall he had praised Goldschmidt and Kierkegaard in the same breath], since no one could tell whether it might not have moved him to come out with that confession.

Now that he his dead without having made the confession everything is changed; all he has left behind is the fact that he has preached Christianity to a standstill in an illusion.

The situation is also changed regarding my melancholic devotion to my dead father's pastor. For it would be too much if even after his death I were unable to speak less reservedly about him, although I know very well that I will always be susceptible in my old devotion and my aesthetic admiration.

Originally I wanted to turn my whole thing into a triumph for Mynster. As later I came to see things more clearly it remained my wish, but I was obliged to require this little confession and, it not being something I desired on my own behalf, I thought it might be done in a way that made it a triumph for Bishop M.

From the time a secret misunderstanding arose between us my wish was at least to succeed in avoiding coming to attack him while he was alive; I thought it quite possible I myself might die.

And yet it came very close to my thinking I would have to attack him. I missed just one of his sermons, the last; it wasn't illness that kept me, I went to hear Kolthoff preach.[45] I took this to mean: now's the time, you must break with the tradition from Father. It was the last time M preached. God be praised, is it not like a guidance?

If Bishop M could have given way (which could after all have been kept from everyone, for whom it would have come to be his triumph) my outward circumstances could also have been more free of concern than they were; for in his worldly wisdom Bishop M, who I am sure privately conceded enough to me in regard to spirit, counted on its having to end with my giving in to him in one way or another, because I would be unable financially to hold out against him.

To me, a saying he frequently came up with in our conversations, although not directed at me, was very apt: It depends not on who is the strongest but who can hold out longest.[46]

Mynster's death meant that Kierkegaard's fanciful goal of converting Denmark's primate reverted to a realm of lost chances where its unrealism could remain undetected. For it wasn't a might-have-been that only formed itself in Kierkegaard's mind once it had become impossible to put it to the test. All those abortive visits to the living Mynster had been linked with Kierkegaard's hope that Mynster would prove to be that 'ideal reader' who saw the point of what he was saying.

While the politics of the aftermath of Mynster's death unfolded under his sharp eye, Kierkegaard kept his cards close to his chest, at least in public. In private he made visits to his brother-in-law, Ferdinand Lund, using the opportunity to vent his feelings about Mynster. The record of these lunch visits by Troels Frederik Troels-Lund, the youngest son of the remarried Lund (first married to Petrea) are of Kierkegaard needling Lund's wife, Anna Cathrine, who had a high opinion of Mynster. Was he just letting off steam in one of the few private contexts still available to him, or genuinely trying to convince those members of his family to whom he had always been particularly attached? Troels-Lund thought it was all a rehearsal, a test of what might come when he went public. The insistent confrontations, which the family found acutely embarrassing and did all they could to avoid by getting Uncle Søren to talk of other things, reached a climax one day when Anna Cathrine finally got up and said: 'You know that the man you speak so ill of is one for whom we here cherish the greatest respect and profoundest gratitude. I cannot sit here and hear him continually abused. If *you* won't stop the only way I can avoid it is by leaving the room', which she then did.[47]

That was shortly before Easter 1854. But it was not until the end of the year that Kierkegaard saw that he could use his meticulously maintained freedom to act. By then the main obstacles had been removed. Efforts at hindering Martensen's succession had failed. Supported by the majority of the clergy and the radically conservative prime minister, A. S. Ørsted (brother of the scientist), Martensen had narrowly beaten the National-Liberal contender, H. N. Clausen (who had been supported also by the king), to the post. Once Martensen had been named to the see, on 15 April 1854, Kierkegaard's continued opposition to Martensen and the church could speak for itself now that the purely political issue of the succession was decided. That he still held his fire was perhaps due to the powerful political feelings afoot and the possibility of an attack at this stage being used to lend strength to others in their efforts to remove Ørsted's ministry. In December, however, these efforts had succeeded. There was a change of government in which the National-Liberal opposition gained power. Kierkegaard published his article on the eighteenth in *Fædrelandet*.

Instead of provoking instant reaction, the effect was one of stunned incomprehension. The delay itself was partly to blame but also the fact that no disagreement between Kierkegaard and Mynster had been suspected. An attack on Martensen, yes; that would have been more in keeping, though a eulogy at a burial was hardly the appropriate occasion. That Kierkegaard should come out and desecrate the memory of this noble anti-Hegelian individualist and friend of his family was shocking. Many people were scandalized. Among the words his former teachers used were 'sickly', 'ecstatic', 'sectarian', and 'unjust'. Only Rasmus Nielsen, whose support Kierkegaard had earlier more or less declined, came to his defence. Madame Heiberg, a long-standing admirer who rather more than her husband was inclined to think of Kierkegaard as 'on our side', called him an 'unfaithful beast'.[48]

Of course, only those who had read Kierkegaard's works and understood them, or were privy to the journals, could have appreciated the reasons for the collision, perhaps even seen a kind of logical inevitability in Kierkegaard's response to Martensen's address. But at that time there were few such readers and the journals were still private, though there was much there to scandalize them even more. The late journal entries make the whole of society sound as if riddled with the malaise Kierkegaard saw in its church and found mirrored in the primate. Like the true Messiah who would be spat upon, as against the Messiah whom society would receive with open arms and invite to a convention, the once-conservative Kierkegaard was now expressing himself in revolutionary rather than 'evolutionary' terms. Society's institutions, even marriage, were to go the way of all that was merely *humanly* ethical, as mere refuges for that vast majority that fails to live a life in the category of spirit.

But we know to be wary about jumping too quickly to conclusions. We can read, as his contemporaries at that time could not, that Kierkegaard saw the excess in what he said and justified it as being offered in the spirit of a corrective. The term 'corrective' is Kierkegaard's own and stems from as early as 1849. It suggests a dialectical relationship between the established and what is needed to bring it further. Thus a corrective must be understood, not on its own, but in terms of what has to be rectified.[49] For example, 'beneath the holy gloss' of actual marriage, as against the ideal painted by Victor Eremita, he saw mere 'worldliness and cowardice'.[50] This entry too is from 1849. What one might say on Kierkegaard's behalf is that society had failed to make even the first of the two movements of faith expounded in *Fear and Trembling*, resignation and withdrawal from the worldly. In another entry, from 1850, under the heading 'The Turning-point in the World', Kierkegaard had also said that 'the time of immediacy is past'. Not in the sense that the world has gone beyond it, but rather in the sense that now there is no going back and 'everyone has to learn in earnest to be himself the master, to guide himself without the intercession of guides and leaders'. Just as Quidam, in the psychological experiment in *Stages*, 'sees that the matter is comic and yet tragically clings to it on the strength of something else',[51] so too is social life as we know it a manifestation of the fear of taking the next step and a desperate clinging to the forms that protect individuals from entering upon the life of spirit. A corrective is necessary. As a corrective, however, it is necessarily one-sided, but, as Kierkegaard remarks, to anyone complaining about that all you can say is that it is easy enough to 'add the other side' again, but then the corrective 'ceases to be the corrective' and you become the establishment once more.[52]

Even without benefit of this inside knowledge there were, in liberal circles, some private pockets of support.[53] Later, it would grow and become public. Now, however, public reaction of any kind was sparse. Martensen published a reply ten days after the article appeared, and Kierkegaard immediately delivered another salvo to which Martensen never replied, and indeed he took no further part. Some few clergy entered into what was to become a familiar tradition in responding to Kierkegaard, protesting that the standard against which Kierkegaard judged Mynster as failing to be a witness to the truth was eccentrically exaggerated. In general, however, the clergy simply let the incident pass them by. At first Kierkegaard did little, replying only to some snide comments from a curate from Alborg who had previously rubbished *Either/Or* and *Fear and Trembling*. As Mynster began to gain in respect among people who, usually, hardly spared him a thought, Kierkegaard was coming close to having made himself look a fool – the more so now that Martensen, for all the manoeuvring against his becoming Mynster's successor, was sitting decidedly pretty.

Kierkegaard's frustration is evident in the journals. Martensen's silence was a 'fearful prostitution'. To 'what depths of misery, philistinism, mediocrity and lies the establishment [had] sunk'.[54] An entry from the time which fairly sums up Kierkegaardian thought in the version that peaked in *Practice in Christianity*, and which carried him through to the onslaught on the church, gives us a clear enough picture. Before the turn of the year and under the heading 'Imitation' he wrote:

Christ comes to the world as the prototype, constantly insisting: follow my example.

People soon turned the relation around, they preferred to *worship* the prototype; and finally in Protestantism it became presumption to want to emulate the prototype – the prototype is only the redeemer.

The apostle imitates Christ and insists: follow my example.

Soon the apostle was turned around, people worshipped the apostle.

Thus the slippery slope.

Among us there lived the now departed Bishop Mynster – Christianly quite plainly a criminal though in another context an exceptionally gifted man, and I am sure there were many among us who felt Mynster was too high-up to emulate and who were therefore content to worship him.

.The divine invention is one thing, that the only kind of worship God demands is imitation, the one thing man wants is to worship the prototypes.[55]

There was eventually some debate in the newspapers. Rasmus Nielsen defended Kierkegaard's 'good deed' and, on receiving no reaction, in another article challenged Martensen to reply to Kierkegaard. Still no reply. On 29 January Kierkegaard published another piece, 'The Issue with Bishop Martensen'. To no avail. February went by and March was almost through when, on the twentieth, he published yet another article, a short one, suggesting there would be no cause for complaint if Mynster had only admitted that it was not the Christianity of the New Testament that he represented but 'if you will, a pious extenuation, a slurring, shrouded in a host of ways in illusion'. Two days earlier Regine had contrived to meet him on the street, just before she and her husband were to depart for the West Indies, where Schlegel was to take over a governorship. 'I said to him under my breath as he passed, "God bless you – may it go well with you!" He was sort of taken aback and greeted me for the first time since the break and for the last time here on earth!'[56] Whether or not he took this friendly gesture as a sign that his first collision was now resolved, and this was the spur he needed, Kierkegaard now launched a series of articles, on 21 and 22 and then on 26, 28, 30, and 31 March, the last of which bore the title 'What Do I Want?'. The answer was 'honesty'; he was not, as he had been represented, either a spokesman for or a representative of a strict Christianity in the face of a milder form. All he wanted to say was that 'in a world where millions and millions call themselves Christians, one person there conveys: I dare not call myself a Christian', and that he knew he had God's consent to say it.[57]

At this point Grundtvig entered the fray, directing a sermon at Kierkegaard on Palm Sunday though referring only to the 'blasphemer'. Kierkegaard saved his reply for what was just about to come. For after a few more articles and a reply to a cleric who had accused him of contradicting not just himself but also the Lord, Kierkegaard launched his own broadsheet, *The Instant* (*Øieblikket*).

In this publication Kierkegaard pilloried the State Church, or more particularly the People's Church instituted in 1849, in terms that readers of *The Corsair* would have appreciated. The first issue begins by reminding its readers that, according to Plato, nothing worthwhile will be done until those who rule are people who have no desire to do so.

The heading of one piece in the first issue reads: 'Is it defensible for the State, the Christian State!, to do what it can to make Christianity impossible?' Another short article talks of those who, though they realize there is something utterly pitiful about the whole of religious life, resist the thought because they find the usual way of things so attractive. They are likened to people with coated tongues, a bad taste in their mouths, and with the shivers, who are advised by the doctor to take an emetic. Kierkegaard says to them: 'Take an emetic and get out of this half-hearted condition.' A short piece in the second issue, entitled 'We Are All Christians', says how difficult it would be for anyone to try to declare himself a non-Christian, however vehemently, because he thought Christianity was a lie. 'What nonsense', the state would say, 'where will it all end if we allow one person to declare himself a non-Christian, they'll all end up doing the same, no, no, *principiis obsta* and stand firm by the principles. We now have the statistics in order, everything in its place, everything correct, always provided that we are all Christians – *ergo* he is a Christian too: a conceit like that just to want to be different must not be indulged, he is a Christian and will remain one.' Among a collection of more aphoristic contributions under the title 'Short and to the Point', we read: 'Is it the same teaching when Christ says to the rich young man: Sell all you have, and then give it to the poor, and when the priest says: Sell all you have and give it to me?' Another, under the title 'The Theatre – the Church', says:

Essentially the difference between the theatre and the Church is that the theatre honestly and openly admits to being what it is; the Church on the other hand is a theatre that in every way fraudulently conceals what it is. . . . An example: on the billboard outside the theatre it always says straight off: Money will not be returned. The Church, this solemn sanctity, would shudder at the offensiveness and scandal of having this put plainly over the church door or printed under the list of preachers on Sunday. But the Church nevertheless does not shudder at insisting perhaps even more strongly than the theatre that you will not get your money back. . . . So how fortunate that the Church has the theatre beside it, for the theatre is a scoundrel, a real kind of witness to the truth, that betrays the secret that what the theatre says openly the Church does clandestinely.

In the following issue, the seventh, a 'kind of short story' entitled 'First God's Kingdom' begins:

Theology graduate Ludvig Piety – is seeking. To hear that a 'theology' graduate is seeking, it needs no lively imagination to grasp what he seeks, the kingdom of God of course, what one *first* has to seek.

No, that isn't it. What he seeks is a royal living as a pastor, and as I shall briefly sketch, a great deal has happened before he comes that far.

First he has been to grammar school from which he is then discharged. After that he has *first* taken two exams and, after four years' reading, *first* taken his degree.

So now he is a theology graduate and one might think that after *first* having got all that behind him, now at last he can start doing something for Christianity. Why not? No, *first* he must attend the Seminary for half a year, and after that's gone there's no question of seeking for the first eight years, which *first* must be put behind him.

And now we are at the beginning of the novel: the eight years have gone, he seeks.

His life which up to now cannot be said to have had any relationship to the unconditioned, suddenly acquires such a relationship. He seeks everything unconditionally, fills one stamped sheet of paper after another, runs from Herod to Pilate, recommends himself to both the cabinet minister and the janitor, in short he is totally in the service of an unconditioned. Yes, an acquaintance who hasn't seen him the last two years, says he has found to his surprise that what happened to Münchausen's dog, which was a greyhound but with all that running turned into a badger, has also happened to [Ludvig]. . . .

The last piece in the final issue to be published was entitled: 'The Priest Not Only Proves the Truth of Christianity but at the Same Time Refutes It.'

There can be only one relationship to revealed truth: belief.

That one believes can be proved in just one way, by being willing to suffer for one's faith, and how much one believes is proved only by how willing one is to suffer for one's belief. . . .

Now, on the contrary, the priest as good as wants to make proving the truth of Christianity through there having been those who have given all, risked life and blood for Christianity, into a source of income (but having that is after all the exact opposite of the suffering, of the sacrificing, wherein the proof lies).

Proof and refutation in one! The proof of Christianity's truth being that people have risked everything for it, is refuted or made suspect by the priest, in delivering the proof, doing the exact opposite. . . .[58]

Among some leftover unpublished material we read of 'one more death sentence over all official Christianity: this enormous castle in the air, a Christian world, Christian states, kingdoms, countries; this sporting with millions of Christians who mutually acknowledge one another in their mediocrity yet are all believers; this whole thing rests on a foundation which according to Christ's own words makes faith impossible'.[59]

A classic of satirical literature, *The Instant* caused a furor. At last Kierkegaard found himself in the field of action, as a journalist again, just as he had begun back in 1835. To those who knew him he seemed to be bearing the strain well. One suspects he was rather enjoying it all. When Brøchner met Kierkegaard on the street at this time and walked back with him to his new home in Klædeboderne, he was surprised to find how he managed to retain 'not just his usual equanimity and cheerfulness but even his sense of humour'.[60] But this was to be their last meeting. Kierkegaard fell ill before the tenth issue of *The Instant* went to press. His last journal entry is dated 25 September 1855, the same day, as it happened, as the publication of the ninth issue. A week later, on 2 October, he collapsed in the street. He was taken by carriage first to his home and then, at his own request, to Frederik's Hospital, where his condition steadily worsened. He died six weeks later, on 11 November.

There are three characteristic records from that time. One is an account by his niece, Henriette Lund,[61] who together with her father rushed to the hospital on hearing of Kierkegaard's collapse. She recounts that she had heard someone say that, on being brought to the hospital, Kierkegaard had said – echoing Tasso's words – that he had come there to die. Yet on seeing him she saw radiating from his face, 'mixed with the pain and sorrow', a 'blissful feeling of triumph'. Never before had she seen 'the spirit break through the earthly sheath in such a way and convey to it a lustre as though it were itself the body transfigured in the dawn of the resurrection'. But on a later visit 'the pain of the illness had come more to the fore'.[62] Although Henriette Lund's *Recollections from Home*, first published in 1880, where this account belongs, was written with an eye to promoting an alternative picture of her uncle to the one still widely current at that later time, there is no reason to doubt its accuracy in terms of what William Afham calls 'remembrance'.

Of the body's deterioration we have a detailed account in the hospital record. This begins by noting that the patient had suffered the usual childhood diseases but had, as a rule, been in good health since, except for a long period of constipation. The patient was unable to offer any specific reason for his present sickness. However,

he does associate it with drinking cold seltzer water in the summer, with a dark dwelling, together with the exhausting intellectual work that he believes is too taxing for his frail physique. He considers the sickness fatal. His death is necessary for the cause which he has devoted all his intellectual strength to resolving, for which he has worked alone, and for which alone he believes that he was intended;

hence the penetrating thought in conjunction with so frail a physique. If he is to go
on living, he must continue his religious battle; but in that case it will peter out,
while, on the contrary, by his death it will maintain its strength and, he believes, its
victory.[63]

The patient also recounted how, two weeks earlier at a party at
Giødwad's, he had slid off the sofa while leaning forward. The occasion
is recorded by Israel Levin, who had assisted Kierkegaard with several
chores, including taking manuscripts to the printers and helping with
the proofreading of *Sickness*.[64]

He was sitting on the sofa and had been so gay, amusing, and charming, and then
he slid from the sofa onto the floor; we helped him up, but he stammered: 'O-h-h,
j-j-just l-l-leave it t-t-till the m-maid sweeps it out in the morning,' and fainted
shortly afterwards.[65]

The same had happened the following day when he was about to get
dressed but without any dizziness, cramp, or loss of consciousness, 'just
a feeling of utter weakness'. So it went until he collapsed in the street.
Once in hospital, Kierkegaard became increasingly unable to stand on
his own feet or to get up, or to move to either side when sitting up. He
was also unable to raise his legs when lying down. There was expecto-
ration, difficulty in sleeping, and also in urination. Regarding the latter,
Kierkegaard noted that he always had an aversion to passing water in
the presence of others, and whether flippantly or not, remarked that
this defect may have had a decisive effect on him and have been a
reason for his becoming an oddity. He asked on 6 October, for religious
reasons, to go without his half-bottle of beer a day. A pain in his left
hip developed and he lay with his left leg tilted over the right, bent at
the hip and knee. They tried electric treatment on his legs but with
only very slight results. Constipation was added to his inability to move
his limbs, and by 4 November his condition had become aggravated by
bed-sores. By the ninth his condition had visibly worsened and now he
lay in a half coma, said nothing, and took no food. The pulse was 'weak
and unsteady', having risen to 130. On the tenth he remained in a half-
coma, his breathing 'rapid'. On the eleventh the condition was much
the same, the breathing 'heavy and short'. He died at 9 P.M. He was
forty-two years old. The tentative diagnosis was 'paralysis-(tubercul?)',
probably tuberculosis of the spine marrow. There was no autopsy.

Two of Kierkegaard's nephews were on hand during his final illness, employed in the hospital at the time as interns.[66] One of them felt himself a close ally of Kierkegaard. Several other members of the family paid him visits, and his brother tried but was refused. In fact the only member of the church allowed to talk with him was his lifelong friend Emil Boesen, who paid almost daily visits during the final illness and recorded their conversations.

In what is probably a resumé of the first two visits,[67] Kierkegaard responds to Boesen's opening question, 'How are things going?', by saying:

Badly; I am dying, pray for me that it comes quickly and easily. I am in low spirits. . . . I have my thorn in the flesh, like St Paul; so I couldn't enter into ordinary relations, and so I concluded that my task was out of the ordinary. I then tried to carry it out as best I could. I was a toy in the hands of Guidance which tossed me out and I was to be used. Then several years went by, then slap-bang!, Guidance reaches out its hand and takes me on board the Ark; that's always the life and fate of the emissary extraordinary. That's also what was wrong with Regine; I'd thought it could be changed but it couldn't, then I dissolved the relationship. How odd, the husband became Governor,[68] I don't like it . . . it would have been better if it had ended quietly. It was right that she got Schlegel, that was the first understanding and then I came along and disturbed things. She suffered a great deal with me. . . .

Boesen says that Kierkegaard spoke of her with great affection and sadness. 'I was afraid she'd become a governess, she didn't but now she's that in the West Indies!' To the question whether he had been angry and bitter, Kierkegaard said:

No, but to a great degree distressed and anxious and indignant, for instance at my brother Peter; I didn't receive him when he last came to my home, after his speech at Roskilde. He thinks that as the elder brother he must take precedence. He'd been flogged when I was still getting it on the a . . . , I wrote a piece against him, very caustic, which is in the desk at home.'

Boesen then asked him if he had decided anything about his papers. 'No', replied Kierkegaard, 'let it be as it may.' But

it depends on what dispensation it receives from Providence, whichever way it goes. But there's also the fact that I'm financially ruined and now have nothing, just enough for the burial. I began with a little, something over twenty thousand, and saw it could only last so long, ten to twenty years. Now it's seventeen, it was a big thing. I might have applied for an appointment, as an old graduate I could have got one, but I couldn't accept it (there was my thorn in the flesh), so the matter was decided. I understood that very quickly. What matters is to come as close to God as possible. And there are people who to be doing that need others, lots, all that nonsense about the majority. And then there's someone who needs only one. He stands highest among those who need anyone. The person who needs most stands lowest. It needs only one to say that.

To Boesen it seemed that Kierkegaard wanted to talk about the thorn in his flesh. He said,

The doctors don't understand my illness. It is mental, now they want to take it in the usual physician's manner. – It is bad; pray for me that it is soon over.

Miss Ilia Fibiger, the night nurse,[69] had sent him some flowers, and Kierkegaard had them put in a glass-faced cabinet; he looked at them but wouldn't have them put in water. 'It is the fate of flowers to bloom, be fragrant, and die.' If he could have faith that he was to live, then that is what would happen; he could go home. If he could have a glass of water and put on his boots he might get out of there again, not be in hospital; still it was all right for one whose life had been that of an exception to die in the category of the common.

On Thursday, 18 October, Boesen records that Kierkegaard was very weak, his head hung down on his chest, and his hands shook. He fell into a doze, but was awakened by his own coughing. He kept dozing off, particularly after taking his meals.

Now I've eaten . . . and everything is prepared to receive you, I do that with open arms.

Boesen asked if he found it possible to collect his thoughts, or were they confused? Kierkegaard replied that for most of the time he had control of them, sometimes at night they got rather confused. Could he pray in peace to God? 'Yes, I can!' Did he have anything he wanted to say?

No; yes, greet everyone, I've been very fond of them all, and tell them my life is a great, to others unknown and incomprehensible suffering. It all looked like pride and vanity but wasn't. I am not at all better than others, I have said that and never anything else. I had my thorn in the flesh, and therefore did not marry and was unable to take on an official position. I am after all a theology graduate, and had a public title and private favour; I could have got what I wanted, but I became the exception instead. The day went in work and excitement and in the evening I am put aside, out of the way – it was the exception.

When Boesen asked him again if he could pray in peace, Kierkegaard answered, 'Yes, I can; then I pray first for the forgiveness of sins, that everything may be forgiven; then I pray to be free of despair at the time of my death, and the saying frequently occurs to me that death must be well pleasing to God; and then I pray for what I would so much like to be the case, that I know a little in advance when death comes'.

It was a fine day, that Thursday, and Boesen said: 'When you sit and talk like that you seem healthy enough just to get up and leave with me.' Kierkegaard replied:

Yes, there's just one problem, I can't walk. But then there's another means of transport: I can be lifted up. I have had a feeling of becoming an angel, getting wings, that too is what's going to happen, sitting astride a cloud and singing Hallelujah, Hallelujah, Hallelujah! I know any idiot can say that; it all depends how it is said.

And all that was because he believed and took refuge in God's mercy through Christ? 'Yes, of course, what else?' Would he want to have changed anything he had said? He had, after all, expressed himself in unreal and strict terms. 'That is how it should be, otherwise it doesn't help. What good would it do first to speak for awakening and then for appeasement? Why do you bother me with this?'

Kierkegaard would not even receive Jens Giødwad, whose party he had been at and who had helped him so much as the go-between protecting his pseudonymity. 'Giødwad', he said,

did me personal favours but disowned me in public. I can't put up with that. You have no idea what a poisonous plant Mynster has been, no idea; it's monstrous how widely it has spread its corruption. He was a colossus; strong forces were needed to topple it, and the one who did it had to pay. When they hunt wild boar, the hunters have a specially selected hound and they know quite well what is going to happen: the wild boar is felled but the hound pays the price. I will die gladly, so I am sure that I solved the task put before me. People would often listen to what someone dead has to say rather than to whatever comes from someone still living.

Boesen said he would rather Kierkegaard lived a while yet; he had been so stringent and gone so far; there must be something left for him to say.

Yes, but then I won't die either. I have had to forget all the *Instants* and the rest to get peace, and feel I've had a fitting, important and hard enough task. Remember that I have seen things from the very core of Christianity; everything is procrastination, procrastination – You must have had enough ups and downs because of knowing me?

'Yes', said Boesen, 'but I have said nothing about it to others, and where people knew about it and discussed it, it was respected.' Kierkegaard then said, 'Was it, now? – I'm so happy you came, thank you, thank you!'

On Friday, 19 October, Kierkegaard had slept for a few hours in the evening and was wide awake. His brother had been at the hospital but had not been allowed in. Peter had travelled from his parsonage in Pedersborg-by-Sorø, some distance away in west central Zealand, after hearing of Søren's worsening condition. This matter, according to Kierkegaard, could not be stopped through debate but by taking action,[70] and he had stopped and acted. Boesen asked Kierkegaard whether he would like to receive the last rites. 'Yes, indeed', said Kierkegaard, 'but from a layman, not a pastor.' That would be hard to arrange. 'Then I'll die without.' 'That's not right!', said Boesen.

The matter is not in debate, I have made up my mind, my choice is made. The priests are royal functionaries, royal functionaries have nothing to do with Christianity.

Boesen said that couldn't be right.

Indeed; it is God, you see, who is sovereign, but then there are all these people who want to arrange everything so conveniently, so they are all served up Christianity and there are the thousand pastors so that no one in the land can die blessed without belonging; so it is they who are sovereign and it is all over with God's sovereignty; but he must be obeyed in everything.

After this spirited defence, Kierkegaard collapsed and Boesen left, concerned about the consequences if Kierkegaard's wish to receive the final rites at the hands of a layman were acceded to. It would be a symbolic act of considerable significance and could easily be abused. What if the view gained currency that to be a good Christian you must not be a pastor?

When Boesen visited the next day, Kierkegaard was unable to hold his head up and asked Boesen to support it. When Boesen said that he would see him the next day, Kierkegaard said they might as well say goodbye today and asked Boesen to forgive him for the problems he would have avoided but for knowing him. The following days there was little response. On 25 October, Boesen replied to Kierkegaard's question of whether his refusal to see his brother had provoked a scandal by trying to convince Kierkegaard that people were genuinely concerned for him and that those who did not agree with his total rejection of the established church must be entitled to their view; and in any case was it not possible to reach salvation that way as well? Kierkegaard dismissed their good intentions with a 'get thee behind me, Satan!' quotation which, in its full form in a journal entry from the previous year, shows where the land now lay: 'Christianity is on such a high level that even humanity of the best-intentioned kind . . . is not just a misunderstanding, a false view, but is of Satan.' Indeed Christendom was 'Satan's invention.'[71] Now, on his death-bed, Kierkegaard said he couldn't bear to talk about it, it was a great strain. Boesen had brought with him a sermon by the chairman of the Pastoral Convention, a gesture of friendship if not support from the latter. Kierkegaard asked him to send it back. Boesen said it was not intended that he should read it. But Kierkegaard replied that the man, Fenger, had spoken against him in public, so what was the meaning of sending this to him in private? Boesen also said that he had seen Peter, who was on his way home. Kierkegaard said he expected his refusal to see Peter would cause a scandal. Boesen said he didn't think it would, in fact they thought of him with the greatest sympathy. What they said in public was in self-defence. Kierkegaard found this line of conversation too strenuous, so Boesen then asked him whether there had been bad air in the bedroom of his previous apartment. 'Yes', said Kierkegaard; the thought exasperated him. Then why hadn't he moved?

I was under too great a strain. I still had some issues of the *Instant* to get out, and a few hundred rixdollars left to be used for that. So either I could let it be and conserve my energies or keep going and drop. And I rightly chose the latter; then I was through.

Boesen then asked if he had got all the issues he wanted out. He had. To which Boesen replied: 'How remarkable that so much in your life has worked out.' 'Yes', said Kierkegaard, 'that is why I am very happy and very sad, because I cannot share my happiness with anyone.'

Boesen visited Kierkegaard again on 26 October, but nothing important was discussed, and likewise on the twenty-seventh. On that day, a Saturday, there were larger than usual crowds on the street.

Yes, that's what once made me feel so good.

Boesen reproached Kierkegaard for never coming to visit him (in Horsens, south of Aarhus on the east of Jutland).

No, how could I find time for that!

The last time Boesen saw his friend, Kierkegaard could scarcely talk. He had to leave town, and Kierkegaard died soon after.

※

We know that already in 1846, as he was approaching his thirty-third birthday, Kierkegaard had detailed requirements for the repair, that spring, of the family burial site at Assistens Graveyard:[72]

The small upright support (with the text about Father's first wife) is to be removed. The fence behind should be closed.

The fence should be nicely repaired.

Just inside the fence, where that small column stood, a carved gravestone with a marble cross should be placed. The face of this gravestone should carry the words that were formerly on that small column.

Leaning against the gravestone should be placed that slab with Father's and Mother's names together with the rest, which of course Father himself drew up.

Then another slab corresponding with this one should be made and on it written (but in smaller letters so that there will be more space left) what is now written on the large flat stone that covers the grave, and said large stone be removed altogether. This slab too should lean against the gravestone.

The whole burial plot should then be levelled and seeded with a fine low grass, except for a very tiny spot of bare soil showing in the four corners, and in each of these corners should be planted a little bush of Turkish roses, as I believe they are called, some very tiny ones, dark red.

On the slab (on which is to be written what was on the large flat stone, that is, the names of my late sister and brother)[73] there will thus be enough room for my name to be placed there as well:

Søren Aabye, born 5 May 1813, died ——

And then there will be enough space for a little verse which may be done in small type:

> In yet a little while
> I shall have won;
> Then the whole fight
> Will at once be done.
> Then I may rest
> In bowers of roses
> And unceasingly, unceasingly
> Speak with my Jesus.[74]

In his desk, locked and under seal, Kierkegaard's brother found a
will marked to be opened after his death. It is assumed to have been
written in 1849 along with related correspondence.

Dear Brother,

It is, of course, my will that my former fiancée, Mrs. Regine Schlegel, inherit
unconditionally whatever little I can leave behind. If she will not accept it for
herself, she is to be offered it on the condition that she be willing to administer it
for distribution to the poor.

What I want to express in this way is that to me an engagement was and is just
as binding as a marriage, and that therefore my estate is her due exactly as if I had
been married to her.

Your brother,
S. Kierkegaard[75]

Regine declined the inheritance, asking only that her letters be returned along with a few personal items. However, it is reported, in an
interview in 1896 with Regine, that it was Schlegel who had declined it
on her behalf, wanting to avoid a stir. Although there was next to no
capital, the inheritance did include a large collection of books, and of
course author's rights.[76]

'Poor Kierkegaard'?

IT isn't just because of what they produce and survives them that biographies of significant figures don't end with the *bios* itself. The works of artists, especially great ones, can take on lives of their own that may eclipse those of their authors, to such an extent that they may even leave the latter in total biographical obscurity. The reason why biographies don't end with the deaths of their subjects is rather that the aftermath of a life can teach us more about the life itself. In this respect a life not illuminated by the death would be hardly worth recording. Not least of the clues to the meaning of a life, for instance, can be the light cast on it by the way in which surviving contemporaries responded to the death. This would be especially so in the case of a person who thought his death might help to give his life the meaning he meant it to have.

Hans Christian Andersen, in a letter dated 24 November, briefly summed up the events on the day of the burial.

> Søren Kierkegaard was buried last Sunday, following a service at the Church of Our Lady, where the parties concerned had done very little. The church pews were closed and the aisles unusually crowded. Ladies in red and blue hats were coming and going; ditto dogs with muzzles. At the grave-site itself there was a scandal: when the whole ceremony *there* was over (that is, when Tryde had cast earth upon the coffin), a son of a sister of the deceased stepped forward and denounced the fact that he had been buried in this fashion. He declared – and this was his point more or less – that Søren Kierkegaard had resigned from our society, and therefore we ought not to bury him in accordance with our customs! I was not out there, but it was said to have been unpleasant. The newspapers say little about it. In last Thursday's number of *Fædrelandet* this nephew has published his speech along with some afterthoughts. To me the entire affair is a distorted picture of Søren K.: I don't understand it![1]

It was Henrik Lund, the nephew who had attended Kierkegaard in hospital, who held the protest speech at the grave-side. As one bystander in whose memory the 'distasteful scene' stuck for many years put it: the 'young physician, visibly upset and with a New Testament in his hand, mocked the clergy represented by P. Kierkegaard and by [Archdeacon Eggert Christopher] Tryde, who had buried with pomp a man who had renounced all fellowship with the "plaything Christianity of the pastors" '. That may be a reference to the talk of Christianity as a castle in the air in *The Instant*.[2] Henrik said that over the years he had become bound by ties of friendship, as well as blood, to his uncle, who 'stands and falls with his writings and the opinions and views that he presents in those'. He complained that on this occasion there had not been a single mention of them. As Andersen's description implies, he took that typically caustic passage from *The Instant* about 'our all being Christians' to point out that in no other religious society would someone who had 'left it so decisively' and 'with no prior recantation' be nevertheless looked upon 'after his death as a member of that society'. Perhaps unadvisedly, also prompted by comments in *The Instant*, he also suggested that the church had taken over the proceedings just for the money, and (a gibe directed at his uncle Peter) for the sake of the family's reputation. Lund ended by saying, 'I have spoken and freed my spirit!'[3]

Martensen was naturally not in attendance. He did, however, write down something on the day. He strongly disagreed that it had been done to save the family's reputation: 'the like of anything so *tactless* as the family having him buried on a Sunday, between two religious services, from the nation's most important Church, is hard to imagine.' There was no way of stopping this by law, but plain respect for 'proper conduct' should have been enough to prevent it. That, however, was something 'Tryde lacked here as always when it is required of him'. He had heard that 'a large cortège of mourners (in full pomp, what irony!)' had followed the coffin, but also that it was mainly made up of the young and 'a mass of obscure personages', not a single dignitary among them – 'unless one wants to include R. Nielsen and Magister Stilling [the young man who once asked Brøchner's elder relative to tutor him in as short a time as it had taken Kierkegaard to cram for his exams] in this category. . . .' Word had just come to him that 'there was a big scandal at the grave, a student named Lund came on with *The Instant* and the New Testament as a witness for the truth against the church which had buried S. Kd "for money" etc.' He predicted that the newspapers would soon be full of these stories. So far, confirmation from 'official channels' had not reached the new primate, but it 'was a great offence' which he realized called for 'serious measures'.[4]

Martensen also mentions that 'Kierkegaard's brother spoke at the church (as a brother, not a pastor)'. Though at the time Martensen knew nothing of 'what he said and how', a theology student who recalled that the church was 'full to bursting' had recorded on that very day that, in his eulogy, Peter Kierkegaard

explained the family circumstances, how their father, who had once herded sheep on the moors of Jutland, had loved the children with the most heartfelt love, that by and by all but two of them had departed this life, and now his brother had also left him, so that he alone remained. He then said it was neither the time nor the place to discuss Søren's activities; we neither dared nor could accept much of what Søren had said, but his true intention had been to clear away all the rubble that had collected at the door of the Church; that he [Søren] himself had not been aware of how far he had gone, and of the fact that he had gone too far. He [Peter] could not thank this great gathering on his deceased brother's behalf, since the latter had always withdrawn into solitude, and it was against his principles and opinions to be surrounded by the crowd. Nor could he thank the gathering on his own or the family's behalf, since they had been enticed there by various motives which he didn't want to go further into. He finished with a fervent prayer that Søren's efforts and achievement might not be misunderstood but that the truth in them might become apparent and be a positive influence in the service of Christ.[5]

Peter subsequently lost the notes of his eulogy, but on trying on request to reconstruct them twenty-six years later he recalled that it had included a 'confession' that he was not only deeply regretful but 'also felt

a sincere shame and remorse, because during recent years none of us had understood that the vision of the deceased had become partially darkened and distorted from exertions and suffering in the heat of battle, causing his blows to fall wildly and blindly, as did Ølver's in the Norwegian saga; and that we should have acted as Ølver's friends did, and with the confident gaze and the mild embraces of love, lured him or compelled him to take a long and quiet rest. . . .'[6]

The implication of Peter's choice of this analogy from Snorri Sturluson's account of the kings of Norway is well observed by Kirmmse. What it means is that in his last year Søren had been mad (in the saga Ølver had been drunk at the time). Also, Ølver's full name (Olvir miklimunnr) means 'bigmouth'. Earlier that year in July, and about half-way through the series of issues of *The Instant*, Peter had repeated his performance of five years earlier. He had again criticized Søren publicly, suggesting that the signed works represented just another point of view, like the pseudonyms.[7] It was this that Kierkegaard had referred to, in his last conversations with Boesen, as the reason he had refused to welcome his brother to his home, as later to the hospital. Peter had heard of Søren's reactions to his speech (some of which are recorded in the journals),[8] and had come to town to seek a reconciliation – unless of course it was to try to persuade him to go abroad and take a rest.

The poignancy of Peter's recollection is not in an elder brother's memory of his younger brother as someone who had lost his mind. It is in the distinct possibility that the memory of what he had done to his brother was instrumental in Peter losing his. How much this owed to a bad conscience in this one matter or was a manifestation of some deeper, more permanent sense of guilt, is hard to say. What *is* true is that Peter, a character far better deserving the 'gloomy Dane' sobriquet than his younger brother, had been prone to self-doubt from childhood. It is paradoxical that Søren, so anxious in his pseudonymous guises to urge total responsibility for one's selfhood, should devote so much space in his journals to blaming his own suffering on his father, while for Peter the very thought of doing so would merely have reinforced his self-reproach. In his many years as sole survivor of that Chekhovian trio who had once lived at Nytorv, while the royalties inherited from the sales of new editions of his dead brother's books steadily accumulated, two of them published by himself, the overwhelming conviction seems to have grown in Peter that he had taken his brother's life. He donated the money to charity and even started paying back insignificant debts long forgotten by those to whom the small sums were still due. He decided finally that he no longer deserved his bishopric, if indeed he ever had. He resigned it in 1875 and four years later returned his royal decorations. In February 1883 Peter sent a letter to the Probate Court, later returned opened to the family but now lost. According to Peter's own record it began with the text of I John 3:15: 'Anyone who hates his brother is a murderer, and you know that no murderer has eternal life abiding in him.' In 1884, one-time member of parliament, cabinet minister, and finally bishop of Aalborg, Peter Christian Kierkegaard renounced his legal right to take care of his own affairs. He ended his days as a ward of the state and died on 24 February 1888 at the age of eighty-two, in, as Kirmmse quotes his biographer, 'the darkness of insanity'.[9]

By this time Bishop Mynster had been dead for twenty-eight years.

His star had in the meantime faded if not fallen. That fact raises the question of whether Kierkegaard may not be said to have won this contest too. Although Mynster was not entirely forgotten, it seems clear that among those who still held him in respect there was a felt need to defend his name. In 1884 there appeared a compact defence of the bishop, *Har S. Kierkegaard fremstillet de christelige Idealer – er dette Sandhed?* ('Has Kierkegaard Portrayed the Christian Ideals – Is This the Truth?'), the title recalling Kierkegaard's notorious article. Its author, who had just recently died, was one of Mynster's sons, though not the pastor to whom Kierkegaard had written when returning that book. This was the author and editor C. L. N. Mynster. The manuscript had been found among unpublished writings by a nephew, Jakob Paulli, son of Just H. V. Paulli, whose second wife was Marie Elisabeth Mynster, Bishop Mynster's eldest daughter. Provoked by the recently published *Concise History of Danish Literature for Use in School and at Home*, her author-editor brother had begun the manuscript in the summer of 1881, but then pressure of other work had forced him to put it aside.

This short pamphlet is an important document for an appreciation of the reception of Kierkegaard at the time. By then at least a selection of the journals had become available. They had first been catalogued by Henrik Lund, who discovered them in Kierkegaard's apartment among a huge collection of unpublished material in folders, notebooks, and piles of carefully marked and dated journals. Lund's father sent these to Peter Kierkegaard, who in 1859 published *The Point of View* and in 1876 *Judge for Yourself!* The rest of the material he handed over to an editor named Barfod, who between 1869 and 1877 put out three volumes of papers and journals, which included the comments on Mynster. The increasing vilification of the primate revealed in those pages was clearly a provocation for the son, and in the pamphlet he defends Bishop Mynster, claiming him as the real source of whatever is true in Kierkegaard's ideas. In doing so he is of course acknowledging what was by now generally accepted as Kierkegaard's genius, but hoping to correct the image he had left of the primate. The author of the *Concise History*, one Sigurd Müller, was a member of the up-and-coming generation of writers who clearly took Kierkegaard's side in the attack on the church. A phrase quoted by Mynster, Jr. gives us a clear enough clue to the state of cultural play. It refers to the 'two greatest religious movements of the time', the Grundtvigians and the Kierkegaardians. In the end, however, the latter never left any lasting mark in the Danish Church, though Kierkegaardian ideas were to be re-imported in the form of a local Barthianism between the two world wars. The Grundtvigian mixture of Christianity, populism, and national idealism proved, on the other hand, if not more heady at least more catching, and it left its powerful evangelical imprint, still visible today in both Denmark and Norway, not just on the church but in many ancillary and educational institutions.

Was there then no constituency for the conservative viewpoint expressed in the pamphlet? Or was this a lone call from the past and a son's attempt to rescue the memory of his father? Later on, from about 1900, there was indeed to be a moderately high-church current in Denmark, one which looked to Mynster and Martensen as its spiritual fathers. At the moment, however, the division was more cultural than theological. We shall return to that in a moment. In these terms it is easy enough to see where Mynster, Jr.'s allegiance lay. The pamphlet's last sentence acknowledges that, by being accorded the status these young textbook writers believed he deserved, Kierkegaard was alive and well but corrupting the youth. '[A]bove all', Mynster concludes, 'the verdict on S. Kierkegaard, and on his verdict on his contemporary teachers, is by no means so clear that any definitive word on the matter should be put before young people.'[10]

The document is valuable as a conservative's estimate of Kierkegaard's judgment on Mynster, a judgment that, thanks also to the journals, had now played its part in defining the distance at which the young radicals wanted to place themselves from the past. It challenges Kierkegaard's own grasp of Christian truth, pointing out that Kierkegaard's vision leaves no room for a sense of joy in God's creation, and that the charity he spoke of is evident in neither his own words nor his deeds. The journals gave no indication of 'the fruit of the spirit', that is to say of 'love, joy, peace, patience, gentleness, kindliness'. Certain passages may show a spiritual relation to God, but none shows a spiritual relation to Kierkegaard's fellow humans. Admitting that the journals make it clear that Kierkegaard himself made no claims to be a true Christian, the author says that a writer who sharpens Christianity's demands should at least show signs of having been strict with himself; otherwise what he writes is just a game. In a neat posthumous riposte to Kierkegaard, Mynster cites Bishop Mynster's comment that Kierkegaard 'made sport of the holy' and aimed at something it was impossible but also undesirable to put into practice, however impressive on paper. In *Either/Or* the Assessor says that things are easy enough 'on paper' but not in life. Again employing Kierkegaard against himself, Mynster describes Kierkegaard as a Don Quixote, suffering from the illusion that what once was true for the age of Christian persecution was still true for the nineteenth century. His father, the bishop, had given more than sufficient attention to the suffering that Kierkegaard stressed was part of being witness to Christian truth. Kierkegaard had also been unfair to Mynster personally. As he called on the busy primate at all hours, it wasn't surprising he couldn't always be given an audience. In fact the bishop had frequently welcomed Kierkegaard and shown him every respect. One need only read his published comments on *Fear and Trembling* to see that Mynster appreciated Kierkegaard's early work and saw 'what Kierkegaard was after'. As for Mynster's praising Kierkegaard and Goldschmidt in the same breath, that was based on the later Goldschmidt of *North and South* and the story 'A Jew', not on *The Corsair*. In fact Mynster had never seen Kierkegaard's 'martyrdom' in *The Corsair*. As for Kierkegaard himself, both Sibbern and Martensen had concluded that he was 'sickly' and that his morbid condition had worsened with the years. The word 'exalted' also reappears in the pamphlet, but Mynster's son does admit, and perhaps not simply in deference to Kierkegaard's newly won place in the Danish literary canon, that it might not be such a bad thing for all young theologians to 'have had a Kierkegaardian period'.[11]

This remark echoes similar sentiments to be found in Martensen's *Christian Ethics*, the supplement to his *Christian Dogmatics* of 1849.[12] Martensen, whose book gained wide publicity and was published in English translation in Edinburgh in two parts (1878 and 1881), gives an account of Kierkegaard's works, especially *The Sickness unto Death*, detailed enough to show that he had now studied these closely and, especially in a section entitled 'Sin Against the Holy Spirit', even profited from them. But, in a chapter on 'Socialism and Individualism', Martensen provides Kierkegaard with a neat pigeon-hole; he is an individualist. In thus classifying him, Martensen appears to be doing to Kierkegaard what Climacus claimed that the paragraph-ploughers had been unable to do to Lessing: have him killed and 'world-historically jointed and salted in a paragraph'. Martensen goes further. Kierkegaard is not a genuinely philosophical individualist, or if he is, then in world-historical terms he is not a significant one. Individualism had received its theoretical (systematic) explication and justification before Kierkegaard, in the work of one Alexander Vinet. Demonstratively praising the latter for his love of humanity, Martensen nevertheless finds fault with the theory itself. It 'represses the sympathetic element in human nature' and 'lead[s] every individual to labour autopathically for his own perfection'. The fault of individualism is that it demands only 'individual philanthropy, love towards human individuals, since these are the only actual existences, but not universal philanthropy, love towards the nation, fatherland and church, love towards humanity and its ideal aim, and above all devotion to the kingdom of God which is coming, and is to be perfected through history'. Martensen's verdict, noisily silent on the subject of his tormentor's humanity and back-handed in its praise, is that 'S. Kierkegaard's support of Individualism', undertaken with 'great talent and powerful one-sidedness', 'forms a remarkable episode in Danish literature'.[13]

We remember how Johannes Climacus deplored the ease with which the hospitable System had accommodated original thinkers. Poor Hamann, poor Jacobi! Are we not inclined here to say 'poor Kierkegaard'?

Many of those who have claimed basic agreement with Kierkegaard patronizingly defend themselves against the threat of extremism in the way Peter Christian tried to defend the honour of his family. They attribute his 'hard' thoughts to derangement. Thus Martensen too talks of 'ecstasy' and 'intoxication'.[14] Rumours that Kierkegaard suffered from a form of epilepsy, which may or may not be true, were seen by Sibbern among others as a possible cause of his alleged 'exaltation'.[15] Others, Georg Brandes in the first rank, suggested sexual sublimation. But perhaps a fate worse than this for the reception of Kierkegaard's thought was for his works to be selectively and badly read.[16] Once the politically involved critics and literary theorists took over, the pattern of superficial reading and expropriation was to become the norm. Brandes himself, that very Brandes whose nanny had told him to make sure he pulled his trousers down evenly over his boots, was to weave Kierkegaard into his own anti-establishment campaign against Denmark's cultural isolation.[17] Even if the project had been one Kierkegaard might have had reason to support, it is hard to say whether he would have done so on Brandes's terms. By that time the division between the believers, the romantics, and the politically conservative who opposed Brandes and the free-thinking cultural and politicians liberals of the left who took his side had become one in which Kierkegaard cannot easily be placed. It was nevertheless Brandes who espoused Kierkegaard's 'cause' and spread the word. He himself, scorned by the conservatives in Denmark as an 'atheist Jew' and debarred from a professorship in aesthetics because of his anti-establishment activities, moved to Berlin. There, influenced by Nietzsche, he was just on the point of interesting the latter in Kierkegaard's work when the German philosopher became mentally ill.

In Germany, however, Kierkegaard was to find other readers. In fact he had already had one for some time, an itinerant Scandinavian whose travels took him to Munich and Dresden and who had begun assimilating Kierkegaardian motifs ever since, in the later 1840s acquiring a copy of *Either/Or* while still an apothecary's apprentice in a small town on the Norwegian coast. Whether Henrik Ibsen (1828–1906) had his copies of Kierkegaard with him on his travels between 1864 and 1892, or just kept the motifs in his head, it is remarkable to think that among the many works Ibsen wrote in far-off Rome was a verse play heavily loaded with Kierkegaardian symbolism, *Brand*.

Though it produces some surprising results, the sharp division in Denmark between conservatives and liberals provides a useful frame for charting the further course of the reception of Kierkegaard in Europe and the world at large. One fairly surprising result is that what rightly deserves to be put on the conservative side embraces positions as far apart except in their shared illiberalism as communism and National Socialism, defenders of which on either side would appeal to the same division in stressing their mutual difference. Georg Lukács and Emanuel Hirsch illustrate the point. Hirsch, whose translations of Kierkegaard did much to further interest and research in Germany, biased both his readings and his translations in favour of an existence theology favourable to the National Socialist movement. Lukács (1885–1971), the Hungarian writer who later became the twentieth century's leading Marxist intellectual, although later to criticize the 'self-mortifying subjectivism' of Kierkegaard's critique of Hegel, in his youth idolized Kierkegaard. Having encountered his works in the intellectual circles of his (like Kierkegaard's) prolonged student days in Heidelberg, Lukács even saw his own late radical choice of communism as a case of a Kierkegaardian leap.

Lukács's case is particularly interesting for the insight it affords into the relation between Kierkegaard and the existentialism of Sartre and Merleau-Ponty.[18] In his confrontation with *Existenzphilosophie* after World War II, Lukács poured scorn on what he called this 'permanent carnival of fetishized inwardness' which continued, he said, to 'mesmerize and mislead bourgeois intellectuals'.[19] He held Edmund Husserl (1859–1938) and Martin Heidegger (1889–1976) historically as well as morally accountable, but also Kierkegaard. Both Kierkegaard and Nietzsche he described as 'antidemocratic', and he held them responsible for the 'destruction of reason'.

However, Lukács's pupil Lucien Goldmann considered Lukács himself to be the true father of *Existenzphilosophie*. Lukács's first book, *Soul and Form* (1910), contains a decidedly appreciative though critical piece on Kierkegaard, entitled 'The Foundering of Form on Life',[20] and much of Lukács's earlier work reads as though it were an attempt to bring Kierkegaardian themes to bear on social problems in pre–World War I Europe. In asking ourselves what happened in the intervening years to cause this change of mind or heart, it is worth noting how tempered is the later criticism. According to Lukács, Kierkegaard (and Schopenhauer too) still had some of that 'good faith' and 'consistency' which the existentialist philosophers were engaged in 'casting off' as they 'increasingly became apologists of bourgeois decadence'.[21] Perhaps what the later Lukács saw in these earlier writers was some kind of heroic example that allowed them to escape the charges of decadence that he now levelled at their works. Or was there even something in Kierkegaard's writings themselves that positively protects them, even in Lukács's eyes, from those charges?

In that early essay, Lukács accuses Kierkegaard of having made a poem out of his life. It all began with that act both of renunciation and deception, the 'gesture', by which Kierkegaard jilted Regine and, by adopting the role of cynical reprobate, tried in furtherance of his love for her to expunge from her mind all traces of his own life. Lukács points out that, as an attempt on Kierkegaard's part to free Regine for a future untrammelled by vestiges of their common past, it was futile from the start. But what Kierkegaard had really done, Lukács says, was

to sacrifice ordinary life for a poet's existence. He suggests that Kierkegaard's religiosity derives from his poetic need for a transcendental locus
of an idealized love, beyond the fluctuations and pettiness of ordinary
human relationships, a fictive relationship in which the actual object of
love no longer stands in the way of that love.[22] The ordinary and
everyday is sacrificed to creativity, but with the love itself preserved in
a purified and 'unreal' form. The religiosity in Kierkegaard's works is
thus not, as Kierkegaard presents it, a 'second movement' *back* to reality
for which resignation of one's love to a higher being is a necessary
preliminary; it is simply a requirement of resignation itself: to preserve
the love in an unreal form there must be a transcendent God to preserve
it. A line can be traced directly from Regine to the transcendental God
of love 'above' and 'beyond' the everyday 'sometimes-you're-right-
sometimes-I'm-right' world, a God for isolated human beings against
whom they are always in the wrong.

As Lukács sees it, Kierkegaard was forcing an intractable infinity into
a mould formed of personally significant but life-defying choices. If
true, that suggests that Kierkegaard failed, in his own life, to practise
the view we have seen that he preached from the start, namely that
form should not be imposed on life but be held onto as it emerges from
life through experience. Lukács might be right here, and we noted the
difficulty in reconciling Kierkegaard's conservatism in this respect with
his demand for unified (formed) action. For Lukács, Kierkegaard
bravely froze objective time with its plethora of possibilities into moments which purported to disambiguate an inherently ambiguous reality. In his subsequent *Theory of the Novel* (1916) Lukács was to say that
the novelist fabricates forms embracing subject and world where the
world itself offers no such visible unities.[23] But if the novelist's passion
is in this way a useless one, how much more so is the passion with
which one makes a novel of one's own life! Kierkegaard's 'heroism',
says Lukács, was that he wanted to 'create forms from life', that he
lived 'in such a way that every moment of his life became rounded into
the grand gesture'.[24] His 'honesty' was that he 'saw a crossroads and
walked to the end of the road he had chosen'. But his 'tragedy' was that
he wanted to live 'what cannot be lived', since, although the whole of
life is the poet's raw material, by trying to give limit and significance to
'the deliquescent mass of reality', he simply spites that reality. The
choice the poet makes is never a choice of an absolute, and the choice

never makes him absolute, never a 'thing in itself and for itself'.[25] In short (and as Kierkegaard himself would in principle agree), the poet as such never touches bottom. Kierkegaard's greatness, then, according to the young Lukács, lay in the special situation and talents that enabled him to conduct his outwardly successful campaign against life's necessity. Yet, really, by giving 'every appearance of victory and success', all that these specious advantages did was to lure him 'deeper and deeper' into 'the all-devouring desert', as Lukács says, 'like Napoleon in Russia'.[26]

In the belief that he was aligning himself constructively with an historical process of humanization, Lukács himself was later to be lured quite literally into Russia, the real Russia which proved a far more consuming desert. So one wonders whether some countercharge might be made on Kierkegaardian premises. Might it be said that, in spite of his life being politically engaged in a way that Kierkegaard's never was, Lukács scarcely touched bottom either? As the title indicates, *Soul and Form* was influenced by the neo-Kantian notion that human subjectivity impresses forms on an inchoate manifold, not in the limited 'transcendental' context within which Kant himself worked, but in the wider post-Hegelian (but also neo-Kantian) context of historical forms of consciousness, which include everything from anthropology to culture and art. In a central chapter, Lukács gives pride of place to the concept Kierkegaard appeals to so insistently in forming a picture of his life, namely tragedy. Among all the forms that consciousness can take, tragedy is privileged in something like the traditional epistemological sense, as it is the self-conscious form of the soul in which reality is faced most fully and openly, with 'death – the limit in itself' as an 'ever immanent reality', a thought that was at that same time forming itself in the mind of Heidegger as the notion of 'being-towards-death'.

Interpreting and responding to the full acknowledgement of finitude, which is where Romantic irony leads, can be done in several ways. Kierkegaard's way is to describe the form of consciousness in which it occurs as one of total isolation in which the self, conscious of finitude as a limit, interprets itself as poised before possibilities that transcend that limit. Heidegger's is to insist that the self has no such possibilities and that mankind is circumscribed by its ongoing finite projects. Lukács represents a third response: the overcoming of tragedy. It is customary, following Goldmann, to see this as the gist of Lukács's path-breaking

History and Class Consciousness (1923).[27] But if so, it is a special kind of overcoming. Tragic consciousness here is not a privileged position from which the solution to tragedy first comes into view then, as in Kierkegaard, to be embraced or rejected. On the contrary, genuinely overcoming tragedy means discovering that the tragic form of consciousness is neither essential nor privileged. So the later Lukács in effect revises his early notion of the sense of finitude as affording privileged access to reality, now rejecting as too 'narrow' the access to reality implied by the notion of the anxious individual consciousness. *History and Class Consciousness* widens the epistemological base to embrace the shared, collective perspective of the proletariat. Thus the mature Lukácsian view is that what is needed for establishing an authentic relationship to reality is not the individual soul's tragic insight but insight into the actual disrelationships – provisional, contingent tragedies one might say – to be found in existing societies. Lukács thus came to deny that anxiety and despair afford a fundamental perspective on the human condition, seeing them as a psychopathological detour which can and should be avoided.

In Lukács's thought there is a clear and acknowledged Hegelian element, also to be found in Kierkegaard. A Hegelian would find any attempt to provide a solution to the tragic consciousness that simply takes that form of consciousness for granted to be totally 'undialectical'. It is as though the sense of tragedy could be conceived as in some way an eternally valid cognitive vantage-point at which humanity has finally arrived and must take at its face value. Any proposed solution must regard it as an unsurpassable spiritual fact, a fact which itself lays down the conditions for human fulfilment. It is precisely an assumption of this kind that provokes cries of 'decadence' from Hegelians.

Wolf Lepenies nicely expresses this point of view: '[T]he element of reflection in bourgeois melancholy was not a phenomenon of rational thought; rather, it represented a return of dis-empowered subjectivity to itself and the attempt to make a means of self-confirmation out of the inhibition of action.'[28] This is the conventional critique of decadentism: the philosophy that seeks subjective solutions to subjective problems, and tries in this way to legitimate the condition in which the problem itself arises. For the Hegelian, since the solution reflects the problem, it does not constitute a genuine escape. Reinterpreting the problem as a necessary precondition of the solution is really nothing more than a narcissistic reflection of melancholy itself. It isn't hard to see how a Hegelian might read Kierkegaard too in this light, for we see once again how Kierkegaard's concept of faith might be diagnosed as a de facto acceptance of despair, an attempt to legitimate despair rather than to 'overcome' it. To overcome despair in the style proper to Hegelians, one must locate and define the 'limited' forms of consciousness out of which it emerges. Subjectivity and its travails can be pinpointed as bourgeois and in the long term as surpassable contingencies of the human condition. Thus idleness and ennui – along with the novel – arise in a certain phase of capitalist society. But, inside the frame of that society's own self-image, these negative features are given positive interpretations. The subjectivity in which they arise secures its own legitimacy as the medium of authenticity, martyrdom, suffering for the truth, sin, personal redemption, or just plain decadence which now acquires metaphysical status. But, says this rationale, whatever the flavour of the positive philosophies erected on it, the solutions here are no less decadent than the problems.

It should be clear that Kierkegaardian subjectivity is not at all undialectical in this way. The successive 'spheres' do not form solutions to problems defined by their predecessors. The 'solution' provided by the religious stages, for example, diagnoses melancholy and despair in religious terms, and therefore as problems of a quite different kind and description. Thus there is a deep divide between the ersatz heroisms of authenticity, or 'positive' decadence of the kind Lukács finds in twentieth-century existentialism, and the Kierkegaardian notion that the Good can materialize only in individual wills aligned to tasks done consistently and in good faith. The latter amounts to an entirely *new* form of consciousness, as new and radical as the one that Lukács adopted when he chose a transindividual solution to tragic consciousness. It is this genuinely revolutionary feature that made other left-wing thinkers like Adorno and Marcuse take Kierkegaard seriously as a genuinely edifying thinker, as when Marcuse concedes that Kierkegaard's existentialism 'embod[ies] many traits of a deep-rooted social theory'.[29] By the same token it was just this revolutionary feature that post–World War II existentialism lacked. Without the religious point of view and its heroic promise of a world socialized by individual conscience in a distributive relationship to God, there remained only 'authenticity' or the cult of subjectivity as an end in itself, what Lukács calls 'bourgeois decadence'.

In a way then, although Lukács is right about the existentialists, he is much closer to Kierkegaard than he allows, also in the way in which he prosecutes his version of 'reality' against their common foe, the bourgeoisie. Lukács and Kierkegaard are both martyrs to the cause of what they assume is the Good. Even the terms of their cultural criticism run parallel. Most of what Lukács says about decadent literature can be paraphrased in terms of Anti-Climacus's typology of despair, except that what Kierkegaard calls despair Lukács calls irrationality. But since what Lukács calls irrationality is the failure to face the possibility of a humanized world in the way *he* believed that must be done, the real disagreement is about the method and content of humanization. What sets the later Lukács apart most decisively from Kierkegaard is that he systematically ignored the possibility of an *un*fetishized subjectivity. True to Marxist form and what it derives from turning Hegel upside down, he assumed that the answer to all the travails of subjectivity can be given indiscriminately in terms of some trans-individual realm of forces to be controlled and diverted so as to produce some special state of human being, a state in which tragedy and despair no longer occur. As a self-appointed custodian of the 'subjectivities' of the great writers – Dante, Shakespeare, Balzac, Mann, Tolstoy – whose works he interpreted as sources of insight into the course that the historical process should take, Lukács felt that by preserving a heritage that would one day be the property of the people he was saving communism from its antihumanistic image. A noble and humanistic aim. If this was Lukács's heroism, *his* honesty might lie in a proved commitment to the belief that literature is the irrational soul's striving for expression with mankind as its topic, and that in order to be 'really', rather than fictitiously and decadently, about mankind, literature must catch onto history. In this way, it can be said of Lukács, too, that he walked to the end of the road he had chosen.

Although for Lukács to overcome tragedy meant overcoming the aesthetics of subjectivity, something that sounds Kierkegaardian, their notions of the role of the eternal differ profoundly. To have the eternal become a feature of the self is, for Lukács, to lift the self *out* of reality and leave it in stasis. The eternal is what, if you yourself bring it into time, brings you yourself, not a history, but to a stop. For Kierkegaard, however, that would be what Hegelians would call a 'bad' eternal. Stasis and sterility, boredom and ennui, take over only when the aesthetic is developed into a cult that *refuses* any kind of continuity and declines to take on a form in life – though not, we must bear in mind, by imposing it on what is already a form in the making. To Lukács, Kierkegaard's idea of the 'eternal' in one's self looks like that of fixing a path for oneself ahead of history in defiance of reality. What we gather from the pseudonymous works, from *Either/Or* to *The Sickness unto Death*, however, as well as from the signed *A Literary Review*, is the idea or ideal of a constant readiness to solve ethical tasks, precisely by providing a dimension of inner time or continuity which allows human (and other) value originally to manifest itself. Form does not *founder* on life, it is what makes the life of value possible.

Lukács wanted to live a life for humanism, but when he found his bourgeois clothes ill-suited to the better self, he reached resolutely into the wardrobe and seized a commissar's uniform. Choosing the part of a militant 'we', he embarked on his own inner history, choosing to be directed by the 'dialectic of the historical process'.[30] Certainly he saw better than Kierkegaard the tragedy of human exploitation, and his contribution was to bring humanizing insights to bear on the prevailing Marxist interpretation of that tragedy. But it remained an essentially intellectual contribution. In Kierkegaardian terms that would mean it was also an aesthetic one. Lukács managed to live most of his revolutionary life in a world of literature, in the belief that there lay humanity's insight into its own humanization. In reality, having appointed himself its guardian, he was taking the European heritage hostage. Such a life is a doubly vicarious participation in the life of poetic subjectivity, and Kierkegaard might have pointed out that it was Lukács's own way of making a poem of his life. Lukács's tragedy, he might have said, was to fail to see through the myth of the universal 'we' and to detect *its* dehumanizing power.

Yet there is much that left-wing thinkers like Lukács and Adorno have in common with Kierkegaard, among them the idea that the 'aesthetic' is a growth point, not just a locus of sterility and decadence. Another shared motif is *Bildung*. Art provides exemplars of character, or rather exemplary art does so. It would be interesting to know what Lukács made of that in many other ways admirable author Hans Christian Andersen. Lukács much admired the *Bildung* aspect of Thomas Mann's work, and indeed it makes sense to say that the influence of Kierkegaardian motifs in early twentieth-century literature is quite ac-

curately mirrored in what Lukács approved of in it. An early apprentice
to the kinds of self-conscious sensitivity and self-questioning that was
an inheritance from the Romantics, Lukács himself had an appreciation
not only of the character-building side, where he distances himself from
Kierkegaard's religious emphasis, but also of the emotional intensity
and dramatic 'collisions' of inner experience as these come to expression
in Dostoevsky and Kafka. Of the latter's works Lukács wrote that they
'symbolize art's helplessness, the terrifying vision of anxiety based on
the conviction that man is completely at the mercy of the incomprehensible and impenetrable terror', and he says that Kafka 'expresses an
elemental Platonic horror at the sight of an alien reality'.[31] As for his
regard for Ibsen, Lukács, like Kierkegaard a rich man's son, as reward
for graduating with distinction from the gymnasium in 1902 was given
a ticket by his father to visit the ailing Norwegian dramatist in Christiania. The great man left an indelible impression on the seventeen-year-
old, who travelled there with his tutor.[32] Later Lukács wrote a seminal
essay on Ibsen and even staged *The Wild Duck* in Budapest in his own
Hungarian translation from a German version. On leaving Heidelberg
he took with him his enthusiasm for Kierkegaard too, to a group of
friends (which included Bartok) who met regularly, and whom in 1918
he informed of the leap of faith that transformed this member of the
intellectual nobility into a people's commissar.[33]

In matters of literary and cultural history one must be wary in
accepting either claims or disclaimers of allegiance. The case of Lukács
shows that this is true even when the allegiance is at what might be
called firsthand. It takes a thorough look at the thought of the thinkers
themselves to see where similarity and difference lie. An important
feature of cultural development, whether it is considered to be growth
or decadence, is the absence of any guarantee of transitivity in the
influence on one author who again influences another. Just as Hamann
was one of Kierkegaard's literary mentors, so Kierkegaard has become
that of another generation, indeed several. One may be as suspicious of
the relationship of influence in one single link as one should be of the
whole chain. How much of Hamann, for instance, do we see in Kierkegaard? Very likely much less than a superficial appraisal suggests. We
may have to say the same of those now described, even by themselves,
as following in Kierkegaard's footsteps. It is interesting to speculate, on
the evidence of his response to Schopenhauer (1788–1860), how Kier-

kegaard would have taken to Nietzsche (1844–1900) or to Dostoevsky (1821–1881), both names with which he came to be closely linked at the beginning of the twentieth century. Nor must we forget the extraordinarily influential Swiss Protestant theologian Karl Barth (1886–1968), who provides a welcome counterweight to the attentions of the National Socialist Hirsch. Barth, who rejected natural theology and its implied basis in the belief that there is some similarity between creatures and God, once said that if he had a system it was limited to Kierkegaard's infinite qualitative distinction between time and eternity.

There is a tendency among literary and cultural historians to place artists and writers in groups when all that links them are certain things in the air. Whether a dramatist and novelist like Arthur Schnitzler (1862–1931), who has many Kierkegaardian traits, actually read Kierkegaard is largely academic, as is whether, if he did do so, he read him well. Many of the ideas of an original writer gain currency, and ideas once current catch on anyway. Would the Spanish existentialist philosopher Miguel de Unamuno y Jugo (1864–1936) have produced something recognizably Kierkegaardian even if he had not read Kierkegaard in his early days (as witness his *Tragic Sense of Life* [1913])?[34] The answers can differ from case to case, as with the comparatively early influence of Kierkegaard in Japan, where there is a long tradition of careful Kierkegaard scholarship. Among the many writers who clearly did read Kierkegaard, from Joyce to Updike, or from de Beauvoir and Sartre to Derrida and beyond, apart from the degree of influence there also arises the question of symmetry: if it is true that they are all influenced by and not just interested in Kierkegaard, how much of Kierkegaard is there in what *they* write? As for the 'existentialists' themselves, some like Sartre denied being influenced by Kierkegaard at all, and Heidegger, who denied being an existentialist, was only sparingly appreciative. Yet, in their cases, as in the critical appreciation of a Lukács, one may be more inclined to disagree with these claims and judgments just because they clearly shared with Kierkegaard so much of the background on which their criticism and the reasons for their disclaimers build.

With regard to the wide appreciation Kierkegaard has received at the hands of the descendants of those liberals and realists who backed Brandes, we should be more chary. There is a huge ambiguity here. The symmetry may on the one hand be less evident than ever; the

Kierkegaard these writers and readers know is the one they find of themselves in what they read of Kierkegaard. Yet on the other hand, they can claim that this is exactly what the Kierkegaard of the pseudonymous authorship with its indirect communication wanted of his reader, so that what we have here is maximal symmetry, and they may claim instead to be the authentic Kierkegaardians.

A book like the present one can only take note of the continuing influence of its subject's writings as that which makes the biography worth writing. It cannot judge, let alone adequately describe, the life of the works. Whether and how far their continuing influence, now spreading under the patronage of Wittgenstein even into the philosophy of language, combines symmetry with transitivity is a matter for much discussion and no doubt for unending research. As for why Kierkegaard's writings are so variously appreciated (or in some quarters vilified), no single straightforward answer seems possible.

Irony with its alienating influence may be one clue. But the ironical stance is open to many interpretations and can be responded to in many ways: aesthetically, ethically, religiously. Looking at that stance, as well as from it, may provide a focus that reveals more of the core of Kierkegaard's thought than the hitherto-preferred concentration on his historical role as an important critic of the Hegel of·the *Encyclopedia*. There may be more to our advantage in the challenge that Kierkegaard mounts to Hegel's crucial claim that nothing good ('justice, morality, and truth') can come of irony.[35] At least such a focus makes better sense of the wide range of uses to which Kierkegaard has been put, and it may explain why people see in his writings things so apparently far apart as the revitalizing of religion and anticipations of postmodernism.

The causes Kierkegaard has been identified with are as legion as they are as little representative of what, when we read him in connection with his life, seems to have given depth and breadth to his own thought. The designations and headings under which he is made to fall often belong to a wide-angled view of the cultural terrain – places, or even whole continents, on maps whose coordinates are the inventions of a new generation of paragraph-ploughers. Apart from testifying to the continued life of the works, the existence of these maps and their locations does, however, contribute in its way to that continuation, and therefore also to the interest a reader may have in a work like the present one. No biography is definitive and every biography is inescapably fictional, but a reader who has reflected on the writer's life may feel better placed to judge the claims people make for the writings. We will know better how to judge those who find in Kierkegaard's writing an 'astonishing reassertion of the radical pietistic vision' that finally shattered the fortifications of 'critical reason' put up by Fichte, Hegel, and Schelling.[36] We may know better how to conceive his 'brilliant discovery of the concept of radical choice', and what to make of such claims as that Kierkegaard introduced single-handedly the now typically confrontational mode of 'moral discourse',[37] or that it was his intention in the dissertation to 'expose the root of irony in Western thought and to uncover the hidden source of both Romantic irony and the Hegelian rejection of it, in the uniquely personal contribution of Socrates to the foundation of the dialectical imagination'.[38]

Acute and perceptive as these and other thumbnail attributions often are, they invite us to read Kierkegaard from somewhere quite far from his elbow. The nearer we approach his elbow and catch glimpses of what steered it both to and on the page, the less easy it is to be convinced by the picture sometimes conveyed of an astute manipulator of world culture working from a self-imposed exile in his own land. One benefit of a biography is to make it easier to winnow the unintended consequences of a writer's thought from those that motivated his writing, and in the end to make better-informed judgments about where Kierkegaard himself would feel at home among the many trends with which his name has been connected.

It is always tempting, under the aegis of one's respect for an author from the past, to edit away the 'outdated' and local elements, either just in order to highlight his prescience or simply – though it may prove a back-handed compliment – to show how much of what *we* appreciate is to be found in his works, if clothed in another style. But the deliberate domestication of an author in this way – a form of preemptive appropriation – can lead to absurd results. If, to be welcome in one home, the author must shed habits that make him welcome in another – and that process is repeated for as many movements as claim his sponsorship – in the end there may be no more to the brand name everyone cherishes than a heterogeneous sampling of what is local to themselves.

But how else, some will ask, can we deal with the past except in the language and from the perspective of the present? It's a good question, and the answer may be that we cannot do otherwise. But surely we can try, and surely we should. The belief that the present enjoys a vantage-point that enables it to grasp the past better than the past grasped itself is, after all, extraordinarily complacent – it is also, of course, Hegelian. But cultural historians themselves distinguish between history, on the one hand, and heritage on the other. Our heritage is the past seen as continuous with our present, a past we feel at home in since it is those large parts of it that are still around us, even in us, that acquire that name; in uncovering our heritage we need not greatly concern ourselves with what the past was really like. Historians, however, do concern themselves with that; for them history is a quest for truth to which any possessive hold on the past must be considered an obstacle.[39] So it is also, and however sketchily and imperfectly, with biography. You could of course say, adopting a heritage point of view, that what the author means to us is nothing over and above the meaning his writings have for us, and that applies to any present that is now past. Works too have their own history, as acknowledged in the hermeneuticist's concept of a text's *Wirkungsgeschichte* (effective history). There could be a history of the effective history of a text, the *bios* of the *grafé*, and in the case of Kierkegaard's writings that might make for a fascinating study. Our own concern has been with the life of the author, but also with the texts – in the context of their author's life, his present. That this concern with history has a point can be illustrated. In the twenties a Scandinavian cultural historian wrote:

Behind Ibsen's *Brand* stands one of the mightiest philosophical figures of the nineteenth century – Søren Kierkegaard, one of the greatest moral anarchists of all time. He is a pure product of the German Romantic situation and thus a thorough-bred Romantic, as well as a clear-minded know-all, a fearless experimenter of the soul, a savourer of every kind of psychological possibility and state, prepared for a boundless life's flux almost suggestive of some of Bergson's ideas. He tried to unite the Romantic notion of individuality with radical, personal inwardness in order to reach the absolute by an act of will through the paradox. In opposition to classical pietism with a kind of Platonic Eros concept at its centre, we get a Romantic pietism which with him develops a completely morbid and revolutionary disposition. . . .[40]

Learned statements like these appear to cast light on the past, but do they? Didn't Kierkegaard strive mightily to distance himself from the Romantics? Or has the author concluded that Kierkegaard protested too much, enough to suggest that at heart he really was a Romantic? That would be to go further than history. What history tells us is that Kierkegaard, though greatly interested in the Romantics, found it a fatal flaw of Romanticism that it gave no foothold for his 'category of the individual'.

The author in this case was writing of his present, and it is quite natural for him to view his antecedents in the light of the cultural conflicts of his own time. Yet these may differ significantly from those of the time in which the antecedents wrote. How they differ is for cultural historians to decide or endlessly debate. The task of this book has been to treat its subject historically, which among other things means accepting that there may be serious *dis*continuities with the present. There may even be voices as yet unheard, and things that we are even unable to hear – for reasons Kierkegaard himself has not been slow to give. He spoke of wanting to preserve his 'heterogeneity' as an author, thinking first and foremost of his relationship to his contemporaries. He would surely wish to extend that same wish to us. Can we claim to know any better than they what that difference was that he wished to preserve? Do we really have any idea at all of what it was he was driving at? The thin, slightly piping voice murmurs from the grave,

Here I lie, poor Kierkegaard, buried whole by generations of gravediggers, but as for my works – sorry, I mean my *work*, it has been world-historically jointed and salted, not just in a single § in the way they couldn't manage with Lessing, but scattered in a seemingly endless number of §§.

He may have himself to blame, and it is still a question whether the works make one work, and if so what. But I hope he would have appreciated this one attempt among many possible others to collect the *disjecta membra* of his life and work in the light of some idea of what it was that drove him to write.

Notes

1. IV A 85 (see references to the journals that follow).

Chapter 1

1. See George Pattison, *'Poor Paris!': Kierkegaard's Critique of the Spectacular City* (Kierkegaard Studies: Monograph Series 2, edited by Niels Jørgen Cappelørn and Christian Tolstrup), Berlin and New York: Walter de Gruyter, 1999, p. 144.
2. See Bruce H. Kirmmse, *Kierkegaard in Golden Age Denmark*, Bloomington and Indianapolis: Indiana University Press, 1990, p. 12.
3. Though of less interest economically, Greenland, the second largest island in the world after Australia, had also become a Danish colony. And until 1814, when Norway was ceded to Sweden according to the terms of the Treaty of Kiel in 1813 (as a reward for assisting Napoleon), that country too had, for four hundred years, been a province of Denmark. Not a few 'Danish' celebrities (for instance the eighteenth-century poet, playwright, and philosopher Ludvig Holberg) were Norwegian by birth, though because until 1811 (when the present University of Oslo was founded in what was then Kristiania [and later Christiania]) the province's administrators were educated in Copenhagen, the distinction between Dane and Norwegian in those social circles was not always clear, and the language they spoke was called Dano-Norwegian.
4. See Kirmmse, *Kierkegaard in Golden Age Denmark*, pp. 81–4.
5. See Paul Johnson, *The Birth of the Modern: World Society 1815–1830*, New York: HarperCollins, 1991.
6. See Kirmmse, *Kierkegaard in Golden Age Denmark*, pp. 12 ff., for an account of the historical background.
7. See Kirmmse's excellent survey, ibid., Chapter 4, especially pp. 47–50.
8. *Encounters with Kierkegaard: A Life as Seen by His Contemporaries*, collected, edited, and annotated by Bruce H. Kirmmse, translated by Bruce H. Kirmmse and Virginia R. Laursen, Princeton, NJ: Princeton University Press, 1996, p. 63. My translations sometimes differ, and page references to the originals are

given in parentheses to *Søren Kierkegaard truffet. Et Liv set af hans Samtidige*, collected, edited, and annotated by Bruce H. Kirmmse, Copenhagen: C. A. Reitzels Forlag, 1996 (pp. 98–9).

9. Kirmmse, *Encounters*, p. 64 (99).
10. Ibid., p. 22 (43). The letter gives Ostermann's account of the circumstances of the talk.
11. Ibid., p. 63 (99).
12. Ibid., p. 21 (42).
13. Where it was published 22 January 1836; ibid., p. 20 (42).
14. *Søren Kierkegaards Papirer* (*Papirer*), edited by P. A. Heiberg and V. Kuhr, second and enlarged edition by Niels Thulstrup, København: Gyldendal, 1968, I A 75, dated 1 August 1835 (also in Søren Kierkegaard, *Papers and Journals: A Selection*, Harmondsworth: Penguin, 1996, p. 36).
15. Kirmmse, *Encounters*, p. 22 (42)
16. Ibid., p. 20 (42).
17. *Papirer*, I B 2, p. 157. The talk is reproduced on pp. 157–78.
18. Matt. 13:31; Mark 4:30; Luke 13:18.
19. *Papirer*, I B 2, pp. 158–9.
20. Ibid., p. 159.
21. Ibid., p. 160.
22. Ibid., pp. 160–1.
23. Ibid., p. 161.
24. Ibid. See *Papirer*, I A 12, 17 September 1834 (*Papers and Journals: A Selection*, p. 12).
25. *Papirer*, I B 2, p. 162.
26. Ibid., pp. 163–4.
27. See Teddy Petersen, *Kierkegaards polemiske debut. Artikler 1834–36 i historisk sammenheng*, Odense: Odense Universitetsforlag, 1977, pp. 55, 103, and 161 n.8. The translations are my own.
28. *Papirer*, I B 2, p. 173.
29. Ibid.
30. Ibid., pp. 172–3.
31. *Papirer*, I A 75, p. 56, 1 August 1835 (*Papers and Journals: A Selection*, p. 35).
32. *Papirer*, I B 2, p. 174.
33. Ibid., pp. 174–5.
34. Ibid., p. 172.
35. For useful references see Frederick C. Beiser, *Enlightenment, Revolution, and Romanticism: The Genesis of Modern German Political Thought 1790–1800*, Cambridge, MA: Harvard University Press, 1992. Heiberg had translated Scribe's libretto to the French composer Daniel Auber's three-act opera *The Bride*. Auber (1782–1871) wrote lively and piquant music. George Pattison, to whom I owe the reference to Schlegel, cites Schlegel's comment that the great events of the age were the French Revolution, Fichte's *Science of Knowledge*, and Goethe's *Wilhelm Meister*.
36. Frederik Christian Sibbern, one of Kierkegaard's teachers in a textbook entitled

Theory of Thought or Logic (third and enlarged edition, Copenhagen, 1866, pp. 279–80), and in a style mercifully never adopted by his student, defines science's (or knowledge's) 'idea' in a typically Germanic construction almost impossible to render into English. A literal translation would be roughly as follows: an 'all-encompassing, first-moving and constitutive-of-the-essence-of-the-self-building-and-continually-educating-and-freshly-renewing wholeness of cognitions, especially insofar as an Ideal or image of fulfilment, an exemplar, hovers before one's eyes.'

37. *Papirer*, I B 2, p. 172.
38. Ibid.
39. See George Pattison, 'Art in an Age of Reflection', in Alastair Hannay and Gordon D. Marino (eds), *The Cambridge Companion to Kierkegaard*, Cambridge University Press, 1997, pp. 80–1.
40. J. L. Heiberg, *Om Philosophiens Betydning for den nuværende Tid*, in *J. L. Heibergs prosaiske Skrifter*, Kjøbenhavn: C. A. Reitzels Forlag, 1861, p. 385.
41. Ibid., pp. 384–5.
42. Ibid., pp. 391–2.
43. Cf. J. L. Heiberg: 'The speculative idea in its immediate expression is the beautiful or the aesthetic idea' ('Indledning til Philosophien i Alimindelighed og Logik i Saerdeleshed' [Guide to the Lectures on the Philosophy of Philosophy or Speculative Logic at the Royal Military College Academy], 1831–32, in *J. L. Heibergs Samlede Skrifter. Prosaiske Skrifter*, I. Bind, Kjøbenhavn: C. A. Reitzel, 1861, p. 369). The volume is not listed among the works sold at the auction of Kierkegaard's library on his death, but it is unthinkable that he had not dipped into it. In his early student days Kierkegaard held Heiberg to be superior as an aesthetician to any German author.
44. *Papirer*, I B 2, p. 172.
45. Ibid., pp. 177–8.
46. See Petersen, *Kierkegaards polemiske debut*, p. 59.
47. Orla Lehmann, 'Trykkfrihedssagen V', *Kjøbenhavnsposten*, 12 February 1836, reprinted in Petersen, *Kierkegaards polemiske debut*, p. 62.
48. Petersen, *Kierkegaards polemiske debut*, pp. 64–5. The summary to be given of the exchange draws on the same source; see pp. 60–102.
49. Ibid., pp. 105–8.
50. See Goethe's *Faust*, vv. 2322 ff.
51. This is recounted by Kierkegaard himself in a note added later to the papers from this period. See *Papirer*, I B 7.
52. In 1837 the then thirty-seven-year-old Hage took his own life. Shortly before, he had been sentenced by the government to lifelong censorship for publishing a number of liberal articles. See Kirmmse, *Encounters*, p. 275. The quotations from Hage's article are from Petersen, *Kierkegaards polemiske debut*, pp. 73–8.
53. Quotations from Kierkegaard's two-part article are from Petersen, *Kierkegaards polemiske debut*, pp. 78–88.
54. O'Connell (1775–1847), the well-known Irish leader of the time, whose astute activities in British politics did much for the nationalist cause.

55. Quotations from Lehmann's article are from Petersen, *Kierkegaards polemiske debut*, pp. 88–93.
56. Quotations from Kierkegaard's article are from Petersen, *Kierkegaards polemiske debut*, pp. 94–102.
57. The scholastic Buridan said that if a hungry ass were placed exactly between two haystacks in every respect equal, it would starve to death, because it would have no motive for going to one rather than the other.
58. *Papirer*, I B 6.
59. See Petersen, *Kierkegaards polemiske debut*, p. 149.
60. Kirmmse, *Encounters*, pp. 22–3 (43). The letter is dated 23 February 1836.

Chapter 2

1. See Kirmmse, *Kierkegaard in Golden Age Denmark*, pp. 23–5.
2. See Flemming Christian Nielsen, *Ind i verdens vrimmel: Søren Kierkegaards ukendte bror* (Into the World's Tumult: Søren Kierkegaard's Unknown Brother), Copenhagen: Holkenfeldt, 1998. Nielsen cites Henrik Stangerup's essay collection, *Tag din Seng og gå* (Take Up Thy Bed and Walk), Copenhagen: Gyldendal, 1986.
3. See the account in Carl Weltzer, *Peter og Søren Kierkegaard*, Kjøbenhavn: G. E. C. Gads Forlag, 1936, pp. 48ff.
4. *Papirer*, I A 331 from 1836.
5. *Papirer*, I A 68, dated 29 July 1835 (*Papers and Journals: A Selection*, p. 26)
6. From Michael Pedersen Kierkegaard's papers in the Royal Library. See Thompson, *Kierkegaard*, p. 24.
7. See *Papirer*, IV B 1 (*Johannes Climacus eller de omnibus dubitandum est*), pp. 106–7. The castle was Frederiksberg. See Josiah Thompson's biography, *Kierkegaard*, New York: Knopf, 1973, pp. 30–1 and 245.
8. *Papirer*, XI¹ A 299, p. 240.
9. The Moravian Church originated in the fifteenth-century Hussite movement (not to be confused with the Hutterites, named after Jakob Hutter, who was tortured and burned as a heretic and who also had a Moravian connection, the sect having gone to Moravia to seek refuge from persecution). Herrnhutism became a worldwide movement based on a theocratic conception of a combined church and civic life, of which the local Moravian communities were treated as anticipatory models.
10. See Kirmmse, *Kierkegaard in Golden Age Denmark*, pp. 31–5, for an account of Herrnhutism in Denmark.
11. J. P. Mynster, *Meddelelser om mit Levnet* (Communications about My Life), second printing, Copenhagen: Gyldendal, 1884, p. 24. Cited in Kirmmse, *Kierkegaard in Golden Age Denmark*, p. 102. See Kirmmse's Chapter 10 in *Kierkegaard in Golden Age Denmark* in general on Mynster.
12. See Kirmmse, *Kierkegaard in Golden Age Denmark*, pp. 34–5.
13. See Frederik Hammerich, *Ett Levnetsløb* (A Life), Copenhagen: Forlagsbureauet i Kjøbenhavn, 1882, p. 59. Cited in Thompson, *Kierkegaard*, p. 43.

14. *Papirer*, IX A 411 (*Papers and Journals: A Selection*, p. 342).

15. See Kirmmse, *Kierkegaard in Golden Age Denmark*, p. 236.

16. N. F. S. Grundtvig, *Værker i Udvalg*, vol. II, edited by Georg Christensen and Hal Koch, Copenhagen: Gyldendal, 1940, p. 326. See Kirmmse, *Kierkegaard in Golden Age Denmark*, p. 212.

17. *Verdens krønike* (World Chronicle), 1812.

18. See Weltzer, *Peter og Søren Kierkegaard*, p. 42, and Kirmmse, *Kierkegaard in Golden Age Denmark*, p. 218.

19. *Papirer*, I A 72, dated 1 June 1835 (*Papers and Journals: A Selection*, p. 29).

20. *Breve og Aktstykker vedrørende Søren Kierkegaard*, vols. I–II, edited by Niels Thulstrup, Copenhagen: Munksgaard, 1953 (English translation by. H. Rosenmeier, *S. Kierkegaard: Letters and Documents*, Princeton, NJ: Princeton University Press, 1978, page references in parentheses), I, p. 4 (5) (see *Papers and Journals: A Selection*, p. 4).

21. See Kirmmse, *Encounters*, pp. 8 and 9 (23–6).

22. Ibid., pp. 4–5, 7, 8, 10, 11 (20, 22, 24, 26–8).

23. *Papirer*, IV B 1, pp. 108–9. See Josiah Thompson, *Kierkegaard*, p. 31, where the opponent is taken to be a friend of his brother, from the university, brought home to meet his father.

24. The remark is by Meïr Aron Goldschmidt, with whose journal Kierkegaard had later become embroiled. See Kirmmse, *Encounters*, p. 84 (125).

25. See Weltzer, *Peter og Søren Kierkegaard*, p. 25.

26. *Papirer*, I A 72, 1 June 1835 (*Papers and Journals: A Selection*, p. 31).

27. *Breve og Aktstykker*, I, p. 4 (4) (see *Papers and Journals: A Selection*, p. 4).

28. See Kirmmse, *Encounters*, pp. 10 and 12 (26 and 27).

29. *Breve of Akstykker*, I, pp. 7–8 (9).

30. Ibid., p. 7 (8–9).

31. I owe these details to Jon Stewart.

32. The lectures on logic and psychology were published in *Menneskets aandelige natur og væsen* (Man's Spiritual Nature and Being), 2 vols., 1819–28, and republished in 1885 as *Læren om de menneskelige følelser og lidenskaber* (Theory of Human Emotions and Desires).

33. Kirmmse, *Encounters*, p. 19 (40).

34. See A. N. B. Fica's Introduction to a later edition of *En dansk students Eventyr*, Copenhagen: Gyldendalske Boghandel/Nordisk Forlag, 1934, pp. 27–8.

35. Poul M. Møller, *Efterladte Skrifter*, of 3 vols., Copenhagen: Bianco Lunds Bogtrykkeri, 1842, vol. 2, pp. 273–527.

36. *Søren Kierkegaard: Samlede Værker*, edited by A. B. Drachmann, J. L. Heiberg, and H. O. Lange (1901–6), revised edition 1920–36, revised again 1962, referred to as the third edition (SV^3), vol. 9, pp. 33–4 (*Concluding Unscientific Postscript*, translated by David F. Swenson and Walter Lowrie, Princeton: Princeton University Press, 1941, p. 34fn.), cf. p. 153; also in *Kierkegaard's Writings* [KW], translated by Howard V. Hong and Edna H. Hong, Princeton, NJ: Princeton University Press, 1992, vol. XII:1, p. 34, cf. p. 172,) in connection with a discussion by Møller of immortality, published in 1837 ('Tanker over Mulig-

heden af Beviser for Menneskets Udødelighed' [Thoughts on the Possibility of Proofs of Human Immortality], *Maanedsskrift for Litteratur*, no. 17, Copenhagen 1837, pp. 1–72 and 422–53). See P. M. Møller, *Efterladte Skrifter*, op. cit., vol. 2, pp. 158–72.

37. Lund was twice Kierkegaard's brother-in-law, both Nicolene and Petrea having married brothers of his. Weltzer notes that Søren's sense of affinity with Wilhelm Lund was due not necessarily to his absence abroad but to Lund's eirenic theism (Weltzer, *Peter og Søren Kierkegaard*, p. 21).

38. See Kirmmse, *Kierkegaard in Golden Age Denmark*, pp. 49, 59ff.

39. Kirmmse, *Encounters*, p. 196 (273).

40. See Carl Jørgensen, *Søren Kierkegaard. En Biografi*, København: Nyt Nordisk Forlag Arnold Busck, 1964, vol. I, p. 36.

41. See Kirmmse, *Kierkegaard in Golden Age Denmark*, p. 169.

42. 'One of Christian Lund's office staff was sent to Gilleleje to fetch Søren (the 30th of July), who couldn't return however until the next morning' (P. C. Kierkegaard, *Dagbogen*, p. 58).

43. Kirmmse, *Encounters*, p. 228 (314).

44. Ibid., p. 196 (273).

45. Ibid., p. 216 (295). Sibbern said that Kierkegaard had 'basically a very polemical nature, inclined to opposition' ('Han var i Grunden en meget polemisk Natur, tilbøjelig til Opposition'), but said he was surprised that someone who so hated newspaper agitation should 'end up an out-and-out journalist agitator himself'. This reference is to a later polemic.

46. He mentions Møller's comment in journal entries (e.g., *Papirer*, A 275 and 276 [*Papers and Journals: A Selection*, pp. 593]).

47. See Kirmmse, *Encounters*, p. 205 (283). The remark is attributed by Martensen to a friend (of Martensen's).

48. *Papirer*, V A 3, from 1844 (*Papers and Journals: A Selection*, p. 179). 'I was born the wrong fiscal year, in which so many other bad banknotes were put in circulation, and my life seems best compared to one of them. There is something of greatness about me, but because of the poor state of the market I am not worth much. And at times a banknote like that became a family's misfortune.' The reference is to unbacked currency issued by the government to meet the costs of rebuilding Copenhagen after the British bombardment in 1807 and other needs arising from the Napoleonic wars. See Chapter 1 of this volume.

49. *Papirer*, I C 20 and 23, from 1834.

50. The record of the Kierkegaard's family attendance at Communion, identifying those present and explaining absences, is due to Niels Jørgen Cappelørn. See Bruce H. Kirmmse, ' "Out With It!": The Modern Breakthrough, Kierkegaard and Denmark', in Hannay and Marino (eds), *The Cambridge Companion to Kierkegaard*, pp. 37–8.

51. See Weltzer, *Peter og Søren Kierkegaard*, p. 15.

52. It has been suggested (by Emanuel Hirsch, *Kierkegaard Studien*, vols. I-II, Gütersloh, 1933, II, pp. 490–2) that this letter included in the journals is part of a literary project Kierkegaard had in mind to write on Faustian themes with

which he was preoccupied both then and later. But it could also be an elaboration of a real letter. At least Kierkegaard received a letter from Lund several weeks later (see *Papirer*, I A 187) which was possibly a reply but is not preserved. Whether or not an indication of a general lack of interest in theology at the time, in *Papirer* (I C 19) there is a heading, 'H. N. Clausen's "Dogmatic Lectures'", dated 1834–5 but with no notes. There are, however, remarks inserted in Kierkegaard's own translation of Schleiermacher's *Christian Faith*, second edition (1830), pp. 3–70, which could stem from the lectures, though they may equally be the result of the tutoring session with Martensen.

53. See *Papirer*, I A 11, 12, 13, 15, 16, 18, 21, and 22 (*Papers and Journals: A Selection*, pp. 11–14).
54. *Breve og Aktstykker*, p. 37 (47–8) (letter no. 4).
55. *Papirer*, I A 75, dated 1 August 1835 (*Papers and Journals: A Selection*, p. 32).
56. *Papirer*, I A 75, dated 1 August 1835 (*Papers and Journals: A Selection*, p. 33).
57. *Papirer*, I A 72, dated 1 June 1835 (*Papers and Journals: A Selection*, p. 29).
58. *Papirer*, V B 47:13.
59. *Papirer*, I A 96, from 1835 (*Papers and Journals: A Selection*, p. 43).
60. *Papirer*, I C 61; cf. 46–53, 62–5.
61. *Papirer*, V A 108, from 1844 (*Papers and Journals: A Selection*, p. 183).
62. P. C. Kierkegaard, *Dagbogen*, p. 65; cf. Weltzer, *Peter og Søren Kierkegaard*, p. 87.
63. Thompson, *Kierkegaard*, p. 44.

Chapter 3

1. *Papirer*, I A 114, January 1836 (*Papers and Journals: A Selection*, p. 48).
2. *Papirer*, I A 13, 29 January 1835 (*Papers and Journals: A Selection*, p. 12).
3. Kirmmse, *Encounters*, pp. 207–8 (285–6).
4. *Papirer*, I A 12, 17 September 1834 (*Papers and Journals: A Selection*, p. 12).
5. *Papirer*, I A 51, 16 March 1835 (*Papers and Journals: A Selection*, p. 17).
6. Kirmmse, *Encounters*, p. 3 (19).
7. See Kirmmse, ' "Out with It!": The Modern Breakthrough, Kierkegaard and Denmark', in Hannay and Marino (eds), *The Cambridge Companion to Kierkegaard*, pp. 24 and 30 f.
8. *Papirer*, XI² A 439, from 1855 (*Papers and Journals: A Selection*, p. 647). That the entry may have less bearing on the circumstances discussed here is suggested by the possibility noted to me by George Pattison that the idea of coming into existence being a crime could be an allusion to Calderon de la Barca's *Life Is a Dream*, a work known in Copenhagen at the time.
9. *Papirer*, II A 605, from 1837 (*Papers and Journals: A Selection*, p. 108).
10. *Papirer*, II A 491, from 1839 (*Papers and Journals: A Selection*, p. 104).
11. Poul M. Møller, *Efterladte Skrifter*, Copenhagen: Bianco Lunos Trykkeri, 1843, vol. 3, p. 329. Ahasuerus is the subject of several of Møller's *Strøtanker* (Aphorisms); see Børge Madsen's selection, in Poul Martin Møller, *Strøtanker*, København: Steen Hasselbachs Forlag, 1962, pp. 55–7.

12. *Papirer*, I C 64, from 1835; see I C 62 for Kierkegaard's source.

13. *Papirer*, I C 58, December 1835 (*Papers and Journals: A Selection*, p. 47).

14. *Papirer*, I A 150.

15. *Papirer*, I A 181, from 1836.

16. A figure in the play of the same name by Holberg.

17. *Papirer*, I A 333, from 1836–37 (*Papers and Journals: A Selection*, pp. 69–71).

18. *Papirer*, I A 91 and 89, 11 and 9 October 1835 respectively (*Papers and Journals: A Selection*, p. 39).

19. *Papirer*, I A 94, 17 October 1835 (*Papers and Journals: A Selection*, pp. 40–1).

20. *Papirer*, I C 73, March 1836, and I A 153, April 1836 (*Papers and Journals: A Selection*, p. 50).

21. *Papirer*, I A 162 (*Papers and Journals: A Selection*, p. 51).

22. *Papirer*, I A 154, April 1836 (*Papers and Journals: A Selection*, p. 50).

23. *Papirer*, I A 164, April 1836 (*Papers and Journals: A Selection*, p. 51).

24. *Papirer*, I A 161, from 1836 (*Papers and Journals: A Selection*, p. 50).

25. *Papirer*, I A 166, April 1836 (*Papers and Journals: A Selection*, p. 51).

26. *Papirer*, II A 520, 28 July 1839.

27. *Papirer*, VII[1] A 221.

28. *Papirer*, IV A 65.

29. *Papirer*, I A 331–2.

30. See Kirmmse, *Encounters*, p. 218 (297). The remark by Møller is mentioned in *Papirer*, XI[1] A 275 and 276. See Chapter 2, note 45, of this volume.

31. See Petersen, *Kierkegaards polemiske debut*, pp. 125 (where the passage is included in the article in question), 146–7.

32. Kirmmse, *Encounters*, p. 226 (311–12).

33. Ibid., p. 216 (295).

34. Ibid., p. 65 (102). Meïr Aron Goldschmidt, whose memory this is, was the former editor of *The Corsair*, about which more later. This occasion of their first meeting was in the summer of 1837 at the house of the mother of Goldschmidt's former teacher, and a friend of Kierkegaard's, Peter Rørdam. It was during the same summer, and at the same place, that Kierkegaard first met Regine Olsen. See Chapter 4.

35. Kirmmse, *Encounters*, pp. 229, 230, 249 (316, 343).

36. Ibid., p. 84 (125).

37. *Papirer*, I A 225, 19 August 1836 (*Papers and Journals: A Selection*, pp. 53–4).

38. *Papirer*, I A 242, 14 September 1836.

39. *Papirer*, I A 174, 13 June 1836.

40. *Papirer*, I A 177 (*Papers and Journals: A Selection*, p. 52).

41. P. M. Møller, *Statistisk Skildring af Lægsgaarden i Ølseby-Magle*, by a young geographer, Copenhagen and Kristiania: Gyldendalske Boghandel/Nordisk Forlag, 1919.

42. *Papirer*, II A 75, from 1837.

43. *Papirer*, II A 102, 6 July 1837. To which, somewhat curiously, he adds 'it is the haemorrhoid *non fluens*–the higher life's *molimina* [strainings to enable a discharge]'.

44. *Papirer*, I A 207, 19 July 1836 (*Papers and Journals: A Selection*, p. 52); I A 256, 36 August 1836, and I A 265, 27 October 1836.

45. *Sämtliche Werke. Historisch-Kritische Ausgabe*, edited by J. Nadler, Vienna: Herder, 1949–57, vol. II, pp. 40–1. See Frederick C. Beiser's account of Hamann in *The Fate of Reason*, pp. 16–29.

46. *Papirer*, XI¹ A 299 and IX A 411 (*Papers and Journals: A Selection*, p. 342).

47. Poul Martin Møller, 'Tanker over Muligheden af Beviser for Menneskets Udødelighed' (Thoughts on the Possibility of Proofs of Human Immortality), *Maanedsskrift for Litteratur*, no. 17, Copenhagen, 1837, pp. 1–72, 422–53.

48. *Papirer*, I A 273 (*Papers and Journals: A Selection*, p. 56). See page 52 of this volume.

49. *Papirer*, I A 305 (*Papers and Journals: A Selection*, p. 59).

50. *Papirer*, I A 285, 20 November 1836 (*Papers and Journals: A Selection*, p. 57).

51. *Papirer*, I A 304 (*Papers and Journals: A Selection*, p. 59).

52. *Papirer*, II A 37 (*Papers And Journals: A Selection*, pp. 81–2); cf. *Papirer*, I A 238.

53. *Papirer*, I A 239, 13 September 1836 (*Papers and Journals: A Selection*, pp. 54–5).

54. *Papirer*, I A 328, from 1836–37 (*Papers and Journals: A Selection*, pp. 66–9).

55. J. L. Heiberg, 'Inlednings-Foredrag til det i November 1834 begyndte logiske Cursus paa den kongelige militaire Høiskole' (Introductory Lecture to the Course in Logic Begun in November 1834 at the Royal Military College), first published in 1835 in Copenhagen by J. H. Schubothe's Bookstore (reprinted in Heiberg, *Prosaiske Skrifter* [*J. L. Heibergs samlede Skrifter*], vols. I–II, Copenhagen: C. A. Reitzel, 1861–62, I, pp. 461–516).

56. See Martensen in *Maanedsskrift for Litteratur*, no. 16, 1836, pp. 515 ff. ('If instead of seeking the eternal thought, which man himself did not imagine, [Hegel] had sought the eternal word, which man himself did not utter to himself, then he would have come to the Christian *logos*, and instead of finding only the Concept and reason in existence, he would have found the word and revelation.' [p. 527]), and later Sibbern, in *Maanedsskrift for Litteratur*, no. 19, 1838, pp. 283, ff., 424 ff., 546 ff.; no. 20, pp. 20 ff., 103 ff. 193 ff., 293 ff., 405 ff.

57. Kirmmse, *Encounters*, p. 217 (295–6); cf. p. 215 (294), where Kierkegaard's question asks 'what relation philosophy stands in to life in actuality [*i Virkeligheden*]'. Johan Sebastian Cammermeyer Welhaven (1807–1873), a Norwegian poet-philosopher with antinationalistic views and political attitudes very similar to Kierkegaard's, became lecturer in philosophy in Kristiania in 1840 and later professor. In a phrase Kierkegaard would have appreciated, Welhaven once said in a lecture that philosophizing for the Hegelian was just 'playing with auxiliary verbs'. The conversation with Sibbern may have taken place in 1848, the year hostilities broke out between Denmark and Germany, during which Welhaven is known to have visited Copenhagen. Whether the term 'existentially' was his own coinage is unclear. See Arne Løchen, *J. S. Welhaven: Liv og skrifter*, Kristiania: H. Aschehoug (W. Nygaard), 1900, p. 521. Norwegian letters were

strongly influenced by Danish authors at the time. Although Welhaven, whose mother was a niece of Heiberg's father, ridiculed Hegel, he was nevertheless, like Kierkegaard, an enthusiastic supporter of Heiberg's aesthetics (see Löchen, *J. S. Welhaven*, p. 124). In religion he remained a fairly orthodox Schleiermacherian. See Löchen, *J. S. Welhaven*, pp. 506, 508.

58. *Papirer*, III C 31, 6 December 1841.

59. Kirmmse, *Encounters*, p. 251 (345).

60. *Papirer*, X² A 155, from 1849 (*Papers and Journals: A Selection*, p. 439). See *Papirer*, II C 11–36 (from 1837–40) and C 26 and 27 (from 1838–39) in *Papirer*, XIII (a record of the lectures).

61. Kirmmse, *Encounters*, pp. 198–9 (275).

62. Ibid., pp. 196–7 (274).

63. Ibid., p. 199 (275).

64. *Papirer*, II, A 108. In one of several other entries he says it was the 'kaleidoscopic shaking together of a certain compendium of ideas' in Jean Paul (*Papirer*, II A 118, p. 70, 13 July 1837 [*Papers and Journals: A Selection*, p. 87]) that may have put him off writing down his own thoughts. Jean Paul had considerable influence in Denmark as a poet, literary theorist, and aesthetician (*Vorschule der Ästhetik*, bd. 1–3, 2nd edition, Stuttgart/Tübingen 1813). See SKS, K1, p. 84.

65. *Papirer*, II A 52.

66. *Papirer*, I C 126, 27 January 1837.

67. See *The Sickness unto Death*, Harmondsworth: Penguin Books, 1989, p. 85.

68. She had been confined in a brazen tower by her father, Acrisius, king of Argos, in a typically vain attempt to defeat the oracle's pronouncement that she would give birth to a son who would kill his grandfather.

69. *Søren Kierkegaards Skrifter* (SKS), edited by Niels Jørgen Cappelørn, Joakim Garff, Johnny Kondrup, Alastair McKinnon, and Finn Hauberg Mortensen, København: Søren Kierkegaard Forskningscenter/Gads Forlag, 1997–, bind 2 (SKS 2), p. 216 (*Either/Or*, Harmondsworth: Penguin, 1992, p. 214). The passage alludes to Hegel's notion of the 'unhappy consciousness' in *Phenomenology of Spirit*, but ideals framed in terms of self-centredness were common. Cf., e.g., Johann Gottfried Herder (1744–1803): 'Each nation has the *centre* of its happiness *within itself*, just as a ball has its centre of gravity within itself' (*Auch eine Philosophie der Geschichte zur Bildung der Menschheit*, 1774, Frankfurt am Main, 1967, pp. 44 ff.). Kierkegaard briefly mentions Herder in *Papirer* as early as 1835 (I C 55); see also I A 121, from February 1836.

70. See note 54.

71. See note 55.

72. Martensen's Latin dissertation was translated into Danish in 1841 and into German in 1844. As 'The Autonomy of Human Self-Consciousness' it is included in a collection of translations, *Between Hegel and Kierkegaard: Hans L. Martensen's Philosophy of Religion*, by Curtis L. Thompson and David J. Kangas (American Academy of Religion: Texts and Translations Series), Atlanta: Scholars Press, 1997.

73. Martensen, 'The Autonomy of Human Self-Consciousness', p. 135.

74. 'Review of *Perseus, Journal for den speculative Idee, nr. 1, Juni 1837*', in *Maaneds-skrift for Litteratur*, nos. 19 and 20; see note 55.

Chapter 4

1. *Papirer*, II A 597 (*Papers and Journals: A Selection*, p. 108).
2. *Papirer*, II A 29 and 30 (*Papers and Journals: A Selection*, pp. 80–1).
3. *Papirer*, II A 50; II A 56 (*Papers and Journals: A Selection*, p. 83)
4. 'Betragninger over Ideen af Faust, med hensyn paa Lenaus Faust' (Delibera-tions on the Idea of Faust with Reference to Lenau's Faust), in *Perseus*, no. 1 (June 1837), pp. 91 ff.
5. Weltzer, *Peter and Søren Kierkegaard*, p. 99. The remark is from a letter from Peter Kierkegaard to Frederik Pedersen, dated 13–15 January 1877; see Thompson, *Kierkegaard*, p. 87.
6. See Weltzer, *Peter and Søren Kierkegaard*, p. 107. Maria ends a letter to her mother: 'Good old Kierkegaard also sends his friendly greetings, he is well and in good spirits this winter.'
7. *Papirer*, II A 132, 14 July 1837; II, A 127; II A 125 (*Papers and Journals: A Selection*, pp. 89, 88).
8. See Weltzer, *Peter and Søren Kierkegaard*, p. 117 (*Dagbog*, 90).
9. *Papirer*, II A 67, 8 May 1837 (*Papers and Journals: A Selection*, p. 84).
10. Kirmmse, *Encounters*, p. 34 (59). The words are those of a Hanne Mourier, who formulated Regine's memories in a letter to Regine to verify the accuracy of an interview between them.
11. *Papirer*, II A 68, from 1837 (see *Papers and Journals: A Selection*, p. 85, trans-lation revised).
12. *Papirer*, II A 66, from 1837.
13. See Leif Bork Hansen, *Søren Kierkegaards Hemmelighed og Eksistensdialektik* (Søren Kierkegaard's Secret and Dialectic of Existence), Copenhagen: C. A. Reitzel Forlag, 1994.
14. See *Peter and Søren Kierkegaard*, p. 75 (see Hjalar Helweg, *Søren Kierkegaard, en psykiatrisk Studie*, Copenhagen: Farleigh, 1933, p. 386).
15. A rixdaler was a coin minted by the Danish State Bank (*Riksbank*) in Denmark in 1813 (the year of Kierkegaard's birth) to stay the monetary chaos that had arisen following the bombardment of Copenhagen by the British navy in August 1807. A rixdaler at this time was worth between three and four crowns but its purchasing power today would be thirtyfold.
16. *Papirer*, II A 150 and 151, 31 August 1837.
17. *Papirer*, II A 166, 25 September 1837.
18. *Papirer*, II A 163, 20 September 1837 (*Papers and Journals: A Selection*, pp. 91–2). Baron Ludwig Holberg (1684–1754) was a Norwegian-born poet, a professor of metaphysics, eloquence, and history at Copenhagen, and a renowned satirist.
19. *Papirer*, II A 640, from 1837.
20. *Papirer*, II A 155, 4 September 1837; II A 156, from 1837; II A 171, 7 October 1837 (*Papers and Journals: A Selection*, p. 92).

21. *Papirer*, II A 159, from 1837 (*Papers and Journals: A Selection*, p. 91).
22. *Papirer*, II C 12–24, from 1837.
23. *Papirer*, II A 209, April 1838 (*Papers and Journals: A Selection*, p. 96).
24. Kirmmse, *Encounters*, p. 241 (332).
25. *Papirer*, II A 216, 2 April 1837 (*Papers and Journals: A Selection*, p. 97).
26. *Papirer*, V B 46, from 1844: 'Min Opvaagnens mægtige Basune, min Stemnings forønskede Gjenstand' (my awakening's mighty trombone [lit. sackbut], my mood's wished-for object), and (quoted here) 'min Ungdoms Begeistring; min Begyndens Fortrolige; min tabte Ven; min savnede Læser.'
27. *Papirer*, II A 210, 1 April 1838.

Chapter 5

1. SKS, Kommentar bind 1 (K1), 1997, pp. 70–1.
2. Kirmmse, *Encounters*, p. 12 (29–30). See SKS, K1, pp. 71–2.
3. SKS, K1, pp. 73–4.
4. See SKS, K1, pp. 72–3.
5. See Kirmmse, *Encounters*, p. 28 (50).
6. *H. C. Andersens Almanakker*, 1833–73, edited by Helga Vang Lauridsen and Kirsten Weber, Copenhagen: Det danske Sprog-og Litteraturselskab and G. E. C. Gads Forlag, 1990, pp. 23, 24. The reference to the favourable review is on p. 22.
7. *Af en endnu Levendes Papirer*, SKS 1 (1997), p. 14.
8. Reply to Objections II, see, e.g., *René Descartes Meditations on First Philosophy in Focus*, edited by Stanley Tweyman, London and New York: Routledge, 1993, p. 103.
9. SKS, 1, pp. 18–19.
10. Ibid., pp. 20–3.
11. Ibid., pp. 24–5.
12. Ibid., pp. 35–9, 41, 55.
13. Ibid., p. 32. Cf. Rom. 8: 38–9.
14. See Friedrich Schleiermacher, *Hermeneutics: The Handwritten Manuscripts*, edited by Heinz Kimmerle, translated by James Duke and Jack Fortsman, Missoula, MT: Scholars Press, 1977.
15. SKS, 1, pp. 32–3. The reference is found not in Karl Daub (contemporary German theologian, see p. 82 of this volume), but in Fr. Baader, *Vorlesnungen über speculative Dogmatik* (Lectures on Speculative Dogmatics), vol. 1, Stuttgart/Tübingen, 1828, p. 80. See SKS, K1, p. 100.
16. J. L. Heiberg, 'Autobiographiske Fragmenter' (Autobiographical Fragments), in Heiberg, *Prosaiske Skrifter*, vols. 1–11, Copenhagen: C. A. Reitzel, 1861–62, vol. 11, pp. 485–504.
17. *Papirer*, IV B 124 (in XIII, p. 364); cf. V C 3, p. 373: 'Who has not forgotten that fine Easter morning when Prof. Heiberg got up to grasp the Hegelian philosophy, in the way he himself so edifyingly explained – was this not a leap? Or did someone dream that up?' (See *Journals and Papers: A Selection*, p. 187; and VI B 40.14.)

18. See *Papirer*, III B 1. The expression occurs here in a comment Kierkegaard wrote in 1840 on a play Andersen had written where one of the characters cited passages from *From the Papers of One Still Living*.

19. J. W. Goethe, *Italian Journey* (1796–98), translated by W. H. Auden and Elizabeth Mayer, London: Collins, 1962, pp. 363–4; cf. pp. 251–2, 305–6.

20. *Papirer*, I A 8, 11 September 1834 (*Papers and Journals: A Selection*, pp. 9–10).

21. *Papirer*, II A 228, 10:30 A.M., 19 May 1838 (*Papers and Journals: A Selection*, p. 97).

22. *Papirer*, II A 77, from 1837 (*Papers and Journals: A Selection*, p. 85).

23. See Kirmmse, *Encounters*, p. 28 (50).

24. *Papirer*, II A 231 and 232, 9 July 1838 (*Papers and Journals: A Selection*, p. 97); and II A 229, 4 June 1838.

25. These remarks are owed to the useful guidance of George Pattison.

26. *Papirer*, II A 29, 19 March 1837 (*Papers and Journals: A Selection*, pp. 80–1).

27. *Papirer*, II A 30, inserted with entries dated 19 March 1837 (*Papers and Journals: A Selection*, p. 81).

28. See Kirmmse, *Encounters*, p. 213 (292), and Weltzer, *Peter and Søren Kierkegaard*, p. 126.

29. *Breve og Aktstykker vedrørende Søren Kierkegaard*, I, pp. 40–1, dated 17 July 1838 (51–2) (letter no. 8). See Weltzer, *Peter and Søren Kierkegaard*, pp. 125, 127 (the latter citing Søren's brother's diary, which relates that Søren dined with his father and brother just two days before his father's death). The letter to Boesen is dated 17 July and begins: 'Dear Emil!!, the *only* one by whose intercession I endured the world that for me was in so many ways unbearable, the only one who remained when I let doubt and mistrust like a rushing storm wash away and destroy everything – *my Ararat*, how are things going? . . .' and it goes on to say 'how everything has changed since that time . . . the world has taken very much from me but, thank God, not more than it has given'.

30. *Papirer*, II A 231, talks of Michael Pedersen Kierkegaard being a father a second time. A note written on 10 July 1838 (II A 233) says, 'I hope it will be the same with the peace I enjoy *here at home* as with the man I once read about who also wearied of his home and rode off; after covering a short distance the horse stumbled and he fell off, and on getting up he caught sight of his home which now seemed to him so pretty that he immediately remounted and rode home to stay. If only you get the right view of it'. The emphasis is in the original and does suggest that Kierkegaard wrote the entry at Nytorv. He may well have been staying there, now and then, while his father was becoming weaker. Peter talks of them both being 'called down' just after he had died but also that on the Monday, two days before, Søren had dined with them ('*hos oss*', which has the same implication as the French '*chez nous*', that is, 'at our home' rather than his, though the fact that they inhabited separate apartments in the family home leaves scope for a kind of in-house visiting (see Weltzer, *Peter and Søren Kierkegaard*, p. 128).

31. *Papirer*, II B 3 and 1–21. The original title translates as *The Conflict between the Old and the New Soap-Cellar: A Heroic-Patriotic-Cosmopolitan-Philanthropic-Fatalistic Drama in Several Scenes*. Remarking on the hint of an 'unseemly

coquetry' in this title, Kierkegaard suggests as an alternative: 'The All-Embracing Debate by Everything against Everything, or the Crazier the Better, from the Papers of One Still Living, Published against His Will by S. Kierkegaard.' Carl Roos, *Kierkegaard og Goethe* (Kierkegaard and Goethe), Copenhagen: Gad, 1955, thinks the play is a parody of Goethe's *Faust* with local personalities in the parts (Heiberg as Springgaasen and Martensen as Phrase). Soap cellars were places where soap was manufactured; '*Sæbekoger*' (soap-cook, or soap-maker) was a term of abuse ('nitwit' or 'blockhead').

32. *Papirer*, II A 241, 11 August 1838 (*Papers and Journals: A Selection*, p. 98).

33. See Weltzer, *Peter and Søren Kierkegaard*, p. 139.

34. *Papirer*, II A 802–6, from 1838 (the last four in *Papers and Journals: A Selection*, pp. 117–18). The Orlepp translation of *King Lear* did not appear until 10 March 1839, and Jens Himmelstrup ('Den store Jordrystelse', *Kierkegaardiana*, vol. IV, 1962) concludes that the autobiographical entries were written between 3 and 30 September 1839 (the Goethe quote also appears as journal entry II A 557 dated 9 September 1839).

35. Weltzer, *Peter and Søren Kierkegaard*, pp. 138–9.

36. Carl Jørgensen *Søren Kierkegaard. En Biografi* (Søren Kierkegaard: A Biography), Copenhagen: Nyt nordisk Forlag/Arnold Busck, 1964, places the 'earthquake' entries in the autumn of 1839, not contemporaneously with the 'earthquake' as in Peter's account. But Jørgensen explains the earthquake in terms of Kierkegaard's decision earlier *not to return* home, due to the realization that the two brothers and their father formed a destructively dialectical trio, which would not favour his project or his peace of mind. If Jørgensen is correct we could call the earthquake Kierkegaard's final weaning. But Peter's account seems more plausible.

37. The story of the curse on the Jutland heath was first publicized after Peter's death (he wept when Barfod, the editor of the first collected journal entries, showed it to him, and withheld it from publication). Søren notes it in an entry from 1846: 'How dreadful, the thought of that man who as a small boy tending sheep on the Jutland heath, in much suffering, starving and exhausted, once stood up on a hill and cursed God! – and that man was unable to forget it when he was eighty-two years old' (*Papirer*, VII¹ A 5 [*Papers and Journals: A Selection*, p. 204]).

38. *Papirer*, II A 807, from 1838 (*Papers and Journals: A Selection*, p. 118, translation altered).

39. Kirmmse, *Encounters*, p. 218 (297–8).

40. Ibid., p. 29 (51–2).

Chapter 6

1. See Kirmmse, *Encounters*, p. 229 (315).

2. *Papirer*, VIII¹ A 640, 19 April 1848; and VI A 8, from 1844–45 (*Papers and Journals: A Selection*, pp. 295, 187).

3. Kirmmse, *Encounters*, p. 228 (314).

4. *Papirer*, III A 35, from July 1840 (*Papers and Journals: A Selection*, p. 132).

5. Kirmmse, *Encounters*, p. 228 (314).

6. *Papirer*, II A 305, 17 December 1839.

7. *Papirer*, II A 335, 20 January 1939 (*Papers and Journals: A Selection*, p. 100, translation altered).

8. *Papirer*, II A 755, from 1838 (*Papers and Journals: A Selection*, p. 115).

9. *Papirer*, II A 523, 30 July 1839 (*Papers and Journals: A Selection*, p. 106); J. P. Mynster, 'Rationalisme, Supranaturalisme', *Tidsskrift for Litteratur og Kritik*, vol. 1, 1839, pp. 249–68. In an article replying to Mynster, 'Rationalisme, Supranaturalisme og *principium exclusi medii*', in the same issue (pp. 456–73), Martensen repeatedly refers to this disjunctive form and categorizes Mynster's position as an 'Either/Or' (*Enter/Eller*), and he asks rhetorically whether it isn't the task of the age to overcome 'this unfortunate aut aut?' (p. 467).

10. *Papirer*, II A 347, 2 February 1839. The sovereign mistress's name appears in latinized form 'Regina' (queen) (*Papers and Journals: A Selection*, pp. 100–1).

11. *Papirer*, X^5 A 149:3, from 1849.

12. Kirmmse, *Encounters*, pp. 217 (296). Those asked to record their memories of Kierkegaard are almost unanimous in remembering an outwardly sociable person with none of the traits of the depressive. Although Sibbern, we remember, recalled his 'witty, somewhat sarcastic' look (p. 216 [295]), and others too saw another side, detecting malice (Israel Levin, who being himself not immune may not be the best judge, claims that Kierkegaard was 'in general not very likable' and that 'his pupils did not like him', and that he was 'sarcastic and could bear a grudge' [p. 13 (291)]), Brøchner talks of a 'singularly winning expression' and of how there could be something 'infinitely gentle and loving in his eye, [though] also something stimulating and exasperating' (p. 229 [316]).

13. *Papirer*, IX A 70, from 1848 (*Papers and Journals: A Selection*, p. 310). From that later perspective he could add: 'and then that God in heaven should help me as he has.'

14. *Papirer*, II A 495, 509, and 423, from 1839, the two latter from 22 July and 14 May respectively (*Papers and Journals: A Selection*, pp. 103–5).

15. *Papirer*, II A 576, from 1839–40.

16. *Papirer*, II A 497, from 1839. The text says 'en Mils Vei'. A Danish *mil* is ten kilometres and so in fact closer to seven miles. The river rises in the Sierra de Cazorla in Andalusia and was known in antiquity as Baetis.

17. Kirmmse, *Encounters*, pp. 143–4 (204). Nathanael of Cana in Galilee; See John 1:45–51, 21:2.

18. See Weltzer, *Peter og Søren Kierkegaard*, pp. 155–6, for details of the examiners' questions, and Kirmmse, p. 228 (pp. 314–15) for Brøchner's account.

19. See *Papirer*, III A 53, from 1840 (footnote).

20. The relevant journal entries are *Papirer*, III A 51–85, from July 1840 (a selection can be found in *Papers and Journals: A Selection*, pp. 133–7).

21. *Papirer*, A 54, 77, from July 1840 (*Papers and Journals: A Selection*, pp. 134, 136)

22. *Papirer*, A 82, from 1840 (*Papers and Journals: A Selection*, p. 137).

23. *Papirer*, X⁵ A 149, from 1849 (*Papers and Journals: A Selection*, pp. 412–13).

24. *Den isolerede Subjektivitet: dens vigtigste Skikkelser*, Copenhagen, 1840; see vol. I, pp. 77 ff., 13 ff., 18 ff.

25. J. L. Heiberg, 'Det logiske System. Første Avhandling, indeholdende: paragrapherne 1–2', *Perseus, Journal for the den speculative Idee*, no. 2, 1838, pp. 1–45. A. Adler, 'J. L. Heiberg, "det logiske System (a) Intet, (b) Vorden, (c) Tilværen" ', *Tidsskrift for Litteratur og Kritik*, vol. 1, 1840, pp. 474–82.

26. *Papirer*, III A 1 and A 3, 4 and 5 July 1840 (*Papers and Journals: A Selection*, pp. 127–8).

27. *Papirer*, III A 11, 18 July 1840 (*Papers and Journals: A Selection*, p. 130).

28. *Papirer*, III A 5, 10 July 1840 (*Papers and Journals: A Selection*, p. 129).

29. See Kirmmse, *Encounters*, p. 213 (292–3).

30. See *Papirer*, III C 5, on the 'Edifying in the Thought that against God We Are Always in the Wrong'.

31. *Breve og Aktstykker*, I, pp. 14–15 (17–20). The sermon had Philippians 1:19–25 as its text, focusing on verse 21: 'For me to live is Christ, and to die is gain.' The text also contains the words: 'But if I live in the flesh, this is the fruit of my labour: yet what I shall choose I wot not. For I am in a strain betwixt two. . . .' The either/or in this case is not between living with and living without Christ but between living with Christ and dying. The complete text of the sermon itself is printed in *Papirer*, III C 1. See C 2–25 for drafts of other sermons, including one on Abraham and Isaac, and other material relating to the seminary.

32. *Papirer*, II A 163, 20 September 1837 (*Papers and Journals: A Selection*, pp. 91–2). See Chapter 4 of this volume.

33. See Ernst Behler, 'Kierkegaard's *The Concept of Irony*', in *Kierkegaard Revisited* (Kierkegaard Studies: Monograph Series 1), ed. Niels Jørgen Cappelørn and Jon Stewart, Berlin/New York: Walter de Gruyter, 1997, p. 28.

34. *Papirer*, I C 69, from 1835–36.

35. See SKS, K1, p. 126, which also refers to a 'highly interesting' conversation Kierkegaard records (*Papirer*, II A 102) having had with Møller on the subject of irony and humour in 1837. The aphorism first appeared in the second edition of Møller's *Efterladte Skrifter* (edited by C. Winther, F. C. Olsen, C. Thaarup, and L. V. Petersen, Copenhagen: 1848–50 (the first edition appeared from 1839 to 1843). Of relevance to another aspect of Kierkegaard's dissertation are other entries in the journals from 1837 and 1838 (*Papirer*, II A 186, 1 November 1837; and A 240, 2 August 1838). These refer to the Tübingen theologian Ferdinand Christian Baur's *Das Christliche des Platonismus oder Sokrates und Christus* (1837), part of which had been translated in *Tidsskrift for udenlandsk theologisk Litteratur* (Journal for Theological Literature Abroad), edited by two of Kierkegaard's teachers, Clausen and Hohlenberg, 1837, no. 3, pp. 485–534. In the first entry Kierkegaard remarks that Baur's dissertation 'enters right into my investigation on irony and humour', though apparently not in the part translated. The later entry describes Baur's view as gnostic, and Kierkegaard considers whether the recent revival of Chiliasm (the doctrine of Christ's

thousand-year reign) might be a useful counterweight to that. The gnostic view that the world is worthless is very like that expressed in *Either/Or*'s 'Diapsalmata' and has interesting associations with Romantic irony. There are several entries on these themes during this period.

36. *Papirer*, I A 75, 1 August 1835 (*Papers and Journals: A Selection*, p. 35).

37. See Chapter 3, note 52, in this volume; and *Papirer*, II A 627 (*Papers and Journals: A Selection*, p. 109).

38. *Om Begrebet Ironi med stadigt Hensyn til Socrates* (On the Concept of Irony with Constant Reference to Socrates), SKS, 1, p. 353 (*The Concept of Irony with Continual Reference to Socrates*, translated by Howard V. Hong and Edna H. Hong, Kierkegaard's Writings [KW], vol. II, p. 324).

39. SKS, 1, pp. 312, 313 (KW, II, pp. 276, 277).

40. *Papirer*, I A 125, from February 1836 (*Papers and Journals: A Selection*, p. 49).

41. *Papirer*, II A 627 (*Papers and Journals: A Selection*, pp. 109–10).

42. *Papirer*, I A 307, 11 December 1836 (*Papers and Journals: A Selection*, pp. 59–60).

43. SKS, 1, p. 337 (KW, II, p. 305). In its focus on Socrates rather than Christianity, the dissertation all but ignores the distinction between irony and humour.

44. *Papirer*, X 3 A 477, from 1850 (*Papers and Journals: A Selection*, p. 506).

45. SKS, 1, pp. 270, 276 (KW, II, pp. 228, 235).

46. Ibid., p. 277 (KW, II, p. 236).

47. Ibid., pp. 294, 295 (KW, II, pp. 256, 257).

48. *Papirer*, I A 75, 1 August 1835 (*Papers and Journals: A Selection*, p. 35).

49. SKS, 1, p. 306 (KW, II, p. 269).

50. Ibid., p. 307 (KW, II, p. 270).

51. Ibid., p. 308 (KW, II, p. 271).

52. See Friedrich Schlegel, *Kritische Friedrich Schlegel Ausgabe*, edited by Ernst Behler in collaboration with Jean-Jacques Austettner et al., 35 vols., Paderborn: Schöningh, 1958–, vol. 2, p. 152.

53. Immanuel Kant, *Critique of Pure Reason*, translated by Norman Kemp Smith, London: Macmillan, 1980, p. 59.

54. *Kritische Friedrich Schlegel Ausgabe*, vol. 2, p. 204. Here I draw heavily on Ernst Behler's essay, 'Early German Romanticism: Friedrich Schlegel and Novalis', in *A Companion to Continental Philosophy*, edited by Simon Critchley and William R. Schroeder, Oxford: Blackwell, 1998, see p. 78.

55. Kirmmse, *Encounters*, p. 234 (322); see also p. 167 (233).

56. *Kritische Friedrich Schlegel Ausgabe*, vol. 10, p. 357.

57. *Papirer*, I A 302 and 91, from 1835 (*Papers and Journals: A Selection*, pp. 59, 39).

58. *Papirer*, III C 33, from 1841–2. Kierkegaard refers to *Aesthetics* in the collection of Hegel's writings edited by Marheineke et al., Berlin, 1832–., vol. 3, p. 440.

59. See note 25 to this chapter.

60. The dissertation's first part, of over two hundred pages, argues the case for Socrates as an ironist, charting irony's emergence in the way Socrates is understood in the works of Xenophon, Plato, and Aristophanes. This is an interesting

but well-selected assortment. As a youth, Xenophon, who accompanied Cyrus into Asia, had been a pupil of Socrates, who is reputed to have saved his life at the battle of Delium in 424 B.C. Xenophon later wrote an account of Socrates to defend his teacher's memory against charges of irreligion and of corrupting the Athenian youth. Plato, on the other hand, was about fifteen years Xenophon's junior and his memories of Socrates, from a later stage in the latter's life, became embellished in the parts assigned to him in the dialogues. Aristophanes, the comic poet and almost exactly Xenophon's contemporary, wrote a famous play, the *Clouds*, in which Socrates appears as a Sophist.

61. *Papirer*, II A 627 (*Journals and Papers: A Selection*, p. 109).

62. G. W. F. Hegel, *Aesthetics: Lectures on Fine Art*, translated by T. M. Knox, Oxford: Clarendon Press, 1975, vol. I, p. 68.

63. Ibid., p. 69.

64. See Chapter 3, note 43, in this volume.

65. SKS, 1, p. 297 (259).

66. Kirmmse, *Encounters*, pp. 29–32 (52–3); and SKS, K1, pp. 124–5, 129–46.

67. After his theology exams, Brøndsted (1780–1842) had studied philology, and on graduating in 1806 he travelled to Greece, a land that captivated him and which presented itself to him in a quite different light (also literally) to that of Roman antiquity. On the way there, as was not untypical of Danish scholars at the time, he visited the celebrated, including Goethe. He also joined Oehlenschläger, first in Dresden and then in Paris. On his return he gave a celebrated series of lectures on Greece and its ancient monuments and sights. Brøndsted died after a riding accident the year after Kierkegaard's defence of his dissertation.

68. This information is recorded in a letter found in Peter's archives from H. Ferdinand Lund to his brother P. Wilhelm in Brazil, dated 2 April 1841. See Weltzer, *Peter og Søren Kierkegaard*, p. 162, and Kirmmse, *Encounters*, pp. 44, 300 (71, 404). The letter says Kierkegaard had 'begun to spit blood *again*' (emphasis added). To put Regine's mind at rest Kierkegaard told her it was due to recurring back pains caused by a fall from a tree in childhood.

69. The dissertation gave him the title *Magister*, but some years later the title for the degree was changed to Doctor.

70. See SKS, K1, pp. 144–5.

71. SKS, 1, p. 292 (254). Cf. Ludwig Wittgenstein in *Tractatus Logico-Philosophicus*, translated by D. F. Pears and B. F. McGuinness, London: Routledge & Kegan Paul, 1961, 6.45, where he says that 'viewing the world *sub specie aeterni*' is to view it 'as a whole, a limited whole'.

72. Roger Poole (*Kierkegaard: The Indirect Communication*, Charlottesville and London: University Press of Virginia, 1993, p. 60) reads the first part of the dissertation as a subtle emptying of the Hegelianisms that leaves Hegel's words intact but gives them new, Kierkegaardian transcriptions. It is only with the help of a Derrida and a Le Man that we are able to 'read Hegel as [Kierkegaard] read Hegel'. Referring to the literary 'device' we need to decipher this way of reading Hegel (the idea that there is nothing beyond the text), Poole says: 'Russell and Moore, in carrying out their deposition of Hegel in the early

years of this century, were merely bringing to an end a century of agony in which serious men and women of good intelligence had tried to apply Hegel to reality and consistently failed . . . [But] Kierkegaard had seen to the bottom of the device in 1841 and triumphantly defeated Hegelianism by refusing to accord it referential status' (ibid., p. 52). My own view is that it took Kierkegaard some time to grasp the implications of his thought for Hegel and that some aspects of Hegel's thought, its structures in particular, remained with him to the end. In this connection, see Jon Stewart, *Hegel's Relations to Hegel Reconsidered* (forthcoming). Ernst Behler perceptively refers to the dissertation as 'an immensely complex text developing under the surface of a massive Hegelianism' ('Kierkegaard's *The Concept of Irony*', p. 29). In support of this, the whole of the first part of the dissertation can be seen as an exercise in the Hegelian art of understanding life, or a concept, backwards, reading its genesis into the historical origins and culminating, fittingly for the method, with Hegel's own understanding of Socrates.

73. SKS, 1, pp. 352–4 (KW, II, pp. 324–5).
74. Ibid., p. 355 (KW, II, p. 326).
75. Kirmmse, *Encounters*, p. 29 (51–2).
76. Ibid., pp. 235, 334 (323, 441).

Chapter 7

1. *Papirer*, X⁵ A 149, from 1849 (*Papers and Journals: A Selection*, p. 413).
2. *Papirer*, IX A 67, from 1848: 'The few days I have been really happy, humanly speaking, I have always longed indescribably for her, her whom I have loved dearly and who with her entreaty also touched me so deeply.' (*Papers and Journals: A Selection*, p. 310, translation altered).
3. *Papirer*, X² A 68 and X⁵ A 149, from 1849 (the latter in *Papers and Journals: A Selection*, p. 414).
4. *Papirer*, X² A 83 (*Papers and Journals: A Selection*, p. 431).
5. See *Papirer*, X⁵ A 149, from 1849 (*Papers and Journals: A Selection*, p. 413): 'A person like me, doing penance, my *vita ante acta* [life before actions], my melancholy – that was enough' (for him to realize the mistake). Kierkegaard writes: 'Had I not been a penitent, not had my *vita ante acta*, not been melancholic, marriage to her would have made me happier beyond my dreams. But even I, being the person I unfortunately am, had to say that without her I could be happier in my unhappiness than with her – she had touched me deeply, and I would so much, ever so much, have done everything. . . . [In the margin: Yet she must have had some inkling of how it was with me. For the following remark came up quite often: You will never be happy anyway, so whether I get to stay with you can't really matter one way or the other. She once also said that she would never question me about anything if only she might stay with me.]' (ibid. [*Papers and Journals: A Selection*, p. 414]).
6. *Papirer*, X² A 3, from 1849 (*Papers and Journals: A Selection*, p. 421).
7. *Papirer*, X⁵ A 149, from 1849 (*Papers and Journals: A Selection*, p. 415).

8. *Papirer*, X¹ A 24, from 1849.

9. *Papirer*, X² A 3, 7 September 1849 (*Papers and Journals: A Selection*, p. 421).

10. *Papirer*, X¹ A 667 and X⁵ A 150 (the latter in *Papers and Journals: A Selection*, p. 419).

11. *Papirer*, X⁵ A 150: 1–2, from 1849 (*Papers and Journals: A Selection*, p. 419).

12. Johannes *de silentio*, *Frygt og Bæven*, SKS, 4, p. 138 (*Fear and Trembling*, Harmondsworth: Penguin, 1985, p. 72).

13. *Papirer*, X² A 3, 7 September 1849 (*Papers and Journals: A Selection*, pp. 421–2).

14. See Hegel, *Aesthetics*, II, pp. 1159 ff.

15. *Papirer* X⁵ A 149, from 1849 (*Papers and Journals: A Selection*, p. 415).

16. *Papirer*, X⁵ A 149, from 1849 (*Papers and Journals: A Selection*, pp. 415–16).

17. Kirmmse, *Encounters*, pp. 162–3 (227).

18. *Papirer*, III A 185 (where Kierkegaard comments that, if 'my good Jonas Olsen really could hate like no one else,' he would have valued being his contemporary, since passion is the 'real gauge' of human energy) and X⁵ A 149 (*Papers and Journals: A Selection*, p. 417). That Peter said his brother was 'done for' is reported by Kierkegaard himself (*Papirer*, VI A 8, from 1844–45 [*Papers and Journals: A Selection*, p. 187]). See Carl Jørgensen, *Søren Kierkegaard. En Biografi*, Copenhagen: Nyt Nordisk Forlag/ Arnold Busck, 1964, vol. I, p. 137.

19. One of several letters to Emil Boesen (1812–1879). See *Breve og Aktstykker*, I, p. 107 (138) (letter no. 68).

20. For Marx's possible attendance see Gregor Malantschuk, *Den kontroversielle Kierkegaard*, Copenhagen: Vinten, 1976. Regarding the other actual and possible attendants I am indebted to George Pattison.

21. *System of Transcendental Idealism*, translated by Peter Heath, introduction by Michael Vater, Charlottesville: University Press of Virginia, 1978.

22. *On University Studies*, translated by E. S. Morgan, edited by N. Guterman, Athens, Ohio: Ohio University Press, 1966.

23. *Papirer*, II C 25, from 1838–39, included in XII, pp. 313–18.

24. A letter to Pastor Spang dated 18 November. *Breve og Aktstykker*, 1, p. 77 (98) (letter no. 51).

25. Dated 14 December, ibid., p. 82 (104) (letter no. 54).

26. Dated 15 December, ibid., p. 84 (107) (letter no. 55).

27. *Papirer*, III 27 (in XIII, pp. 253–329), November 1841–February 1842. Record [*Referat*] of Schelling's lectures in Berlin, 1841–42, on 'Philosophy of Revelation', translated by Howard V. Hong and Edna H. Hong, in KW, II (the same volume as their translation of *The Concept of Irony*), pp. 331–412.

28. *Breve og Aktstykker*, I, pp. 109–10 (141) (letter no. 70).

29. Ibid., pp. 92–3 (118–19) (letter no. 80).

30. Heinrich (also 'Henrik' and 'Henrich') S. Steffens, *Caricaturen des Heiligsten* (Caricatures of the Most Holy), Leipzig, 1819. Steffens, a naturalist and philosopher, was born in Norway in 1773; he was a close relation of Grundtvig as well as more indirectly of Mynster. After studying at Kiel and coming under the influence of Schelling in Jena, he returned to Copenhagen and became

instrumental in introducing a (Nature) Romanticism to Denmark, but returned quite soon (in 1804) to teach in Halle and then in Berlin. For the impact of Steffens on Danish culture, see Kirmmse, *Kierkegaard in Golden Age Denmark*, esp. pp. 80–84. See *Papirer*, I A 250, 28 September 1836 (*Papers and Journals: A Selection*, p. 55).

31. In a letter to Sibbern dated 15 December, *Breve og Aktstykker*, pp. 83–4 (106–7) (letter no.55). The other friend was Pastor Spang (see pp. 77, 93 [97, 119] [letters nos. 51 and 61, dated 18 November and 8 January]). Both Marheineke and Werder had been in Copenhagen, and Martensen had visited Marheineke during his German stay in 1834–35. Werder was said to be exceedingly hospitable to Danish visitors (see vol. 1, p. 45).

32. The treatise, in the form of a letter, is entitled 'Equilibrium between the Aesthetic and the Ethical in the Development of Personality.' See note 46 following.

33. *Breve og Aktstykker*, I, p. 95 (123) (letter no. 62).

34. See p. 168 of this volume.

35. *Papirer*, X^5 A 146, 11 October 1853 (*Papers and Journals: A Selection*, p. 558).

36. *Breve og Aktstykker*, I, p. 90 (115) (letter no. 60).

37. Ibid., p. 74 (93) (letter no. 50).

38. Ibid., p. 81 (102) (letter no. 54).

39. Ibid., p. 83 (105) (letter, no. 54).

40. See Helmut Müller-Sievers, *Self-Generation: Biology, Philosophy, and Literature around 1800*, Stanford, CA: Stanford University Press, 1997, Chapter 5.

41. *Papirer*, X^1 A 658, from 1849; VIII^1 A 642, from 1848; IV A 234, from 1843 (*Papers and Journals: A Selection*, pp. 409, 295, 165).

42. Both history 'in a deeper sense' and mood are mentioned in the dissertation, the former briefly as something that love based on 'sensuousness' cannot have (SKS, 1, p. 333 [KW, II, p. 300]), and the latter ('succumbing to mood') in connection with mood and 'boredom' being the ironist's 'only continuity' (SKS, 1, pp. 319, 320 [pp. 284, 285]).

43. *Synspunktet for min Forfatter-Virksomhed: En Ligefrem Meddelelse, Rapport til Historien* (The Point of View for My Activity as an Author), SV^3 18, p. 89.

44. *Papirer*, IV A 234 (*Papers and Journals: A Selection*, p. 165). See *Enten-Eller. Et Livs-Fragment*, edited by Victor Eremita, SKS, 3, p. 304 (*Either/Or: A Fragment of Life*, Harmondsworth: Penguin, 1992, p. 582).

45. Phalaris ruled in Agrigentum in Sicily from about 570 to 564 B.C. He is said to have burnt his victims alive in a brazen bull, the first victim being the bull's inventor. Reeds were placed in the nostrils of the bull to turn the cries into music.

46. SKS, 2, p. 27 (*Either/Or*, p. 43).

47. *Papirer*, IV A 216, from 1843 (*Papers and Journals: A Selection*, pp. 163–4).

48. *Papirer*, IV A 221 (*Papers and Journals: A Selection*, p. 164).

49. For the origins and possible dating of the material that went into *Either/Or*, see SKS, K2–3, pp. 38–58.

50. See the opening of Chapter 3 of this volume.

51. See, e.g., *Papirer*, II A 406, 414, 415, 417, 420, 421, and 435, all from April and May 1838 (A 415, 417, 420, and 435 in *Papers and Journals: A Selection*, pp. 102–3).

52. *Papirer*, II A 491 (*Papers and Journals: A Selection*, p. 104).

53. *Papirer*, IV A 215 (*Papers and Journals: A Selection*, p. 163).

54. *Papirer*, IV B 59, from 1844 (*Papers and Journals: A Selection*, p. 170).

55. *Papirer*, IV A 214 (*Papers and Journals: A Selection*, p. 163).

56. See p. 193 of this volume.

57. *Breve og Aktstykker*, I, p. 107 (137) (letter no. 68).

58. *Papirer*, X^1 A 192, from 1849 (*Papers and Journals: A Selection*, p. 376).

59. *Synspunktet for min Forfatter-Virksomhed* ('The Point of View for My Activity as an Author'), SV^3 18, p. 90. See also an unpublished 'Post-Scriptum to *Either/Or*', *Papirer*, IV B 59, from 1844, where Kierkegaard (Victor Eremita) suggests that the title is to be read as belonging not to the book or its publisher/editor, but to the reader. See Chapter 10 of this volume.

60. Thompson, *Kierkegaard*, p. 165.

61. See *Papirer*, III C 5, from 1840–41 (*Papers and Journals: A Selection*, p. 150).

62. See *Papirer*, IV A 87, p. 33, where Kierkegaard writes that it seems to be his lot to teach the truth, as far as he can find it, but in a way that destroys all his authority. But for someone ready to learn, he says, it doesn't matter whether he is spoken to by 'a Bileam's donkey or a guffawing crosspatch or an apostle or an angel' (cf. Numbers 22–24).

63. *Papirer*, I C 69, from 1835–36. Interest in Schlegel's *Lucinde* had been reawakened by the Young Germany movement, to which Karl Gutzkow belonged, and plays an important part in the crucial direction in which Kierkegaard turns Romantic irony in his dissertation.

64. Johannes Climacus, *Afsluttende Uvidenskabelig Efterskrift*, SV^3 9, 1963, pp. 208–9 (KW, XII, 1, p. 249).

Chapter 8

1. *Papirer*, X^5 A 149, from 1849 (*Papers and Journals: A Selection*, pp. 417–18).

2. Alternatively 'Gjødvad' and 'Gjødwad', also 'Finsen'.

3. SKS, K2–3, p. 59. See Kirmmse, *Encounters*, p. 56 (88).

4. See Kirmmse, *Encounters*, pp. 56, 107, 112, 300 (89, 156, 163, 403).

5. See ibid., p. 56 (88).

6. See Weltzer, *Peter og Søren Kierkegaard*, pp. 167–8 (*Dagbog*, 121).

7. *Breve of Aktstykker*, I, p. 113 (145) (letter no. 73), 18 January 1843.

8. Weltzer, *Peter og Søren Kierkegaard*, p. 178.

9. Kirmmse, *Encounters*, p. 232 (320).

10. My references and acknowledgements here are due to George Pattison, 'The Initial Reception of *Either/Or*', in Robert L. Perkins (ed.), *Either/Or, Part II*, International Kierkegaard Commentary, Macon, GA: Mercer University Press, 1995, pp. 291–305.

11. *Papirer*, IV B 22, from 1843 (*Papers and Journals: A Selection*, p. 168).

12. *Intelligensblade*, 2/24 (1843), pp. 288, 290, 291. See Pattison, 'The Initial Reception of *Either/Or*', pp. 295–6.

13. *Papirer*, IV B 39 and 45, from 1843 (*Papers and Journals: A Selection*, pp. 169–70).

14. *Fædrelandet*, 5 March 1843. See Pattison, 'The Initial Reception of *Either/Or*', pp. 296–8.

15. *Papirer*, IV B 49, from 1843 (*Papers and Journals: A Selection*, p. 170).

16. *Forposten*, 1/11–15 (12 and 19 March, and 2 and 19 April). See Pattison, 'The Initial Reception of *Either/Or*', pp. 297–8.

17. *Fædrelandet*, 7, 14, and 21 May 1843. See Pattison, 'The Initial Reception of *Either/Or*', pp. 299–30.

18. *Fyenske Tidsskrift for Literatur og Kritik*, 1/4 (843). The review was signed K.-H. but, as Pattison observes, this is the fairly easily penetrable nom de plume of the pastor and author H. P. Koefoed-Hansen, an exact contemporary of Kierkegaard.

19. *Breve of Aktstykker*, I, pp. 120–1 (154–5) (letter no. 82), 25 May 1843.

20. *Papirer*, IX A 175, from 1848; X 1 A 266, from 1849 (*Papers and Journals: A Selection*, pp. 319–20, 382).

21. SKS, 3, p. 318 (*Either/Or*, Harmondsworth: Penguin, p. 594).

22. *Afsluttende uvidenskabelig Efterskrift*, SV³ 9, p. 214 (KW, XII, 1, p. 256).

23. *Frygt og Bæven*, SKS, 4, p. 201 (*Fear and Trembling*, Harmondsworth: Penguin, 1985, p. 137).

24. SV³ 9, p. 215 (KW, XII, 1, pp. 257–8).

25. I discuss this and related questions in 'The Judge in the Light of Kierkegaard's Own Either/Or: Some Hermeneutical Crotchets', in Robert L. Perkins (ed.), *Either/Or, Part II*, pp. 183–205.

26. See SV³ 9, pp. 215–16 (KW, XVII, 1, pp. 257–8).

27. *Papirer*, X² A 14, from 1849 (*Papers and Journals: A Selection*, p. 425).

28. *Papirer*, IV A 76, from 1843.

29. For a selection of the positions from which Abraham's intention has been interpreted see Ronald M. Green, ' "Developing" *Fear and Trembling*', in Hannay and Marino (eds), *The Cambridge Companion to Kierkegaard*, Chapter 10. See also the references given in Alastair Hannay, *Kierkegaard*, London/New York: Routledge, 1999, pp. 347–8, and the translator's introduction to *Fear and Trembling*.

30. *Papirer*, X² A 14, from 1849 (*Papers and Journals: A Selection*, p. 425).

31. SKS, 2, p. 47 (*Either/Or*, p. 54).

32. Hegel, *Aesthetics*, II, pp. 1193, 1198 (translation altered).

33. *Papirer*, IV A 76, from 1843. For the published version see *Frygt og Bæven*, SKS, 4, pp. 107–8 (*Fear and Trembling*, pp. 45–6). See note 28 to this chapter.

34. SKS, 4, p. 114 (*Fear and Trembling*, p. 51).

35. SKS, 4, pp. 131, 141 (*Fear and Trembling*, pp. 65, 75).

36. The metaphor of blackening the breast is applied explicitly to his attempt to repel Regine in *Papirer* X⁵ A 146, 13 October 1853 (*Papers and Journals: A Selection*, p. 558).

37. *Papirer*, X⁵ A 146, 13 October 1853 (*Papers and Journals: A Selection*, p. 558).
38. *Papirer*, X⁵ A 149, from 1848–49 (*Papers and Journals: A Selection*, p. 417).
39. Immanuel Kant, 'The Quarrel among the Faculties' (1798); cf. *Religion within the Limits of Reason Alone*, translated and with an introduction and notes by Theodore M. Greene and Hoyt H. Hudson, New York: Harper and Brothers, 1960, p. 175, where Kant invokes Abraham in connection with the Inquisition.
40. Hegel, *Aesthetics*, I, p. 466.
41. G. W. F. Hegel, *Lectures on the History of Philosophy*, translated by E. S. Haldane and Frances H. Simon, London: Routledge & Kegan Paul, 1968, pp. 10–11.
42. SKS, 4, p. 160 (*Fear and Trembling*, p. 96).
43. SKS, 4, pp. 148, 160, 172 (*Fear and Trembling*, pp. 83, 96, 107).
44. Hegel, *Aesthetics*, II, pp. 1229–30.
45. *Papirer*, VII¹ B 83 (*Papers and Journals: A Selection*, p. 246).
46. SKS, 4, pp. 12–15 (*Repetition* [KW, VI], translated, edited, and with an introduction and notes by Howard V. Hong and Edna H. Hong, Princeton, NJ: Princeton University Press, 1983, pp. 133–9).
47. SKS, 4, p. 17 (KW, VI, p. 140).
48. See *Papirer*, IV B 1, esp. pp. 146–50. For the genesis of the text of *Repetition*, see SKS, K4, pp. 12–28.
49. SKS, 4, p. 27 (KW, VI, p. 150).
50. SKS, 4, pp. 56–7 (KW, VI, p. 186, translation altered).
51. SKS, 4, p. 93 (KW, VI, p. 229, translation altered).
52. SKS, 4, p. 179 (KW, VI, p. 212) (original emphasis).
53. SKS, 4, p. 75 (KW, VI, p. 207).
54. SKS, 4, pp. 95–6 (KW, VI, pp. 229–30, translation altered).
55. According to Regine herself, in an interview in 1896, she had told Kierkegaard on the day that he proposed and had followed her uninvited into her house that one of her former schoolteachers, Candidat Schlegel, 'was evidently fond of her'. (See Kirmmse, *Encounters*, p. 52 [83].)
56. *Papirer*, IV A 152, from 1843.
57. SKS, 4, p. 57 (KW, VI, p. 187). See my *Kierkegaard*, pp. 69–72.
58. *Papirer*, X¹ A 266, from 1949 (*Papers and Journals: A Selection*, p. 383).
59. *Papirer*, IV A 97, from 1843 (*Papers and Journals: A Selection*, p. 156).
60. See Kirmmse, *Encounters*, p. 60 (94).
61. *Papirer*, X⁴ A 540, from May 1852 (*Papers and Journals: A Selection*, p. 540). For Sibbern's intercession see, e.g., Kirmmse, *Encounters*, p. 37 (62).
62. SKS, 5, pp. 13, 63, 113, 183, 289.
63. See *Papirer*, IV C 1. The text goes: 'Howbeit we speak wisdom among them that are perfect: yet not the wisdom of this world, nor of the princes of this world, that come to nought: but we speak the wisdom of God in a mystery, even the hidden wisdom which God ordained before the world, unto our glory. Which none of the princes of this world knew: for had they known it, they would not have crucified the Lord of glory. But as it is written, Eye hath not

seen, nor ear heard, neither have entered into the heart of man, the things that God hath prepared for them that love him.'

Chapter 9

1. For an account of the origins of the text see SKS, K 4, pp. 317–32.
2. See Chapter 8, pp. 184–5, in this volume.
3. *Intelligensblade*, nos. 41–42: 'Kirkelig Polemik' (Church Polemics). See again George Pattison's 'The Initial Reception of *Either/Or*', in Robert L. Perkins (ed.), *Either/Or, Part II*, pp. 301 – 3.
4. See Kirmmse, *Encounters*, pp. 63, 288 (98, 390).
5. *Kjøbenhavnsposten*, 4 January 1844.
6. *Papirer*, II C 25 and 54 (in XII and XIII).
7. *Papirer*, II (XII, p. 331).
8. Mynster, 'Rationalisme,' pp. 262, 266. See p. 129 of this volume.
9. Ibid., p. 254. Jon Stewart and Arild Waaler first drew my attention to the relevance and details of Mynster's 1839 essay and of Martensen's response to it; see note 70, this chapter.
10. SKS, 4, p. 460 (KW, VIII, p. 162).
11. G. W. F. Hegel, *Phenomenology of Spirit*, translated by A. V. Miller, Oxford: Clarendon Press, 1977, §80, p. 51. *Phänomenologie des Geistes, Gesammelte Werke*, vol. 9, edited by Wolfgang Bonsiepen and Reinhard Heed, Hamburg: Felix Meiner, 1980, p. 57.
12. G. W. F. Hegel, *Faith and Knowledge*, translated by W. Cerf and H. S. Harris, Albany: State University of New York Press, 1977, p. 58.
13. SKS, 4, p. 365 (KW, VIII, p. 61).
14. SKS, 1, p. 292 (254). See Chapter 6, note 71, this volume.
15. *Papirer*, III A 3, July 1840 (*Papers and Journals: A Selection*, p. 128).
16. *Papirer*, V B 47.13, p. 104.
17. *Papirer*, V B 53.29, p. 119 (*Papers and Journals: A Selection*, p. 185).
18. SKS, 4, p. 359 (KW, VIII, pp. 44–5).
19. See Roger Poole, *Kierkegaard*, p. 86: '*The Concept of Anxiety* labors to represent itself at once as an impeccably academic work and as the undoing of all such work.'
20. SKS, 4, p. 352 (KW, VIII, p. 47).
21. Johann Karl F. Rosenkranz, *Psychologie oder die Wissenschaft vom subjectiven Geist*, Königsberg, 1837. See Poole, *Kierkegaard*, pp. 94–6. As a matter of interest, Kierkegaard also possessed Rosenkranz's *Encyclopädie der theologischen Wissenschaft*, Halle, 1831–   .
22. SKS, 4, p. 337 (KW, VIII, p. 30).
23. SKS, 4, p. 347 (KW, VIII, p. 41).
24. SKS, 4, p. 323 (KW, VIII, p. 16).
25. SKS, 4, p. 365 (KW, VIII, p. 61).
26. SKS, 4, p. 366 (KW, VIII, p. 61).

27. SKS, 4, pp. 381–2 (KW VIII, pp. 78–9). In the case of Kierkegaard's use of the term 'self' it is as well to think of selfhood as a matter of there being, over a certain threshold, more or less. In the sense in which by the self's 'possibilities' one understands its possibilities of fulfilment, as Kierkegaard usually does, one should put this by saying that, once the 'synthesis is posited', the self can either fail to fulfill or succeed in fulfilling its possibilities. The term 'self' applies, one can say, when selfhood is at issue for itself, whether standing before its possibilities and facing them or just anxiously inhabiting the space of tensions in which its possibilities of fulfilment are presented less or more clearly.

28. SKS, 1, p. 207 (KW, II, p. 259).

29. SKS, 4, p. 386 (KW, VIII, p. 83).

30. SKS, 4, pp. 402–3 (KW, VIII, pp. 99–100).

31. SKS, 4, p. 388 (KW, VIII, p. 84).

32. SKS, 4, pp. 388–96 (KW, VIII, pp. 76–83).

33. SKS, 4, p. 399 (KW, VIII, p. 96).

34. SKS, 4, p. 420 (KW, VIII, p. 118).

35. SKS, 4, pp. 447–8 (KW, VIII, pp. 147–8).

36. See SKS, 4, p. 363 (KW, VIII, p. 59).

37. See *Papirer*, I A 2, 30 May 1834 (*Papers and Journals: A Selection*, p. 9); II A 31, 1837; SKS, 4, pp. 362–3 (KW, VIII, pp. 58–9).

38. See SKS, K 4, p. 173, and for a general account of the text's origins, pp. 181–94.

39. *Papirer*, V A 98, from 1844 (*Journals and Papers: A Selection*, p. 183). The occasion for the entry was Kierkegaard's reading Aristotle for the first time. It was 'strange' to find that the motivating concept of Book 3, Chapter 3, of *De anima* was 'error' – as it had been for him in 'De Omnibus Dubitandum Est'.

40. *Papirer*, IV A 2, from 1842–43.

41. New York: Harper, 1959.

42. *Papirer*, II A 335, 20 January 1839 (*Papers and Journals: A Selection*, p. 100, translation slightly altered). 'Rationalism and Supernaturalism', which may have appeared at about the time of this entry, describes supernaturalism in terms of 'breaking' the 'chains of all the syllogisms and all natural laws' (p. 262).

43. H. L. Martensen, *Grundrids til Moralphilosophiens System*, Copenhagen: C. A. Reitzel, 1841, translated as 'Outline to a System of Moral Philosophy, by Curtis L. Thompson and David J. Kangas, *Between Hegel and Kierkegaard: Hans L. Martensen's Philosophy of Religion*, Atlanta, GA: Scholars Press, see p. 248.

44. 'Johannes Climacus, or De Omnibus Dubitandum Est', *Papirer*, IV B 1, from 1842–43, p. 116. See Chapter 2, note 7, of this volume.

45. *Papirer*, IV B 10.10 and 10.18 ('When I am ignorant [*uvidende*] I do not doubt [in] uncertainty. I let the matter rest, I do not know if there are ghosts. Doubt is the higher moment of uncertainty, I decide my relation to the matter, in uncertainty I do not do that'.)

46. *Papirer*, IV B 2.9.

47. *Papirer*, IV B 2.19. Emphasis added.

48. *Papirer*, IV B 1, pp. 146–8.
49. 'De Omnibus' has Johannes Climacus (who we remember is the innocent hero of the story and not its author) put it in a typically Hegelian way: since consciousness is neither reality nor ideality and yet, without either, would be nothing, both its coming into being and its nature are a 'contradiction'. This contradiction is the 'first form' of the actual relation between ideality and reality, as opposed to its possible or theoretical relation. Consciousness turns out, in Climacus's philosophical terminology, to be 'spirit', and we find here the makings of Kierkegaard's notion (in *Either/Or*, *Anxiety*, and *The Sickness unto Death*) of the self as a relation to the psychosomatic synthesis (also a relation) that it simultaneously is.
50. *Papirer*, IV B 1, pp. 149.
51. *Papirer*, I A 60, 28 May 1835 (*Papers and Journals: A Selection*, pp. 18–21).
52. *Papirer*, I A 62. 1 June 1835 (*Papers and Journals: A Selection*, p. 21, translation altered).
53. *Papirer*, IV B 1.9.
54. *Papirer*, IV B 1.9.
55. G. E. Lessing, 'Über den Beweis des Geistes und der Kraft', *Theologische Streitschriften*, GW, 9, p. 82. The short piece (only eight pages) also includes an occurrence of a favourite phrase of Climacus's: 'metabasis eis allo genos' (Greek, literally, shift to another kind, or qualitative change). Kierkegaard refers to a 'leap' as early as 1835, in a journal entry (*Papirer*, I A 99 [*Journals and Papers: A Selection*, p. 44]), proposing that it is because Christianity is a 'radical cure' that people shrink from it and 'lack the strength to make the despairing *leap*' (original emphasis).
56. G. E. Lessing, *Sämtliche Werke*, edited by K. Lachmann and F. Muncker, Berlin: Walter de Gruyter, 1979, p. 428.
57. SKS, 4, p. 218.
58. *Papirer*, V B 10; cf. SK4, K4, p. 190.
59. *Papirer*, V B 3.2 (*Papers and Journals: A Selection*, p. 184, translation altered).
60. SKS, 4, p. 305.
61. SKS, 4, p. 243.
62. SKS, 4, p. 248.
63. SKS, 4, pp. 272–84; the 'jest' reference is on p. 272 (*Philosophical Fragments*, translated by David Swenson, revised by Howard V. Hong, Princeton, NJ: Princeton University Press, 1962, p. 89).
64. See SKS, K4, pp. 262–86; and Arild Waaler, 'Aristotle, Leibniz and the Modal Categories in the Interlude of the Fragments', in *Kierkegaard Studies: Yearbook 1998*, edited by Niels Jørgen Cappelørn and Hermann Deuser with Jon Stewart and Christian Tolstrup, Berlin and New York: Walter de Gruyter, 1998, pp. 276–91, and 'Philosophiske smuler – En liten parentes', *Bøygen. Tidsskrift for nordisk språk og litteratur* (1997), 4, pp. 2–7.
65. SKS, 4, pp. 285–6 (*Philosophical Fragments*, pp. 107–10).
66. SKS, 4, p. 306.

67. *Papirer*, V A 96, from 1844 (*Papers and Journals: A Selection*, pp. 182–3); cf., e.g., *Papirer*, II A 379: 'With Christianity everything has become a step lower in so far as a higher moment has entered. . . .'

68. See, e.g., Arnold B. Come, *Trendelenburg's Influence on Kierkegaard's Categories*, Montreal: Inter Editions, 1991.

69. KW, XII, 1, p. 17.

70. H. L. Martensen, 'Rationalisme, Supranaturalisme og *principium exclusi medii*', *Tidsskrift for Litteratur og Kritik*, vol. 1, 1839, p. 46. Heiberg had responded to Mynster in the same issue. A few years later ('Herbart og Fichte om de logiske Prinsiper', vol. 7, 1842, pp. 325–52) Mynster had repeated that the issue was still in no way outdated (p. 325). See Chapter 6, note 9, of this volume.

Chapter 10

1. For an account of the origins of the manuscripts and of the occasion for their revision, see SKS, K4, pp. 540–62.

2. See *Papirer*, IV B 110–11 and 116.

3. *Papirer*, IV B 125–39, officially dated 1844 but more likely from late 1843. See SKS, K4, p. 542.

4. SKS 4, p. 477.

5. SKS, 4, p. 480.

6. SKS, 4, p. 484.

7. *Intelligensblade*, edited by J. L. Heiberg, Copenhagen, vol. 4.

8. SKS, K4, p. 546.

9. SKS, K4, p. 492.

10. SKS, 4, p. 493.

11. *For Literatur og Kritik. Et Fjerdingaarsskrift*, edited by Fyens Stifts literære Selskab, 1843, vol. 1, no. 4, pp. 384 f.

12. See SKS, K4, p. 552.

13. SKS 4, p. 497.

14. SKS, 4, pp. 501–2.

15. SKS, 4, p. 503.

16. *Papirer*, IV A 2, 1842–3; see p. 229 of this volume.

17. *Papirer*, V A 100–101. See SKS, K4, pp. 552–4.

18. SKS 4, p. 509.

19. The idea that philosophy is what the age demands and that it calls 'doubly' to the 'chosen, whose destiny it is to hasten ahead of the masses, each in his individual circle of activity, and plant the flag of culture in heretofore untrodden soil', was promoted in Heiberg's 'Introductory Lecture to the Course in Logic', p. 35 in the 1835 edition. Heiberg continued: 'To say more about the recommendations of philosophical knowing I take to be unnecessary at least in this group.' In a reply to an anonymous review of the lecture (in fact by Eggert Christopher Tryde), Heiberg (*Dansk-Litteratur-Tidende*, 1833, no. 46, p. 770) had said: 'And theology is philosophy; otherwise it is nothing.'

20. SKS, 4, pp. 511–12.

21. SKS, 4, p. 515.
22. SKS, 4, p. 515.
23. SKS, 4, p. 515.
24. SKS, 4, p. 516.
25. This was the first of Hippocrates' *Aphorisms*. The physician was born ca. 460 B.C. on Cos and died at Larissaa in Thessaly ca. 357 B.C., more than one hundred years later. The full aphorism: 'Life is short, art is long; the occasion fleeting, experience deceitful, and judgment difficult.'
26. SKS, 4, p. 516.
27. The expression 'going beyond Hegel' is attributed to Sibbern, who used it appreciatively in a review of Heiberg to mark a certain independence of the master in Heiberg. Kierkegaard's use of the expression 'going further than Socrates' in *Fragments* may contain some allusion to this. Kierkegaard is himself alluding to Martensen as well as to Heiberg. In a review of Heiberg's logic course (*Maanedsskrift for Litteratur*, vol. 16) he complains that the Hegelian system doesn't have the resources to embrace life's fulness, including the freedom expressed in poetry and religion. See notes 55, 56 in Chapter 3 of this volume. See SKS, K4, p. 620.
28. By all accounts a reference to Martensen, who, in a review of Heiberg's *New Poems*, advances a theory of the comic which is to be found in Hegel's *Aesthetics*. See SKS, K4, pp. 620–1.
29. SKS 4, p. 518. A reference to Heiberg's treatise, 'The Logical System', in *Perseus*, no. 2, where the author claims to supplement Hegel's exposition, which 'lacks certain details'. See SKS, K4, p. 621
30. SKS, 4, p. 518.
31. SKS, 4, p. 519.
32. SKS, 4, p. 520.
33. SKS, 4, p. 521.
34. SKS, 4, p. 522.
35. SKS, 4, p. 523.
36. SKS, 4, p. 523.
37. SKS, 4, pp. 523–4.
38. SKS, 4, p. 525.
39. SKS, 4, pp. 525–6.
40. Rahbek (ed.), *Dansk og Norsk Nasjonalværk, eller ældgammel Moerskabslæsnng*.
41. *Papirer*, II A 432, 17 May 1839. See SKS, K4, p. 540. The ode is from Horace's *Carminum liber*, I (9.19), singing of an evening rendezvous.
42. SKS, 4, pp. 471–2, 474.
43. *Papirer*, V B 192, from 1844.

Chapter 11

1. *Papirer*, IV B 59, from 1844.
2. Ibid.
3. Ibid.

4. *Papirer*, V A 109, 27 August 1844.
5. See Kimmse, *Encounters*, pp. 209–10, cf. pp. 109, 220–1 (287–8, cf. 159, 299–300).
6. SKS, 6, p. 32. For an account of the genesis and origins of the text see SKS, K6, pp. 7–89.
7. 'Caricatures of the Most Holy'; see Chapter 7, note 30.
8. A reference to William Afham.
9. *Papirer*, V A 110, from 1844 (*Papers and Journals: A Selection*, pp. 183–4).
10. SKS, 6, p. 66. Translations are my own.
11. SKS, 6, pp. 37, 38.
12. SKS, 6, pp. 80–4.
13. See SKS, K4, p. 541.
14. SKS, 6, p. 87.
15. SKS, 6, p. 94.
16. SKS, 6, p. 103.
17. SKS, 6, p. 158.
18. SKS, 6, p. 164.
19. *Papirer*, X¹ A 139, from 1849 (*Papers and Journals: A Selection*, p. 372, translation altered).
20. See SKS, K5, pp. 393–4. At one point Kierkegaard had envisaged six such discourses, but in the event the original plan of three was followed. The discourses were published just one day before *Stages*. See the following discussion.
21. See SKS, 6, p. 391.
22. SKS, 6, p. 368.
23. SKS, 6, p. 369.
24. SKS, 6, p. 439.
25. SKS, 6, p. 427; and see, e.g., p. 416.
26. See SV³10, pp. 223 (KW XII, 1, p. 553).
27. SKS, 6, pp. 415, 427.
28. *Papirer*, I A 154, from 1836 (*Papers and Journals: A Selection*, p. 154).
29. SKS 6, p. 396.
30. SKS, 6, p. 403.
31. SKS, 6, p. 403.
32. SKS, 6, p. 439. The term 'prius' occurs in Schelling, and Kierkegaard's use of it can be traced to the notes he took at Schelling's lectures.
33. *Phenomenology of Spirit*, §77, p. 49.
34. SKS, 6, p. 424.
35. For example, concerning the letter he sent to Regine (*Papirer*, X⁵ A 149 [*Papers and Journals: A Selection*, p. 415]; cf. X¹, A 667 [p. 416]) with reference to Quidam's saying he had a murder on his conscience.
36. SKS, 6, p. 368.
37. *Papirer*, IV A 234, from 1843 (*Papers and Journals: A Selection*, p. 165).
38. SKS, 6, pp. 96–7.
39. SKS, 6, pp. 404–12. See SKS, K6, p. 356.

Chapter 12

1. *Papirer*, VI A 79, from 1845 (*Papers and Journals: A Selection*, p. 190). See SKS, 6, pp. 446, 451, 454.
2. For an account of the origins of the texts, see SKS, K5, pp. 293–402.
3. Kirmmse, *Encounters*, pp. 240, 336 (331, 443–4). For Kierkegaard's expression of surprise at having reached thirty-four, see *Papirer*, VIII¹ A 100 (*Papers and Journals: A Selection*, pp. 260–1).
4. *Papirer*, VI A 75, 10 June 1845 (*Papers and Journals: A Selection*, p. 189).
5. *Breve og Aktstykker*, I, p. 20 (26–7). The passage is translated in *Papers and Journals: A Selection*, pp. 656–7.
6. SV³ 9, p. 20 (KW, XII, 1, p. 17).
7. SV³ 9, p. 19 (KW, XII, 1, p. 16).
8. Ibid.
9. See SV³ 9, p. 26 (KW, XII, 1, pp. 25–6).
10. N. F. S. Grundtvig, *Værker i Udvalg*, vol. II, edited by Georg Christensen and Hal Koch, Copenhagen: Gyldendal, 1940, p. 326. See Bruce Kirmmse, *Kierkegaard in Golden Age Denmark*, p. 212.
11. SV³ 9, p. 37 (KW, XII, 1, pp. 38–9).
12. SV³ 9, p. 44 (KW, XII, 11, p. 47).
13. SV³ 9, p. 36 (KW, XII, 1, p. 37).
14. SV³ 9, p. 46 (KW, XII, 1, p. 50).
15. SV³ 9, p. 49 (KW, XII, 1, p. 53).
16. SV³ 9, p. 48 (KW, XII, 1, p. 52).
17. SV³ 9, p. 51 (KW, XII, 1, p. 56). See, e.g., Aristotle, *Nicomachean Ethics*, 1177 a.
18. *Papirer*, V B 8.
19. SV³ 9, p. 62 (KW, XII, 1, p. 72).
20. SV³ 9, p. 59 (KW, XII, 1, pp. 67–8).
21. SV³ 9, p. 56 (KW, XII, 1, pp. 64–5).
22. 'Eine Duplik' (1778), *G. E. Lessing's gesammelte Werke* (GW) (new revised edition), Leipzig: G. J. Göschen'sche Verlagshandlung, 1857, vol. 9, p. 98.
23. What could Kierkegaard make of a thinker who at one time or another held (1) that individuals can get a head-start at birth by bringing their spiritual gains with them from a previous existence (and generation), (2) that freedom was *not* such a good idea *because* it induced anxiety (*Philosophische Aufsätze*, 1776) – Lessing thanked his God that he was 'under necessity, that the best must be' – and who ended up believing (3) that the resort to religion was in any case a sign of human immaturity (*Die Erziehung des Menschengeschlechts* [1780], GW, 9, pp. 399–425). But in mitigation and in the context of the fourth thesis attributable to Lessing, it would be perfectly in order to doubt that Lessing considered any of these to be 'results'.
24. Henry Chadwick, 'Lessing', in Paul Edwards (ed.), *Encyclopedia of Philosophy*, New York: Macmillan. 1967, vol. 4, p. 445.
25. SV³ 9, p. 90 (KW, XII, 1, p. 106).

26. *Papirer*, V B 1.2 and 1.3, from 1844. For Lessing's use of the word *Sprung*, see GW, 9, pp. 84–5.

27. For an informative account of this aspect of the period, see Frederick C. Beiser, *The Fate of Reason: German Philosophy from Kant to Fichte*, Cambridge, MA: Harvard University Press, 1987.

28. See *Papirer*, e.g., I A 100, 10 September 1836; A 237, 12 September 1836; A 340, from 1836–37; II A 2; A 623, from 1837.

29. See *Papirer*, V B 55.14, from 1844; and J. G. Hamann, *Sokratische Denkwürdig-keiten*, edited by Sven-Aage Jørgensen, Stuttgart: Reclam, 1968.

30. J. G. Hamann, *Sämtliche Werke, Historisch-kritische Ausgabe*, edited by J. Nadler, Vienna: Herder, 1949–57, vol. II, p. 74.

31. Moses Mendelssohn, *Morgenstunden oder Vorelesungen über das Daseyn Gottes*, Berlin, 1785, revised edition, 1876. See Beiser, *The Fate of Reason*, pp. 72, 78, 94.

32. Friedrich Heinrich Jacobi, *Werke*, edited by F. H. Jacobi and F. Köppen, Leipzig: Fleischer, 1812, vol. IV/1, pp. 210–11, 223.

33. See Carl Ludwig Michelet, *Geschichte de letzten Systeme der Philosophie in Deutschland von Kant bis Hegel*, vols. I–II, Berlin: 1837–38, vol. I, pp. 302–18.

34. SV³ 9, p. 209 (KW, XII, 1, p. 250).

35. SV³ 9, pp. 83, 82 (KW, XII, 1, pp. 96, 95); and p. 209 (KW, XII, 1, p. 251).

36. SV³ 9, p. 82 (KW, XII, 1, p. 95).

37. SV³ 9, p. 91 (KW, XII, 1, p. 107).

38. SV³ 9, p. 84 (KW XII, 1, p. 93). G. E. Lessing, 'Über den Beweis des Geistes und der Kraft', see Chapter 9, note 55, of this volume. The familiar Aristotelian expression 'metabasis eis allo genos' occurs, e.g., at SV³ 9, p. 84 [KW XII, 1, p. 98]).

39. SV³ 9, pp. 83, 82 (KW, XII, 1, pp. 96, 95).

40. G. E. Lessing, *Axiomata*, GW, 9, pp. 210, 211. Cf. Beiser, *The Fate of Reason*, p. 58. Lessing's remarks here are part of his dispute with H. M. Goeze (see *Anti-Goeze*, GW, 9, pp. 241–322), an orthodox Lutheran pastor in Hamburg, who had reacted against Lessing's publication (with commentary) of an attack on positive religion by H. S. Reimarus (*Apologie oder Schützschrift für die vernunftige Veregrer Gottes*). Lessing had received the manuscript, withheld by its author during his lifetime because he feared the effect of its publication, from Reimarus's daughter, Elise (cf. SV³ 9, p. 89 [KW, XII, 1, p. 103], where Kierkegaard refers to her as Emilie).

41. G. E. Lessing, 'Über den Beweis des Geistes und der Kraft', GW, 9, p. 85.

42. SV³ 9, p. 85 (KW, XII, 1, p. 99).

43. I. Kant, 'Gedanken bei dem frühzeitigen Ableben des Herrn Friedrich von Funk', *Werke, Akademie Text Ausgabe*, edited by W. Dilthey et al., Berlin: de Gruyter, 1979, vol. II, pp. 37–44. See Beiser, *The Fate of Reason*, p. 333, n. 49.

44. SKS, 4, p. 136 (*Fear and Trembling*, p. 70).

45. SV³ 9, p. 85 (KW, XII, 1, p. 99).

46. Ibid.

47. SV³ 9, p. 90 (KW, XII, 1, p. 105).

48. SV³ 9, p. 88 (KW, XII, 1, p. 102).

49. SV³ 9, p. 57 (KW, XII, 1, p. 65).

50. SV³ 9, p. 59 (KW, XII, 1, p. 69).

51. F. H. Jacobi, 'Über die Lehre des Spinoza in Briefen an den Herrn Moses Mendelssohn' (LS), in *Jacobis Spinoza Büchlein*, edited by Fritz Mauthner, München: Georg Müller Verlag, 1912, pp. 63–80.

52. LS, pp. 79 and 80, quoted in German in SV³ 9, pp. 87–88 (KW, XII, 1, p. 12).

53. SV³ 9, p. 85 (KW, XII, 1, p. 99).

54. SV³ 9, p. 62 (KW, XII, 1, p. 71).

55. *Papirer*, X² A 130, from 1849 (*Papers and Journals: A Selection*, p. 436).

56. *Papirer*, III C 33, from 1841–2. Kierkegaard refers to *Aesthetics*, in the collected edition of P. Marheineke et al., Berlin, 1832, vol. 3, p. 440.

57. Hegel, *Aesthetics*, II, pp. 1229–30.

58. In Hegel, tragic heroes find themselves 'violat[ing]what, if they were true to their own nature, they should be honouring'. In Antigone's case it was her uncle's royal command, but in the bereaved Creon's case 'the sacred tie of blood' (ibid., p. 1217). Cf. p. 1218, where Hegel says that '[o]f all the masterpieces of the classical and modern world', with its multiple tragedies 'the *Antigone* seems to him to be of its kind 'the most magnificent and satisfying work of art'.

59. Ibid., p. 1214.

60. 'Hjertets Reenhed er at ville Eet', in *En Leiligheds-Tale*, SV³ 11, pp. 30 f. (*Purity of Heart Is to Will One Thing: Spiritual Preparation for the Office of Confession*, translated and with an introductory essay by Douglas V. Steere, New York, Harper Torchbooks, 1958, p. 53).

61. SKS, 4, pp. 447–51 (KW, VIII, pp. 148–51).

62. SV³ 9, p. 127 (KW, XII, 1, p. 153).

63. SV³ 9, pp. 13, 132 (KW, XII, 1, pp. 158, 159).

64. SV³ 9, pp. 137–51 (KW, XII, 1, pp. 165–81).

65. SV³ 9, pp. 154–6 (KW, XII, 1, pp. 185–7).

66. SV³ 9, pp. 163–4, 166 (KW, XII, 1, pp. 196, 199).

67. SV³ 9, pp. 169–70 (KW, XII, 1, p. 203).

68. SV³ 10, p. 10 (KW, XII, 1, p. 302).

69. SV³ 10, p. 19, see pp. 18–22 (KW, XII, 1, p. 312, see pp. 311–14).

70. SV³ 10, p. 23 (KW, XII, 1, pp. 317).

71. SV³ 10, pp. 27–28 (KW, XII, 1, pp. 321–2).

72. SV³ 10, p. 29 (KW, XII, 1, p. 324).

73. SV³ 10, p. 52 (KW, XII, 1, p. 351).

74. SV³ 10, p. 46 (KW, XII, 1, pp. 343–4).

75. SV³ 10, p. 52 (KW, XII, 1, p. 351).

76. SV³ 10, p. 57 (KW, XII, 1, p. 357).

77. SV³ 10, p. 56 (KW, XII, 1, p. 356).

78. Ibid.

79. SV³ 10, p. 181 (KW, XII, 1, pp. 503–4).

80. SV³ 10, p. 179 (KW, XII, 1, pp. 501–2).

81. SV³ 10, pp. 181–2 (KW, XII, 1, pp. 504–5).

82. SV³ 10, p. 178 (KW, XII, 1, p. 500).

83. SV³ 10, p. 133 (KW, XII, 1, p. 447).

84. *Papirer*, II A 140, from 1837 (*Papers and Journals: A Selection*, p. 90).

85. SV³ 10, p. 189 (KW, XII, 1, p. 513).

86. SV³ 10, p. 134 fn. (KW, XII, p. 448).

87. SV³ 10, p. 223 (KW, XII, 1, p. 553).

88. *Papirer*, X⁶ B 78, from 1850 (*Papers and Journals: A Selection*, p. 459). The passage goes on to say that 'offence is the negative criterion which fixes the quality separating God and man'. The believer is not offended, indeed the opposite, but always has 'the possibility of offence as a negative category'. Kierkegaard puts into the mouth of his later pseudonym, Anti-Climacus, a series of pronouncements about faith and the absurd which he also ascribes to the earlier pseudonyms and means Anti-Climacus to inherit, among them the following: 'The absurd is not simply the absurd or absurdities indiscriminately . . . the absurd is a category . . . the negative criterion of the divine . . . the absurd marks off the sphere of faith, a sphere unto itself, negatively . . . it is the category of courage and enthusiasm . . . [there is] nothing at all daunting about it. . . .' (*Papirer*, X⁶ B 79).

89. *Papirer*, X² A 592, from 1850 (*Papers and Journals: A Selection*, p. 482).

90. Harvie Ferguson, *Melancholy and the Critique of Modernity: Søren Kierkegaard's Religious Psychology*, London/New York: Routledge, 1995, p. 167.

91. Ibid.; cf. James Conant, 'Kierkegaard, Wittgenstein, and Nonsense', in Ted Cohen, Paul Guyer, and Hilary Putnam (eds.), *Pursuits of Reason*, Lubbock: Texas Tech University Press, 1992, p. 215; and Henry E. Allison, 'Christianity and Nonsense', *The Review of Metaphysics*, vol. 2. (1967), no. 3, reprinted in Josiah Thompson (ed.), *Kierkegaard: A Collection of Critical Essays*, Garden City, NY: Anchor Books, 1972, p. 446.

92. See Conant, 'Kierkegaard, Wittgenstein, and Nonsense', p. 215. That subjective reflection is presented as a conspicuously unsuccessful method of arriving at truth is Allison's reason for taking the 'argument' of *Postscript* to be deliberately 'misologistic'.

93. SV³ 10, p. 226 (KW, XII, 1, p. 556).

94. *Papirer*, I C 100, 7 September 1836.

95. *Papirer*, II A 29 and 30 (*Papers and Journals: A Selection*, pp. 80–81). See Chapter 4, note 2, in this volume.

96. William Heinesen, *The Doomed Fiddlers (De fortabte Spillemænd)* (1950), Copenhagen: Gyldendal, 1965, p. 144, my translation.

97. *Papirer*, X² A 130, from 1849 (*Papers and Journals: A Selection*, pp. 436–7).

98. According to Brøchner; see Kirmmse, *Encounters*, p. 235 (323–4).

99. Johan Ludvig Heiberg, 'Det logiske System', *Perseus, Journal for den speculative Idee*, 1838, no. 2, pp. 1–45.

100. SV³ 10, pp. 278–9 (KW, XII, 1, pp. 617–18).

101. SV³ 10, pp. 280–1 (KW, XII, 1, pp. 620–1) (emphasis added).

102. *Papirer*, VI B 83.3, from 1845.

103. SV³ 10, pp. 280–2 (KW, XII, 1, pp. 620–1) (emphasis added).

104. SV³ 10, pp. 285–6 (KW, XII, 1, pp. 625–6).

105. SV³ 9, p. 65 (KW, XII, 1, p. 75).

106. *Papirer*, VII¹ A 4, 7 February 1846 (*Papers and Journals: A Selection*, p. 204).

Chapter 13

1. Josiah Thompson, *Kierkegaard*, pp. 188–9.

2. *Papirer*, VI B 192 (*Papers and Journals: A Selection*, p. 197).

3. *Papirer*, VI B 193 (*Papers and Journals: A Selection*, p. 198).

4. P. L. Møller (ed.), *Gaea, Aarbog*, 22 December 1845. See Jørgensen, *Kierkegaard. En Biografi*, II, pp. 130–1.

5. See Jørgensen Carl, *Kierkegaard. En Biografi*, II, p. 131.

6. 'Where there is spirit, there is the Church; where there is P. L. Møller, there is *The Corsair*.' *Faedrelandet*, 1845, no. 2078, 27 December 1845.

7. *Fædrelandet*, 1845, no. 2078.

8. *Fædrelandet*, 1846, no. 9.

9. *Papirer*, VII 1 A 97 and 98, 9 March 1846 (*Papers and Journals: A Selection*, pp. 213–17).

10. SV³ 14, p. 29 (*A Literary Review*, Harmondsworth: Penguin, 2001, p. 24).

11. SV³ 14, p. 25 (*A Literary Review*, p. 20).

12. SV³ 14, p. 31 (*A Literary Review*, p. 26).

13. SV³ 14, p. 28 (*A Literary Review*, p. 24).

14. SV³ 14, p. 34 (*A Literary Review*, p. 30).

15. SV³ 14, p. 32 (*A Literary Review*, p. 28).

16. SV³ 14, p. 43 (*A Literary Review*, p. 39).

17. SV³ 14, p. 33 (*A Literary Review*, pp. 28–9).

18. SV³ 14, pp. 92–3 (*A Literary Review*, p. 90).

19. SV³ 14, p. 92 (*A Literary Review*, pp. 86 and 90).

20. SV³ 14, p. 61 (*A Literary Review*, p. 58).

21. SV³ 14, p. 60 (*A Literary Review*, p. 57).

22. SV³ 14, pp. 58–59 (*A Literary Review*, p. 55).

23. SV³ 14, p. 59 (*A Literary Review*, pp. 55–6).

24. SV³ 14, p. 77 (*A Literary Review*, pp. 74–5).

25. SKS, I, p. 137 (KW, II, p. 79).

26. *Papirer*, X³ A 477, from 1850 (*Papers and Journals: A Selection*, p. 506).

27. SV³ 14, p. 46 (*A Literary Review*, p. 42).

28. SV³ 14, p. 46 (*A Literary Review*, p. 44).

29. M. Heidegger, *History of the Concept of Time: Prolegomena* (HCT), translated by Theodore Kisiel, Bloomington: Indiana University Press, 1985, p. 247.

30. HCT, p. 244 (my italic, original italic removed). What Heidegger refers to is the way we not only measure ourselves against one another but also the way we identify ourselves by our proximity or apartness (better or worse than) in these respects. So *Abständigkeit* is not the presence or measure of any specific distance between oneself and others, or others in general; it is concern with

difference *überhaupt*, whether with measuring up to or even seeing oneself as superior to others, or the concern to be just like them, whether they are higher or lower, even the concern that everyone should be like everyone else. *Abständigkeit* is, in short, a way or mode we have of being with others, a structural feature of *Dasein* as such. In Kierkegaard's more vivid language, it is the quagmire of selfish and mutual other-regarding opposition, where gossip, rumour, specious importance, and apathetic envy govern our relations with one another. Kierkegaard would happily have agreed that the nature of this concern with difference is to draw *Dasein* in the direction of the 'average and everyday', with a resulting absorption in *das Man* in which there is a 'levelling of all differences' (ibid., p. 426).

31. See my 'The Dialectic of Proximity and Apartness', in Harald Jodalen and Arne Johan Vetlesen (eds), *Closeness: An Ethics*, Oslo: Scandinavian University Press, 1997, pp. 167–84. That Heidegger does not put the term to this use surely has to do with his concern to establish the 'phenomenon' as in some way structural to human being, while Kierkegaard is interested in seeing under what conditions its bad influence can be avoided.

32. SV^3 14, p. 63 (*A Literary Review*, p. 60).

33. As I did in Chapter 7 of my *Kierkegaard* ('Arguments of the Philosophers'), London/New York: Routledge, 1982 (rev. ed. 1991, new ed. 1999).

34. *Papirer*, VII^1 B 135, from 1846 (*Papers and Journals: A Selection*, p. 251).

35. *Papirer*, VII^1 B 43, from 1846.

36. SV^3 14, p. 77 (*A Literary Review*, p. 73).

37. See SV^3 14, p. 87 (*A Literary Review*, p. 84).

38. SV^3 14, pp. 86–7 (*A Literary Review*, p. 85).

39. HCT, pp. 246–7.

40. SV^3 14, pp. 89–94 (*A Literary Review*, pp. 86–92).

41. SV^3 14 p. 78 (*A Literary Review*, p. 75).

42. Klaus-M. Kodalle, 'The Utilitarian Self and the "Useless" Passion of Faith', in Niels Jørgen Cappelørn and Hermann Deuser (eds), *Kierkegaard Studies: Yearbook 1999*, Berlin/New York: Walter de Gruyter, 1999, e.g., pp. 400–2.

43. SV^3 14, p. 79 (*A Literary Review*, p. 76). 'Glittering vices' is a notion attributed to Augustine's *City of God*, but the actual expression itself is not found there.

44. SV^3 14, p. 80 (*A Literary Review*, pp. 77–8).

45. SV^3 14, p. 98 (*A Literary Review*, p. 97).

46. SV^3 14, p. 99 (*A Literary Review*, p. 97).

47. SV^3 14, pp. 79–80 (*A Literary Review*, pp. 76–7).

48. *Papirer*, X^2 A 394, from 1850 (*Papers and Journals: A Selection*, p. 466).

49. *Papirer*, X^1 A 107, from 1849 (*Papers and Journals: A Selection*, p. 365, translation altered, original emphasis).

50. SV^3 14, p. 101 (*A Literary Review*, p. 100).

51. See, e.g., Hubert L. Dreyfus and Jane Rubin, 'Kierkegaard on the Nihilism of the Present Age: The Case of Commitment as Addiction', *Synthese*, vol. 98, no. 1, (1) January 1994, pp. 3–19; Alastair Hannay, 'Kierkegaard's Present Age and Ours', in Mark Wrathall and Jeff Malpas (eds.), *Heidegger, Authenticity and*

Modernity: Essays in Honor of Hubert L. Dreyfus, Volume 1, Cambridge MA: MIT Press, pp. 105–22, notes pp. 354–6; and the collection of essays devoted to *A Literary Review* in Niels Jørgen Cappelørn and Hermann Deuser (eds.), *Kierkegaard Studies: Yearbook 1999*.

Chapter 14

1. Kirmmse, *Encounters*, p. 335 (442).
2. See *Papirer*, VII¹ A 182, 186, 189 191, 197, 198, 200, from 1846 (*Papers and Journals: A Selection*, pp. 235–43).
3. Kirmmse, *Encounters*, p. 237 (326–7).
4. *Papirer*, VII¹ A 2 and 3, from 1846 (*Papers and Journals: A Selection*, p. 203). From a journal that runs parallel with the first NB journal.
5. *Papirer*, VII¹ A 9, 9 February 1846 (*Papers and Journals: A Selection*, p. 204).
6. *Papirer*, VII¹ A 97 and 98, 9 March 1846 (*Papers and Journals: A Selection*, p. 215).
7. *Papirer*, VII¹ A 5, from 1846 (*Papers and Journals: A Selection*, p. 204).
8. Kirmmse, *Encounters*, p. 138 (198).
9. *Papirer*, VII¹ A 107, from 1846 (*Papers and Journals: A Selection*, p. 223).
10. *Papirer*, VII¹ Ibid. A 107, from 1846 (*Papers and Journals: A Selection*, pp. 223–4)
11. *Papirer*, VIII¹ A 99, from 1847 (*Papers and Journals: A Selection*, p. 260).
12. Thompson, *Kierkegaard*, p. 191.
13. Kirmmse, *Encounters*, p. 97 (142).
14. W. Kaufmann (ed.), *From Dostoevsky to Sartre*, New York: Random House, 1956, p. 20. This reference is thanks to an internet encounter with Mike Bool.
15. Kirmmse, *Encounters*, p. 195 (271–2).
16. Thompson, *Kierkegaard*, p. 139. The quotation is from Steven Crites, 'The Author and the Authorship: Recent Kierkegaard Literature', *Journal of the American Academy of Religion*, vol. 38 (March 1970), p. 38. Thompson gives Lieutenant, later Colonel Barth, the initials that were in fact his son's.
17. Kirmmse, *Encounters*, p. 100 (p. 146).
18. Ibid., pp. 95, 295 (pp. 139, 397–8).
19. Ibid., p. 238 (328).
20. *Papirer*, VII¹ A 147, 7 September 1846 (*Papers and Journals: A Selection*, p. 231).
21. *Papirer*, VII¹ A 107 (*Papers and Journals: A Selection*, p. 224).
22. *Papirer*, VII¹ A 229, 24 January 1847 (*Papers and Journals: A Selection*, p. 245, translation altered).
23. SV³ 14, p. 87 (KW, XIV, pp. 95–6).
24. See Thompson, *Kierkegaard*, p. 190. An intriguing novel based on Møller's life is Henrik Stangerup's *The Seducer: It is Hard to Die in Dieppe*, translated by Sean Martin, London: Marion Boyars, 1990.
25. *Papirer*, VII¹ A 109, from 1846 (*Papers and Journals: A Selection*, p. 225).
26. Kirmmse, *Encounters*, pp. 65–67, 72–75 (102–3, 110–13).
27. *Papirer*, X¹ A 98, from 1849 (*Papers and Journals: A Selection*, pp. 362–3).

28. The latter expression is from a prayer by Mynster on dedicating a new church building. (J. P. Mynster, *Kirkelige Leiligheds-Taler*, 2 vols., Copenhagen: Reitzel, 1854, vol. 1, p. 383. This and other prayers are quoted in Chapter 6 ('Kierkegaard Goes to Church') of George Pattison's excellently scene-setting *'Poor Paris': Kierkegaard's Critique of the Spectacular City*, Kierkegaard Studies: Monograph Series 2 (1), Berlin and New York: Walter de Gruyer, 1999, p. 111.

29. *Papirer*, X² A 589, from 1850.

30. *Papirer*, VII¹ A 169, 5 November 1846 (*Papers and Journals: A Selection*, pp. 233–4).

31. *Papirer*, IX A 240, from 1848 (*Papers and Journals: A Selection*, pp. 327).

32. *Papirer*, VII¹ A 221, 20 January 1847 (*Papers and Journals: A Selection*, p. 243).

33. See *Papirer*, VII¹ A 97 and 98, from 1846 (*Papers and Journals: A Selection*, p. 215), for a comment to the effect that in the Preface to *Postscript* written in May 1845, he had omitted a reference to P. L. Møller's connection with *The Corsair* precisely so that Mynster should not think Kierkegaard would stoop so low as to 'bother with a thing like that'.

34. *Papirer*, X² A 96, from 1849 (*Papers and Journals: A Selection*, pp. 432–3).

35. *Papirer*, VIII¹ A 482, from 1847 (*Papers and Journals: A Selection*, pp. 277–8).

Chapter 15

1. *Papirer*, IX B 63.8, from 1848.

2. *Papirer*, VIII¹ A 390, 4 November 1847; cf. *Papirer*, X⁴ A 511, from 1852 (*Papers and Journals: A Selection*, pp. 274, 536).

3. *Papirer*, VIII¹ A 231, from 1847. The earlier entry (*Papirer*, II A 469) is dated 7 July 1839.

4. See Chapter 6 of this volume.

5. *Papirer*, VIII¹ A 9, from 1847 (*Papers and Journals: A Selection*, p. 254).

6. *Papirer*, VIII¹ A 293, from 1847 (*Papers and Journals: A Selection*, p. 272).

7. *Papirer*, II A 130, 18 July 1837 (*Papers and Journals: A Selection*, p. 89); cf. *Papirer*, II A 127, 1 July 1837; II A 128 (marginal comment); and II A 131, 7 October 1837.

8. SV³ 12, p. 210 (KW, XVI, pp. 216–17).

9. Immanuel Kant, *Fundamental Principles of the Metaphysic of Morals*, in *Kant's Critique of Practical Reason and Other Works on the Theory of Ethics*, translated by T. K. Abbott, London: Longmans, Green, 6th edn., 1954, p. 15; cf. Matthew 22:37 and Luke 10:25 and 10:27.

10. SV³ 12, p. 188, original emphasis removed (KW, XVI, p. 194). See Philip L. Quinn, 'Kierkegaard's Christian Ethics', in Hannay and Marino (eds), *The Cambridge Companion to Kierkegaard*, pp. 349–69, see pp. 361–2; see also Chapter 7 in Hannay, *Kierkegaard*.

11. Kant, *Metaphysical Elements of Ethics*, in *Kant's Critique*, p. 312.

12. Matthew 22:37–40; Mark 12:29–31; and Luke 10:25 and 10:27–28. See Deuteronomy 6:5.

13. Kant, *Critique of Practical Reason*, in *Kant's Critique*, p. 176.

14. SV³ 12, p. 56 (KW, XVI, p. 56).

15. SV³ 12, p. 23 (KW, XVI, p. 17).

16. Kant., *Fundamental Principles of the Metaphysic of Morals*, in *Kant's Critique*, p. 18.

17. William Shakespeare's 'Love is not love which alters when it alteration finds' (sonnet 116), frequently quoted in this connection.

18. See Tracy Strong, *Friedrich Nietzsche and the Politics of Transfiguration*, Berkeley: University of California Press, 1975, pp. 192–202, and Keith Ansell-Pearson, *Nietzsche contra Rousseau*, Cambridge University Press, 1991, pp. 214–15.

19. Cf. Nietzsche's claim, in his unpublished essay on 'Homer's Weltkampf' from 1872, that natural talent must develop through struggle.

20. Cf. Nietzsche's unpublished essay from 1871 on 'The Greek State'.

21. *Papirer*, VIII¹ A 299, from 1847 (*Papers and Journals: A Selection*, p. 272); and SV³ 12, p. 312 (KW, XVI, p. 326).

22. SV³ 12, p. 132 (KW, XVI, p. 134). See Rom. 13:10: '[L]ove is the fulfilment of the law'; and Philip L. Quinn, 'Kierkegaard's Christian Ethics', p. 354.

23. SW³ 12, pp. 260–1 (KW, XVI, p. 271).

24. *Papirer*, VIII¹ A 4, from 1847 (*Papers and Journals: A Selection*, p. 253).

25. SV³ 12, pp. 281, 276 (KW, XVI, pp. 293, 288).

26. SV³ 12, pp. 88–9 (KW, XVI, pp. 87–8). See Quinn, 'Kierkegaard's Christian Ethics', p. 365.

27. SV³ 12, p. 107 (KW, XVI p. 107).

28. SV³ 12, p. 62 (KW, XVI, p. 58).

29. SV³ 10, p. 283 (KW, II, 1, p. 622).

30. *Papirer*, VIII¹ A 390, 4 November 1847 (*Papers and Journals: A Selection*, pp. 274–5).

31. E.g., *Papirer*, VIII¹ A 551, from 1848 (*Papers and Journals: A Selection*, p. 292).

32. A. P. Adler, *Nogle Prædikener*, Copenhagen, 1843.

33. See Thompson, *Kierkegaard*, pp. 195–6; and Kirmmse, *Kierkegaard in Golden Age Denmark*, p. 331.

34. *Breve og Aktstykker*, I, p. 122 (155–6) (letter 83).

35. Kirmmse, *Encounters*, p. 234 (322–3).

36. E.g., *Papirer*, VIII¹ A 252, from 1848.

Chapter 16

1. A. P Adler, *Nogle Digte* (Some Poems), *Studier og Eksempler* (Studies and Examples), *Theologiske Studier* (Theological Studies), and *Forsøg til en kort systematisk Fremstilling af Christendommen i dens Logik* (Attempt at a Short Systematic Presentation of Christianity and Its Logic), all published in Copenhagen in 1846. Later, in August, Kierkegaard also bought Adler's *Skrivelser min Suspension og Endledigste vedkommende* (Writings Concerning My Suspension and Dismissal), which had appeared the previous year.

2. *Papirer*, VIII¹ A 440, 1 December 1847.

3. SV³ 15, p. 53. The drafts and various used and unused fragments appear in *Papirer*, VII 2, and are published as KW, XXIV, in Julia Watkin's translation from her own Danish edition, *Nutidens religieuse Forvirring. Bogen om Adler*, Copenhagen: C. A., Reitzel, 1984.

4. *Papirer*, IX A 189, from 1848 (*Papers and Journals: A Selection*, p. 322).

5. *Papirer*, IX A 302, from 1848.

6. See Kirmmse's discussion in *Kierkegaard in Golden Age Denmark*, pp. 331–9.

7. See *Papirer*, VIII¹ A 219, dated 2 August 1847; VIII¹ A 227, dated 3 August 1847; VIII¹ A 249, dated 15 August (*Papers and Journals: A Selection*, pp. 269–71); and VIII¹ A 250, dated 16 August.

8. *Papirer*, X¹ A 41 and 42, from 1849 (*Papers and Journals: A Selection*, pp. 355–6). For Levin's comments, see Kirmmse, *Encounters*, pp. 211–12 (289–90).

9. *Papirer*, VIII¹ A 497, 28 December 1847.

10. *Papirer*, X¹ A 281, 25 April 1849; and X⁵ A 146, 13 October 1853 (*Papers and Journals: A Selection*, pp. 383, 559).

11. Though recall that Kierkegaard had also demanded, and therefore allowed, that political parties or newspapers that do express opinions and claim to act should do so in the decisive and integrated way that he required of individuals.

12. See *Papirer*, IX A 375, from 1848; X¹ A 202 and X² A 10, from 1849 (*Papers and Journals: A Selection*, pp. 339–40, 377–8, 423). The apartment was in no. 156 A, now 7, at the corner with Tornebuskegade.

13. The desire to speak out is mentioned in *The Point of View*, SV³ 18, p. 119, and referred to as a 'need' (*Trang*) rather than a decision, just as the 'need' to write (*Produktivitetens Trang*) (see ibid., p. 133).

14. *Papirer*, VIII¹ A 640 and 645, 19 and 24 April 1848 *(Papers and Journals: A Selection*, pp. 295–6).

15. *Papirer*, X¹ A 583, from 1849; X⁶ B 249, from 1849–50.

16. *Papirer*, IX A 293, November 1848 (*Papers and Journals: A Selection*: pp. 332–3).

17. SV³ 18, pp. 104–6, 125–6, 133.

18. See *Papirer*, X¹ A 122, 508, 510, 513, 517, and 530 (*Papers and Journals: A Selection*, pp. 368, 390–4).

19. *Papirer*, X¹ A 147, from 1849 (*Papers and Journals: A Selection*, pp. 373–4).

20. SV³ 15, p. 67 (*The Sickness unto Death*, p. 35); *Papirer*, VIII¹ A 18, from 1837. He had got hold of Adolf Trendelenburg's *Geschichte der Kategorienlehre. Zwei Abhandlungen* (History of the Theory of Categories: Two Treatises), published in Berlin in 1846.

21. *Papirer*, IX A 390, from 1848 (*Papers and Journals: A Selection*, pp. 340–1).

22. SV³ 10, p. 195 (KW, XII, 1, p. 520).

23. Hegel, *Phenomenology of Spirit*, § 78, pp. 49, 50. Doubt and despair are also distinguished in *Either/Or*; see p. 515 (SKS 3, p. 204).

24. Hegel, *Phenomenology of Spirit*, p. 50, emphasis removed.

25. SKS 3, pp. 188, 203, 209 (*Either/Or*, pp. 502, 513, 520).

26. SKS 3, pp. 188 and 200 (*Either/Or*, pp. 502, 511)

27. SKS 3, pp. 239–40 (*Either/Or*, pp. 542–3).

28. SV³ 15, pp. 122 and 112 (*The Sickness unto Death*, Harmondsworth: Penguin Books, 1989, pp. 99, 89).

29. SV³ 15, pp. 98–99, 146, 102 (*The Sickness unto Death*, pp. 72, 125, 76).

30. SV³ 15, pp. 133, 87 (*The Sickness unto Death*, pp. 111, 59).

31. See SV³ 15, pp. 131, 132, 135; see also p. 133 (*The Sickness unto Death*, pp. pp. 109, 110, 113; see also p. 111).

32. SV³ 15, pp. 101, 122 (*The Sickness unto Death*, pp. 75, 99).

33. SV³ 15, p. 118 (*The Sickness unto Death*, p. 94).

34. See Hegel, *Aesthetics*, I, p. 155.

35. SV³ 15, pp. 122–3, 74 (*The Sickness unto Death*, pp. 99–100, 44).

36. SV³ 15, p. 87 (*The Sickness unto Death*, p. 59).

37. SV³ 15, p. 133 (*The Sickness unto Death*, p. 111).

38. See Kirmmse, *Kierkegaard in Golden Age Denmark*, pp. 152–3.

39. SV³ 10, p. 269 (KW, XII, 1, p. 606).

40. *Fædrelandet*, nos. 188–91, 24–27 July 1847, in SV³ 14. It was signed 'Inter et Inter' (Between and Between Acts), a subtle double entendre.

41. *Papirer*, IX A 175, from 1848 (*Papers and Journals: A Selection*, pp. 319–20); and SV³ 18, p. 90.

42. SV³ 10, pp. 52, 57 (KW, XII 1, pp. 351, 357).

43. *Papirer*, X¹ A 510, A 548, A 557, and A 508, from 1849 (*Papers and Journals: A Selection*, pp. 392, 399, 400, 390).

44. *Papirer*, X¹ A 567, from 1849 (*Papers and Journals: A Selection*, p. 402).

45. *Papirer*, X² A 273 and A 256, from 1849 (the latter *Papers and Journals: A Selection*, p. 449).

46. *Papirer*, XI¹ A 47, from 1854 (*Papers and Journals: A Selection*, p. 571).

47. *Breve og Aktstykker*, I, pp. 220–1 (280–1) (letter no. 196).

48. In May 1849 the Swedish writer, traveller, and literary critic Frederikke (or Frederika) Bremer (1801–1869), wanting to interview Kierkegaard and include him in her survey of contemporary Scandinavian literature, began 'To Victor Eremita . . .'. See ibid., pp. 225–7 (286–8) (letters no. 201, 203, 204). See Kirmmse, *Encounters*, p. 295.

49. *Papirer*, X¹ A 553 and A 556, from 1849 (*Papers and Journals: A Selection*, p. 400).

Chapter 17

1. *Papirer*, X¹ A 234, A 258, and A 260, from 1849 (*Papers and Journals: A Selection*, pp. 379–81).

2. Kirmmse, *Encounters*, p. 42 (68).

3. *Papirer*, IX A 216, from 1848 (*Papers and Journals: A Selection*, p. 325).

4. *Papirer*, IX A 262, from 1848 (*Papers and Journals: A Selection*, pp. 328–9).

5. *Papirer*, X¹ A 568, from 1849 (*Papers and Journals: A Selection*, p. 402).

6. *Breve og Aktstykker*, I, pp. 262–3 (334–5) (letter no. 239).

7. *Papirer*, X² A 210, from 1849 (*Papers and Journals: A Selection*, p. 445). Kirmmse, *Encounters*, p. 53 (83).

8. *Papirer*, X¹ A 533, from 1849 (*Papers and Journals: A Selection*, p. 395).

9. *Papirer*, X¹ A 497, from 1849, and X⁴ A 605, from 1852.

10. *Papirer*, XI² A 219, 29 June 1855 (*Papers and Journals: A Selection*, p. 642).

11. See Bruce H. Kirmmse, ' "Out With It!": The Modern Breakthrough, Kierkegaard and Denmark,' in Hannay and Marino (eds.), *The Cambridge Companion to Kierkegaard*, p. 27.

12. *Papirer*, VIII¹ A 394, from 1847 (*Papers and Journals: A Selection*, p. 275).

13. I owe to George Pattison the clear biographical reference in the last paragraph of Part Two, section B, subsection A ('The Sin of Despairing over One's Sin') of *The Sickness unto Death*. An 'idiot minister' (Mynster) admires, for the depth of his soul, the melancholy man (Michael Pedersen Kierkegaard) who despairs of forgiveness. That the passage also mentions the deep-souled man's 'wife' as one who feels 'deeply humble in comparison with such a serious and saintly husband who is able to grieve thus over sin' would then be a rare but significant reference in the authorship to Kierkegaard's mother. Resentment of the father is also evident. See SV³ 15, pp. 162–3 (*The Sickness unto Death*, pp. 145–6).

14. *Papirer*, X¹ A 167 (*Papers and Journals: A Selection*, p. 375).

15. *Papirer*, X⁴ A 604, from 1852.

16. *Papirer*, X¹ A 510, from 1849 (*Papers and Journals: A Selection*, pp. 392–3); and SV³ 15, p. 125 (*The Sickness unto Death*, pp. 102–3).

17. SV³ 15, p. 164 (*The Sickness unto Death*, p. 147).

18. SV³ 16, pp. 108, 107 (*Practice in Christianity*, KW, XX, pp. 107, 106). See Philip L. Quinn, 'Kierkegaard's Christian Ethics', pp. 368–74, and Kirmmse's extended discussion (pp. 379–404) in his *Kierkegaard in Golden Age Denmark*.

19. E.g., *Papirer*, X⁵ A 98, from 1853; and XI¹ A 62, from 1854.

20. SKS 4, p. 329 (KW, VIII, p. 21).

21. SV³ 16, p. 13 (KW, XX, p. 7).

22. SV³ 16, pp. 45, 51–60, 85 (KW, XX, pp. 35, 42–53, 81).

23. SV³ 16, p. 86 (KW, XX, p. 82).

24. SV³ 16, p. 138 (KW, XX, p. 143).

25. SV³ 16, p. 162 (KW, XX, p. 167). See Ettore Rocca, 'Kierkegaard's Second Aesthetics', in Niels Jørgen Cappelørn and H. Deuser (eds), *Kierkegaard Studies: Yearbook 1999*, Berlin/New York: Walter de Gruyter, 1999. The author's account of the use of religious imagery in the later discourses is very germane to the latter part of *Practice*.

26. Among these sources is Johann Arndt (1555–1621), a Lutheran writer whose penchant for medieval mysticism led him to oppose systematic theology. Kierkegaard was early acquainted with Arndt's work, in German as well as in Danish translation (see, e.g., *Papirer*, X⁶ C 1:89, where Kierkegaard cites Arndt as saying that life is more important than doctrine but that doctrine is really his life). Another is H. A. Brorson (1694–1764), whose hymns provide frequent parallels with Kierkegaard's own turns of phrase. He chose some lines from one of them to be inscribed on the family grave. See note 74 to this chapter.

27. Mynster, in *Yderligere Bidrag til Forhandlingerne om de kirkelige Forhold i Danmark* (Further Contributions to the Negotiations Concerning the Ecclesiastical Situation in Denmark), Copenhagen, 1851, p. 44, had referred to Goldschmidt as 'one of our most talented writers' and described Kierkegaard using a term (*Fremtoning* [phenomenon]) coined by Goldschmidt.

28. *Papirer* X^4 A 167, A 168, from 1851, the latter from June (*Papers and Journals: A Selection*, p. 524); and A 270, after 2 May 1851.

29. *Papirer*, X^1 A 302, dated both 4 and 5 May 1849; and X^1 A 309.

30. 'Now for something different.'

31. Topics for his sermons.

32. *Breve og Aktstykker*, I, pp. 280–1 (357–8) (letter no. 263).

33. See *Papirer*, X^4 A 6, from 1851 (*Papers and Journals: A Selection*, pp. 517–18); and X^5 A 125, 27 May 1853.

34. SV^3 17, pp. 76–7.

35. SV^3 17, p. 65.

36. See Carl Jørgensen, *Søren Kierkegaard. En Biografi*, IV, pp. 9–10; and Carl Koch, *Søren Kierkegaard og Emil Boesen*, Copenhagen, 1901, p. 35.

37. Kirmmse, *Encounters*, p. 195 (272).

38. *Papirer*, X^4 A 551, from 1852 (*Papers and Journals: A Selection*, pp. 535–7).

39. *Papirer*, X^4 A 663, from 1852 (*Papers and Journals: A Selection*, p. 552).

40. *Papirer*, XI^1 A 74, from 1854 (*Papers and Journals: A Selection*, pp. 572–3).

41. *Papirer*, XI^1 A 144, from 1854 (*Papers and Journals: A Selection*, pp. 581–5).

42. *Fædrelandet*, no. 295, 18 December 1854.

43. See *Papirer*, XI^3 B 188, from 1855, in which Kierkegaard stresses his need to distinguish his own position from the Grundtvigians, this 'most demoralizing' form of Christianity 'we have'.

44. *Breve og Aktstykker*, I, pp. 327–8 (357–8) (letter no. 299).

45. Ernst Wilhelm Kolthoff (1809–1890), the Church of the Holy Spirit (*Helligaandskirke*) in Copenhagen.

46. *Papirer*, XI^1 A 1, 1 March 1854 (*Papers and Journals: A Selection*, pp. 568–9).

47. Kirmmse, *Encounters*, p. 186 (256).

48. See Kirmmse, *Kierkegaard in Golden Age Denmark*, pp. 482–3 and notes, for sources for the expressions of disapproval (from Clausen, Sibbern, the jurist Ørsted, and Joanne Louise Heiberg). It is interesting to note in passing that Clausen, Sibbern, and Ørsted had all been elected members of the Royal Danish Academy of Science and Letters, as also had Martensen and Mynster. Kierkegaard was never even proposed. See Olaf Pedersen, *Lovers of Learning*, Copenhagen: Munksgaard, 1992, pp. 206–8, 256.

49. *Papirer*, X^1 A 658, from 1849; X 4 A 596, from 1852 (*Papers and Journals: A Selection*, pp. 411, 545); and X^5 A 106

50. *Papirer*, X^2 A 14, from 1849 (*Papers and Journals: A Selection*, p. 425).

51. *Papirer*, X^2 A 622, from 1850 (*Papers and Journals: A Selection*, p. 487).

52. *Papirer*, X^1 A 640, from 1849 (*Papers and Journals: A Selection*, p. 408).

53. See, again, Kirmmse, *Kierkegaard in Golden Age Denmark*, p. 483, concerning

the rare insight into the revolutionary implications of Kierkegaard's writings shown by one Hansine Andræ, wife of mathematician and liberal politician C. G. Andræ. See also Kirmmse, *Encounters*, pp. 118–19 (171).

54. *Papirer*, XI^2 A 265, 28 May 1855. See also XI^2 A 411 and XI^2 A 425, from 1855.

55. *Papirer*, XI^1 A 158, from 1854 (*Papers and Journals: A Selection*, p. 585).

56. See Carl Jørgensen, *Søren Kierkegaard. En Biografi*, V, p. 94. Jørgensen cites Hjalmar Helweg's version of Hanne Mourier's account of an interview with Regine late in life, in his *Søren Kierkegaard. En psykiatrisk-psykologisk Studie* (Søren Kierkegaard: A Psychiatric-Psychological Study), Copenhagen: H. Hagerups Forlag, 1933), pp. 385–92. The version in Kirmmse, *Encounters*, p. 42, has 'and returned her wish with a greeting', omitting the last phrase.

57. The articles from *Fædrelandet*, including the original attack on Martensen's eulogy, are to be found in SV^3 19, pp. 9–72.

58. *Øieblikket*, 1–9, Copenhagen: C. A. Reitzels Bo og Arvinger, 2nd and 3rd printings, 1855, 1 (24 May 1855), pp. 1, 9, 14; 2 (4 June 1855), pp. 20–21; 6 (23 August 1855), pp. 5, 25–6; 7 (30 August 1855), p. 13; 9 (24 September 1855), pp. 20–1.

59. A list of contents for the unpublished tenth issue is found in *Papirer*, XI^3 B 326 and 828. This quotation from one of the drafts is translated from *Øieblikket Nr. 1–10, Hvad Christus dømmer, Guds Uforanderlighed, af Søren Kierkegaard*, Copenhagen: Hans Reitzel, 1984, p. 188.

60. Kirmmse, *Encounters*, p. 248 (341).

61. Daughter of Petrea Severine Kierkegaard (1801–1834), who was married to Henrik Ferdinand Lund, the head of the National Bank.

62. Kirmmse, *Encounters*, p. 172 (240–1).

63. *Breve og Aktstykker*, I, p. 21 (28). The following account is a paraphrase of the hospital journal's description on pp. 21–4 (28–32).

64. *Papirer*, X^5 B 15–23, from 1849.

65. Kirmmse, *Encounters*, p. 210 (288). See *Udtalelser*, Søren Kierkegaard Archives, D, *PK*. 5, Læg 31, Royal Library, Copenhagen.

66. Henrik and Michael Lund, sons of Nicolene Christine Kierkegaard (1799–1832) and Johan Christian Lund, clothier and brother of the father of Henriette Lund. See note 62 to this chapter.

67. See translations also in Kirmmse, *Encounters*, pp. 121–8 (175–82), and *Papers and Journals: A Selection*, pp. 651–6.

68. Johan Frederick Schlegel was appointed governor in the Danish West Indies. It is rumoured that this was to enable them to escape the embarrassment that persisted in connection with the broken engagement and its aftermath. He and Regine left Copenhagen on 17 March 1855. According to Hanne Mourier, who interviewed Regine on her return, she and Kierkegaard met on the street the day before their departure and she had said to him, 'God bless you – I hope things go well with you!' Whereupon Kierkegaard drew back and greeted her for the first and last time since the break (Kirmmse, *Encounters*, p. 38 [63]).

69. A philanthropist and author.

70. An allusion, no doubt, to Peter's reputation among his fellow-students in Germany as *der Disputier-teufel aus dem Norden*.

71. *Papirer*, XI¹ A 375, from 1854 (*Papers and Journals: A Selection*, p. 602).

72. *Breve og Aktstykker*, I, p. 20 (pp. 26–7).

73. Maren Kirstine Kierkegaard (1797–1822) and Søren Michael Kierkegaard (1807–1819).

74. From a hymn written by H. A. Brorson (1694–1764).

75. *Breve og Aktstykker*, I, p. 25 (pp. 26–7).

76. See Kirmmse, *Encounters*, p. 53 (84).

Chapter 18

1. Kirmmse, *Encounters*, p. 136 (192–3).

2. Ibid., p. 115 (167).

3. Ibid., pp. 134–5 (189–91).

4. Ibid. p. 135 (191–2).

5. Ibid., p. 132 (188).

6. See Kirmmse, 'Out With It!', in Hannay and Marino (eds.), *The Cambridge Companion to Kierkegaard*, pp. 24, 30 f., 36–7. The source is given as *Kirketidende*, 1881, no. 22; reprinted in *Peter Christian Kierkegaards Samlede Skrifter*, vol. 4, p. 124.

7. *Kirketidende*, 1881, no. 22; reprinted in *Peter Christian Kierkegaards Samlede Skrifter*, vol. 4, p. 125. See Kirmmse, 'Out With It!', in Hannay and Marino (eds.), *The Cambridge Companion to Kierkegaard*.

8. See *Papirer*, XI³ B 154 and 155.

9. Weltzer, *Peter og Søren Kierkegaard*, pp. 358, 255; Kirmmse, 'Out With It!', in Hannay and Marino (eds.), *The Cambridge Companion to Kierkegaard*, pp. 35–9.

10. C. L. N. Mynster, *Har S. Kierkegaard fremstillet de christelige Idealer – er dette Sandhed?* (Has S. Kierkegaard Represented the Christian Ideals – Is This Truth?), published with a foreword by Jakob Paulli, Kjøbenhavn: C. A. Reitzels Forlag, 1884, pp. 18, 46.

11. Ibid., pp. 13, 16, 19, 22, 23, 35, 41, 42, 44.

12. Mynster, Jr., points to several things that identify him as a supporter of Martensen. He quotes, for instance, the latter's *Grundrids til Moralphilosophiens System* from 1841: '[T]he rhythmic exchange of activity and pleasure', and 'it is just as much man's duty to savour as to act'. He also claims that in the many indirect attacks made on Martensen in the pseudonymous works, Kierkegaard had failed to see how far Martensen actually stood from the Hegelians. But then Kierkegaard has also failed to grasp the need for knowledge and faith to progress hand in hand (ibid., p. 20).

13. H. Martensen, *Christian Ethics. Special Part: First Division: Individual Ethics*, translated (from the author's German) by William Affleck, Edinburgh: T. & T. Clark, 1881, pp. 122–3; and *Christian Ethics*, translated (from the Danish 'with the sanction of the author') by C. Spence, Edinburgh: T. & T. Clark, 1873, pp. 215–17.

14. *Christian Ethics* (1873), p. 223.

15. See Leif Bork Hansen, *Søren Kierkegaards Hemmelighed of Eksistensdialektik* (Søren Kierkegaard's Secret and His Dialectic of Existence), Copenhagen: C. A. Reitzels Forlag, 1994. For Sibbern, see Kirmmse, *Encounters*, p. 216 (295).

16. Mynster's son sets a rather sorry example. Telling us that the catch-phrase 'all or nothing' had now become popular more than any other, he asks: 'But just because the Lord wants us to do his will in everything, does it follow that he always asks "everything" of us?' 'Isn't "something" rather than "all" sometimes enough?' This, if a reference to *The Instant*, no. 6 (23 August 1855), may be apt enough. There, in 'What Does the Fire-Chief Say?', Kierkegaard scorns compromise and again stresses either/or. This would, however, be a serious misunderstanding of the salient use of the same motto, in the form '*Aut Caesar aut nihil*' (Caesar or nothing) in *The Sickness unto Death*, which sides not with Caesar but with nothing. This sort of confusion persisted in the image of Kierkegaard's ideas and is expressed in Ibsen's *Brand* (it would be nice to think that the title derives from that of Kierkegaard's essay; the Danish for fire-chief is 'Brand-Major'). Mynster himself refers to 'the Norwegian poet's tightening of the requirement in *Brand*' as a poor indication of what 'true, humble Christianity' should be (Mynster, p. 29).

17. When Brandes went to Oslo to give a lecture on Kierkegaard, he was refused an official lecture hall.

18. For an interesting account of Lukács's relation to Kierkegaard, see Andras Nagy, 'Abraham the Communist', in George Pattison and Steven Shakespeare (eds.), *Kierkegaard: The Self in Society*, Basingstoke: Macmillan, 1998, pp. 196–220

19. G. Lukács, *Existentialisme ou marxisme?*, Paris: Nagel, 1948, p. 84.

20. G. Lukács, *Soul and Form*, Cambridge, MA: MIT Press, 1971.

21. G. Lukács, *The Destruction of Reason* (1954), Atlantic Highlands, NJ: Humanities Press, 1981, p. 296.

22. Lukács, *Soul and Form*, p. 24.

23. G. Lukács, *Theory of the Novel* (Cambridge, MA: MIT Press, 1971).

24. Lukács, *Soul and Form*, p. 41.

25. Ibid., p. 40.

26. Ibid., pp. 40–1.

27. G. Lukács, *History and Class Consciousness*, Cambridge, MA: MIT Press, 1971.

28. W. Lepenies, *Melancholy and Society* (1969), Cambridge, MA: Harvard University Press, 1992, p. 153.

29. H. Marcuse, *Reason and Revolution: Hegel and the Rise of Social Theory* (1941), Boston: Beacon Press, 1960, p. 264.

30. Stephen Spender, 'With Lukács in Budapest', *Encounter* (December 1964), p. 55.

31. G. Lukács, 'A kritikai realizmus jelentösége ma' (The Meaning of Critical Realism Today), Budapest: Szépirodalmi, 1985, p. 6, quoted in Arpad Kadarkay, *Georg Lukács: Life, Thought, and Politics*, Oxford: Blackwell, 1991, p. 425.

32. Kadarkay, *Georg Lukács*, pp. 28–9.

33. Ibid., Chapter 8.
34. I have it from George Pattison that Unamuno learnt Norwegian in the late 1890s in order to read Ibsen, and that he had been reading Kierkegaard by 1903. A letter of 1904 has him currently reading the *Samlede Værker*.
35. Hegel, *Aesthetics*, I, p. 67.
36. John Milbank, 'Knowledge: The Theological Critique of Philosophy in Hamann and Jacobi', in John Milbank, Catherine Pickstock, and Graham Ward (eds.), *Radical Orthodoxy: A New Theology*, London/New York: Routledge, 1999, p. 22.
37. Alasdair MacIntyre, *After Virtue: A Study in Moral Theory*, London: Duckworth, 1981, pp. 41, 38.
38. Harvie Ferguson, *Melancholy and the Critique of Modernity*, p. 42.
39. See David Lowenthal, *The Heritage Crusade and the Spoils of History*, Cambridge University Press, 1998.
40. Harry Fett, *Vort nationale Enevælde. Ethos og Eros* (Our National Autocracy: Ethos and Eros), Oslo: H. Aschehoug & Co. (W. Nygaard), 1925, p. 62, my translation. To indicate just how radical Kierkegaard's influence had been in Norway, Fett cites the Norwegian theologian Christopher Bruun (1839–1920), said to be the model for Ibsen's Brand. On intellectual life (*aandsliv*) in the late nineteenth and early twentieth centuries, Bruun said: 'Most of what we have here in Norway in the way of independence points either through Ibsen back to Kierkegaard or through Bjørnson to Grundtvig' (ibid.). Bjørnstjerne Bjørnson (1832–1910), politician and poet, was Norway's most influential writer of the time, in spite of being Ibsen's contemporary. On Pietism's connection with an intense inner life, see Isaiah Berlin, *The Roots of Romanticism*, edited by Henry Hardy, London: Chatto & Windus, 1999, pp. 37–8. I owe both these references to Brit Berggreen.

Index

490